Time Out
New Orleans

Penguin Books

PENGUIN BOOKS

Published by the Penguin Group
Penguin Books Ltd, 27 Wright's Lane, London W8 5TZ, England
Penguin Putnam Inc., 375 Hudson Street, New York, New York 10014, USA
Penguin Books Australia Ltd, Ringwood, Victoria, Australia
Penguin Books Canada Ltd, 10 Alcorn Avenue, Toronto, Ontario, Canada M4V 3B2
Penguin Books (NZ) Ltd, 182–190 Wairau Road, Auckland 10, New Zealand

Penguin Books Ltd, Registered offices: Harmondsworth, Middlesex, England

First published 1998
10 9 8 7 6 5 4 3 2 1

Colour reprographics by Precise Litho, 34–35 Great Sutton Street, London EC1
Printed and bound by William Clowes Ltd, Beccles, Suffolk NR34 9QE

Edited and designed by

Time Out Magazine Limited
Universal House
251 Tottenham Court Road
London W1P OAB
Tel +44 (0)171 813 3000
Fax +44 (0)171 813 6001
E-mail guides@timeout.co.uk
http://www.timeout.co.uk

Editorial

Managing Editor Peter Fiennes
Editor Caroline Taverne
Deputy Editor Cath Phillips
Consultant Editor Harriet Swift
Researchers Shana-Tara Regon, Rich Wilson
Proofreaders Tamsin Shelton, Phil Harriss
Indexer Jackie Brind

Design

Art Director John Oakey
Art Editor Mandy Martin
Designers Benjamin de Lotz, Scott Moore, Lucy Grant
Scanner Operator Chris Quinn
Advertisement Make-up Paul Mansfield
Picture Editor Kerri Miles
Picture Researcher Emma Tremlett

Advertising

Group Advertisement Director Lesley Gill
Sales Director Mark Phillips
Advertisement Sales (New Orleans) *OffBeat*
Advertising Assistant Ingrid Sigerson

Administration

Publisher Tony Elliott
Managing Director Mike Hardwick
Financial Director Kevin Ellis
Marketing Director Gillian Auld
General Manager Nichola Coulthard
Production Manager Mark Lamond

Features in this guide were written and researched by:

History John Kemp, Harriet Swift (Battle of New Orleans). **New Orleans Today** Harriet Swift. **Architecture**
Doug MacCash. **Literary New Orleans** Harriet Swift. **By Season** Christi Daugherty, Alex Oliver (Jazz Fest).
Mardi Gras Alex Rawls. **Sightseeing** Roberts Batson, Christi Daugherty, Alex Rawls, Harriet Swift. **Museums
& Galleries** Doug MacCash, Harriet Swift. **Accommodation** Harriet Swift. **Restaurants, Cafés &
Coffeehouses** Christi Daugherty, John DeMers, Harriet Swift. **Shops & Services** Patricia Saik, Dorothy
Waldrup. **Children** Margaret Woodward. **Film** Rick Barton. **Gay & Lesbian** Roberts Batson. **Media** Harriet
Swift. **Nightlife** Alex Oliver. **The Performing Arts** Christi Daugherty. **Sport & Fitness** Alex Rawls. **Trips Out of
Town** Christi Daugherty, Harriet Swift. **Directory** Michael Greene, Beverly Rainbolt.

The Editors would like to thank the following:

Melanie Ruddle at Continental Airlines, Melanie Tennyson (for postal services), Beverly Gianna and
Christine DeCuir at the New Orleans Convention & Visitors Bureau, Susan Hybart Alsup (Mobile, Alabama),
Barbara and Bill Johnson (Pensacola, Florida), Georgia Wade McDaniel (Gulf Shores, Alabama), Maggie
Cantwell, Karen Gildea, Gail Glassman, Sara Hare, John Kaine, Elizabeth Ann Kelly, Elaine Kolp, Michael
Marshall, Madeleine Claire Moise, Ed McCaughan, Jane Rosborough, Janet Rudolph, Diana Smith, NJ
Stevenson, Wade Welch and Christina Vella.

The Editor flew to New Orleans courtesy of Continental Airlines.

Maps by JS Graphics, Hill View Cottage, 17 Beadles Lane, Old Oxted, Surrey RH8 9JG.
Photography by Sydney Byrd except for pages 5, 6, 9 **AKG**; page 10 **Bridgeman Art Library**; pages 11, 193 **Redferns**;
pages 12, 40 **Frank Gordon & Son**; page 172 **Movie Store Collection**; page 215 **David Haymon**; page 217 **All Sport
USA**; page 238 **Linda S Reineke**; page 243 **Brian Gassel**; page 247 **Mike Clemmer**. Pictures on pages 63, 101, 117,
127, 167, 193, 212, 225, 226, 235, 244, 246, 248, 249, 250 were supplied by the featured establishments.

Contents

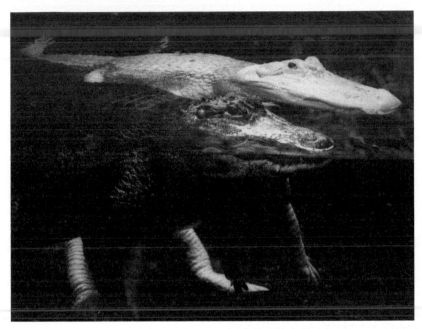

About the Guide

The *Time Out New Orleans Guide* is one of an expanding series of city guides produced by the people behind London and New York's successful listings magazines. Our hard-working team of local writers has striven to provide you with all the information you'll need to explore the Big Easy.

As befits the birthplace of jazz and a town with 24-hour licensing laws, we've included an extra large Nightlife chapter, covering all the best bars, and music clubs, as well as a Sightseeing chapter that details all the sights, both on and off the beaten track, arranged by neighbourhood. We've included the most up-to-date advice on what to see (and what to avoid), as well as information on where to eat, drink, sleep and shop. And, when you've had enough of the city, there's a chapter covering all the best trips out of town – to nearby Louisiana, Mississippi, Alabama and Florida.

CHECKED AND CORRECT

Above all, we've tried to make this book as useful as possible. Addresses, telephone numbers, transport information, opening times, admission prices and credit card details are all included in our listings. And, as far as possible, we've given details of facilities, services and events, all checked and correct at the time we went to press. However, owners and managers can change their arrangements at any time. Before you go out of your way, it's always best to telephone and check opening times, dates of exhibitions, and other particulars.

THE LIE OF THE LAND

Greater New Orleans covers some 363.5 square miles (941.5 square kilometres), just under a third of which is on dry land. It is divided into three parishes (counties) called Orleans, Jefferson (where the airport is located) and St Bernard. Because the city is defined by waterways – the great curves of the Mississippi River to the south, east and west, and vast Lake Pontchartrain to the north – the streets form less of a grid pattern than in many US cities.

We've included cross streets in all our addresses, so you can find your way about more easily; we've also included zip codes for any venue you might want to write to, as well as e-mail and website addresses where possible. And there's a series of fully-indexed colour street maps, a map of the surrounding countryside and a transport map at the back of the guide, starting on *page 275*.

PRICES

The prices we've supplied should be treated as guidelines, not gospel. Fluctuating exchange rates and inflation can cause charges, in shops and restaurants particularly, to change rapidly. If prices vary wildly from those we've quoted, ask whether there's a good reason. If not, go elsewhere. Then please write and let us know. We aim to give the best and most up-to-date advice, so we always want to know if you've been badly treated or overcharged.

CREDIT CARDS

The following abbreviations have been used for credit cards: **AmEx**: American Express; **DC**: Diners' Club; **Disc** (Discovery); **JCB**: Japanese credit cards; **MC**: Mastercard (Access); **V**: Visa (Barclaycard). Virtually all shops, restaurants and attractions will accept dollar travellers' cheques issued by a major financial institution (such as American Express).

TELEPHONE NUMBERS

The area code for New Orleans is 504. All telephone numbers printed in this guide take this code, unless otherwise stated. Numbers preceded by 1-800 can be called free of charge from within the US, and some of them can be dialled (though not all free of charge) from the UK.

RIGHT TO REPLY

It should be stressed that the information we give is impartial. No organisation has been included in this guide because its owner or manager has advertised in our publications. We hope you enjoy the *Time Out New Orleans Guide*, but we'd also like to know if you don't. We welcome tips for places that you think we should include in future editions and take notice of your criticism of our choices. There's a reader's reply card at the back of this book.

There is an online version of this guide, as well as weekly events listings for several international cities, at http://www.timeout.co.uk.

Introduction

If you approach New Orleans by car from the east, one of the first exit signs you see on the interstate reads 'ELYSIAN FIELDS/NEXT RIGHT'. Despite the landscape of decrepit rooftops and commercial billboards, this is one of the truest road signs ever posted. Virgil's 'deathless abode of the spirits of the blessed' is echoed in New Orleans, an ageless city whose residents relish life in such a marvellous make-believe land.

Visitors would do well to adopt the attitude of the native New Orleanians. It's a relaxed, unhurried attitude that moves slowly, laughs at everything and never looks at a clock. While the 'later, darlin'' atmosphere has been known to push Type A executives and parents dedicated to wholesome family vacations over the edge of sanity, it has been successfully embraced by millions. A moment of reflection on the attractions of New Orleans brings the realisation that one is here, after all, not for sightseeing or cultural events but to experience New Orleans itself. The hordes who visit the Crescent City every year don't just come for the Mardi Gras, Jazz Fest or the museums, food, sacred relics, sport, natural wonders or history. Even those fabulous jewels in the crown are only a part of New Orleans, not the whole. What is here is a release from the ordinariness of daily life, a sense of sinking into a world of sensuality and freedom, a languid place of music, laughter and unfettered individualism.

New Orleans has all the equipment of a late twentieth century post-modern urban area, of course. There are ambitious entrepreneurs, pushy car salesmen, equivocating politicians, AA meetings, yuppie gyms, shopaholic wives, wandering husbands, alienated teenagers, and the rest. But the city remains outside the conventional forces of history. New Orleans retains a medieval cast of mind that operates in terms of feasts and holidays, family ties and human relationships, pleasure and sin. Its reputation for tolerance and indulgence has been variously traced to the French and Spanish settlers, the Catholic church, the climate and the unpredictability of the Mississippi River. All the elements that have gone into making New Orleans are widely known, but the city's unquenchable *joie de vivre* – despite a turbulent history of war, poverty, disease, natural disasters and plain bad luck – remains a mystery.

The spirit of New Orleans is infectious, easy for even the two-day visitor to catch. The plan for a great visit is simplicity itself: have no plan.

The more you open yourself up to possibility in New Orleans, the more the city will deliver. New Orleanians have been having fun for almost 300 years and are generous about showing how it's done. It's a talent that seems to have been present from the first. During yellow fever periods of the 1790s, New Orleanians left the city in droves hoping to avoid the 'night airs' that caused the fever. They piled into each other's plantation villas for long house parties that revolved around card games and raucous pranks. If they were going to die or lose their families, the Creoles were determined to go out with plenty of laughs.

Join the party that never stops. Exit onto Elysian Fields and repeat the New Orleans mantra, 'laissez les bons temps rouler'. Let the good times roll, taking you where they will.
Harriet Swift

In Context

History

Tales of the Big Easy – from muddy estuary to 1990s Bohemia.

A New York journalist once described New Orleans as the northernmost Caribbean city, a cross between Port-au-Prince, Haiti, and Paterson, New Jersey, with a culture not unlike that of Genoa, Marseilles or Egyptian Alexandria. French and Spanish New Orleans was very much a part of the French and Spanish Caribbean. Its earliest populations consisted of lesser French and Spanish gentry, criminals, soldiers, debtors, tradesmen, merchants, prostitutes, priests and nuns, farmers from the fields of France and Germany, Acadian exiles from Canada, Canary Islanders, American Indians, Africans, Englishmen, Irish, and Anglo-Americans from the British colonies (later American states) along the Atlantic seaboard. Others came – Sicilians, Greeks, Eastern Europeans, Cubans, Central Americans, Chinese and Vietnamese.

For almost three centuries, New Orleans has survived yellow fever epidemics, Indian wars, slave revolts, economic depressions, conspiracies, hurricanes, floods, the American and French revolutions, Civil War and Reconstruction, racial riots and oppression, political corruption and, alas, Americanisation. Today its jazz, French Quarter, cuisine and Mardi Gras are world famous.

Actually, the lower Mississippi River Valley came within weeks of being a British rather than a French colony, and New Orleans was founded on the insistence of a Scotsman who practically ruled the economy of early eighteenth-century France.

Colonial beginnings

It all began in 1682 when a French-Canadian, Robert Cavelier, Sieur de La Salle, descended the Mississippi River to its mouth and claimed the entire Mississippi Valley for Louis XIV of France. La Salle, however, failed to establish a colony and was later assassinated by his own men. Colonisation was left to two other French Canadians.

In the early 1690s, prominent Canadians (still governed by France) convinced Louis XIV that a strong colony in Louisiana was in his interest. They had good reasons: to protect and expand France's colonial possessions; to block the British who were moving west from the Atlantic seaboard; and finally, to capitalise on prosperous Spanish trade in the Gulf of Mexico.

In September 1698, the French Government dispatched the Canadian, Pierre Le Moyne, Sieur d'Iberville, with his younger brother, Jean Baptiste

Le Moyne, Sieur de Bienville, and five small ships. After a brief encounter with the Spanish in nearby Pensacola, Florida, the expedition dropped anchor at the mouth of the Mississippi on 3 March 1699. It was Mardi Gras day and New Orleanians have been celebrating ever since.

France wasted little time in building a series of posts along the Mississippi and Gulf Coast, including Mobile, Alabama, and Biloxi, Mississippi. By 1718, French officials knew they had to have a permanent settlement on the river to protect their claim. From the beginning, however, Louisiana had been a drain on the royal purse.

Enter John Law, an adventurous Scotsman, with a new scheme. In 1716 Law created the Banque Generale de France and then convinced Philippe, Duc d'Orleans, regent for young Louis XV, that Louisiana had potential for great wealth. Law formed a joint stock company to develop the colony and sold shares to the Duke and other investors. The Crown then granted Law's company an exclusive charter to Louisiana.

Law, a master at public relations, flooded southern Germany, France and Switzerland with posters, encouraging farmers to emigrate to Louisiana. Thousands grabbed at the opportunity to make a fresh start in the New World. Most settled upriver from New Orleans in an area that to this day is called the Côte des Allemands (the German Coast). During the first four years of Law's control, the colony's population grew from about 400 to 8,000, including African slaves.

In building his city on the river, Law again showed himself to be a masterful politician. Working through Bienville in the colony, Law named the city 'Nouvelle Orleans' in honour of the Duc d'Orleans. He gave instructions that the streets of the new city be named after members of the royal family, their ancestors, patron saints, cousins (including bastards), and major stock holders in the company. Hence streets in the French Quarter (the original French settlement) bear lofty names such as St Ann, St Louis, Royal, Bourbon, Chartres, Conti, Dauphine, Burgundy, Du Maine and Orleans. Law's bold venture did not last long. By the early 1720s, the company went bust and he eventually fled to France, narrowly escaping a good stoning in the streets. He died in complete obscurity.

Opposite: eighteenth-century spin-doctor and adventurer, John Law.

Imperial squabbles

The history of New Orleans is inseparable from its port. France had hoped to reap great riches from the interior of North America, but gold and silver did not pour from the wilderness. Tobacco, lumber, indigo, animal hides and other goods were floated downriver on flatboats to the new city, where ships from France, Spanish Florida, the West Indies and the British colonies waited to trade with spices, cloth, wine and other items. New Orleans became a commercial centre, connecting Europe and the West Indies with the upper regions of the Mississippi.

But international storms were brewing. For over a century, the three major European colonial powers – France, Spain and Britain – had been at each others' throats in North America. By the early 1750s, both France and Britain had staked a claim to the Ohio River Valley. In 1754 war broke out in North America (started by the young British-American militia officer George Washington) and quickly spread to Europe. Dubbed 'The French and Indian War' in the British American colonies and the 'Seven Years War' in Europe, the conflict was to eliminate France as a colonial power in America. Despite an alliance with Spain a year before the war ended, France was finally defeated in 1763. It ceded to Britain all of Canada and French territory east of the Mississippi River. France also lost India to Britain. Spain ceded both East and West Florida to Britain.

New Orleans and Louisiana west of the Mississippi, however, were not included in the package. In 1762, Louis XV, realising that he was losing the war, convinced his cousin, King Carlos III of Spain, to enter the war on the side of France. As a token of appreciation, Louis gave Louisiana to his cousin. The colony was costing him his royal shirt. Carlos III, however, accepted Louisiana as a buffer to keep the British away from nearby Mexico.

Louisiana Frenchmen were not happy about the deal. They brooded for almost six years while petitioning the king to revoke the gift, but Louis refused. Hope received a further knock when Don Antonio de Ulloa, a military officer and respected scientist, was appointed governor. He arrived in 1766 and met a cool reception. Two years later, the colonists staged a bloodless coup and drove Ulloa from the colony. Again, they begged the French Crown to take them back and again Louis refused.

Spain's retaliation was quick and complete. In July 1769 Spanish forces arrived under the command of General Alexander O'Reilly, an Irishman in Spanish service. O'Reilly crushed the short-lived rebellion, set up a new government and executed the coup's ringleaders.

Revolution

Though the fact is ignored by most history books, Spanish New Orleans played a major role in the American Revolution against the British Crown. Through the Louisiana colony, the Spanish sent supplies and munitions to the American rebels and allowed American raiding parties to launch forays into British West Florida. While the British were busy with their upstart American colonials, Spanish Governor Bernardo de Galvez drove the British from East and West Florida.

Galvez and his successors practised an open immigration policy that gave refuge to both loyal and rebel British-Americans fleeing the Revolution, and to the Acadians (whose descendants are Louisiana's French-speaking Cajuns) driven from Nova Scotia by the British after they refused to renounce their Catholic faith and pledge allegiance to England. Canary Islanders settled in the swamps and bayous south of New Orleans, where their descendants live today, many still speaking an archaic Spanish dialect.

During the final decades of the eighteenth century, Spanish New Orleans prospered despite fires, plagues, rebellions, pressure from Americans expanding westward, and the French Revolution. While the revolution in France was in progress, mobs of French New Orleanians roamed the streets calling Spanish Governor Carondelet a *cochon de lait* (suckling pig). Carondelet kept the mobs in hand and then, diplomatically, gave refuge to French aristocrats fleeing the revolution.

Carondelet also had troubles with restless Americans heading west (usually Kentuckians or 'Kaintocks' as they were called by New Orleans Creoles). During the American Revolution, the Continental Congress assured the Spanish that it had no designs on Louisiana. After the war, however, pressure and tension mounted between the infant United States and Spain as American commerce on the Mississippi River grew. Americans wanted free navigation of the river and Spain,

A flourishing port was vital to the growth of eighteenth-century New Orleans.

which controlled both sides of the river below Natchez, prevented free trade. Spanish officials seized American flatboats and Americans clamoured for an invasion of Louisiana. War was averted in 1795, but the tensions remained.

By the end of the eighteenth century, New Orleans had become a major North American port with a population of almost 10,000. Unfortunately, three fires in the 1780s and early 1790s almost destroyed the old colonial city. Most buildings in today's French Quarter were constructed during the Spanish colonial days and after the 1803 Louisiana Purchase.

As a result, the French Quarter has a unique mixture of nineteenth-century architectural styles, including Spanish with strong Caribbean influences, Greek Revival, English townhouse and American Victorian. The oldest building in the French Quarter, and the only one remaining from French colonial days, is the former **Ursuline Convent** on Chartres Street, completed in the early 1750s (*see chapter* **Sightseeing**).

The Louisiana Purchase

In the early 1800s, political events in Europe once again drifted up the Mississippi. In 1800 Napoleon forced Spain to return Louisiana to France. The news did not sit well with US President Thomas Jefferson, who feared a war with France was inevitable. The issue that concerned him most was free navigation of the Mississippi from the Ohio and Illinois territory to New Orleans. To solve the problem, he wanted to buy New Orleans and a portion of Spanish West Florida bordering the Mississippi. This would put the entire east bank of the river in American hands, but Napoleon had

a better deal in mind. Needing money to fight Britain and knowing he could not hold on to the colony when war came, Napoleon decided to sell not only New Orleans, but the entire Louisiana colony. In other words, in 1803, for $15 million, the USA bought the entire central section of North America from the mouth of the Mississippi north to Canada and west to the Rockies.

Victory over the British

The first decade or so of the American era has been described by one historian as one of 'excitement, uproar, flux, boom and bust, disasters, disappointments, and achievements'. Thousands of people died in the yellow fever epidemics. American and foreign sailors frequently slugged it out on the river levees and in taverns, while the Creoles saved their contempt for Anglo-Americans. Statehood came in 1812, as well as the arrival of the first steamboat, the *New Orleans*, captained by Nicholas Roosevelt, an ancestral kinsman of two American presidents.

The year 1812 also brought war with Great Britain. Events didn't reach Louisiana until December 1814 when the British decided to invade the lower Mississippi. In December and January Andrew Jackson, with a rag-tag army of Tennessee and Kentucky frontiersmen, Louisiana militiamen, and Louisiana's Baratarian pirates under the command of Jean Lafitte, stopped the far superior British army in a bloody battle at Chalmette Plantation just downriver from the city (*see page 8*). Ironically, the battle took place two weeks after the USA and Britain had signed a treaty ending the War of 1812.

Antebellum prosperity

The five decades between the Battle of New Orleans and the American Civil War were the city's golden years. It pulsated with the energy of commerce, business, change and expansion. Tensions between newly arriving Anglo-Americans and Creoles heightened. Competition and rivalry thrived not only among merchants and other fortune seekers, but also between two radically different cultures. By the early 1830s the city was divided into two well-defined sections: the American Sector upriver of Canal Street and the French Quarter below Canal Street.

Prosperity and the competitive spirit between the two sections dramatically changed the landscape of New Orleans. Americans, wanting to emulate other prosperous cities on the East Coast, and Creoles, with their eyes to their beloved France and to their own architectural heritage, built antebellum New Orleans. Above Canal Street stood **Gallier Hall**, a Greek Revival temple facing Lafayette Square; blocks of three-storied, red-brick row houses; and the new Customs House at the foot of Canal Street. Below Canal Street, Creoles boasted of the newly rebuilt **St Louis Cathedral** and the magnificent **Pontalba Buildings** facing the Place d'Armes *(for details of all three, see chapter* **Sightseeing***)*.

The arts also flourished during these years. New Orleans had one of the first opera houses in the USA. Blacks and whites, rich and poor – strictly segregated – could hear a Bellini, a Meyerbeer or a Donizetti opera at one of several opera houses in the city. Patrons filled the St Charles Theater in the American Sector and the Théâtre d'Orleans in the French Quarter and later the new French Opera House on fashionable Bourbon Street (destroyed by fire in 1919).

MARDI GRAS PARADES

Without question, the city's most famous pastime came once a year: Mardi Gras. Mardi Gras balls are as old as the city itself, but Mardi Gras parades, for which the city is so well known, didn't arrive on the scene until the 1820s. They were pleasant, colourful events featuring costumed and masked Creoles, who made their way through the streets from the opera house to some grand salon for an evening ball. These 'cavalcades' gradually degenerated into packs of masked thugs who roamed the streets throwing flour into unsuspecting faces. The first parade using vehicles or 'floats' was in 1839 when an odd assortment of wagons and carriages paraded through the American and Creole sections of the city.

The city's first carnival organisation was formed not by Creoles but by upper crust Anglo-American businessmen, who were quickly succumbing to 'decadent' Creole ways. In 1857 they founded the Mistick Krewe of Comus, adopting the spelling 'krewe' because they felt it had an Old English flavour. Comus held its first parade that year with Milton's *Paradise Lost* as its theme. By the end of the nineteenth century, Mardi Gras was celebrated by everyone: white, black, American, Creole, as well as new immigrants from Europe, Catholics, even Protestants.

DISEASE

New Orleans was indeed a place where one could make a fortune and enjoy life's pleasures. But poverty and disease were never far away. Yellow fever took thousands of lives. In 1856 some 2,700 people died of the fever, more than 1,000 from cholera, and 652 from tuberculosis. By far the most devastating yellow fever epidemic hit the city in the summer of 1853. Over 8,000 men, women and children died that summer. Hardest struck were the destitute Irish and German immigrants just arriving in America. The Irish had survived the Potato Famine and a treacherous Atlantic crossing only to end up in shallow mud graves along the levee. They died in such staggering numbers that open wagons rode through the streets picking up heat-swollen bodies. In stacks of 50 or more they were carted to cemeteries and shallow graves.

THE MULTICULTURAL METROPOLIS

In the decades immediately preceding the Civil War, Irish and German immigrants arrived in the city by the thousands. Most came by ship from Liverpool, Le Havre, Bremen and Hamburg, on voyages lasting up to six weeks. Packed into steerage, many did not survive the crossing. By 1860 the Irish population in the city had reached 25,000. Both Irish and Germans found homes in the newly emerging political parties. Pitched street battles between the anti-immigrant Native American Party, 'Know-Nothings' (former Whigs) and Democrats were common. A section of Uptown New Orleans is still called the Irish Channel for its once large concentration of Irish immigrants and their descendants. Every year, those of Irish extraction still hit the streets with their New Orleans-style St Patrick's Day parade, a spectacle that would make the lads back home blush (*see chapter* **By Season**).

Two unique segments of the New Orleans population were the Creoles and the 'free people of colour'. In colonial times, the term Creole (from the Spanish *criollo*) meant a person of European ancestry born in the colonies. The term altered as times changed, shifting from a purely racial meaning. In early nineteenth century New Orleans, 'Creole' came to mean anyone descended from European colonists, black or white, creating the overlapping and confusing castes of Creoles, Creoles of colour and free people of colour (who

The Battle of New Orleans

If the Americans had lost the Battle of New Orleans (depicted, right), it would have meant total devastation for the city. Not from the invading British but from winner-take-all US commandant Andrew Jackson who was ready to burn New Orleans rather than lose it. Luckily, Jackson's ragamuffin army prevailed in the 1814-15 battle and New Orleans was untouched. The irony of the battle was that a peace treaty had been signed two weeks before it was fought, but word only reached America a month later.

The battlefield is now at the edge of the town of Chalmette, in St Bernard Parish, about a 15-minute drive from the French Quarter (for details, see chapter **Sightseeing**), with a hulking industrial smokestack looming to the south and oil refineries dotting the river landscape. Still, it's easy to imagine the battlefield as it appeared to Jackson and the British commander, Major General Sir Edward Pakenham (Wellington's brother-in-law). Pakenham brought his 10,000 battle-tested redcoats downriver of New Orleans through an overland route and planned to march into the city.

Jackson checked the British juggernaut with a daring night-time attack on 23 December 1814.

The two armies faced each other nine miles (14.5 km) south of the city, amid sugarcane fields and swamps. Jackson established a fortified line at a natural bottleneck on the Rodriguez Canal between the Chalmette and Villere plantations. With the river on one side and cypress swamp on the other, the Americans lined up behind a mud rampart and carefully placed artillery.

The British attacked on 8 January 1815, counting on superior numbers, strong artillery and disciplined troops to overwhelm the Americans. Instead, the assault was a disaster, with confusion on the field and the loss of key commanders. Pakenham and his second-in-command, Major General Samuel Gibbs, were killed, and the number three man, General John Keane, was badly wounded. British losses were more than 2,000 while the Americans reported only 13 killed. British troops on the West Bank did put the Americans to rout but Jackson had clearly carried the day.

---

were not necessarily Creoles). With the changeover to US government, the designation took on a new edge, separating the Creoles from the *arriviste* Americans.

The most fascinating segment of the New Orleans community were the free people of colour. They included tradesmen, shopkeepers, cabinetmakers, plantation owners, artists, journalists, land speculators and investors. One such was Norbert Rillieux, a Paris-educated engineer and cousin of the French Impressionist painter Edgar Degas. Degas's mother was born in New Orleans. One of his great uncles had a long-lasting liaison with a free woman of colour that produced several children, all of whom became prominent in their own fields. The lifestyles of the free blacks paralleled that of their white counterparts and relatives. Ironically, many volunteered to fight for the Confederacy during the early years of the Civil War.

The Civil War

New Orleans was riding high on a wave of prosperity by the end of the 1850s. Banks were strong, cotton and sugar crops were setting new records, and British textile mills were buying all the cotton they could get. The nation, however, was racing towards civil war. New Orleans's adherence to the Southern cause was a bit confusing. Not only had

it prospered under US economic protection, but its commercial and family connections with the northeast were greater than in any other Southern city.

By the time the Civil War came in 1861, most New Orleanians fully supported the Confederacy. In January of that year, Louisiana seceded from the Union. Less than three months later, war began when Southern troops under the command of New Orleans-born General Pierre Gustave Toutant Beauregard opened fire on Fort Sumter in Charleston, South Carolina. A month later the Union fleet blockaded the mouth of the Mississippi River.

New Orleans remained in the Confederacy for little more than a year. In April 1862, Union warships, commanded by 'Damn the Torpedoes' David Glasgow Farragut, came up the river, bypassing the two protecting forts and dropped anchor in front of the city. Farragut trained his guns on the city and demanded its surrender. When city officials refused, Farragut sent a detachment ashore, cut down the rebel flag and hoisted the Stars and Stripes. For the remainder of the war, New Orleans was under military rule.

The most colourful character to emerge from this era was the Yankee military commander, Major General Benjamin 'Silver Spoons' or 'Beast' Butler, a Massachusetts politician turned army general. New Orleanians hated him for insulting the women of New Orleans in his infamous General Order 28.

Apparently, the ladies snubbed Union soldiers at every opportunity. To remedy this problem, Butler issued an order that any woman who insulted a Union soldier or officer would be 'treated as a woman of the town plying her avocation'. Butler was roundly denounced in Congress and in Britain's Parliament. He got the nickname 'Silver Spoons' because his subordinates, including his brother, made fortunes by confiscating and selling the property of 'disloyal' citizens.

Reconstruction

New Orleans had the distinction of being under Reconstruction longer than any other Southern city. It began in May 1862 and lasted until April 1877 when the last Union soldier withdrew from the city. New Orleans's port and nearby plantations were a source of great wealth for corrupt politicians, 'scalawags' (Southern collaborators) and 'carpet-baggers' (Northern opportunists). The social and political upheaval brought on by Reconstruction was bloody and violent, often leading to open street battles between armies of unreconstructed white New Orleanians and the Reconstruction state government backed by US troops and the largely black Metropolitan Police Force.

But not all was gloomy during the Reconstruction. The French Opera House and the St

Charles Theater played to large audiences. Gambling halls and saloons were full, while temperance societies continued their pre-war struggle against the demon rum. Mardi Gras became even grander. Rex, the grandest of all Mardi Gras parades even today, first rolled in 1871 in honour of the Russian Grand Duke Alexis's visit to New Orleans. Freed slaves and the pre-war free people of colour gained full civil rights, including the right to vote and hold public office. With the withdrawal of federal troops in April 1877, one of the most romanticised periods in the city's history was over.

The Gilded Age

The 1880s and 1890s in New Orleans was an era of boom and bust, corruption and reform, racial retrenchment and labour unrest among former slaves, native whites and newly arriving immigrants. No longer backed by federal troops, blacks lost most of the civil rights gained during Reconstruction. The US Supreme Court in its famous *Plessy v. Ferguson* decision upheld the state's 'separate but equal' segregation laws and the state's 1898 constitution effectively removed most black voters from the roles. White and black New Orleanians would live together but apart for almost half a century until the civil rights movement in the late 1950s and 1960s ended legal segregation.

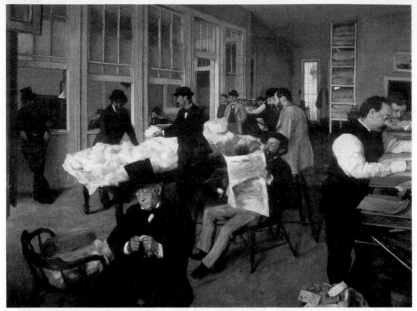

Degas' 'The Cotton Exchange, New Orleans', painted during his visit in the 1870s.

With a population of more than 216,000, the Crescent City was still the South's largest conurbation and officials worked hard at selling it to the nation's business community. The World's Industrial and Cotton Centennial Exposition of 1884-85, held on the site of what is today Audubon Park, showed how far the city had come since Reconstruction.

Despite real social and racial problems, New Orleans was booming. There was a conscious air of what is known as 'boosterism'. Grand mansions sprang up along major avenues; the visual and literary arts flourished; Carnival emerged bigger than ever; government reformers created Storyville, the red-light district, in an attempt to curb widespread prostitution (it was later closed down by the authorities in 1917 for it's corrupting influence on soldiers); and the old American Sector above Canal Street began its transformation into a modern American city.

But not all New Orleans marched hand-in-hand down the booster trail. These years of rapid modernisation inspired in many artists a keen sense for the new city that was emerging around them and a sensitivity to the old city that was slowly passing. Writers George Washington Cable and Grace King drew heavily on old New Orleans for their stories *(see pages 32-33* **Literary New Orleans***)*. Painters drew inspiration from unspoiled swamps, decaying plantations and French Quarter buildings packed with newly arriving Sicilian immigrants.

MAFIA & MOBS

The Gilded Age brought tensions to a familiar subject: immigration. Thousands of poor Sicilians entered the city through its port in the 1880s and 1890s. By 1890, the Sicilian population had reached 30,000. While most of these laboured hard along the docks and in other jobs, a new menace festered in their ranks – the Mafia.

Tensions turned violent in October 1890 with the murder of New Orleans Police Chief David Hennessy, who had declared war on the secret crime society. In his dying breath, Hennessy reportedly said he had been shot by the 'Dagoes'. On the night of the shooting, the city's mayor ordered the arrest of every Sicilian and Italian found in the streets. Nineteen were brought in, but only ten were actually charged. Nine others were indicted as accessories.

When a trial failed to convict any of them, outraged newspapers urged New Orleanians to turn out in force and avenge the murder of Chief Hennessy. Mobs led by prominent citizens stormed the city gaol where they shot and hanged over a dozen Sicilians, including those who had been acquitted by the jury.

New Orleans newspapers generally praised the day's work, but the US government eventually paid the Italian government $25,000 to soothe its indignation over the event. In May 1891, however, a New Orleans grand jury concluded that the Mafia did exist in New Orleans – and that it had murdered Hennessy.

The twentieth century

New Orleans entered the twentieth century with an air of optimism. The nation had just defeated Spain in the Spanish-American War. At home in Louisiana, the Democrats had become the dominant political party. The US Army-backed carpetbaggers and scalawags were gone. But even by the late 1890s, New Orleans had begun to fall behind other American cities. Its national standing by population dropped from ninth to twelfth in 1900 and to sixteenth by 1918.

During this period, jazz was born in the bordellos of Storyville and in the music halls along the city's lakefront. World War II boosted the city's economy, especially in shipbuilding. The famous Higgins landing boat that put millions of Allied troops on beaches from Normandy to Saipan was invented and built at the Higgins Shipyard in New Orleans. After the war, the city assumed a leading role in the nation's petrochemical industry.

In the early 1960s, New Orleans began to change. The civil rights movement hit New Orleans square in the face in 1960 when a federal court finally ordered the city's public schools to desegregate. Six years earlier, the US Supreme Court had declared the 'separate but equal' doctrine unconstitutional, but the city – and the rest of the South – resisted for years.

In November 1960, the city held its breath as four black children, escorted by US federal marshals, broke the colour line for the first time since Reconstruction. The most poignant scene in that dramatic episode was the picture of little six-year-old Ruby Bridges, holding her mother's hand as the two of them walked with armed marshals past a shouting mob.

Civil rights also extended to the ballot box. Beginning in the early 1970s, political power in the city slowly shifted to black voters as their numbers grew. In 1977, in a dramatic break with the past, New Orleanians elected their first black mayor, long-time civil rights advocate Ernest N 'Dutch' Morial. Dutch's son, Marc Morial, was elected to the same office in 1994.

The 1960s and 1970s also saw major changes in the city's demographics as middle-class white and black families moved to the suburbs. New techniques in draining the surrounding marshlands, a new interstate highway system connected to the nearby countryside and new affordable housing opened vast tracts of undeveloped land for city dwellers. Coupled with racial tensions and rising crime rates, this lead to more and more families moving to the 'burbs, leaving the inner city mostly to the poor.

At the same time, however, some young and affluent white and black families remained behind to buy and renovate the 'gingerbread' Victorian cottages Uptown. Since then, entire neighbourhoods have given way to the restoration movement.

THE OIL BOOM...

Throughout the 1970s and early 1980s, the city's port and its petroleum industry primed New Orleans's economic pump. The city entered the 1980s as upbeat as a young priest on the first day of Lent. Good times were ahead, or so its population thought. The **Louisiana Superdome** (*see page 40* **Architecture**) had been built; Poydras Avenue attracted new high-rise office buildings and hotels; oil companies moved in their corporate offices; and the 1984 Louisiana World Exposition 'The World of Rivers', managed the intensity of a six-month-long Mardi Gras. Flags, balloons and street musicians led visitors to the main entrance to be greeted by buxom papier-mâché mythological river deities wrestling with alligators. At night, searchlights, fireworks and green laser beams traced across the sky.

...AND BUST

Unfortunately, the high-flying optimism of the early 1980s crashed and was burnt out by 1986. The state's once-rich petrochemical industries collapsed when OPEC nations dramatically increased oil production, sending prices plummeting. The 1984 World Exposition was an artistic success but a financial flop. The dramatic increase in inner-city crime and crack cocaine chased even more middle-income families to the suburbs. Daily

1920s jazz pioneer Jelly Roll Morton.

St Charles Avenue at the junction of Poydras in the 1920s, before the highrise of the CBD.

newspaper headlines told sobering and depressing stories of a dwindling population, poverty, corrupt policemen, record-breaking murder rates, video poker, failed gambling riverboats, the ups and downs of a permanent land-based casino, shady politicians and cronyism, and political shenanigans in the new gambling industry.

Another event struck at the heart of traditional New Orleans Mardi Gras. In 1992, the city council passed a tough anti-discrimination ordinance, denying parade permits to carnival and social organisations that were not open to all races, genders or ethnic groups. The ordinance was later softened, a bi-racial commission formed, and compromises struck. Yet, the city's oldest carnival krewes – Comus, Momus and Proteus – refused to follow the order and cancelled all parades. Only Rex opened its ranks and continued its parade.

1990s RENAISSANCE

By late 1996 and early 1997, the city's and state's economies, which had diversified somewhat during the oil and gas bust, had begun to make a strong comeback. Tourism and employment were up, crime was down, manufacturing increased, oil and gas prices rose sharply and other industries showed healthy growth.

Despite the city's darker side of life – its assorted wags and reprobates, its crime and poverty – New Orleans has awoken during the past few years to its own creative spirit. It will never be the largest city in the South again, but it has reclaimed its position as a leading centre for the arts. Once home to William Faulkner, Tennessee Williams, Truman Capote and Louis Armstrong, New Orleans now claims a new generation of artists and writers. The Jazz and Heritage Festival, the Tennessee Williams Literary Festival, and the Essence Music Festival (*see chapter* **By Season**) attract thousands of people each year from all over the world. The city now has more art galleries, artists and writers, world-class restaurants and hotels than at any other time in its history. The 'Big Easy', a name for the city coined by black jazz musicians years ago, has experienced a cultural renaissance not seen since its glory days in the 1850s.

In May 1997, a visiting architect eloquently described New Orleans for a local newspaper: 'Here, beyond the streets and buildings, there are neigh-

Key events

1682 French-Canadian Robert Cavelier, Sieur de La Salle, arrives at the mouth of the Mississippi River and claims the territory for France. He names it Louisiana in honour of Louis XIV, King of France.

1699 French-Canadian Pierre Le Moyne, Sieur d'Iberville, arrives with a small fleet and begins French colonisation of the region.

1718 New Orleans founded and named after France's regent, Philippe, Duc d'Orleans.

1719 Large groups of African slaves and German and Swiss families begin arriving.

1722 Hurricane destroys much of the early city.

1727 Ursuline nuns open a school for girls, a tradition that continues to this day.

1751 Jesuits introduce sugarcane to Louisiana.

1762 In the secret Treaty of Fontainebleau, France cedes New Orleans and all of Louisiana west of the Mississippi River to Spain.

1763 France cedes Louisiana east of the Mississippi to Britain.

1768 French Louisiana colonists rebel and drive Spanish governor from Louisiana.

1769 New Spanish governor Alexander O'Reilly executes rebel leaders.

1777 Spanish governor Bernardo de Galvez begins aid to the American Revolution effort against Britain.

1788 Much of New Orleans destroyed by fire.

1792 & 1794 Devastating fires again destroy parts of the city.

1794 St Louis Cathedral dedicated.

1800 Spain cedes Louisiana back to France.

1803 France sells Louisiana to the United States.

1812 (January 10) The steamboat *New Orleans*, the first on the western waters, arrives in New Orleans.

1812 (April 30) Louisiana becomes the 18th state of the Union.

1815 US forces under Andrew Jackson defeat British at the Battle of New Orleans.

1832 Yellow fever and cholera kill more that 5,000 New Orleanians.

1839 First Mardi Gras parade held.

1853 Yellow fever epidemic kills more than 8,000.

1857 First Comus Mardi Gras parade rolls.

1861 Louisiana secedes from the US and later joins the Confederacy.

1862 US fleet captures New Orleans during the Civil War.

1865 Civil War ends.

1868 Louisiana rejoins the Union.

1872 First Rex Mardi Gras parade rolls.

1874 Street battle between White League and Metropolitan Police on Canal Street.

1877 Reconstruction ends in New Orleans as federal troops withdrawn.

1878 Yellow fever epidemic kills over 5,000 in Louisiana.

1891 Mob lynches Italians in aftermath of the murder of Police Chief Hennessy.

1897 City creates Storyville red-light district.

1915 New Orleans devastated by hurricane and flood.

1929 Great Depression begins.

1941 World War II brings to New Orleans's shipbuilding industry.

1960 New Orleans's public schools desegregated.

1965 Hurricane Betsy heavily damages the city.

1975 New Orleans Superdome completed.

1978 Ernest N 'Dutch' Morial becomes New Orleans's first black mayor.

1984 New Orleans's world's fair, 'The World of Rivers', held.

1991 Legalised gambling returns to New Orleans when voters approve new state lottery.

1992 Three of the city's oldest carnival organisations boycott Mardi Gras when the City Council passes an anti-discrimination law.

1994 Marc Morial, son of former Mayor Dutch Morial is elected Mayor.

1995 Harrah's Casino abruptly closes, shutting down the only non-floating casino in New Orleans and calling into question the whole issue of the city as a gambling centre.

1998 Marc Morial re-elected Mayor.

---

bourhoods and communities, people and personalities and lives and experiences that are… the very things some critics regret that modern America left behind as it paved the expressways, fled to the suburbs, protected property values and shut out the world… There is pride of ownership here, but this is also a city of rental property – singles, doubles, four-plexes, townhouses, carriage houses, flophouses, slave quarters. The residential buildings are tight together, close to the street, enveloped with porches and balconies, patios and courtyards. Sounds and smells drift from household to household. People visit and mingle, and truly there is cultural richness, vibrancy and diversity.'

New Orleans has a soul unlike any other city in North America. Like a heavily rouged old diva, she charms you, seduces you and manipulates you. She is raw emotion behind a tattered veil of elegance.

New Orleans Today

Crime, poverty and ineptitude dog the city, but New Orleans retains its special magic while managing to reinvent itself in ways no one could predict.

'I speak with pain of her decay. [New Orleans] is fading, moldering, crumbling – slowly but certainly... in the midst of the ruined paradise of Louisiana.' (Lafcadio Hearn, 1877)

The fading, moldering, crumbling and decay of New Orleans so sadly trumpeted by Lafcadio Hearn more than 120 years ago continues apace. Without fail, each passing year, every new decade provides more evidence of the impossibility of the city's survival. Certainly the 1990s have tested the soul of New Orleans. In 1994 New Orleans was the murder capital of the US. Not only was crime dangerously out of control but the city's police force was part of the crime wave. From 1993 to 1998 more than 50 NOPD officers were charged with felonies. Other ominous signs include more than 37,000 abandoned buildings within the city limits, a school system with the lowest statewide scores in a low-literacy state, an economy far too dependent on the high-volume, low-paying service industry, and, as if to seal the doomsday predictions for New Orleans, the city has been declared America's most obese, meaning the metropolis with the most candidates for heart attack and early death.

Typically, it was the 'most obese' label that stung New Orleanians to the quick.

'It's because of the quality, and the quantity of great food,' one indignant citizen told a *New York Times* reporter, hinting heavily that the rest of the nation was simply jealous of the great cuisine in New Orleans.

CAPITAL OF CRIME

Which is not to say that the other problems have been ignored. It's just that in the New Orleans view of life, the eternal virtues are food, music, family and fun. First things first, in other words. The enormity of the troubles that loomed over New Orleans from every angle also made it easier to deal with smaller issues. Crime, always a concern in American cities, seemed to many to have exploded in New Orleans in the mid-1980s. It went fairly quickly from a place where hardly any middle class people (black or white) ever experienced crime, to a city of fear. Carjackings, house break-ins, muggings, rapes, murders and other horrors crept out of the back streets into previously inviolate neighbourhoods. Burglar bars were standard in every New Orleans home by the early 1990s. A cottage industry of designer bars even grew up among local decorators.

Urban crime is an old and sadly familiar story in the US but it took on a particular edge in New Orleans when the police force was shown to be thoroughly compromised. Unlike the Machiavellian machinations of 'the Godfather' cop corruption, New Orleans police were shockingly small-minded and stupid. One of the most scandalous cases involved a vice cop who was recruited to protect

---

A city called...

Talk show host David Letterman wanted to bring his New York-based program to New Orleans for a week, but was overridden by accountants who deemed the trip too costly. Instead, Letterman flew in more than 400 New Orleanians to be the entire show audience on 15 May 1998. In honour of their visit, the famous Letterman Top Ten list was devoted to renaming the Big Easy:

10. Planet Hangover
9. The Topless Metropolis
8. The Least Annoying French Place on Earth
7. Your Buddy on the Big Muddy
6. John Goodman's Favourite Hangout
5. Where the Saints go 6 and 10
4. Attack of the Drunken Fraternity Boys
3. The Small Difficult
2. The City that Sobriety Forgot
1. Jambalayapalooza

Multi million-dollar gamble: the shell of the land-based casino stands empty.

an illicit drug warehouse. Easily seduced by big money, the cop didn't have a clue that the 'criminals' he was dealing with were actually federal officers investigating NOPD corruption. In between his warehouse guarding and actual police duty, he arranged for a small-time criminal to kill a prostitute who had filed a complaint against him. The corrupt officer talked freely about the arrangements over the mobile phone given to him by the ersatz drug criminals. He was arrested, tried and convicted along with several other officers he had enlisted in the drug warehouse protection team.

Even more bizarre was the case of a rookie policewoman who teamed up with a teenage felon to rob a Vietnamese grocery store. She boasted that it would be the perfect crime because she had worked there as a security guard during her off-duty hours. Instead, it was a complete botch, with the inept Bonnie and Clyde killing two members of the Vietnamese family *and* the policewoman's partner who was working as an off-duty guard at the store.

Even the most unforgiving, Old Testament foe of crime recognised that the city's poverty was at the root of the crime rate's steep increase. New Orleans was particularly desperate at the dawning of the 1990s, after the oil business collapse of the 1980s and the erosion of the port, historically the anchor of the New Orleans economy.

GAMBLING ON THE FUTURE

Legalised gambling was presented as the answer to all the city's troubles. Although many areas in Louisiana were eager for gambling, New Orleans was lukewarm to the idea. Still, casinos were dying to set up shop in the city despite the restrictive laws that decreed all gambling venues must be onboard vessels that would actually sail. It was somehow thought that riverboats would isolate gambling from the larger community and, in the case of New Orleans, would not drain customers from already established entertainment businesses. Governor Edwin Edwards, the wily Cajun and self-professed lover of gambling, was able to engineer a deal that allowed for one 'land-based' casino in New Orleans. The competition for that licence was very heated, with Harrah's, the famous Nevada gambling business, finally named winner. The land-based casino, promised its supporters, would reinvent New Orleans with jobs, ripple-effect affluence and tourists!

New Orleanians, sceptical by nature, were unconvinced, but in the time-honoured passive way of the South, shrugged and carried on.

In many ways, 1995 seemed to be a breaking point for New Orleans. Legalised gambling was failing, despite the millions of dollars poured into the riverboats and land-based casino, and police-crime scandals were so bad many citizens refused to even read about the newest one. Mayor Marc Morial

The symbols of the Crescent City light up City Hall at night.

Louisiana lingo

For a list of culinary terms, *see p115* **Restaurants**.

bayou: (pronounced 'bye-yew'), a marshy tributary of a river or lake.

Cajun: a descendant from the Acadians – French exiles from Nova Scotia who settled in Louisiana in the 1760s; also the French dialect, the food and the music they popularised.

crawfish: freshwater crustacea, also known as mudbugs and sometimes spelt crayfish.

Creole: a descendant of European (especially French and Spanish) settlers of the Caribbean basin; 'Creole of colour' was used for those with black ancestors. The term is beginning to re-emerge in local vocabulary, in cooking for example.

debris: served with your roast beef po-boy; all the delicious bits and pieces of meat and gravy that pile up during preparation. Always say 'yes' when asked in a cafe, 'You want debris wit dat?'

Dixie: geographically, the Old South; as an adjective for anything of the South. The term may have come from *dix*, the French word for ten, which appeared on the first $10 bills issued by the Citizen's Bank of Louisiana, or may have been derived from the Mason-Dixon Line, the surveyors' 1767 line between Pennsylvania and Maryland that became the demarcation of North and South between the states.

Faubourg: means 'suburb' in French and 'neighbourhood' in New Orleans.

go cup: plastic cups handed out at bars for patrons to take their drinks away with them.

gris-gris: powders used in the voodoo charms; a spell.

king cake traditional ring-shaped oval pastry, decorated in Mardi Gras colours (purple, green and gold) and containing a small plastic baby Jesus.

krewe: Mardi Gras parade organisation or 'club'.

lagniappe: a baker's dozen – something extra. The title of the *Times-Picayune*'s weekend entertainment supplement.

laissez les bons temps rouler: let the good times roll: a popular Cajun expression.

levee: embankments built up along the Mississippi River to control or, at least, limit flooding.

makin' groceries: shopping for groceries.

Mardi Gras: while the term can be used to mean both the pre-Lenten season and 'Fat Tuesday' itself (the last day of celebration before Ash Wednesday, the first day of Lent), New Orleanians usually use Mardi Gras to mean Fat Tuesday and **Carnival** to denote the season. *See also chapter* **Mardi Gras**.

neutral ground: the strip of land that divides the lanes of a street or highway (the median). Usually grassy or landscaped.

pirogue: (pronounced 'pee-roe') Cajun flat-bottomed boat, ideal for the shallow waters of the bayou.

quadroon: an archaic, romanticised term for a person of mixed black and white parentage, meaning they are one-quarter black. There are similar terms such as **octoroon**, meaning one-eighth black.

second line: (noun and verb) the friends and family members who follow behind the coffin and band in a jazz funeral.

shotgun house: small, wood-frame house built with rooms one behind another, with no hallway. So called because a shotgun (supposedly) could be fired through the front door and out the back without ever hitting anything. A **double shotgun** is a duplex (maisonette) and a **camelback shotgun** means a partial second storey (usually bedrooms) has been added at the back of the structure. *See also chapter* **Architecture**.

streetcar: in New Orleans the public transport electric cars are always 'streetcars', never 'trolleys' or 'trams'.

street name pronunciation: New Orleanians have their own way of pronouncing fairly common street names. For example, Bienville is 'bee-en-vil', Burgundy is 'Bur-GUN-dee', Calliope is 'callie-ope', Chartres is 'charters', and Milan 'millen'.

With Orleans, when referring to the parish, it's pronounced 'Or-leens'; when it's the city, it's always 'Noo Or-lins'. The mysterious Tchoupitoulas Street is pronounced 'chop-a-TOOL-us'.

throw: the largesse of Mardi Gras; the trinkets thrown from the parade floats – plastic beads, cups, toys, candy.

Vieux Carré: literally the 'old quarter', the French name for the French Quarter.

where y'at? typical New Orleanian greeting. Native Orleanians who speak with the local Brooklynesque accent are known as **Yats** from this greeting.

yeh, you right: Yat small-talk response to almost any comment.

zydeco: dance music of south-western Louisiana's black, French-speaking Creoles; thought to be a corruption of the first two words of the old dance tune 'les haricots n'est pas salé'.

---

brought in a new police chief, the avuncular Richard Pennington from Washington, DC, to a general attitude of 'what difference can one man make?'

Meanwhile, Harrah's abruptly closed down the new casino, temporarily located in the city auditorium in Armstrong Park, and halted work on the multi million-dollar new building taking shape at the foot of Canal Street.

THE CLEAN-UP BEGINS

Although not related, the two events marked a turning point. Pennington, with the help of anti-crime consultants, set about cleaning house at the NOPD while launching a campaign for higher pay, the employment of more police officers and the installation of a sophisticated computer tracking system for crime. The gambling bust ironically gave the city a sense of purpose and righteousness. Local citizens interviewed randomly about Harrah's failure told TV interviewers that they knew all along gambling wouldn't work in New Orleans. The crime rate began to drop after 1995 and, after some peaks caused by laid-off casino workers, so did the unemployment rate, although it's still high.

Tourism continues to thrive in the French Quarter, making the service industry the city's biggest employer.

People now talk about the bad times of 'the '90s' as if they were years away. There's a renewed sense of security, though laced with the usual urban wariness. Crime, always at its most brutal and intense at the lower rungs of society, has retreated somewhat to drug dealers shooting each other and grudge matches between always explosive young men. While the tourism-convention business still provides the bulk of blue collar jobs, there's hopeful talk of modest advancements such as training the young unemployed to be chefs rather than fast-food workers and the increasing solidity of the oil and gas business with its higher-paying jobs.

But the promising signs of urban flowering and recovery aren't the real story of New Orleans. The remarkable thing about the city is that it has always survived despite all the odds stacked against it: climate, terrain, history, acts of God (hurricanes, yellow fever epidemics). And, it has not only survived, but kept its loony genius for generating pleasure intact. New Orleans has gone through colonisation, war, poverty, racial turmoil and the merciless demands of late twentieth-century 'progress', yet has celebrated the world's best Mardi Gras for almost 300 years and invented jazz.

In some kind of collective unconscious drive to power, the city has always excelled at what it truly values. Anyone who has dealt with the famously inefficient bureaucracy of the city government is stunned to see the well-oiled municipal machine

that handles the spectacle of Carnival and the crushing crowds of Jazz Fest, the Super Bowl and other gargantuan annual events. This is a place that can't figure out how to install left-turn lanes in traffic but can put a police officer on every block for a Mardi Gras parade and then move it along as neatly as NASA launching a moon shot. New Orleans is ages behind even the most backward rural hamlets in curbside recycling but deploys SWAT teams of street cleaners during Carnival, often giving city streets their best cleaning all year.

REJUVENATING JAZZ

At the close of the twentieth century, the New Orleans talent for reinventing itself is at it's most impressive. While jazz is sometimes thought to be in danger of becoming a calcified art form relegated to Preservation Hall, young black working-class kids have found new paths into the old medium through the revival of brass bands and school jazz programs. They may play with a hip hop sensibility and combine the music with rap, but unlike their peers in most US cities they're not slaves to radio, MTV and other received music. They see themselves as creators – all potential heirs to the Neville Brothers.

Similarly, in other areas, the New Orleans sense of hubris works in unexpected ways. A lack of capital and conservative ways kept the city from ripping itself up and turning old neighbourhoods into urban renewal experiments, one of the greatest American city-killers. New Orleans isn't sliced up by expressways and freeways. In fact, neighbourhood activists were able to have one odious on-ramp to the Crescent City Connection bridge dismantled after many years of lobbying. Now an area once blighted by traffic and the sheer ugliness of the girders has come back to life and Coliseum Square on Camp Street is poised to regain its old prestige.

FOOD, GLORIOUS FOOD

New Orleans cooking has become some of the most exciting in America, another unexpected display of brilliance. Though it is affectionately called the city of '500 restaurants and five recipes' by foodies, local chefs and restaurants moved boldly into new ideas in the late 1980s and their supposedly traditional customers happily followed. While it may seem odd to point to cooking as a sign of urban health, it's an important New Orleans yardstick. The indignant New Orleanian who protested to the *New York Times* reporter that the city's corpulence was a badge of honour suggested he go to the St Thomas housing project where he would find red beans and rice as fabulous as in any restaurant in the city. New Orleans, he was saying, is rich in all the important ways.

While New Orleans continues to lose population to the suburbs, it continues to draw young people from all over the US – and the world – to find themselves as artists. Musicians, writers, painters, sculptors and those with vague ideas of just being creative are drawn to New Orleans, giving the city a continual infusion of new ideas, new art and new energy. Their art remains mostly below the mainstream eye-level but it keeps small clubs going, quirky art galleries opening and fuels the boom in coffeehouses.

Unlike other magnet cities, this energy and yearning and growing-up doesn't translate into political terms. In the history of New Orleans there are periodic calls for reform and reorganisation, demands to throw the bums out and start anew. Since the 1970s the city has been a black majority municipality, and it has had a black mayor since 1978 and a black-majority city council since the 1980s. Yet this change hasn't really altered New Orleans. The changes are literally cosmetic (white skin to black skin). The reason for this is that no one really wants the city to change very much. A safe city would be nice, a prosperous city would be lovely, but these are details. Everyone, native and newcomer, wants the essential New Orleans of sensuality and hyper-individuality to continue, wherever it leads. As Lafcadio Hearn said: 'Better to live here in sackcloth and ashes than own the whole state of Ohio.' It's a wish that New Orleans takes all too literally.

The towers of the Central Business District, seen from Algiers Point across the river.

By Season

There's more to celebrate in New Orleans than Mardi Gras: festivals devoted to strawberries or goats share the calendar with those highlighting music, art and literature.

Before visiting south Louisiana it's worth considering the weather, and how it might affect your physical and mental health. New Orleans is located in the subtropics, but saying that doesn't even begin to sum up just how miserably hot and humid the summer and autumn can be. A favourite local cry is, 'It's not the heat, it's the humidity;' yet so far does that come from describing the breathless, dripping summers that a popular play on the saying is, 'It's not the heat; it's the stupidity.'

Whatever the problem, with humidity factored in, temperatures in New Orleans during July, August and September can hover well above 100°F: suddenly, you understand why Tennessee Williams's characters are so neurotic and grumpy.

And yet, for some, this is the best time to visit the city. A steamy New Orleans summer night is simultaneously sensual and oppressive, almost physically heavy. It's hard to breathe, or to think, and that's sort of what it's all about. A long, cold cocktail might be nice… and now you're really in the Big Easy. If romanticism doesn't mean as much to you as comfort, stick to winter and spring. In winter the temperature rarely drops below 55°F and in spring the warm days are breezy and the city blooms with tropical flowers.

Whenever you visit, you are likely to hit one of the dozens of jamborees that fill the Louisiana and New Orleans calendar. From festivals of French heritage to those celebrating berries (blue and straw) and even ones that herald goats and frogs, there is truly something for everyone.

Below we have included an address and phone number for each event, together with a date, where possible; for the most up-to-date information on seasonal events, consult the **New Orleans Visitors Bureau** (566 5011/1-800 672 6124/www. nawlins.com). For out-of-town information, try the **Louisiana Department of Culture, Recreation & Tourism** (342 8119), or check local newspapers.

Spring

For the **New Orleans Jazz & Heritage Festival**, *see page 22*. For **Mardi Gras**, *see page 25*.

Black Heritage Festival
Audubon Institute, 6500 Magazine Street, New Orleans, LA 70118 (861 2537). **Date** 2nd weekend in March.
This is the city's biggest celebration of its strong African-American roots. The Black Heritage Festival is, pretty much, exactly what it says. The festival includes music, food and art, as well as spoken word presentations and performances at a variety of locations throughout the city, including Audubon Zoo, Riverwalk and the Louisiana State Museum.

St Patrick's Day
Molly's at the Market, 1107 Decatur Street, at Ursulines Street (525 5169). **Date** weekend before the 3rd Tue in March.
There is simply nothing like St Patrick's Day in New Orleans. The city's Irish heritage is surprisingly long and the town brings its own unique twist to the celebration of Ireland's patron saint. There is a block party on the day itself (17 March) based around **Parasol's Bar & Restaurant** (*see p195* **Nightlife**), but the first parade starts on the previous Friday at 6pm at **Molly's at the Market** (*see p189* **Nightlife**) and covers the French Quarter. On Saturday, a parade starts at 1pm at the corner of Magazine and Race Streets and goes down Magazine Street through the Irish Channel. Ingredients for making Irish stew are tossed from massive floats. Cabbages, turnips, carrots and onions hurtle through the air to an eagerly waiting crowd. Bring a bag and you can take home dinner. Bizarre – and great fun.

St Joseph's Day
New Orleans Visitors Bureau, 1520 Sugar Bowl Drive, New Orleans, LA 70112 (566 5011/1-800 672 6124). **Date** weekend after 17 March.
Italian life in New Orleans is as important and unusual as its Irish heritage. The two cultures are in many ways inextricably intertwined in the city, so it is appropriate that the celebrations of the two patron saints fall close together. St Joseph's Day is celebrated with the creation of massive altars

National holidays

New Year's Day (1 Jan)
Martin Luther King Day (third Mon in Jan)
Presidents' Day (third Mon in Feb)
Memorial Day (last Mon in May)
Independence Day (4 July)
Labor Day (first Mon in Sept)
Columbus Day (second Mon in Oct)
Veterans' Day (11 November)
Thanksgiving Day (last Thur in Nov)
Christmas Day (25 Dec)

*The block party begins: the city has its own bizarre version of **St Patrick's Day** (page 19).*

made of food inside Italian churches and homes. Huge free dinners are served to all takers at Italian churches and there are several parades.

Tennessee Williams
New Orleans Literary Festival
5500 Prytania Street, suite 217, New Orleans, LA 70115 (581 1144/fax 529 2430/twfest@gnofn.org). **Date** end March.
Writers famous and not so famous take part in this celebration of the works of Louisiana's beloved author. *See p34* **Literary New Orleans**.
Website: www.gnofn.org/~twfest

French Quarter Festival
French Quarter Festival Office, 100 Conti Street, at S Peters Street, New Orleans, LA 70130 (522 5730/ fax 522 5711). **Date** early April.
The French Quarter Festival is how many people (visitors and locals) like to imagine the French Quarter: bands playing, wonderful smelling food being cooked in Jackson Square, well-behaved people dancing in the streets. The festival is a tourism gimmick designed to stir up the slow patch between Carnival and Jazz Fest but it has developed its own personality. The crowds are older than the Jazz Festers and the music is heavily tilted toward trad jazz but it's a Very Nice time in the Quarter all the same.
Website: www.fqfestivals.org

Crescent City Classic
8200 Hampson Street, suite 217, New Orleans, LA 70118 (861 8686/fax 861 8687).
Date 2nd Sat in April.
The New Orleans version of the Boston Marathon. The Crescent City classic is a 10,000m race from Jackson Square to Audubon Park. It passes some of the city's most famous architecture along the way, but everybody's moving too fast to enjoy it. Most of the city turns out to cheer the runners on.

Julia Street Jump
Information from Contemporary Arts Center, see p92.
Date 1st Sat in May.
Dozens of art galleries in the Warehouse District open their doors and wine bottles in honour of the city's artists at this annual event. The area boasts New Orleans's largest concentration of art galleries, so it offers a great opportunity to see a wide variety of local art. Some of the city's top bands turn out to play during the street party and food and drink are sold during this arty street fête.

Summer

Reggae Riddums Festival
PO Box 6156, New Orleans, LA 70174 (367 1313).
Date 2nd weekend in June.
This is a mini-Sun Splash (*very* mini), with three days of sun and music celebrating the culture of the Caribbean. Held out-of-doors in the festival area of City Park, the turnout is generally fairly small, but the crowd is a lot of fun. In addition to reggae music performed by artists from around the world, the festival features art, crafts and food from the islands.

Go 4th on the River
New Orleans Visitors Bureau, 1520 Sugar Bowl Drive, New Orleans, LA 70112 (566 5011/1-800 672 6124).
Date 4 July.
New Orleans celebrates the nation's independence with characteristic individuality. Rather than a backyard barbecue, there are jazz bands on Bourbon Street, thousands of people throng the narrow streets from shop to bar and back again and, at sunset, there's a huge fireworks show on the river by the French Quarter.

Essence Music Festival
Black Tourism Network, 1520 Sugar Bowl Drive, New Orleans, LA 70112 (523 5652). **Date** early July.

Essence, a slick magazine for African-American women, decided to take its message on the road in 1995, organising the Essence Festival. The magazine brought in big names in music, bestselling writers, famous personalities and mixed all the elements into a frothy four days of concerts, panel discussions, book signings and shopping sprees. 'I think every black middle class woman in America is here', said one startled hotel manager. Held in July, when the hotels are usually empty, Essence has become an important date on the New Orleans calendar. It's *Waiting to Exhale* [illegible] in New Orleans in recent years, but might change city in the future.

White Linen Night
Information from Contemporary Arts Center, see p92.
Date 1st Sat in Aug.
This is an elegant version of Julia Street Jump, with all the city's artists, art lovers and thousands of hangers-on turning out to celebrate the New Orleans art scene at the CAC. The event is a play on Tennessee Williams-style Southernness, with everybody draped in white fabric, particularly linen. The result combines timeless elegance with a very modern frivolity, a half-dozen bands, crowded bars, sultry heat and humidity. Loads of fun.

Autumn

For the annual **New Orleans Film and Video Festival** in October, *see page 174* **Film**.

Southern Decadence
Information from the Lesbian & Gay Community Center, see p177. **Date** weekend before Labor Day (1st Mon Sept).
Just five years ago, this parade and weekend-long party was a tiny, tacky, hysterically funny but local affair. Today it's an enormous, tacky, hysterically funny event drawing participants from around the globe. Decadence is one of the city's largest gay events and its Sunday afternoon parade is a spectacle not to be missed. It's really nothing more than a French Quarter-wide drag show, but the costumes are astonishing, with cut-outs in all the wrong places leaving absolutely nothing to the imagination. Throughout the weekend the city's gay bars are in high fever and dancing continues until everyone passes out. The parade takes all afternoon, so if you missed it you were drunker than they were.

New Orleans Lesbian & Gay Pride Festival
New Orleans Alliance for Pride (phone/ fax 949 9555/NGaypride@aol.com).
Date end Sept/early Oct.
A small but ever-growing celebration of gay life. In 1998 the festival moved to Armstrong Park – a change of venue from Washington Park where it has been held for almost two decades.

Art for Arts' Sake
Information from Contemporary Arts Center, see p92.
Date 1st Sat in Oct.
The scene: the city streets. The time: end of summer. The shriek: 'Darlin' I love your tan!' Kiss, hug, move on, whisper to companion: 'South of France my ass! She got that tan freeloading at some tacky condo in Gulf Shores!' Art is not just for art's sake at this end-of-summer street party but an excuse to check out who's been where, doing what and with whom all summer long. Galleries go to great efforts to showcase their best and/or splashiest art and the art community organises really good parties. The hot spots are in the Warehouse District around the Julia Street-CAC axis and on Magazine Street between Antonine and Napoleon. There's free food and drink in the galleries and bands in the street, demonstrating the great New Orleans art form, partying.

Hallowe'en
Information from Hallowe'ens in New Orleans (945 5546).
Date Sat nearest to 31 October.
The city goes full-throttle at Hallowe'en, with a huge variety of options ranging from hanging out with Anne Rice to costume-watching in the French Quarter. Anne Rice's Hallowe'en party, called the Gathering of the Coven, has been an annual event since 1989, with thousands coming from all over the country to meet at one of her many houses. The Vampire Queen herself always attends, as do various celebrities in disguise (phone Anne Rice's Lestat the Vampire fan club on 897 3983 for details; *see also page 34* **Literary New Orleans**). Even larger than that ghoulish happening is the Julia Street Wharf fundraiser for the local AIDS hospice Lazarus House. As many as 10,000 people show up every year for this event, one of the biggest in New Orleans's gay community. Costumes are outrageous, but admission is by invitation only.

Average monthly climate

	high temp		rainfall	% poss sunshine	relative humidity
Jan	69°F	20°C	4.97in	49%	67%
Feb	65°F	18°C	5.23in	51%	64%
March	71°F	21°C	4.73in	57%	60%
April	79°F	26°C	4.50in	65%	59%
May	85°F	29°C	5.07in	69%	59%
June	90°F	32°C	4.63in	67%	60%
July	91°F	32°C	6.73in	61%	62%
Aug	90°F	32°C	6.02in	63%	63%
Sept	87°F	31°C	5.87in	64%	62%
Oct	79°F	26°C	2.66in	72%	59%
Nov	70°F	21°C	4.06in	62%	60%
Dec	64°F	18°C	5.27in	48%	66%

Jazz Fest

The New Orleans Jazz and Heritage Festival, which celebrated its 28th year in 1998, started as a small, four-stage production at Congo Square in Armstrong Park. Since this inauspicious beginning, Jazz Fest has grown into what many consider the premier live music event in the world, featuring over 4,000 musicians on ten stages spread out over the infield of the New Orleans Fair Grounds (*see page 78* **Sightseeing**).

Held annually over the last Friday, Saturday and Sunday in April and the first Thursday to Sunday in May, Jazz Fest attracts music fans from as far abroad as Australia and Japan. Apart from Mardi Gras, the festival draws more visitors to New Orleans than any event and yet maintains a distinctly local feel thanks to the considerable number of local musicians and supporters who attend every year. Despite some big-name acts, the festival draws about 80 per cent of its talent from the large and diverse pool of New Orleans and Louisiana musicians.

Since almost 50 bands and musicians are scheduled to play each day between 11am and 7pm, each stage is empty only long enough for one band to remove their gear and the next to set up. There is no lull in the music and usually the big dilemma for fans is not so much finding a good act to see, but working out how to catch a bit of all the great bands playing simultaneously.

There are essentially two groups of fans: the squatters and the rovers. While fans are not allowed to bring ice chests, tents or large camping equipment with them, blankets, tarps, beach chairs and umbrellas are allowed through the gates. Squatters take advantage of this and park themselves in one spot for the afternoon, usually in front of one of the two stages that feature the big-name acts. This can occasionally lead to minor confrontations – some rovers have been heard to refer to the squatters as 'blanket Nazis' – but as the crowds get more dense, standing shoulder to shoulder becomes the only option anyway.

For the real music fan, however, roving is the only way to go. At a festival where it's possible to see a dozen top bands in the space of eight hours, travelling fast and light is the best choice and is worth the effort of wading through the dense crowds from stage to stage.

The two stages at either end of the Fair Grounds are the biggest, have the largest areas in front of them and typically feature larger-name, nationally touring acts. On the stages between these can be found the WWOZ Jazz Tent, offering contemporary jazz; the Fais

Do-Do Stage, which mostly features Cajun and zydeco bands; Economy Hall, for New Orleans traditional jazz; the Rhodes Gospel Tent, featuring gospel singers, bands and choirs from throughout the south-eastern United States; and Congo Square, showcasing African and Caribbean music. Other stages offer a mixed bag of music ranging from Celtic to klezmer and the Music Heritage stage is the place for interviews with musicians and short performances highlighting the history of music in New Orleans and throughout the world.

As any Jazz Fest veteran knows, great music is not the only reason to visit the Fair Grounds. It also offers a huge selection of local culinary offerings at dozens of small booths. Portions are small enough to allow a good serving of crawfish bread, étouffée, boudin, andouille, cochon du lait or any number of other south Louisiana delicacies. A special section associated with Congo Square offers African and Caribbean foods – usually the best port of call for vegetarians. And recent additions in the Grandstand include booths serving sushi, falafel, houmous, tabouleh and other global dishes. Also to be found in the Grandstand are cooking demonstrations from local chefs, history and folktales from Cajun balladeers and knowledgeable locals and art exhibitions.

When heading out to Jazz Fest, remember that New Orleans can be hot, humid and sunny in the spring, so dress accordingly. Hats and sunscreen are recommended and sunglasses are a must. Sandals and sneakers are the most appropriate footwear, but if it rains the infield gets muddy and since it's the infield of a horse track, the 'mud' isn't really something you want oozing between your toes. There's little cover from either the sun or the rain and when either becomes unbearable the few tents get crowded quickly. Often a brief shower can be a welcome respite from the heat and humidity of late spring.

Performance schedules are available in the Jazz Fest Program on sale at the Fair Grounds, or pick up a copy of *OffBeat*, distributed free outside the gates, which contains feature stories and interviews with Jazz Fest performers as well as complete schedules and club listings for later in the evening. The daily *Times-Picayune* also prints schedules, as does the weekly alternative paper, *Gambit*.

New Orleans Jazz & Heritage Festival
Jazz Fest, PO Box 53407, New Orleans, LA 70153 (522 4786). **Date** last Fri in April to 1st Sun in May.

A New Orleans brass band heralds the beginning of another fiesta.

Winter

Opening Day at the Fair Grounds

New Orleans Fair Grounds Race Course, 1751 Gentilly Boulevard, New Orleans, LA 70119 (944 5515/1-800 262 7983/fax 944 2511).
Date Thanksgiving Day.
Only in New Orleans is the country's Thanksgiving holiday – the symbolic anniversary of the pilgrim's first meals on the continent – universally celebrated at a racetrack. Following a 100-year-old tradition, the New Orleans horse racing season opens on Thanksgiving Day and locals turn out in large family groups by the thousands. The mood is festive, the racetrack is beautiful and a good time is had by all horse or gambling lovers. Beats the hell out of television and family quarrelling all afternoon.

Celebration in the Oaks

City Park, 1 Palm Drive, New Orleans, LA 70124 (482 4888/fax 483 9379).
Date Fri after Thanksgiving until first Sun in Jan.
At Christmastime the giant oaks in City Park are bedecked with lights, huge luminous displays seem to float over the park's bayous and Christmas music fills the air. This is essentially a drive-thru experience, though you can park and walk through the Christmas tree garden to the amusement park and the antique carousel. Christmas lights like you've never seen them before.
Website: www.neworleans.com/citypark

Christmas Eve Bonfires Along the Levee

St James Historical Society, PO Box 426, Gramercy, LA 70052 (869 9752). Fires begin in Gramercy and continue upriver to Convent, along Hwy 44.
Date 24 Dec; fires lit 7pm-midnight.
In a tradition dating back to Christmas during the settlers' days, fires are lit up and down the Mississippi River levee outside New Orleans just after dark to help Santa find his way to the area. Residents in the area spend weeks gathering firewood and build elaborate structures that they then set ablaze, creating huge fires that line the enormous levees on either side of the river. The atmosphere is festive and the fires lining the slow-moving river under a dark sky are a beautiful sight.
Website: www.stjamesla.com

New Year's Eve

In Jackson Square and throughout the city.
Date 31 Dec.
In a city that will take any excuse for a party, this is a big one. Upmarket hotels and restaurants schedule complete evening festivities, bars are decked out in gaudy decorations and at midnight the whole town gathers in Jackson Square to watch a glowing Baby New Year descend to signal the end of the year, followed by fireworks on the Riverwalk. For something a little more out of the ordinary, head over to Bourbon Street at St Ann Street, where much of the gay community gathers at midnight for the tongue-in-cheek 'Drop a Drag Queen', wherein Velma, a rather large drag queen, is slowly lowered down the side of the New Orleans Pub. For years a mostly local event, New Year's Eve is becoming a more organised tourist happening as the city begins to realise that visitors see it as an alternative to New York. Recent festivities have been broadcast live on VH1 and other cable television stations.

Sugar Bowl

Louisiana Superdome, 1500 Sugar Bowl Drive, New Orleans, LA 70112 (525 8573/fax 525 4867).
Date on or near New Year's Day.
One of the plums of American college football, the Sugar Bowl was once held in an old stadium called the Sugar Bowl. Now it's at the Superdome, of course, with two of the leading US collegiate teams fighting it out for post-regular season glory. One team is always from the southeast. Fans of both teams (usually announced in early December) flood into town wearing their college colours and braying team chants as they roll around the French Quarter. Tickets are impossible to get except from scalpers.

Out of town

Audubon Pilgrimage

West Feliciana Historical Society, PO Box 338, St Francisville, LA 70775 (635 6330/1-800 789 4221/fax 635 4626). **Date** 3rd weekend in March.
Tour some of the state's most beautiful antebellum homes in this spring tour that coincides with the blooming of the lush plantation gardens. Virtually all the historic homes in the area are open for touring during the pilgrimage and it's a good time to see some homes that are rarely open to outsiders (admission is $15). Don't miss the gardens at Afton Villa, which are only open in spring and summer.
Website: www.saintfrancisville.la.us

Amite Oyster Festival

Amite Chamber of Commerce, 101 SE Central Avenue, Amite, LA 70422 (phone/fax 748 5537). **Date** 3rd or 4th weekend in March.
The biggest, freshest oysters ever can be sampled at this festival (if, that is, it's a good oyster year). Fresh from the sea, these salty, gooey creatures can be found in every form imaginable – fried, stuffed, baked and, of course, raw. A small-town festival and a good way to mingle with bayou residents. Admission is free.

Ponchatoula Strawberry Festival

PO Box 446, Ponchatoula, LA 70454 (386 6677). **Date** 2nd weekend in April.
Just 30 minutes north-west of New Orleans, Ponchatoula is a tiny bayou town that is home to a large contingent of strawberry growers. It is, in fact, the strawberry capital of Louisiana. Every year the town celebrates its bumper crop with a carnival and a startling variety of foodstuffs made with the berries. Strawberry daiquiri, strawberry pie, strawberry pizza and strawberry sandwiches. You betcha.
Website: www.Ponchatoula.com/strawberry/

Louisiana International Goat Festival

457 Zydeco Road, Opelousas, LA 70570 (1-318 942 2392/fax 1-318 942 9201). **Date** mid-April.
Yes, this is a festival in celebration of goats. Small and admittedly odd, it includes a goat meat cookoff, followed by a goat show, educational seminars and demonstrations and is based in Opelousas, about 30 minutes' drive from Lafayette. The 1998 festival was disrupted when lightning struck the judging tent; fortunately, the only casualty was a goat. There's festive zydeco and Cajun music, too. Yee-haw.
Website: www.zydeco.org

Festival International de Louisiane

PO Box 4008, Lafayette, LA 70502 (1-318 232 8086/fax 1-318 291 5480. **Date** last week in April.
Lafayette is the self-proclaimed Capital of French Louisiana and every year the Cajuns celebrate their roots with a French-oriented international festival. The event has grown to include hundreds of dancers, musicians and artisans from around the world. Great music and terrific Cajun food abound. Well worth investigating.

Breaux Bridge Crawfish Festival

PO Box 25, Breaux Bridge, LA 70517 (1-318 332 6655/fax 1-318 332 5917). **Date** end April/early May.
This is the big daddy of crawfish festivals. This is where they're grown, this is the best place to eat 'em and this is what they call the Crawfish Capital of the World (it's about a 15-minute drive from Lafayette, in the heart of Acadiana). Piles and piles of the little crustaceans are consumed during the weekend. It is also one of the centres for Cajun music, so great bands can often be heard here. People come from all over Louisiana to join in the crawfish-peeling, head-sucking, beer-drinking hysteria. A sight to be seen.
Website: www.crawfest@iamerica.net

FestForAll

730 North Boulevard, at St Joseph Street, Baton Rouge, LA 70802 (1-800 527 6843). **Date** mid-May.
This festivity in the state capital centres around music, art, food and beer. The crowd is considerably different from that which frequents New Orleans' more tourist-oriented events and the festival has a small-town feel. A great place to catch area blues acts and to grab some shrimp bread.
Website: www.bracvb.com

Louisiana Catfish Festival

St Gertrude Catholic Church, PO Box 767, Des Allemands, LA 70030 (758 7542/fax 758 7591). **Date** mid-July.
A festival in celebration of that beloved, bottom-feeding, long-whiskered fish that makes up a substantial portion of the local cuisine. A good excuse to visit this small bayou town south of New Orleans, which was settled by Germans (hence the name) in the midst of French Louisiana. This is, of course, catfish po-boy heaven.

Rayne Frog Festival

PO Box 383, Rayne, LA 70578 (1-318 334 2332/ fax 1-318 334 8341). **Date** early Sept.
This tiny town in the heart of Acadiana, just west of Lafayette, calls itself the Frog Capital of the World. To prove it there are frog murals all over town and this festival of frogness every spring. You can chase frogs, race frogs, call frogs and even eat frogs if you're so inclined. A quirky small-town fest that must be seen to be believed. The date of the festival changes each year, so check before setting out.

Original Southwest Louisiana Zydeco Music Festival

Southern Development Foundation Farm, 457 Zydeco Road, Opelousas, LA 70570 (1-318 942 2392/fax 1-318 942 9201). **Date** Sat before Labor Day.
The place to hear zydeco. Some 13 bands from Texas and Louisiana take to the stage at this one-day outdoor extravaganza in front of crowds of more than 15,000. There are food booths serving Creole dishes, arts and crafts stalls and demonstrations of everything from basket-weaving to storytelling.

Festivals Acadiens

PO Box 52066, Lafayette, LA 70505 (1-318 232 3808/ from US 1-800 346 1958/from Canada 1-800 543 5340/ fax 1-318 232 0161/info@ lafayettetravel.com). **Date** 3rd weekend in Sept.
This is actually a combination of festivals celebrating Cajun culture and heritage, based in Lafayette. The festive weekend includes the Bayou Food Festival, the Festival de Musique Acadienne, the Louisiana Native Crafts Festival and the Acadiana Fair and Trade Show. Cajun food, music and art are the pull and the festival is justifiably renowned, both for its fun and its educational aspects. Eat cochon du lait and then fais-do-do until you drop.

Mardi Gras

Krewes, king cakes and costumes: the Carnival season laid bare.

Mark Twain compared explaining a joke to dissecting a frog: it can be done, but the frog dies in the process. Similar rules apply to Mardi Gras. Too much thinking ruins the fun and blinds visitors to an essential characteristic of New Orleanians – they pretend very well. They pretend being in costume changes everything, that plastic beads look good on everybody and that there's nothing unsettling about wealthy riders throwing cheap trinkets to the rabble below. Even the mayor plays, naming the king of the Krewe of Rex mayor for Fat Tuesday, Mardi Gras day.

For two weeks every year, New Orleans celebrates Mardi Gras, a name that awkwardly describes the whole fortnight and the Tuesday that is the climax of the carnival season, also known as Fat Tuesday. Parades roll every night and riders throw beads, cups, doubloons and toys to the crowds below. While one version of Mardi Gras takes place along St Charles Avenue or Canal Street, another version exists in the French Quarter, a version that more resembles an exotic Spring Break than a tradition-steeped celebration.

HISTORY OF CARNIVAL

Some form of Mardi Gras celebration has been a part of New Orleans life since the early eighteenth century. Under French rule, masked balls were held during the pre-Lent season, though this practice was discontinued under Spanish rule. Even as an American city, masking remained illegal until Creoles petitioned for permission in 1823 to resume masked balls. The first parade took place in 1837, but became a focus for social unrest, making Mardi Gras a controversial celebration for years to come.

In 1857, the **Mistick Krewe of Comus** formed to put on a safer, more stylised parade, calling their organisation a 'krewe' to give it an ancient flavour. It became the prototypical Mardi Gras krewe, holding private, ceremonial balls and creating costumes and a different carnival theme each year. **Rex**, arguably the most famous krewe, was formed in 1872. It has defined Mardi Gras for many years, giving it many of its traditions – the king cake, the purple, gold and green colour scheme, the flag and – perhaps the only tradition New Orleans ignores – its theme song, 'If Ever I Should Cease to Love'. The first satirical krewe, the **Knights of Momus**, formed in 1872, mocking the Reconstruction carpetbaggers in Baton Rouge and the government in Washington DC that had installed them. **Zulu**, the

first and largest black krewe, formed to satirise Rex in 1916. Of these founding krewes, only Rex and Zulu continue to parade, with Zulu preceding Rex down St Charles Avenue on Fat Tuesday.

In 1969, **Bacchus**, the first of the 'superkrewes' was formed by wealthy men brought to town by the oil boom but barred from joining the Establishment krewes who shunned the newcomers for lacking upper-class *je ne sais quois*. Like **Endymion** and **Orpheus** after it, Bacchus aspired to the biggest floats, the longest parades and the most generous 'throws'. The superkrewes found their kings in the entertainment world – rather than New Orleans society – and Danny Kaye led the first Bacchus parade. These parades were seen by the older krewes as challenges not only to the dominance of their organisations, but to the dominance of the old money they represented in New Orleans.

The older krewes received a further challenge in 1992 when the City Council passed an ordinance requiring krewes that used public streets and services to integrate along racial and gender lines. Since secrecy had been a cornerstone for Comus, Rex and Momus, any discussion of their membership would involve making the private public. Momus and Comus quit in protest. Rex continued, as did Zulu, which already included black and white, men and women.

PARADE INFORMATION

Fat Tuesday is always 47 days before Easter, which the Catholic church determined would be on the first Sunday after the full moon after the Spring Equinox. Dates for the next three years are as follows: **16 February 1999**; **7 March 2000**; **27 February 2001**.

Parades maintain a fairly regular schedule; for details of times and routes, check the *Times-Picayune*, or buy a copy of Arthur Hardy's annual *Mardi Gras Guide* ($3.50), which lists krewe information and parade times and routes, as well as details on the history of Carnival.

THE FIRST WEEKEND

Parades once went through the French Quarter, but that practice ended because of the fragile state of the buildings. Now the only parade in the Quarter is the **Krewe du Vieux Carré**, which marches a Saturday or two before the Mardi Gras season. It's an irreverent walking parade with the emphasis on the downscale and the distasteful. Floats – such as they are – are built on wagons and grocery carts, and like the costumes they look as if they'll come apart when the spit dries or the tape peels. The Krewe du Vieux Carré likes its satire raw and juvenile and the best throws at the parade are often the handouts or printed parody items. One handbill passed out after the break up of the USSR advertised a Russian 'Going Out of Business Sale', while another featured the Next Ten Commandments, the last of which was 'Call Your Mama'.

Survival tips

The most important thing to remember is that Mardi Gras is a marathon, not a sprint. Hangovers and exhaustion will eventually become a problem anyway, so there is no need to start that fight on the very first night.

After alcohol-related challenges, the biggest test for visitors is getting around. Everybody wants a parking spot somewhere near the parade route, so, if you're driving, allow plenty of time for the maddening hunt and consider hiring a bike (*see page 219* **Sport & Fitness**). Streetcars, buses, cabs and bicycles are by far the best ways to travel during Mardi Gras. Parking in or near the French Quarter is virtually impossible.

The rule of thumb for parking is to pass on any spot where there is any question about its legality. You must allow three feet (92cm) on either side of a driveway, 14 feet (4.3m) in front of a stop sign, eight feet (2.4m) from a corner, and always park in the direction of the traffic. The parking police will ticket and/or tow anybody for the slightest parking infraction and nothing screws up Mardi Gras like a trip to the impound lot.

Next, bring some food. Ironically, this is hard to find on Fat Tuesday when most restaurants are closed and those that are open have limited menus. Variety stores are open, so junk food is available, but it isn't the sort of fare that will keep a drinker on his or her feet into the night. The creative may be able to talk their ways into private parties hosted by residents or business owners, where sandwiches and bathrooms are more valuable than money, but the conventional and shy should plan ahead.

Tempting as it may seem, Quarter visitors should avoid starting early by stunt-drinking because the day is long and bathrooms can be hard to access. There are public toilets on Decatur Street, but for the most part the facilities in bars are the only option.

The Mardi Gras season can be thought of as the two weekends preceding Fat Tuesday, though there are parades almost every night between the weekends. The first weekend is a good time for families because the crowds are manageable. The party gladiators and mobile homes have yet to come to town and the throws are neither so spectacular or so rare that they merit tussles over ownership. **Canal Street** and **St Charles Avenue** are closed for parades, so kids can have the rare thrill of playing in the middle of two of New Orleans's busiest streets.

Sparta, which rolls on the first Saturday night, is notable for having the old-line parade feel and for being one of the parades that still uses flambeaux. Parades were once lit by torches carried beside the floats, but street lights made them unnecessary. In a city that will turn anything done more than twice into a tradition, flambeaux were deemed crucial to Mardi Gras and the practice continued. They are carried by white-robed black men who are thrown money as they dance with their torches, but the danger of dancing with butane-fuelled fires caused most krewes to abandon using flambeaux. For many though, fire adds an element of the real to a parade and the lighting of the torches beforehand is a great spectacle.

THE SECOND WEEKEND

The second weekend is the big show, with two parades on the Friday night, two on Saturday during the day and Endymion at dusk in Mid City. Three parades on Sunday culminate with Bacchus. Friday is an easy night because **Hermes**, a traditional parade and the only one with stilt-walkers, is followed down St Charles Avenue by the new, satirical **Krewe d'Etat**, rumoured to be composed of former Momus and Comus members.

Saturday, however, forces some tough choices. **Iris**, the only all-women's parade in the city, is long and generous in throws to those who can get close to the floats, but those stuck at the back may find its members help reinforce the stereotypes about women and throwing. **Tucks** follows Iris and is one of the must-see parades. Its satire isn't as blue as the Krewe du Vieux Carré, but its king's throne is a toilet and the royal sceptre a toilet brush. Tucks works hard to be unlike the old-line parades, generating as much undignified energy as possible. The riders are throwing fools, offloading beads as if the parade only had to get to the end of the block rather than the five more miles to the end, and their energy and enthusiasm are contagious.

Across town, **Endymion** begins to form while Tucks rolls. Actually, Endymion crowds start forming three, four, even five days before the parade. The neutral (median) grounds on Orleans Avenue have become the Mayfair and Park Lane of Endymion viewing, so suburbanites drive in and stake out plots, camping for days in advance.

Mardi Gras Indians

Few elements of New Orleans pull together as many central themes as Mardi Gras Indians. They are rarely seen on Mardi Gras itself and they aren't actually American Indians, but tradition, secrecy, money, community, music and race all play interesting parts in the Indian story.

Their origins are a matter of conjecture, since few of the original Indians were literate and the accounts that have been passed down vary. It is generally agreed that black New Orleanians first paraded as Indians in the 1880s, when Chief Becate formed the Creole Wild West. They might have chosen to be Indians because Becate and others had Indian blood, or because of the influence of Buffalo Bill's Wild West Show, which wintered in New Orleans in 1884. There might be a West African influence derived from Caribbean Carnival. Whatever the case, working-class blacks formed tribes in their neighbourhoods and met to perform a ritualised fight, doing war dances and singing boastful songs.

Dressing as Indians gave poor blacks a way to express themselves and bring Carnival to their neighbourhoods. Every Mardi Gras, tribes set out on routes known only to the chiefs and their 'Spy Boys', who led the parades on the lookout for rival tribes, and this practice continues today. They are accompanied on their journey by the 'second line' – friends and family members who play rhythm instruments and sing the response to the chief's songs.

The songs are largely stories – of battles, wild nights or lost friends – but they are told in a private slang whose origins, like most Indian rituals, are now obscure. New songs are written, but songs that have been sung for generations still make up the core of the repertoire. They are passed on as part of the tradition to younger Indians and weren't set down until the 1970s when tribes like the Wild Magnolias (*pictured*) and the Wild Tchoupitoulas made recordings (though these aren't very representative).

Today, costumes are what the Indians are best known for – huge, elaborate explosions of colours that are best understood as folk art. Victory in ritual battles goes to the chief with the most beautiful, most elaborate costume ('beautiful' and 'elaborate' become synonyms during Mardi Gras). Every year, each Indian makes a new suit, sometimes recycling bits of beadwork or decorative patches from a previous year's suit but never re-using any old one. The size and elaborateness of a suit is determined by the rank of the member, scaling up from Spy Boy and Flag Boy to the bus stop-sized creations worn by the Big Chief.

The best time to see the Indians is when the tribes meet on the Sunday closest to St Joseph's Day (19 March) and again two Sundays later. These parades are more accessible and on safer, more reliable routes than the more neighbourhood-oriented ones on Mardi Gras day.

Adventure New Orleans

Cruise the Mississippi...

Cruise back into time on the authentic Paddlewheeler Creole Queen or the Riverboat Cajun Queen through one of America's busiest ports. Five cruises departing daily. Enjoy our nightly Dinner Jazz Cruise, complete with a Creole Buffet, live Dixieland Jazz, dancing, and a sparking city skyline as a backdrop.

Call (504) 524-0814 or 800-445-4109

Sights & Sounds of New Orleans

Architecture, history, nightlife - New Orleans Tours offers the best of New Orleans.

- The Complete City Tour
- Historic Plantation Tour
- River & City Combination Tour
- French Quarter Walking Tour
- Garden District Walking Tour
- Pete Fountain's Jazz Extravaganza

Call (504) 592-0560 or 800-543-6332

Explore the Wilder Side of New Orleans...

Our swamp boats will take you on an adventure into the wilds of Louisiana's meandering, moss-draped bayous. The gators are wild, the owls are a hoot, and Bandit the raccoon will steal your heart.

Call (504) 529-4567 or 800-445-4109

Group and private charter rates are available.
http://www.visitnola.com

The practice irritates the locals who get shut out of prime viewing spots, but the police have allowed it to continue. A stage is now set up on Saturday morning so bands can entertain the growing village of police-tape interlopers, coolers, barbecues and lawn chairs. Some defend their plots in Cooler City like mama bears defending their cubs, losing sight of the fact that Mardi Gras is, after all, about playing. A better bet is to see Endymion on the sidewalk side of Canal Street, where the crowds aren't so thick or immobile.

Endymion and the other superkrewes put on consistently good shows, each with their own strengths. Endymion specialises in excess, never throwing one string of beads when there are 11 more in the bundle, never throwing little beads when bigger ones exist, and never throwing one cup when a whole sleeve would make a bigger splash. Where other krewes boast one celebrity, Endymion has two or three and while the other big parades last almost two hours, Endymion can stretch on into the night.

Sunday's **Bacchus** is best known for its floats, which are among the most ornate and handsome. The krewe has developed a stable of signature floats that appear every year regardless of the theme. The Bacchagator and the Baccha-Whoppa

each hold more than 100 riders, while the Bacchusaurus is a significant deviation from the standard riders-on-a-shoebox float model.

The **Kong** family also rolls each year, with three floats whose riders don't throw, but invite the crowd to enjoy the otherwise-illegal act of throwing their lousier beads back at a float.

LUNDI GRAS

Monday, or Lundi Gras was once a day of rest. The quiet, traditional Proteus once paraded in the evening, but it shut down in 1992 in protest at the Mardi Gras Ordinance; the only daytime event was the arrival of the King of Rex at Spanish Plaza at the foot of Poydras and Canal Streets. In the last few years though, Lundi Gras has become an event all its own. **Zulu** hosts an all-afternoon party at Woldenberg Park near the Aquarium, while **Rex** has expanded its celebration at Spanish Plaza to include more music by the likes of the Neville Brothers, Dr John and the Radiators. Uptown, Harry Connick Jr's **Orpheus** is the third superkrewe parade and after only five years, has become one of the season's best. It features the most marching bands and has floats to rival Bacchus. Its newest float, the Leviathan, is the most elaborate and expensive to date – a rolling Las Vegas casino marquee. By any Mardi Gras standards, it's bee-you-tiful.

Superkrewe **Bacchus** *has become famous for its huge and elaborate floats.*

Show us your tits!

The practice of women baring their breasts for beads has become a sad commonplace during the Mardi Gras festivities – though it's nowhere near the epidemic the national media have portrayed it to be (the traditional Carnival cry used to be 'throw me something, mister!', now it's 'show us your tits!').

As a rule of thumb, proximity to the French Quarter determines how frequent and how tolerated the practice is: at Napoleon and St Charles Avenues in Uptown, it's unusual to see bare breasts, but it's far more common between Lee Circle and Canal Street. The French Quarter is ground zero for breast exposure, and tourists will walk the Quarter looking up at the balconies for attractive women who might agree to lift their tops in exchange for a string of beads.

In recent years, women have responded by encouraging men to drop their trousers and expose themselves, but the New Orleans Police Department takes a very dim view of this. Men caught exposing themselves can be busted for indecent exposure. Women who expose themselves, on the other hand, are often lectured but not charged with an offence, the argument being that the problem they pose is not moral but practical – they attract a crowd, which jams up the street.

FAT TUESDAY

Fat Tuesday begins as early as 4am or 5am, when an Endymion-like second city springs up on the neutral grounds along St Charles Avenue. The day is officially underway when **Zulu** begins at 8.30am on Jackson Avenue. It's a matter of some debate whether Zulu has ever started on time, so smart parade-goers figure it will make it to St Charles some time after 9am, though the lateness isn't always Zulu's fault. One year vandals deflated the tyres of the floats overnight, delaying the parade by over an hour.

When it eventually arrives, Zulu riders – black and white, male and female – are in their traditional make-up, the jungle blackface of natives in Tarzan movies. Since 1909 Zulu has parodied Rex, creating low parallels to Rex's high-class pretensions, mocking white stereotypes of blacks by wearing fright wigs and black paint. The jungle theme is continued in the most prized Zulu throw – the coconut – each of which is hand-decorated by the rider. Actually, they aren't truly 'throws' since a law passed in 1987 banned their throwing for safety reasons, but they are intermittently handed down to those zealous and determined enough to hang on to a front row spot for the duration of a parade. Further touches of the absurd Zulu sense of humour involve painting white figures built onto the front of floats black for the occasion: a black Heidi and a black King Arthur have both appeared in Zulu parades.

Rex begins Uptown on Napoleon Avenue and follows Zulu along St Charles and while it is a pretty parade, its pomp and old-fashioned attitude seem too restrained after a weekend of parades that throw beads that could double as skipping ropes. Members' careful distribution of small, cheap beads and their gentlemanly demeanour are anticlimactic after the slapstick of Zulu, so many skip the event and head on to the French Quarter. Rex is followed by the truck parades: over 300 trucks pass with groups and families in costume throwing whatever can be thrown for the duration of the afternoon. The occasional cool item gets thrown, but mostly it's beads recycled from other parades and after days of catching these all but the most dedicated have had enough.

IN THE FRENCH QUARTER

At some point, all revellers make it to the French Quarter. It lures everyone throughout Mardi Gras like a low-rent siren, beckoning college students and other weak minds to the cheap pleasures and enduring pain inflicted by a night spent jammed hip-to-haunch on Bourbon Street. It has become the popular image of Mardi Gras, so most people have to experience at least once for themselves the joys of flat draught beer and naked breasts it promises. By Fat Tuesday, even the resolute break down, devise costumes – the worse taste, the better – and head for the Quarter. The wise will get their fill on Royal or Chartres Streets, both of which feature the usual madness but with more manageable crowds.

The day begins ending at **Café Brasil** (*see page 204* **Nightlife**) around dusk, when would-be drummers play extended rhythm jams for anyone still able to dance. The grooves are sporadic but well-meant and the scene is a nice antidote to Bourbon Street for those not bothered by the relentless pounding. Every year, the police symbolically end Mardi Gras and close down Bourbon Street with an impressive show of force at midnight, marching horses through the streets and forcing the remaining lost souls onto the sidewalks or into the bars for yet more beer. The party goes on all night, but those still out on the streets at this point are the equivalent of house guests who can't take a hint and go home.

Literary New Orleans

'My greatest instinct is to be free. I found that in New Orleans' –
Tennessee Williams.

One of the remarkable things about New Orleans's extensive literary heritage is its resonance in everyday life. People who have never seen *A Streetcar Named Desire* quote Blanche DuBois and Stanley Kowalski at the drop of a hat: 'I have always depended on the kindness of strangers', 'I have this attorney friend', and, of course, 'STELLLaaaa!'

Visitors to the city want dinner reservations at **Antoine's** restaurant (*see page 119*) because the title of Frances Parkinson Keyes's 1948 novel still resonates, although *Dinner at Antoine's* is long out of print. Young men in black leather jackets roar into New Orleans on cross-country road trips because that's what Jack Kerouac did in *On the Road*. John Rechy's 1963 novel *City of Night* remains the starting point for unapologetic gay literature, while Ellen Gilchrist's insouciant stories of the 1970s and 1980s introduced a new breed of sexually exuberant women to fiction. From Mark Twain to Kate Chopin to William Faulkner to Tennessee Williams to Anne Rice, New Orleans has nurtured and fed the literary imagination.

Although New Orleans was one of America's richest cities before the Civil War, the concentration of wealth, a leisure class and a cosmopolitan atmosphere did not produce lasting literature. Mark Twain's intoxication with New Orleans began in the antebellum period when he was a steamboat pilot, but he wrote about it later in *Life on the Mississippi*. Walt Whitman came to New Orleans, too, before the Civil War. New Orleans was not a major influence on his poetry, but his later biographers have suggested he enjoyed the gay *demi-monde*. Alexis de Tocqueville was in New Orleans during his 1831-2 pilgrimage through America. His remarks about the city in *Democracy in America* were in the context of his discussion about slavery.

New Orleans, famous for its exoticism since its earliest days, has always been a magnet for writers and artists. Many of them, however, were (and remain) 'experience tourists', alighting in the city briefly (usually in the French Quarter) to soak up material or inspiration, then moving on. Native writers, and many who became permanent residents, often slipped into the seductive trap of 'local colour', producing artificial, affected work in everything from novels to folklore.

There was actually a huge market for Southern writing after the War Between the States. The plantation Eden with its hoop-skirted beauties and gallant young cavaliers in Confederate grey were the staples of a 'belles and beaux' genre (of which the apotheosis is *Gone With the Wind*) that has not completely disappeared. There were plenty of writers, in New Orleans and elsewhere, happy to churn out books to fill the need.

In the booming literary market of the last century, New Orleans did produce two fiction writers of lasting importance: George Washington Cable (1844-1925) and Kate Chopin (1851-1904). Cable was a native New Orleanian, but not a Creole. He was a staunch Presbyterian and a Confederate veteran who worked as an accountant. As a kind of hobby, he wrote sketches and essays for the local papers. Cable gradually worked his way through the ideas of the Lost Cause and the Southern Way of Life to discover that none of it made any sense. In New Orleans, with its always bizarre colour line, a society based on racism was even more absurd than in its other Southern applications.

Cable has been called 'the first modern Southern writer', a title that sometimes baffles today's readers who find his *Old Creole Days* stories burdened with dialect, paternalism and sentimentality. Cable's most popular stories, such as *Madame John's Legacy*, often involve beautiful young women who are persecuted for having a drop or two of Negro blood. However, his work is underpinned by a bracing clarity in its perception of racial realities.

Cable's writing was praised by critics and his books were bestsellers, but he became uncomfortable with life in New Orleans. The polite distaste that his friends and neighbours began to show towards Cable and his family eventually prompted him to move to Northampton, Massachusetts, where he found continued critical acclaim and refuge in the friendship of Mark Twain.

*Once home to the writer, **Faulkner House Books** celebrates his birthday with a festival.*

In fact, Cable's work was so despised it pushed a young New Orleans woman, Grace King (1852-1932), to begin writing books to present a 'true' portrait of Southern life. King achieved a measure of success with fiction such as *Balcony Stories*. Her efforts at recording and preserving local history were important, but she never wavered in her pre-occupation with white supremacy.

The writer that Grace King aspired to be, the woman who gave voice to the true New Orleans, was actually born in St Louis. Kate Chopin married into a Louisiana Creole family at 21. Despite running a large household and giving birth to six children, Chopin pursued writing. She achieved some attention in her lifetime, but was ultimately assigned to the 'local colour' trashbin. Her fortunes rose again with the women's movement as women readers and feminist critics grasped that the lush New Orleans settings for her masterpiece, *The Awakening* (1889), were not mindless embroideries but the counterpoint to the heroine's arid inner life.

Though not quite in the same class, Lafcadio Hearn (1850-1904) did much to enhance the city's mystique. His essays and stories about New Orleans dwelt on the Creoles, American Indians, Italians and Cajuns. A newspaperman of English-Greek extraction, Hearn spent ten years in New Orleans, most of it in the French Quarter. His Creole cookbook and guide to Creole sayings, *Gombo Zhebes*, is overshadowed by his later work on Japan and his translations, but Hearn's great rubric about New Orleans is still widely quoted: 'Better to live here in sackcloth and ashes than own the whole state of Ohio.'

In the 1920s, New Orleans showed signs of becoming a Greenwich Village South as writers, poets and artists began to gather around the Midwestern novelist Sherwood Anderson (*Winesburg, Ohio*) who had settled at the Pontalba Apartments. William Faulkner (1897-1962) was part of the circle around Anderson, a melancholy young man from Mississippi whom many remembered more for his drinking than his writing.

Others in and out of the city in those years included Scott Fitzgerald, who spent several months in New Orleans while working on the galleys to his first novel, *This Side of Paradise*, in 1920. Author John Dos Passos (*USA*) also lived in the city briefly. More permanent were novelist and anthropologist Oliver Lafarge, composer Genevieve Pitot and local colourists Lyle Saxon and Roark Bradford.

The literary renaissance of New Orleans was heralded through its own magazine, *The Double Dealer*, one of the famous literary 'little magazines' of the pre-World War I and 1920s period. Neither the Greenwich Village atmosphere nor *The Double Dealer* lasted very long, but both were far more influential than their duration would suggest.

Faulkner used his New Orleans experience most directly in *Pylons*, a minor novel. But New Orleans opened up Faulkner in many ways, according to Kenneth Holditch, the genial scholar who has turned his encyclopaedic knowledge of New Orleans's literary history into popular books and tours. Holditch compares Faulkner's experience to that of his character Henry Sutpen in *Absolom, Absolom!*, Faulkner's magnum opus. Both were

Hail the writer

New Orleans honours its literary heritage with festivals, tours and even a shouting contest.

Anne Rice's Voicemail

(522 8634).
The vampire's friend records a new five-minute message every few weeks to share her thoughts on anything from her newest book launch to President Clinton's legal problems. Fans are then invited to leave their own message, which Rice comments on in her next tape.
Websites: www.randomhouse.com/annerice
alt.books.anne-rice.

Desire Street

ftp.etext.org/pub/Zines/DesireStreet
This New Orleans poetry magazine is only available online.

Kenneth Holditch's Literary Tour

PO Box 50986, New Orleans, LA 70150 (945 6789/ fax 945 1586). **Tours** by appointment Mar-July. **Tickets** $15. **Credit** AmEx, MC, V.
Holditch is one of the pioneers of the literary walking tour. His New Orleans walks set a standard of erudition, storytelling and accuracy that other cities strive to match. This tour is one of the great pleasures of a visit to New Orleans. For more organised sightseeing tours, *see chapter* **Sightseeing**.

New Orleans Popular Fiction Conference

PO Box 740113, New Orleans, LA 70140-0113 (391 1320). **Date** 2nd weekend in Nov. **Admission** $150. **Credit** MC, V.
This annual winter conference used to be for romance writers only, but now it includes all genre writing: mystery, science fiction, westerns and fantasy. Published writers, established agents and well-known publishing house editors make themselves available to the aspiring authors who want to be the next Danielle Steel – or Louis L'amour. The conference lasts two days and is usually based at a downtown hotel.

Pirate's Alley Faulkner Society

632 Pirate's Alley, at Royal Street, New Orleans, LA 70116 (586 1612). Bus 3 Vieux Carré, 55 Elysian Fields, 81 Almonaster, 82 Desire. **Membership** $35 per year. **Credit** MC, V.
An annual celebration of Faulkner's birthday by Faulkner House Books grew into the Society that spun off the **Words & Music Festival** (*see below*) and publishes *Double Dealer Redux*, a journal of New Orleans writers and writing.

Tennessee Williams New Orleans Literary Festival

5500 Prytania Street, suite 217, New Orleans, LA 70115 (581 1144/fax 529 2430/twfest@gnofn.org). **Date** end March. **Admission** $35 weekend panel discussion pass; $25 concessions. **Credit** MC, V.
One of the best all-round literary festivals in the USA, this five-day event runs the gamut from master classes for writers taught by first-rate authors, to the hilarious Stella Shouting Contest with would-be Stanleys (male and female) giving the famous 'STELLLaaaa' wail their best shot. Held in mid-March every year, the festival is based at Le Petit Théâtre du Vieux Carré (*see p212* **Performing Arts**).
Website: www.gnofn.org/~twfest

Walker Percy Symposium

St Tammany Parish Library, 310 West 21st Avenue, Covington, LA 70433 (871 1220). **Date** end Sept. **Admission** free.

Mississippi men, bred in a puritan culture and then exposed to 'that city foreign and paradoxical with its atmosphere at once fatal and languourous, at once feminine and steel-hard… a place created for and by voluptuousness, the abashless and unabashed senses'.

Faulkner lived in several apartments during his residence in the French Quarter (1924-6). One of his former homes now contains Faulkner House Books in Pirate's Alley, behind St Louis Cathedral. Owners Joe DaSalvo and Rosemary James have renovated the building and follow the old New Orleans custom of living over the store. DaSalvo and James are founders of the **Pirate's Alley Faulkner Society** and its spin-off, the **Words & Music** literary festival (*see above*).

Truman Capote (1926-84) is often linked with New Orleans, but his contact with the city was minimal. He was born there, but his young, feckless parents soon sent him away to live more or less permanently with relatives in Alabama. Capote visited the city off and on throughout his life, most importantly at the age of 20 when he was struggling with his first novel. He later said his New Orleans sojourn, living in an apartment at 811 Royal Street for several months, cleared his head. He gave up on a breezy novel about New York socialites and turned to his Alabama youth, producing his first major work, the Gothic Southern novella, *Other Voices, Other Rooms*.

Like Capote, playwright Lillian Hellman was born in New Orleans but was not as much a daughter of the city as she liked to suggest. Her plays (*The Little Foxes, The Children's Hour, Watch on the Rhine*) have been overshadowed by her memoirs and long involvement with writer Dashiell Hammett, both of which have been going through a revision that throws serious doubt on Hellman's ability to tell the truth.

Vampire's friend: the ubiquitous Anne Rice.

Suburban Covington honours its most famous resident with a one-day conference at the local library. Percy scholars talk then mingle with the audience. It's all very low-key and quite nice. The date has recently been changed from March to September; phone or write to the Director for more information.
Website: www.stpl.com

Words & Music Festival
See above, Pirate's Alley Faulkner Society. **Date** last week Sept. **Admission** varies.
An ambitious new festival, launched in 1997, that will be held every autumn. Big-name writers, musicians and actors headline the four days of panels, talks, readings, concerts and parties.

Tennessee Williams (1911-83) is the city's genuine literary icon. His 1947 play *A Streetcar Named Desire* has fixed New Orleans in the literary and popular landscape for all time. Williams, who was born in Mississippi and raised in St Louis by Southern parents who considered themselves in exile, used many Southern settings in his work, but his name is completely entwined with New Orleans – which was fine with the playwright. Throughout his life he referred to New Orleans as 'home', a city he came to in 1938 as a sexually and artistically frustrated young man. Escaping from a suffocating family and dead-end job in St Louis, Thomas Lanier Williams reinvented himself as 'Tennessee' in New Orleans. He acted on his sexual attraction to men and began to find his writing voice.

In 1961 he said: 'If I can be said to have a home, it is in New Orleans where I've lived off and on since 1938 and which has provided me with more material than any other part of the country.'

Williams lived in an attic room at 722 Toulouse Street during his first period in New Orleans. Later, when he was well off, he favoured the Monteleone Hotel for short stays. Later still, he bought a building at 1014 Dumaine Street, which was his longest-lasting home in New Orleans, although he sold it shortly before his death in 1983.

A contemporary of Williams's, but someone he most surely never met, was Frances Parkinson Keyes (1885-1970), a one-woman publishing industry in the 1930s and 1940s. Her hackneyed romances, *Crescent Carnival*, *Blue Camellia* and *Steamboat Gothic*, among others, sold millions of copies, making her the Danielle Steel of her era. Keyes came to New Orleans in 1939 and eventually bought the former residence of Confederate General PGT Beauregard in the French Quarter. Keyes's literary efforts are all but forgotten now, but like Grace King, she continues to be admired for her preservation efforts. She restored the Greek Revival mansion in Chartres Street (now called the Beauregard-Keyes House) and established a foundation for its care. The house is open to the public (*see chapter* **Sightseeing**).

New Orleans is usually mentioned in any discussion of the Beat poets and writers, but the city was definitely a minor outpost in the Beat world. Jack Kerouac and Neal Cassady passed through New Orleans during William Burroughs's 1948-9 stay in Algiers on the West Bank. Kerouac, in typical style, was thrilled with New Orleans: 'At dusk we were coming into the humming streets of New Orleans... The air was so sweet in New Orleans it seemed to come in soft bandannas; and you could smell the river and really smell the people, and mud, and molasses, and every kind of tropical exhalation.' Burroughs was less impressed. Arrested for drugs, he left New Orleans to avoid prosecution. In later years he described the city as 'a preserved artificial museum' and labelled the residents as 'surly'.

By the 1960s, New Orleans had several important writers in residence. In addition to the peripatetic Tennessee Williams, novelists Shirley Ann Grau, Walker Percy and John Kennedy Toole were living and working in the city.

Grau, who still lives quietly in Metairie, has written a string of acclaimed novels, including *Keepers of the House*, which won the Pulitzer Prize. Walker Percy (1916-90), a non-practising doctor, was instantly recognised as a major American writer on the publication of his first book, *The Moviegoer*. Percy, a convert to Catholicism, used fiction to grapple with the big philosophical questions that absorbed him. Like the handful of novels that were to follow, *The Moviegoer* approaches the human condition with humour, compassion and a steely dedication to discovering principles worth living for.

The New Orleans area figures strongly in many of Percy's books, but not always the city itself, which he found a little too precious. 'The occupational hazard of the writer in New Orleans is a variety of the French flu, which might also be called the Vieux Carré syndrome,' Percy later wrote in a piece for *Esquire* magazine. 'One is apt to turn fey, potter about a patio, and write feuilletons and vignettes or catty romans à clef, a pleasant enough life, but for me too seductive.'

Percy, whose books include *Lancelot, The Last Gentleman* and *Love in the Ruins*, lived contentedly with his family in suburban Covington until his sudden death in 1990.

Unlike Grau and Percy, Toole laboured in obscurity. In 1969 he killed himself, in part because he could not get his novel, *A Confederacy of Dunces*, published. After his death, Toole's mother – the model for the half-mad mother of the book's amazing hero, Ignatius O'Reilly – focused all her energy on her son's neglected manuscript. In one of the great tales of American literature, she hounded Walker Percy until he agreed to read the tattered typewritten pages. Percy, shocked that the book was not only good but brilliant, became its advocate. 'Confederacy' was finally brought out by Louisiana State University Press after commercial publishers rejected it. The book was a publishing triumph, a bestseller, and winner of the 1980 Pulitzer Prize. In 1997 a statue of Ignatius was put up on Canal Street, near one of his favourite haunts, the old Holmes Department Store.

Ellen Gilchrist, who lived in New Orleans during the 1960s and '70s, gained readers' and critical praise for her short stories about funny, resilient Southern women with voracious appetites for sex, love and trouble. Her collection of short stories, *Victory Over Japan*, won the National Book Award in 1984. She moved on to Arkansas but New Orleans continues to figure heavily in the lives of her characters.

In the past couple of decades, New Orleans has been home (literally and figuratively) to a wide range of well-known writers, including novelists Richard Ford and Robert Olen Butler, and poet Yusef Komunyakaa – all Pulitzer Prize winners. Other notables include: Stephen Ambrose, Douglas Brinkley, Emily Toth and Christina Vella (history and biography); Tom Piazza, Jason Berry, Andrei Cordescu, Michael Lewis, Bethany Bultman and Rodger Kamenetz (non-fiction); and Sheila Bosworth, Poppy Z Brite, Moira Crone, Louis Edwards, Tim Gatreaux and Valerie Martin (fiction). Mystery writers based in New Orleans include Julie Smith, James Lee Burke, Jean Redmann, Tony Dunbar, Christine Wiltz, James Sallis and Tony Fennelly.

Yet all of these writers' prizes, glowing reviews and sales are dwarfed by the high profile of Anne Rice, who has become a combination of tourist attraction and professional eccentric. Rice is associated with New Orleans in the public imagination in a way that rivals and maybe surpasses even Tennessee Williams's fame.

The author of a pile of bestsellers, beginning with *Interview With the Vampire* (1976), Rice moved back to New Orleans in 1989 after more than 20 years spent in San Francisco with her husband, poet-painter Stan Rice. Anne Rice comes from a working-class Irish Channel family. Her early output of well-received fiction has grown into a literary machine that publishes at least a book a year. Rice's work is eagerly anticipated and devoured by fanatical readers. Her fans come to New Orleans in droves, not only to catch a glimpse of their heroine but to walk in the footsteps of her characters – the witches, vampires and mortals whom Rice carefully places in the city's houses, cemeteries, churches and dark alleys.

Rice's move back to New Orleans coincided with the explosion of her popularity. She quickly moved from being a well-known writer to an international celebrity with bodyguards, several residences, a large staff and a shifting public image. Rice embraces her fans on her own terms. She has a voicemail number that will record messages after a five-minute monologue by Rice on her thoughts about everything. While the city cashed in on the *Vampire Lestat* and *Mayfair Witches* fans who flocked to New Orleans for Hallowe'en, Rice took over and improved the 'coven ball'. For a while she operated a selection of 'Anne Rice Tours' but discontinued them after she was annoyed by the adverse newspaper coverage they received.

New Orleans looks on Rice with a mixture of admiration and amusement. In 1997 she ignited a public brawl with flamboyant restaurateur Al Copeland. Rice, like many Garden District residents, was upset by Copeland's plans for a high-profile, neon-lit restaurant on St Charles Avenue. What had been neighbourhood grumbling became a national news story when Rice took out a full-page ad in the *Times-Picayune* attacking Copeland's Straya restaurant as 'absolutely hideous'. Copeland struck back with his own ad and offered customers a discount if they brought in Rice's *Times-Picayune* screed.

The incident came not long after Rice had incensed her Catholic neighbours by buying their small community chapel from the Catholic Church. When they complained, Rice took out an ad saying they only went to the chapel because they were a bunch of elitists who were avoiding the nearest Catholic church located next to the St Thomas housing project.

Rice, like Grace King and Frances Parkinson Keyes, has a powerful urge for preservation. She has bought and improved at least seven historic properties in New Orleans. Although her newspaper ads and antics – such as arriving at book signings in a coffin – have given her a reputation as a clown with dark overtones, in New Orleans it is by no means a drawback to have a bizarre streak.

Tennessee Williams had his character Stella put it this way: 'New Orleans is not like other cities.' In life or literature.

Architecture

Filling in the background on the buildings of the Big Easy: Creole cottages, millionaires' mansions and a minimalist sports dome.

Most visitors to New Orleans will probably be chiefly interested in the indigenous Creole architecture that developed in the oldest sections of the city: the French Quarter and its immediate suburbs, Tremé and Faubourg Marigny.

Admittedly, even the most aged structures in New Orleans are absolutely youthful by Old World standards. Most French Quarter buildings date from 1795 or later. The wonder of the Vieux Carré is not its age, but rather that it is a relatively intact example of a colonial New World city shaped as surely by the natural environment of south Louisiana as it was by European antecedents. The real architects of New Orleans buildings past and present are the sodden ground, the lack of bedrock (or any locally available stone, for that matter), copious rain, wilting heat, occasional hurricanes and fire. Old New Orleans structures tilt wearily on their foundations, leaning against one another at the shoulder for support; beneath them lie scores of feet of silt. Most roofs, be they tile, slate or asphalt shingle, are steeply pitched to shed the five

or six feet (1.5-1.8 metres) of rainfall the city routinely receives each year, though, unpractically, flatter roofs were a Spanish Colonial design vogue.

The broad overhangs that shade the streets in the older parts of town against the relentless summer sun also provided a strip of negotiable, dry ground for pedestrians at a safe distance from the sloppy, unpaved streets. The eight to ten foot- (2.4-3 metres) spaces beneath raised dwellings served as storage and utility areas, but also protected the structures from periodic flooding, a feature that became more practical as the city outgrew the natural levees of the river and the barely discernible ridges. The enormously high ceilings in New Orleans townhouses, often 14 feet (4.3 metres) above the floor, helped dissipate the debilitating summer heat before the days of air-conditioning, as did the tall french doors and triple-hung windows that slice through the upper storeys of dwellings, taking advantage of every faint breeze.

The force of tropical winds soon taught New Orleans colonial designers to overbuild to some

One of the stars of St Charles Avenue: the **Orleans Club** (see page 42).

extent. At least one early plan for a tall building included timber buttresses reinforcing the exterior walls against the wind, though no such structure survives. However, the attics of even modest French Quarter cottages hold webs of beams that are heavier than would have been necessary to support the weight of the roof alone.

Fire was another problem. The rapidly spreading fires that devoured the original wooden settlement on the site of the French Quarter in 1788 and 1794 dramatically demonstrated the need to use non-combustible materials in the closely spaced community. Hence, the Spanish Colonial government decreed that all rebuilt structures were made of wooden frames, filled between the uprights with brick and coated with an inch (2.5 centimetre)-thick layer of stucco to prevent further conflagration.

In the early twentieth century, the French Quarter was mainly a low-income sector bordered on the river side by less-than-picturesque shipping warehouses. The area was not generally revered for its architectural significance and without the farsightedness of a handful of preservationists, including architects Sam Wilson and Richard Koch, the area might have fallen to the wrecker's ball, like so much of early urban America. However, the Vieux Carré was saved from wholesale demolition in the 1960s when the freeway, which was planned to pass through the river side of the old city, was re-routed. In 1965, the whole French Quarter became a National Historic Landmark, thereby keeping the area intact without requiring that it become a sterile museum piece.

Shotgun houses

The neighbourhood between Esplanade and the Fair Grounds racetrack – a typical working-class enclave – is enchanting, with its rows of closely spaced 'shotgun' houses adorned with various stylistic embellishments to the façades: Italianate, Craftsman and even Gothic Revival. The rooms in these modest-framed structures are lined up one after another, with room opening into room, without the benefit of a hallway (though side hall shotguns do exist). The name shotgun house may have originated with the assertion that it was possible to fire a barrel of shot in the front door and out through the back without hitting anything in between. Double shotgun houses, with twin lines of rooms side by side, are as common if not more common than singles.

When a second floor is added to the rear rooms of a shotgun house, it is known as a 'camelback'. 'Raised shotguns' are shotgun houses with lower ground floors that are usually used as garages or apartments. Shotgun houses were commonly built from the mid-1800s to the early 1900s and can be found in neighbourhoods like Bywater, the Irish Channel, Mid City and Carrollton. Shotgun houses demand a certain immodesty from those who dwell within them, as family members and visitors alike must pass through each room to travel from one end of the house to the other.

A relatively recent threat to the French Quarter – and to all of New Orleans's wooden architecture – is the Formosan termite, a rapacious little pest that came to the Mississippi Gulf ports in shipments of material during World War II. Many locals agree that no wooden structure in the French Quarter remains completely unaffected by the plague and even a short-term lack of vigilance can allow a building to be virtually ruined.

Eighteenth-century survivors

Visitors don't need to be helped to find historic structures in the Vieux Carré; they're everywhere. But it may help to be steered to older buildings of particular historic and architectural significance.

Painted in a ghostly absinthe-laced grey, the **Old Ursuline Convent** (1112 Chartres Street, at Ursulines Street) almost disappears behind its protective walls into the mist on the river side of the Quarter. Built between 1749 and 1753, this graceful two-storey structure, with its steep stepped roof terminating in a gentle flair, is the only surviving building from the French Colonial period. No longer a convent, it is now the repository of the archives of the Archdiocese of Louisiana and open for tours (*see page 53* **Sightseeing**).

Nearby is **Madame John's Legacy** (632 Dumaine Street, between Royal and Chartres Streets), which got its name from a story by George Washington Cable, a nineteenth-century writer who recorded much of the factual history of the times but was also one of the great myth-makers of New Orleans. The building dates from the late 1700s – later than the French Colonial period – but is reportedly a faithful replica of the original structure on the site, which was destroyed in the fire of 1788. A raised structure, with a deep gallery and thin columns, it is the only remaining French Quarter dwelling that echoes plantation structures from the same period. It is now the property of the Louisiana State Museum and has been respectfully restored and maintained, down to the use of the original, odd, olive-coloured trim paint (*see page 56* **Sightseeing**).

The exact date of construction of **Lafitte's Blacksmith Shop** (941 Bourbon Street, at St Philip Street) is not known, but it is believed to have been built in the decade before the 1788 fire and therefore is the earliest known example of one of the most common types of New Orleans building: the Creole cottage. Essentially, the Creole cottage is a more or less square building divided into four rooms of equal size without a hall. French doors and windows open directly on to the sidewalk and the steep roof is often perforated with dormer windows.

Lafitte's, which is now a bar, is a particularly good example to visit, for two reasons. First, the surfaces of the stuccoed walls have been allowed

*The Spanish Colonial **Merieult House**.*

to deteriorate sufficiently to expose the underlying diagonal beam and brick structure. Second, it is a cool, dark, romantic saloon in which to rest and contemplate Creole building methods over a gin and tonic. Incidentally, the building was neither a blacksmith's shop nor a meeting place for Lafitte (the pirate) and Jackson (the future president) to plot the defence of the city against English invaders. Again, the fiction of George Washington Cable has become popular history. *See page 187* **Nightlife**.

The **Merieult House** (533 Royal Street, at St Louis Street) is an early example of the most typical of French Quarter architecture: the Spanish Colonial-style townhouse. This two-storey structure has a ground floor dedicated to storefronts, a deep balcony, an upper storey for living quarters and an arched carriageway that leads from the street to the stairs and rear courtyard. But like so many other Vieux Carré structures, the Merieult House does not abide by any strict set of stylistic rules. The stepped roof, for instance, is more typical of the French Colonial period and the lower façade was redesigned in the early nineteenth century in a crisp geometric style suggesting Greek Revival taste. (A typically shallow-angled Spanish Colonial roof, complete with decorative tile grill can be seen atop the weather-worn cottage at 709 Dumaine Street, a few blocks away.)

Modern masters

No American city looks to its history more than New Orleans, but even there modernity has found a foothold. In the 1970s, New Orleans enjoyed a booming oil-based economy and corporate construction exploded in the old American sector of the city, just above Canal Street. Poydras Street, in particular, became a canyon of high-rise office buildings in mirrored glass and marble, which were in large measure indistinguishable from buildings of similar vintage in Dallas, Houston or Atlanta. At either end of the new corporate row are two structures of architectural importance, both for their own characteristics and because they define the struggle between cultural uniqueness and homogenisation in New Orleans architecture: the Louisiana Superdome and the Piazza d'Italia.

Near the river end of Poydras Street, on Commerce Street, the **Piazza d'Italia** (*pictured below*) was designed by Charles W Moore, Allen Eskew and Ron Filson to celebrate the contribution of the Italian – particularly the Sicilian – community to the culture of New Orleans. Completed in 1978, it is walled on one side with a series of overlapping building façades that suggest abstractly both the Italianate features of much of New Orleans architecture and genuine Old World architectural components. A fountain delivers water to a pool in the shape of Italy, surrounded by concentric tile circles implying the spread of Italian influence throughout the world. Every sort of construction material was used to decorate the plaza: brightly painted stucco, chrome, glazed tiles,

marble, brick and coloured lights. The design is deliberately lively, even gaudy in its decorative excess. But there is a certain harmony in the visual racket, and above all, the Piazza certainly reflects the riotous spirit of life in New Orleans.

The architects' decoration of the plaza soon earned the design a place in textbooks as an example of postmodern architectural sensibility. However, shops and restaurants did not spring up around the plaza as was originally envisioned and within a very short time – coincident with the bust in the oil industry – the Piazza d'Italia

fell into disrepair. Though it has been refurbished occasionally, the deterioration has continued more or less unabated. A recent visit was particularly discouraging. The water in the reflecting pool had gone green with algae and islands of floating rubbish dotted the surface. Tiles had fallen, cement cracked, metal tarnished and all functioning elements had ceased to work. The once-entertaining plaza is now an embarrassment. Still, if you're hunting for a bona fide example of postmodernism in a town that barely acknowledges modernity, the Piazza exists.

At the other end of Poydras Street, springing up like a colossal mushroom, is the **Louisiana Superdome** (*pictured above; see page 60* **Sightseeing**). Designed by the architecture firm of Curtis and Davis and completed in 1975, it is the biggest enclosed sports arena ever built. The white cap of the Superdome – 680 feet (207 metres) in diameter, with an area of 9.7 acres (3.9 hectares) – is the world's largest continuous roof, unobstructed by upright supports. To stand on the playing field (as visitors are allowed to do), with the ceiling arching 273 feet (83.2 metres) above, is undeniably a humbling experience. It is equally undeniable that the Superdome has a relentlessly sterile, generic design. From the unadorned stainless-steel exterior to the grey on grey interior décor – relieved only by a smattering of colour in the upholstery of the 73,000 seats and the impossibly green artificial playing field – the Superdome nowhere reflects the joyous character of the city it serves. Yet it remains a fantastic structure to behold in all its minimalist glory.

The Mericult House was built in 1791 on the rubble of a building lost in the first conflagration. Though all else was destroyed around it, the house survived the second catastrophic fire in 1794. Today it is the home of the Historic New Orleans Collection, a museum and research centre (*see page 90* **Museums & Galleries**). Guided tours are available around the carefully restored upper floors of the house and rear courtyards.

The nineteenth-century legacy

The French Quarter (which has always been a residential neighbourhood) assumed its present appearance in the early to mid-nineteenth century, with townhouse after townhouse lining the narrow streets (often with shared walls), displaying a variety of stylistic impulses: Spanish Colonial, French Colonial, Greek Revival, Federal and other less common fashions. Above the streets, balconies webbed with cast and wrought iron railings protrude from the regular, rectangular façades like beards and moustaches. At one time, the ground floors buzzed with commerce of every kind, from barber shops painted in slashes of red and white, to numerous small, corner groceries, to some light manufacturing. The rows of townhouses were punctuated here and there with cottages and, much later, the narrow-faced shotgun house, which is ubiquitous throughout New Orleans. Behind the townhouses, at the back of each lot, were half-buildings (which served as slave quarters in antebellum times), utility outhouses and rental apartments. You can still find these hidden buildings peeking from between taller structures throughout the Vieux Carré.

It's difficult to list the features that distinguish the Creole townhouse from the earlier Spanish-style townhouse. Perhaps the distinctions are more an issue of degree: those structures considered Creole townhouses were in many cases larger and built in greater abundance than their colonial predecessors.

The **Pedesclaux-Le Monnier House** (417 Royal Street, at St Peter Street), touted as a 'Creole skyscraper' by carriage-driving tour guides (known better for their hyperbole than their history), was – at four full storeys – the tallest townhouse in the French Quarter. The building has small shops on its ground floor, with apartments above. It was begun just after the 1794 fire but not finished until 1811. The design was started by Barthelemy Lafon and completed by Hyacinthe Laclotte, who also designed another of the French Quarter giants, the **Napoleon House** (500 Chartres Street, at St Louis Street). This was designed as the residence of New Orleans's Mayor Nicholas Girod in 1815 and is apocryphally reported to have been offered as the New World refuge for Napoleon Bonaparte. Today, its ground

floor is occupied by a bar and restaurant, making it another wonderful spot to postpone sightseeing long enough to study the architecture from behind a sandwich and beer (*see page 189* **Nightlife**).

Jackson Square

Jackson Square, the centre of the French Quarter is surrounded by the best-known buildings in New Orleans. The varied styles of these structures is a metaphor for the multi-ethnic Creole culture of early nineteenth-century New Orleans itself.

St Louis Cathedral, the focal point of Jackson Square, was completed in 1850 from plans by JNB de Pouilly. Visitors who have beheld the great churches of Europe will certainly not be awed by this building, but its lance-like spires are taller by far than any architectural feature of the period. The design is essentially Greek Revival, with dozens of vertical half-columns and pilasters striping the cathedral's façade. But the style is compromised by a similar number of arched windows and entry ways and the towers. The checked floor was designed by Eugene Warburg, a free man of colour (the local term for the large population of free blacks who made up much of the artisan trade in antebellum New Orleans).

Flanking the cathedral at each shoulder are the **Cabildo** (on the west) – designed as the seat of the Spanish Colonial government – and the **Presbytère** (on the east) – envisioned as housing for priests. These imposing structures are perfect anchors for the tall cathedral between them. Both buildings were designed by Gilberto Guillemard and built just before and after the second fire: the Presbytère in 1791-1813 and the Cabildo in 1795-9. The high, rather incoherent mansard roofs were added in 1847 and serve to detract from the two-tiered horizontality of the original Spanish Colonial appearance. Both buildings are now part of the Louisiana State Museum (*see page 89* **Museums & Galleries**).

The upper and lower **Pontalba Apartments** (completed in 1850) form the upriver and downriver arms of the square. Built by the infamous Baroness Pontalba, who spend most of her life in Paris, these huge red brick structures bear features of the classic Creole townhouse and hints of later American influence. But above all, the long, continuous apartments mirror the elegant terraced houses of nineteenth-century Paris. The **1850 House**, one of the apartments in the Pontalba buildings, is open to the public (*see page 52* **Sightseeing**).

American mansions

St Charles Avenue is one of the best preserved, if least spectacular, of the great avenues that sprang up around the USA to demonstrate industrial-era wealth. The mercantile section of New Orleans above Canal Street was known as the 'American' sector, both to reflect the influx of business interest that followed the Louisiana Purchase and to distinguish it ethnically from the Creole enclave of the Vieux Carré.

A good place to begin investigating this more recent architecture is **Gallier Hall** at the eastern end of St Charles Avenue, at Lafayette Street (*see page 60* **Sightseeing**). Built by New York architect James Gallier in 1850-51 as a second city hall (to accommodate American interests), this Greek Revival temple is remarkable in the New Orleans cityscape for its size and grandeur. It boasts ten Ionic columns rising to seven times the height of the average man, surmounted by a tremendous pediment.

The merchant, manufacturing and banking kings of New Orleans around the turn of the century expressed their individuality, their world-consciousness and – of course – their enormous wealth in the wildly eclectic, preposterously large dwellings that line St Charles further uptown. The four-block stretch from Valence Street to Robert Street is a wonderful slice of what was New Orleans's millionaires' row. It includes the **Brown House** (4717 St Charles Avenue), built in 1905, a weighty, broad-footed Romanesque Revival mansion constructed of sandstone and roofed in red tile. The structure seems to sink into its expansive, shaded lawn, reflecting perhaps the gravity of the original occupant's self-image. On the other hand, the 1866 **Aldrich-Genella House** (at No.4801) is an airy, vertical, Second Empire construction that seems to leap up from the ground with a certain genteel *joie de vivre* – especially as it is currently coated in cotton candy-pink paint.

The **Rosenberg House** (No.4920) is a 1911 Colonial Revival anomaly, as stylistically suited to the south of England as south Louisiana. Designed by Emile Weil, it has an exposed wooden framework between stucco and a ground-floor stone wall that looks as though it should be surrounded by a moat. The mansion at 5005 St Charles Avenue, now the **Orleans Club**, was originally a residence and is of particular interest amid the mixed romanticism of the Avenue. Built in 1868, it is a splendid, if austere, retelling of the American-style townhouse, with subtle Italianate flourishes and ironwork. In context, it seems just as exotic as any of the other eclectic designs. It's a private and very exclusive women's club these days and the mansion is the setting for countless wedding receptions, engagement parties and dinner-dances.

Unfortunately, you can't see the interiors of any of the above mansions, but both the **Columns Hotel** (No.3811, *see page 197* **Nightlife**) – designed in 1883 by Thomas Sully, one of the principal architects of St Charles Avenue – and the **Latter Library** (No.5120) were originally residences and

are open to the public. For more on St Charles Avenue mansions and the surrounding area, *see page 72* **Sightseeing**.

The Creole avenue

Heading away from the French Quarter towards the lake is Esplanade Avenue, the other of the city's golden roads of the past. Esplanade is remembered as the great Creole avenue, rivalling the American avenue, St Charles. It is also rumoured to have been the road of industrial-age illicit romances: the great houses on St Charles were built for rich men's wives; the mansions on Esplanade for their mistresses. The legend is probably baseless, but in New Orleans, history is always the step-child of the well-told falsehood. It is a fact, though, that while St Charles is a reasonably well-preserved strand of architectural pearls, Esplanade has been allowed in large part to fall into gross disrepair. Oddly, this only adds to the shadowy road's allure.

For much of its length, Esplanade is lined with two-storey, free-standing townhouses of the American type. In addition to these typical mid- to late-nineteenth-century homes, the street is punctuated by marvellous architectural eccentricities (sadly, the only house you can go inside is the Degas House).

About half way between the Vieux Carré and City Park stands the somewhat dishevelled **Dufour-Baldwin House** (1707 Esplanade Avenue, at North Derbigny Street). This Greek Revival mansion was built in 1859 from a design by Henry Howard and Albert Diettel. The 16 Corinthian columns that support the broad balcony and entablature make this the most impressive façade on Esplanade. The forlorn grandeur of the house is only enhanced by the current mustard-yellow paint that harmonises with the oak leaves and resurrection ferns on the ground below.

The typical townhouse further up Esplanade, at No.2306 (at Tonti Street) decorated in a popular Italianate pattern of wooden appliqué, is remarkable for two things. First, the house was the brief residence of the Impressionist master Edgar Degas on his visit to New Orleans in 1872 – it is generally known as the **Degas House** (*see page 81* **Sightseeing**). The other peculiarity is that early drawings of the structure indicate that half of it has now gone. No explanation of the disappearance is recorded, but at least one scholar theorises that the house to the left is the missing part, which was moved and redesigned at an unknown time.

The **Sharpy House** (No.2326, at N Tonti Street) is eye-catching, not only for its dramatic façade but for the peculiar, galvanised metal sculpture in the shape of shotgun houses stacked in the front yard. These large silver shapes, crowded into the rather small area in front of the house, are the satirical sculpture of artist and city planner Robert Tannen. The **Dunbar House** (No.2453, at N Dorgenois Street) is a rare, incongruous example of a mansard design, with its tall roof and elaborate dormers. This anomalous structure illustrates the Esplanade Avenue manifestation of the eclectic, cosmopolitan tastes that prevailed in the late nineteenth century, as does the Queen Anne style **Grosson House** (No.0000, at 11 White Street).

Hiding a half-block off the Avenue at 1438 Leda Street is the Luling Mansion or the **Jockey Club**, as it is popularly if spuriously known. Designed and built in 1865, it is remembered as James Gallier's masterpiece in the Italianate style, with two wrap-around balustraded balconies, arched ground-floor openings and a fourth-storey cupola.

Places of worship

New Orleans is said to have more bars per capita than any other city, but it is also supposed to have more churches. Here are a few of the best.

Touro Synagogue (4224 St Charles Avenue, at General Pershing Street) is one of the signature accomplishments of Emile Weil (who also designed the Rosenberg House on St Charles Avenue). The bone-coloured brick structure, completed in 1909, is ribboned with strips of brightly coloured ceramic tiles in geometric patterns and capped with a huge gleaming dome of reflective tiles.

St Augustine's Catholic Church (1200 Gov Nicholls Street, between N Rampart Street and St Claude Avenue) in the Tremé neighbourhood, adjacent to the French Quarter, is remarkable for its Italianate frame design. But it is also of note as the first Catholic church in the US to be built by an African-American congregation, in 1842. St Augustine's served the unique community of free blacks in New Orleans before the Civil War and was also the first church where slaves were allowed to worship with free men.

St Joseph's Catholic Church (1802 Tulane Avenue, at S Prieur Street), massive though it is, now seems lost in the urban wasteland of highways, parking lots and generic modern buildings that share its Mid City locale. Built in 1869-92 by two separate architects, Carl Kaiser and Patrick Keeley, this glorious Romanesque giant is the largest brick building in the city.

Best of the rest

For every building we've mentioned, there's a dozen others also worth seeing. But don't fear: architecture is a passion in New Orleans and there is no shortage of texts and tours for those interested (*see pages 85-88* **Sightseeing**). Here are some other sights that should not be missed.

Canal Street has a continuous string of nineteenth-century storefronts, decorated like wedding cakes with Italianate and Beaux Arts ornamentation. In the upper storeys of its buildings, the street provides a wonderful vision of the elegance of an earlier age; at street level, it reminds us of the gaudiness of contemporary retailing. The whole of the **Garden District**, with its glorious homes embedded in jungles of wisteria and spider lilies, is many visitors' favourite locale for architecture. The splendid residences on Prytania Street and the numbered streets (First, Second, Third and so on) are of particular note (*see page 68* **Sightseeing**).

The city-side bank of Bayou St John (the stretch of water that skirts the eastern edge of City Park) is the location of **Pitot House** (1440 Moss Street, *see page 80* **Sightseeing**) and the **Old Spanish Customs House** (1300 Moss Street). Built in 1805 and 1807 respectively, these two beautiful structures provide a glimpse of the plantation homes that were once scattered across the outlying areas.

Far downriver in Bywater lie two buildings that require special mention: the **Doullut houses** (400 Egania Street, at Douglas Street), also known as the Riverboat Houses. Designed by River Captain Milton Doullut in 1905 and 1913, these charming houses have oriental roofs, decorative strands of wooden balls hung above the porches and cupolas made to mimic riverboat pilot houses.

Overgrown oaks dominate the Garden District.

Sightseeing

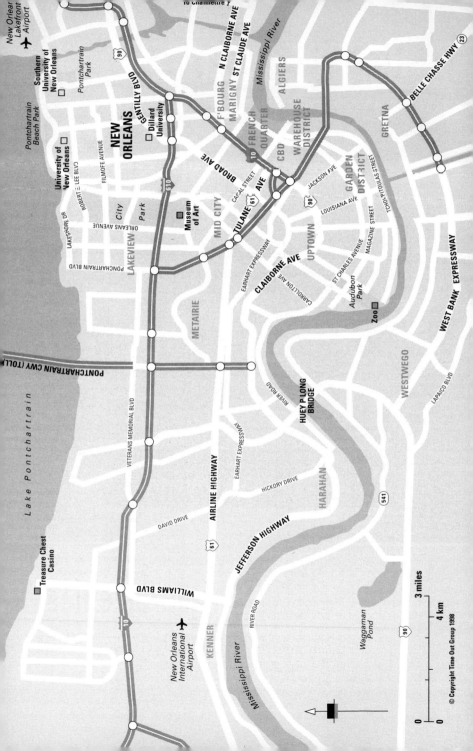

Sightseeing

Opulent mansions, witch-led walking tours, crumbling cemeteries and the mighty Mississippi are just the starting points for seeing New Orleans

New Orleans is somehow larger than the sum of its sights. The city has museums and significant architecture and quirky localisms but those aren't what you'll remember about it. Rather it will be the delight of a city steeped in the pursuit of pleasure amid a semi-tropical cityscape that has mostly eluded the wrecking ball of the twentieth century.

Sightseeing is a way to structure your immersion into the life of New Orleans. Waiting for the St Charles Streetcar on Canal Street you might see a mini-Mardi Gras parade, even though it's September, put on for a film company or a convention or because some folks got tired of waiting for Carnival. Walking between historic house tours in the Quarter you'll pass corner bars, lone musicians and even uniformed Catholic schoolgirls. Strolling through Audubon Park you'll overhear power-walking Uptown socialites comparing notes on the new débutante crop. Looking for an address in Marigny you'll come across the oldest gay bookstore in the South. Think of sightseeing as the stitches that pull together the rich, sometimes elusive tapestry of New Orleans. See the sights, but don't forget to look between the lines and around the corner.

The French Quarter

See Map 7

The Quarter, or 'Quawduh' as the locals say, is the heart of the city and its soul. And its libido, as well. It is a place of romance and sensuality, mystique and undecipherable strangeness. Louisiana novelist Walker Percy wrote – disparagingly – that prostitutes ply their trade in the very shadow of St Louis Cathedral, the oldest Roman Catholic cathedral in the US. Other observers, however, have found this mixture of the sensual and the spiritual to be the Quarter's principal attraction.

For writers and artists, lovers and outcasts of all sorts, the French Quarter – officially called the Vieux Carré – has long been more than an inspiration; it has also been a refuge. Tennessee Williams called it 'the last frontier of bohemia'. Particularly for those escaping the narrow minded parochialism of small Southern towns, the French Quarter's attitude of tolerance has provided a first safe haven.

Pleasures of the flesh abound, with opportunities ranging from the demure to the most spectacular. And although it isn't often spoken aloud, the reason many come to the French Quarter is, quite frankly, to get laid. But the area provides an array of visual experiences as well, most especially architectual.

Newcomers who expect the Quarter to look like Paris are confounded by an architecture that more closely resembles Havana. This is because the early French colonial buildings, mostly modest frame cottages, were almost all consumed in the great fires of 1788 and 1794. The Spanish, then controlling Louisiana, rebuilt the town from the ground up, so the new buildings reflected their own culture rather than the styles of their French predecessors. As the Spanish administrators were mainly Creoles rather than Europeans ('creole' comes from the Spanish word 'criollo' meaning 'born in the colonies'), the new town was more Caribbean than European. What one sees today reflects that style to a large extent: plaster-over-brick buildings painted in a palette ranging from pastel to bright; decorative ironwork on the balconies that provide shelter from both tropical rains and the torrid sun of summer; and hidden patios filled with lush tropical foliage.

Everywhere there is music. From an open window floats a wisp of Brahms or a bamboula by Louis Gottschalk, the native-born nineteenth-century Creole pianist and composer. But not surprisingly in the birthplace of jazz, the music heard most is contemporary: R&B, rock, gospel, Cajun, zydeco, country, reggae, rap. From solitary horn players on street corners to the open doors of music clubs on Bourbon Street, music fills the air.

The French Quarter is still a residential neighbourhood, although as property values escalate it has become less affordable to the waiters, bartenders, artists and writers who used to inhabit it. However, its residents continue to defend the neighbourhood against encroaching commercial interests (with varying degrees of success), and it was this impulse that ignited the preservation movement earlier this

St Louis Cathedral: *parish church of the Quarter and centrepiece of Jackson Square.*

century, which resulted in the designation of the Quarter as a historic district under the protection of the Vieux Carré Commission.

What is protected today is still a village, its street pattern very much as Adrien de Pauger, engineer of the French colony, designed it in 1722, four years after the establishment of the little settlement in the bend of the Mississippi River.

Around Jackson Square

Hugging the river are some of the city's oldest and newest attractions. On the downriver side of the Quarter are a series of buildings called, collectively, the **French Market**. Running from St Ann Street to Barracks Street, the market begins with the **Café du Monde**, open 24 hours a day throughout the year except Christmas Day, and famous for

coffee and square doughnuts called beignets (*see page 142* **Cafés & Coffeehouses**). At the other end of the Market are the open-air farmers' markets and flea markets. In between are a number of disappointingly touristy shops and restaurants. At the lower end of the Market stands the impressive **Old United States Mint** (*see page 89* **Museums & Galleries**).

On the upriver edge of the Quarter lie two of the area's newest additions, the riverfront Woldenberg Park and the **Aquarium of the Americas** (*see page 51*). In the middle of the Quarter, between Woldenberg and the Café du Monde, is a river promenade named the **Moon Walk** (in honour of former mayor Moon Landrieu).

It was at this place that the city was founded. The French settled here because the bend in the river provided an excellent lookout in both directions.

If you only have two days…

For the traveller on a tight schedule, New Orleans can be easily distilled into several must-see experiences that comprise the best of the Big Easy.

DAY ONE

Up early (before 8am) to see the **French Quarter** at its best. This fabled den of iniquity has another personality in the mornings. It's a close-knit neighbourhood of dog-walkers, schoolchildren and open-air shops. Residents try to get to the French Market for the day's fresh produce before the tourists arrive and Café du Monde and other breakfast places belong to the natives. At this hour the Quarter is relatively empty and traffic free, giving walkers a good view of everything.

Finish your walk before 9am and stroll over to **Café du Monde** (*p142*) for a suitably decadent breakfast of café au lait and sugar-drenched beignets. To stretch out breakfast through several reorders of beignets and coffee, pick up an armful of US and European newspapers next door at **French Quarter News** (*p181*). Around 10am or 11am join one of the walking tours that emanate from the Quarter. Good bets are the **Friends of the Cabildo walks**, **Rob Florence's cemetery tour** or **Le Monde du Creole** (*p86 and p87*).

Lunch! Possibly the day's biggest decision: where to eat? For working-class cuisine raised to art, try **Mother's** (*p128*) a block from the Quarter, or for top-of-the-line cuisine there's Emeril Lagasse's lovely **NOLA** (*p116*). Walk off some of that stuffed feeling (if you don't feel you've overeaten, you've gone to the wrong place) strolling down Royal Street now that the shops are open.

Take in one of the museums in the Quarter. The **Old US Mint** (*p89*) provides a good grounding in jazz and Mardi Gras, while the hushed **Historic New Orleans Collection** (*p90*) combines a house tour and Louisiana artefacts. Or, for a meta-museum experience, there's the unapologetically lurid **Musée Conti** (*p91*).

It's been a full day. Go back to the hotel, take a nap. This is a vacation. Emerge refreshed and hungry in the early evening. Dine at **Antoine's** (*p119*) or **Galatoire's** (*p120*) for a big dose of Old New Orleans. Then cross Esplanade Avenue into the music land of **Frenchmen Street** – here's where the real music is happening, not in

the Bourbon Street bars. Try **Snug Harbor** (*p204*) for jazz and headliners, **Rubyfruit** (*p177*) for lesbian dance club atmosphere, **Café Brasil** (*p204*) for anything from unannounced music stars trying out new material to poetry readings to jazz fusion and beyond. Finish the day with a nightcap at **Lafitte's Blacksmith Shop** (*p187*), one of the oldest neighbourhood bars in the US.

DAY TWO

Sleep late. Order room service for breakfast. When you're ready for the bright New Orleans sun, put on your shades and head out to the Mississippi River and board one of the steamboats headed downriver to the **Audubon Zoo** (*p74*). Disembark at the Audubon Park/Zoo stop. At the zoo, go directly to the Louisiana Swamp site. Check out the alligators, replicated Cajun village, lots of water and swamp – now you've seen Louisiana in the wild, you don't have to take an all-day swamp tour. Linger at the zoo longer or make a beeline for **Audubon Park** (*p74*). Cross Magazine Street and walk through the park up to St Charles Avenue. The pathways are clearly marked and it will take less than 30 minutes.

At St Charles, catch the streetcar headed towards the Riverbend area; get off when the streetcar turns on to Carrollton Avenue at **Riverbend**. Lunch can be a hamburger at the **Camellia Grill** (*p131*) or a full meal at **Franky & Johnny's** (*p135*), the Italian-Creole restaurant. Catch the streetcar heading back downtown. The slow-moving car is a window on St Charles Avenue, with its exuberant display of conspicuous architectural consumption.

Rest at your hotel or in a dark bar, say the **Napoleon House** (*p189*) or the Monteleone's famous **Carousel Room** (*p185*) or the **Columns** (*p197*) if you're staying Uptown. **Irene's** (*p123*), a Creole restaurant beloved by locals, is a good spot for dinner.

For evening entertainment drop by **Tipitina's** (*p209*), the archetypal New Orleans music club. Although Tip's now has a place in the Quarter, make the pilgrimage Uptown to the original, riverside Tip's where the spirit of Professor Longhair lives on. Finish the night back in the Quarter at **Café du Monde**, where you'll probably run into the rest of the audience and some of the band.

Near the river they laid out a public place that they called the Place d'Armes because its principal purpose was as encampment and drill field for the soldiers manning the outpost. Later, the Spanish would call the square Plaza de Armas, and still later, Americans renamed it **Jackson Square** in honour of General (later US President) Andrew Jackson, hero of the Battle of New Orleans in 1815.

Facing the square, on the opposite side from the river, the French erected a simple chapel, which promptly blew down during the first major storm. The second church on the spot burned down on Good Friday 1788. The third church, begun in 1789, designated a cathedral in 1793 and considerably enlarged and redesigned in the 1850s, is the **St Louis Cathedral** that still stands today (*see page 52*).

The Spanish built two imposing buildings on either side of the church and today the three form one flank of the square. The **Cabildo** was the seat of government for the Spanish colony of Louisiana. On the other side, the **Presbytère** was planned as the residence for the priests of the church. Both served mainly as government buildings until they became part of the Louisiana State Museum system (*see page 89* **Museums & Galleries**).

Flanking the square, upriver and down, are the imposing red brick **Pontalba Apartments**, built in the 1850s by one of New Orleans's many dynamic women, the Baroness Michaela Pontalba. Often called the first apartment buildings in the country, they have always been used as they are

Voodoo

Shortly after the French settled New Orleans, African slaves began to be imported. The colonial government promptly enacted a set of laws called the Code Noir, or 'Black Code', which in 1724 was designed to regulate slavery in the Louisiana Colony and to define the rights and responsibilities of all parties: slaves, slave owners and free people of colour. The Code Noir also specified that the Roman Catholic faith was the only religion allowed in the colony and slave owners were required to see to it that all their slaves were instructed in Catholicism and baptised.

The practice of other religions was illegal in the colony, so much of African religious culture was eventually lost, though more of it survived in New Orleans than anywhere else in North America. It would seem that the French colonial government, along with the French Catholic Church, adopted a laissez-faire policy towards the problem and many Africans in Louisiana continued – illegally – to practise African religious rituals.

Since many Africans became Catholics while secretly keeping alive their native faiths, eventually the language and rituals of both religions blended together, helped by some of the similarities shared by the two traditions. Africans, like Christians, were monotheistic: the word for 'One God' in the language of the Fon tribe was *Voudon*. Another shared practice was the belief in life after death. A third was the African concept of *loas*, minor deities who functioned very much as saints do in Catholicism.

A major difference concerned the souls of the dead. Unlike Christian theology, where the spirits depart earth for heaven or hell, Africans believed that spirits could remain on earth among the living. This belief is what makes New Orleans a 'city of spirits'. Since everything and every place is inhabited by the spirits of the dead, every house in New Orleans is 'haunted', one of the reasons there are so many so-called 'ghost' tours today.

But this also proves that some aspects of African religious culture still survive in the city. There are plenty of people of all races who still draw from both Christian and African religious traditions in the practice of their faith – and the mixture of the two is called voodoo.

The only authentic voodoo house of worship (as opposed to commercial voodoo shops and 'museums') easily accessible to the visiting public is the **Voodoo Spiritual Temple**. The 7.30pm Thursday service is open to the public and visitors are welcomed by Priestess Miriam Chamani and her staff, who provide information about the temple and voodoo in general. An African bone reading costs $45.

Another important voodoo historical site nearby is **Congo Square** (in Armstrong Park, between St Peter and St Ann Streets), where slaves and free people of colour were allowed to congregate by the French colonial government. Also of interest are places associated with Marie Laveau, the most famous of the nineteenth-century voodoo priestesses, including her long-time residence at 1020 St Ann Street and her tomb in St Louis Cemetery No.1 (*see page 70*).

Voodoo Spiritual Temple
828 N Rampart Street, between St Ann & Dumaine Streets (522 9627/voodoo@gnofn.org). Bus 3 Vieux Carré, 88 St Claude. **Open** 10am-8pm daily. **Admission** free. **Map 7 C1**

Signs of the times: the railings of Jackson Square provide an impromptu open air gallery.

today: with shops on the ground floor and residential apartments above. Of note is the elaborate cast iron work on the balconies, thought to be the first cast iron balconies in New Orleans. The letters 'A' and 'P' are woven into each section of the iron design after the baroness's maiden (Almonester) and married names. One of the apartments, the **1850 House** (*see page 52*), is open to the public.

Once the Pontalba buildings were completed – and the incongruous third floors incorporated into the Cabildo and the Presbytère – the design of the square was established and it has changed very little since then.

Today Jackson Square is still a vital centre of the city's culture. Every day the place is filled with buskers and street performers, palm and tarot readers, and it's used as a site for civic events ranging from the French Quarter Festival in April to carol-singing on the Sunday before Christmas. It also serves as a sort of dividing point in the Quarter. There are exceptions, but the Canal Street half of the Quarter (known as the upper Quarter, because it's upriver) is largely commercial, whereas the lower Quarter is quieter and more residential.

Aquarium of the Americas & IMAX Theater

1 Canal Street, at the Mississippi River (581 4629/ 1-800 774 7394). Bus 41 Canal. **Open** *Aquarium 9.30am-6pm (last ticket sold 5pm) Mon-Thur, Sun; 9.30am-7pm (last ticket sold 6pm) Fri, Sat; IMAX 10am-6pm daily; shows every hour.* **Admission** *Aquarium* $10.95; $8.50 seniors; $5 2-12s; *IMAX* $7.50; $6.50 seniors; $5 2-12s. **Credit** AmEx, MC, V.
Map 7 A3

Aquariums are all the rage in American cities but it actually makes sense for New Orleans to have one. Located in a soaring glassy blue building beside the Mississippi River, the aquarium fittingly concentrates on the places close at hand: the Mississippi, the Gulf of Mexico and the Caribbean. Authenticity extends to a replica of an offshore oil rig in the Gulf of Mexico section, which green-sensitive visitors may see as a little too tolerant in its attitude to sharing the seas. The Caribbean Reef installation is spectacular: visitors walk through a 30ft (9m) glass tunnel underneath the sea world that moves all around them.

Next door is the **IMAX Theater**, a state-of-the-art film experience that virtually puts viewers on Mount Everest or at the bottom of the sea with its high-definition giant screen and multi-speaker sound system. The films usually deal with some dramatic aspect of the natural world, though the programmes aren't co-ordinated with the Aquarium or the Audubon Zoo (which is operated under the same auspices).
Disabled: toilet. Website: www.auduboninstitute.org

1850 House

523 St Ann Street, on Jackson Square (568 6968/ 1-800 568 6968). Bus 3 Vieux Carré, 55 Elysian Fields, 81 Almonaster, 82 Desire. **Open** 9am-5pm Tue-Sun. **Admission** $4; $3 students, seniors; free under-12s. **Credit** MC, V. **Map 7 C2**

'House' is a little misleading for this museum as it's actually an apartment in the stately Pontalba buildings. This makes a tour all the more interesting because it's the only chance you'll have to see the residential upper floors of the Pontalbas. The ground floor houses an office and gift shop while the second and third floors have been recreated as a Victorian Creole townhouse with dining room, master bedroom and nursery.

Website: www.crt.state.la.us/crt/museum/lsmnet3.htm

St Louis Cathedral

725 Chartres Street, on Jackson Square (525 9585). Bus 3 Vieux Carré, 55 Elysian Fields, 81 Almonaster, 82 Desire. **Open** 7am-6.30pm daily; tours approx every ½hr. **Admission** free. **Map 7 C2**

St Louis Cathedral is modest in comparison to the great cathedrals of Europe but is quite rightly seen as the symbol of New Orleans. Its three-steepled façade crowns Jackson Square with an uncluttered elegance. Tours are available throughout the day, arranged around masses and church activities. It is the parish church for the French Quarter. *See also p41* **Architecture**.

Decatur & Chartres Streets

Decatur Street separates Jackson Square from the river. Originally called Rue de la Levee, for many years it contained rough sections such as the infamous Gallatin Alley, reportedly so dangerous in the nineteenth century that police refused to enter it (the alley has since been demolished). In the 1960s it was still largely unrenovated, and became the centre for New Orleans's hippie culture. Now

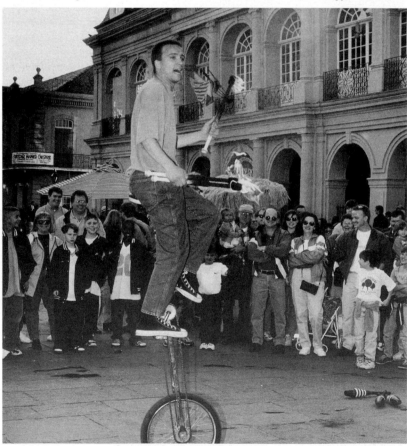

The French Quarter is a busker's paradise, complete with captive audience.

largely gentrified, the street includes shops, restaurants and clubs such as Jimmy Buffet's **Margaritaville** and **House of Blues** (*see page 203* **Nightlife**), as well as the local outposts of the **Hard Rock Café**, **Planet Hollywood** and the **Fashion Café** (*see page 134* **Restaurants**).

Parallel to and north of Decatur Street is Chartres Street (pronounced 'chartors'). Interrupted by St Louis Cathedral at its centre, Chartres is a mixture of galleries, shops, flats and houses. On lower Chartres stands the oldest building in the Mississippi River valley, the convent of the **Ursuline** nuns (*see below*), which now serves as a museum of the Catholic Church. Facing the convent is the **Beauregard-Keyes House**, an 1826 Greek Revival home open to the public (*see below*).

Further upriver, flanking the Hotel Ste Hélène on Chartres Street, stands the bar, restaurant and scene of Napoleonic intrigue, the **Napoleon House** (*see page 189* **Nightlife**) and the **New Orleans Pharmacy Museum**, site of an early nineteenth-century drugstore run by America's first licensed pharmacist (*see page 91* **Museums & Galleries**).

During the 1920s and 1930s, when the Quarter had deteriorated into little better than a slum, it attracted a number of struggling young artists and writers drawn by the charm of the area and the cheap rent. Among these were William Faulkner, who lived across from the cathedral in Pirate's Alley (in what is now **Faulkner House Books**, *see page 152* **Shops & Services**). Novelist Sherwood Anderson lived around the corner at 708 Royal Street. Later, Tennessee Williams would live variously at 431 and 538 Royal Street, 722 Toulouse Street, 710 Orleans Street and 623 St Peter Street. Truman Capote wrote most of his first novel, *Other Voices, Other Rooms*, in an apartment at 811 Royal Street.

Beauregard-Keyes House

1113 Chartres Street, at Ursulines Street (523 7257). Bus 3 Vieux Carré, 55 Elysian Fields, 81 Almonaster, 82 Desire. Open 10am-3pm Mon-Sat; tours on the hour. Admission $4, $3 seniors, students; $1.50 under-12s. No credit cards. Map 7 C2

This 1826 house reflects both the Creole and American building styles, with its American central hall and Creole veranda and courtyard. The house is furnished and decorated in the style of the mid-nineteenth century. Some of the furniture and items are from the family of Confederate General PGT Beauregard, who briefly lived in the house after the Civil War. In the 1940s, bestselling novelist Frances Parkinson Keyes (pronounced 'Kize') took over the house, then in great disrepair, gradually returning it to its old beauty, if not improving it. The back courtyard is very handsome and the side garden has been restored to a formal Creole garden. Keyes's doll and costume collections are on display in the courtyard buildings where she had quarters and living quarters. The gift shop is one of the few places to find Keyes's books, which are now all out of print.

Old Ursuline Convent

1112 Chartres Street, at Ursulines Street (529 3040). Bus 3 Vieux Carré, 55 Elysian Fields, 81 Almonaster, 82 Desire. Open Tours 10am, 11am, 1pm, 2pm, 3pm Tue-Fri; 11.15am, 1pm, 2pm Sat, Sun. Admission $5; $4 seniors; $2 students; free under-8s. No credit cards. Map 7 C2

The grande dame of New Orleans architecture, this serene-looking convent was built between 1745 and 1760, replacing an earlier compound built in the 1100s. It is the oldest surviving building in New Orleans – being one of the few structures left standing after the devastating fires of 1788 and 1794. The only complete French colonial building in New Orleans, it retains some details of the first structure. Especially lovely are the hand-hewn cypress stairs. The Ursuline nuns arrived in the city in 1727 from France and set about their work of teaching and healing. The order was prosperous and shrewd. They were notable for not only teaching the daughters of the bourgeoisie but black and Indian children as well. The convent was sold to the church in the nineteenth century and used as the archbishop's residence. The adjacent St Mary's Church was built in 1845 as the archbishop's chapel. Today the compound houses the archdiocese's archives. Visits are limited to regularly scheduled tours. *Disabled: toilet.*

Royal Street

Royal Street, which runs behind the cathedral, was the main street of the original town. The banking district developed in the early nineteenth century around Conti Street and historic bank buildings remain today at 334, 343, 403 and 417 Royal. The 417 Royal building, today **Brennan's** (*see page 119* **Restaurants**), was built by a grandfather of the painter Edgar Degas.

No.431 Royal, next door to Brennan's, was the site of New Orleans's possibly most significant contribution to civilisation. In the 1790s an apothecary named AA Peychaud operated his business there. Legend has it that Peychaud, who had concocted a mixture he called bitters, blended it with some cognac and *voilà!*, the first mixed drink was created. Since Peychaud had created his potion in an egg cup (*coquetière* in French) the new drink became known as a 'cocktail' by Americans whose enthusiasm for alcoholic options exceeded their fluency in French pronunciation.

Down the street at 533 Royal is a very early building, the **Merieult House** (circa 1794), which houses the **Historic New Orleans Collection** (*see page 90* **Museums & Galleries**), an important museum and archival collection of New Orleanian documents, maps, prints and artefacts.

The first eight blocks of Royal Street contain some of the grandest Spanish-styled townhouses, displaying particularly fine examples of intricate cast iron balconies, and at No.915 is an example of one of the city's 'cornstalk fences'. Today most of these buildings house art galleries, antique shops and upmarket boutiques, as well as restaurants and cafés. A few steps off Royal on St Louis Street is the famous **Antoine's Restaurant**, which has

Balcony scene: Royal Street has some of the finest cast ironwork in the city.

been operated by the same family since 1840 (*see page 119* **Restaurants**). Nearby is the Omni Royal Orleans Hotel (621 St Louis Street; 529 5333) whose open-air rooftop bar provides one of the best views of French Quarter rooftops, the river and the city skyline.

Behind the cathedral is a small garden that contains a memorial to yellow fever victims and a statue of Christ with uplifted arms. Tennessee Williams, who once lived in a house at 710 Orleans that looked out on to the garden, wrote that the statue seemed to be embracing all of humankind. Less reverential passers-by have noted that the shadow cast by the statue resembles the gesture of American football referees and have dubbed it the 'Touchdown Jesus'.

Just off Royal Street, on Dumaine Street, is a rare example of early French colonial architecture. For years the house has been known as **Madame John's Legacy** (*see page 56*), after a fictional character – though most locals, used to the make-believe world of Mardi Gras, have long forgotten that there never was a Madame John, nor any such legacy.

Further down Royal are two other famous houses. At No.1132 is **Gallier House** (*see below*), built in 1857 by architect James Gallier Jr as his home. Open to the public for tours, it contains some interesting innovations, including Gallier's design for the first indoor plumbing system in New Orleans. Two doors down, at the corner of Gov Nicholls Street, is the **Lalaurie House** (1140 Royal Street), probably the most famous 'haunted house' in the city. Although the story is enthusiastically embellished by companies providing 'ghost tours', the infamy of the place is documented. Madame Lalaurie was fined for mistreating slaves and it is the slaves who are alleged to haunt the place.

Between Royal and Bourbon Streets, on Orleans Street, is the site of the old **Orleans Ballroom**, where many elegant nineteenth-century galas were held, including balls where white gentlemen seeking mistresses were introduced to beautiful women of colour. The ballroom, also known as the Quadroon Ballroom, has been lovingly incorporated into the design of the Bourbon Orleans Hotel (717 Orleans Street; 523 2222), which occupies most of the block. Ascend the grand double staircase to the second floor and you might be able to peer inside the ballroom.

Gallier House

1132 Royal Street, between Gov Nicholls & Barracks Streets (525 5661). Bus 3 Vieux Carré, 48 Esplanade, 55 Elysian Fields, 81 Almonaster, 82 Desire.
Open 10am-3.30pm Mon-Sat; tours every ½ hour.
Admission $6; $5 seniors, students; $4 8-18s;
free under-8s. **Credit** MC, V (gift shop only).
Map 7 D2
James Gallier Jr, son of key New Orleans architect James Gallier Sr, designed this side-hall, Greek Revival townhouse. The house has been carefully restored and furnished in the style of an upper-class family of the 1860s. Furnishings change with the seasons, with mosquito netting added in summer and Christmas decorations in the winter.

Madame John's Legacy

632 Dumaine Street, at Royal Street (1-800 568 6968). Bus 3 Vieux Carré, 55 Elysian Fields, 81 Almonaster, 82 Desire. **Map 7 C2**
This raised Creole cottage dates from 1788, making it one of the oldest buildings in New Orleans. Its longevity renders the house one of the most architecturally and historically significant structures in Louisiana, but a writer gave the house its enduring fame and name. George Washington Cable used the house in his novella, *Madame John's Legacy*, the story of how a quadroon mistress used her inheritance from her white lover, the father of her children. Historians insist the house has no such tangled history, but it has become a symbol for the New Orleans subculture of 'shadow families'. The house is owned by the Louisiana State Museum and has been under renovation. It is due to reopen to the public at the end of 1998 and will house a folk art museum.
Website: www.crt.state.la.us/crt/ museum/lsmnet3.htm

Bourbon Street

The next street north of Royal is Bourbon Street. It didn't become the famous nightlife spot and tourist trap it is today until the middle of this century. Nowadays there isn't much authentic Dixieland jazz to be heard in the clubs and bars and their offerings change quickly, so you'll hear a whole range of musical styles along the street. It's closed to traffic after 7pm, when the first eight blocks (from Canal Street to St Ann Street) become a walker's mall and most clubs leave their doors open so strollers can hear the music without even going inside.

Bourbon Street is an adult entertainment area. Among the music clubs are saloons, strip shows – and their pricey, newer incarnations called 'Gentlemen's Clubs' – female impersonator shows, and tacky T-shirt shops. The best show on the street tends to be the free one provided by its weird and wild habitués.

The street is strictly segregated by sexual orientation. The first seven blocks (to Orleans Street) are 'straight Bourbon' and the next two are 'gay Bourbon'. Although gay bars are scattered throughout the Quarter and the suburbs, three of the largest are in this area. Facing each other at St Ann Street are the two largest dance bars, the **Bourbon Pub & Parade Disco** and **Oz**. At the corner of Dumaine is **Café Lafitte**, one of the oldest gay bars in America, with a principally male clientele. *See chapter* **Gay & Lesbian** for more on these.

A block further down Bourbon, at St Philip Street, is a quaint old building called **Lafitte's Blacksmith Shop** (*see page 187* **Nightlife**), which was a gay bar in the 1940s and 1950s but now is not. Although probably apocryphal, the legend persists that the shop was a base for the privateering activities of local pirate Jean Lafitte in the eighteenth century.

Towards Rampart Street

The next two streets are Dauphine and Burgundy (pronounced 'Bur-GUN-dy'). While they are pleasant parts of the Quarter and some hotels and restaurants are located here, they are mostly quiet, residential areas. On St Louis Street is the **Hermann-Grima Historic House** (*see page 57*), with its working 1830s kitchen.

The final street in the Quarter is Rampart Street, once the site of turn-of-the-century jazz joints. Today a few clubs offering New Orleans music have reopened, including the **Funky Butt** and **Donna's Bar & Grill** (*see page 201* **Nightlife** *for both*), which presents New Orleans's brass bands nightly.

From the river to North Rampart Street, the Quarter is filled with pleasures of every sort. And surprises. It can be noisy – maddeningly or exhilaratingly so – or scene and peaceful. And often the difference is just around a corner. Explore. This is the French Quarter and it's like nowhere else on earth.

Hermann-Grima Historic House

820 St Louis Street, between Bourbon & Dauphine Streets (525 5661/hggh@gnofn.org). Bus 3 Vieux Carré **ᵖᵐ** ~~.....~~ **Open** 10am-3.30pm Mon-Sat; tours every ½ hour. **Admission** $6; $5 seniors, students; $4 8-18s; free under-8s. **Credit** MC, V (gift shop only). **Map 7 B2**

This Federal-style house is especially interesting for its fully restored and working 1830s kitchen. Every Thursday, from October until May, skilled volunteers cook an entire meal using the tools, foods and methods that would have been used at the time. The house is also notable for its living history programmes, during which the house is 'dressed' as it would have been in the mid-nineteenth century for a major event such as a family funeral or wedding. *Disabled: toilet.*

Faubourg Tremé

Across Rampart Street from the French Quarter is a section of town known as the Tremé, originally the Tremé family plantation. The area has deep roots in New Orleans's cultural history, but is not safe to wander around on foot. It's worth joining an organised walking tour that covers the nearby St Louis Cemetery No.1, Congo Square and Armstrong Park (*see page 87* **Tours**).

The square facing Rampart Street between St Peter and St Ann Streets is called **Congo Square**. In the earliest days of the colony, this area was designated by the French government as a place where slaves could congregate. French colonial law, as set down in the Code Noir, said that slave owners could not make their slaves work on Sunday, to encourage them to go to church and become good Catholics. With a day off each week and a place provided where they could meet and interact, slaves in Louisiana were able to retain much more of their African language, music, dance and religion than anywhere else in North America. Elements of African culture survived long enough to become blended into European culture and with time New Orleans became the most African of North American cities.

It is this blend that created jazz. And gumbo. And voodoo. In terms of the preservation of

The Creole courtyard and verandas of the **Beauregard-Keyes House**. *See page 53.*

African culture in the New World, Congo Square is one of the most important sites in North America. Sadly, most of the surrounding neighbourhood was levelled during the first half of this century at a time when African culture wasn't appreciated. To make amends, somewhat belatedly, the resulting park was named after **Louis Armstrong** and a large arch erected at St Ann Street with his name on it. Also in the park is a statue of Armstrong and a bust of jazz pioneer Sidney Bechet. And the city-owned theatre in the park was recently named after native daughter Mahalia Jackson.

At Conti and Rampart Streets is **Our Lady of Guadaloupe Chapel** (411 N Rampart Street, 525 1551), one of the oldest in New Orleans. Now a very active Catholic parish church, it was originally built on the edge of the little town in 1826 as the mortuary chapel, to handle the great number of funerals resulting from yellow fever epidemics. To the rear of the chapel is a statue that has come to be known as 'St Expedite'. Much beloved and venerated in a neighbourhood that has historically had a vibrant African culture, St Expedite is sometimes referred to in whispers as 'the voodoo saint'. Behind the chapel is **St Louis Cemetery No.1**, the oldest cemetery in New Orleans (*see page 70* **Cities of the dead**).

Adjacent to the cemetery is where **Storyville**, the infamous red-light district, flourished from 1896 to 1917. Nothing remains of the grand brothels that ran from the cemetery to Canal Street. They were purposefully demolished after the district was shut down at the beginning of World War I. The only surviving building from the era is a sad little corner store at Basin and Bienville Streets, and even this lost its second floor years ago during a hurricane. The residential area behind Armstrong Park has deteriorated terribly during this century, although recent efforts have been made to reclaim the part of Tremé near Esplanade Avenue.

Faubourg Marigny

As Esplanade Avenue heads towards the river, it becomes the downriver boundary of the French Quarter. The old French Creole families of the nineteenth century hoped Esplanade would be the grandest residential avenue of the city. Wonderful homes were built here, but the more numerous – and richer – Americans in their Uptown section made St Charles Avenue even grander (*see page 72*). Today most of these grand homes have been divided into apartments, but a few are still single homes. Most notable is the Matilda Grey house at 704 Esplanade. Painted what neighbours call Matilda Grey Pink, the house was acquired by the oil heiress earlier this century and is now one of the homes of her niece and namesake Matilda Stream.

Two hundred years ago, Esplanade Avenue marked the edge of town. On the other side was the plantation of the prominent Marigny family. Scion of this great family (his father and grandfather are buried in St Louis Cathedral), Bernard de Marigny was one of the richest millionaires in the history of America. In around 1800 he was orphaned and inherited a fortune, then valued at $7 million. By the time Bernard came to the end of his long life, he had spent the entire fortune. He timed it well. Bernard is what Orleanians call a good role model. He lived his life fully and enjoyed what he had, though his heirs didn't see it quite that way. At some point, Bernard decided that the plantation would be more valuable as real estate than as farm land, so he sold it off as lots, creating what is often described as New Orleans's first suburb.

It is still a distinctive neighbourhood. The section between Esplanade Avenue and Elysian Fields Avenue is very much like the adjacent French Quarter. Below Elysian Fields, the properties are more modest. A less transient area than the Quarter, its residents have forged a strong neighbourhood identity. The Marigny is the site of a number of B&Bs, ranging from the **Claiborne Mansion** (2111 Dauphine Street; 949 7327), the most historically significant building in the neighbourhood, to very modest establishments. B&Bs have proliferated in the Marigny because they are officially illegal across Esplanade Avenue in the French Quarter.

Most of the neighbourhood is rather quiet, but three blocks on Frenchmen Street have become a very hip entertainment strip. From Esplanade to Royal are music clubs **Igor's Checkpoint Charlie**, **Café Brasil**, and **Snug Harbor** (*see chapter* **Nightlife**); **Rubyfruit Jungle** (a lesbian bar, *see page 177* **Gay & Lesbian**) and numerous restaurants and shops. Also on this strip is the **Faubourg Marigny Bookstore**, the oldest gay, lesbian and feminist bookstore in the South (*see page 176* **Gay & Lesbian**).

Beyond the French Quarter

Below the Marigny is Bywater, a working-class neighbourhood largely settled by Irish and German immigrants in the nineteenth century, where the **Jackson Barracks** is located (*see page 91* **Museums & Galleries**). Towards Lake Pontchartrain is Gentilly, a twentieth-century suburb, and further east, a modern suburban sprawl called New Orleans East.

There's not much of interest in these 'burbs, except perhaps some of the newer colleges that are located there. The **University of New Orleans** is on the Lakefront at Elysian Fields; **Southern University in New Orleans** is on Press Street; and **Dillard University** is located on Gentilly Boulevard; *see page 262* **Directory** for more on all three.

CBD & Warehouse District

See Map 6

The CBD

The downtown section of New Orleans – stretching from Canal Street to the interstate and from Camp Street to Tulane Avenue – is known with business-like precision as the Central Business District, or CBD. Inexplicably, no locals refer to it as downtown. While most of the tallest skyscrapers are nondescript structures built during the hazy, crazy oil boom days of the 1970s and 1980s, there are a number of remnants of the city's earlier days, when architecture was grand and Gothic.

In the early eighteenth century, most of what is now the CBD was sugarcane plantation and Canal Street was a strip of dirt nearly 200 feet (61 metres) wide marking the edge of the city and the beginning of farmland. As the area's population grew, Canal Street became critical as a meeting place in a city that was divided along national lines. By the nineteenth century, descendants of the French lived and worked in the French Quarter, while the American residents sprawled out over what is now the CBD and the Garden District and was then known as the American Sector. Canal Street was the border between the two.

The paths of the two groups rarely crossed. In those days, the French ran the city and when the American residents wanted to meet them the meetings occurred in the middle of Canal Street. The area was designated as a neutral ground between the two cultures and New Orleanians today still refer to the grassy space in the centre of any boulevard as a 'neutral ground'.

As the city became a centre for shipping, the downtown section gradually became a business centre and the Americans moved their residences further up St Charles Avenue, forming the basis for the neighbourhoods that exist today.

Because much of what is notable in the CBD is on St Charles Avenue, one of the best ways to see the area is to take the streetcar from Canal Street down St Charles to Lee Circle, and then walk back through the streets to catch the sites that aren't on the trolley route.

On the first block of St Charles from Canal Street is the **Crescent Billiard Hall** (115 St Charles Avenue), which was built in 1826 as a rather massive structure for which the sole purpose was the playing of billiards. The building is now the private Pickwick Club. Two blocks further along is the old **United Fruit Company Building** (321 St Charles Avenue), now the home of a bank. The beautiful Greek Revival building was once the

local outpost of the infamous company that, with the help of the CIA, made a fortune in the 1940s and 1950s off the fruit and political misfortune of Central America. The name is still emblazoned across the building.

Two blocks later is a small, somewhat dingy square surrounded by official-looking buildings. This is **Lafayette Square**, one of the oldest public squares in the city and now a favourite sleeping area for the homeless. The buildings around it are mostly federal buildings – including the federal courthouse, which is directly across the square from the streetcar line.

On the corner of Lafayette Square sits one of the city's most popular upmarket restaurants, **Mike's on the Avenue** (*see page 127* **Restaurants**). It serves what is known as 'fusion' cooking (read yuppie modern) and has wide windows that provide a grand view of the avenue. On the opposite side of St Charles from the square is **Gallier Hall** (*see page 60*), an 1850s structure that was used as City Hall for more than a century (it's a pity it isn't still, because the current City Hall at the edge of the CBD is a 1960s architectural nightmare).

A few blocks further down St Charles is **Julia Row**, the block of Julia Street between St Charles and Camp Street. American bigwigs occupied the 13 brick townhouses on the uptown side between the 1830s and the Civil War, when it was one of the most fashionable areas to live.

Further along sits one of the city's most beloved fixtures, the **Hummingbird Hotel** (804 St Charles Avenue; 523 9165). For more than half a century the Hummingbird has thrived. Today it is a flophouse in the 1940s style, popular with both skid-row types and backpacking college students – for years its public phone had a hand-made sign above it that stated firmly, 'No talking to imaginary people.' Its $24 rooms are spare, noisy and smelly and people love them. Best of all is the grill downstairs where the eccentric staff make some of the best fast food in the city at absurdly low prices, 24 hours a day. Breakfast, lunch or dinner will cost you less than $5 (best bets are the eggs and hamburgers). Even celebrities line up at the 'Bird – Tom Cruise and Nicole Kidman ate here while he was in town filming *Interview with the Vampire*.

At the foot of St Charles Avenue is **Lee Circle**, where the statue of Confederate General Robert E Lee has sat since 1884 (14 years after his death), atop a marble pedestal. Knowledgeable locals will point out that Lee's statue, sculpted by New Yorker Alexander Doyle, faces north, so that his back is never turned to his enemies.

Also at Lee Circle is one of the city's true hidden treasures. The **Sydney & Walda Bestoff Collection** is an impressive array of modern art belonging to a foundation created by members of the local Katz and Besthoff families who, until 1997, owned the K&B chain of drugstores. For more than 30 years the foundation collected art from acclaimed artists, placing much of it on the concrete plaza outside the K&B Building (at K&B Plaza). Inside the office building is more art, and visitors are invited to wander at will, uncovering the hundreds of treasures that sit in such workaday sites as next to elevators and outside toilets.

It is bizarre and wonderful, but too good to last. The K&B chain was recently sold to a national company (Rite-Aid) and much of the collection will be moved in 2000 to the New Orleans Museum of Art. Until then, the plaza and office is open during weekday business hours (*see page 94* **Museums & Galleries**).

One significant CBD site not on St Charles Avenue is the **Church of the Immaculate Conception**, also known as the Jesuit Church (130 Baronne Street). This extraordinary structure combines a myriad of architectural influences includ-ing Moorish, Arabian and Gothic. The building is a precise 1930s replica of the original church, which stood on the site from 1857 but was demolished in 1926 because of structural weakness. It contains the furnishings of the original, including cast iron pews and a gilt altar designed by local architect James Freret. The statue of the Virgin Mary inside was constructed in France for the royal chapel in the Tuileries, but the French Revolutionary War of 1848 put paid to that idea. It was later sold to the New Orleans church.

At the northern end of the CBD rises the hulk of the **Lousiana Superdome** (*see below*), built in 1975. Encircled by elevated highways, the dome now seems as natural a part of the New Orleans skyline as any church spire. Covering 52 acres (21 hectares) and rising 27 storeys high, the structure has aged surprisingly well. South of the Superdome, on Loyola Avenue, is the unusual memorial-cum-art installation known as the **Richard & Annette Bloch Cancer Survivors Plaza** (*see below*).

Gallier Hall

545 St Charles Avenue, at Lafayette Street. St Charles Streetcar. **Not open to the public. Map 6 C1**
Gallier Hall is constructed of creamy-looking marble and fronted by two rows of Ionic columns. It has long been one of the city's most important buildings, where visiting heads of state are received and deceased leaders traditionally lay in state – Confederate President Jefferson Davis and Confederate General PGT Beauregard both lay in state here. Today it is a ceremonial building, often rented out for special events. It is also the centre of all Mardi Gras activities, where every parade stops for review.

Louisiana Superdome

Sugar Bowl Drive, at Poydras Street (box office 587 3800/tour information line 587 3808). Bus 16 S Claiborne. **Open** 9am-4pm daily; tours hourly depending on other scheduled events. **Tours** $6; $5 concessions; $4 under-12s. **Credit** MC, V. **Map 6 A/B 1**
When the Superdome was completed in 1975 it was considered a modern marvel. Louisianans loved it. People drove hundreds of miles to see it, whether or not there was an event on. It's home to the New Orleans Saints football team as well as touring superstars, but is worth visiting at any time. Tours are given daily. *See also p40* **Architecture.**
Disabled: toilet. Website: www.superdome.com

Richard & Annette Bloch Cancer Survivors Plaza

Neutral ground of Loyola Avenue, between Poydras & Lafayette Streets. Bus 16 S Claiborne. **Map 6 B1**
This wildly colourful sculpture and garden installation was plopped down in the middle of a busy street in 1995. Midwestern philanthropists Richard and Annette Bloch wanted to share his two-time triumph over cancer with the American public and decided to do so by honouring 'cancer survivors' with outdoor sculptures in 54 American cities. A pavilion and fountain are linked by a group of frolicking sculptures representing presumably cancer-free men, women and children, and 14 soaring towers that carry 'positive mental attitude' aphorisms about cancer. Hardly anyone goes to the plaza because it's difficult to get to and off the beaten track, yet the sightlines down Loyola are striking and for all its earnestness there is a certain serenity about the place. A few homeless people catch some sleep on the benches, but it's a safe place to visit during the day.

Robert E Lee faces his enemies at **Lee Circle.**

Warehouse District

One block towards the river from St Charles Avenue is Camp Street. This is the outer edge of the CBD and the beginning of the Warehouse District. The district runs the same length as the CBD, between Camp Street and the river. It was long the location of dozens of cavernous warehouses, designed primarily for the storage of cotton, coffee and sugar destined to be shipped up the river or overseas. When modern shipping practices and the expansion of the port upriver eliminated the need for all that storage space, the Warehouse District was essentially abandoned. From the 1960s to the 1980s it sat empty and ramshackle, an eyesore on the edge of the CBD, with pigeons and bums the only regular residents.

But the 1984 Worlds Fair changed all that, with the development of a massive fair site on the edge of the district. Several warehouses were converted to public use, holding nightclubs and restaurants for the visiting fair-goers. Although the fair wasn't a financial success (falling in the middle of the recession, it was the first Worlds Fair ever to lose money), it changed the city's perspective toward the Warehouse District. Developers began seeing the rotting, window-covered behemoths for what they really were – gold mines.

The conversion process begun then continues today. Upmarket apartments and condos paved the way, with the lofts' high ceilings and enormous windows attracting scores of young professionals. The conversion of several warehouses into museums and art galleries meant the area also became know as the Arts District. Walking is the best way to see the tightly packed district, as parking spaces are at a premium and galleries are lined up virtually door to door.

The **Contemporary Arts Center** (*see page 92* **Museums & Galleries**) is a focal point of the district. It was built in an abandoned warehouse in 1976 with the stated mission of providing space for alternative arts in the city, which then had a very conservative art scene. The CAC specialises in modern works by local and national artists and hosts plays in its three small auditoriums. It also houses a popular cybercafé.

From the new to the old: across Camp Street from the CAC is the rust-coloured, castle-like structure that for 100 years has housed the **Confederate Museum**. Many visitors (and New Orleanians) write off the museum as a retro shrine to slavery and white supremacy without ever visiting the place, but Civil War buffs will enjoy the large collection of memorabilia – including part of General Robert E Lee's wartime silver service and flags and uniforms still dotted with nineteenth-century blood – in what turns out to be a restrained coverage of the War Between the States.

The Confederate Museum is poised to become the centre of a new museum community as the nearby **Ogden Museum of Southern Art** and **D-Day Museum** near completion (*see chapter* **Museums & Galleries** for details of all three). The former – housed in a restored late-nineteenth-century library designed by Henry Hobson Richardson – will house the large collection of Southern art donated to the University of New Orleans by millionaire collector Roger Ogden, while the latter will present the D-Day experience through film, exhibits and interactive displays.

The majority of art galleries in the area are located on **Julia Street**, which bounds the CAC on one side; for details, *see page 97* **Museums & Galleries**. The galleries are open to the public and close enough together to be comfortably explored on foot. One of the best ways to see them is on the first Saturday of every month when many hold art openings in the evenings (usually 6-8pm), complete with wine and cheese. Note that on those Saturdays, most galleries are closed during the day while setting up their new shows.

Buried in among the warehouses and galleries is a museum that is aimed at children but great fun for adults. The **Louisiana Children's Museum** (*see page 167* **Children**) is jam-packed with hands-on exhibits, most of which are less art than

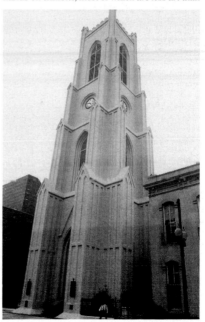

St Patrick's Cathedral. See page 62.

toys. For the littlest tykes there is a play kitchen, a radio station, a grocery store and even a port, all in miniature.

Back on Camp Street are several more art-related shops, while at the corner of Camp and Girod Streets is the city's weekly **Crescent City Market**. Area farmers and bakers bring in fresh produce, herb plants, freshly baked bread and jams on Saturday mornings, and the locals crowd in to snatch it all up. Nearby, squeezed in between modern structures, is the soaring form of **St Patrick's Cathedral** (*see below*), long the centre of Irish Catholicism in New Orleans.

The Warehouse District is also home to a number of the city's more popular restaurants and bars. At the corner of Poydras and Camp Streets is **Mother's** (*see page 128* **Restaurants**), world-famous for its po-boy sandwiches and red beans and rice. At peak times, locals and tourists line up for hours and put up with Mother's counter service just to get some of that home cookin'.

The **Mermaid Lounge** (1100 Constance Street) is a popular hole-in-the-wall music bar favoured by the alternative local music scene. Rainbow-coloured hair and multiple piercings are the predominant style, although the mood is a friendly one even to the un-tattooed. Located in a tiny old house surrounded by towering warehouses and the massive underpinnings of the interstate, the Mermaid is a great place on a hot night for hanging around outside, listening to music and drinking cold beer (*see page 206* **Nightlife**).

At 828 S Peters Street, you'll find one of the best venues for regional and national bands. The **Howlin' Wolf** club offers live music nightly, along with a wide selection of international beers, including a dozen different choices on tap. *See page 206* **Nightlife**.

For something completely different, head for the very tip of the district in front of the Riverwalk Mall, at the foot of Poydras Street. Between Poydras and Canal Streets on the river is an odd, 1960s-style skyscraper with a round top. This is the optimistically named **World Trade Center** (*see below*). While the building houses mainly offices and is due for conversion into a hotel, on the thirty-third floor the **Top of the Mart** bar offers a stunning bird's-eye view of New Orleans and the Mississippi River.

From the vantage-point offered by Top of the Mart you can clearly see the hub of one of New Orleans's top industries: conventions. Past the Riverwalk, the recently expanded **Ernest N Morial Convention Center** (*see 254* **Directory**) sprawls alongside the river from Julia Street to the other side of the Crescent City Connection bridge. It's a typical example of undistinguished late-twentieth-century convention architecture, strictly utilitarian. The centre is named after the

first black mayor of New Orleans, the father of current mayor Marc Morial.

Most conventioneers, in their eagerness to get away from business and to the fun of the French Quarter, miss the surrounding neighbourhood, taking shuttle buses or taxis to and from their hotels. This is a sensible idea at night, but during the day walking is the only way to explore the less obvious pleasures of the surrounding Warehouse District, which lacks the neon signs, barkers or long queues of the Quarter.

A short walk from the Convention Center is the decorative hulk of the planned, land-based casino, which at the time of writing was still empty and the subject of intensive litigation (*see chapter* **New Orleans Today**).

Taking up a full downtown block, the only really noteworthy thing about the building is what it hides on its far side. Behind it, on the riverside, sits a petite, golden helmeted figure astride a golden steed: a statue of Joan of Arc. Much beleaguered, the statue was given to the people of New Orleans by the French and has been moved from pillar to post ever since. France recently protested the treatment of its gift and the city assured the country that in its new location next to (that is, behind) the massive casino, the statue would receive the attention it deserves. In fact, the small gold-leafed statue is charming, rare and almost never noticed.

St Patrick's Cathedral

724 Camp Street, at Girod Street (525 4413).
Bus 11 Magazine. **Open** *Mass* 11.30am, noon Mon-Fri; 4pm, 5.30pm Sat; 8.15am, 9.45am (Tridentine Latin Mass), 11.30am Sun; tours by arrangment.
Map 6 C1/2
When waves of Irish immigrants flooded into the city during the early nineteenth century, one of their earliest moves was to construct a religious home. Most of the services in the city at that time were conducted in French and the Irish felt – and generally were – unwelcome. Work began on St Patrick's in 1838 by architects James and Charles Dakin; its Gothic style was loosely based on York Minster in England. The building was eventually completed by James Gallier, the respected local architect responsible for Gallier Hall. The interior of the church is impressive, with vaulted ceilings and a dramatic altar. The elaborate murals were painted in 1840 by artist Leon Pomarade.

World Trade Center

2 Canal Street, at the Mississippi River (Top of the Mart 522 9795). Bus 41 Canal. **Open** *Top of the Mart* 10am-11pm Mon-Thur; 10am-midnight Fri; 11am-1pm Sat; 2-11pm Sun. **Credit** AmEx, DC, Disc, MC, V.
Map 6 C1/2
This ugly International-style high-rise offers the best view of the city. From the Top of the Mart bar on the 33rd floor, the contours of New Orleans and the Mississippi River are clearly visible, making the city's quirky street grid and geography understandable. The Top is one of those bars – inexplicably so popular in the 1960s – that revolve slowly, making the 360° circuit in about 90 minutes. Its faded, red-velvet slinkiness makes up for the watery drinks (one-drink minimum) and indifferent service.

Uptown

See Map 4 and Map 6

Uptown is the term used to describe the entire area on the other side of the Pontchartrain Expressway from the CBD, an area that stretches upriver as far as the next huge bend in the Mississippi. It encompasses the **Lower Garden District**, the **Garden District** – one of the most picturesque neighbourhoods in New Orleans – the student area around **Loyola** and **Tulane Universities**, and **Audubon Park** and **Zoo**.

People who live Uptown are accused of being snobs, but they came by their snobbery honestly. When Americans from the north-east began to migrate to New Orleans during the first half of the nineteenth century, they preferred to settle in what

is now Uptown rather than in the French 'downtown' – the French Quarter – or in the Creole Faubourg Marigny. The Uptown area, which was essentially rural, was developed between 1840 and the turn of the century as the plantations between what is now Howard Avenue and the country retreat community of Carrollton were broken up into suburbs.

The flavour of Uptown is most easily picked up by a drive or streetcar ride down St Charles Avenue. On the lake side of St Charles – 'lake side' and 'river side' being more useful than compass references in a city oriented like New Orleans – dull, boxy buildings from the 1950s stand within a mile of opulent, ornate houses from the mid-nineteenth century. These near-mansions exist as monuments to the wealthy, but stand in close proximity to such working-class institutions as Shoney's, Burger King and Walgreens.

Part of **Loyola University***'s extensive Uptown campus. See page 76.*

A streetcar named St Charles

There really is something romantic and charming about the streetcars in New Orleans. They puuu with a rumble and a clamour, bells ring and sparks fly. During the day they chug past purposefully; at night they seem to float like ghost cars with windows full of golden light. There is something about those slow-moving, eminently Southern cars that just gets to you.

The rumbling of the streetcar outside his window supposedly inspired playwright Tennessee Williams to write *A Streetcar Named Desire*. There's only a bus named Desire now, which doesn't really have the same resonance. But Williams would still feel at home on a streetcar today – the St Charles Avenue cars are painted the same olive-green shade they've always been and the design is unchanged from those that rumbled along the line in the 1920s.

But, when you get past that coat of paint, the streetcar system is really just a shadow of what it once was. The St Charles Avenue line started in 1835 as a critical transport artery connecting the city of New Orleans with the surrounding area. In those days it was the New Orleans and Carrollton Railroad and its mule-drawn cars took passengers from New Orleans to the tiny burgs of Lafayette, Jefferson City and Carrollton. That may not seem far today, now that the town of Carrollton is merely part of Uptown and Jefferson City just a suburb, but back then it was a daylong trip. Things continued that way for nearly 60 years, when the railroad line was expanded and converted to electricity in 1893 and the streetcars came into operation.

But the tracks that once crisscrossed the city and the streetcars that were once as ubiquitous as barges on the river were gradually put out of use after the 1950s, as the automobile took over the nation. Here and there throughout the city (look along the brick sections of Royal Street), remnants of old car tracks give some indication of how pervasive the network once was. But since then the streetcar line has become a single one, travelling from Canal Street along St Charles Avenue to Carrollton Avenue, then down Carrollton Avenue to Claiborne Avenue, where the line ends.

In the 1980s a short stretch of tourist-oriented track was added along the riverfront – called, unsurprisingly, the Riverfront line – which stretches from the Convention Center to Esplanade Avenue at the edge of the French Quarter. But it's not particularly useful, since the distance is easily walked.

However, the streetcar pendulum is swinging back again. A massive extension of the system is under way and the city has begun to restore the Canal Street line. Reportedly by the end of the century, the St Charles Streetcar, the Riverfront line and the route along Canal Street will form a convenient loop. Riders will be able to travel on the streetcar along Canal Street to City Park in Mid City, then travel through Uptown and return to the French Quarter.

In the meantime, the St Charles line is still one of the best (and at $1 a trip, the cheapest) ways to see the mansions along the grand boulevard. The creaky wooden seats aren't comfortable, but the wide windows let in a constant flow of air, the cars are usually crowded with local characters – and you'll be riding in a piece of romantic history.

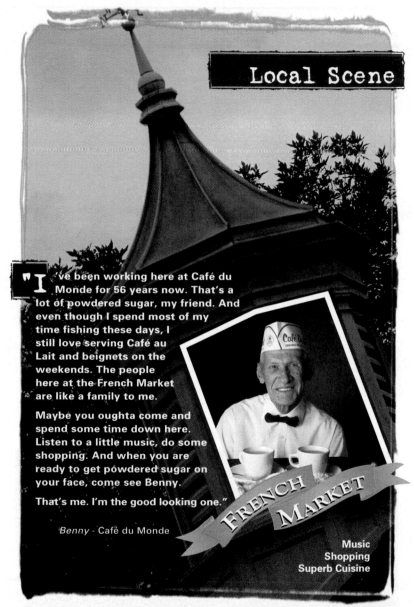

"I've been working here at Café du Monde for 56 years now. That's a lot of powdered sugar, my friend. And even though I spend most of my time fishing these days, I still love serving Café au Lait and beignets on the weekends. The people here at the French Market are like a family to me.

Maybe you oughta come and spend some time down here. Listen to a little music, do some shopping. And when you are ready to get powdered sugar on your face, come see Benny.

That's me. I'm the good looking one."

Benny - Café du Monde

FRENCH MARKET

Music
Shopping
Superb Cuisine

From Café du Monde through the farmers' and community flea markets. 504-522-2621 • 504-596-3424

Such franchises and commercial enterprises are found between the Pontchartrain Expressway and Jackson Avenue; between Jackson and Carrollton Avenues is a trip back in time along a street almost untouched by the twentieth century. It's worth remembering, however, that like wood panelling, rows of beautiful houses do not indicate uniformly wealthy neighbourhoods. In many cases, humble cottages and shotgun houses are less than a block away.

Lower Garden District

In the 1830s, the area around Annunciation and Melpomene Streets – now known as the Lower Garden District – was a particularly desirable 'American' neighbourhood, but the opening of the Orleans Cotton Press in 1833 on Front Street (between Thalia and Terpsichore Streets) changed that. The combination of industrial activity and European immigrants who settled near the Mississippi kept the area from becoming as fashionable as people hoped. Estates were quickly surrounded by cottages on lots that had been divided and redivided. Working-class immigrants settled near the river because work was available there, just as they did in so many other US cities.

Today, one of the most striking aspects of the Lower Garden District is its virtual embarrassment of beautiful Victorian homes, along with the equally striking fact that many of them are in an advanced state of disrepair and decay. The neighbourhood has a downtrodden appearance and can be downright dangerous for casual strollers. Sightseers are urged to travel in groups, avoid walking in the area at night and keep alert. This is one of those neighbourhoods where if it looks like trouble and feels like trouble, you're probably in trouble.

Nonetheless, the area has its attractions. One side effect of the poverty is that rents are low and the young and artistic have flocked to the area. The neighbourhood was recently dubbed the 'Hippest Neighborhood in America' by a national magazine (the *Granta*-like *Utne Reader*), because of the abundance of spacious apartments, art and antique shops that have recently sprung up. The area is both beautiful and tawdry, delicious and dangerous.

The stretch of St Charles Avenue that runs through the Lower Garden District is generally the most disappointing part of that grand avenue, so start by getting off it. Turn towards the river on any one of the cross streets (many are named after Greek muses, *see page 68*) and head towards **Magazine Street** (*see page 73*), which runs parallel to St Charles about eight blocks away.

Along the way the side streets are a lesson in architectural history. The houses were original-

The St Charles confection known as the *'Wedding Cake House'*. See page 72.

ly built further apart but over time other structures filled the gaps and the original antebellum plantation houses are now surrounded by Victorian and Gothic building, with dashes of Italianate and Greek Revival style adding a touch of class.

From Magazine Street, turn on to Jackson Street to discover some of the neighbourhood's largest and most elaborate homes, many of which are still owned by individual families. Four blocks north is **Prytania Street**, one of the city's grand, residential boulevards. The most impressive of Prytania Street's offerings are further uptown in the **Garden District** itself (*see below*), but there is one section that should be visited first.

Heading down Prytania Street toward the CBD and the interstate, the buildings become older – the product of the late eighteenth and early nineteenth centuries. For dozens of years this neighbourhood suffered from the effects of an interstate off-ramp planted right up against the houses, which destroyed property values and eventually left the area virtually abandoned. But a united effort by local conservationists resulted in the removal of the ramp, which has utterly revitalised the neighbourhood. If it looks familiar, it may be because the area was widely used in the movie *Interview with the Vampire*.

At the centre of the neighbourhood, at Camp and Terpsichore Streets, sits the heavily fenced statue of local philanthropist **Margaret Gaffney Haughery**. When erected in 1884, it was the first statue of a female ever dedicated in the US. Haughery was illiterate and widowed as a young woman, but she started her own bakery and dairy business that eventually made her a wealthy woman. Once successful, she dedicated her life to helping children and is credited with working with every charitable institution in the city that cared for orphans. When she died, she left her lifetime earnings to the charities she supported, signing her will with an 'X' since she never learned to write. Her statue shows her seated with a child at her side and is labelled simply 'Margaret', as the children called her.

Garden District

While the poor and middle class settled near the river, the more affluent settled around Prytania, St Charles Avenue – which was called Nayades in the early nineteenth century – and Carondelet Street. Areas such as the Garden District – bordered by St Charles Avenue, Louisiana Avenue, Magazine Street and Jackson Avenue – were safely removed from commercial activity and the lots were still large enough to sustain substantial houses and tree-lined streets. The houses here are some of the most remarkable and some of the old-

The muses

When the first plantations were divided into faubourgs (suburbs) between 1806 and 1810, the streets were named after Greek deities. Some have since disappeared and some names have changed, but many of these streets still exist in the Lower Garden District. The city has fought changing those named after the muses because New Orleans is the only city in America with streets named after all nine of them – Clio, Calliope, Melpomene, Terpsichore, Thalia, Euterpe, Harmony, Urania and Polymnia. New Orleans also has the distinction of being the only city to pronounce many of them wrongly, rarely bothering with the final 'e'.

est in Uptown and the best way to see them is on foot. Where possible, walk around the houses to get a sense of their size because some are larger than they first appear or have hidden interesting features not visible at first glance. (There are a number of good walking tours of the district, including a free one led by rangers from the Jean Lafitte National Park office: *see page 86* **Tours** for details.)

On **Prytania Street**, facing the river and close to the streetcar stop at First Street, is the **Louise S McGehee School** (No.2343), a school for 'proper young ladies' built in 1872 by architect James Freret. Constructed in the Renaissance style, the mansion is notable for its Corinthian columns and for being one of the few houses in New Orleans with a basement (admittedly largely above ground), since the high water table usually makes them impracticable. The interior can be seen in the movie *The Kingfish*, which stars John Goodman as former state governor Huey P Long.

The oldest house in the Garden District is the **Toby House** (across the street at No.2340 Prytania), a plantation-style home built by a Philadelphian in 1838. Like many of the Garden District's residents, Toby was subject to the city's cycles of financial boom and bust; at one point, he was so financially strapped that he appealed to the Texas government for repayment of money he had advanced to the state in support of Texan independence.

Intricate ironwork is a particular feature of many Garden District homes. The cast iron grillework at nearby **1331 First Street**, designed by architect Samuel Jamison, is worth a look, while a few doors down at **No.1315**, is a Greek Revival house virtually unchanged from when it was built, down to the oak trees and its lush garden.

On the corner of First and Chestnut Streets is one of the Garden District's most visited sights: **Rosegate**, home of Anne Rice (*see page 72*) – one of several properties she ownes in the area.

Further along Chestnut Street (starting at No.2305 and continuing onwards) are the **Seven Sisters**, a row of seven shotgun houses that are dwarfed by the surrounding mansions. Popular legend has it that a father built these houses for his seven daughters to live in side-by-side, but it's more likely that a land speculator built them hoping someone would want to live in the ritzy Garden District badly enough to move into such small dwellings.

Back on First Street, continuing down towards Magazine, **No.1239** has rose-motif grillework on its gallery and a woven-iron fence – not the more common cast iron or wrought iron version. By today's standards, these houses were steals when they were built; in 1857, this one cost a mere $13,000.

One of the best examples of Greek Revival design in the area is also on First Street, at **No.1134**. Built in 1849, the property has clean, simple lines and a beautiful garden. Jefferson Davis, the president of the Confederacy, died here on 6 December 1889.

One block up from First Street, on Phillip Street, **No.1220** was once the home of Isaac Delgado, founder of the Delgado Community College and an art collector whose bequest began the New Orleans Museum of Art in City Park. The house has a semi-octagonal bay – an unusual feature at the time – and fluted Corinthian columns. **1238 Philip Street** is another Greek Revival house, built in 1853 with 14-foot (4.3-metre) high ceilings – typical of the area. Both properties have fabulous gardens.

Peer through the dense shrubbery at **1213 Third Street** to glimpse an Italianate villa, a style that was much more common along the Atlantic seaboard in 1867, when it was built, than in New Orleans. The Italian villa at **1331 Third Street** was built by James Gallier Sr in 1853 for Michael Musson, the postmaster and uncle of painter Edgar Degas. Its cast iron galleries are among the most impressive in the area and the garden adjoining it is unmissable. **No.1415 Third Street** is one of the largest houses in the Garden District. Constructed in the late 1850s for tobacco merchant Walter Robinson, it is also one of the most elaborate, with a wide gallery and central parapet.

Colonel Short's Villa (1448 Fourth Street) – named after its first owner, Robert Short – was built in 1859 for less than $25,000. This showpiece has remarkable ironwork on its columns, framed galleries and a cast iron cornstalk fence that is its trademark. Walk around both sides to get the full effect.

It's not the house (or the dog) but Anne Rice they've come to see. **Rosegate**, *page 72.*

Cities of the dead

The great nineteenth-century humorist Mark Twain is credited with coining the term 'Cities of the Dead' to describe New Orleans's cemeteries filled with above-ground tombs. Twain was amused by what appeared to be tiny houses laid out on miniature streets and like many visitors to New Orleans over the centuries, probably thought it was a bit much – a symptom of a society known for its excesses as well as its unhealthy preoccupation with death and dying. Couldn't Orleanians simply bury their dead in the ground like everyone else?

Well, no, actually. The early French tried in-ground burial, but with distressing results. New Orleans is very low-lying – today approximately half the city lies below sea level – and swampy.

The only reason Orleanians aren't up to their waists in water moccasins is due to a remarkable system of levees, drainage canals and pumps that push the rainwater up to sea level to get it over the levees and into Lake Pontchartrain and the Mississippi River. In the early days, the city was even swampier than now.

The climate posed a further problem: New Orleans is inundated with over 60 inches (152.4 centimetres) of rain a year, a condition aggravated by spring floods, when melting snow and ice flow down the Mississippi River from the north.

Swamps are not good places to bury your loved ones, because the buoyancy of wooden coffins brings them back up. While there is no reason to believe that this unhappy fact of nature was the origin of the saying 'you can't keep a good man down', it did provide the early French colonists with a challenge. Early solutions included drilling holes in the caskets, hoping they would fill with water and stay submerged, or weighing them down with a cargo of bricks and rocks. Neither was successful and there were many unhappy returns.

Because of these problems of terrain and climate, the Spanish government decreed that burial should be in vaults constructed above ground and substantial enough (brick covered with a layer of plaster) to contain the earthly remains of the dead even during storm and deluge. Thus began a practice that continues today. Although the area is sufficiently well drained now to allow in-ground burial, many locals elect to continue interring in old family tombs.

What makes New Orleans's cemeteries unique, however, are the old burial customs. The brick tombs became very hot under the tropical sun. This solar heat, together with the high humidity, caused the interred bodies to quickly disintegrate into ash through a process of natural cremation. When the local authorities realised this was happening, they passed a law requiring that burial vaults remain sealed for a year after interment. One year and a day after interment, however, the vault could be opened. Ashes would be moved to the rear of the vault and a new corpse then placed into the vault.

The oldest and most historically interesting cemetery is **St Louis Cemetery No.1** just north of the French Quarter, founded by the Spanish in 1789. Earlier burial sites are now unmarked and lost, but the remarkable range of size, style and condition of the remaining tombs is interesting. Some family tombs are quite small, while others are large, elaborate architectual monuments. Indeed, some of the city's foremost architects designed tombs here, including JNB de Pouilly, who designed the façade of St Louis Cathedral. While most resemble little chapels in style, a few are more eccentric, such as the pyramid-shaped **Varney** tomb inside the cemetery gate.

Sadly, many tombs are in an advanced state of deterioration. The Catholic Church, which has always owned the cemetery, does not include the upkeep of family tombs as part of the sale of plots – families were required not only to pay for the construction of their tombs, but also to maintain them. So when no descendants are left to take care of family tombs, the church allows them to disintegrate.

Of particular note are the large 'society' tombs, constructed as joint efforts by groups who formed burial associations or societies. The largest of these, the **Italian Benevolent Society** tomb, was the site of a scene in *Easy Rider* that scandalised and angered many locals who felt that the sanctified ground of the cemetery was not an appropriate place for nudity, rape and copious dope-smoking.

Among the noted Orleanians buried in St Louis No.1 are bon vivant **Bernard Marigny**, known as the richest teenager in American history; civil rights pioneer **Homer Plessy**; mayors **Etienne de Boré** and **Ernest Morial** (*pictured left*); chess genius **Paul Morphy**; the first two wives of **Governor Claiborne**; and artist **George Ferbres**.

However, the most famous tomb – probably in all Louisiana – is that of voodoo priestess **Marie Laveau** (*pictured right*). Today people of all races visit the tomb, pray and leave offerings of candles and flowers, or, following the African tradition, coins, food or other amulets and totems. Recently, though, an unfortunate custom has developed of marking Xs on the tomb, an act of vandalism that has no historical basis.

Other cemeteries worth visiting include **Lafayette Cemetery No.1** in the Garden District, which contains the graves of French, German and Irish settlers, among others. A scene from *Interview with the Vampire* was filmed here, as well as the chase scene from John Woo's *Hard Target* (Anne Rice likes the place so much she was carried through it in a coffin to mark the publication of her 1995 novel, *Memnoch*). **Metairie Cemetery** in

Mid City contains some of the grandest tombs in the city.

Finally, not all New Orleans cemeteries are safe places. Although there have been no incidents of crime in St Louis No.1 recently, it's best to visit any cemetery in groups or to try one of the many excellent walking tours (*see page 87* **Tours**).

The cemeteries

St Louis Cemetery No.1 *Basin Street, between Conti & St Louis Streets. Bus 57 Franklin.* **Open** 9am-3pm Mon-Sat, 9am-noon Sun.
Lafayette Cemetery No.1 *Washington Avenue, between Prytania & Coliseum Streets. St Charles Streetcar/bus 11 Magazine.* **Open** times vary.
Metairie Cemetery *Metairie Road, at I-10. Bus 27 Louisiana.* **Open** times vary.

In the centre of the Garden District is **Lafayette Cemetery No.1** (*see pages 70-71* **Cities of the dead**). The first 'American' cemetery, it was opened in the early 1830s for the Anglos who had begun settling into the uptown area. Located across the street from the **Commander's Palace**, one of the best-known and most expensive restaurants in the city (*see page 131* **Restaurants**) and the bustling Rink shopping complex, many visitors can't resist walking into the cemetery when they find the gates open. Don't do it! Robberies are not unknown and maintenance workers sometimes lock people in by mistake. Take a guided tour instead.

Back on Prytania Street is a rare **Gothic Revival house** at No.2605 – note the pointed arches over the doors and windows of both the house and adjoining guest cottage. While the Gothic Revival style was popular in the North, it never caught on in New Orleans. The house was built in 1849 by James Gallier Sr on a commission from gambler Cuthbert Bullitt; when Bullitt rejected the house (probably because of the financial problems that plagued many Garden District businessmen) it was snapped up by Londoner Charles Briggs.

No.2521 Prytania is now the chapel of **Our Mother of Perpetual Help**, but it originally belonged to coffee merchant Henry Lonsdale. Lonsdale's story was typical: he made a fortune and went broke twice before his coffee business stabilised his finances. The house was one of the most expensive in the Garden District when it was built in 1856 and has intricate wrought ironwork on the gallery.

If you want to see inside a Garden District house, visit the headquarters of the **New Orleans Opera Association Women's Guild** at 2504 Prytania Street (899 1845), where tours are available.

Rosegate

1239 First Street, at Chestnut Street. St Charles Streetcar/ bus 11 Magazine. **Not open to the public. Map 6 B3**
Called Rosegate after the interwoven design of its striking iron fence, this house, built in 1857, is an official Orleans Parish landmark but the small, reverent crowds who gather on the sidewalks around it aren't interested in architecture. They've come to pay homage to Gothic author Anne Rice. A huge fake German Shepherd dog stands guard on the upper balcony, to general mystification, although neighbours suggest this is Rice's message to fans that she has state-of-the-art security. Much further Uptown, at No.1314 Napoleon Avenue and Prytania Street is another Rice property, the 1865 Italianate **St Elizabeth's Orphanage** (899 6450). The building is open to the public (Rice's doll collection is on display) and visitors are shown around by staffers who will give details of other Rice properties open to visitors.

St Charles Avenue

The period between the 1860s and the 1880s saw the building of St Charles's signature mansions, such as the **Columns Hotel** (*see page 111* **Accommodation** *and page 197* **Nightlife**), built in 1883 as a home for Simon Hernsheim, then one of the nation's most successful cigar manufacturers.

Many houses were built by Northern entrepreneurs who used their business connections and the growth of New Orleans as a port to amass fortunes; as business picked up after the Civil War, so did development. In 1882, St Charles residents – tired of the swampy mess created by heavy rain – paid to have the avenue paved; it was one of the first streets in America to be covered in asphalt.

While New Orleans was expanding toward Carrollton, the Carrollton community was expanding along St Charles Avenue towards New Orleans, although at a slower pace. As the nineteenth century closed, development from each end had begun to meet and surround Audubon Park.

A good way to explore the avenue is to take the **St Charles Streetcar** from the CBD (*see page 65*). You can see how the street developed historically from Canal Street towards Carrollton Avenue, and the streetcar's leisurely pace is ideal for picking out the sights. The whole journey will take about 45 minutes (if you don't get off) and costs $1; pay the extra 10¢ for a transfer and you can jump on and off.

For information on the first stretch of St Charles, between Canal Street and Lee Circle, *see page 59* **The CBD**. The section of St Charles after Lee Circle is not particularly picturesque or interesting until you reach Josephine Street. The corner of St Charles and Josephine Street is easily spotted because the glass and iron building there is painfully out of place amid the surrounding mansions. When the Eiffel Tower in Paris began to sag, its restaurant was broken down, shipped in pieces to New Orleans and reconstructed on St Charles. It is now the location of the **Red Room** (*see page 206* **Nightlife**), a plush music club where both the chichi and lounge kids can feel at home.

A couple of blocks later, on the left (at No.4010), is **Sully House**, built by Thomas Sully, one of the city's most prominent architects in the late 1800s. He built this modest Queen Anne house for his family. Though many of his houses are no longer standing, he was one of the architects who helped create the look that St Charles Avenue is famous for. The grander **Castle's House** (further along at 6000 St Charles) was also built by Sully and is more typical of his work.

Across Napoleon Avenue and on the right is the distinctive **Sacred Heart Academy** (4521 St Charles Avenue). It's a Catholic girls' school and one of the more formal-looking buildings on a very formal street. Further along, on the left, at the junction with Soniat Street, is the **Milton Latter Memorial Library** (*see page 73*) where one of the biggest second-hand book sales in the city is held every year.

One of the more unusual St Charles Avenue houses is at No.5809. Known as the '**Wedding Cake House**', the building barely toes the line between extravagant and over-the-top. No architectural ornament, flourish or geegaw has been left out, with the possible exception of balloons decorated with Disney figures.

Other notable buildings include the **Touro Synagogue** (No.4224), named after philanthropist Judah Touro, son of a Rhode Island rabbi. During Mardi Gras, its steps become a playground for kids waiting for parades to pass. Also look out for the **Brown House** (No.4717), built in 1905 by cotton magnate WP Brown as a wedding gift for his wife, and the **Orleans Club** (No 5005), which was built just after the Civil War. For details of these, *see chapter* **Architecture**.

Milton Latter Memorial Library
5120 St Charles Avenue, at Soniat Street (596 2625). St Charles Streetcar. **Open** 11am-6pm Mon-Thur; 11am-5pm Sat. **Admission** free.
Map 4 C9
A 1907 stone mansion, once the home of pioneer aviator Harry Williams and his wife Marguerite Clark, star of silent films. The neo-Italianate house is now the Uptown branch of the public library. It's a good spot to take a break while exploring the neighbourhood and is the only grand old house on St Charles with easy public access. The chandeliers and beautiful decorative work are clues to the scale and style of other St Charles homes, although much of the interior has been massively remodelled to accommodate the library's needs.
Disabled: toilet. Website: http://home.gnofn.org/~nopl

Magazine Street

Translating from the French as 'street of shops', Magazine Street was for many years New Orleans's central street of commerce. Today it is a long, winding, narrow road, banked on both sides with colourful shops from its start at Canal Street all the way uptown, past the zoo in Audubon Park, to River Road.

The street became the centre of Irish activity in the nineteenth century, and part of the neighbourhood on the river side of Magazine is still known as the **Irish Channel**. The homes in the Irish Channel – originally those of the labouring classes – are substantially different from those on the lake side of Magazine Street. They are generally smaller, and narrow 'shotgun' houses are plentiful.

Between the Warehouse District and Sophie Wright Place, Magazine is pretty humble, with only **Rue de la Course** at the corner of Race Street (*see page 143* **Cafés & Coffeehouses**) to give anyone a reason to slow down. A fine example of the lifestyle of the Lower Garden District can be experienced at this small, neighbourhood coffeeshop, which offers a dizzying array of coffees, teas and pastries and is packed throughout the day with arty types drawing, reading and dreaming. There's another branch further Uptown.

Across the street from the café is the former St Vincent's Orphanage, now reworked into **St Vincent's Guesthouse** (*see page 112* **Accommodation**). And at St Mary Street is **Jim Russell Records** (*see page 164* **Shops &**

Services), a good place to look for old vinyl and second-hand CDs.

Around the corner is the **Half Moon** bar (*see page 195* **Nightlife**). It shut down for a while, but reopened a few years ago, larger and remodelled. It still attracts old guys who nurse their beers and flirt outrageously with the female bartenders, but also brings in a very mixed crowd at night. Its jukebox is one of the best in the city.

Back on Magazine Street, the primary attraction is the cluster of a dozen or so antique stores that start in the 1900 block and spread up another three blocks to Jackson Avenue. The definition of 'antique' is tested here, as items range from genuine fine furniture and collectibles to stuff that's only a notch or two above junk. For antique shoppers, though, the hunt is part of the thrill and if you have the patience to work the block there are unquestionably good finds to be had and the buildings themselves are interesting.

OJ Hooter Furniture (1938 Magazine Street; 522 5167) is one of those in-between stores where, on a good day, lucky deals can be found. The store rambles over two storeys and tens of thousands of square feet of high-quality mahogany and attic junk. **Audubon Antiques** (2025 Magazine Street; 581 5704) is another, slightly more expensive version along the same theme, which offers the opportunity to wander for what seems like miles through stacks of glorious old stuff.

The river side of the block between St Andrew Street and Jackson Avenue is a countercultural oasis. The **Positive Space Gallery** (*see page 98* **Museums & Galleries**) specialises in experimental art shows that the Julia Street galleries wouldn't consider; while the **Zeitgeist Alternative Arts Centre** (*see page 174* **Film**) offers a combination of alternative theatre, film and art. It specialises in showing highly independent films and documentaries, along with local, contemporary art.

Also in the same block are second-hand clothing store **Mariposa Vintage Clothes** (2038 Magazine Street; 523 3037), and **Juan's Flying Burritos** (2018 Magazine Street; 569 0000) which serves good Mexican food to those who don't mind that there is more ink on the cook's body than appeared on his high school final exams.

You could also investigate the deep blue walls of the **Mystery Café** (3226 Magazine Street; 891 1992). The food leans towards the Middle East with houmous and pitta sandwiches, but includes other sandwiches and salads, too. Next door to Mystery is **Café Roma** (1901 Sophie Wright Place; 524 2419), one of a local chain of Italian restaurants. It's a breezy place with wide windows opening on to the street and ceiling fans wafting the garlic-heavy air.

Back on Magazine Street, the antique shop parade continues towards Washington and Louisiana Avenues, although this stretch is fairly

Audubon Park & Zoo

The area now known as Audubon Park was originally the Foucher plantation, but it was bought by the city and named Upper City Park in 1871. In 1886 it was renamed Audubon Park after the Haitian-born painter and ornithologist John James Audubon, who lived in New Orleans in the 1820s. At the time it extended from the river, through what is now Audubon Zoo and across St Charles Avenue to the current site of Tulane University and Audubon Place. Much of the building and development of the park was carried out for the 1884 Cotton Centennial Exposition, though none of the initial buildings has survived.

Today the park also includes a small golf course, riding stables and the zoo. Winding through these grounds is over a mile of path on which no one ever died of loneliness. Those grim, gaunt runners who seem to embrace their solitude find more emotionally barren places to run because Audubon's path is used by walkers, runners, rollerbladers and cyclists who like the shade and the fact that there are other people around.

Audubon Golf Course has been a source of controversy at times: some argue that an exclusive sport has no place in such an egalitarian space as a public park and that the land could be better used. But those who complain of elitism cannot have played the course, paid its dirt-cheap green fees or waited behind people who are picking up clubs for the first time and beer for the tenth time that day. Audubon is a part of the wild and woolly world of public golf, where no swing is too shameful and no place is safe.

Audubon Zoo, a short walk through the park from the St Charles Streetcar stop, is generally ranked among the top zoos in the US. 'Zoo' here doesn't mean just lions and tigers and bears. The place has wisely adopted a regional focus, promoting Louisiana swamps as a land as exotic as any African savannah. In fact, the meticulously recreated 6.5-acre (2.6-hectare) swamp installation, complete with alligators and a Cajun fishing camp, has been known to dissuade visitors from bothering to take a fully fledged swamp tour. Also popular are the Embracable Zoo, which encourages visitors to make contact with domestic animals; the Butterflies in Flight pavilion where you can walk through an indoor glade of butterflies; and the sea lion show in a lovely 1920s outdoor amphitheatre.

North of the park, between St Charles Avenue and Tulane University, is **Audubon Place**, a gated community designed in 1895. The idea was to create a small neighbourhood of millionaires, which is largely what happened, though the

residential, with only a few businesses. The area between Seventh Street and Louisiana Avenue has experienced growth in the past few years and now has its share of antiques and collectible shops, though more care has been taken to make them feel like shops rather than attics or basements with cash registers. There are also a number of vintage clothing stores including **Creative Native** (3116 Magazine Street; 899 6485), a few doors down from another branch of Rue de la Course at Magazine and Eighth Streets. Across the street is **Big Life Toys** (3117 Magazine Street; 895 8695), which specialises in strange and nostalgic toys loved by adults. Children will probably prefer its other shop, at 5430 Magazine Street.

Part of the growth in the neighbourhood is due to the influx of bars and restaurants. **Semolina** (3242 Magazine Street; 895 4260) is a local pasta chain with moderate prices and equally moderate food, but it's full on week nights. Next door is a more traditional Italian restaurant, the recently renovated **Café Italiano** (3244 Magazine; 891 4040). In the same block is the **Bulldog** (*see page 195* **Nightlife**), a dive that was renovated into a beers-of-the-world joint. As the night wears on, it becomes more of a college hangout and its narrowness can be a problem for the claustrophobic, but those who want to be where the action is will love it. Diagonally across the street is another newish joint, the **Balcony Bar** (*see page 193* **Nightlife**), named, well, after its balcony.

As Magazine Street heads further Uptown, you'll find plenty of small boutiques that cater to a limited audience. In the block that ends at Louisiana Avenue – the boundary of the Garden District – is **Underground Sounds** record store (*see page 164* **Shops & Services**). Laura is clearly running a labour of love here, actively supporting local music by selling local bands' CDs and showing up at their gigs. It operates as a kind of drop-in centre for fans of underground music.

The land of coffeeshops is further Uptown between Jefferson and Nashville Avenues. Between Louisiana and Jefferson Avenues is a stretch of arts and crafts boutiques, then a residential stretch, but at Jefferson, coffee is in the air. **PJ's Coffee & Tea** (5432 Magazine Street; 895 0273) on the river side of the street is now faced by **CC's Gourmet Coffee House** (*see page 143* **Cafés & Coffeehouses**) on the lake

houses weren't built until the early 1900s. Bob Dylan is rumoured to have a house on Audubon Place, but the armed guard and Dylan's own talent for privacy makes it hard for anyone to know for sure.

Audubon Park

St Charles Avenue to Mississippi River, between Walnut Street & Exposition Boulevard (information 581 4629/1-800 774 7394/ Audubon Park Golf Course 865 8260/ Cascade Stables 891 2246). St Charles Streetcar/

bus 11 Magazine. **Open** 6am-10pm daily. **Admission** free. **Map 4 A/B 9/10** *Disabled: toilet. Website: www.auduboninstitute.org*

Audubon Zoo

6500 Magazine Street, Audubon Park (581 4629/ 1-800 774 7394). St Charles Streetcar/ bus 11 Magazine. **Open** *winter* 9.30am-5pm daily; *summer* 9.30am-6pm daily. **Admission** $0.50, $4.50 seniors, 2-12s. **Credit** AmEx, MC, V. **Map 4 B9** A free shuttle bus runs from the St Charles Streetcar stop to the zoo.

side of the street. Both cafés have outdoor seating and both belong to local chains. PJ's is based in New Orleans and CC's is owned by Community Coffee in Baton Rouge. Coffee giant Starbuck's has identified New Orleans as the target for its next locust-like invasion, so it will be interesting to see how the local chains survive the onslaught.

A few blocks down on the lake side at the corner of Magazine and Nashville, is **Café Luna** (8022 Nashville Avenue; 899 3723), one of the nicest of the coffeeshops. Oh, and there are still more antique shops mere doors away, but as the shops move further Uptown, they graduate up in price and pretension. The stores here sell objets d'art.

Finally, New Orleans has not escaped cigar mania, and two of the better stores are on Magazine Street. The **Mayan Import Company** (3009 Magazine Street; 269 9000) is one of the newest cigar stores and features some lesser known but solid cigars for smokers more interested in taste than showing off their cigar's band. Two blocks past the coffeeshops is **Dos Jefes** (5700 Magazine; 899 3030), a store that

predated the boom by two or three years. It not only operates an interesting and varied humidor but also runs a cigar-friendly bar on Tchoupitoulas (*see page 197* **Nightlife**). Smokers with a taste for Americana will love the earnest piano nights.

Riverbend

Riverbend, based around Oak Street and S Carrollton Avenue where the streetcar turns off St Charles Avenue, was originally a cottage community called Carrollton outside the city. Now an area of shops and bars, it caters primarily for Loyola and Tulane university students.

Down where Carrollton meets the levee, **Cooter Brown's** (*see page 197* **Nightlife**) is as well-known for its wide selection of beers and cheese fries as it is for the number of guys wearing baseball caps there. Further up Carrollton, at St Charles, is the famous **Camellia Grill** (*see page 131* **Restaurants**), perhaps the best-known diner in the city. When customers want a slice of pie heated up, it goes on the grill just like everything else. It's a local institution not to be missed by those whose diet and constitution can handle it.

Most of Oak Street, a few blocks up S Carrollton, feels like small town America, with the Whitney bank clock at the corner as a reminder of the days when people used to meet under the Whitney clock. Further up the street is the **Maple Leaf Bar** (*see page 209* **Nightlife**), a watering hole by day but one of the best places in town for blues and zydeco at night.

The Universities

Across St Charles Avenue from Audubon Park, **Tulane University** and **Loyola University** sit next to each other, and because they are so close together and were built around the same time, they look like one large campus. Though the area they occupy might look compact from St Charles Avenue, this is deceptive: the campuses reach almost to Claiborne Avenue.

Loyola was founded by the Jesuits, who opened the College of Immaculate Conception downtown in 1849. In 1904, the order opened a second university on the current site on St Charles and in 1911 united the two schools at the St Charles address. The campus is dominated by the Gothic Holy Name of Jesus Church, built in 1914. A state-of-the-electronic-arts library is scheduled to open here in 1999.

Tulane came about through a gift of wealthy New Orleans businessman, Paul Tulane, in 1883. He wanted to fund a technical school to train mechanics but in typical Louisiana style, politicians saw this windfall as a chance to revive the bankrupt University of Louisiana. Tulane was talked into the deal and the state university was rechristened 'Tulane' and given a second chance. The ramshackle downtown campus was abandoned in 1888 for a more spacious one Uptown, on the site of a former sugarcane plantation on the lake side of St Charles Avenue. Since then, Tulane has expanded north past Willow Street and the heart of the campus is now on Freret Street near Broadway. The campus architecture is generally undistinguished but a walk through it is a pleasant diversion.

The most interesting feature of Tulane's campus may be its research collections. It is home to the **Amistad Research Center**, one of the most important collections of African-American history in the world. The stacks, with more than ten million documents, are available only to scholars but the modest reading room has changing displays from the collection. A big bonus, however, is the Amistad art collection, which includes major works by Jacob Lawrence, Henry O Tanner, Elizabeth Catlett and other important black artists. Some paintings and sculpture are always on display and

visitors are free to walk through the offices looking at the work.

Tulane also houses the **Howard-Tilton Memorial Library**, which includes the Southeastern Architectural Archive, dedicated to the architecture of New Orleans and the Gulf South, and the **William Ransom Hogan Archive of New Orleans Jazz**, devoted to preserving the history of jazz. The **Newcomb Art Gallery**, located in the Woldenberg Art Center on campus, is a hidden jewel (*see page 92* **Museums & Galleries**).

Unlike campus areas in other college cities, the Tulane/Loyola district has not spawned any sort of commercial area catering to the young and groovy. Of the three places where students traditionally waste their student loans – bookshops, record shops and bars – only bars flourish in this neighbourhood and those are party gladiator havens, hardly places for young rebels to cultivate their dissatisfaction with society at large.

Popular among them are **The Boot**, **Phillip's** and **TJ Quills** (for all, *see chapter* **Nightlife**). What rebels exist write in expensive hardback notebooks at the coffeeshops on Maple Street, **PJ's Coffee & Tea** and **Coffee & Company** (*see pages 142 and 143* **Cafés & Coffeehouses**).

Perhaps the only true counterculture outpost is the **Mushroom** record shop (*see page 164* **Shops & Services**), upstairs from The Boot. Secondhand record and CD stores have opened and closed on Maple Street, but only Mushroom has survived.

The **Maple Street Book Shop** (*see page 153* **Shops & Services**) is the only independent bookstore here, but it lives in spite of students, who show no signs of being interested in reading. It's particularly good on local poetry and its children's shop next door is one of the better place for kids' books in the city. For more on student life, *see page 262* **Directory**.

Loyola University New Orleans
6363 St Charles Avenue, at Calhoun Street (865 2011). St Charles Streetcar. **Open** *offices* 8.30am-4.45pm Mon-Fri.
Map 4 B/C8
Website: www.loyno.edu

Tulane University
6823 St Charles Avenue, at Audubon Park (865 5000). St Charles Streetcar. **Open** *offices* 8.30am-5pm Mon-Fri.
Map 4 B/C8
Disabled: toilet. Website: www.tulane.edu
Amistad Research Center *Tilton Hall, Tulane University campus (865 5535/fax 865 5580/amistad@ mailhost.tcs.tulane.edu). St Charles Streetcar.* **Open** 9am-4.30pm. **Admission** free.
Website: www.arc.tulane.edu
Howard-Tilton Memorial Library *7001 Freret Street, at Audubon Street (865 5605). Bus 15 Freret, 22 Broadway.* **Open** 8am-12.45pm Mon-Thur; 8-10.45am Fri; 8am-8.45pm Sat; 10am-12.45pm Sun. **Admission** free.

Mid City & Beyond

See Map 5

This is one of the sections of the city that most tourists overlook, and more's the pity. The area of town known as Mid City stretches from the edge of the French Quarter to Lake Pontchartrain, and its neighbourhoods are considered by many to be closest in feel to the old New Orleans. Until the mid-nineteenth century, Mid City was dominated by swamps and a handful of plantations. Bienville established one of the earliest settlements at Bayou St John, which he named after his patron saint. Many of the streets here are built on top of the original dirt trails used by settlers and Indians; for example, Bayou Road sits on top of an ancient Indian trail that led from Bayou St John to the Mississippi River.

Around the time of the Civil War, plantation owner John McDonough donated his massive property to the city. His one condition was that it be used to provide schools for the city's poor children. To a large extent the city did just that and many schools in town are still named after the antebellum philanthropist, but the city also twisted the law in its own favour, and, with the help of some sympathetic jurisprudence, turned much of McDonough's property into City Park. Once the city had taken over the property, draining the swamps to make the land usable accelerated and over the next half-century more and more property in the area dried out sufficiently to become the residential neighbourhoods that exist today.

Mid City is large, but it's possible to explore sections of it on foot. The most useful bus is **48 Esplanade**, which goes from the French Quarter along Esplanade Avenue to the foot of City Park.

City Park

City Park is the fourth largest urban park in the US. Its 1,400 acres (566.6 hectares) are permeated by streams and bayous crossed with charming, arched bridges under the shade of enormous oaks, many draped in Spanish moss, providing a luxuriant green canopy for most of the park. Some of the trees are believed to be 1,000 years old. Swans and ducks paddle on its waterways, as do visitors who rent canoes and boats. The network of bayous give the park the feel of an island, a kind of Neverland place.

Most of the park's structures and many of its sculptured waterways were constructed as part of the federal Workers Project Administration (WPA) put into place by President Franklin Delano Roosevelt to provide jobs during the Depression. WPA artists designed the bridges and

details, while hundreds of construction workers put it all together. The WPA insignia can still be seen on many structures and the main drive through the park is still called Roosevelt Drive.

Today, City Park contains riding stables, baseball diamonds and lagoons for boating and fishing, all open to the public. The **Bayou Oaks Golf Course** has four 18-hole courses as well as a sophisticated driving range, while the **Tennis Center** has lighted courts and a pro staff available for lessons. The **Stables** offer trail rides and riding lessons (for all, *see chapter* **Sport & Fitness**). There's even a tiny amusement park, **Carousel Gardens**, with a 100-year-old carousel. The lush **Botanical Gardens** abut **Storyland**, a colourful children's playground (for all, *see below*).

Also inside City Park, on Collins Diboll Circle near the Esplanade Avenue entrance, is the **New Orleans Museum of Art** (*see page 92* **Museums & Galleries**). While NOMA is not large, it has a good collection, including a valuable Degas completed while the painter was living in New Orleans in 1872. It also hosts touring exhibitions. The 1911 building itself is beautiful and its wide front porch, with massive columns, is a cool and comfortable place to rest during a walking tour. There aren't many cafés or fast food places around the perimeter of the park, so the museum café is the best place to eat.

Admission to the park is free, but you have to pay for some of the facilities. For more information about where things are and what to do, visit the Casino Building at the centre of the park near the tennis courts. The park is reasonably safe but night-time visits are not a good idea.

City Park

Between Bayou St John, City Park Avenue, Orleans Avenue & Robert E Lee Boulevard (general information 482 4888/Bayou Oaks Golf Course 483 9397/City Park Stables 483 9398/City Park Tennis Center 483 9383/ canoe & boat rental 483 9371 Sat & Sun only). Bus 46 City Park, 48 Esplanade, 90 Carrollton. **Map 5** Disabled: toilet. Website: www.neworleans.com/citypark

Botanical Gardens

Victory Avenue, at the southern end of City Park (483 9386). **Open** 10am-4.30pm Tue-Sun. **Admission** $3; $1 5-12s; free under-5s. **Map 5 D4**
A 10-acre (4-hectare) plot including a conservatory, gift shop and garden study centre. Visitors are free to walk through the grounds; there are no guided tours but garden staff and volunteers are friendly, plant-loving types who enjoy talking about the gardens. Especially lovely are the rose garden and azalea and camellia garden.

Storyland & Carousel Gardens

Victory Avenue, at the southern end of City Park (483 9382/Carousel 483 9356). **Open** *Storyland* 10am-12.30pm Wed-Fri; 10am-4.30pm Sat, Sun; *Carousel Gardens* 10am-2.30pm Wed-Fri; 11am-5.30pm Sat, Sun. **Admission** *Storyland* $2; free under-2s; *Carousel Gardens* $1; free under-2s; $8 unlimited rides. **Map 5 D5** This pre-Disney children's playground, with its storybook characters and a small amusement park next door with a rare wooden carousel, are great favourites with children. They're attractive to grown-up children, too, who love the tranquil beauty of the carousel (called 'the flying horses' by New Orleanians) and the unfrenzied attitude of Storyland toward childhood.

Around Esplanade Avenue

From Esplanade Avenue at the foot of City Park, head past the large statue of beloved local Confederate General PGT Beauregard at the park gates to Bayou St John, the inlet that runs along the west side of the park from Lake Pontchartrain. This is the original bayou where early settlers set up camp, where there are now a number of beautiful houses in a variety of local architectural styles. Bayou St John is a pleasant place to linger and is designed for leisurely reflection with regular concrete staircases leading down to the water.

Walk alongside the bayou and after several blocks you will arrive at **Pitot House Museum** (*see page 80*). Constructed in the late eighteenth century in typical West Indies style, its period furnishings offer a realistic look at how the early French residents lived.

Back on Esplanade Avenue, about two blocks away from Bayou St John is **St Louis Cemetery No.3** (*see page 70* **Cities of the dead**). Established in 1835, this is a typical New Orleanian cemetery. Admission is free. The city's tombs are among its most distinctive and striking architecture and this is one of the safer cemeteries to visit. Tour buses stop regularly throughout the day and you can pick up a brochure from the cemetery office near the gates. Nearby is the **Fair Grounds Racecource** (*see below*), New Orleans's horse racing track, which opened in 1872.

Just a few blocks further along tree-lined Esplanade is a small collection of charming restaurants, coffeeshops and boutiques. **Whole Foods Market** (*see page 161* **Shops & Services**) is a large, progressive health food store with a produce section, freshly baked goods and a deli with an emphasis on vegetarian food. Nearby is **Café Degas** (*see page 139* **Restaurants**), which specialises in French food at reasonable prices. On sunny days, its patio is a great place to while away an hour or so. Around the corner is the coffeeshop **True Brew** (3133 Ponce de Leon Street; 947 3948), a good spot to load up on gourmet coffees and pastries.

More beautiful homes can be seen further along Esplanade Avenue, although after about ten blocks the neighbourhood gets noticeably dodgy, and travelling by car or bus is highly recommended. But first, note No.2306 Esplanade, known as the **Degas House** (*see page 81*), where Edgar Degas stayed during his visit to New Orleans in the 1870s. At the end of the same block, at the

intersection of Esplanade Avenue and Bayou Road in a triangular-shaped park, is a monument called 'the Goddess of History: Genius of Peace'. The original statue was donated to the city by a wealthy local, George H Dunbar, but was destroyed in 1938. The existing figure is an exact replica of the original.

To see the rest of Mid City will require a car. Head north, towards the lake, along Wisner Boulevard (which parallels the eastern side of City Park), turn left on to Robert E Lee Boulevard and right on to Lakeshore Drive. Lakeshore is where New Orleans turns into beachfront property. Dotted with palm trees and with a distinctive salt-flavoured breeze, Lakeshore Drive runs along the shores of **Lake Pontchartrain** and its colourful marinas. At 40 miles (64 kilometres) long and 24 miles (39 kilometres) wide, the lake has long acted as beach for New Orleans. But while boating is still a popular pastime, for nearly 20 years the waters of the lake have been deemed too polluted for swimming, and people with sense avoid close contact with its waters.

Lakeshore Drive ends at **West End Park**, a popular outdoors area where locals run, walk and cycle. West from here are the suburbs of Metairie and Kenner. This is a utilitarian area, with little to attract visitors – unless you need to shop at K-Mart. However, at the entrance to the Lake Pontchartrain Causeway is a well-marked birdwatching area. In late July thousands of purple martins nest under the bridge; the best time for viewing is sunset, when the birds return for the night.

Fair Grounds Racecourse

1751 Gentilly Boulevard, near Esplanade Avenue (944 5515/fgno@accesscom.net). Bus 48 Esplanade. **Open** Mon, Thur-Sun but hours vary; call for details. **Map 5 E/F5**

The Fair Grounds isn't one of America's top tracks but in many respects it is one of the most successful. The disastrous clubhouse fire of 1993 didn't put a stop to the racing, and a new grandstand was built and opened in 1997. With horse racing marginalised in many states because of the expansion of the gambling industry, the Fair Grounds fire proved how committed New Orleanians are to their ponies. The importance of the Fair Grounds as an inner-city park and centre has been solidified by the creative use of the complex for Jazz Fest every spring. The racing season, which runs from November to March, offers a haven during stressful times; many locals go to the races on Thanksgiving Day to escape problematic family dinners, and during Carnival season it's a popular respite from the all-encompassing Mardi Gras machine. Parking isn't a problem during the season (with the exception of the opening day). For Jazz Fest it's best to take a taxi or a bus or get dropped off by a friend. *See also p218* **Sport & Fitness**. *Disabled: toilet.*

Paddle a pedalo on the waterways of **City Park***, the Neverland of Mid City. See page 77.*

The **Cresson House** (see page 43), one of **Esplanade Avenues**'s eclectic creations.

Pitot House Museum

1440 Moss Street, between Esplanade Avenue & Grand Route St John (482 0312). Bus 48 Esplanade. **Open** 10am-3pm (last tour at 2pm) Wed-Sat. **Admission** $5; $4 seniors, students; $2 under-12s. **No credit cards. Map 5 E4**
When Pitot House was built in the late 1790s, Bayou St John was in the country and the land nearby was plantation fields. The bayou, which connected Lake Pontchartrain to the Mississippi River, was lined with plantation houses. Pitot House is the lone survivor of that era, a graceful West Indies- style structure with brick-between-posts construction and a double-pitched roof, built for a family of merchants. It was sold in 1810 to James (formerly Jacques) Pitot, a refugee from the Haitian slave rebellions who resettled in New Orleans. Pitot was an early mayor of New Orleans. The house was restored in the 1960s and is now furnished with post-Louisiana Purchase, pre-Victorian pieces from the early nineteenth century. Fitting so naturally into its landscape and painted with the soft reds and yellows favoured by the Creoles, this is one of the prettiest houses in New Orleans.

Kenner

Among New Orleanians, suburban Kenner is often used as a shorthand term for all that is plastic, second-rate and boring. 'She got married and moved to Kenner' is the same as saying someone has dropped off the edge of the earth. Yet Kenner, too, has a historic past and some surprisingly interesting mini-museums in its old town area, Rivertown, which occupies the site of an old sugarcane plantation at the edge of the Mississippi River. Among the museums are the **Mardi Gras Museum** (*see page 91* **Museums & Galleries**); the **Saints**

Hall of Fame (*see below*) and the **Louisiana Toy Train Museum** (519 Williams Boulevard, next to the railway tracks; 468 7223), which houses several rooms of model trains.

Rivertown is also the home of the **Louisiana Wildlife & Fisheries Museum** (303 Williams Boulevard; 468 7232). Even with Louisiana's relaxed attitude towards the environment, it's a shock to see a scale model of an offshore oil drilling platform and a video praising oil companies as enlightened environmentalists in a museum devoted to the outdoors. The displays also include a 15,000-gallon freshwater tank of marine life.

On the lake side, Kenner houses one of the few surviving casinos in the Greater New Orleans area, the **Treasure Chest Casino** (*see page 185* **Nightlife**).

Saints Hall of Fame Museum

409 Williams Boulevard, between Short & Fourth Streets, Rivertown, Kenner (468 7231). Bus Kenner Loop. **Open** 9am-5pm Tue-Sat. **Admission** $3; $2 seniors, under-12s. **Credit** MC, V (gift shop only).
'Saints' and 'Hall of Fame' might be thought contradictory terms, but this museum provides a perhaps unintended insight into sports fanaticism. The Saints, the local football team, have never won a play-off game and usually have losing seasons, but New Orleans is addicted to the team. The museum, surprisingly, takes a wide view of the Saints phenomenon, with uniforms, game balls, photos and installations and even an Aints display (Saints' anti-fans). At the team's lowest points, fans become anti-fans, showing up at the Superdome with paper bags over their heads to show their collective embarrassment. Vintage bags are on display.
Disabled: toilet. Website: www.kenner.la.us

Degas in New Orleans

The Degas House on Esplanade Avenue is an 1852 Italianate structure built for the Musson family, Edgar Degas' American cousins. Degas' mother was raised in New Orleans and the extended French-American clan was remarkably close – some of the Musson cousins sat out the Civil War in France with the Degases. Degas made his only visit to the US in 1872-3, spending five months in New Orleans. He did some painting and made sketches for other pictures but was not completely at home in the city, which he found too sun-soaked and foreign. He wrote plaintively to his dealer in Paris that there was too much to paint in New Orleans. Their mutual friend Manet, he said, would know what to do with this exotic place.

The Musson household also included Degas' younger brother René, who had come to New Orleans to go into business and marry their cousin Estelle Musson. Several years after Edgar Degas' visit, René deserted his wife and children for another woman, one of their Esplanade neighbours, and eloped to France. The event caused a fatal rift in the Degas-Musson family.

The Mussons sold the house in the 1880s. At some point the house was split in two. It is possible that the next-door house (to the left of the Degas House) is the other half of the original, but no one knows. A local couple bought what was still called the Musson house in the 1990s, restored it and turned it into a B&B (*see page 113* **Accommodation**). The house is open to the public, although there is little to see directly connected to Degas's visit or even the Musson family. The owners have hung reproductions of Degas' major works in the house, turning it into a kind of virtual Degas gallery.

In 1999 Degas' brief stay in Louisiana will be celebrated with a major exhibition at the New Orleans Museum of Art. The Degas House will be heavily involved in the events surrounding this.

Degas House

2306 Esplanade Avenue, at Tonti Street (821 5009/ degas@bellsouth.net). Bus 48 Esplanade.
Open *9am-5pm Mon-Fri; 10am-2pm Sat-Sun.*
Admission *suggested donations $6; $4 seniors; $3 students, under-12s. Credit AmEx, MC, V.*
Map 5 F5
Website: www.degashouse.com

EDGAR GERMAIN HILAIRE
DEGAS
French "Impressionist" master whose mother and grandmother were born in New Orleans. Painted many famous subjects on a visit here in 1872-1873 at Musson Home on Esplanade. His "Portrait of Estelle" bought by Delgado Museum.
ERECTED BY THE LOUISIANA TOURIST DEVELOPMENT COMMISSION. 1975

Greater New Orleans

See Map 2

The West Bank

The land just across the Mississippi River from New Orleans actually lies east of the city, but is nonetheless universally known as the West Bank. It is made up primarily of sleepy and generally uninviting 'bedroom communities', but there are a handful of attractions that make some sections worth a visit.

One of the most pleasant – and free – attractions is the ferry at the foot of Canal Street, which takes riders directly to **Algiers Point** on the West Bank. The ride itself is worth the trip, as passengers watch New Orleans shrink behind them and feel the incredible tug of the river's mighty current as it grabs the ferry and threatens to spin it around. The ferry looks like a toy on the water next to the enormous ships that ply the waterway. On the other side is a charming little neighbourhood of historic homes and wide front porches that looks as though it has been plucked out of Uptown New Orleans and plopped in its current location. During the day, the streets are quiet and make a pleasant stroll in which to admire the architecture and the gardens upon which many residents pride themselves.

Have a look at **Behrman House** (228 Pelican Avenue), a Queen Anne cottage built in 1896. This was the childhood home of Martin Behrman, who served as mayor of New Orleans from 1894 to 1920. A short distance away, on the corner of Olivier and Pelican Avenues, is the **Mount Olivet Church**. Constructed in 1866, it is the oldest church in Algiers. Also on Pelican Street is the **Algiers Point Public Library**, housed in a charming Italianate structure that was built in 1907 as the community's library; it has served that purpose ever since. Also, notice the very decorative houses on the 300 block of Delaronde Street. These were built in the 1890s, and have been restored to shining Victorian style.

At the foot of the ferry landing in Algiers is a pleasant place to stop for a beer or some lunch. The **Dry Dock Café** (133 Delaronde Street; 361 8240) offers good, inexpensive home cooking and has wide-open windows through which to watch the ebb and flow of ferry riders. On sunny days chairs and tables are set out on the sidewalk.

Also worth visiting in Algiers is **Blaine Kern's Mardi Gras World** (*see below*), where many of the Mardi Gras floats are designed and built. Shuttle buses take you direct from the ferry terminal to the warehouses. Beat fans also make their way to Algiers to pay homage to the house where **William Burroughs** lived briefly in the 1940s (*see below*).

Algiers Point/Canal Street Ferry

Algiers Point or Canal Street, at the Mississippi River (364 8114). Bus 41 Canal, 108 Algiers Local. **Open** 5.45am-midnight daily; ferries depart Canal Street on the hour and ½ hour, and Algiers Point at ¼ past and ¼ to the hour. **Admission** free pedestrians; $1 per vehicle (paid on the Algiers side). **No credit cards. Map 4 G/H7**

Blaine Kern's Mardi Gras World

233 Newton Street, at Brooklyn Street (361 7821/ 1-800 362 8213/briankern@mardigrasworld.com). Bus 108 Algiers Local. **Open** 9.30am-4.30pm daily; tours every ½hr. **Admission** $8.50; $6.50 seniors; $4 children. **Credit** AmEx, DC, Disc, MC, V.
Blaine Kern is more crucial to Carnival than Rex. Kern's establishment designs floats and oversees more than 40 parades. The complex of warehouses ('dens' in Carnival ese) and workrooms welcomes visitors. Take the ferry from the foot of Canal Street across the river to where a brightly marked Mardi Gras World van picks up visitors for a free shuttle to the den. Visitors enter the eerie world of Carnival make-believe, getting close-up looks at the floats and decorations, sometimes watching the designers at work.
Disabled: toilet. Website: www.mardigrasworld.com

William Burroughs House

509 Wagner Street, Algiers. **Not open to the public.**
This unassuming little house on the West Bank is a shrine to Beat fans who in turn are a mystery to the family that has lived here since 1951. A historic marker sits in the front yard, paying homage to novelist William Burroughs's 1948-1949 residency. Burroughs was visited here by Jack Kerouac, Neal Cassady and others from their bi-coastal circle, one of the mini-adventures of *On the Road*. The house was changed substantially after Burroughs left in a hurry in 1949 to avoid prosecution for drugs.

Chalmette

An easy 15-minute drive from the French Quarter, in St Bernard Parish, is **Chalmette Battlefield**, the site of the Battle of New Orleans on 8 January 1815, when Andrew Jackson and a ragtag army of frontiersmen, militiamen and pirates defeated a superior British force, led by General Sir Edward Pakenham (*see page 8* **History**). At the end of the two-hour dawn battle, 2,000 British troops lay dead or dying in the field. American casualties are remembered variously from a low of nine to a high of 77. The battlefield is now run by the National Park Service and open to the public.

A very good 30-minute video shown in the visitor centre explains the political climate that sparked the War of 1812 and gives a basic outline of the battle. Self-guided walking tours are an easy 1.5 mile (1 kilometre) loop through the park. The 150-foot (48-metre) Chalmette Monument provides an excellent view of the battlefield but is sadly only open to visitors on rare occasions. Across the field, behind the site of the British lines, is the **National Cemetery**, a poignant Civil War burial ground lined with rows of tiny marble headstones.

The easiest way to reach the battlefield is by car

Swamp life

The other worthwhile West Bank sites are located considerably further afield in the tiny town and large bayou known as **Lafitte**. Located about 30 minutes' drive from New Orleans, Lafitte takes its name from the notorious pirate who once used the thick tangle of the swamp as one of his hideouts. Today, the small town of Lafitte remains a fishing village. Crab nets are frequently spread in back yards that abut the bayou. Houses are perched on stilts that stand a minimum of 10 feet (3 metres) high, to keep them safe from the floods that occur in any heavy rain. Children here have frequently been given their own boats by the age of ten, and the water is the most common means of transport. For visitors, the water and the swamp are the main attractions as well.

The town of Lafitte lies south of the **Jean Lafitte National Historical Park & Preserve**. About 15 miles (24 kilometres) south of New Orleans, here you can wander among exotic swamp trees draped in Spanish moss, while all around grow wild the kind of tropical plants that city folk spend a fortune on in inner-city plant stores. The park offers guided walking tours (2pm daily) with a qualified botanist who tells visitors about the history of the area, and the wildlife and plants. Guided canoe treks leave the park every Sunday at 8.30am and, best of all, moonlight canoe treks take off at sunset at every full moon; reservations are essential. The park's visitor centre in the French Quarter (916 N Peters Street; 589 2636) has maps and information.

To charter a fishing boat, try **Ripp's Inland Charters** (689 2665), which will introduce you to the wide variety of fish that can be seized from the state's swamps. Self-starters can rent boats from **Joe's Landing** (689 7966) for reasonable hourly fees that range widely depending upon the size of the boat and the amount of equipment rented. Canoes can be rented from **Bayou Barns** (689 3889) or from **Earl's Bar** (689 3271), where you can also get a beer and advice on where the best wildlife can be found.

If all this isn't adventurous enough for you, try an airboat tour, which will show you much the same territory only at great speed and with terrific noise. One of the best can be found in Des Allemands, about 30 miles (48 kilometres) from New Orleans off US 90. **Captain Arthur Matherne** will take you on an informative and occasionally hair-raising trip through the bayous around the old German community, and give you a thorough look at how the state's fishing families make their living today (call 758 2365 for bookings).

While you're in the area, though, don't just watch the sea life, eat some, too. Several small, friendly restaurants dot the area, all offering seafood so fresh it's barely dead. In Crown Point, try the **Restaurant des Familles** (corner of Highways 45 and 3134; 689 7834). **Boutte's** in Lafitte (Boutte's Street; 689 3889) is another good local find, with an upstairs room that overlooks the bayou.

Jean Lafitte National Historical Park & Preserve
7400 Highway 45 (Barataria Boulevard), Marrero (589 2330). No public transport. **Open** *park* 7am-7pm daily; *visitor centre* 9am-5pm daily. **Admission** free.

---

but you can also go by boat. The **Creole Queen** paddlewheeler cruise (phone 524 0814), which embarks from the Riverwalk mall dock, lands at the park twice daily and is met by park rangers who give a brief talk on the battle – but these are quick on-and-off stops, with no walking about. If you go under your own steam, plan to have lunch at **Rocky & Carlo's**, the legendary Creole Sicilian restaurant nearby (613 W St Bernard Highway, Chalmette; 279 8323).

The battle is celebrated every January with American and British encampments on the original site. In London, it is quietly remembered by a statue in St Paul's Cathedral of Pakenham and his second-in-command, Major General Samuel Gibbs. Both are dressed in the uniforms they were wearing during the New Orleans campaign.

Chalmette Battlefield & National Cemetery
8606 W St Bernard Highway (Highway 40), Chalmette (589 4430). No public transport. **Open** 8.30am-4.30pm daily. **Admission** free.

The North Shore

Across Lake Pontchartrain from New Orleans is a slice of wilderness still intact enough to give some indication as to how wild and woolly the area once was. The North Shore, as the entire region is generally known, includes a few small towns worth visiting, a burgeoning bedroom community worth avoiding and miles upon miles of wilderness, swamps and wildlife.

Just crossing the **Pontchartrain Causeway** is a monumental experience. At 23.6 miles (38

*Westward ho! The **Canal Street Ferry** (page 82) ploughs its way across the Mississippi.*

kilometres) long, the Causeway is the world's longest bridge, and is listed as such in the Guinness Book of World Records. The first span of the bridge was constructed in 1956, the second in 1969. What at first seems like fun, though, soon grows tedious since it provides 23.6 miles of precisely the same view – two slim strips of white concrete above greyish-blue water. The Causeway is a toll bridge ($1.50 each way).

Immediately across the bridge are two small towns that have survived from the nineteenth century – when the journey to New Orleans took hours – to the present day when they are struggling to retain some air of rural charm as a mass of urban 'white flight' heads their way.

Mandeville and **Covington** are very close together and similar in style. Both are distinctive for the soaring pines that line their streets. Both are tiny towns with original downtowns filled with shops and restaurants, and both are surrounded by a growing modern sprawl that is, so far, well hidden by woods. Of the two, Covington has the most to offer a casual traveller. Its downtown is walkable and distinguished by pricey clothing stores and elegant gift shops together with small restaurants and coffeeshops usually filled to the brim with bored, wealthy housewives left behind by husbands who make the daily commute to downtown New Orleans.

Located at the conjunction of two rivers – the Bogue Falaya and the Tchefuncte – Covington is a virtual wilderness of trees, swamps and greenery. Next to all that swampland, downtown Covington seems to pop up incongruously and out of nowhere. It is so charming it verges on the museum-like, with streets bejewelled with perfectly restored nineteenth-century raised cottages. It was in Covington that author and existentialist Walker Percy made his home for many years. He once described the town to *Esquire* magazine as 'a pleasant non-place'.

Just outside Covington and Mandeville is another, similarly charming little burg, and the birthplace of the area's best beer. In the nineteenth century, **Abita Springs** was a popular getaway for New Orleanians weary of the urban struggle. Today, the town is as peaceful as ever, to the point of having a sort of lost-in-time feel. Its houses are old and so surrounded by forest as to be lost to one another. Its downtown consists of only a handful of structures, with two real sights. The **Abita Springs Brewery** (21084 Highway 36; 893 3143; website: www.abita.com) is the most popular micro-brewery in Louisiana, offering a wide variety of brews including seasonal beers such as the much-loved Christmas Ale. Opened in 1996, the brewery offers free tours at the weekend. Its sister restaurant, the **Abita Brew Pub** (*see page 141* **Restaurants**) is a popular place on the North Shore to stop for lunch or dinner.

The other Abita Springs attraction is the venerable **Piney Woods Opry** (838 9063), held in the tiny, quaint town hall near the brewery on Saturday nights during spring and autumn. This little local event has become regionally popular and is broadcast live on many radio stations. Most of the musicians are old-style bluegrass players, although the entertainment is never predictable. The musicians tune up in the mayor's office, and the mayor starts the show promptly at 7pm. The hall only holds 400 and those in the know show up an hour early to get a seat. And since this isn't New Orleans, no alcohol is allowed inside or out (bear in mind that the police don't have much to do here besides pestering overly exuberant tourists).

An even more refreshing alternative to New Orleans's urban sprawl is the **Tammany Trace** (it's signposted from Abita Springs). The trace is an old railroad bed that is being converted into a nature path for walking, cycling, rollerblading and horse riding. At its current length, the trace is 31 miles (50 kilometres) long, running through bayous and forests and over 31 bridges. Work is under way to extend the path, which is planned to be about a third longer than it is now and could one day stretch for more than 100 miles (161 kilometres). Toilets and picnic areas are located at strategic spots. A renovated, stationary caboose parked near the entrance to the trace is the official information centre where you can pick up maps and tips on the best parts of the wilderness path.

The birds of Louisiana were exotic enough to fascinate naturalist John James Audubon during his stay in the region, so twitchers are likely to see species on the trace that they've never encountered before in the wild. Interested ornithologists should explore the **Great Louisiana Bird Fest** (871 9272), held every April on the North Shore. The festival includes a variety of bird-watching tours, photographic safaris through the woods and seminars with local wildlife experts. Everything from the bald eagle to the pileated woodpecker are likely to be seen, photographed, analysed and even tagged by wildlife preservationists.

If you weary of seeing wildlife at the traditionally cautious distance one usually encounters, head about 10 miles (16 kilometres) west of Abita Springs to the **Global Wildlife Center** in Folsom (*see page 168* **Children**), where you can go toe-to-toe with a giraffe, a zebra or a camel, depending on your preference. Global is a 900-acre (364-hectare) exotic wildlife preserve where the animals have been conditioned to think of man primarily as the 'Holder of a Cup of Corn'. This is an incredibly exalted position among the beasts and huge bison will willingly stick out their very long tongues in an absurd and childish fashion so that corn can be poured down their throats. It's all very weird and almost a forbidden pleasure to get that close to a dangerous-looking longhorn steer or a large, ambling camel.

Another way to get close to nature, albeit in a somewhat less intimate fashion, is to take one of the many **swamp tours** offered in the Honey Island Swamp in nearby Slidell. Honey Island is considered by many conservationists to be one of the state's most perfectly preserved swamp areas. More than 70,000 acres (28,350 hectares) are in a permanently protected wildlife area. One of the best tours is offered by Dr Paul Wagner, a wetland ecology expert (*see page 87* **Tours**).

Those in search of more civilised activities should head further afield to **Ponchatoula**, which prides itself on its large collection of antique stores. Ponchatoula is another of those North Shore communities with a quaint old downtown, although this one is more 1920s than 1890s. Here the antique shops stand shoulder to shoulder along the main streets and prices can be slightly lower than in New Orleans. You'll also find locally made art and pottery in some stores.

Tours

African Legacy Tour
Information 945 6789/fax 945 1586. Tour starts at Louisiana Products, 507 St Ann Street, on Jackson Square. Bus 3 Vieux Carré, 55 Elysian Fields, 81 Almonaster, 82 Desire. **Tours** 2pm Fri, Sun. **Tickets** $15. **Credit** AmEx, MC, V.
The African experience in Louisiana, free people of colour, the privileged world of Creoles of colour and the black Mardi Gras experience are highlighted in this tour, led by Greg Osborn, a noted researcher and historian of black Louisiana.

Bicentennial Commemorative Cocktail Tour
Information 945 6789/fax 945 1586. Tour starts at Louisiana Products, 507 St Ann Street, on Jackson Square. Bus 3 Vieux Carré, 55 Elysian Fields, 81 Almonaster, 82 Desire. **Tours** 5.30pm daily. **Tickets** $15 (adults only). **Credit** AmEx, MC, V.
The cocktail was invented in New Orleans and this walking tour uses that fact as a symbol of the city's sordid yet highly entertaining past. Participants bring their own go cups, but the tour doesn't actually go from bar to bar loading up on cocktails – sorry.

Carriage tours
Every day, usually from 8am to midnight, mule-drawn carriages line up on Decatur Street, in front of Jackson Square. Carriage tours of the French Quarter are a staple of New Orleans tourism but their allure is a mystery. They are smelly, slow, some of the mules wretched and the drivers are notoriously inaccurate storytellers. However, if you're determined to see the Quarter by mule, there are several things to bear in mind. Unlike taxi stands, passengers aren't required to take the first carriage in line, so walk up and down and ask about prices. This also gives you a chance to pick a driver you like and can understand. Nipping into Quarter bars for a drink isn't unknown among drivers and the thick New Orleans accent and the Southern penchant for mumbling can render a driver unintelligible. Also ask how long the mule has been out; a fresh animal makes for a much snappier drive. Prices vary widely, from $5 a person to $40 for a supposedly romantic tour for a couple. Also find out how long the tour will last and how many people will be in the carriage, before the driver starts stuffing in as many people as he can.

Crescent Star Magick & Mystery Tour
Information 895 8494/crescen@aol.com. Magick & Mystery tour starts at Café du Monde, Decatur Street, Jackson Square; Romantic New Orleans tour starts at Earth Savers, 434 Chartres Street, at St Louis Street. Both Bus 3 Vieux Carré, 55 Elysian Fields, 81 Almonaster, 82 Desire. **Tickets** $15; $12 under-20s. **No credit cards.**
Tours *Magick & Mystery* 8pm daily, *Romantic New Orleans* April-Sept 5pm Mon, Wed-Sun; Oct-March 3pm Mon, Wed-Sun.
Two separate tours led by New Orleans native Hannah, a Gestalt therapist by day with an interest in comparative religions, who also cheerfully describes herself as a 'good witch'. The night-time Magick & Mystery tour is infused with New Age acceptance and tempered by Hannah's funny stories of local voodoo practitioners and the spells they cast on troublesome neighbours. The daytime Romantic New Orleans tour is a lively revisiting of legendary love affairs and infamous lovers. Book in advance for both.
Website: http://members.aol.com/crescen

French Quarter Walking Tours with Friends of the Cabildo

Information 523 3939/fax 524 9130/cabildo@gnofn.org. Tour starts at the 1850 House Museum Store, 523 St Ann Street, on Jackson Square. Bus 3 Vieux Carré, 55 Elysian Fields, 81 Almonaster, 82 Desire. **Tours** 1.30pm Mon; 10am, 1.30pm Tue-Sun. **Tickets** $10; $8 students, seniors; free under-12s. **Credit** AmEx, DC, Disc, MC, V.
Led by trained volunteers, these two-hour walks are strong on architecture and historical fact.

Gay Heritage Tour

Information from the Bienville Foundation (945 6789/ fax 945 1586). Tour starts at Alternatives, 907 Bourbon Street, at Dumaine Street. Bus 3 Vieux Carré, 55 Elysian Fields, 81 Almonaster, 82 Desire. **Tours** 2pm Thur, Sun. **Tickets** $15 (adults only). **Credit** AmEx, MC, V.
Roberts Batson, the New Orleans gay history laureate (and writer of our **Gay & Lesbian** chapter), leads a 2½-hour walk around the Quarter tracing the lives and struggles of gays and lesbians from colonial days to the present. Ellen DeGeneres and Tennessee Williams are among the legion who came out in New Orleans.

Great Women of New Orleans

Information 945 6789/fax 945 1586. Tour starts at Louisiana Products, 507 St Ann Street, on Jackson Square. Bus 3 Vieux Carré, 55 Elysian Fields, 81 Almonaster, 82 Desire. **Tours** 10.15am Sat. **Tickets** $15. **Credit** AmEx, MC, V.

Baroness Pontalba, voodoo queen Marie Laveau, the pioneering Ursuline nuns and other remarkable New Orleans women are included in this lively walking tour.

Jazz Tour: Its Roots and Its Future

Information 945 6789/fax 945 1586. Tour starts at Armstrong Arch, N Rampart Street, at St Ann Street. Bus 3 Vieux Carré, 57 Franklin. **Tours** 2pm Tue, Sat. **Tickets** $18. **No credit cards.**
Donald M Marquis, long-time jazz curator of the **Old US Mint** (*see p89* **Museums & Galleries**), discusses the roots of jazz and points out landmarks associated with the music. A bonus is visiting the superb jazz exhibition at the Old Mint (the tour ticket includes museum admission).

Jean Lafitte National Historical Park & Preserve Tours

Information 589 2636. Tours start at French Quarter Visitors Center, 916 N Peters Street, at Decatur Street. Bus 3 Vieux Carré, 55 Elysian Fields, 81 Almonaster, 82 Desire. **Tours** 10.30am daily. **Tickets** free.
Universally called 'the ranger walks', these 90-minute tours by rangers from the French Quarter office of the Jean Lafitte Park are a little shorter than most tours – but they are free and have the added bonus of being very good, particularly on history and architecture. Each walk takes only 30 people, and passes are handed out at the office from 9am each morning. There are no proxy passes; each person going on the tour has to pick up a pass in person.
Website: www.nps.gov/jela

*For **carriage tours**, see page 85. You have been warned...*

Le Monde Creole French Quarter Courtyard Walking Tour

Information 568 1801/fax 528 9426/creolwrld@aol.com.
Tour starts at Le Monde Creole, 624 Royal Street, at
Toulouse Street. Bus 3 Vieux Carré, 55 Elysian Fields,
81 Almonaster, 82 Desire. **Tours** *10.30am, 2.30pm*
Tue-Sun (tours also available in French). **Tickets** $16;
$15 under-18s. **Credit** MC, V.

The Locouls, a Creole family based at Laura Plantation in
Vacherie (*see p224* **Trips Out of Town**), are used as a kind
of upper-class Every Family to acquaint visitors with daily
Creole life in New Orleans, following in their footsteps
around the Quarter. The tour deals with the 'shadow' Locouls
– the white mens' black mistresses and children – with
insight and sensitivity.

Literary Tour by W Kenneth Holditch

Information 945 6789/fax 945 1586. Tour starts at
Louisiana Products, 507 St Ann Street, on Jackson
Square. Bus 3 Vieux Carré, 55 Elysian Fields, 81
Almonaster, 82 Desire. Tours 10.30am Sun.
Tickets $15. **Credit** AmEx, MC, V.

Holditch is the acknowledged expert on Tennessee
Williams's French Quarter years and also an expert on the
entire literary history of the city. An outstanding New
Orleans literary experience.

Garden District

Rangers from the New Orleans unit of the **Jean
Lafitte National Historical Park & Preserve**
(*see page 86*) also lead a free, daily, 90-minute walking tour of the Garden District. The tour starts at
the corner of Washington Avenue and Prytania
Street, at 2.30pm. Note that there are only 30 places.

Historic New Orleans Walking Tours: Garden District/Cemetery Tour

Information 947 2120/fax 947 2130/rflo@worldnet.
att.net). Tour starts at Garden District Bookshop,
The Rink, 2727 Prytania Street, at Washington Avenue.
St Charles Streetcar. **Tours** 11am, 1.45pm daily.
Tickets $14; $12 students, seniors; free under-12s.
No credit cards.

If cemetery expert and writer Rob Florence isn't leading this
tour, then one of his very knowledgeable associates will be.
The Garden District walk hits all the highlights including
architecture, celebrities' homes (from the sidewalk only) and
a tour of Lafayette Cemetery No.1.
Website: www.tourneworleans.com

Cemetery tours

For haunted house tours, *see page 168* **Children**.

Historic New Orleans Walking Tours: Cemetery/Voodoo Tour

Information 947 2120/fax 947 2130/rflo@worldnet.
att.net. Tour starts at Café Beignet, 334B Royal Street,
at Conti Street. Bus 3 Vieux Carré, 55 Elysian Fields,
81 Almonaster, 82 Desire. **Tours** 10am, 1pm Mon-Sat;
1pm Sun. **Tickets** $15; $13 students, seniors; free under-
12s. **No credit cards.**

This is unquestionably the best way to see St Louis No.1, the
city's oldest cemetery. Rob Florence, who has written two
books on the cemeteries and is a passionate cemetery preservationist, has organised a walk through St Louis that takes
visitors to the key sights, then moves on to a voodoo temple,
churches and Congo Square.
Website: www.tourneworleans.com

Save Our Cemeteries

Information 525 3377/1-888 721 7493/fax 525 6677/
soc@gnofn.org.
Tickets *Lafayette Cemetery No.1* $6; $5 seniors,
students; free under-12s; *St Louis Cemetery No.1* $12; $10
seniors; $6 students; free under-12s.
Credit AmEx, MC, V (advance booking only).

This exemplary non-profit group works to preserve the city's
remarkable burial grounds. The group schedules several
volunteer-led tours of Lafayette No.1 cemetery in the Garden
District and St Louis No.1 cemetery in Tremé each week.
Reservations are essential.
Website: www.gnofn.org/soc

Bus tours

Gray Line of New Orleans

Information 569 1401/1-800 535 7786/fax 587 0742/
tours@graylineno.com. Tours start at Gray Line Ticket
Booth, Toulouse Street, at the Mississippi River.
Bus 3 Vieux Carré, 55 Elysian Fields, 81 Almonaster,
82 Desire. **Tours** phone for schedule. **Tickets** $15-$59;
$7.50-$21 6-12s. **Credit** AmEx, DC, Disc, MC, V.

Always reliable if rarely exciting, Gray Line offers several
tours around New Orleans. The New Orleans Loop bus travels
to all the major sights between 9am and 5.45pm and allows you
to get on and off the bus en route. It's a good way to cover a lot
of ground without feeling tied to a tour group. Gray Line's other
excursions include riverboat and walking tours; phone for a
full list.
Website: www.graylineno.com

New Orleans Tours

Information 592 0560/1-800 543 6332/fax 592 0549).
Tours start at various locations around the city. **Tours**
9am-7.30pm daily; phone for schedule. **Tickets** $10-$39;
$5-$23 3-12s. **Credit** AmEx, MC, V.

The schedule includes a variety of tours, including an over-
all city tour and some combination tours using riverboats
and streetcars. Phone for more information.
Website: www.visitnola.com

Plantation tours

Various outfits including **Gray Line** (*see above*)
run tours to the River Road plantations; check the
Visitors Bureau (*see page 264* **Directory**) for
the full range. If you want to explore the plantations yourself, *see page 224* **Trips Out of Town**.

Swamp tours

Note that, with all these tours, costs vary depending on whether you need transport to and from
New Orleans. *See also page 170* **Children**.

Dr Wagner's Honey Island Swamp Tours

Crawford Landing, at West Pearl River, Slidell
(242 5877/fax 643 3960/swamp@cmq.com).
Tours daily; times arranged by reservation. **Tickets**
with transport $40; $20 under-12s; *without transport* $20;
$10 under-12s. **No credit cards.**

Dr Wagner's tours give you a real feel for the wilderness
through which you travel because the small, 12-seater
boats used can penetrate far into the tiny bayous and
streams where much of the wildlife hides. During spring,
summer and autumn you will almost certainly see alligators, bald eagles and herons and possibly otter, deer or
black bears.

Jean Lafitte Swamp Tours

Information 689 4186/689 4187/fax 689 2038.
Tours 10am, 2pm daily. **Tickets** *with transport* $38; $23
3-12s; *without transport* $20; $10 3-12s. **Credit** AmEx,
Disc, MC, V.

Louisiana Swamp Tours

Information 689 3599/1-888-307 9267/fax 689 3380/
swamp@accesscom.net. **Tours** 9.30am, noon, 2pm daily.
Tickets *with transport* $39; $18.50 4-12s; *without transport*
$20.50; $16.50 4-12s. **Credit** AmEx, MC, V.
Both these outfits take visitors through the waters of Lafitte in
search of alligators; during the heat of summer, you are virtually
guaranteed to see some. The guides are usually colourful locals
with a rapport with the gators, and an encyclopedic knowledge
of the local flora and fauna.
Website: www.louisianaswamp.com

Other tours

Bicycle tours

Michael Hamner gives two bicycle tours of New Orleans,
a three-hour, 10-mile (16-km) Basic Tour ($25) that includes
the French Quarter, Warehouse District and Uptown, and a
five-hour, 25-mile (40-km) Grand Tour ($40) that does 'the
basic' plus City Park, Lake Pontchartrain and Metairie
Cemetery; phone 945 9505 to arrange a booking. Bikes and
helmet hire cost extra. The **Bienville Foundation** (945
6789), which runs many of the most interesting tours in the
city, also offers guided bike tours, as does **Olympic
Bicycles** (*see p219* **Sport & Fitness**).

Preservation Resource Center

Information 581 7032/prc@ iamerica.net).
The PRC, founded in 1974, is a hands-on, creative force in
New Orleans preservation. Eschewing the white gloves
route, it deploys a wide range of strategies to keep New
Orleans habitable. In addition to innovative schemes such
as selling decrepit houses for almost nothing to people who
will fix them up, the PRC sponsors several high-profile
annual architectural events such as the **Holiday Home
Tour** (in December), which opens up showy private homes
for public tours; **Shotgun House Month** (in March),
which celebrates the archetypal New Orleans dwelling
with a number of events; and the **Stained Glass in
Sacred Places Tour**, which takes place in spring and
autumn and looks at the magnificent windows in New
Orleans churches. The PRC will also arrange an architectural tour of the city. Costs depend on the type of tour
requested and number of participants, so phone them for
more information.
Website: www.prcno.org

Sea-Saint Recording Studio

3809 Clematis Avenue, at Lavender Street (949 8386).
Bus 55 Elysian Fields, 57 Franklin, 90 Carrollton.
Open 10am-6pm Mon-Fri; tours by appointment only.
Tickets free.
Located in a working-class neighbourhood in New Orleans
East, this 24-track recording studio has been host to some of
the biggest names in music: Paul McCartney, Tom Jones,
Fats Domino, Michelle Shocked, Boz Scaggs, Paul Simon,
Patti LaBelle, Joe Cocker and a legion of others have worked
here. Owned by New Orleans music legend Allen Toussaint
and his partner Marshall Seahorn, visitors are welcome but
must phone in advance for an appointment. Manager Sandy
Labayen happily shows visitors around the modest one-
storey building while apologising that there really isn't much
to see. For true believers, just standing in the studio where
the stars record and studying the autographs on the walls
of the games room is more than enough. It's possible to run
into a major star but unlikely: Sea-Saint is closed to outsiders
during major recording sessions.
Disabled: toilets.

Spring Fiesta Association
Tour of Homes

Information 826 St Ann Street, New Orleans, LA 70116
(581 1367). **Tours** phone for details.
Since 1937 this pioneering preservation group has opened
private homes to the public to spotlight New Orleans culture
and raise funds. There are usually three tours in the third
week of March, each for one day only, of French Quarter
houses, Garden District houses and a bus tour to River Road
plantations. Most people will see these palatial homes only
in the pages of *Southern Living* or *Architectural Digest*, so
it's a big weekend for house-worshippers.

The paddle-steamer 'Natchez', one of the many riverboats offering tours.

Museums
& Galleries

Exploring the history of jazz, voodoo or the Confederacy; showing post-impressionists, cubists or abstract expressionists: the city's collections are a diverse bunch.

At times it may seem as if New Orleans itself is a museum. The unique vernacular architecture, the native residents of so many varied backgrounds, the carnival and holy day traditions, the indigenous foods, the music and to a large extent the visual arts – all seem absolutely redolent with the past. This means that, unlike US cities of more recent vintage or with more progressive self-images, it is not necessary to visit New Orleans's history museums to access the city's past. The true function of these museums is to bring understanding to the great heap of artefacts and attitudes that is the Crescent City.

Note that many museums are closed on Mondays. For details of the **Louisiana Children's Museum**, see page 167 **Children**.

Louisiana State Museum sites

No institution does a better job of untangling the threads of the region's complicated past than the Louisiana State Museum, which is housed in four locations: the **Old United States Mint** on Esplanade Avenue, at the Mississippi River; the **Presbytère** on Jackson Square in the heart of the French Quarter; the **Cabildo** – a twin of the Presbytère – also on Jackson Square, and the **Arsenal**, which is nestled behind and connected to the Cabildo.

All four museums
Information (568 6968). **Open** 9am-5pm Tue-Sun.
Admission $4; $3 concessions; free under-12s; 3-day ticket to all 4 sites $10; $7.50 concessions; free under-12s.
Credit MC, V.
Disabled: toilet. Website: www.crt.state.la.us/crt/museum/lsmnet3.htm

Old United States Mint
400 Esplanade Avenue, at Decatur Street. Bus 3 Vieux Carré, 48 Esplanade, 55 Elysian Fields, 81 Almonaster, 82 Desire. **Map 7 D3**
This huge, ox blood-coloured, Greek Revival structure, built during the presidency of Andrew Jackson to produce coins for the rapidly expanding American West, served as a mint from 1838 to 1909 (you can buy examples of all the paper currency and coins once produced here). The building sits on the spot where Jackson reviewed his troops before the

Battle of New Orleans. The Mint is now used to showcase the two touchstones of New Orleans identity: jazz and Mardi Gras. The jazz exhibit features a collection of instruments played by the progenitors of this uniquely American art form, from the primitive home-made percussion kits of the first street 'spasm' bands, to one of Dizzy Gillespie's signature, modified horns. But jazz pilgrims travel to the Mint to behold one relic above all: the well-worn cornet upon which the young Louis Armstrong learned to play.

The Mardi Gras exhibition is a wonderful initiation into the city's Carnival traditions – particularly the costuming. Of particular interest are the costumes of the Acadian or Cajun Mardi Gras, which takes place in the wetland communities west of Baton Rouge. These hand-made jesters' outfits, with conical hats and painted masks, are often worn by horse-back revellers and are entirely different from New Orleans Mardi Gras costumes – and practically never seen in the city.

Presbytère
751 Chartres Street, at St Ann Street. Bus 3 Vieux Carré, 55 Elysian Fields, 81 Almonaster, 82 Desire. **Map 7 C2**
The Presbytère holds consistently excellent changing exhibitions drawn from the Louisiana State Museum's expansive holdings; recent shows have ranged from an exploration of the cultural impact of the alligator to a celebration of two centuries of evening wear. But the single most interesting artefact on display is actually outside the building. The nameless, pumpkin seed-shaped, Confederate navy submarine, which was discovered scuttled in Lake Ponchartrain 13 years after the Civil War, remains a magnetic maritime enigma, like something from the writings of Jules Verne.

Cabildo
701 Chartres Street, at St Peter Street. Bus 3 Vieux Carré, 55 Elysian Fields, 81 Almonaster, 82 Desire. **Map 7 C2**
Louisiana history is an aggregate of ironies, and no place exposes the unexpected aspects of the state's past better than the permanent collection at the Cabildo. For instance, the first display in the exhibit – dedicated to the Native American peoples of what would become Louisiana – is titled 'The First Families of Louisiana', a wry jab at history museum traditions of the past, which acknowledged the importance of a locale's social elite while neglecting the contributions of its first inhabitants. In another subtle commentary, the portrait of Iberville, who established the first permanent European settlement in the area, is paired with a vintage firearm, in an irresistible illustration of the adage 'might makes right'.

Louisianans of African descent are again and again featured for their role in the formation of the culture, not just for their victimhood under slavery and antebellum segregation. Here is Gabriel Gerome, a 'free man of colour' (as blacks who were not slaves were known) who fought beside

Guns and lost causes: the fascinating and anachronistic **Confederate Museum**.

Andrew Jackson to prevent the English from seizing the city during the Battle of New Orleans in 1815. Here is Norbert Rillieux, a free man of colour who invented an early method of distilling sugar cane sap into sugar. And here is Edmund Dede, an internationally renowned composer who entertained audiences before the Civil War to great acclaim. The ironies of the New Orleans social and racial mix is poignantly emphasised in one room, in which a slave auction block in all its hideousness is juxtaposed with memorabilia from Melrose plantation, which was the property of a family of free blacks who themselves owned slaves. It is this sort of collision of expectations that makes the Cabildo history display the most penetrating in the city.

Arsenal

619 St Peter Street, at Chartres Street. Bus 3 Vieux Carré, 55 Elysian Fields, 81 Almonaster, 82 Desire.
Map 7 B2
The museum housed in the old State Armory (built in 1839) is actually an extension of the Cabildo, and is entered from Chartres Street, not St Peter Street. But visitors should not miss going around the corner to see the fascinating façade, which is perforated by tall, broad windows to admit light, but also criss-crossed with iron straps to protect it from insurgents. Like the Presbytère, the Arsenal houses rotating exhibitions, including a recent show dedicated to one of the town's favourite vices: coffee.

Other museums

Confederate Museum of the Louisiana Historical Association

929 Camp Street, at Howard Avenue (523 4522).
St Charles Streetcar. **Open** 10am-4pm Mon-Sat.
Admission $5; $4 concessions; $2 under-12s.
Credit MC, V. **Map 6 B/C2**
This redstone, Romanesque revival structure is the oldest history museum in the city and now poised to become the centre of a new museum community as the **D-Day and**

Ogden museums (*see p91 and p92*) near completion. It is of interest to visitors for two reasons. First, it houses a splendid collection of artefacts from the War of Succession (as the American Civil War was known in the South). Here are all the sinister death-dealing devices, the uniforms and poignant personal mementoes of war that any such museum interesting to history buffs. The political forces of the war are not discussed, although there is an affecting exhibit about the black Confederate units, a minor but much debated element of the Civil War organised in its final desperate months.

In addition, the Confederate Museum is a time capsule of another era's museum practices and social attitudes. The beautiful 1891 structure, purpose-built to house the collection, is a museum piece itself, with long skylights to admit the sun, warm wooden panelling on every wall and rows of built-in display cabinets, all in excellent repair. Today, the Confederacy is commonly viewed as a deeply flawed – if not altogether evil – institution, based as it was on agrarian slavery. Still, the men who fought and died for the South were as often as not simple patriots, not political theoreticians. So, any view of the Confederacy is now an emotional maelstrom of historic chagrin and ancestral pride that can still cause tempers to rise. The Confederate Museum takes no particular stand on these social issues, even as the city it serves has become at least half African-American in population – this in itself makes the museum an anachronism. But that irony only adds to the fascination of a visit to this odd institution – don't miss it.

Historic New Orleans Collection

533 Royal Street, at St Louis Street (523 4662).
Bus 3 Vieux Carré, 55 Elysian Fields, 81 Almonaster, 82 Desire. **Open** 10am-4.45pm Tue-Sat. **Admission** Williams Gallery free; Louisiana History Galleries & Williams House (by guided tour only) $4. **No credit cards. Map 7 B2**
Low-key to the point of invisibility to the less-than-alert visitor, this compound of eighteenth- and nineteenth-century buildings, including the 1794 Merieult House (*see p39* **Architecture**) offers art, culture and history in several

attractive forms. The HNOC grew out of wealthy philanthropist Kemper Williams's interest in collecting documents and memorabilia connected to the War of 1812. His hobby expanded to include almost anything connected with Louisiana history, a passion shared by his wife, Leila. The Williamses established a foundation for their collection with an endowment to continue the work of collecting, cataloguing and studying Louisiana. The ground-floor Williams Gallery has excellent changing shows – past exhibits include photographs by New Orleans's mid-century Surrealist Clarence John Laughlin, and the musical memorabilia of Bill Russell, a producer and archivist of traditional jazz – while the permanent exhibits in a suite of upstairs galleries provide a genteel overview of the history of the city. Among the highlights are the documents used to negotiate the Louisiana Purchase; a large and detailed painting by John Antropus from 1858 of a slave funeral; and an iron ball – once manacled to a slave's leg as punishment – that visitors can lift to feel its weight. There are guided tours (10am, 11am, 2pm, 3pm, Tue-Sat), one of the 1889 Trapolin House, remodelled in the 1940s as a home for the Williamses, and another of the upstairs galleries. The latter tour, given by excellent volunteer guides, is the city's best short course in local history.
Disabled: toilet. Website: www.hnoc.org

Jackson Barracks
National Guard Installation & Museum
6400 St Claude Avenue, between Delery & Angela Streets (278 8242/jbmuseum@cmq.com). Bus 88 St Claude. **Open** 7.30am-4pm Mon-Fri; tours by appointment. **Admission** free.
Anyone devoted to the history of war, particularly World War II, will be interested in this out-of-the-way military museum. It has been a military installation since the 1830s and is now the headquarters of the Louisiana National Guard. The museum has weaponry from the War of 1812 as well as other nineteenth-century pieces, but the main focus is contemporary, with updates from the Gulf War.
Disabled: access to theatre & 1st floor only; toilet. Website: www.jbmuseum@cmq.com

Mardi Gras Museum
421 Williams Boulevard, at Short Street, Rivertown, Kenner (468 4038). Bus Kenner Loop. **Open** 9am-5pm Tue-Sat. **Admission** $3; $2 concessions. **Credit** (shop only) MC, V.
What is this marvellous little museum about Mardi Gras doing way out here in Kenner? Small but complete, the museum gives a close-up view of Carnival. There is the obligatory video, of course, but the real value of the museum is its thoughtful yet fun overview of Mardi Gras. There are costumes worn by the Mardi Gras Indians, Carnival queens and kings and float riders, and a wide range of memorabilia and photographs. There's also a recreated float where wannabe riders can get the feel of krewedom.

Musée Conti Wax Museum of Louisiana
917 Conti Street, at Dauphine Street (525 2605). Bus 3 Vieux Carré, 57 Franklin. **Open** 10am-5.30pm Mon-Sat; noon-5.30pm Sun. **Admission** $6.25; $4.75 children. **Credit** MC, V. **Map 7 B1/2**
Another somewhat anachronistic institution, the Wax Museum comprises, as you might expect, a labyrinth of dimly lit hallways bordered by kitsch tableaux played out by waxen mannequins. It doesn't rival the Cabildo or the Historic New Orleans Collection in its presentation of New Orleans's history, but it actually does a very credible job of illustrating the factual incidents and myths that make up the city's self-image. Opened in 1964, there are a few rather dated displays – including the visit of the Duke and Duchess of Windsor to Mardi Gras in the mid-1950s (a moment that must have had great cachet 35 years ago, but is now totally obscure) – as well as a scene from the Eisenhower-era movie *Creature from the Black Lagoon*, complete with monster and

shrieking female victim mired in mud. But the exhibits have been kept in remarkably good shape and, like the Confederate Museum, part of the fun is stepping back in time to an earlier sensibility.
Disabled: toilet. Website: www.get-waxed.com

National D-Day Museum
945 Magazine Street, at Howard Avenue (527 6012/ ddaymus@gnofn.org). **Map 6 C2**
Although this museum, housed in a nineteenth-century warehouse building, is not scheduled to open until June 2000, it is already considered part of the growing downtown museum community. It will present the D-Day experience through film, exhibits and interactive displays, and the severe, geometric façade is highlighted in military colours: brown, olive green and khaki. New Orleans is the natural site for an American D-Day museum as the place where the inexpensive but efficient Higgins landing craft that made the invasion of Normandy possible were built.

New Orleans Fire Department Museum
1135 Washington Avenue, at Magazine Street (896 4756). St Charles Streetcar/bus 11 Magazine. **Open** 9am-4pm Mon-Fri. **Admission** free. **Map 6 A/B3**
A fire station since 1850, this two-storey brick building on a quiet stretch of Washington Avenue now houses an array of vintage firefighting equipment and memorabilia, including an 1838 hand pump and an 1860 hand-drawn truck. Best of all, though, are the retired firefighters who are on hand as guides. Visitors are welcome to wander at will, but the friendly, knowledgeable firefighters bring this museum to life.
Disabled: access to 1st floor only; toilet.

New Orleans Historic Voodoo Museum
724 Dumaine Street, at Royal Street (523 7685). Bus 3 Vieux Carré, 55 Elysian Fields, 81 Almonaster, 82 Desire. **Open** 10am-8pm daily. **Admission** $6.30; $5.25 concessions; $4.20 11-18s; $3.15 5-11s; free under-5s. **Credit** AmEx, Disc, MC, V. **Map 7 C2**
The Voodoo Museum is hardly the spot for scholarly edification on the indigenous integration of Roman Catholicism and Afro-Caribbean religions known as Voodoo – but it is a wonderfully seedy, spooky French Quarter experience nonetheless. Visitors will find room after room of weird, macabre artefacts, from a desiccated cat to baby coffins, skulls, turtle shells and alligator skins. No visit would be complete without a palm or card reading. Lots of cheesy fun.
Website: www.voodoomuseum.com

New Orleans Historic Pharmacy Museum
514 Chartres Street, at St Louis Street (565 8027). Bus 3 Vieux Carré, 55 Elysian Fields, 81 Almonaster, 82 Desire. **Open** 10am-5pm Tue-Sun. **Admission** $2; $1 concessions; free under-12s. **Credit** (shop only, minimum $20) **Map 7 B2**
This storefront museum occupies the original site of the first licensed pharmacy in the US, opened in 1823. The old wooden counters, cases and shelves have been restored to jewel-like perfection, and on display are the beautiful handmade glass vessels and ceramics that were the tools of the profession in the nineteenth century. The second floor includes a sickroom and library. Here, you return to a time when cocaine might have been dispensed over the counter for a toothache, a lithium potion was taken for nervousness, and live leeches swam in a porcelain bowl that looked as innocent as a soup tureen – you can easily imagine Dr Jekyll having a flavoured soda water at the soda fountain. The museum is most notable for its calm, old-fashioned approach to museumery: there are no interactive displays, no characters in costumes, no straining for relevance. The courtyard (popular with local brides) is lovely.
Disabled: toilet. Website: www.kenner.la.us

Williams Research Center of the Historic New Orleans Collection

410 Chartres Street, at Conti Street (598 7100). Bus 3 Vieux Carré, 55 Elysian Fields, 81 Almonaster, 82 Desire. **Open** 10am-4.30pm Tue-Sat. **Admission** free. **Map 7 B2**

Housed in a gorgeously renovated turn-of-the-century police station, the WRC (part of the HNOC) is not a museum per se – though it always has wonderful displays of historic objects, documents and art. A recent exhibition displayed artefacts related to the local myth that grew up around Longfellow's epic poem *Evangeline*, including the original manuscript. But its real function is as a public library and archive for serious students of any aspect of the region's culture or history. The WRC is a 'closed stack' facility; that is, visitors are not allowed to browse through the collection, but must ask research assistants for help.
Disabled: toilet.

Fine art museums

It is difficult to determine exactly where history leaves off and fine art begins. Art is a document of its time as much as any piece of correspondence or photograph: thus, a portrait of a historical figure by the eighteenth-century transplanted Englishman Thomas Sully would be considered principally a historical record at the Historic New Orleans Collection, while at the New Orleans Museum of Art it would first be considered an early American oil on canvas. Visitors will find wonderful examples of visual art at practically all the city's history venues, while for those seeking art for its own sake, New Orleans is extremely rich in art of all periods.

Contemporary Arts Center

900 Camp Street, at Howard Avenue (523 1216). St Charles Streetcar. **Open** 10am-5pm Mon-Sat; 11am-5pm Sun; cybercafé 7am-8pm Mon, Tue, Sun; 7am-11pm Wed-Sat. **Admission** Louisiana Galleries free; upstairs galleries $5; $3 concessions; free under-12s; free Thur. **Credit** AmEx, MC, V. **Map 6 B/C2**

A cornerstone of the arts in New Orleans, the CAC (as it is universally known) is housed in a dramatically redesigned warehouse building downtown. It has no permanent collection but is instead the city's most vital rotating show space, with four, large, ground-floor galleries where shows change ten times a year, and a larger upstairs hall where exhibitions change five times a year. The centre specialises in showing the newest, most experimental work – whether regional, national or international. Recent shows have highlighted master glass-maker Dale Chihuly, photographer William Wegman, Haitian flag-makers, and New Orleans visual artists such as Willie Birch, John Scott and Douglas Bourgeois whose art is based on their love of the region's indigenous music. The CAC is also a venue for contemporary theatre, dance productions, films and occasional musical events (*see p209* **Nightlife** for more information on this). It has a cybercafé where visitors can sip cold-dripped iced coffee (a must in the delta heat) while surfing the net free of charge.
Disabled: toilet. Website: www.cacno.org

Newcomb Art Gallery

Woldenberg Art Center, Tulane University campus, at Willow Street (865 5328). St Charles Streetcar. **Open** 10am-5pm Mon-Fri; noon-5pm Sat. **Admission** free. **Map 4 B8**

Tulane University's recently renovated and enlarged Newcomb Gallery clearly transcends the other university showplaces in town. It's rather out-of-the-way, on the Willow Street side of the Uptown campus, but the quality of its exhibitions have certainly put the place on the map. It houses a permanent display of Newcomb Pottery, the famous pottery made by Newcomb students and professors from 1895-1940. Newcomb, a women's college, was an important link in the American Arts and Crafts movement, inspired by the Ruskin-Morris Arts and Crafts movement in England. Changing shows have also recently included early works by Abstract Expressionist masters Mark Rothko and Adolph Gottlieb, a marvellous selection of contemporary glass-makers and a wonderful group show of Japanese print makers.
Disabled: toilet.

New Orleans Museum of Art

1 Collins DiBoll Circle, City Park (488 2631). Bus 46 City Park, 48 Esplanade. **Open** 10am-5pm Tue-Sun. **Admission** $6; $5 concessions; $3 children. **Credit** AmEx, MC, V. **Map 5 D/E4**

The New Orleans Museum of Art – or NOMA, as it is often abbreviated – is located at the lake end of Esplanade Avenue in City Park. Its collection is as eclectic as most metropolitan museums, including everything from a few Renaissance paintings to a Warhol or two; from pre-Columbian ceramics to interactive computer displays; from ephemeral Chinese ink painting to monumental welded steel sculpture. Just a few of the notable objects in the collection include a stunning academic portrait from the late 1780s of Marie Antoinette by Elizabeth Louise Vigeé LeBurs, which seems to epitomise New Orleans's mania for all things French and all things decadent; a sketchy portrait by Edgar Degas of his blind Creole cousin Estelle Musson, done on the artist's brief visit to the city in 1872; and a gorgeous 1889 allegorical painting by William Bouguereau titled *Whisperings of Love*. Also of note is the Billups glass collection, particularly the ancient and antique glass. Combined with the rest of the museum's holdings, it forms the finest, most inclusive glass collection in the South. NOMA's permanent exhibitions are excellent, and are supplemented by the highest-quality travelling shows and in-house rotating exhibitions.
Disabled: toilet. Website: www.noma.org

Ogden Museum of Southern Art

University of New Orleans, 615 Howard Avenue, at Lee Circle (539 9600/fax 539 9602). **Map 6 B2**

Scheduled to open in 2000, the Ogden Museum is an anxiously awaited addition to the New Orleans art scene. The museum – which is currently being installed in the massive, red sandstone Howard library, built in 1888 (it hasn't been used as a library for decades) – is based on the extensive private collection of real estate magnate and Louisiana art devotee Roger Ogden. It includes everything from nineteenth-century landscapes by William Buck that help us visualise the early Louisiana lifestyle, to scores of cartoon-like wildlife watercolours by Gulf Coast visionary artist Walter Anderson, to contemporary papier mâché sculpture by nationally known artist Willie Birch. Though the exact layout of the institution is still unknown, the quality of the Ogden collection and the splendour of the architecture – to stand in the old library's rotunda and look up at the stunning woodwork of the ceiling will be worth the price of admission – should combine to produce a wonderful experience. The Ogden Museum abuts the Confederate Museum, which is across the street from the CAC.

Ecleticism encapsulated: the **New Orleans Museum of Art** *in City Park.*

Top glass

In the past 15 years the Crescent City has emerged on to the international art scene as a gathering place for glass-makers. The reason for local artists' particular affinity for the medium can be traced to Tulane University's glass programme under the direction of sculptor Gene Koss. The course began in 1976 with a rather primitive studio equipped with a furnace to liquefy broken bottles, an annealer to gradually reduce the temperature of the fiercely hot material, and various grinding and polishing tools to 'cold work' the glass once it was cool. In 1984 the original sponsor of the small studio, Margaret Pace, increased her donation five-fold, which allowed Koss to expand the operation into a state-of-the-art, computerised, quarter-million-dollar facility.

Class after class of fine arts students were exposed to the wonders of the medium but had few or no opportunities to ply their craft, as no public glass shops existed. Then, at the beginning of the 1990s, some of Koss's students opened two glass shops to foster Tulane students and others after graduation. Now practically every contemporary art gallery featuring New Orleans artists has a glass-maker or two in its stable. Visiting artists frequently take advantage of the public facilities to experiment with the medium, and local collectors have supported the new industry by buying glass sculpture with zeal. Coincidentally, the New Orleans Museum of Art's extensive glass collection – which was part of the museum's holdings before the art was practised in the city – provides continued inspiration to the ever-growing number of New Orleans artists who consider glass their principal medium.

RHINO (*see page 157* **Shops & Services**) is a craft co-operative gallery that stocks examples of the finest glass by local artisans, including work made at many of the other glass studios in town, while **Arlodante Contemporary Craft Gallery** (535 Julia Street, at Camp Street; 524 3233; open 11am-5pm Tue-Sat) specialises in work by national artists. The **Nuance Gallery** (728 Dublin Street, at Maple Street; 865 8463; open 9am-5pm Tue-Sat) is the studio and gallery of glass-blower Arden Stewart. At this time there are no glass demonstrations, but Stewart's beautiful perfume bottles and sherry glasses are worth the trip to the Riverbend neighbourhood uptown alone.

The process of sculpting with hot liquid glass is a fascinating ballet of fire and muscle. If you want to watch glass artists at work, there are three studios open to the public:

New Orleans School of Glass Works & Print Making

727 Magazine Street, at Julia Street (529 7277). Bus *11 Magazine.* **Open** 10am-5pm Mon-Sat. **Credit** Disc, MC, V. **Map 6 C2**
This brightly lit storefront gallery displays the widest variety of glass art in the city, from local, national and international glass-makers, and artists give regular demonstrations in the large 'hot shop' behind the gallery. Here visitors can observe the differences between lampworking (where rods of glass are formed and joined with

Sydney & Walda Bestoff Foundation Collection

K&B Plaza, 1055 St Charles Avenue, at Lee Circle (586 2007). St Charles Streetcar. **Open** usually 9am-5pm Mon-Fri. **Admission** free.
Map 6 B2
Formerly known as the Virlane Foundation Collection, this was the art collection of the K&B drugstore corporate headquarters on Lee Circle. The K&B chain has recently been sold to another corporation, so the future whereabouts of the collection is in some doubt – though it was recently announced that the outdoor sculpture in the collection will form the basis of a new sculpture garden near NOMA in City Park. In the meantime, this splendid collection of monumental sculpture – including pieces by Isamu Noguchi, George Rickey, Ida Kohlmeyer, Henry Moore, Barbara Hepworth and Alexander Calder – is continuously on display and free of charge. The indoor collection is scattered around the corporate offices – imagine having your desk decorated with an Yves Klein or a Jim Surles or an Umberto Boccioni – and open to the public during business hours.
Disabled: toilet.

Galleries

The commercial art gallery scene in New Orleans is phenomenal. For a city of such a relatively small population and relatively shallow pockets, which already pours so much of its disposable capital into Mardi Gras (one of the greatest of folk art expressions), it supports an almost unbelievable number and variety of art outlets. The galleries range from the most high-minded exhibition spaces showing intellectually challenging contemporary painting and sculpture to the 'Brie and Chablis' set to countless frame and poster shops selling inexpensive posters to decorate student rooms and pizza parlours. Tourist dollars feed the marketplace to a large extent, particularly in the French Quarter. Still, even considering out-of-town money, the size and vitality of the commercial art community seems to defy logic.

the flame of a gas torch), blown glass (where molten glass is gathered on the end of an iron tube and expanded by blowing air into the molten mass) and casting (where quantities of liquid glass are poured into sand moulds). Demonstrations are given daily, but phone first to check the daily schedule.
Disabled: toilet.

Rosetree Glass Studio & Gallery
446 Vallette Street, at Opelousas Street (366 3602/ brendamark@mindspring.com). Bus 101 Algiers. **Open** 9am-5pm Mon-Fri. **Credit** MC, V.
Map 4 H7
Founded by Mark Rosenbaum, the first artist to graduate from Tulane University's glass course, the studio has a hot shop with a protected spectators' area and a spacious gallery showing the Rosetree line of blown vessels and changing exhibits of glass art. The studio is in a renovated theatre in Algiers Point, directly across the river from the Vieux Carré – it's a seven-block walk from the ferry landing. There are daily glass-blowing demonstrations.
Disabled: toilet.

Studio Inferno
3000 Royal Street, at Montegut Street (945 1878). Bus 82 Desire. **Open** 10am-5pm Mon-Sat. **Credit** AmEx, MC, V. **Map 4 H6**
This corrugated metal warehouse building in the Bywater neighbourhood has been renovated into studio space for a dozen or so artists – including neon light sculptors, painters and photographers – and features a large hot shop. Studio Inferno makes its own drinking glasses, pitchers and cast glass ornaments (for sale in the small gallery), and one of its founders, Mitchell Gaudet, is among New Orleans's premier glass sculptors; his works are inspired by the city's odd, above-ground cemeteries. Glass-making occurs almost daily, except in the hot summer months; phone to check the daily schedule.

French Quarter
Visitors could easily imagine that the French Quarter is the centre of the arts in New Orleans; arguably, they would be correct. The fences surrounding Jackson Square and behind St Louis Cathedral are the amorphous, open-air gallery of New Orleans street artists. Admittedly, the work is hardly of the highest calibre, but that doesn't stop visitors from buying pictures as personalised mementoes of their trip.

The streets of the Quarter – particularly Royal and Chartres Streets – are studded with innumerable antique shops, curio shops, poster shops, clothing stores, jewellery stores and – yes – art galleries. To separate them into distinct categories is not as easy as it might seem. Some 'art galleries' sell nothing more than tourist kitsch, while some curio shops, which do not pretentiously describe themselves as galleries at all, sell objects of the

highest artistic merit by anyone's standards. Certain galleries carry a large quantity of art but cater exclusively to the antique-buying crowd, selling high-priced period paintings to decorate period interiors; then again, perfectly respectable paintings and sculpture can sometimes be found in antique stores.

To try to ferret out every art-selling concern in the Vieux Carré or to rigorously segregate and list these scores of businesses would be daunting. Anyway, the fun is in the hunt, and visitors will doubtlessly enjoy searching these endless storefronts, using their own criteria to distinguish them. Don't miss the following places.

A Gallery for Fine Photography
322 Royal Street, at Bienville Street (568 1313). Bus 3 Vieux Carré, 41 Canal, 55 Elysian Fields, 81 Almonaster, 82 Desire. **Open** 10am-6pm Mon-Sat; 11am-6pm Sun. **Credit** AmEx, Disc, MC, V. **Map 7 B2**
As the name implies, this is the city's premier retailer of art photography, from early-century portraits of prostitutes by Eugene Bellocq to contemporary works by the likes of Annie Leibowitz.

Barrister's Gallery
526 Royal Street, at St Louis Street (525 2767). Bus 3 Vieux Carré, 55 Elysian Fields, 81 Almonaster. **Open** 10am-5pm Mon-Sat. **Credit** AmEx, MC, V. **Map 7 B2**
Barrister's is a twilight zone of African fetishes, Oceanic masks, Haitian voodoo flags, medical specimens, Southern folk art, Eastern Orthodox icons, offender art (a wonderfully descriptive term for art made by prisoners) – and on and on. Don't miss it.

Bryant Galleries of New Orleans
316 Royal Street, at Conti Street (525 5584). Bus 3 Vieux Carré, 55 Elysian Fields, 81 Almonaster, 82 Desire. **Open** 10am-6pm Mon-Thur, Sun; 10am-8pm Fri, Sat. **Credit** AmEx, DC, Disc, MC, V. **Map 7 B2**
Bryant Galleries provides an eclectic selection of fine arts, ranging from pastel paintings to bronzes, most relating to New Orleans.

Carmen Llewellyn Gallery
240 Chartres Street, at Bienville Street (558 9859). Bus 3 Vieux Carré, 41 Canal, 55 Elysian Fields, 81 Almonaster, 82 Desire. **Open** 11am-5pm Mon-Sat. **Credit** AmEx, MC, V. **Map 7 B2**
Shows changing exhibitions of contemporary and modern painting and sculpture by renowned Latin American artists.

Dyansen Gallery
433 Royal Street, at St Louis Street (523 2902). Bus 3 Vieux Carré, 55 Elysian Fields, 81 Almonaster, 82 Desire. **Open** 10am-6pm Mon-Thur, Sun; 10am-8pm Fri, Sat. **Credit** AmEx, DC, Disc, MC, V. **Map 7 B2**
Part of a nationwide operation, Dyansen features a wide variety of art, from soft neo-Impressionist paintings of women in diaphanous gowns to the occasional Picasso print.

Elliott Gallery
540 Royal Street, at Toulouse Street (523 3554). Bus 3 Vieux Carré, 55 Elysian Fields, 81 Almonaster, 82 Desire. **Open** 9.30am-6pm Mon-Sat; 11am-5pm Sun. **Credit** AmEx, DC, Disc, MC, V. **Map 7 B2**
A French Quarter art landmark formerly known as the Nahan Gallery, this is the home of the well-known moderns Max Papart, Theo Tobias and James Coignard.

Hanson Gallery
*229 Royal Street, at Bienville Street (524 8211/
hansongals@aol.com). Bus 3 Vieux Carré, 41 Canal,
55 Elysian Fields, 81 Almonaster, 82 Desire.* **Open**
10am-6pm Mon-Sat; 11am-5pm Sun. **Credit** AmEx, Disc,
MC, V. **Map 7 B2**
In addition to limited edition prints and original paintings
by a galaxy of art stars including Peter Max, Leroy Nieman
and Mark Kostabi, Hanson features the work of local lumi-
nary Adrian Deckbar and occasional group shows of contemporary art by women. Part of a nationwide group.

La Belle Galerie
*309 Chartres Street, at Bienville Street (529 5538/529
3080). Bus 3 Vieux Carré, 41 Canal, 55 Elysian Fields,
81 Almonaster, 82 Desire.* **Open** 10am-7pm daily.
Credit AmEx, DC, Disc, MC, V. **Map 7 B2**
La Belle Galerie has everything African and African-
American, from one-of-a-kind iron sculpture by contemporary artists and limited edition prints to genuine tribal art
and artefacts.

Mann Gallery
*713 Bienville Street, at Royal Street (523 2342)
Bus 3 Vieux Carré, 41 Canal, 55 Elysian Fields,
81 Almonaster, 82 Desire.* **Open** 11am-5.30pm Mon-Sat.
Credit AmEx, MC, V. **Map 7 B2**
A step back in time to the period of French Academic painting and Impressionism. Not the place to shop if you're on a
tight budget.

Peligro
*305 Decatur Street, at Conti Street (581 1706).
Bus 3 Vieux Carré, 55 Elysian Fields, 81 Almonaster,
82 Desire.* **Open** 10am-6pm Mon-Thur; 10am-10pm Fri,
Sat; noon-6pm Sun. **Credit** AmEx, Disc, MC, V.
Map 7 B2
Located near the House of Blues music club, Peligro sells folk
and primitive art, including work by artists from Mexico and
the American South.
Disabled: toilet.

Rodrigue's Studio
*721 Royal Street, at Orleans Street (581 4244/
rgallery@bellsouth.net). Bus 3 Vieux Carré, 55 Elysian
Fields, 81 Almonaster, 82 Desire.* **Open** 10am-6pm daily.
Credit AmEx, MC, V. **Map 7 C2**
Cajun artist George Rodrigue had already established himself as a gifted painter of his Acadiana homeland when he
committed the image of his deceased terrier mutt Tiffany to
canvas. What followed was an almost incomprehensible
ascent into the stratosphere of fortune and notoriety for the
artist. Visitors will either share in the magic of the blue dog
phenomenon or the bafflement.
Website: www.mbay.net

Thomas Mann Gallery I/O
*829 Royal Street, at Dumaine Street (523 5041).
Bus 3 Vieux Carré, 55 Elysian Fields, 81 Almonaster,
82 Desire.* **Open** 11am-6pm daily. **Credit** AmEx, MC, V.
Map 7 C2
This is the French Quarter annex of artist Thomas Mann's
larger Uptown gallery, featuring a wide assortment of what
Mann calls 'techno-romantic' jewellery, household items,
furniture and pure art designs. Geometric abstraction,
excellent craftsmanship and post-industrial humour seem
to be the rules in Mann's own work, as well as in the stable of artists he shows.
Website: www.thomasmann.com

Take a pew at the open-air **Sydney &
Walda Bestoff Foundation Collection**.
See page 94.

Stone + Press Galleries
*238 Chartres Street, at Bienville Street (561 8555).
Bus 3 Vieux Carré, 41 Canal, 55 Elysian Fields, 81
Almonaster, 82 Desire.* **Open** 10.30am-5.30pm Mon-Sat.
Credit AmEx, DC, Disc, MC, V. **Map 7 B2**
An elegant showplace for the finest of the printer's art, par-
ticularly lithography. The selection of prints has recently
included American Regionalists of the 1930s and 1940s.

Julia Street & Magazine Street

A visiting art critic of some renown, commenting
on the predominance of international styles and
the demise of regionalism, once declared that there
is no such thing as Creole art. It is certainly true
that the pervasive styles of the twentieth century
are also the pervasive styles of New Orleans's contemporary art scene: Abstract Expressionism;
Cubism in its various latterday incarnations; faux-
primitive figure painting, and so forth.

But there is nonetheless a particular character
to New Orleans visual art that seems to distance
it to some degree from generic contemporary art.
A macabre sense of humour, a modesty of scale, a
love of the folk or naïve arts and an unusual attention to local subject matter – all seem to be general
characteristics of New Orleans artists. Though, of
course, for every artist that upholds these rules,
there are two others who defy them.

Visitors who are serious about contemporary
art and wish to draw conclusions of their own
should leave the French Quarter and travel to New
Orleans's 'gallery row' on Julia Street and further
uptown on Magazine Street, making a few notable
detours along the way.

Contemporary galleries are usually open from
Tuesday to Saturday, 10am-5pm, though recently
many establishments have opened their doors on
Mondays, too. On the first Saturday of the month,
all the galleries are open from 6-9pm; it's a great
free street party, particularly the season opener in
October (*see chapter* **By Season**).

Academy Gallery
*5256 Magazine Street, at Valmont Street (899 8111).
Bus 11 Magazine.* **Open** 9am-4pm Mon-Fri; 10am-4pm
Sat. **No credit cards. Map 4 C10**
The showplace of the New Orleans Academy of Fine Arts,
a school that specialises in the traditional arts of draughts-
manship, representational painting, ceramic sculpture and
photography. The exhibitions of work by faculty members,
students and invitees from the local community are uniformly excellent.

Arthur Roger Gallery
*432 Julia Street, at Magazine Street (522 1999). Bus
11 Magazine.* **Open** 10am-5pm Mon-Sat. **Credit** AmEx,
MC, V. **Map 6 C2**
By any one's measure this is one of the best contemporary
art spaces in the South. With three separate gallery spaces,
AR shows a large and eclectic group of local and national
all-stars. Included among them is George Dureau, one of
the grand old men of New Orleans art, whose photographs
of dwarves, amputees and other unfortunates have
brought dignity to his subjects as well as international
acclaim to the artist.

Christopher Maier Furniture Design

329 Julia Street, at Commerce Street (586 9079).
Bus 11 Magazine. **Open** 10am-5pm daily. **Credit** AmEx,
MC, V. **Map 6 C2**
Master woodworker Maier is humble in describing his cre-
ations as mere furniture; functional sculpture would perhaps
be a better term for this excellent work.

Carol Robinson Gallery

840 Napoleon Avenue, at Magazine Street (895 6130).
Bus 11 Magazine, 24 Napoleon. **Open** 10am-5.30pm Tue-
Sat. **Credit** AmEx, MC, V. **Map 4 D10**
Newly moved to a lovely former residence on Magazine
Street, Carol Robinson has for more than a decade provided
a showplace for some of the city's finest emerging talent as
well as some of the best old-hands.

Cole Pratt Gallery

*3800 Magazine Street, at Peniston Street (891 6789/
cpgaller@gnofn.org). Bus 11 Magazine.* **Open** *Sept-June*
noon-5.30pm Mon; 10am-5.30pm Tue-Sat; *July, Aug*
10am-5pm Tue-Sat. **Credit** AmEx, MC, V. **Map 4**
D9/10
On the opposite pole of the contemporary art spectrum from
Positive Space (*opposite*), this gallery specialises in genteel, contemplative forms of local art – a wonderful contrast.

The Davis Gallery

*3964 Magazine Street, at Constantinople Street (897
0780). Bus 11 Magazine.* **Open** 10am-5pm Tue-Sat.
No credit cards. Map 4 D9/10
Specialising in authentic African tribal art, the Davis Gallery
has for years presented dignified exhibitions that seem as
much museum-like as gallery-like.
Disabled: toilet.

d.o.c.s./A Studio Gallery of Contemporary Arts

*709 Camp Street, at Girod Street (524 3936). St Charles
Streetcar/bus 11 Magazine.* **Open** 11am-6pm Tue-Sat.
Credit AmEx, MC, V. **Map 6 C1**
Only a short walk downtown from Julia Street, this hand-
some gallery displays the works of emerging talents, who
may very well be the city's next generation of stars.
Disabled: toilet. Website: www.docsgallery.com

Galerie Simonne Stern

518 Julia Street, at Magazine Street (529 1118).
Bus 11 Magazine. **Open** noon-5pm Mon; 10am-5pm Tue-
Sat. **Credit** MC, V. **Map 6 C2**
The oldest of the Julia Street galleries and one of the finest.
Though the rotating show schedule includes a wide variety
of styles, the work here could probably be best categorised
as 'non-objective' (that is, art without subject matter). George
Dunbar's elegant, gilded minimalist paintings, created with
expensive gold leaf, have made him one of New Orleans's
best-known artists.

Heriard-Cimino Gallery

440 Julia Street, at Magazine Street (525 7300).
Bus 11 Magazine. **Open** 10.30am-6pm Mon-Fri; 10am-
5pm Sat. **Credit** AmEx, MC, V. **Map 6 C2**
A newcomer to the Julia Street scene, Heriard-Cimino has
added a contingent of excellent Texas artists to the New
Orleans mix.

LeMieux Galleries

332 Julia Street, at Tchoupitoulas Street (522 5988).
Bus 11 Magazine. **Open** 10am-5.30pm Mon-Sat. **Credit**
Disc, MC, V. **Map 6 C2**
Characterised perhaps by a looser, more celebratory attitude
toward contemporary arts, LeMieux consistently captures
the spirit of New Orleans with a stable of some of the city's
best artists.

Marguerite Oestreicher Fine Arts

626 Julia Street, at St Charles Avenue (581 9253).
St Charles Streetcar. **Open** 10am-5pm Mon-Sat.
Credit AmEx, Disc, MC, V. **Map 6 B2**
This tiny space has one of the most wide-ranging exhibition line-ups of any Julia Street locale: recent shows have
included collages by the world-famous Joseph Cornell and
the first major outing for emerging local sculptor Adam
Farrington. Marguerite O's is always surprising and
always charming.

Mario Villa Gallery

*3908 Magazine Street, near Constantinople Street
(895 8731). Bus 11 Magazine.* **Open** noon-5pm Mon;
10am-5pm Sat. **Credit** AmEx, MC, V. **Map 4**
D9/10
Known mainly as a showroom for designer Mario Villa's
own good-natured, postmodern furniture, this gallery is also
a changing exhibition space that has presented innumerable
excellent shows over the years.

Positive Space: The Gallery

*2022 Magazine Street, at Jackson Avenue (522 9344/
flash@lanyap.com). Bus 11 Magazine.* **Open** 11am-5pm
Tue-Sun. **Credit** AmEx, Disc, MC, V. **Map 6 B3**
Just a short cab ride uptown from the quiet commercial
dignity of the Julia Street gallery row is this aged storefront
gallery containing the city's funkiest, most experimental
exhibitions.
Website: www.lanyap.com/pspace/

Stella Jones Gallery

*1st NBC Center, 201 St Charles Avenue, at Common
Street (568 9050). St Charles Streetcar.* **Open** 10am-6pm
Mon-Fri; noon-5pm Sat. **Credit** AmEx, DC, Disc, MC, V.
Map 6 C1
Located on the ground floor of an office building just uptown
from the French Quarter, this gallery – showing changing exhi-
bitions of the finest contemporary art by African-Americans
– is slightly off the beaten path, but well worth a visit.
Website: www//.stellajones.com

Still-Zinsel Contemporary Fine Art

*328 Julia Street, at Tchoupitoulas Street (588 9999/
stilzinsel@aol.com). Bus 11 Magazine.* **Open** 10am-5pm
Mon-Sat. **Credit** MC, V. **Map 6 C2**
The interior architecture of Still-Zinsel makes it clearly the
best-looking showplace in the city, and the gallery's outstanding stable of artists makes it a Julia Street must.

Sylvia Schmidt Gallery

400A Julia Street, at Tchoupitoulas Street (522 2000).
Bus 11 Magazine. **Open** 10am-5pm Tue-Sat. **Credit**
AmEx, MC, V. **Map 6 C2**
A small gallery that does an excellent job of displaying
local and national artists working in a broad variety of
media and styles.

Thomas Mann Design

*1804 Magazine Street, between Felicity Street & St Mary
Street (581 2113). Bus 11 Magazine.* **Open** 11am-6pm
Mon-Sat. **Credit** AmEx, MC, V. **Map 6 B3**
Like his French Quarter outlet, artist/proprietor Thomas
Mann exhibits his own beautifully made post-industrial
(junk) assemblages, as well as a wonderfully talented stable
of like-minded jewellers, household object designers and
artists. Always excellent.

Wyndy Morehead Fine Arts

*603 Julia Street, at Camp Street (568 9754). St Charles
Streetcar.* **Open** 10am-5.30pm Tue-Fri; 10am-5pm Sat.
Credit AmEx, MC, V. **Map 6 C2**
Wyndy Morehead specialises in a gentler, less wilfully chal-
lenging brand of contemporary art that is broadly pleasing.

Consumer New Orleans

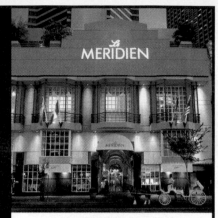

Accommodation

Pillow talk: where to rest your head in historic hotels, cosy cottages or bohemian B&Bs.

There are two things every visitor should know before booking a hotel room in New Orleans: first, the 'real' city extends far beyond the French Quarter, and second, you will pay dearly to stay within the Quarter.

The charms of the French Quarter are many (foremost being the freedom to walk everywhere), but staying there is not the key to an intimate relationship with New Orleans. An old-fashioned St Charles Avenue hotel or a Marigny B&B will also provide a genuine and exciting stay. Every area offers a different perspective on the city, from the business-like perspective of the CBD, to the gay mecca of Faubourg Marigny, or the laid-back residential ambience of Uptown.

WHEN & HOW TO BOOK

Mardi Gras. Jazz Fest. The magic words in the hotel industry. Despite the hype, it's not that difficult to book a room for these events. Getting the room you *want* can be very tough, though. Start early, even if you haven't booked your flight. If you change your mind, you'll lose the deposit but that's a reasonable risk when balanced against finding yourself in a roach infested Kenner motel. Hotels and B&Bs accept bookings a year in advance of Carnival and Jazz Fest and have often booked more than half of all rooms six months ahead. Shop around, but be resigned to high rates and conditions such as a minimum three-, four- or even five-night stay.

There are bargains to be had, but these are strictly for those who like to live dangerously. If attendance happens to be poor, the hotels start making deals, dropping room prices and dispensing with minimum stays. The discounts don't appear until the very last minute, when hotel managers are on the brink of taking a loss, usually on the eve of the second weekend of Jazz Fest or during the final ten days before Fat Tuesday. Look through the *Times-Picayune*'s business page and *City Business* weekly magazine. Both pay close attention to the hotel industry at these crucial times, and both are available online (*see page 182* **Media**). Other high seasons include New Year, when the Sugar Bowl takes place, and early July for the Essence Festival (*see chapter* **By Season**).

The low season is summer, when New Orleans is almost unbearably hot and steamy. For bargain hunters, it's the best time of year because of the

Splash out at the grand **Pavilion** *(page 109).*

fabulous deals. Every hotel has some kind of summer special but the savvy traveller can cut his or her own deal with a little pushing and prodding. Be careful, however, not to let the prices overwhelm good sense. For anyone who doesn't like hot weather or has never experienced a semi-tropical climate, New Orleans is hard work in the summer.

AND BEAR IN MIND

When budgeting for your stay, remember to add in the 11 per cent hotel room tax. If a hotel includes 'parking' in its amenities, check what this means. In the French Quarter you might be charged more than $8 a day to park in a nearby carpark, since on-site facilities are rare. If you have a car, you'd be better off outside the Quarter. Also find out if a hotel charges for local phone calls. Some hotels have dropped this appalling policy (noted in our listings) while others use it to gouge every extra penny from travellers.

Travellers seeking hotels that are fully accessible for the disabled should look to fairly new (post-1990) hotels built with a barrier-free mindset (*see page 255* **Directory** for more information).

ABOUT THE LISTINGS

All the hotels listed in this chapter are air-conditioned unless otherwise stated. Some of the more modest older houses should air-condition rooms but leave bedrooms while the common areas are cooled only by fans. If you're visiting in summertime, AC is crucial to comfort. Unless otherwise noted, all rooms have a telephone and a TV.

We've divided the hotels into price categories according to the cost of a double room – but remember this is just a guide because room rates can fluctuate enormously during the year.

French Quarter

Above $150

Chateau Sonesta Hotel

800 Iberville Street, New Orleans, LA 70112, at Dauphine Street (586 0800/1-800 766 3782/fax 586 1987/in UK 0800 898 410). Bus 3 Vieux Carré, 41 Canal, 57 Franklin. **Rates** *single $145-$225; double $165-$255; suite $370-$800.* **Credit** *AmEx, DC, Disc, MC, V.* **Map 7 A1**

Many New Orleanians hold a grudge against the Sonesta hotel chain for taking over the much-loved DH Holmes department store and turning it into a hotel. However, the Chateau Sonesta has somewhat redeemed itself by paying homage to the Holmes legacy and reinstalling the famous clock (as centrepiece of the Clock Bar) as well as commissioning a lifesize sculpture of Ignatius J O'Reilly, the slovenly hero of *A Confederacy of Dunces*. Ignatius, like most people in New Orleans, used the old store as a landmark, as in: 'Meet me at the clock for 4.30pm' – no further directions needed. The hotel has further allied itself with local tradition

by persuading the Brennan family to open one of its restaurants within the complex, Ralph Brennan's Red Fish Grill. The hotel is heavily tied to convention business and provides the amenities expected by the exacting corporate market. The rooms are tasteful and the service good. Some rooms have balconies that open on Bourbon Street, which can be fun but not if you are overly sensitive to noise. **Hotel services** *Babysitting. Bar. Concierge. Conference facilities. Fax. Fitness centre. Laundry. No-smoking rooms. Parking. Restaurants. Rooms for the disabled. Swimming pool. Safe.* **Room services** *Cable TV. Dataport. Hairdryer. Minibar. Radio. Room service (24 hour). Voicemail.*

Hotel Maison de Ville & the Audubon Cottages

727 Toulouse Street, New Orleans, LA 70130, at Royal Street (561 5858/1-800 634 1600/fax 528 9939). Bus 3 Vieux Carré, 55 Elysian Fields, 81 Almonaster, 82 Desire. **Rates** *single $195-$225; suite $325; cottage $245-$830.* **Credit** *AmEx, DC, Disc, MC, V.* **Map 7 B2**

Tennessee Williams is just one of the multitude of celebrities who have loved this oasis of luxury and civility a block from Bourbon Street. Non-celebrities adore Maison de Ville, too, but perhaps they don't savour the quietude and discretion in the way that Elizabeth Taylor, Ed Bradley, Dan Aykroyd and other famous folk do. The hotel is actually two units in two places: Maison de Ville is a compound of townhouse, slave quarters, courtyard and carriage house on Toulouse Street, while the Audubon Cottages is a very private enclosure of seven self-sufficient cottages a few blocks away on Dauphine Street. At Maison de Ville, the rooms are on the small side but decorated and maintained with great care. At the cottages (artist John James Audubon lived and worked in No.1 during his New Orleans stay), the rooms are larger and the furnishings grander. A stay at Maison de Ville is a serious financial investment but has the rare virtue of a guaranteed return, paid out in dream-like surroundings and faultless service. The Bistro at Maison de Ville, one of the city's best restaurants, is the hotel café. No under-12s are allowed.
Hotel services *All rooms no-smoking. Bar. Concierge. Continental breakfast. Fax. Laundry. Restaurant. Safe. Swimming pool. Valet parking.* **Room services** *Hairdryer. Minibar. Modem. Radio. Refrigerator. Room service (11.30am-10pm). VCR.*

Best hotels for...

backpackers:
the bargain-priced **Marquette House** (*p112*) is well maintained and close to public transport.

fitness buffs:
Mackie Shilstone's famous Pro Spa makes the **Avenue Plaza** (*p111*) nirvana for sweat-lovers.

romantics:
Soniat House (*p104*) sets the scene for romance better than Hollywood.

graduation:
proud matriarchs and patriarchs settle into the stately **Pontchartrain Hotel** (*p111*) each spring.

celeb-spotting:
not all the famous folk stay at the **Maison de Ville** (*above*), but if Robert Redford is in residence, it's small enough to ensure you'll bump into him.

French Quarter funkiness:
the **Olivier House Hotel** (*p105*) is an unpretentious hotel with romantic nooks and crannies and a patchwork of styles and spaces.

Mardi Gras:
the **Hotel Intercontinental** (*p108*) is a quick walk to the madness of the French Quarter and even has it own viewing stand.

Jazz Fest:
The grand **Nicholas M Benachi House Bed & Breakfast** (*p113*) is an easy stroll to the Fair Grounds.

an affair:
Al Copeland's **Grand Boutique Hotel** (*p109*) is ideal for an assignation and with room service from the Straya Restaurant, you'll never have to leave the room.

The relaxed **Hotel Ste Hélène**: handy for the Quarter and all it has to offer. See page 105.

Royal Sonesta Hotel

300 Bourbon Street, New Orleans, LA 70140, at Bienville Street (586 0300/1-800 766 3782/fax 586 0335/in UK 0800 898410). Bus 3 Vieux Carré, 41 Canal. **Rates** single $145-$280; double $185-$320; suite $550-$1,200. **Credit** AmEx, DC, Disc, MC, V. **Map 7 B2**
The Royal Sonesta is a little village within the village of the Quarter. Covering almost an entire block, bounded by Royal, Conti, Bourbon and Bienville Streets, the majority of the 500 rooms look out on the multi-level courtyard hidden at the centre of the complex. Within the sprawling hotel are bars, restaurants, shops, meeting rooms and the lively ebb and flow of a crossroads hotel. The Royal Sonesta has an excellent business centre (for the travellers who needs more than a place to plug in their laptop) and all rooms have enhanced communications outlets. The staff are friendly and easygoing. Staying here one has a sense of being at the heart of the Quarter without the overwhelming noise, clutter and confusion that is the reality of a big night on Bourbon Street. **Hotel services** *Babysitting. Bars. Business centre. Concierge. Conference facilities. Continental breakfast, evening coffee & tea. Fax. Fitness centre. Interpreting services. Laundry. No-smoking rooms. Parking. Restaurants. Rooms for disabled. Swimming pool.* **Room services** *Hairdryer. Dataport. Minibar. Radio. Room service (7am-2am). Safe. Voicemail.*

Soniat House

1133 Chartres Street, New Orleans, LA 70116, at Ursulines Street (522 0570/1-800 544 8808/fax 522 7208). Bus 3 Vieux Carré, 48 Esplanade, 55 Elysian Fields, 81 Almonaster, 82 Desire. **Rates** room $160-$250; suite $275-$495; two-bedroom suite $625. **Credit** AmEx, MC, V. **Map 7 C2**
Since opening in 1983, this elegant little inn has been on a million 'best' lists but the praise for the beautiful setting usually overlooks the real power of the Soniat House – its effortless, seamless service. Providing world-class service is no easy thing in New Orleans with its pervasive 'Later, darlin" attitude. Comprised of two 1830s Creole townhouses that face each other across Chartres Street, the inn is a creation of Rodney and Frances Smith. Hands-on owners, the Smiths have decorated the 25 rooms and suites with French, English and Louisiana antiques, good artwork, old books and a soothing palette of colours. This is a very beautiful hotel. Each compound is entered through a flagstone carriageway that opens on to a lush, green courtyard. Although there's no restaurant or bar, a home-made breakfast is served in guests' rooms or the courtyard (for an extra fee) and the well-stocked honour bars take care of the cocktail hour.
Website: www.soniathouse.com
Hotel services *Breakfast. Concierge. Fax. Laundry. No-smoking rooms. Safety deposit boxes. Valet parking.* **Room services** *Hairdryer. Dataport. Radio.*

$100-$150

Andrew Jackson Hotel

919 Royal Street, New Orleans, LA 70116, at St Philip Street (561 5881/1-800 654 0224/fax 596 6769). Bus 3 Vieux Carré, 55 Elysian Fields, 81 Almonaster, 82 Desire. **Rates** $109-$169. **Credit** AmEx, DC, Disc, MC, V. **Map 7 C2**
Although there's no connection between the historical Andrew Jackson and this hotel, it's probably a place he would have liked. Jackson preferred a simple approach to life but didn't live a spartan existence. The Andrew Jackson Hotel is attractive and well maintained, with a minimum of fussiness. The lovely T-shaped courtyard and its fountain are the hotel's main contribution to guest luxury. The 22 rooms are decorated in unremarkable hotel style with modern bathrooms. **Hotel services** *Continental breakfast. Fax. Safe. Valet parking.* **Room services** *Cable TV. Radio.*

Bienville House

320 Decatur Street, New Orleans, LA 70130, at Bienville Street (529 2345/1-800 535 7836/fax 525 6079). Bus 3 Vieux Carré, 41 Canal, 55 Elysian Fields, 81 Almonaster, 82 Desire. **Rates** room $120-$270; suite $375-$650. **Credit** AmEx, DC, Disc, MC, V. **Map 7 B3**

Bienville House offers that rarest of New Orleans amenities: a view. In flat, below-sea level New Orleans, a bird's-eye view of anything is unusual. The hotel, only a block from the Mississippi River, has several river-facing rooms with lovely views of the crescent that makes the Crescent City. A former warehouse, the hotel underwent a complete renovation in 1997 and feels like a new place. If you don't get a room with a view, there's always the rooftop sundecks, another rarity in local hotels. Rooms are stocked with more details than usual (coffeemakers, ironing boards) and decorated in soft colours.
Hotel services *Business meeting rooms. Continental breakfast. Fax. Laundry. No-smoking floors. Rooms for disabled. Safe. Sundecks. Swimming pool. Valet parking.* **Room services** *Cable TV. Hairdryer. Iron & ironing board. Modem. Radio.*

Hotel Provincial

1924 Chartres Street, New Orleans, LA 70116, at Ursulines Street (581 4995/1-800 535 7922/fax 581 1018). Bus 3 Vieux Carré, 48 Esplanade, 55 Elysian Fields, 81 Almonaster, 82 Desire. **Rates** *single or double $150-$175; small suite $215; suite from $275.* **Credit** AmEx, DC, Disc, MC, V.
Map 7 C2
Business travellers like the Provincial because they can stay in the Quarter *and* have the necessities of the trade: on-site parking, sophisticated in-room communications and meeting rooms. Non-biz travellers who want something a bit more upscale than the smaller hotels, but don't want to pay top-dollar for the very plush places, find the family-owned Provincial just right. Two storeys of rooms encircle the inner courtyards, which are made up of pleasant sitting areas with a pool. The hotel's 105 rooms are spacious and decorated in a neo Victorian style that mixes antiques and handsome reproductions. The hotel restaurant is NuNu's, which offers traditional New Orleans cuisine.
Hotel services *Babysitting. Bar. Concierge. Conference rooms. Fax. Laundry. No-smoking rooms. Parking. Restaurant. Rooms for disabled. Safe. Swimming pool.* **Room services** *Cable TV. Hairdryer. Modem. Radio. Voicemail.*

Hotel Ste Hélène

508 Chartres Street, New Orleans, LA 70116, at St Louis Street (522 5014/1-800 348 3388/fax 523 7140). Bus 3 Vieux Carré, 55 Elysian Fields, 81 Almonaster, 82 Desire. **Rates** *single $130; double $150; suite $175-$225.* **Credit** AmEx, V. **Map 7 B2**
The Ste Hélène is a cosy little hotel next door to the Napoleon House. It's convenient for the activities of the Quarter and has a relaxed atmosphere. There are 26 rooms on three floors, many overlooking the interior courtyard, where free champagne is served every evening. Rooms are pleasantly decorated but some are on the dark side (which can be a bonus after too many cocktails). The suites are enormous and well worth laying down some cash for a special occasion.
Hotel services *Continental breakfast. Fax. No-smoking rooms. Safe.* **Room services** *Cable TV. Hairdryer. Radio. Refrigerator.*

Hotel St Marie

827 Toulouse Street, New Orleans, LA 70112, at Bourbon Street (561 8951/1-800 366 2743/fax 571 2802/hotels@frenchquarter.com). Bus 3 Vieux Carré. **Rates** *single $115; double $135; suite $195.* **Credit** AmEx, DC, Disc, JBC, MC, V.
Map 7 B2
A smallish hotel with all the French Quarter requisites: tropical courtyard, pool, balconies. The St Marie is owned by the same group that operates the much larger **Prince Conti Hotel** nearby (*see below*). It's the same idea on a reduced scale, offering few frills but reliable rooms, a good front desk staff and a better-than-average hotel restaurant,

the Northern Italian-oriented Grana. Rooms facing the courtyard are sunnier and quieter than those overlooking Toulouse Street.
Website: www.frenchquarter.com
Hotel services *Bar. Conference rooms. Continental breakfast. Fax. Laundry. Restaurant. Rooms for disabled. Room service (11am-6pm). Safe. Swimming pool. Valet parking ($12 a night).* **Room services** *Radio.*

Hotel St Pierre

911 Burgundy Street, New Orleans, LA 70116, at Dumaine Street (524 4401/1-800 225 4040/fax 524 6800). Bus 3 Vieux Carré, 57 Franklin. **Rates** *single $109; double $129; suite $139.* **Credit** AmEx, DC, Disc, MC, V. **Map 7 C1**
Tucked away at the back of the Quarter, the St Pierre is a jumble of buildings that anywhere else would be a mess. But in New Orleans the elements coalesce into a pleasing compound that feels like a swinger's hideaway. Room sizes and furnishings vary, with a few antiques mixed with 1950s tile bathrooms, exposed brick and french doors. There's a bordering-on-boho quality about the place and every room is named after a musician – Duke Ellington, Ella Fitzgerald et al – the staff insist they all stayed here or played here when this building was a jazz club. Or was it an after-hours joint? The stories don't jibe, but so what.
Hotel services *Continental breakfast. Fax. Parking. Safe. Swimming pool.* **Room services** *Cable TV. Radio.*

Olivier House Hotel

828 Toulouse Street, New Orleans, LA 70112, at Bourbon Street (525 8456/fax 529 2006). Bus 3 Vieux Carré, 41 Canal. **Rates** *single $105; double $145; suite $160-$250; cottage $350.* **Credit** AmEx, DC, MC, V.
Map 7 B2
The kind of place that most people imagine when they try to picture a 'typical' French Quarter hotel. Housed in an 1836 Creole townhouse, the hotel is the hands-on operation of the amiable Danner family. They are innkeepers in the old sense, managing to keep everything running smoothly with no need to tell you how 'unique' their hotel is nor how special they are for running such a 'quaint' place. The rambling hotel reflects their attentive care. Rooms are furnished with antiques and second-hand store finds. The garden room, a renovated stable, is full of sunlight (rare in New Orleans) and the cottage is an adorable Victorian dollshouse with its own tiny courtyard. The French Quarter is at its authentic, unself-conscious best.
Hotel services *Fax. Laundry. No-smoking rooms. Parking. Swimming pool. Pets allowed. Safe.* **Room services** *Radio. Refrigerator (some rooms).*

Prince Conti Hotel

830 Conti Street, New Orleans, LA 70112, at Bourbon Street (529 4172/1-800 366 2743/hotels@frenchquarter.com). Bus 3 Vieux Carré, 41 Canal. **Rates** *single $120; double $140; suite $195.* **Credit** AmEx, Disc, MC, V.
Map 7 B2
A New Orleans standby, the Prince Conti has been the favoured hotel of visiting Southerners for decades. There's an austere quality about the place, whose 58 rooms seem hidden behind a monotonous façade. The carpeted hallways encourage quiet conversation and the antique-laden rooms seem to call for bedtime sips of absinthe. The service is personal in an old-fashioned way; no one has been through a corporate training session to learn to say 'Good morning' or 'Let me take that bag for you'. The hotel attracts an older clientele, making it a good choice for the traveller looking for a quiet, restful hotel in the Quarter.
Website: www.frenchquarter.com
Hotel services *Business meeting rooms. Continental breakfast. Fax. Laundry. Parking. Restaurant. Rooms for disabled. Safe.* **Room services** *Radio. Modem. Daily newspaper.*

$50-$100

Bon Maison Guesthouse

*835 Bourbon Street, New Orleans, LA 70116, between
St Ann & Dumaine Streets (phone/fax 561 8498/bmgh@
acadiacom.net). Bus 3 Vieux Carré.* **Rates** $75-$145.
Credit MC, V. **Map 7 C2**
To book a room in this 1833 townhouse is to become a French
Quarter resident for a few days or weeks. The guesthouse
managers are friendly but leave the guests alone, providing
housekeeping needs and a key to the barely marked front
gate. Bon Maison is a typical private Quarter compound,
with entry through a gated narrow alley that opens into a
leafy brick courtyard. There are five rooms for rent, all with
private baths, three with full kitchens. Nicely decorated and
furnished with queen-sized beds, the rooms open on to balconies that overlook the courtyard. Bon Maison is gay-
oriented, but straight guests are welcome and will feel at home.
Website: www.bonmaison.com
Hotel services *Fax. Safe.* **Room services** *Cable TV.
Coffeemaker. Microwave.*

Hotel Villa Convento

*616 Ursulines Street, New Orleans, LA 70116, at
Chartres Street (522 1793/fax 524 1902/convento@
aol.com). Bus 3 Vieux Carré, 48 Esplanade, 55 Elysian
Fields, 81 Almonaster, 82 Desire.* **Rates** $89-$155.
Credit AmEx, Disc, MC, V. **Map 7 C2**
Please disregard any mention by carriage drivers that this
is the 'original House of the Rising Sun'. It's an oft-repeated
myth that ranks with 'the pirate Jean Lafitte slept/schemed/
swashbuckled here', said of every eighteenth-century structure in New Orleans. What *is* here is a relaxed, family-run
hotel that provides clean, unfussy rooms in a pleasant atmosphere. Some member of the cheerful Campo family is almost
always at the front desk, ready to help with questions and problems. The hotel is a bit dull aesthetically, but has the feel of an
old-fashioned boarding house with hallways and stairs leading off in several directions. Try to book one of the rooms on
the upper floors that have views of the Quarter and balconies.
Hotel services *Continental breakfast. Fax. Free local
phone calls. Safe.* **Room services** *Cable TV.*

Le Richelieu Hotel

*1234 Chartres Street, New Orleans, LA 70116, at
Barracks Street (529 2492/1-800 535 9653/fax 524
8179). Bus 3 Vieux Carré, 48 Esplanade, 55 Elysian
Fields, 81 Almonaster, 82 Desire.* **Rates** room $85-$150;
one-bedroom suite from $170; two-bedroom suite from
$280; VIP suite $475. **Credit** AmEx, DC, Disc, MC, V.
Map 7 D2
Le Richelieu is on the Esplanade side of the French Quarter,
housed in buildings that date from the eighteenth century –
although it's only been a hotel since 1969. Its main claim to
fame is that Paul McCartney lived here with his family for
two months in 1977 while recording at Sea-Saint Studios.
Other celebs have checked in, too, doubtless impressed with
the hotel's discretion. Beyond keeping a secret, the Richelieu
is attractive for its attention to service, handsome rooms and
a great rarity in the Quarter: a free parking lot.
Hotel services *Babysitting. Bar. Concierge. Free local
phone calls. Interpreting service. Laundry. Parking (free).
Restaurants. Room service (7am-11pm). Swimming pool.*
Room services *Hairdryer. Refrigerator.*

Rue Royal Inn

*1006 Royal Street, New Orleans, LA 70116, at St Philip
Street (558 0566/1-800 776 3901/fax 524 3900).
Bus 3 Vieux Carré, 55 Elysian Fields, 81 Almonaster, 82
Desire.* **Rates** room $75-$120; suite $145. **Credit** AmEx,
DC, JBC, MC, V. **Map 7 C2**
Resident Persian cats rule this small, friendly hotel. They
allow themselves to be petted and fussed over, but acknowl-
edge admirers with the barest tilt of the head. The cats are

The atmospheric **Columns Hotel** *(page 111).*

the only sniffy element of the Rue Royal, which prides itself
on a helpful, accessible staff. Most of the 17 rooms open on
to the central courtyard. All feature exposed brick walls, high
ceilings and nineteenth-century decorative touches and some
have balconies overlooking Royal Street, a big plus during
Carnival. A better-than-usual continental breakfast is another
positive feature.
Hotel services *Continental breakfast. Fax. Laundry.
No-smoking rooms. Parking. Rooms for disabled. Safe.*
Room services *Hairdryer. Radio. Refrigerator. VCRs.*

St Peter House

*1005 St Peter Street, New Orleans, LA 70116, at
Burgundy Street (524 9232/1-800 535 7815/fax 523
5198). Bus 3 Vieux Carré, 57 Franklin.* **Rates** single
$59; double $100; suite $150. **Credit** AmEx, Disc, MC, V.
Map 7 B1
Located in the more residential back-of-the-Quarter area, this
is the sort of place that is becoming increasingly rare in the
Quarter as upmarket hotels and inns threaten to take over.
While it offers more than a hostel or youth guesthouse, the
St Peter is definitely on the basics-only side of the hotel
ledger. There are some Victorian furnishings but the flowers are all plastic, it's that kind of mix. The inn's best feature
is the broad, shaded, second-storey balcony that accommo-
dates chairs, tables and many conversations. Be aware,
though, that it also overlooks a loud, late-hours bar and a
room facing Burgundy can mean a noisy night.
Hotel services *Continental breakfast. Fax. Safe.*

Ursuline Guest House

*708 Ursulines Street, New Orleans, LA 70116, at Royal
Street (525 8509/1-800 654 2351/fax 525 8408).
Bus 3 Vieux Carré, 48 Esplanade, 55 Elysian Fields, 81
Almonaster, 82 Desire.* **Rates** $85-$125. **Credit** AmEx,
MC, V. **Map 7 C2**

There are only 13 rooms in the Ursuline Guest House, a small hotel on a quiet stretch of Ursulines Street. Most open on to the back courtyard where the Jacuzzi purrs softly behind greenery. The rooms are dark and quiet, good places to recover from too many drinks and too much dancing. Modern bathrooms and the occasional antique are nicely mixed for a feeling of the Old French Quarter without a case of the cutes. No children are allowed – which is another bonus if you plan on too much partying. The Ursuline has a large gay clientele, but straight couples will enjoy its easygoing atmosphere, too.
Hotel services *Continental breakfast. Evening drinks. Fax. No-smoking rooms. Parking (limited). Jacuzzi. Safe.* **Room services** *Cable TV. Radio.*

Faubourg Marigny & Bywater
$50-$100

Lamothe House
621 Esplanade Avenue, New Orleans, LA 70116, at Royal Street (947 1161/1-800 367 5858/fax 943 6536). Bus 3 Vieux Carré, 48 Esplanade. **Rates** $90-$195. **Credit** AmEx, Disc, MC, V. **Map 7 D2**
On the lower end of Esplanade, directly across from the French Quarter, the Lamothe House is an 1840s townhouse that also counts several small houses as part of its offerings. The inn is a mixture of faded elegance and practical considerations, such as arrangements of plastic flowers in the stately entrance hall. Some suites are furnished with rare Louisiana antiques. Rooms at the back of the house open on to the long courtyard. The **Marigny Guesthouse**, situated behind the Lamothe compound on Kelerec Street, has six rooms and three suites, all slightly larger than in the Lamothe House. Prices are the same, and all bookings and arrangements are made through the Lamothe office.
Website: www.travelbase.com/destinations/new-orleans/ lamothe
Hotel services *Continental breakfast. Fax. Kitchen. Parking. Safe.* **Room services** *Alarm clock. Hairdryer.*

Sun Oak Bed & Breakfast
2020 Burgundy Street, New Orleans, LA 70116, between Frenchmen and Touro Streets (phone/fax 945 0322). Bus 55 Elysian Fields, 82 Desire. **Rates** $75-$125. **No credit cards. Map 4 G6**
Architecture professor Eugene Cizek and art teacher Lloyd Sensat are devoted to historic preservation through art. They teach classes, organise seminars, travel and do a multitude of other good works. In private life, they have restored and revived an early-nineteenth-century Creole cottage in the Marigny. There are only two guestrooms (both with bath) in a compound that includes a wonderfully big garden. Cizek and Sensat have used antiques to great effect. Staying here is like checking into the Gallier House or the Beauregard-Keyes House: you are staying in a house museum with the benefit of hosts who are two of the best-known preservationists in Louisiana.
Hotel services *Continental breakfast. Kitchen. No-smoking rooms. Parking.* **Room services** *Radio.*

Under $50

Mazant Guesthouse
906 Mazant Street, New Orleans, LA 70117, at Burgundy Street (944 2662). Bus 82 Desire, 89 St Claude. **Rates** $29-$39. **No credit cards.**
Bywater is an old working-class neighbourhood near the docks. Sprinkled through the single- and double-shotguns are big, spreading houses such as the 1883 Mazant Guesthouse, once home to the prosperous bourgeoisie. Popular with young Europeans and travellers of all ages

with a bohemian inclination, the Mazant offers the basics (bed, bath, shelter from the elements) with an unaffected congeniality. There are 11 rooms, six that use the hall bathrooms. Furniture includes some period pieces and sturdy 1950s survivors. Only the bedrooms are air-conditioned; the rest of the house is cooled by big windows and ceiling fans. Nearby attractions include funky music bars such as **Vaughan's Lounge** (*see p210* **Nightlife**).
Hotel services *Continental breakfast. Kitchen. Laundry. No-smoking rooms. Parking.*

CBD & Warehouse District
Above $200

Hotel Intercontinental
444 St Charles Avenue, New Orleans, LA 70130, at Poydras Street (525 5566/1-800 327 0200/fax 523 7310). St Charles Streetcar. **Rates** single $210-$270; double $230-$290; one-bedroom suite $1,500; two-bedroom suite $2,000. **Credit** AmEx, DC, Disc, MC, V. **Map 6 C1**
The Intercontinental is huge and shiny, with all the expected services and specialities of a hotel catering to the corporate and deep-pocketed tourist trade – it even has six 'environmental rooms', equipped with special water- and air-filtration systems. But at Carnival time the hotel goes to the head of the class. It has a very special geographical connection to Mardi Gras since it's not only a prime spot on the downtown parade route, but on Mardi Gras Day is home to the Queen of Carnival, the debutante chosen to be consort to Rex, King of Carnival. The Rex parade halts at the viewing stands erected at the hotel's side on St Charles Avenue for the king to toast the queen and her ladies-in-waiting, all sitting attentively in the royal box. The viewing stands are a great spot to watch parades. You actually get to take in many of the visual thrills lost to the crowds on the ground, and, perhaps most important, you have complete, unrestricted access to many, many bathrooms in the hotel. There's also an all-day buffet in a dining room, which eliminates trying to fight your way into a crowded café. The downside is that tickets are sold for the viewing stand (around $40) and buffet ($40) – they are not free with your very expensive room. Yet in the madness of Mardi Gras, this is perhaps the most civilised way to participate, having the freedom to hit the streets or watch from the stands, party 24 hours or rest up in high hotel style in the midst of it all.
Hotel services *Babysitting. Bar. Business centre. Concierge. Conference facilities. Fax. Fitness centre. Hair salon. Interpreting services. Laundry. No-smoking floors. Parking. Restaurants. Rooms for disabled. Room service (24-hour). Swimming pool.* **Room services** *Hairdryer. Minibar. Modem. Radio. Safe. VCR.*

$150-$200

Queen & Crescent Hotel
344 Camp Street, New Orleans, LA 70130, at Natchez Street (587 9700/1-800 975 6652/fax 587 9701/ qandc@neworleans.com). St Charles Streetcar/ bus 11 Magazine, 41 Canal. **Rates** single $99; double $179. **Credit** AmEx, DC, Disc, MC, V. **Map 6 C1**
Despite its rococo name, the Queen & Crescent is a new hotel, opened in early 1998. It's a good choice for the business traveller who has more to do than work. The hotel is well placed in the CBD and the rooms are equipped with more than the usual business amenities, all having two phone lines and dataports. Faxes are available on request and there's easy help with your wardrobe (full-size ironing boards and irons, shoe shine if you ask). The hotel is also well situated for Carnival,

*Take a break in one of the **McKendrick-Breaux**'s well-appointed rooms (page 112).*

with Canal Street parades and the French Quarter two blocks away. The handsome building dates from 1913, when it was the headquarters of the Queen & Crescent Railroad. The rooms are attractive and comfortable, decorated with chintz and antique replicas. Rooms facing Camp Street tend to be smaller (but cost the same).
Website: www. queenandcrescent.com
Hotel services *Bar. Conference facilities. Continental breakfast. Fax. Fitness centre. Laundry. No-smoking rooms.* **Room services** *Cable TV. Coffeemaker. Dataport. Hairdryer. Iron & full-size ironing board. Minibar. Radio. Safe. Two phone lines.*

$100-$150

Le Pavilion Hotel

833 Poydras Street, New Orleans, LA 70140, at Baronne Street (581 3111/1-800 535 9095/fax 522 5543).
St Charles Streetcar/bus 3 Vieux Carré. **Rates** single $115-$250; double $115-$275; suite from $695.
Credit AmEx, DC, Disc, JBC, MC, V. **Map 6 B1**
Built in 1907, Le Pavilion has never been anything but a grand hotel. The lobby, with chandeliers the size of small ponies, masses of gilt and marble and gardens of fresh flowers, is grand but not intimidating. The staff, while professional, dispense with the haute hotel archness. The affable attitude is perhaps summed up in the nightly lobby buffet of peanut butter and jelly sandwiches set out on silver platters with elegant coolers of fresh milk. Le Pavilion is smiling at itself, but with great style. The hotel's excellent dining room, the Crystal Room, is often overlooked and the rooftop swimming pool is a beauty. The single rooms can be on the small side, but there are antiques and eighteenth- and nineteenth-century artworks in almost all rooms.
Hotel services *Bar. Concierge. Conference facilities. Fax. Interpreting services. Laundry. No-smoking rooms. Parking. Restaurants. Rooms for disabled. Room service (24-hour). Swimming pool.* **Room services** *Cable TV. Hairdryer. Modem. Radio. Safe.*

Under $50

YMCA Lee Circle

920 St Charles Avenue, New Orleans, LA 70130, at Lee Circle (561 9622/fax 523 7174). St Charles Streetcar. **Rates** single $29; double $35; triple $41; quad $46.
Credit MC, V. **Map 6 B2**
The location is excellent, with the streetcar's happy bells telling you you're in the heart of New Orleans, and the rates are unbeatable. In addition, the perks of the YMCA are great, even for the non-fitness freak. But all this must be balanced against the actual hotel facilities: 40 rooms, spread out over two floors, all uniformly dingy, dark and tired. The rooms vary from doubles (two single beds) to 'quads', a bunk bed and a double bed and all have window-unit air-conditioning. The bath/shower rooms on the hall are adequate, but the shower/changing rooms at the fitness centre are sparkling. The place is booked far in advance for Mardi Gras and Jazz Fest.
Hotel services *Café. Fax. Full use of fitness centre.*
Room services *TV.*

Uptown & Garden District

Above $200

Grand Boutique Hotel

2001 St Charles Avenue, New Orleans, LA 70130, at St Andrew Street (558 9966/1-800 976 1755/fax 571 6464). St Charles Streetcar. **Rates** suites $199-$259.
Credit AmEx, DC, Disc, MC, V. **Map 6 B3**
Restaurateur Al Copeland has brought his flamboyant touch to hotels with this new (1997) 44-room inn above his flashy Straya restaurant. The large, comfortable suites come with a range of amenities, including microwave and two phones, tied up in an art-deco-goes-1990s look. The Jacuzzis, in the most expensive, are actually in the room, not the bathroom. Somehow not surprising at Al Copeland's where everything is big, bright and cheerfully over the top.

Welcome to New York.
Now get out.

The obsessive guide to impulsive entertainment

On sale at newsstands in New York
Pick up a copy!

To get a copy of the current issue or to subscribe, call Time Out New York 212 539 4444

Hotel services *Bar. Continental breakfast. Guest membership Mackie Shilstone Pro Spa. No-smoking floor. Parking ($10 a night). Restaurant. Room service (11am-11pm). Rooms for disabled.* **Room services** *Cable TV. Clock radio. Dataport. Hairdryer. Microwave. Refrigerator. Safe.*

$150-$200

Pontchartrain Hotel

████ █ ██████ ██████, New Orleans, LA 70130, at Josephine Street (524 0581/1-800 777 6163/fax 529 1165). *St Charles Streetcar.* **Rates** queen bed $145; two queen beds or one king bed $180; deluxe king bed $200; suite $225-$275. **Credit** AmEx, DC, Disc, MC, V.
Map 6 B3
The Pontchartrain sits on St Charles Avenue like one of the street's more discreet mansions. Confident and poised, it has no reason to call attention to itself, knowing that people who matter know that the Pontchartrain is the right place to stay in New Orleans. The hotel has a tiny lobby but most of the socialising takes place in the dim Bayou Bar or in the venerable Caribbean Room restaurant. The legendary suites are perfect for entertaining rock stars or debutante teas, but the other rooms are quite nice, too, with high ceilings, deep carpets, antiques and big windows.
Hotel services *Babysitting. Bar. Concierge. Continental breakfast. Fax. Free shuttle to French Quarter & Convention Center. Laundry. Meeting rooms. No-smoking rooms. Parking. Restaurant. Room service (24-hour). Safe.* **Room services** *Hairdryer. Modem. Radio.*

$100-$150

Prytania Park Hotel

1525 Prytania Street, New Orleans, LA 70130, at Terpsichore Street (524 0427/1-800 862 1984/fax 522 2977). St Charles Streetcar. **Rates** single $99; double $109; room with loft & suite $109, $119. **Credit** AmEx, DC, Disc, JCB, MC, V. **Map 6 B2**
The Prytania Park is a complex of old and new buildings hidden from the street. Although it's not an authentic replication of an Old New Orleans household or compound, the Prytania Park *feels* very Old New Orleans, with its open galleries, jumble of stairways, small courtyards and atmosphere of privacy. The rooms are nicely furnished, which comes as no surprise when one learns that the hotel is owned by the Halperin family, who also own an old-line New Orleans furniture store across the street (and site of a very good café). Exposed brick, high ceilings, fans and warm wood tones give the rooms a nineteenth-century feel, but all are equipped with new amenities such as 27-inch TVs and fridges, and, in some, microwaves. The hotel shuttle bus (shared with other Uptown hotels) is a big plus.
Website: www.gardendistrict.com
Hotel services *All rooms no smoking. Continental breakfast. Fax. Free shuttle to French Quarter & Convention Center. Parking. Safe.* **Room services** *Hairdryer. Radio. Refrigerator.*

$50-$100

Avenue Plaza Hotel

2111 St Charles Avenue, New Orleans, LA 70130, at Jackson Street (566 1212/1-800 535 9575/fax 525 6899). St Charles Streetcar. **Rates** $89-$249. **Credit** AmEx, DC, Disc, MC, V. **Map 6 B3**
A favourite with business people for its subdued Garden District setting, parking, rooms with kitchens and other extras. Most prominent is the full use of Mackie Shilstone's Pro Spa, located in the hotel (*see p220* **Sport & Fitness**). The hotel is an all-suite operation, with 256 rooms. All have

a full (if small) kitchen. The 'junior suites' are one big room with a kitchen alcove and bathroom, while the 'one-bedroom suites' have two rooms: a bedroom and a sitting-dining room.
Hotel services *Babysitting. Bar. Beauty salon. Business services. Café. Concierge. Fax. Conference facilities. Fitness centre. Kitchenette. Laundry. No-smoking floors. Parking. Safety deposit boxes. Swimming pool.* **Room services** *Coffeemaker. Hairdryer. Kitchen. Microwave. Radio. Voicemail.*

The Columns Hotel

3811 St Charles Avenue, New Orleans, LA 70115, at General Taylor Avenue (899 9308/fax 899 8170). St Charles Streetcar. **Rates** $90-$200. **Credit** AmEx, MC, V.
Map 4 D9
Romantic and atmospheric, the Columns Hotel strikes most first-time visitors as eerily familiar. That's because they've probably seen it many times – on film. Every movie made in New Orleans seems to have at least one scene set on the hotel's spacious veranda overlooking St Charles Avenue. The Brooke Shields/Susan Sarandon film *Pretty Baby* was made here – the 1883 Italianate mansion was cast as their bordello home. Visitors return to the Columns year after year for its nineteenth-century elegance of stained glass, sweeping staircases and mahogany woodwork. Guests are housed in a variety of rooms in the upper floors with wonderful furnishings including huge nineteenth-century beds and clawfoot bathtubs. Six rooms have shared bathrooms. The front desk can be a bit rigid in dealing with problems, but the repeat customers give the hotel a hearty thumbs-up. There are no TVs in the rooms.
Hotel services *Bar. Continental breakfast. No-smoking rooms.*

Chainful choices

Chain hotels, as we all know, are sterile, cookie-cutter boxes of sameness, only for the timid, unimaginative and unevolved. Well, yes, until you discover everything with local colour is booked and you desperately need a place to stay that has a working bathroom, central heating, air-conditioning and a reliable phone. New Orleans counts almost every major chain in residence. Listed here are some of the possibilities.

Holiday Inn, Middle America's favourite, has seven hotels in the metro area, including two in the French Quarter: the **Chateau LeMoyne** (301 Dauphine Street; 581 1303) and at **124 Royal Street** (529 7211). For Holiday Inn reservations, call 1-800 465 4329.
La Quinta Inns is another mid-range motel chain. There are seven in the Greater New Orleans area, mostly in outlying communities, but an all-suites La Quinta is scheduled to open in the Warehouse District at the end of 1998. For reservations, call 1-800 678 6667.
Hilton has a hotel at the airport and also at the foot of Poydras Street in the CBD. Call 1-800 445 8667 for details.
There's a **Marriott** in Metairie (832 0888) and also in the CBD (522 1300).
Or try the **Sheraton** New Orleans, 500 Canal Street (525 2500).

Hampton Inn – Garden District

3626 St Charles Avenue, New Orleans, LA 70115, at Foucher Street (899 9990/1-800 426 7866/fax 899 9908). St Charles Streetcar. **Rates** $89-$129.
Credit AmEx, DC, Disc, MC, V. **Map 4 D9**
Opened in 1997, the blush-coloured Hampton Inn blends in so well with old St Charles that most people don't realise it wasn't always here. It's handy for the streetcar, but also offers free parking. A narrow lap pool is wedged into a small but appealing courtyard. The rooms still have that brand-new aura.
Hotel services *Continental breakfast. Free local phone calls & incoming faxes. Parking. Swimming pool.*
Room services *Hairdryer. Radio.*

Lefevre-Martin House Bed & Breakfast

6022 Pitt Street, New Orleans, LA 70118, at State Street (899 3111/1-800 729 4643/fax 899 6467). St Charles Streetcar. **Rates** $55-$75. **No credit cards. Map 4 B9**
Staying at Barbara Lefevre-Martin's Uptown home is like visiting Auntie Mame. Warm and welcoming to her guests, she fits them into her schedule around harp playing (she often performs for guests) and a passionate involvement in Welsh culture (sounds bizarre, but it's true). Four bedrooms are available to guests, all with shared baths. Situated in an affluent neighbourhood near Tulane and Loyola universities, the house is popular with parents visiting their student children and Europeans who want a more personal introduction to New Orleans. There are no phones or TVs in the rooms, but there is a TV in the communal sitting room.
Hotel services *All rooms no-smoking. Breakfast. Fax. Kitchen. Laundry. Parking.* **Room services** *Radio.*

McKendrick-Breaux House Bed & Breakfast

1474 Magazine Street, New Orleans, LA 70130, at Race Street (586 1700/fax 522 7138). Bus 11 Magazine. **Rates** $85-$125. **Credit** MC, V. **Map 6 B3**
Eddie and Lisa Breaux are ardent house restorers and their expertise and passion shows in this 1860s Greek Revival townhouse, which is preservationist in spirit and modern in practicalities. The McKendrick-Breaux House is the rare B&B that makes sense for a business traveller. The inn provides in-room voicemail for guests, fax access and off-street parking. Located on a reviving area of Magazine Street, the inn has well-designed rooms (all with private baths) in two adjoining houses, linked by a pretty garden. The Breauxs are excellent hosts who intuitively know the difference between helping guests and imposing on them.
Hotel services *Continental breakfast. Fax. Kitchen. Laundry. No-smoking rooms. Parking. Safe.*
Room services *Cable TV. Hairdryer. Radio. Voicemail.*

St Charles Inn

3636 St Charles Avenue, New Orleans, LA 70115, at Foucher Street (899 8888/1-800 489 9908/fax 899 9908). St Charles Streetcar. **Rates** single $55-$70; double $65-$90. **Credit** AmEx, MC, V. **Map 4 D9**
A big 1950s-style box on St Charles Avenue, the St Charles Inn is a good buy for the traveller who values bargains more than aesthetics. The hotel is clean and well run, while the hallways and boxy rooms call up memories of early Holiday Inns. Two restaurants are on the ground floor and more eateries are within a block. Another convenience is the streetcar, which practically stops at the front door.
Hotel services *Café. Continental breakfast. Fax. Laundry. Parking. Rooms for disabled. Safe.*
Room services *Radio.*

St Vincent's Guesthouse

1507 Magazine Street, New Orleans, LA 70130, at Race Street (566 1515/fax 566 1518/peterschreiber@ compuserv.com). Bus 11 Magazine. **Rates** single $39; double $69. **Credit** AmEx, DC, Disc, JBC, MC, V.
Map 6 B3

St Vincent's, an 1861 red brick pile, has been transformed from Victorian orphan asylum to contemporary guesthouse, an unusually happy adaptation of an old and apparently useless building. Peter and Sally Schrieber, who operate three other modest inns, have turned the hulking three-storey complex into a hip hotel, installing a tearoom, pool and upbeat white furnishings. The redecoration and restoration is modest, but has created a comfortable, affordable inn, popular with younger travellers and Europeans. St Vincent's is notable for being a historical site that is fully accessible for the disabled, with elevators, new wide-door bathrooms and exterior ramps. The neighbourhood is on the rise – the **McKendrick-Breaux B&B** (*see above*) and **Rue de la Course** (*see p143* **Cafés & Coffeehouses**) are across Magazine Street – but it still merits caution.
Hotel services *All rooms for disabled. Continental breakfast. Fax. No smoking rooms. Parking. Safe. Swimming pool.*

Whitney Inn

1509 St Charles Avenue, New Orleans, LA 70130, at Melpomene Street (521 8000/fax 521 8016/whitney. inn@worldnet.att.net). St Charles Streetcar. **Rates** single $75; double $90; suite $90-$200; penthouse suite $250. **Credit** AmEx, MC, V.
Map 6 B2
Two late nineteenth-century townhouses have been connected to form the Whitney Inn, a back-to-basics small hotel. It's on a semi-commercial stretch of St Charles Avenue and fits in with the utilitarian neighbourhood. Rooms have been retrofitted for usefulness and easy maintenance. What they lack in charm, they make up in modest prices and accessibility.
Hotel services *All rooms no-smoking. Continental breakfast. Deck. Fax. Parking. Rooms for disabled.*
Room services *Cable TV. Kitchenettes (some rooms). Radio.*

Under $50

Longpre Guest House

1726 Prytania Street, New Orleans, LA 70130, at Euterpe Street (581 4540/fax 521 8016/longprezoo@ webtv.net). St Charles Streetcar. **Rates** dorm $12; room with shared bath $35; room with private bath $40.
No credit cards. Map 6 B2
Does MTV know about this place? It would be perfect for one of the network's ersatz documentaries about twentysomethings. The Longpre House is a meta-hostel, no memberships, curfews or adults. Staffers and residents proudly wear T-shirts advertising the 'Longprezoo'. The 1850s townhouse is dingy and worn, but often fully booked. There are four dorm rooms, each sleeping eight, and five private rooms, all with shared baths. The maximum stay is three weeks.
Website: www.angelfire.com/la/longprezoo
Hotel services *All rooms no-smoking. Hall phones. Kitchen. Lockers. TV room.*

Marquette House

2253 Carondelet Street, New Orleans, LA 70130, at Jackson Street (523 3014/fax 529 5933/HINewOrle@ aol.com). St Charles Streetcar. **Rates** dorm room $13.97-$16.97; apartments $39.95-$45.95. **Credit** MC, V.
Map 6 B3
The hostel of choice for most backpackers and under-30s, this compound includes dormitory buildings and, most interestingly, a separate building of apartments. The dorms are fine, with plenty of locker space, while the apartments offer outstanding value-for-money. Housed in a vaguely plantation-style, two-storey building, they have kitchenettes, ceiling fans, several beds and sitting areas. The décor is garage-sale utilitarian, but at this price who cares? Members of Hostelling International (including the AYH and the YHA)

pay reduced rates. A good portion of the guests are greying baby boomers who just can't pass up the great deal. The atmosphere is dorm-friendly, but mutterings are sometimes heard that the staff are less than warm and empathetic in dealings with guests. No TV.

Hotel services *Lockers.*

St Charles Guesthouse

*1748 Prytania Street, New Orleans, LA 70130, at Polymnia Street (523 6556/fax 522 6340). St Charles Streetcar. **D.** Single room $60, double with shared bath $65-$75; double with private bath $85.*
Credit AmEx, MC, V. **Map 6 B2**

A block away from St Charles Avenue, the St Charles Guesthouse is well worth seeking out. The rates are modest, the rooms comfortable and the atmosphere casual and genuinely friendly. Owner-manager Dennis Hilton is a steady and welcome presence, chatting with guests, taking detailed phone messages and making arrangements for any special needs. Hilton enjoys surprising his guests with spontaneous parties, such as a crab boil on the last night of Jazz Fest. Hilton's philosophy is that his guests are at his hotel to see New Orleans, not to watch TV or keep up with the office back home. Consequently, there are no phones in the rooms and no TV. (He will, however, make arrangements for guests to check their e-mail.) Europeans return year after year to the rambling old inn, often starting out as students using the clean but spartan 'backpacker' rooms with ceiling fans, then moving up as they can afford it to the more expensive rooms with creature comforts such as double beds, old-fashioned tiled bathrooms and air-conditioning.

Website: www.neworleans.com
Hotel services *All rooms no-smoking. Continental breakfast. Kitchen. Swimming pool.*

Old World Inn

*1330 Prytania Street, New Orleans, LA 70130, at Thalia Street (566 1330/fax 566 1074/trips@angelfire.com). St Charles Streetcar/bus 11 Magazine. **Rates** single $39-$85; double $49-$85; triple $69-$95; quadruple $79-$85.*
Credit MC, V. **Map 6 B2**

A charmingly shabby inn in the grey area between the Warehouse District and the Lower Garden District. Run by musician-entertainers Charlie and Jean Matkin, the Old World is a friendly, low-key place. The décor combines old family pieces with yard sale finds, but the big dining room-lounge is inviting and often the scene of music-making. The place is almost completely no-tech: hairdryers can only be plugged into certain outlets so as not to overload the 100-year-old building's resources.

Websites: www.angelfire.comb/biz/OldWorldInn or www.earthlink.net/~oldworldinn
Hotel services *Continental breakfast. No-smoking rooms. Safe.*

Mid City

$100-$150

Nicolas M Benachi House Bed & Breakfast

2257 Bayou Road, New Orleans, LA 70119, at Esplanade Avenue (525 7040/1-800 308 7040/fax 525 9760/cotton@nobabb.com). Bus 48 Esplanade.
Rates $105-$125. **Credit** AmEx, DC, Disc, JBC, MC, V.
Map 5 F5

The Benachi House is a mini-estate within the city limits. The 1858 Greek Revival mansion sits on a landscaped half-acre lot with a carriage house, patio and gazebo. Attorney and owner Jim Derbes has meticulously restored the house and furnished it with period pieces. There are four guestrooms, two with private baths, two with shared baths. Derbes, an authority on preservation law and a well-known activist both in New Orleans and nationally, is an interesting host, always happy to discuss the house. A full breakfast is served in the elegant dining room and the kitchen is well stocked with drinks and munchies for guests. A particularly good bet for Jazz Fest, since the Fair Grounds are a short walk away. There are TVs in most rooms.

Website: www.nolabb.com
Hotel services *All rooms no-smoking. Breakfast. Fax. Kitchen. Laundry. Parking.*

Esplanade Villa Bed & Breakfast

2216 Esplanade Avenue, New Orleans, LA 70119, at Bayou Road (525 7040/1-800 308 7040/fax 525 9760/cotton@nobabb.com). Bus 48 Esplanade.
Rates $125-$135. **Credit** AmEx, DC, Disc, JCB, MC, V.
Map 5 F5

Also restored by Jim Derbes of the Benachi House, the Villa is a newer project, across Esplanade Avenue. The 1880 house offers five suites, each with recreated Victorian bathrooms, complete with clawfoot tubs, antiques and parlours. Guests walk across to the Benachi House for breakfast.

Website: www.nolabb.com
Hotel services *Fax. Free local phone calls. Full breakfast. Kitchen.*
Room services *Cable TV.*

Degas House Bed & Breakfast

2306 Esplanade Avenue, New Orleans, LA 70119, at N Tonti Street (821 5009/1-800 755 6730/fax 821 0870/degas@bellsouth.net). Bus 48 Esplanade.
Rates $125-$200. **Credit** AmEx, MC, V.
Map 5 F5

In 1873, Edgar Degas visited his mother's Creole family in New Orleans for several months and lived here, in the Musson family's 1852 Italianate villa. Now a B&B and semi-shrine to Degas, the house has seven guestrooms on the second and third floors, all with private baths. The bedrooms are furnished with handsome period pieces but in a minimalist style; no cosy B&B clutter here. Degas' art is everywhere in prints and reproductions. The house will be busy in 1999 when it links up with the New Orleans Museum of Art to promote a major exhibition, 'Degas in New Orleans'.

Website: www.degashouse.com
Hotel services *All rooms no-smoking. Continental breakfast. Fax. Safe.* **Room services** *Cable TV. Radio.*

Reservation services

Several reservation services provide a helping hand for negotiating the hotel maze. Because they charge the hotels and B&Bs a fee for making bookings, travellers get their advice and help for free. Also on hand with helpful booking advice is the **New Orleans Visitors Bureau** (*see page 264* Directory).

Bed & Breakfast and Beyond

3225 Napoleon Avenue, New Orleans, LA 70125 (822 8525/1-800 886 3709/fax 822 8547/Mshimon@lhm net).
Maggie Shimon takes pride in matching the traveller to the B&B in her highly personalised service. She will also help in booking tours, special events and other requests of visitors.

Website: www.nolabandb.com

New Orleans Bed & Breakfast

PO Box 8163, New Orleans, LA 70182 (838 0071/1-888 240 0070/fax 831 0140/info@neworleansbandb.com).
Sarah-Margaret Brown represents more than 200 hosts. She will also recommend houses, apartments and condos for travellers who want to live like a local for a while.

Website: www.neworleansbandb.com

Restaurants

As the saying goes, 'There are two times of day in New Orleans: mealtime and in between.'

'A paradise for gluttons', one early twentieth-century visitor said of New Orleans. Despite cultural, social, medical and lifestyle revolutions in the ensuing decades, New Orleans remains much the same. Food, glorious food, continues to be a local obsession at every level.

The local cuisine has changed over the years, but only because it's good, not because it's healthy. The Creole, Cajun, Italian, African, Spanish and Caribbean influences that conjured up New Orleans food to begin with have been recast and reinterpreted into some of the most exciting restaurant cooking around. The **Commander's Palace** (*page 131*), **Emeril's** (*page 126*), **Bayona** (*page 115*), along with a handful of other restaurants, have helped turn the city into a New American cooking centre. Yet the genius of the old ways hasn't been abandoned: red beans and rice is still on every Monday menu and best friends come to blows

over who makes the best fried shrimp po-boy sandwich in Orleans Parish. For food, New Orleans is a paradise.

For bars and restaurants with live music, *see chapter* **Nightlife**. The prices quoted below are the average or price range for a main course. Lunch tends to be about 20 per cent cheaper than dinner. Between 15 and 20 per cent extra should be added to the final bill as a tip.

French Quarter

American

Crescent City Brewhouse
527 Decatur Street, at St Louis Street (522 0571). Bus 3 Vieux Carré, 55 Elysian Fields, 81 Almonaster, 82 Desire, 92 Express. **Open** 11am-midnight (food served until 10pm) Mon-Thur, Sun; 11am-1am (food served until midnight) Fri, Sat. **Main courses** $10. **Credit** AmEx, DC, Disc, MC, V. **Map 7 B3**
In an ideal location : mid the bustle of Decatur Street, the Brewhouse offers a combination of good beers (all made in-house) and great food. The balcony has become a popular tourist gathering point and on breezy afternoons is a good place in the Quarter to sit, enjoy a fine beer and watch the world go by. The beers are created by the restaurant's German-born brewmeister-owner, while the cuisine mixes American and European influences in dishes like Louisiana bouillabaisse, braided salmon and asparagus pasta. *See also* **p201 Nightlife**.
Disabled: toilet.

Rib Room
Omni Royal Orleans Hotel, 621 St Louis Street, at Royal Street (529 7045). Bus 3 Vieux Carré, 55 Elysian Fields, 81 Almonaster, 82 Desire. **Breakfast served** 6.30-10.30am, **lunch served** 11.30am-2.30pm, **dinner served** 6-10pm, daily. **Main courses** $14-$20. **Credit** AmEx, DC, MC, V. **Map 7 B2**
Louisiana-born chef Raymond Toups is making his home state and its bounty proud. The Rib Room is a beloved local institution, a bastion of Martinis and red meat.
Disabled: toilet.

Asian

Shalimar Indian Cuisine
535 Wilkinson Row, at Chartres Street (523 0099/ shalmar@ix.netcom.com). Bus 3 Vieux Carré, 55 Elysian Fields, 81 Almonaster, 82 Desire. **Lunch served** 11am-2.30pm, **dinner served** 5.30-10.30pm, Mon-Sat. **Main courses** $10-$15. **Credit** AmEx, DC, MC, V. **Map 7 B2**
The Keswanis have brought their highly praised Indian cooking from Metairie to the French Quarter. The new location has inspired them to incorporate some 'New Indian' dishes onto the menu of classics.
Disabled: toilet. Website: www.shalimarno.com

Best...

breakfast: Brennan's (*p119*); Bluebird Café (*p134*).
beignets & café au lait: Café du Monde (*p142*); Morning Call (*p143*).
budget meal: Café Atchafalaya (*p131*); Michael's Mid-City Grill (*p139*).
Cajun: Alex Patout's Louisiana Restaurant (*p115*); K-Paul's Louisiana Kitchen (*p115*).
contemporary: Brigtsen's (*p133*); Emeril's (*p126*).
Creole: Arnaud's (*p119*); Galatoire's (*p120*).
hotel dining room: Windsor Court Grill Room (*p127*); Sazerac (*p126*).
Italian: Irene's Cuisine (*p123*); Mosca's (*p141*).
Gospel brunch: Praline Connection II Gospel & Blues Hall (*p126*).
jazz brunch: Commander's Palace (*p131*).
neighbourhood: Mandina's (*p139*); Domilise's Po-Boys (*p135*).
po-boy: Acme Oyster House (*p123*); Mother's (*p128*).
romantic spot: Bella Luna (*p115*); Upperline (*p133*).
soul food: Dooky Chase (*p139*).
seafood: Andrew Jaeger's House of Seafood (*p119*); Casamento's (*p134*).
wine list: Brennan's (*p119*); Dominique's (*p116*).

Useful terms

See also p124 **New Foods** *and p117*
Neighbourhood Restaurants.

andouille: spicy Cajun sausage used in gumbo and other dishes.

beignet: square doughnut covered in icing (powdered) sugar; as served by Café du Monde and other cafés (*see p142*).

biscuits: scones – eaten for breakfast with bacon, gravy, egg, etc.

crawfish: Louisiana's official crustacean; also called mudbugs or – outside the state – crayfish.

dirty rice: a relation of jambalaya involving a mix of rice and meat (giblets, sausage) and seasoning.

étouffée: spicy tomato sauce served typically with crawfish or shrimps. Literally means 'smothered'.

filé: ground sassafras leaves used to season – typically – gumbo.

grits: ground wheat or corn, served like mashed potato. A staple of the Southern breakfast table, usually served with butter and salt, or gravy.

gumbo: a soup-stew made with a variety of ingredients that can include shrimp, chicken, okra, tomatoes and rice; seasoned with filé.

jambalaya: tomatoes and rice, flavoured with anything the chef feels like tossing in (ham, shrimp,

chicken) and flavoured with celery and onions – a Creole pilaff.

mirliton: hard-skinned pear-like vegetable usually served stuffed with ham or shrimp.

muffuletta: a giant sandwich made with seeded muffuletta bread stuffed with any combination of ham, cheese, sausage and olive salad.

pain perdu: ('lost bread') French toast.

praline: brown sugar and pecans, caramelised into a dentist's worst nightmare of an all-sugar, can't-eat-just-one confection.

po-boy: (from 'poor boy') sandwich made with French bread and containing anything from fried oysters or shrimps to roast beef and gravy. 'Dressed' means it is served with lettuce, tomato and a dressing.

red beans and rice: traditional New Orleans Monday-night meal made up of kidney beans with a sauce containing ham or sausage.

rémoulade: a spicy red sauce flavoured with spring onion, cayenne, mustard, lemon, paprika and parsley; usually served cold with shrimp or crabmeat.

roux: cooked mixture of butter and flour used for thickening sauces. Central to Creole and Cajun cooking.

tasso: smoked and spiced ham.

Cajun

Alex Patout's Louisiana Restaurant
221 Royal Street, at Iberville Street (525 7788). Bus 3 Vieux Carré, 41 Canal. **Dinner served** 5.30-10pm daily. **Main courses** $18. **Credit** AmEx, DC, MC, V. **Map 7 A2**
Under the direction of a talented south Louisiana chef, Cajun meets Creole in the heart of the Quarter. The cochon de lait is a hit, along with its side order of sweet potatoes with praline sauce.

K-Paul's Louisiana Kitchen
416 Chartres Street, at Conti Street (596 2530). Bus 3 Vieux Carré, 55 Elysian Fields, 81 Almonaster, 82 Desire. **Lunch served** 11.30am-2.30pm, **dinner served** 5.30-10pm, Mon-Sat. **Main courses** $7-$20.95. **Credit** AmEx, DC, MC, V. **Map 7 B2**
This is the culinary home of world-famous chef Paul Prudhomme. It is not unusual to see a crowd lined up around the block, waiting for a seat at one of the casual, red-and-white checked cloth-covered tables. A decade ago, Prudhomme spread the word about blackened seafood and the public has never ceased to love him for it. A recent expansion has made the restaurant much more accessible and ensured a shorter wait for a table. You know what to order here.
Disabled: toilets.

Patout's Cajun Cabin
501 Bourbon Street, at St Louis Street (529 4256). Bus 3 Vieux Carré. **Open** 11am-midnight daily. **Main courses** $12-$20. **Credit** AmEx, DC, MC, V. **Map 7 B2**
Chef Gigi of the famous Patout family (originally from New Iberia in Tabasco Country) holds sway on this corner of Bourbon Street. Having expanded the space, she continues to maintain a high quality of family-style Cajun cooking.
Disabled: toilet.

Rémoulade
309 Bourbon Street, at Bienville Street (523 0377). Bus 3 Vieux Carré. **Open** 11.30am-midnight daily. **Main courses** $12. **Credit** AmEx, DC, MC, V. **Map 7 B2**
Unbelievably good burgers and fried seafood po-boys are served at this casual outcropping of **Arnaud's** around the corner (*p119*), along with the same soups as the parent restaurant. This is also a good place for quick boiled seafood with a beer.
Disabled: toilet.

Contemporary

Bayona
430 Dauphine Street, at Conti Street (525 4455/ info@ bayona.com). Bus 3 Vieux Carré, 57 Franklin. **Lunch served** 11.30am-1.30pm Mon-Fri. **Dinner served** 6-9.30pm Mon-Thur; 6-10.30pm Fri, Sat. **Main courses** $13-$30. **Credit** AmEx, DC, MC, V. **Map 7 B1**
This is the restaurant home of one of the city's top culinary superstars, Susan Spicer. She oversees the creation and production of the food, which is in a style she calls 'New World Cuisine'. Whatever its origin, her cooking has been wowing food critics since she first opened her chic eatery a few years ago. Try the cream of garlic soup, the Thai shrimp salad and the grilled shrimp with black bean cakes. Or try anything else the knowledgeable staff recommend.
Booking essential. Disabled: toilet. Website: www. bayona. com

Bella Luna
914 N Peters Street, at Dumaine Street (529 1583/ belaluna@gs.net). Bus 3 Vieux Carré, 55 Elysian Fields, 81 Almonaster, 82 Desire. **Open** 6-10.30pm Mon-Sat; 6-9.30pm Sun. **Main courses** $35. **Credit** AmEx, DC, MC, V. **Map 7 C3**

*Old-fashioned New Orleans dining at its best at **Antoine's** (page 119).*

Bella Luna has won over many diners simply on the look of the place, which is undeniably fine. With huge windows overlooking the Mississippi River and an ambience that must be what the rich think of when they think of romance, this is the place where New Orleans café society gets engaged. Chef Horst Pfeifer's food is as beautiful as the view and can be startlingly adventurous, mixing world flavours with New Orleans spice. The menu changes regularly, but has an emphasis on seafood.
Disabled: toilet.

Bistro at the Maison de Ville

Hotel Maison de Ville, 727 Toulouse Street, at Bourbon Street (528 9206). Bus 3 Vieux Carré. **Lunch served** 11.30am-2pm Mon-Sat; 11am-2pm Sun. **Dinner served** 6-10pm daily. **Main courses** $8-$25. **Credit** AmEx, DC, MC, V. **Map 7 B2**
This very Parisian bistro has seldom been better, thanks to New Orleans native chef Greg Piccolo. His Creole touch is fused to a palate of fresh herbs. The menu always includes a vegetarian dish, a pleasant surprise in such lush surroundings. The Bistro is the in-house restaurant for the intimidatingly elegant Maison de Ville hotel, but the dining room atmosphere is welcoming and friendly thanks to maître d' Patrick Van Hoorebeek's light touch.
Website: www.maisondeville.com

Dominique's

Maison Dupuy Hotel, 1001 Toulouse Street, at N Rampart Street (586 8000). Bus 3 Vieux Carré, 57 Franklin. **Dinner served** 6-10pm daily. **Main courses** $18-$25. **Credit** AmEx, DC, MC, V. **Map 7 B1**
Superstar Dominique Macquet (whose CV has included a stint in the kitchens of Kensington Place in London) has taken up residence at the Maison Dupuy. Everything has been upgraded from the hotel's old days, especially the brilliant tastes and textures flowing from the kitchen. Dinner is a five-star treat in formal surroundings.
Disabled: toilet.

G&E Courtyard Grill

1113 Decatur Street, at Ursulines Street (528 9376). Bus 3 Vieux Carré, 55 Elysian Fields, 81 Almonaster, 82 Desire. **Lunch served** 11.30am-2.30pm Fri-Sun. **Dinner served** 6-10pm Mon-Thur, Sun; 6-11pm Fri, Sat. **Main courses** $9.25-$24. **Credit** AmEx, DC, MC, V. **Map 7 C3**
Built around a courtyard, G&E is one of the city's more charming, if somewhat crowded bistros. As the name implies, grilled foods are central to the menu. Chef Michael Uddo calls his cooking New Cuisine, yet he owes at least as much to his Sicilian roots and European training as to anything created recently in California. Check out the Orient-tinged salads, or anything from the rôtisserie, which can be seen from the main dining room.
Disabled: toilet.

Mr B's Bistro

201 Royal Street, at Iberville Street (523 2078). Bus 3 Vieux Carré, 41 Canal. **Jazz brunch served** 10.30am-3pm Sun. **Lunch served** 11.30am-3pm Mon-Sat. **Dinner served** 5.30-10pm Mon-Fri, Sun; 5-10pm Sat. **Main courses** $12-$32. **Credit** AmEx, DC, MC, V. **Map 7 A2**
The very first entry of the bistro concept into New Orleans, B's (as it's known) dishes up just about the best business lunch anywhere, as well as a dinner of relaxed sophistication. The dining room is kept dim, but diners glow with satisfaction provided by the reliably good, Creole-influenced food and the excellent wine list. The gumbo is legendary and the roast meat entrées and creative seafood dishes rule the day.
Disabled: toilet. Website: www.mrbsbistro.com

NOLA

534 St Louis Street, at Chartres Street (522 6652). Bus 3 Vieux Carré, 55 Elysian Fields, 81 Almonaster, 82 Desire. **Lunch served** 11.30am-2pm Mon-Sat. **Dinner served** 6-10pm Mon-Thur, Sun; 6pm-midnight Fri, Sat. **Main courses** $9.50-$30. **Credit** AmEx, DC, MC, V. **Map 7 B2**

Neighbourhood restaurants

In the late nineteenth century, as the French Quarter was developing as a centre of Destination Dining in New Orleans, dozens of pockets were forming around the city for mealtimes more casual and more affordable – but no less intriguing.

Though few of today's neighbourhood restaurants were even imagined in the golden age of Antoine's and Galatoire's, the notion of an ethnically tangled synthesis of French Creole cooking was beginning to emerge. It was most heavily influenced by local Sicilians, but also by Germans, Greeks and Croatians, all striving to place their favourite dishes on the menu.

From the beginning, and quite logically, neighbourhood restaurants developed both from and for their neighbourhood. This meant they reflected the ethnic and financial make-up of their surroundings in interesting ways. And it was primarily the curving riverfront geography that constantly threw one group in with another, followed by the fact that over relatively short times neighbourhoods changed their ethnic mix as one group moved up and out. Before long, there were Sicilian eateries dishing up 'paneed meat', as though it were something other than Wiener schnitzel once removed.

These days, much of the neighbourhood notion remains, if you know where and how to look for it, though there's nothing guaranteed or permanent about these places. Today, one of New Orleans's richest areas for neighbourhood restaurants is Mid City. Our favourites there include both really old places and newer places doing really old things, among them **Mandina's** and **Michael's Mid-City Grill** (*see page 139 for both*).

All of these eateries shine culinarily, both for their à la carte menus and their sometimes-crazy daily specials. Don't fear ordering an Irish classic in a place with an Italian name; in true New Orleans fashion, it'll probably come out part-French and part-African anyway.

Even the French Quarter has seen its 'neighbourhood' developments, as with the renewal of long-tawdry Decatur Street into something much more classy. So, in addition to the well-known staples of gumbo, red beans and rice and jambalaya – here are half a dozen terrific neighbourhood dishes to try in New Orleans:

Oysters Bonne Femme
There are several variations of this classic baked oyster dish – anointed with the French phrase for 'good woman' – plus an extremely popular chicken and garlic fest that's completely different but travels by the same name. **Antoine's** (*p119*) pioneered one of the oyster versions, and there are countless others.

Shrimp-stuffed artichoke
The influence of New Orleans's large Sicilian population is felt in any dish involving the stuffing of artichokes – and almost every restaurant has some such dish. Here's one that's both extra simple and extra good.

Barbecued shrimp
This dish was created at the restaurant called **Pascal's Manale** (*p135*)– don't try to figure out the grammar, that's just what it's called. And speaking of what things are called, barbecued shrimp aren't barbecued at all. They're basically a butter, garlic and pepper combo, all waiting to be sopped up with slices of French bread.

Chicken Creole
The old Creoles took the basic chicken fricassée and made it something all their own. Served with white rice, it makes a colourful and satisfying family dinner.

Paneed veal
Breaded veal sautéd in butter (from the Italian *pane*, or bread). Only a generation ago, this was known simply as 'paneed meat' and cooked all over New Orleans because veal was less expensive than beef.

Boiled brisket of beef
It was **Tujague's** (*p120, pictured above*) that made this dish famous, though there was nothing original among the Creoles about finding new uses for foods that otherwise would be thrown out. Originally, the brisket was used simply for making beef stock for soups and sauces – and then discarded.

*Get caffeinated at **Rue de la Course** (see page 143). Laptops are optional.*

This is a secondary restaurant owned by well-known chef and TV whiz Emeril Lagasse. Lagasse established NOLA as his outpost in the French Quarter – a slightly more affordable version of his **Emeril's** in the Warehouse District (*p126*). The food here – served up in hip surroundings – is in similarly over-the-top style and it rarely disappoints. *Disabled: toilet.*

Palace Café

605 Canal Street, at Chartres Street (523 1661). Bus 3 Vieux Carré, 41 Canal Blues b───l 1 A ll.00am-2.30pm Sun. **Lunch served** 11.30am-2.30pm Mon-Sat. **Dinner served** 5.30-10pm daily. **Main courses** $12.50-$29. **Credit** AmEx, DC, MC, V. **Map 7 A2**

This is one of several restaurants owned and operated by the famous New Orleans Brennan family, owners of the **Commander's Palace** (*p131*) and **Brennan's** (*see below*). It's a bright, upscale spot, headed by Dick Brennan Jr, from the third generation of the clan. Located on down-at-heel Canal Street, Palace Café is two storeys of vivid windows and cheery murals. The oysters Bienville are suitably luscious and the white chocolate bread pudding a local fave. *Disabled: toilet.*

Pelican Club

615 Bienville Street, at Exchange Alley (523 1504/pelicanclub@earthlink.net). Bus 3 Vieux Carré, 41 Canal. **Dinner served** 5-10pm Mon-Thur, Sun; 5.30-11pm Fri, Sat. **Main courses** $22. **Credit** AmEx, DC, MC, V. **Map 7 B2**

Chef Richard Hughes deserves every accolade he's collected for this stylish palace of modern Louisiana cooking splashed with New American and Oriental accents. Noisy and popular. *Disabled: toilet.*

Peristyle

1041 Dumaine Street, at N Rampart Street (593 9535). Bus 3 Vieux Carré, 57 Franklin. **Lunch served** 11.30am-1.30pm Fri. **Dinner served** 6-9pm Tue-Thur; 6-10pm Fri, Sat. **Main courses** $19 lunch. **Set dinner** $19. **Credit** AmEx, DC, MC, V. **Map 7 C1**

Peristyle is one of the city's old guard restaurants, but with a twist. Three years ago, a 27 year old woman did the unthinkable – she bought the place and installed herself as chef. In the largely male, definitely older New Orleans chef's clan, this was sacrilege. But by 1998, Anne Kearney had become one of the city's nationally acclaimed chefs. Her modern cooking style occasionally sets Creole on its ear, with satisfying results. The service is excellent, too.

Creole

Andrew Jaeger's House of Seafood

622 Conti Street, at Royal Street (522 4964). Bus 3 Vieux Carré, 55 Elysian Fields, 81 Almonaster, 82 Desire. **Open** 5-11.30pm daily. **Main courses** $17.95. **Credit** AmEx, DC, MC, V. **Map 7 B2**

This is one of New Orleans's traditional seafood favourites and it is run by a local seafood dynasty. The Jaeger family has been selling fresh fish for decades and for many years cooking it in their family restaurant. The place has two themes – downstairs is loud and funky with live music on busy nights; upstairs is more subdued and upmarket. *Disabled: toilet.*

Antoine's

713 St Louis Street, at Bourbon Street (581 4422). Bus 3 Vieux Carré. **Lunch served** 11.30am-2pm, **dinner served** 5.30-9pm, Mon-Sat. **Main courses** $12.75-$25.50 lunch. **Set dinner** $50. **Credit** AmEx, DC, MC, V. **Map 7 B2**

Antoine's, which dates from 1840, proudly bills itself as the oldest restaurant in North America. Run by the Alciatore family for six generations, the restaurant is part of New Orleans's Old Guard. This is the kind of place where you can picture dozens of fat men in white suits gathering on steamy summer nights to make city policy over Oysters Foch, one of the house specialities. Like many of the city's most beloved restaurants, the place is divided into dozens of small rooms. For locals, it's considered a social snub to be seated in the front room (US presidents and royalty have traditionally dined in the back dining room). Antoine's invented many of the great dishes in the Creole repertoire and the style remains traditional, heavy on the seafood and grilled meat. *Disabled: toilet.*

Arnaud's

813 Bienville Street, at Bourbon Street (523 5433/arnauds@arnauds.com). Bus 3 Vieux Carré, 41 Canal, 57 Bourbon. **Open** 11.30am-10pm Mon-Thur; 11.30am-11.30pm Fri, Sat; 10am-2.30pm Sun. **Main courses** $20. **Credit** AmEx, DC, MC, V. **Map 7 B2**

A French Quarter landmark, which has been keeping founder Count Arnaud's memory alive and cooking since 1918. Another of the city's old-guard restaurants, Arnaud's is also among its most famous. Locals consider Shrimp Arnaud (the house version of shrimp rémoulade) to be a mandatory appetiser; try pompano en croûte and the crème brulee to follow. Jackets must be worn.

Brennan's

417 Royal Street, at Conti Street (525 9711/brennansno @aol.com). Bus 3 Vieux Carré, 55 Elysian Fields, 81 Almonaster, 82 Desire. **Open** 8am-2.30pm; 6-10pm daily. **Main courses** $15-$35. **Credit** AmEx, DC, MC, V. **Map 7 B2**

The restaurant that brought the world Bananas Foster – invented by a chef who was bet he couldn't create an elegant dish with the fruit – but most famous for the gargantuan 'Breakfast at Brennan's', which offers eggs 20 different ways alongside eye-opening cocktails. The 12 formal dining rooms patrolled by creaking waiters fill up quickly for this, so book ahead and try the eggs Hussard. At dinner try the bizarre, delicious steak Stanley with bananas and make sure someone else pays. Brennan's has the most extensive wine list in the city and is owned by the Brennan clan, behind other local eateries including the **Commander's Palace** (*p131*) and the **Palace Café** (*see above*). *Disabled: toilet. Website: brennansneworleans.com*

Café Rue Bourbon

241 Bourbon Street, at Bienville Street (524 0114). Bus 3 Vieux Carré, 41 Canal. **Lunch served** 11.30am-3pm Fri-Sun. **Dinner served** 5.30pm-midnight Mon-Thur. **Main courses** $8-$18. **Credit** AmEx, DC, MC, V. **Map 7 B2**

There's never been so much excitement on the plate at Café Rue Bourbon than there is right now. And the fact that many locals profess they've never heard of the place makes the news all the more extravagant. Check out the balcony upstairs for dining with a view of Bourbon Street.

Café Sbisa

1011 Decatur Street, at St Philip Street (522 5565/napoli@access.com). Bus 3 Vieux Carré, 55 Elysian Fields, 81 Almonaster, 82 Desire. **Open** 5.30-10.30pm Mon-Thur; 5.30-11pm Fri, Sun. **Jazz brunch** 10.30am-3pm Sun. **Main courses** $11-$23. **Credit** AmEx, DC, MC, V. **Map 7 C3**

If Brennan' s and Antoine's epitomise old-style New Orleans elegance, Café Sbisa epitomises old-style New Orleans decadence. In a bistro-like setting that includes breezy balcony dining and a courtyard, Sbisa offers jovial staff, a traditional Creole menu and live jazz. A good place to mix and mingle with locals. Note the huge mural above the bar – all the characters are past or present members of staff. And try the trout almondine, the oyster pan roast and the white chocolate bread pudding. *Disabled: toilet. Website: cafesbisa.com*

Court of Two Sisters

613 Royal Street, at Toulouse Street (522 7261). Bus 3 Vieux Carré, 55 Elysian Fields, 81 Almonaster, 82 Desire. **Open** 9am-3pm, 5.30-11pm, daily. **Main courses** $21 lunch. **Set dinner** $37. **Credit** AmEx, DC, MC, V. **Map 7 B2**

New Orleanians joke that this is the best spot in town to conduct an affair because you will never see any one you know, among the tourist clientele. But the restaurant still exerts a strong pull after decades of serving familiar New Orleans dishes. The garden setting is lovely, the service is good and if one orders conservatively, the food isn't bad. Stick to the tried and true such as gumbo, trout almondine and bread pudding and you won't be disappointed.
Disabled: toilet.

Galatoire's

209 Bourbon Street, at Iberville Street (525 2021/ galatoir@iamerica.net). Bus 3 Vieux Carré, 41 Canal. **Open** 11.30am-9pm Tue-Sat; noon-9pm Sun. **Main courses** $20. **Credit** AmEx, DC, MC, V. **Map 7 A2**

For nearly a century, lunch at Galatoire's has been a tradition. This is where the city's business got done more often than not. Standing in line to get in was a less pleasant tradition, but recently Galatoire's simultaneously expanded its dining room to include a waiting area and expanded its traditions to include allowing reservations. The menu, however, hasn't changed much since 1905 and is rich in Creole dishes. Someone at your table should have trout Marguery; someone else should be a rich lawyer who knows everyone in the town.

Redfish Grill

115 Bourbon Street, at Iberville Street (598 1200). Bus 3 Vieux Carré, 41 Canal. **Brunch served** 10am-3pm Sun. **Lunch served** 11am-3pm, **dinner served** 5-11pm, Mon-Sat. **Main courses** $12.95. **Credit** AmEx, DC, MC, V. **Map 7 A2**

This is the Brennan family again, with its newest development, a casual-dining restaurant at the low-end of Bourbon Street. The look is urban cool, verging on cold, with everything concrete marbled to within an inch of its life. The food is a sometimes confusing California-Creole mix that doesn't always work. Prices are slightly lower than at other Brennan's places, but we think some things are worth paying for.
Disabled: toilet. Website: www.redfishgrill.com

Tujague's

823 Decatur Street, at Madison Street (525 8676). Bus 3 Vieux Carré, 55 Elysian Fields, 81 Almonaster, 82 Desire. **Lunch served** 11am-3pm, **dinner served** 5-10.30pm, daily. **Main courses** $7.95 lunch. **Set dinner** $26. **Credit** AmEx, DC, MC, V. **Map 7 C3**

This is one of those amazing, timewarp New Orleans restaurants where things are still done precisely as they were 100 years ago. Tujague's (pronounced 'Two Jacks') offers only three entrées a day – one each of beef, seafood and chicken. But don't let that scare you off. Whether it's the shrimp rémoulade, signature boiled brisket of beef or garlic chicken bonne femme, each is made to an ancient recipe and with strict attention to detail. The service is great fun and the place makes a heavenly bread pudding for dessert.

French/Continental

Begue's Restaurant

Royal Sonesta Hotel, 300 Bourbon Street, at Conti Street (553 2278/586 0300, ext 278). Bus 3 Vieux Carré. **Lunch served** 11.30am-2pm, **dinner served** 6-11pm, daily. **Main courses** $20. **Credit** AmEx, DC, MC, V. **Map 7 B2**

A hotel restaurant with a long memory, Begue's turns out an excellent blend of classical French dishes with plenty of

New Orleans fare in a pleasant garden setting. The place is named after one of the city's earliest dining personalities.
Disabled: toilet. Website:www.sonestano.com

Broussard's

819 Conti Street, at Bourbon Street (581 3866). Bus 3 Vieux Carré. **Open** 5.30-10pm daily. **Main courses** $18-$35. **Credit** AmEx, DC, MC, V. **Map 7 B2**

A graceful Creole palace that has been going since the 1920s, Broussard's seems to have recovered from a recent series of ownership ups and downs. Gunter and Evelyn Preuss have been joined in operating this French Quarter landmark by their European-trained son Marc. Elegant and pricey food in an elegant setting.
Disabled: toilet. Website:www.broussards.com

Louis XVI

St Louis Hotel, 730 Bienville Street, at Bourbon Street (581 7000/sales@stlouishotel.com). Bus 3 Vieux Carré. **Dinner served** from 6pm daily. **Main courses** $10-$25 dinner. **Credit** AmEx, DC, MC, V. **Map 7 B2**

Agnes Bellet is the first woman in the history of the city's first successful French restaurant. Red meats are the specialities, served with immeasurable care and style in formal surroundings. And Bellet has lightened up a few sauces, or at least offered some alternatives.
Disabled: toilet. Website: www.louisxvi.com

Latin

Criollo

201 Decatur Street, at Iberville Street (561 0007). Bus 3 Vieux Carré, 41 Canal, 55 Elysian Fields, 81 Almonaster, 82 Desire. **Open** 11.30am-11pm Mon-Fri; 6pm-midnight Fri, Sat. **Main courses** $6-$15. **Credit** AmEx, DC, MC, V. **Map 7 A3**

Criollo makes a strong play for locals and tourists, covering the spectrum from Cuban black bean and roasted calabaza soups to guava cheesecake and coconut flan. It draws recipes from the entire Spanish colonial experience.
Disabled: toilet.

Italian

Bacco

310 Chartres Street, at Bienville Street (522 2426/ efg@bacco.com). Bus 3 Vieux Carré, 41 Canal. **Bellini brunch served** 10am-2pm Sun. **Lunch served** 11.30am-2.30pm Mon-Sat. **Dinner served** 6-10pm daily. **Main courses** $9-$16. **Credit** AmEx, DC, MC, V. **Map 7 B2**

In surroundings that mix Italianate architecture with baroque flourishes in a dizzying swirl of faux walls and ceilings, yet more members of the Brennan clan of restaurateurs serve up robust Tuscan-influenced food with panache. The mood here is almost absurdly elegant and the food lighter than at many upmarket New Orleanian restaurants, with olive oil replacing butter in many dishes. Pastas, grilled fish and meat are all good choices, as are the salads and decadent desserts.
Disabled: toilet. Website: www.bacco.com

Café Giovanni

117 Decatur Street, at Canal Street (529 2154/ cafegio@ aol.com). Bus 3 Vieux Carré, 41 Canal, 55 Elysian Fields, 81 Almonaster, 82 Desire. **Dinner served** 5.30-10pm Mon-Thur, Sun; 5.30-11pm Fri, Sat. **Main courses** $15. **Credit** AmEx, DC, MC, V. **Map 7 A3**

Well, shucks: the fast-fingered oyster shuckers at **Acme Oyster House**.
See page 123.

The definitive shrimp po-boy gets the finishing touches at **Domilise's**. *See page 135.*

Refresh body and spirit with the **Praline Connection's** *Creole soul food. See page 126.*

Leading the renaissance of upper Decatur Street, New Orleans-born chef Duke LoCicero has come of age at Café Giovanni. Its popularity has led to the expansion of his eatery, where oysters Giovanni and pasta gamberi followed by osso bucco is a feast.
Disabled: toilet.

Irene's Cuisine
539 St Philip Street, at Chartres Street (529 8811).
Bus 3 Vieux Carré, 55 Elysian Fields, 81 Almonaster,
82 Desire. **Dinner served** 5.30-10.30pm Mon-Fri;
5.30-11pm Sat, Sun. **Main courses** $10.50-$18.90.
Credit AmEx, MC, V. **Map 7 C2**
Irene's is the kind of New Orleans restaurant that would be listed as the city's number one eatery, the jewel in the crown, if the city were any other place but New Orleans. In the glut of absolutely fabulous restaurants, a place like Irene's is often overlooked. Locals love it and are happy to keep it a secret, as tables are hard enough to get as it is. Persevere! The Italian-Creole kitchen serves the best roast chicken in town and that's just the beginning. The interior is cosy and cluttered and the waiters are known for their lovely manners. There's an excellent wine list, too.
Disabled: toilet.

Maximo's Italian Grill
1117 Decatur Street, at Ursulines Street (586 8883).
Bus 3 Vieux Carré, 55 Elysian Fields, 81 Almonaster,
82 Desire. **Open** from 6pm daily. **Main courses** $8.95.
Credit AmEx, DC, MC, V. **Map 7 C3**
It's hard to imagine anything more cool or sophisticated than this Roman-style grill, which is home to some of the best pastas and the most wines by the glass anywhere. The chef's signature dish is veal Cattoche, made with garlic and fresh herbs.
Disabled: toilet.

Ristorante Carmelo
541 Decatur Street, at Toulouse Street (586 1414).
Bus 3 Vieux Carré, 55 Elysian Fields, 81 Almonaster,

82 Desire. **Lunch served** 11.30am-4pm, **dinner served** 5.30-11pm, daily. **Main courses** $8-$14. **Credit** AmEx, DC, MC, V. **Map 7 B3**
Complete with a great balcony and an even better wine room at the top of the stairs, this Quarter favourite serves up remarkably fresh Italian flavours, from the antipasto collection to the tiramisu. Check out the veal Sorrentino.
Disabled: toilet. Website: www.restaurantecarmelo.com

Sclafani's French Quarter
301 Dauphine Street, at Bienville Street (524 5475/
sclafani@msm.com). Bus 3 Vieux Carré, 41 Canal,
57 Franklin. **Breakfast served** 7-10.30am, **lunch served** 11am-2pm, **dinner served** 6-10pm, daily. **Main courses** $7-$17. **Credit** AmEx, DC, MC, V. **Map 7 B1**
The younger generation of a local restaurant family brings its handiwork to the French Quarter with some style and some success. Check out the tournedoes Dauphine topped with jumbo shrimp in a port wine sauce.
Disabled: toilet.

Neighbourhood

Acme Oyster House
724 Iberville Street, at Bourbon Street (522 5980).
Bus 3 Vieux Carré, 41 Canal. **Open** 11am-10pm Mon-Sat; noon-7pm Sun. **Main courses** $5.50. **Credit** AmEx, DC, MC, V. **Map 7 A2**
The best thing served up at this landmark is local character. The waiters are fun, the oyster shuckers are entertaining and if only the walls could talk... It's one of the many Quarter restaurants around which legends have built up. Food-wise, raw oysters are central to the menu. Otherwise, there's a wide variety of po-boy sandwiches, a favourite, naturally, being the oyster po-boy.

Clover Grill
900 Bourbon Street, at Dumaine Street (598 1010).
Bus 3 Vieux Carré. **Open** 24 hours daily. **Main courses** $7.95. **Credit** AmEx, MC, V. **Map 7 C2**

New foods

What's old in food may indeed be new again. Yet no one can deny that the local menu looks different from the way it did a decade ago.

This is due, in no small part, to broad trends that have moved Louisiana's Creole and Cajun cuisines into the vanguard of more healthful, more innovative New American cooking. Yet it's also due to a bevy of new or rediscovered dishes that now turn up on menus around the city, the state and even the nation.

We might dub these dishes New Foods – while recognising that there's almost no such thing. Chefs spend far more time borrowing than inventing. A look at local New Foods is, by definition, a look at new ways to borrow, or at least at new sources from which to borrow.

In a few cases, these are dishes that have never been seen before. More often, they are dishes that have appeared elsewhere, waiting for the person, place or thing that would propel them into the New Orleans marketplace.

Some dishes are strongly associated with a single chef or eatery; others just sort of showed up. Still others, like the blackened redfish of the previous decade, earned their reputation under one chef – Paul Prudhomme – but left a handful of others whining about bragging rights.

The New Foods are fuelled by tastes and techniques from the American Southwest, from Asia, from just about anywhere. And contrary to the apparent fears of previous generations, Louisiana cooking has emerged stronger, not weaker, from the mingling.

And since there is no official Registrar of New Foods, this list of ten dishes could be as short or as long as you care to make it. If you argue that

Orient yourself at **Mike's on the Avenue.**

one of these New Foods isn't new at all, that's exactly the point. It simply has been made to look like new, taste like new, and most importantly sell like new. That's why it's on so many menus in the first place.

Onion 'mum

If most dishes considered here are 'gourmet' items with complex components, this is a simple gimmick dish that has conquered at least part of the known world. Fried onion, of course, is no revelation, thanks to the mountains of onion rings devoured everywhere. The trick is the way this oversized onion is cut, so that in frying it opens like the bloom of a graceful chrysanthemum.

Louisiana crabcakes

Contrary to some presumptions, crabcakes are neither new nor indigenous. Yet when they popped onto the menu at chic places like the **Windsor Court Grill Room** (*p127*) and **Bella Luna** (*p115*), you'd have thought no such taste had ever been experienced before. In truth, forming crab, breadcrumbs and seasonings into cakes is an Old South thing; with other seafoods (like New England cod), it has roots in

---

A diner that probably serves more drag queens than any eatery in the US, the Clover Grill is one of the earthy kind of spots that are becoming all too rare in the Quarter. Its hamburgers, fries and sandwiches are perfect post-club food and the gay clientele provides spur-of-the-minute floor shows. It's a genuine neighbourhood spot, not a virtual French Quarter greasy spoon in the way the House of Blues is a Hollywood-imagined blues club. Be sure to pick up the weekly *Visitors Guide*, with its quirky list of 'What to do and NOT to do' ('The Riverfront Street Car: Ride to nowhere! Walk!').

Felix's Seafood Restaurant & Oyster Bar

739 Iberville Street, at Bourbon Street (522 4440). Bus 3 Vieux Carré, 41 Canal. **Open** 10am-midnight Mon-Thur; 10am-1am Fri; 10am-1.30am Sat; 10am-10pm Sun. **Main courses** $10. **Credit** AmEx, DC, MC, V. **Map 7 A2**

Raw oysters on the half-shell are the essential eats in this casual restaurant. All the best local fish and shellfish turn

up as entrées, in some form or other, from oysters Rockefeller to short-order platters.
Disabled: toilet.

O'Flaherty's Irish Channel Center

514 Toulouse Street, at Decatur Street (529 1317). Bus 3 Vieux Carré, 55 Elysian Fields, 57 Franklin, 82 Desire. **Open** noon-3am daily. **Main courses** $7. **Credit** AmEx, Disc, MC, V. **Map 7 B3**

It's not exactly *haute cuisine*, but O'Flaherty's, the city's most elegant Irish pub, does banner business dishing out meat pies and cabbage stew all year round. Shepherd's pie is the big winner here, followed by the corned beef sandwich and Irish stew. You can knock back a pint of Guinness and catch some charming if cloying dancing youngsters at night, too (*see p203* **Nightlife**).
Website: www.CelticNationsWorld.com

QSR (Quarter Scene Restaurant)

900 Dumaine Street, at Dauphine Street (522 6533). Bus 3 Vieux Carré, 57 Franklin. **Open** 8am-midnight Mon,

colonial America. That said, turning out delicate patties of crabmeat and pairing them with a creative, usually herbal sauce turned quite a few heads when Horst Pfeifer carried doing it at the Grill Room.

Crawfish beignets

What a neat idea these were, when the local version of the sugar-covered French Market doughnut merged with the Caribbean seafood fritter in the hands of French chef Daniel Bonnot at **Bizou** (*p128*). Actually, Bonnot had cooked in the West Indies before arriving in New Orleans, so the merger seemed a natural one. The thinking seems to be that if a fritter will inspire people to eat chewy conch in the islands, how much better will it showcase Louisiana crawfish.

Crawfish spring rolls

The Orient is alive and well in new New Orleans cooking; among others, Mike Fennelly of **Mike's on the Avenue** (*p127*) has turned the exploration of Japanese, Chinese, Thai and other Far East fantasies into the heart and soul of his place on St Charles Avenue. And no dish exemplifies his mission better than the crawfish spring rolls, given a Vietnamese spin by the three-chilli dipping sauce with garlic, red pepper and lime.

Shrimp quesadilla

A quesadilla (sometimes described on menus as 'Mexican pizza') is, like its Italian counterpart, no more than a delivery system for tastes and textures. Outside New Orleans, almost anything can and does turn up on a quesadilla. In New Orleans, shrimp makes an inspired choice. The best bet here is **Bella Luna**'s (*p115*) signature pecan wood-smoked shrimp quesadillas, which ride off toward Italy and Mexico in the same breath.

Oysters Gabie

With the inspiration of millions of Rockefellers and Bienvilles before their eyes, New Orleans chefs never seem to tire of the baked oyster scenario. Take an oyster on the half shell, top it with something good, and shove it into the oven. Simple – and glorious. For a new version of this old flame, try Oysters Gabie at **Gabrielle** (*p137*). Here, home-grown chef Greg Sonnier mixes breadcrumbs, artichokes and pancetta.

Maque choux

Don't let the plethora of spellings fool you: this is (or should be) the dish the Cajuns picked up from the local Choctaw Indians. A dish made with corn (or shrimp or crawfish or chicken), it is a signature item at both **Alex Patout's Louisiana Restaurant** and Gigi Patout's (**Patout's Cajun Cabin**, both *p115*) in the French Quarter, and it's hard to find better. Still, places like the **Pelican Club** (*p119*) love coming up with new, multicultural approaches to the standard.

Pasta gambino

In this Age of the Noodle, pasta is being served everywhere and with everything. A favourite 'new' pasta comes from **Café Giovanni** (*p120*). On a single, very decorated plate, penne hook up with rock shrimp, sun-dried tomatoes and herbed peppers in a light sauce of not one but three cheeses.

Bronzed or blackened fish

To everyone's surprise, the great gimmick dish of the early 1980s Cajun Revolution masterminded by Paul Prudhomme, and served at every ersatz Louisiana eatery from Michigan to Madagascar, not only survives but thrives into the 1990s. Bronzed fish pulls back a bit from both the heavy-handed spicing and overbearing char of the original, preserving the best parts of the flavour. Likely to turn up in any restaurant created by a Prudhomme alumni.

White chocolate bread pudding

Elsewhere, the dessert rediscovery of the decade has been crème brûlée, but in New Orleans, a more dramatic innovation has lifted the beloved bread pudding a notch or three up the food chain. First, there was bread pudding soufflé at the **Commander's Palace** (*p131*); then, with the **Palace Café**'s (*p119*) white chocolate bread pudding, a trendy flavouring met a dessert that didn't need much help in the first place.

Wed-Sun. **Main courses** $3.95-$7.95. **Credit** AmEx, Disc, MC, V. **Map 7 C1**
Popular for its late-night dining, the Quarter Scene has long been a neighbourhood place in one of America's quirkiest neighbourhoods, with all that logically implies. Great for omelettes and other breakfast specials, and for home-cooked specials such as meatloaf or roast chicken.

Vegetarian & wholefood

Old Dog New Tricks Café

*307 Exchange Alley, at Bienville Street (522 4569).
Bus 3 Vieux Carré.* **Open** 11.30am-9pm daily.
Main courses $10.95. **Credit** AmEx, MC, V.
Map 7 B2
Old Dog creates vegetarian dishes with a New Orleans touch, proving that the infamously fattening local cuisine doesn't necessarily have to be. The menu is wide-ranging, from meat-free veggie burgers to dozens of sandwiches, salads, soups and entrées including meat-free red beans and rice.

Faubourg Marigny

Latin

Santa Fe

*801 Frenchman Street, at Dauphine Street (944 6854).
Bus 3 Vieux Carré, 48 Esplanade.* **Dinner served**
5-11pm Tue-Sat. **Main courses** $12. **Credit** AmEx, Disc, MC, V.
Why Santa Fe is one of the busiest restaurants in the Marigny is a mystery. A wait for a table is inevitable and although it's pleasantly located in a historic building and the staff are quite friendly, there's not much to the place. A German chef runs this Southwestern-style eatery and anything can happen on the plate. Raisins are startlingly sprinkled on refried beans. Chicken breast is rolled with pumpkin seeds and cheese. And most sauces are very mild by Southwestern standards. Perhaps the secret is the frosty Margaritas and large glasses of Sangría that pave the way for the quirky food.
Disabled: toilet.

*Enjoy the mother of all po-boys at **Mother's**. See page 128.*

Neighbourhood

Port of Call

838 Esplanade Avenue, at Dauphine Street (523 0120).
Bus 3 Vieux Carré, 48 Esplanade. **Open** 11am-1am
daily. **Main courses** $10. **Credit** AmEx, MC, V.
Map 7 D1
When you're looking for a quick, hearty meal near the French
Quarter, Port of Call should be on your list. It's open late and
offers ridiculously huge hamburgers, enormous baked pota-
toes and heavy pizzas. The crowd is eclectic, ranging from
slumming wealthy folk to artists and shop workers. The
Monsoon is the house drink, the Port's version of the
Hurricane: imbibe with caution.
Disabled: toilet.

Praline Connection

542 Frenchman Street, at Chartres Street (943 3934).
Bus 3 Vieux Carré, 48 Esplanade, 55 Elysian Fields.
Open 11am-10.30pm Mon-Thur; 11am-midnight Fri, Sat;
11am-6pm Sun. **Main courses** $4.50-$14.95. **Credit**
AmEx, DC, MC, V. **Map 7 D2**
One of the best and most accessible of New Orleans's many
Creole soul food restaurants. Despite the candy name,
there's nothing snacky about the spicy, soul food served in
the dining room – in giant portions, at very reasonable
prices. Try the perfect red beans and rice with some stewed
chicken and mustard greens. Or sample the crowder peas
with okra for a real taste of the South. At the S Peters Street
branch, the Sunday Gospel Brunch is a New Orleans institution. Tour bus directors send visitors to the slickly packaged House of Blues gospel brunch but at the Praline
Connection you'll see the local African-American power
structure networking and entertaining visitors. The real star
here is the inexhaustible Rev. Raymond Myles Sr, a gospel
music machine that appears to be atomically powered.
Sitting at his electronic keyboard and backed up by a changing line-up of singers, Myles dispenses gotta-dance gospel
with tear-jerker testimonies of God's goodness ('He rewarded
little ole me with a Mercedes-Benz, y'all, that's how good

God is!'). Be warned: Myles periodically orders the audience
to stand up and hug strangers at the next table in the interest of world peace.
**Branch: Praline Connection II Gospel & Blues
Hall** 901 S Peters Street, at St Joseph Street (523 3973).

CBD & Warehouse District

American

Sazerac

*Fairmont Hotel, 123 Baronne Street, at Common Street
(529 4733). St Charles Streetcar/bus 41 Canal.* **Lunch
served** 11.30am-2pm Mon-Fri. **Dinner served** 6-10pm
Tue-Sun. **Main courses** $12-$25. **Credit** AmEx, DC,
MC, V. **Map 6 B/C1**
This hotel classic has, after a couple of years of experimen-
tation, realigned itself with the finest elements of its past:
roasted meat and fowl, decadent desserts and service every
step of the way.

Veranda

*Inter Continental Hotel, 444 St Charles Avenue, at
Poydras Street (525 5566). St Charles Streetcar.*
Brunch served 11am-2.30pm Sun. **Lunch served**
11am-2pm Mon-Sat. **Dinner served** 5.30-10pm daily.
Main courses $8.95-$25.95. **Credit** AmEx, DC, MC, V.
Map 6 C1
Local hero Willy Coln has captured the feeling of both a
Southern plantation and an old Orleans home. Lunch is a
classy buffet, dinner an à la carte wonderland.
Disabled: toilets.

Contemporary

Emeril's

800 Tchoupitoulas Street, at Julia Street (528 9393).
Bus 10 Tchoupitoulas. **Lunch served** 11.30am-2pm
Mon-Fri. **Dinner served** 6-10pm Mon-Thur; 6-10.30pm

Fri, Sat. **Main courses** $7-$25. **Credit** AmEx, DC, MC, V. **Map 6 C2**

These days you're more likely to see Emeril Lagasse on television than behind the stove at his eponymous restaurant. On his regular TV show, broadcast locally on the Food Channel, Lagasse cooks before a relentlessly thrilled New York audience. Here he dishes up hyper-exciting, tirelessly creative cooking with distinctive flare (try to find your plate under all that spice decoration). The barbecue shrimp are out of this world. Leave room for the banana cream pie. *Disabled: toilet. Dress: jacket and tie. Website: www.foodtv.com*

Metro Bistro

200 Magazine Street, at Common Street (529 1900). Bus 11 Magazine. **Lunch served** 11am-2pm daily. **Dinner served** 5.30-10pm Mon-Thur; 5.30-11pm Sat, Sun. **Main courses** $10-$15. **Credit** AmEx, DC, MC, V. **Map 6 C1**

An accurate homage to the bistro concept, Metro comes complete with comfortable setting, unpretentious service and robust, almost-country cooking. Talented local chef Chris Brown gives the French classics just enough creative spin. *Disabled: toilet.*

Mike's on the Avenue

Lafayette Hotel, 628 St Charles Avenue, at Girod Street (523 1709). St Charles Streetcar. **Lunch served** 11.30am-2pm Mon-Fri. **Dinner served** 6-9.30pm daily. **Main courses** $11-$20. **Credit** AmEx, DC, MC, V. **Map 6 B/C1**

With its wide glass windows looking down over the city's best-known street, Mike's is New Orleans's yuppie heaven. It is also a pioneer among forward looking eateries. In the stylish double dining room food lovers can dish over a dizzying sampler of world cuisine heavily influenced by Pacific Rim styles. The food is described as 'fusion', meaning, we think, anything goes as long as it looks good. If you're hungry and looking for somebody beautiful, Mike's is your place. *Disabled: toilet.*

Windsor Court Grill Room

Windsor Court Hotel, 320 Gravier Street, at Tchoupitoulas Street (522 1992). Bus 3 Vieux Carré, 11 Magazine. **Lunch served** 11.30am-2pm, **dinner served** 6-10pm, daily. **Main courses** $20-$25. **Credit** AmEx, DC, MC, V. **Map 6 C1**

The Windsor Court Hotel and its Grill Room restaurant are hugely popular among the hugely wealthy. This is one of those places where the vase on the table in the entryway holds no fewer than 300 perfect pink roses: attention to detail is everything and the prices certainly reflect it. French chef Rene Bajeux provides a chef's-eye view of the globe in his cooking. Creative and personal, it's some of the best food money can buy – made from some of the best ingredients money can buy. *Disabled: toilets.*

Creole

Bon Ton Café

401 Magazine Street, at Poydras Street (524 3386). Bus 11 Magazine. **Lunch served** 11am-2pm, **dinner served** 5-9.30pm, Mon-Fri. **Main courses** $13. **Credit** AmEx, DC, MC, V. **Map 6 C1**

We've never loved this place to the distraction felt by some, but it does serve pure New Orleans and south Louisiana cooking. It's good and filling no matter what you order. When in doubt, head for the crabmeat au gratin and the bread pudding. *Disabled: toilet.*

Mulate's Cajun Restaurant

201 Julia Street, at Convention Center Boulevard (522 1492). Bus 3 Vieux Carré, 33 Tchoupitoulas. **Open** 11am-11pm daily. **Main courses** $7.95-$13.95. **Credit** AmEx, DC, Disc, MC, V. **Map 6 C2**

This is the New Orleans version of a restaurant that is a landmark in the bayou town of Breaux Bridge. Mulate's can take credit for being the first restaurant in the city to incorporate Cajun food with music and dancing, creating the swamp

*We said leave room for **Emeril's** banana cream pie. Not the room.*

Grab a seat at the counter in traditional Uptown diner the **Camellia Grill** (page 131).

equivalent of a dinner club. Two things you can count on at Mulate's: the Cajun band will be loud and the food will be spicy. Mostly for tourists, though generally worth it for the bands. *See also p206* **Nightlife**.
Disabled: toilet. Website: www.mulates.com

French/Continental

Bizou Restaurant
701 St Charles Avenue, at Girod Street (524 4114/ bizou@bellsouth.net). St Charles Streetcar. **Lunch served** 11am-3pm Mon-Fri. **Dinner served** 5-10pm Mon-Sat. **Main courses** $13-$26. **Credit** AmEx, DC, MC, V. **Map 6 B/C1**
This is another restaurant where those who want to see and be seen are sure to be found. The food is elegantly presented, if only mildly creative and service can be chilly. But the location is great – overlooking the Avenue – and one could while away an evening over wine in worse places.
Disabled: toilet. Website: www.bizourestaurant.com

La Gauloise
Hotel Meridien, 614 Canal Street, at St Charles Avenue (527 6712). St Charles Streetcar/bus 41 Canal. **Breakfast/lunch served** 6.30am-3pm, **dinner served** 5.30-10pm, daily. **Main courses** $13-$18. **Credit** AmEx, Disc, MC, V. **Map 6 C1**
A very French hotel that does an admirable job of creating a very French bistro. The fact that it's a neat little perch overlooking the parade of Canal Street adds an extra dash of pleasure to the experience.
Disabled: toilet.

Latin

Liborio
322 Magazine Street, at Poydras Street (581 9680). Bus 11 Magazine. **Lunch served** 11am-3pm Mon-Fri. **Dinner served** 6-9pm Wed-Sat. **Main courses** $8. **Credit** AmEx, DC, MC, V. **Map 6 C1**

The first restaurant to successfully serve Cuban food in New Orleans, Liborio has made the food of the Spanish Caribbean part of the CBD lunchtime routine. The black bean soup, garlicky roast chicken and seafood paella are all excellent.
Disabled: toilets.

Neighbourhood

Mother's
401 Poydras Street, at Tchoupitoulas Street (523 9656). Bus 3 Vieux Carré, 10 Tchoupitoulas. **Open** 5am-10pm daily. **Main courses** $3-$12. **No credit cards.**
Map 6 C1
Mother's is one of those places where everybody – be they tourist or local – is willing to line up in the sweltering summer heat to wait their turn. Located a few blocks outside the French Quarter, Mother's has been the city's busiest and arguably best po-boy joint for more than 50 years. The red beans and rice is true New Orleans. Alternatively, try the combination Ferdi po-boy, or anything using the 'black ham' leftover from breakfast.

Red Bike Bakery & Café
746 Tchoupitoulas Street, at Julia Street (529 2453). Bus 3 Vieux Carré, 10 Tchoupitoulas. **Brunch served** 10am-3pm Sat, Sun. **Lunch served** 11am-3pm Mon-Fri. **Dinner served** from 6pm Tue-Sat. **Main courses** $10. **Credit** AmEx, DC, MC, V. **Map 6 C2**
Walking into this airy, sunlit café is like stepping off Tchoupitoulas Street into California. Chef-owner Beth Miller comes to New Orleans cooking by way of New York's legendary Silver Palate kitchen and chef Paul Prudhomme, but her emphasis on fresh-baked bread and straight-from-the-garden ingredients makes one think of San Francisco. The Red Bike is particularly welcome in the art district where food spots are sparse during gallery tramps. Miller

If you're searching for sushi, head Uptown to **Kyoto** *and watch the experts at work (page 132).*

smokes her own turkeys, bakes her own focaccia and adds a Southwestern touch to many dishes. Salads are particularly good here, and despite the reputation for healthy food, so are the desserts. Vegetarians will count this café a godsend in carnivorist New Orleans.
Disabled: toilets.

Uglesich's

1238 Baronne Street, at Erato Street (523 8571).
St Charles Streetcar. **Open** *summer* 9.30am-4pm Mon-Fri; *winter* 9.30am-4pm Mon-Sat. **Main courses** $10-$10. **No credit cards. Map 6 B2**
Aside from having a virtually unpronounceable name, Uglesich's is most famous for its astonishingly good seafood po-boys and platters, which are served in a no-frills, no-nonsense manner by the restaurant's long-serving staff. Locals sit shoulder to shoulder with those intrepid travellers who have managed to discover the joint. Pat yourself on the back if you make it here: it's a true New Orleans experience.

Vegetarian & wholefood

Back to the Garden

Lee Circle YMCA, 920 St Charles Avenue, at Howard Avenue (522 8792). St Charles Streetcar. **Open** 7am-5pm Mon-Fri; 9am-4pm Sat. **Main courses** $5-$8. **No credit cards. Map 6 B2**
Great prices and simple, healthy food have made Back to the Garden the city's longest-running wholefood restaurant. The carrot juice is squeezed fresh before your eyes and the salads are loaded with fresh veg. Meat eaters can opt for the great chicken salad. Or try the houmous served in a pitta pocket or a club sandwich on wheatberry bread. Check out the exercise classes at the YMCA when you're done.

Garden District

Asian

Kung's Dynasty

1912 St Charles Avenue, at St Mary Street (525 6669). St Charles Streetcar. **Open** 11.30am-10pm Mon-Thur; 11.30am-11pm Fri, Sat; noon-10pm Sun. **Main courses** $4.95-$12.95. **Credit** AmEx, DC, MC, V.
Map 6 B2/3
Despite a Victorian mansion on lower St Charles Avenue as setting, Kung's is a simple, traditional Chinese restaurant. The cooking here is all the Chinese food you know and love, the staff are friendly and you can sit at a window looking out over the streetcar line.
Disabled: toilet.

Contemporary

Chef's Table

2100 St Charles Avenue, at Jackson Avenue (525 2328). St Charles Streetcar. **Lunch served** 11.30am-2.30pm, **dinner served** 5.30-10pm, Tue-Sat. **Main courses** $7-$14. **Credit** AmEx, DC, MC, V. **Map 6 B3**
Mark Uddo has embarked on his own in a space that formerly housed the landmark Versailles restaurant. Once Gunter and Evelyn Preuss shut down their Garden District digs, it only made sense for someone to take over. Dishes are substantial: try the fire-roasted shrimp or risotto.
Disabled: toilet. Website: www.ci-no.com

*A quintessential New Orleans experience: oyster bread and friendly service at **Casamento's**. See page 134.*

Kelsey's Restaurant

3923 Magazine Street, at Louisiana Avenue (897 6722). Bus 11 Magazine. **Lunch served** 11.30am-2pm Tue-Fri. **Dinner served** 5.30-9.30pm Tue-Thur; 5.30-10pm Fri, Sat. **Main courses** $6.95-$14. **Credit** AmEx, DC, MC, V. **Map 6 A4**
This is the comfortable Garden District haven in which to order anything with gingersnap gravy, or anything combining fried green tomatoes with mague choux. Chef Randy Barlow pays homage to mentor Paul Prudhomme, but over the years has created his own spin on Louisiana's cooking.
Disabled: toilet.

Creole

Commander's Palace

1403 Washington Avenue, at Coliseum Street (899 8221). St Charles Streetcar. **Jazz brunch served** 11.30am-12.30pm Sat; 10.30am-1.30pm Sun. **Lunch served** 11.30am-1.30pm Mon-Fri. **Dinner served** 6 9.30pm daily. **Main courses** $22-$30. **Credit** AmEx, DC, MC, V. **Map 6 A3**
One of the best-known restaurants in the city, the Brennan family-owned Commander's Palace is where the wealthy go to dine when they're in town and where New Orleans society goes to celebrate all its great events – or just Saturday night. If you can afford it, a dinner in this distinctive Garden District mansion should not be missed – the food is justifiably renowned, and most of the city's big-name chefs have done a stint at the stove. The menu changes constantly, but can always be counted on for rich Creole fare – from poached oysters with caviar to bread pudding soufflé – served with a gentility that verges on obsequiousness.
Booking essential. Disabled: toilet. Website: www. commanderspalace.com

Neighbourhood

Café Atchafalaya

901 Louisiana Avenue, at Laurel Street (891 5271). Bus 27 Louisiana. **Breakfast served** 8.30am-8pm Sat, Sun. **Lunch served** 11.30am-2pm Tue-Sun. **Dinner served** 5.30-9pm Tue-Thur; 5.30-10pm Fri, Sat. **Main courses** $10-$20. **Credit** MC, V. **Map 6 A4**
A tiny Garden District café, with Formica-topped tables and a blackboard menu. Service is friendly and the food 'mostly Southern' specialities. Don't miss the fried green tomatoes, which will make converts out of sceptics, or the tempting fresh fruit cobbler. Nostalgic and well done.

St Charles Tavern

1433 St Charles Avenue, at Melpomene Street (523 9823). St Charles Streetcar. **Open** 24 hours daily. **Main courses** $6-$7. **Credit** AmEx, DC, MC, V. **Map 6 B2**
A late-night New Orleans tradition, this 24-hour place can get busy at all kinds of unexpected hours. It has an eclectic crowd of insomniac regulars who will talk your ear off at 3am, if you are inclined to listen while munching through a plate of red beans and rice or the restaurant's 'signature' hamburgers and fries.

Uptown

American

Camellia Grill

626 S Carrollton Avenue, at St Charles Avenue (866 9573). St Charles Streetcar. **Open** 9am-1am Mon-Thur, Sun; 8am-3am Fri, Sat. **Main courses** $6-$7. **No credit cards. Map 4 A8**
For decades, this sweetly named restaurant on the streetcar line where St Charles Avenue meets Carrollton Avenue has

*All the crawfish you can eat – and then some – at **Don's Seafood Hut** in Metairie (page 140).*

stubbornly maintained its traditions as time passed it by. There's counter seating only, which often means a wait for a spot to open up. The café is staffed by breezy waiters in white jackets, shouting orders over their shoulders to the fry cooks. It is said that all the staff are the children and grandchildren of former employees and that their jobs are handed down, like legacies, through the generations. Whatever the case, the service is friendly-verging-on-formal and the food is great. Best bets are the burgers, waffles, omelettes and sandwiches. Safety tip: even with the early hours the Grill is a good place to relax because of the seemingly constant flow of police officers. Cops eat free so they usually take their meal breaks here. Mayor Marc Morial is a late-night visitor as well, often with a lady friend.

Asian

Lemon Grass Café

216 N Carrollton Avenue, at Canal Street (488 8335). Bus 40 Canal/Lakeshore Express, 90 Carrollton. **Dinner served** 6-10pm Mon-Thur; 6-10.30pm Fri, Sat; 5.30-9.30pm Sun. **Main courses** $8-$15. **Credit** AmEx, DC, MC, V. **Map 5 D5**

Lemon Grass is one of very few Vietnamese restaurants that lie within the New Orleans city limits – most are located in the suburbs. The ambience is upmarket, the room is always packed and the spring rolls are perhaps the most popular item on the menu. Lemon Grass manages to blend the comfort of a French café with the exoticism of a Vietnamese restaurant.

Kamikaze

3637 Magazine Street, at Antonine Street (897 0002). Bus 11 Magazine. **Lunch served** 11.30am-2.30pm Mon-Fri; noon-3pm Sat. **Dinner served** 5.30-10pm Mon-Thur; 5.30-10.30pm Fri, Sat. **Set lunch** $12.50. **Main courses** $11-$15. **Credit** Disc, MC, V. **Map 4 D9**

With the subtitle 'Noodles to Die For', Kamikaze has a menu based on Asian noodle dishes, fusing the best of Chinese, Japanese, Vietnamese, Thai, Cambodian and Filipino cuisines. The dining room is small and modern.

Kyoto

4920 Prytania Street, at Jefferson Avenue (891 3644). St Charles Streetcar. **Lunch served** 11.30am-2.30pm Mon-Fri; noon-3pm Sat. **Dinner served** 5-10pm Mon-Thur; 5-10.30pm Fri, Sat. **Main courses** $5.95-$15. **Credit** AmEx, Disc, MC, V. **Map 4 C9**

This is one of Uptown's trendiest sushi restaurants. Kyoto is always packed with academics and young professionals, but the food is great and the atmosphere pleasant. You might start with a tabo roll (a jumbo sushi roll with softshell crab tempura, crawfish, crabstick, cucumber and avocado, lightly rolled in sweet caviar). Service is friendly but often sloppy. Don't hesitate to repeat your order or send an unordered dish back to the kitchen.

Contemporary

Brigtsen's
723 Dante Street, at River Road (861 7610). St Charles Streetcar. **Open** 5.30-10pm Tue-Sat. **Main courses** $14-$24. **Credit** AmEx, DC, MC, V. **Map 4 A8**
Setting up shop in a converted cottage in Riverbend, past the turn in the streetcar line, Frank Brigtsen has given New Orleans one of its most creative kitchens, one that takes 'New Cajun' cuisine and personalises it in inventive ways. Book a table in advance.

Sara's
724 Dublin Street, at Maple Street (861 0565). St Charles Streetcar. **Lunch served** 11.30am-2.30pm,

dinner served 6-11pm, Tue-Sat. **Main courses** $7-$12. **Credit** AmEx, DC, MC, V. **Map 4 A8**
This place used to be a humble curry house called Old Calcutta, but the owners recently turned on their culinary heel. There are still some Indian flavours on the menu, but they've been broadened by the globetrotting handiwork of chef John Newcomer. Presentation is impressive.

Upperline
1413 Upperline Street, at St Charles Avenue (891 9822). St Charles Streetcar. **Brunch served** 11.30am-2pm Sun. **Dinner served** 5.30-9.30pm Wed, Thur, Sun; 5.30-10pm Fri, Sat **Main courses** $17. **Credit** AmEx, DC, MC, V. **Map 4 C9**
Owner JoAnn Clevenger's theatre background pays off in the way she has 'produced' a restaurant. She uses colour, light and props such as flowers and art to great effect. None of this would matter, of course, without wonderful food and chef Richard Benz fills this role with flair. The cooking is eclectic, with strong Cajun and Creole ideas. There's often some kind of theme going on, such as the summer garlic festival or homage to Monet to coincide with a museum showing of his work. All fun but built on the bedrock of a great kitchen.
Website: www.upperline.com

Vizard's

5538 Magazine Street, at Joseph Street (895 5000).
Bus 11 Magazine. **Dinner served** 6-10pm Tue-Thur;
6-11pm Fri, Sat. **Main courses** $18. **Credit** AmEx, DC,
MC, V. **Map 4 C9/10**
Kevin Vizard is a local chef who spins excitement wherever
he goes. In the recent past he has kept a low profile, but has
now made up for it by opening a kind of Creole bistro in the
Uptown space that until now served barbecue.

French/Continental

Bouchon

4900 Prytania Street, at Upperline Street (895 9463).
St Charles Streetcar. **Open** from 6pm Mon-Sat. **Main
courses** $8-$16. **Credit** AmEx, DC, MC, V. **Map 4 C9**
The windows are very big here, the better for the beautiful
clientele to watch its own reflection. The menu is focused
on appetisers – tapas with a French twist – but the wine list
is really the heart of this glossy, chic eatery.
Disabled: toilet.

La Crêpe Nanou

1401 Robert Street, at Prytania Street (899 2670).
St Charles Streetcar. **Dinner served** 6-10pm Mon-Thur,
Sun; 6-11pm Fri, Sat. **Main courses** $7. **Credit** MC, V.
Map 4 C9
A popular Uptown cool-down spot, Nanou got rolling with
its namesake thin pancakes, and has expanded its menu with
style and efficiency. In spirit, it's still a pleasant little crêperie.

Italian

Figaro's Pizzeria

7900 Maple Street, at Fern Street (866 0100).
St Charles Streetcar. **Open** 11am-10.30pm Mon-Thur;
11am-11.30pm Fri, Sat; noon-10pm Sun.
Main courses $5.50-$15. **Credit** AmEx, DC, MC, V.
Map 4 A/B8
Located in the trendy Uptown area near Tulane and Loyola
universities, Figaro's is as popular for its comfortable patio
dining area as for its creative pasta and pizza dishes. The food
is reliable, and the Four Seasons pizza goes down a storm.
Disabled: toilet.

Latin

Vaqueros

4938 Prytania Street, at Robert Street (891 6441/
vaqueros@aol.com). St Charles Streetcar. **Brunch**
served 11am-3pm Sun. **Lunch served** 11.30am-2.30pm
Mon-Fri. **Dinner served** 5-10pm Mon-Thur, Sun;
5-11pm Fri, Sat. **Main courses** $9-$17. **Credit** AmEx,
DC, MC, V. **Map 4 C9**
Undoubtedly the city's best purveyor of Latin American
food. Ever since it opened, in the early 1990s, Vaqueros has
been a hit, creating dishes using both Latin American and
Native American ingredients. Specials frequently include
unusual game, such as wild boar, and the daily fish special
is always worth a try. The Tex-Mex dishes are served in
home-made tortillas with savoury beans and rice and the tortilla chips come with a choice of four salsas.
Disabled: toilet. Website: www.vaqueros-restaurant.com

Mediterranean

Jamila's Café

7808 Maple Street, at Burdette Street (866 4366).
St Charles Streetcar. **Lunch served** 11.30am-2pm
Tue-Fri. **Dinner served** 5.30-9.30pm Tue-Thur, Sun;
5.30-10.30pm Fri, Sat; 5.30-9.30pm Sun.
Main courses $6.75-$10.50. **Credit** AmEx, MC, V.
Map 4 B8
This is a fun little eatery owned by a Tunisian family who
aim to showcase popular dishes from their homeland. Much
of the menu is built around couscous, then continues from
there to include other North African specialities. Jamila and
Moncef Sbaa have recently expanded their business into the
next door premises, where they sell Mediterranean and
Tunisian groceries and gifts.
Disabled: toilets.

Neighbourhood

Bluebird Café

3625 Prytania Street, at Foucher Street (895 7166).
St Charles Streetcar. **Open** *winter* 7am-3pm Mon-Fri;
8am-3pm Sat, Sun. **Main courses** $2.95-$4. **No credit**
cards. Map 4 E9
The long queues out of the door tell you this is a good café.
Get here before 9am at weekends and you won't have to wait.
This is a quintessential breakfast spot, where bright sunlight streams through the windows and hot coffee soothes
the aching head. The all-day breakfast is always a hit, especially Bluebird's huevos rancheros – fried eggs served on a
corn tortilla with black beans and tomato salsa – or any of
the home-made pancakes and omelettes. The orange juice is
freshly squeezed and a variety of teas are available for those
not inclined to java.
Branch: 7801 Panola Street, at Burdette Street (866
7577).

Casamento's

4330 Magazine Street, at Napoleon Avenue (895 9761).
Bus 11 Magazine, 24 Napoleon. **Lunch served**
11.30am-1.30pm, **dinner served** 5.30-9pm, Tue-Sun.
Closed June-Aug. **Main courses** $5-$10. **No credit**
cards. Map 4 D10

Chain reaction

If theme's your scene, New Orleans has
prominent and tourist-packed branches of all
the international theme chains, plus a couple
all it's own. If you don't want to eat the burger
without buying the T-shirt, then head for one
of the following.

Fashion Café New Orleans *619 Decatur Street,
at Wilkinson Row (522 3181). Bus 55 Elysian
Fields, 57 Franklin, 82 Desire.* **Map 7 B3**

Hard Rock Café *418 N Peters Street,
at St Louis Street, (529 5617). Bus 3 Vieux Carré,
55 Elysian Fields, 81 Amonaster, 82 Desire.*
Map 7 B3

New Orleans Planet Hollywood
*620 Decatur Street, at Jackson Square (522 7826/
planethollywood@ neworleansrestaurants.com).
Bus 3 Vieux Carré, 55 Elysian Fields,
81 Almonaster, 82 Desire.* **Map 7 C3**

O'Henry's Food & Spirits *301 Baronne Street,
at Gravier Street (522 5241). Bus 41 Canal.*
Map 6 B1 *Branches throughout the city.*

Popeye's *621Canal Street, at Exchange Place
(561 1021). Bus 3 Vieux Carré, 41 Canal.*
Map 7 A2 *Branches throughout the city.*

Old-style glamour at the Brennan family's famous **Commander's Palace**. *See page 131.*

Casamento's is a white-tiled and mirrored, old-fashioned fishmonger's. For more than half a century, Uptown residents have strolled here for oysters, raw or fried, though usually raw (and only in season). Po-boys, oyster plates and gumbo are just about all you'll find here, along with a lot of seriously eccentric N'awlins characters.

Clancy's

6100 Annunciation Street, at Webster Street (895 1111). Bus 19 Nashville Express. **Lunch served** 11.30am-2pm Tue-Fri. **Dinner served** 5.30-10.30pm Mon-Thur; 5.30-11pm Sat. **Main courses** $10.95-$23.95. **Credit** AmEx, DC, MC, V.
Map 4 B10
Night after night, Clancy's bistro goes about its business of winning and keeping friends among its well-heeled, well-educated, well-travelled clientele. It's hard to find, so take a taxi or ride with a regular.

Domilise's Po-Boys

5240 Annunciation Street, at Bellecastle Street (899 9126). Bus 11 Magazine. **Lunch served** 11am-3pm Mon-Sat. **Main courses** $6.06. **No credit cards.**
Map 4 C10
The queen of po-boy cafés. The Domilise family has been making and selling these calorie- and fat-laden sandwiches for god knows how long, but certainly long enough for several generations to learn the trade perfectly. The fried shrimp po-boy is as close to heaven as many of us will come. Customers wait in line while several ladies of the family make your order. You pay the cook when it's ready, then amble over to the bar across the room to get a beer or Barq's rootbeer. It's completely off the beaten path in a working-class neighbourhood near the river, but worth any amount of trouble to find.

Franky & Johnny's

321 Arabella Street, at Tchoupitoulas Street (899 9146). Bus 10 Tchoupitoulas. **Open** 11am-10pm Mon-Thur; 11am-midnight Fri, Sat; 10am-10.30pm Sun.

Main courses $7.95. **Credit** AmEx, Disc, MC, V.
Map 4 B10
Only a few blocks from Domilise's, making this area a kind of food historic preservation area. Franky & Johnny's has one of the greatest jukeboxes in New Orleans, a good bar and a no-frills restaurant that serves first-class food. Fried or boiled, the seafood is always cooked just right. The stuffed artichokes are delicious and the shrimp salad surprisingly light (and also delicious). The crowd is loud but wonderfully diverse – from Uptown socialites to college kids to serious barflies. A happy place.

Martin's Wine Cellar

3827 Baronne Street, at Napoleon Avenue (899 7411). St Charles Streetcar/bus 24 Napoleon. **Open** 9am-7pm Mon-Sat; 10am-2pm Sun. **Main courses** $6-$8. **Credit** AmEx, MC, V. **Map 4 D9**
It should come as no surprise to wine lovers that the deli at one of the city's best wine shops is a classy place. Choose from an array of sandwiches and salads from the self-service counter, but beware the queues at lunchtime. *See also p159* **Shops & Services.**
Branch: 1200 Veterans Memorial Boulevard, Metairie (896 7300).

Pascal's Manale

1838 Napoleon Avenue, at Dryades Street (895 4877). St Charles Streetcar/bus 24 Napoleon. **Open** 11.30am-10pm Mon-Fri; 4-10pm Sat; 4-9pm Sun. **Main courses** $5.95-$9. **Credit** AmEx, DC, MC, V.
Map 4 D9
Manale's is a crush of drinking, loud talking and breathless oyster eating – and that's before you get a table. Sometimes it seems as though everyone in town is standing at Pascal's bar waiting for a table. The dining room atmosphere verges on raucous, with children running around and people shouting across to friends at other tables. It's still an upmarket restaurant, but one in the local tradition. Many consider it the true home of barbecue shrimp in New Orleans.

Vegetarian & wholefood

Chicory Farm Café

723 Hillary Street, at Maple Street (866 2325). St Charles Streetcar. **Lunch served** 11.30am-2pm Thur-Sat. **Dinner served** 5.30-9pm Thur; 5.30-10pm Fri, Sat. **Main courses** $5. **No credit cards. Map 4 B8**

This relatively new restaurant has been earning national attention for its deft combination of gourmet cooking and vegetarian principles. Ingredients hail from Chicory Farm in Washington Parish, about an hour outside the city. Here the owners grow herbs and vegetables and raise goats and cows for the milk used in their highly rated cheeses – they also supply other restaurants in town.

Eve's Market

7700 Cohn Street, at Adams Street (861 1626). Bus 22 Broadway. **Open** 10am-7pm Mon-Sat. **Credit** Disc, MC, V. **Map 4 B7**

Eve's is actually a deli and grocery store that excels at freshly made soups – mostly vegetarian – and a wide variety of sandwiches made with organic and free-range meat and veg. The shop also offers daily specials to take away, including salads made with everything from houmous or rice to carrots, raisins or chicken with egg-less low-calorie mayo.

Mid City

Asian

Bangkok Cuisine

4137 S Carrollton Avenue, at D'Hemecourt Street (482 3606). Bus 90 Carrollton. **Lunch served** 11am-3pm Mon-Fri. **Dinner served** 5-10pm Mon-Fri; 5-11pm Sat, Sun. **Main courses** $4.95-$8.95. **Credit** AmEx, DC, MC, V. **Map 4 D6**

One of the city's best Thai restaurants. The mood is laid-back and the service always good although the waitresses have to wear some extraordinarily silly dresses. The shrimp soup is a great spicy starter, or you can cool off with the squid salad. The vegetable curry is delicious and vegan.

Genghis Khan

4053 Tulane Avenue, at Carrollton Avenue (482 4044). Bus 39 Tulane, 90 Carrollton. **Dinner served** 6.00-11.00pm Tue-Sun. **Main courses** $12.95. **Credit** AmEx, DC, MC, V. **Map 4 C6**

One of the city's weirdest restaurants that must be experienced to be believed. Inexplicably named after one of history's most violent warriors, the place looks like a suburban diner, serves authentic Korean food and is staffed by professional classical musicians. Immediately after setting your whole fried fish on the table, your waitress may well burst into an aria from *Madame Butterfly* while the maître d' accompanies her on the violin. It's as entertaining as it is bizarre and the food is great – kimchee, bulgoki and the ginger fish should win over any first-timer.

Contemporary

Gabrielle

3201 Esplanade Avenue, at Mystery Street (948 6233). Bus 48 Esplanade. **Lunch served** *Oct-May* 11.30am-2pm Fri. **Dinner served** 5.30-10pm Tue-Sat. **Main courses** $16.95-$20. **Credit** AmEx, DC, MC, V. **Map 5 E5**

This romantic little restaurant has become one of the city's many culinary success stories. Owners Greg and Mary Sonnier started out working at such famous restaurants as **K-Paul's** *(p115)* and **Brigtsen's** *(p133)*, but their own place, located a few blocks from City Park and named after their daughter, has taken on contemporary touches of its own. Gulf fish with a shredded potato crust is a winner. *Booking essential.*

Try the best of 'New Cajun' cooking at **Brigtsen's** *in Riverbend. See page 133.*

The *Best* of times...

M R B'S BISTRO

Join us for Lunch, Dinner,
Sunday Jazz Brunch... ANYTIME!

201 Royal Street • French Quarter
504.523.2078

Creole

Christian's Restaurant
3835 Iberville Street, at N Scott Street (482 4924).
Bus 42 Canal, 43 Lake Vista. **Lunch served** 11.30am-
2pm Tue-Fri. **Dinner served** 5.30-9.30pm Tue-Sat.
Main courses $20. **Credit** AmEx, DC, MC, V.
Map 5 D5
Set within a former church and preserving the charm without the stuffiness, Christian's is for many locals a welcome
home away from home. Try the ever-popular crabcakes on
a sauce of green peppercorns and sun-dried tomatoes.
Booking recommended.

Italian

Liuzza's
3636 Bienville Street, at Telemachus Street (482 9120).
Bus 40, 41, 42, 43 Canal. **Open** 10.30am-10.30pm Mon-
Sat. **Main courses** $7.50. **No credit cards. Map 5 D5**
Fried seafood platters, heaped plates of spaghetti, onion
rings, cold beer in frozen mugs: Liuzza's is a 1947 Italian
restaurant that hasn't changed a dot, and thank god. The
waitresses can be snippy but they call you 'dawlin' and
treat you as one of the family. The bar that precedes the
restaurant is dim and cool and someone is always guf-
fawing at a joke that begins, 'A priest, a rabbi and a
Baptist minister went fishing...' Liuzza's is the kind of
place where Stanley Kowalski would take Stella out for a
really big celebration.

Venezia's
134 N Carrollton Avenue, at Canal Street (488 7991).
Bus 40 Canal/Lakeshore Express, 90 Carrollton.
Open 11am-10pm Mon-Thur; 11am-11pm Fri; 5-11pm
Sat. **Main courses** $6.95-$14.95. **Credit** AmEx, Disc,
MC, V. **Map 5 D5**
Venezia's offers that intrinsically New Orleans-style Italian
food that people either love or hate. The 'red' sauces are thick
and meaty, the cream sauces are thick and full of butter. The
staff are like family, which can be good or bad, depending.
The customers all seem to know each other. Check out the
intriguingly named eggplant Vatican, or stick to the
spaghetti with meat sauce, which is always a reliable choice.
Disabled: toilet.

Neighbourhood

Café Degas
*3127 Esplanade Avenue, at Ponce de Leon Street (945
5635). Bus 48 Esplanade.* **Brunch served** 10.30am-3pm
Sun. **Lunch served** 11.30am-2.30pm Mon-Fri. **Dinner
served** 5.30-10pm Mon-Thur; 6-11pm Fri, Sat; 6-10pm
Sun. **Main courses** $5.95-$17.95. **Credit** AmEx, DC,
MC, V. **Map 5 E5**
Named after the artist who briefly lived in the neighbourhood, Café Degas offers laid-back dining al fresco on its
large, breezy patio a few blocks from City Park. The menu
is well-grounded in French bistro food, including salade
Niçoise and vichyssoise.

Dooky Chase
*2301 Orleans Avenue, at Miro Street (821 2294). Bus
46 City Park.* **Open** 11.30am-10pm daily. **Main courses**
$6.50-$25. **Credit** AmEx, DC, MC, V. **Map 4 F6**
Chef Leah Chase has earned a national reputation for her
solid tributes to her native Creole cuisine. This is the place
to order things like fried chicken or stuffed bell peppers. Soul
food at it best. The Chases' admirable determination to
remain a part of a black neighbourhood doesn't alter the reality of the area. Take a cab to the front door of the restaurant.
Disabled: toilet.

Mandina's
3800 Canal Street, at N Cortez Street (482 9179).
Bus 41 Canal. **Open** 11am-10.30pm Mon-Sat; noon-
9.30pm Sun. **Main courses** $6-$13.95. **No credit
cards. Map 5 B5**
As a waiter recently declared, 'Nothing's changed here in 75
years!' Quite a few schemes and dreams have been launched
at Mandina's over plates of stuffed bell peppers with red
gravy, corned beef and cabbage and other down-home
delights. Mandina's is also famous for its stiff drinks. Even
if the crowd looks intimidating, fight your way to the front
of the bar to tell the bartender you want a table. He keeps
the list in his head but never puts a foot wrong in keeping it
moving and in the right order.

Michael's Mid-City Grill
4139 Canal Street, at N Carrollton Avenue (486 8200).
Bus 43 Canal/Lake Vista, 90 Carrollton. **Open** 11am-
10pm Mon Thur; 11am-11pm Fri, Sat. **Main courses**
$6-$12. **Credit** AmEx, DC, MC, V. **Map 5 D5**
Michael's is a true neighbourhood restaurant and bar, where
the food is relatively inexpensive and mostly pub-quality,
with sandwiches, hamburgers and appetisers dominating
the menu. It also turns out very good seafood dishes that are
always served with broccoli (it's been the vegetable of the
day for years) and potato. But the place is perhaps best-
known for its publicity-stunt 'Big Bucks Burger' – a $100
hamburger, topped with caviar and served with a bottle of
Dom Perignon. Anybody who orders this monstrosity has
their photo taken and added to the gallery of other 'Big
Bucks' faces on the wall.

Palmer's Jamaican/Creole Cuisine
135 N Carrollton Avenue, at Canal Street (482 3658).
Bus 43 Canal/Lake Vista, 90 Carrollton. **Lunch served**
11.30am-2pm Tue-Fri. **Dinner served** 6-10.30pm Tue-
Sat. **Main courses** $5.95-$10.95. **No credit cards.**
Map 5 D5
Who knew there was a Jamaican cuisine? Owner Cecil Palmer
contented himself for years with sneaking Caribbean touches into his Continental cooking in restaurants around the city.
Now, in his own no-frills establishment in Mid City, he lets
his native tongue speak loud and clear, with dishes like jerk
pork, chicken or fish, or the even more traditional curry goat.

Vegetarian & wholefood

Whole Foods Market
*3135 Esplanade Avenue, at Ponce de Leon Street (943
1626). Bus 48 Esplanade.* **Open** 8.30am-9.30pm daily.
Main courses $1.99-$7.99. **Credit** AmEx, Disc, MC, V.
Map 5 E5
The city's most popular health-food grocery store, Whole
Food also does good business as a deli-café. The deli section
is packed with daily specials ranging from an enchilada
casserole, to Thai chicken salad or pasta Prima Donna. Try
the crawfish lasagne or the two-bean casserole served in
flour tortillas. Deli sandwiches are made fresh to order, as
are the daily-changing soups and delicious fruit smoothies.

Bywater

Neighbourhood

Bywater Bar-B-Q
3162 Dauphine Street, at Louisa Street (944 4445).
Bus 82 Desire. **Open** 11am-10pm Tue-Thur; 11am-
midnight Fri, Sat; 11am-10pm Sun. **Main courses** $7.
No credit cards.
In a neighbourhood still undergoing regeneration (the
process may take some time), this place serves pleasant barbecued dishes in a casual, bohemian setting.

Jack Dempsey's

738 Poland Avenue, near St Claude Avenue (943 9914).
Bus 88 St Claude. **Lunch served** 11am-1.30pm
Tue-Fri. **Dinner served** 5-8.30pm Wed, Thur; 5-9.30pm
Fri; 4-9.30pm Sat. **Main courses** $5. **Credit** AmEx, DC,
MC, V.
Named after the famous boxer, this is one of few restaurants
within the city limits to offer family-style dining with enormous portions of fried seafood served in great mounds.
Located in Faubourg Bywater – once a suburb and a good
15 minutes' drive from the French Quarter – it's a restaurant with character, where the waitresses call you 'sweetie'
and the walls are decorated with photo after photo of the
eponymous pugilist

Further Afield

Asian

Taj Mahal Indian Restaurant

923 Metairie Road, at Rosa Street, Metairie (836 6859).
Bus 27 Louisiana, 40, 41 or 44 Canal, 48 Esplanade,
then E4 Metairie Road. **Lunch served** 11.30am-2.30pm,
dinner served 5.30-10.30pm, Tue-Sun. **Main courses**
$6.95-$14. **Credit** AmEx, DC, MC, V.
The Taj is located in a nondescript metal building hidden
behind a florist shop, so the name might seem like a joke at
first, but it is one of the area's hidden treasures. Inside, the
atmosphere is soothing and suburban-upscale, with starched
napery and comfortable chairs. Just about everything on the
menu is great, from the complex curries to the nan, which is
made fresh in-house.
Disabled: toilet.
Website: www.shalimarno.com

Trey Yuen

600 N Causeway Boulevard, at Monroe Street,
Mandeville (626 4477). No public transport. **Lunch**
served 11.30am-2pm Wed-Fri. **Dinner served** 5-10pm
Mon-Sat. **Open** 11.30am-9.30pm Sun. **Main courses**
$6-$14. **Credit** AmEx, DC, MC, V.
A jade-green palace on the North Shore (with a sibling oper-
ation in Hammond), Trey Yuen dishes up exemplary Chinese
food that's worth the drive across the lake.
Branch: 2100 N Morrison Boulevard, at Columbus
Street, Hammond (345 6789).

Cajun

Charley G's

111 Veterans Memorial Boulevard, at Lake Avenue,
Metairie (837 6408). Bus 27 Louisiana, 40, 41 or 44
Canal, 48 Esplanade, then E1 Veterans Memorial
Boulevard. **Lunch served** 11am-2pm Mon-Fri.
Dinner served 5.30-10pm Mon-Thur; 5.30-11pm Fri.
Meals served 11am-8pm Sun. **Main courses** $11.
Credit AmEx, DC, MC, V.
This restaurant has single-handedly brought chic urban
dining to the suburbs. Charley G's specialises in creative
grilled dishes served up in a pleasant, upmarket and relaxed
setting. The grilled andouille appetiser is terrific, the gumbo
smoky and savoury and the seafood entrées have become
local favourites.
Disabled: toilet. Website: www.charleygs.com

Don's Seafood Hut

4801 Veterans Memorial Boulevard, at Clearview
Avenue, Metairie (889 1550). Bus 27 Louisiana,
40, 41 or 44 Canal, 48 Esplanade, then E1 Veterans
Memorial Boulevard. **Open** 11am-10pm Mon-Thur, Sun;
11am-11pm Fri, Sat. **Main courses** $7-$15. **Credit**
AmEx, DC, MC, V.

Although this is a bit of a drive from New Orleans, it offers
some of the best just-plain-old-seafood in the vicinity. Don's
is a fun, casual eatery that attracts fans from miles away.
The appetisers make it a grazer's paradise, while the gum-
bos are Lafayette-style, with extra roux for flavour and thickening. The seafood stuffing is fabulous in anything and the
creamy crab au gratin melts in the mouth.
Disabled: toilet.

Contemporary

Dakota

629 US 190, Covington (892 3712). No public
transport. **Lunch served** 11am-2.30pm Mon-Fri.
Dinner served 5-10pm Mon-Thur; 5-11pm Fri, Sat.
Open 11am-8pm Sun. **Main courses** $9-$15.
Credit AmEx, DC, MC, V.
Chef Kim Kringlie makes this restaurant worth the trip
across Lake Pontchartrain to the North Shore. Between its
wine list and the level of service, Dakota is one of the most
sophisticated and satisfying eateries in the metro area. Try
the crabmeat and brie soup.
Disabled: toilet.

Vega Tapas Café

2051 Metairie Road, at Bonnabel Boulevard, Metairie
(836 2007). Bus 27 Louisiana, 40, 41 or 44 Canal,
48 Esplanade, then E4 Metairie Road. **Dinner served**
6-10pm Mon-Thur; 6-11pm Fri, Sat. **Tapas** $4-$10.
Credit AmEx, DC, MC, V.
A veteran of several creative kitchens around New Orleans,
chef Alison Vega has devoted her latest venture to Spanish
tapas. Great wines by the glass add to the pleasure.
Disabled: toilet.

French/Continental

Crozier's

3216 W Esplanade Avenue, at N Causeway Boulevard,
Metairie (833 8108). St Charles Streetcar/bus
16 S Claiborne, 39 Tulane, 90 Carrollton, then E5
Causeway. **Dinner served** 5.30-10pm Tue-Sat. **Main**
courses $16-$20.
Credit AmEx, DC, MC, V.
Resisting the usual temptation of trading real French for
Cajun spices, Gerard Crozier sticks to his Gallic guns in this
lovely restaurant. Our favourite is the rack of lamb, done
simply but perfectly.
Disabled: toilet.

DeVille Bistro

2037 Metairie Road, at Bonnabel Boulevard,
Metairie (837 6900). Bus 27 Louisiana, 40, 41 or
44 Canal, 48 Esplanade, then E4 Metairie Road.
Brunch served 10am-2pm Sun. **Dinner served**
5.30-10pm Mon-Thur; 5.30-11pm Fri, Sat.
Main courses $10-$19.
Credit AmEx, Disc, MC, V.
Chef Christiane Engeran-Fisher and sous-chef Jennifer
Engeran have given a fresh spin to what was Chez Daniel,
without sacrificing its bistro appeal built on flavourful, most-
ly simple food at affordable prices.
Disabled: toilet.

La Provence

US 190, Big Branch (626 7662). No public transport.
Dinner served 5-11pm Wed-Sat. **Open** 1-9pm Sun.
Main courses $16. **Credit** AmEx, MC, V.
After more than 20 years, chef Chris Keragiorgiou continues
to thrive in his romantic French country inn on the North
Shore. Meals are best begun with pâté and not ended until
several courses and several wines have elapsed.
Disabled: toilet.

Italian

Andrea's

*3100 19th Street, opposite Lakeside Shopping Center,
Metairie (834 8583/andrea@aol.com). St Charles
Streetcar/bus 16 S Claiborne, 39 Tulane, 90 Carrollton,
then E5 Causeway.* **Open** 11am-11pm Mon-Fri, Sun;
5-11pm Sat. **Main courses** $8-$14. **Credit** AmEx, DC,
MC, V.

Andrea's has long been a bala____ Metairie landmark and once Andrea Apuzzo fills the role of the suburban Emeril
Lagasse. Apuzzo dominates his attractive dining room, offering gracious Mediterranean hospitality and demanding to
know what the customers think of his cooking, which is
always fine. Pasta dishes are a strength here – and don't miss
the shrimp Caprese.
Disabled: toilet. Website: www.nolaandrea.com

Carmine's

*4101 Veterans Memorial Boulevard, at Lake Villa Drive,
Metairie (455 7904). Bus 27 Louisiana, 40, 41 or 44
Canal, 48 Esplanade, then E1 Veterans Memorial
Boulevard.* **Open** 11am-10pm Mon-Thur; 11am-11pm Fri,
Sat; 11am-9pm Sun. **Main courses** $12-$15. **Credit**
AmEx, DC, MC, V.
You may never have heard of New Orleans-Italian cuisine,
but it really is different from Italian food elsewhere. This is
one of the city's best-loved neighbourhood Italian restaurants, offering thick, creamy sauces and huge plates of
steaming pasta and fish. The place for sustaining Italian
food, American-style.

La Riviera

*4506 Shores Drive, at Clearview Parkway &
W Esplanade Avenue, Metairie (888 6238). St Charles
Streetcar/bus 16 S Claiborne, 39 Tulane, 90 Carrollton,
then E5 Causeway.* **Lunch served** 11.30am-2pm Tue-
Fri. **Dinner served** 5.30-10pm Mon-Sat. **Main courses**
$16. **Credit** AmEx, DC, MC, V.
Valentino Rovere has picked up where his uncle, the personable chef Goffredo Fraccaro, left off. This is a popular
suburban meeting place that's also one of the most successful Italian restaurants in the metro area.
Disabled: toilet.

Mediterranean

Casablanca

*3030 Severn Avenue, at Lakeside Shopping Center,
Metairie (888 2209). St Charles Streetcar/bus
16 S Claiborne, 39 Tulane, 90 Carrollton, then E5
Causeway.* **Open** 11am-10pm Mon-Thur; 11am-4pm Fri;
after Shabbat-11pm Sat; noon-9pm Sun. **Main courses**
$6.95-$12.95. **Credit** AmEx, DC, MC, V.
Designed within the kosher framework observed by the chef-proprietors, Casablanca has been a Metairie Middle Eastern
favourite for nearly a decade. Familiar dishes are given fresh
treatment here, among them falafel, couscous, tanxia fassi
(baked lamb) and gyros.
Disabled: toilet. Website: www.kosherzone.com

Petra

*541 Oaklawn Drive, at Veterans Memorial Boulevard,
Metairie (833 3317). Bus 27 Louisiana, 40, 41 or 44
Canal, 48 Esplanade, then E1 Veterans Memorial
Boulevard.* **Lunch served** 11am-2pm Mon-Fri.
Dinner served 5-9.30pm Mon-Thur; 5-10pm Fri, Sat.
Main courses $10-$15. **Credit** AmEx, DC, MC, V.
Borrowing its name from the ancient city in Jordan, Petra
takes advantage of the growing trend for Mediterranean
cooking. The restaurant is decorated to death with floral fabric from floor to ceiling, but the coolest thing is the little private booths built into the walls and closed off with curtains.

All very romantic if the Laura Ashley patterns don't stifle
your fantasies. The food is a creative mixture of Middle
Eastern, North African and Greek.
Disabled: toilet.

Neighbourhood

Abita Brew Pub

*72011 Holly Street, in the Downtown Square, Abita ____ ____ (____@____.com). No public
transport.* **Open** 11am-10pm Mon-Fri; 11am-11pm Sat,
Sun (drinks served until 1.30am). **Main courses** $6.95-
$14.95. **Credit** AmEx, DC, MC, V.
Attached to the local brewery and creator of many an enjoyable bottle of pilsner and ale, this quaint restaurant at the
edge of 'downtown' Abita can be worth the long trip across
the lake (it's about 35 minutes' drive from New Orleans). The
surroundings are extremely casual, the food less so.
Disabled: toilet. Website: www.abita.com

Barreca's

*3100 Metairie Road, at N Causeway Boulevard, Metairie
(831 4546). St Charles Streetcar/bus 16 S Claiborne, 39
Tulane, 90 Carrollton, then E5 Causeway.* **Open** 11am-
9pm Mon-Thur; 11am-10pm Fri; 3-10pm Sat; 11am-8pm
Sun. **Main courses** $8.95-$22.95. **Credit** AmEx, DC,
MC, V.
This operation serves Creole and Italian dishes that are
sophisticated enough to attract diners from outside its vicinity. Fish and veal entrées tend to rule the roost.
Disabled: toilet.

Byblos

*1501 Metairie Road, at Bonnabel Boulevard, Metairie
(834 9773). Bus 27 Louisiana, 40, 41 or 44 Canal,
48 Esplanade, then E4 Metairie Road.* **Open** 11am-10pm
daily. **Main courses** $9-$15. **Credit** AmEx, DC, MC, V.
Despite its suburban, strip mall location, Byblos is one of
New Orleans's best ethnic restaurants. The food is superb,
the staff is well-trained and helpful and the café itself is
comfortable and well-appointed. All the Lebanese signature dishes are here: houmous, kibbeh, baba ganoush,
lamb, tabbouleh and a multitude of kebabs. The café is a
good spot for vegetarians. The sample platters are an
excellent way to avoid having to choose among many
tempting dishes.

Deanie's Seafood in Bucktown

*1713 Lake Avenue, at Veterans Memorial Boulevard,
Metairie (831 4141). Bus 27 Louisiana, 40, 41 or 44
Canal, 48 Esplanade, then E1 Veterans Memorial
Boulevard.* **Open** 11am-10pm Mon-Thur, Sun; 11am-11pm
Fri, Sat. **Main courses** $7-$12. **Credit** AmEx, MC, V.
Located in the traditional, seafood section of Metairie long
known as 'Bucktown', Deanie's harkens back to the old
days, when New Orleanians drove out to the shores of Lake
Pontchartrain to dine on the freshest seafood cooked just
feet from where it was unloaded from the fishing boats.
Deanie's still specialises in producing absurdly large portions of boiled or fried seafood, all cooked with just the right
amount of spice. In another nod to the past, it serves cold,
spicy boiled new potatoes rather than bread while diners
wait for their food.
Disabled: toilet.

Mosca's

*4137 US 90 West, Waggaman (436 9942). No public
transport.* **Dinner served** 5.30-9.30pm Tue-Sat. **Main
courses** $10-$24. **No credit cards**.
Even the rigours of the Huey P Long Bridge cannot dissuade
devotees from making their way to this funky roadside
Italian pilgrimage point. Oysters Mosca is the mantra,
though the chicken should complete the garlic festival.
Booking recommended Tue-Fri; no bookings accepted Sat.

Cafés & Coffeehouses

Where to suffer a surfeit of beignets and café au lait.

For cybercafés, see *chapter* **Directory**.

French Quarter & Faubourg Marigny

Ben & Jerry's
537 St Ann Street, at Jackson Square (525 5950).
Bus 3 Vieux Carré, 55 Elysian Fields, 81 Almonaster,
82 Desire. **Open** 10am-9pm daily. **No credit cards.**
Map 7 C2
Sometimes, on a hot afternoon strolling through the Quarter, nothing is better than rich, creamy ice-cream. And nobody makes it better than those peace-loving guys from Vermont. The packaged version of this ice-cream can be found in gourmet groceries around the country, but this is where you'll find the hand-served kind, from their own distinctive shop.

Café du Monde
813 Decatur Street, opposite Jackson Square (581 2914).
Bus 3 Vieux Carré, 55 Elysian Fields, 81 Almonaster,
82 Desire. **Open** 24 hours daily. **No credit cards.**
Map 7 C3
For as long as there has been a New Orleans, it seems there has been Café du Monde. This aptly named sidewalk café is a gathering place for everybody who lives in, or visits, the city. Whether it's for a cup of steaming chicory-laced café au lait on a chilly night, or a plate of filling fried beignets (square doughnuts that come smothered with icing sugar) after a late night of drinking, this is the place everybody ends up. Open 24 hours, the café is at its best in the middle of the night, when the crowd is more eclectic and you never know what will happen next.
Website: www.cafedumonde.com

Coffee Pot
714 St Peter Street, at Royal Street (524 3500).
Bus 3 Vieux Carré, 55 Elysian Fields, 81 Almonaster,
82 Desire. **Open** 8am-midnight Mon-Thur, Sun; 8am-1am Fri, Sat. **Credit** AmEx, DC, MC, V.
Map 7 B2
There's a lot more going on at the Coffee Pot than omelettes and other late-night, sober-up breakfasts in the French Quarter. You could try the trout Conti after a starter of pungent shrimp rémoulade.

Croissant d'Or
617 Ursulines Street, at Chartres Street (524 4663).
Bus 3 Vieux Carré, 48 Esplanade, 55 Elysian Fields,
81 Almonaster, 82 Desire. **Open** 7am-5pm daily.
No credit cards. Map 7 C2
Ideal for breakfast or a light lunch, this little shop offers a wide variety of French pastries, with croissants leading the way. These can be huge and stuffed with blueberry sauce, or smaller and filled with cheese and ham. The café au lait is true New Orleans – equal parts strong chicory coffee and scalded milk.

Service with a smile at **Café du Monde.**

Haagen-Daz Ice Cream Parlour
621 St Peters Street, at Chartres Street (523 4001). Bus
3 Vieux Carré. **Open** 11am-midnight daily. **No credit cards. Map 7 B2**
Another option for ice-cream lovers in the French Quarter. If you find yourself a victim of a sudden craving for one of life's ultimate iced pleasures, the shop is near Jackson Square.

PJ's Coffee & Tea
634 Frenchman Street, at Royal Street (949 2292).
Bus 3 Vieux Carré, 48 Esplanade. **Open** 7am-11pm Mon-Thur, Sun; 7am-midnight Fri, Sat. **Credit** AmEx, MC, V.
This is where the local concept of coffeeshops was invented. Owned by coffee maven Phylis Jordan (PJ), these shops almost all have sunny patios for outdoor sipping, great, strong coffee and simple, sweet pastries, or crunchy bagels with cream cheese fillings. Try PJ's Vienna iced coffee (cold-brewed coffee with a hint of vanilla) or the low-calorie

granita on a hot day. There are several branches across town: check the phone book for your nearest.
Website: www.pjscoffee.com

Royal Blend Coffee & Tea

621 Royal Street, at Toulouse Street (523 2716/ royalblendcoffee.com). Bus 3 Vieux Carré, 55 Elysian Fields, 81 Almonaster, 82 Desire. **Open** 7am-midnight daily. **Credit** MC, V. **Map 7 B2**
Another of the city's marvellous coffeeshops, this one is hidden away in a courtyard, and offers light snacks ranging from salads to sandwiches. You might opt for the lox and bagel, or go for the French twist, a cinnamon puff pastry.
Branch: 244 Metairie Road, at Stella Street, Metairie (835 7779).

Local success story **PJ's Coffee & Tea**.

True Brew

200 Julia Street, at Fulton Street (524 8441). Bus 3 Vieux Carré, 10 Tchoupitoulas. **Open** 6.30am-8.30pm Mon-Fri; 7.30am-8.30pm Sat, Sun. **Credit** MC, V.
Map 6 C2
This is an eccentric combination of coffeeshop, lunching spot and theatre. Most of the time it's an arty coffeehouse in the Warehouse District, which also serves healthy sandwiches and soups at lunchtime. In the evenings, however, it converts into a theatre for local acting troupes.
Disabled: toilets.

Garden District

Java News Roasters

1907 St Charles Avenue, at Jackson Avenue (529 5282). St Charles Streetcar. **Open** 7am-7pm daily. **No credit cards. Map 6 B3**
Located on a fairly bland stretch of St Charles Avenue, the Java News is a popular spot with Euro-teens from the nearby Marquette House hostel, giving the place a certain international flair. Coffee is the main event here, backed up by a variety of pastries and rolls. Magazines and a few newspapers are also on sale.

Rue de la Course

1500 Magazine Street, at Race Street (899 0242). Bus 11 Magazine. **Open** 7am-11pm Mon-Thur, Sun; 7am-midnight Fri, Sat. **No credit cards. Map 6 B3**
A small, laid-back coffeeshop with a dizzying array of coffees, teas and pastries, Rue is usually packed with bohemian types hanging out.
Branch: 3128 Magazine Street, at Ninth Street (529 1455).

Uptown

CC's Gourmet Coffee House

1452 Louisiana Avenue, at Prytania Street (899 1866). St Charles Streetcar. **Open** 6.30am-10pm Mon-Sat; 7.30am-10pm Sun. **Credit** AmEx, Disc, MC, V. **Map 6 A3**
Community Coffee (based in Baton Rouge), best known for its packaged coffee which is served in virtually every restaurant and home in town, has opened its own café. The coffees are fine, but the pastries by chef John Folse are even better.
Branch: 900 Jefferson Avenue, at Magazine Street (891 4969).

Coffee & Company

7708 Maple Street, at Burdette Street (861 8843). St Charles Streetcar. **Open** 7am-10pm daily. **Credit** MC, V. **Map 4 B8**
With its trademark combination of coffee and light, deli cuisine, Coffee & Co offers the best of everything. Two of the best bets from the edible selection include the Reuben

sandwich (corned beef, sauerkraut and Muenster cheese with Thousand Island dressing) and the grilled chicken Caesar pasta salad. There's also a huge array of flavoured coffees and tea. Go for the iced coffee on hot days.
Branches: 800 Harrison Avenue, at Canal Boulevard (488 8746).

Hansen's Sno-Bliz

4801 Tchoupitoulas Street (no phone). Bus 10 Tchoupitoulas. **Open** *daily in summer.* **No credit cards.**
In the summer, New Orleanians will go anywhere for 'snowballs' – paper cones filled with finely shaved ice and a rainbow of different heavily sugared syrups. Here's the no-frills stall that invented the machine that shaves the ice that… you get the picture.

Mid City

Angelo Brocato's

214 N Carrollton Avenue, at Canal Street (486 0078). Bus 90 Carrollton. **Open** 9.30am-10pm Mon-Thur, Sun; 9.30am-10.30pm Fri, Sat. **Credit** MC, V. **Map 5 D5**
When it comes to tradition, it doesn't get any better than this. The little shop's name can still be found printed in tile on the sidewalk outside its former location on Dumaine Street. Today, the shop is tucked away deep in the heart of Mid City. All its desserts are steeped in old-Italian traditions, although the shop itself looks like a Norman Rockwell painting of a turn-of-the-century ice-cream shop. Go directly for the cannoli, or the vanilla pudding, or the tiramisu…

Further Afield

Coffee Cottage

2559 Metairie Road, at Labarre Road, Metairie (833 3513). Bus 27 Louisiana, 40, 41 or 44 Canal, 48 Esplanade, then E4 Metairie Road. **Open** 7am-11pm Mon-Thur; 7am-midnight Fri, Sat; 7am-10pm Sun.
The house speciality is the chef-owner John Caluda's white chocolate bread pudding with, what else, white chocolate sauce on top. On a savoury note, try the Rio Grande roasted chicken focaccia.

Morning Call

Lakeside Plaza, 3325 Severn Avenue, at 17th Street, Metairie (885 4068). Bus 27 Louisiana, 40, 41 or 44 Canal, 48 Esplanade, then E4 Metairie Road. **Open** 24 hours daily. **No credit cards.**
New Orleanians can almost say, 'Do you remember what you were doing when Morning Call moved to Metairie?' Well, suffice it to say, the move did bring top-flight beignets and café au lait to a part of the metro area that knew them not.

Shops & Services

Kit yourself out for Mardi Gras, load up on Louisiana spices or join the mall rats, with the help of our essential consumer guide.

New Orleans shopping is very much like the city itself – decadent, festive and with an eccentric suprise around every corner. Don't expect to stock up on bargains in electronics or drop a bundle on Yves St Laurent – shopping is high adventure, rather than high fashion or hi-tech. This is the place to look for the sinful, the impractical, the fun. Shop for Mardi Gras memorabilia, masks and costumes, European antiques, old and new jewellery, voodoo relics, local music and literature, new and second-hand books and records, vintage clothing and local food such as pralines.

Walking is the best way to shop, especially in the French Quarter and the Warehouse District.

You can travel by bus or streetcar to the Riverbend and Magazine Street shopping areas, but you'll need a car to visit the suburban malls or discount stores. Rather than driving, it's more fun to choose one shopping district, then take your time and poke around. You're bound to find something you've never seen before but just can't live without.

SALES TAX

A hefty nine per cent sales tax is added to the displayed price of most goods and services. Foreigners can recoup this by shopping in any of the stores that display a tax-free sign (there're more than 1,100 of them). Get a voucher and a sales receipt

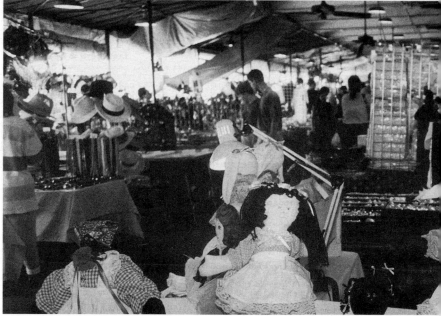

Souvenir-hunters should head for the French Market on Decatur Street, where bric-à-brac stalls ru

when you make your purchase and obtain a rebate at the Louisiana Tax Free Shopping (LTFS) Refund Center at New Orleans International Airport when you leave (568 5323). Refunds of $500 and less are made in cash; refunds of more than $500 will by paid by cheque and posted to you. Phone 467 0723 for more information.

SHOPPING AREAS

The **French Quarter** is the shopping area that everyone visits. Although thronged with tourists and with more than its share of tacky T-shirt and souvenir shops (especially on Bourbon Street), it also houses antique shops and art galleries along Royal Street; funky, new and second-hand clothing stores, many along Chartres Street and Decatur Street; a flea market; new and used book and record shops; clothing boutiques and small specialist shops.

Canal Street was *the* place to shop in the 1950s and 1960s and **Maison Blanche** (*see page 148*) is the last great department store still in business there. The shoppers on the street have changed from ladies clad in hats and gloves to tourists and downtown workers on their lunch break. Now, athletic shoe shops, electronics stores and souvenir shops rub shoulders with longstanding New Orleans merchants. It's worth a stroll just to experience the city's once-famous main street.

Magazine Street comprises six miles (9.7 kilometres) of shops and residences that stretch west from Canal Street all the way up to Audubon Park. The spending opportunities keep growing as new and vibrant shops and galleries pop up all the time. You'll find coffeehouses, bookstores, second-hand clothing, antiques, jewellery, designer shoes and works by local artists, often at prices below those in the French Quarter. The best bargains are on lower Magazine, between Race Street and Jackson Avenue (1300-2100 blocks), while the upper end between Louisiana Avenue and Audubon Park (3400-6000 blocks) is more upmarket.

The **Warehouse District** is an arty slice of New Orleans bounded roughly by Poydras Street, the Mississippi River, St Charles Avenue and the Pontchartrain Expressway. A mix of residential and commercial development since its earliest days as the 'American' section of the city, this area has blossomed into a place to find contemporary artworks by local and regional artists and unusual gifts such as hand-blown glass. At the bottom of Poydras Street, next to the Mississippi, is the **Riverwalk**, a covered shopping mall (*see page 147* **Shopping malls**).

Riverbend can be reached by taking the St Charles Streetcar to the end of St Charles Avenue, where it meets Carrollton Avenue. This compact,

day.

horseshoe-shaped area, surrounding a strip shopping centre, can be walked easily and contains a good mix of upmarket clothing and jewellery stores housed in old-fashioned cottages. From Riverbend, stroll the eight or so blocks down tree-filled **Maple Street**, in the heart of the university area. It's lined with bookstores, clothing and accessory shops and coffeehouses catering to the students who attend nearby Tulane and Loyola Universities.

Old Metairie is a stuffy upper-class neighbourhood that was New Orleans's first modern suburb. The main artery, Metairie Road, is lined with strip shopping centres and speciality shops. Most tourists don't venture this far, but if you've got a car (travelling by bus is possible but unreliable), you can turn up some interesting clothes and household items.

Outside New Orleans, there are discount shops in the suburbs at giant superstores such as Wal-Mart or Sam's Club (where you need a membership card, $35) or at the discount shopping malls in Slidell or Gonzales. But they're not really worth the effort of travelling so far for so little.

Department stores

Dillard
Lakeside Shopping Center, 3301 Veterans Memorial Boulevard, at N Causeway Boulevard, Metairie (833 1075). St Charles Streetcar/bus 16 S Claiborne, 39 Tulane, 90 Carrollton, then E5 Causeway. **Open** 10am-9pm Mon-Sat; noon-6pm Sun. **Credit** AmEx, DC, Disc, MC, V.
Outfit the entire family or decorate the home at this regional store, which has four locations in the greater New Orleans area. It's conservative in feel and geared towards conven-

Shopping malls

DOWNTOWN MALLS
These three downtown shopping malls are conveniently within walking distance of many hotels and tourist attractions, but are smaller than the suburban malls.

Canal Place Shopping Center
333 Canal Street, at Decatur Street (522 9200). Bus 41 Canal. **Open** 10am-6pm Mon-Wed; 10am-7pm Thur-Sat; noon-6pm Sun. **Map 6 C1**
At the foot of 'world-famous Canal Street', this mall is at the top of the shopping food chain in New Orleans, and has a relaxed and elegant atmosphere. The chains – such as Saks Fifth Avenue, Laura Ashley, Pottery Barn, The Limited, Williams Sonoma, The Limited Express, Gucci and Bally – carry the same merchandise as in all their other stores nationwide. Locally owned and operated Weinstein's sells fine and hip but expensive clothing for women (wool sweaters from $300), and an exclusive selection of wonderful Italian designer labels. Linens is a local shop with a good selection of fine linens and clothes for infants and children. For local contemporary arts and crafts, try **RHINO** (*see p156*).
Disabled: toilets.

New Orleans Centre
1400 Poydras Street, next to the Louisiana Superdome (568 0000). Bus 16 S Claiborne. **Open** 10am-8pm Mon-Sat; noon-6pm Sun. **Map 6 B1**
Built in the late 1980s, surrounded by office buildings and anchored by national department stores Macy's and Lord & Taylor (the only branch in New Orleans), this mall caters to business people. The selection of business outfits at Macy's is better here than at its suburban store. Lord & Taylor has a great women's shoe department. Other shops include the usual suspects like Gap and Victoria's Secret.

Riverwalk
1 Poydras Street, at the Mississippi River (522 1555). Riverfront Streetcar/bus 3 Vieux Carré, 10 Tchoupitoulas. **Open** 10am-9pm Mon-Sat; 11am-7pm Sun. **Map 6 C1**

Right on the Mississippi, and worth visiting just for the view of the river, Riverwalk is best known as the mall that was hit by an out-of-control Chinese vessel in December 1996. When not watching for runaway ships, you can shop at over 100 stores, including Banana Republic, Gap, Gap Kids and Abercrombie & Fitch. The shops cater to tourists, so prices for souvenirs and gifts are higher than elsewhere in town.

SUBURBAN MALLS
If you are planning a major shopping trip, consider visiting the suburban malls in Jefferson Parish, where the sales tax is 8.75 per cent, instead of 9 per cent in Orleans Parish.

The Esplanade
1401 W Esplanade Avenue, near Williams Boulevard, Kenner (465 2161). Bus Kenner loop. **Open** 10am-9pm Mon-Sat; noon-6pm Sun.
The largest and busiest mall in town, anchored by Macy's and regional department stores Dillard's and Mervyn's. Mervyn's is the cheaper of the two, without the designer clothes. You'll find just about everything except hardware in the Esplanade's 135 stores. If you're driving, head west on I-10 and take the Williams Boulevard exit.

Lakeside Shopping Center
3301 Veterans Memorial Boulevard, at N Causeway Boulevard, Metairie (835 8000). St Charles Streetcar/ bus 16 S Claiborne, 39 Tulane, 90 Carrollton, then E5 Causeway. **Open** 10am-9pm Mon-Sat; noon-6pm Sun.
One of the oldest malls in the country, refurbished in the 1990s. It lacks the larger stores found in the Esplanade, but the pace is less hectic and the layout more straightforward. You'll find the usual chains, such as Gap, The Limited, The Limited Express, Old Navy and Victoria's Secret. The latest addition is Restoration Hardware, which has stores in 20 states and is full of great stuff, from furniture to hardware. Our favourites include a faux sheepskin dog's toy in the shape of a man, called 'Bite the Man' ($6), and the Tim Allen hammer (star of the US TV series *Home Improvement*) by Hart tools ($32).

tional tastes, but has generally reasonable prices in a wide variety of merchandise. Check the *Times-Picayune* for advertised special deals.

Branches: Belle Promenade Mall, Marrero (348 7100); The Esplanade Mall, Kenner (468 6050); Oakwood Shopping Center, Gretna (362 4800).

JC Penney

Lakeside Shopping Center, 3301 Veterans Memorial Boulevard, at N Causeway Boulevard, Metairie (837 9880). St Charles Streetcar/bus 16 S Claiborne, 39 Tulane, 90 Carrollton, then E5 Causeway. **Open** 10am-9pm Mon-Sat; noon-6pm Sun. **Credit** AmEx, Disc, MC, V.

An old standby in US shopping, offering a decent selection of clothing and housewares at moderate prices. A catalogue sales and phone ordering service is also available.

Macy's

New Orleans Centre, 1400 Poydras Street, next to the Louisiana Superdome (592 5985). Bus 16 S Claiborne. **Open** 10am-8pm Mon-Sat; noon-6pm Sun. **Credit** AmEx, MC, V. **Map 6 B1**

The New York department store with an outpost in New Orleans (and plenty of other US cities). Its basement still yields frequent deals on housewares although the legendary bargain basement is a thing of the past. Macy's is good for moderate to high-end clothing, shoes and make-up, and also has frequent sales, offering 20-40% discounts on men's and women's clothing.

Branch: The Esplanade (465 3985).

Maison Blanche

901 Canal Street, at Dauphine Street (566 1000). Bus 41 Canal. **Open** 9.30am-6pm Mon-Wed, Sat; 9.30am-7pm Thur, Fri; noon-5.30pm Sun. **Credit** AmEx, DC, Disc, MC, V. **Map 7 A1**

'MB' is the last of the great Canal Street department stores, chock full of men's and women's clothing, cosmetics, jewellery, shoes and fashion accessories. The selection in some departments may be more extensive in the newer suburban stores, but they don't have the old charm that still pervades the fancy white building on Canal Street, an architectural eye-catcher and a New Orleans shopping landmark. You'll need a car to reach the other branches.

Branches: Clearview Mall, Metairie (889 7000); Lake Forest Plaza (241 8121); Oakwood Shopping Center, Gretna (362 5300).

Saks Fifth Avenue

Canal Place Shopping Center, 333 Canal Street, at Decatur Street (524 2200). Bus 41 Canal. **Open** 10am-6pm Mon-Sat; noon-6pm Sun. **Credit** AmEx, DC, Disc, MC, V. **Map 6 C1**

Recently expanded, this hoity-toity, upscale store has fine-quality clothing for men and women, a good shoe department and the latest cosmetics from the likes of Bobby Brown.

Antiques

Auction houses

For antiques shopping, New Orleans is right up there with Paris. Designers from Los Angeles and New York make the trip for the wide selection and competitive prices – especially of European antiques. If you're seriously interested in furniture buying, the auction houses offer the best bargains. Even if you're not interested in buying anything, auctions are great fun and browsing the previews gives you a chance to check out European and American treasures from the estates of wealthy Southern families. Contact the auction houses below for sales dates and catalogues (annual subscriptions cost $50-$300) or check their websites. Remember that a buyer's premium of ten per cent is added to the hammer price, and that US residents pay an additional nine per cent sales tax. The auction companies do not ship or pack goods themselves but will work with you and their regularly used services.

Neal Auction Company

4038 Magazine Street, at Marengo Street (899 5329). Bus 11 Magazine. **Open** 9am-5pm Mon-Fri. **Credit** Disc, MC, V. **Map 4 D10**

The older of the two local auction houses and strongest in American and English furniture, porcelain, paintings, prints, sculptures, jewellery and oriental rugs. Anything that isn't sold at the Magazine Street showroom goes to a warehouse in Carondelet Street, where no-minimum-bid auctions are sometimes held.

Website: www.nealauction.com

New Orleans Auction Galleries

510 Julia Street, at Magazine Street (566 1849). Bus 11 Magazine. **Open** 9am-5pm Mon-Fri. **No credit cards**. **Map 6 C2**

The newest auction house, opened in 1991 has a high-end gallery on Julia Street and an outlet for less expensive items at St Charles Avenue. It set a record for Southern art in March 1997 with the sale of 'Steamboats Round the Bend' by John McCrady (1911-68) for an impressive $308,000. The emphasis is on French and European antiques; look for rosewood armoires and cypress linen presses.

Branch: 1330 St Charles Avenue (586 8733).

Website: www.neworleansauction.com

Antique stores

In New Orleans there is a bar or church on every corner and an antique store in between. Most of the established stores are concentrated on Magazine Street and in the French Quarter; those on Royal Street are highly reputable establishments often run by third- and fourth-generation family members. This high concentration translates into competitive prices, while the longevity of the establishments is reflected in the range of stock. However grand the surroundings, the staff and owners are usually friendly and knowledgeable. Here's a selection of the best and most unusual stores.

Animal Arts Antiques

617 Chartres Street, at Wilkinson Row (529 4407). Bus 55 Elysian Fields, 81 Almonaster, 82 Desire. **Open** 10am-5pm Mon-Sat. **Credit** AmEx, Disc, MC, V. **Map 7 B2**

A veritable menagerie, from dead duck paintings to a live dog on the premises.

As You Like It

3025 Magazine Street, at Seventh Street (897 6915). Bus 11 Magazine. **Open** 10am-5pm Mon-Sat. **Credit** AmEx, Disc, MC, V. **Map 6 A3**

An entire store of silver flatware (cutlery), serving pieces and tea sets – it's enough to make your polishing rag do a jig.

The **Neal Auction Company**: *helping to put New Orleans on a par with Paris when it comes to antiques shopping.*

Bep's Antiques
2109 Magazine Street, at Josephine Street (525 7726).
Bus 11 Magazine. **Open** 10am-5pm Mon-Sat.
Credit AmEx, Disc, MC, V. **Map 6 B3**
A small and charming store packed full of rural American
and European pine and oak furniture.

Centuries Old Maps & Prints
517 St Louis Street, at Chartres Street (568 9491).
Bus 3 Vieux Carré, 55 Elysian Fields, 81 Almonaster,
82 Desire. **Open** 10.30am-6pm Mon-Thur; 10.30am-6.30pm
Fri, Sat; 11am-6pm Sun. **Credit** AmEx, Disc, MC, V.
Map 7 B2
In a city that has been governed by three different countries
since the seventeenth century, maps are an important and
interesting link to the past. A great place for history buffs,
but don't rely on the staff; if you have a serious question, ask
the owner.

Charbonnet & Charbonnet
2728 Magazine Street, at Washington Street
(891 9948). Bus 11 Magazine. **Open** 9am-5.30pm Mon-
Sat. **Credit** MC, V.
Map 6 A/B3
A collection of antique pine and cypress cupboards and
tables is complemented by custom-made furniture made
using old cypress wood. Single-bed headboards made from
old cypress pocket doors start at $375.

Civil War Store
212 Chartres Street, at Iberville Street (522 3328).
Bus 3 Vieux Carré, 41 Canal, 55 Elysian Fields, 81
Almonaster, 82 Desire. **Open** 10.30am-6.30pm daily.
Credit AmEx, Disc, MC, V. **Map 7 A2**
Sells anything you can think of from the American Civil War,
from Confederate money to musket balls.

Didier
3439 Magazine Street, at Louisiana Avenue
(899 7749). Bus 11 Magazine. **Open** 11am-5pm Mon-Fri;
by appointment Sat. **No credit cards.**
Map 6 A4
A green shuttered cottage with stencilled floors houses a collection of American city furniture, paintings and prints from
the nineteenth century. The prices are not for the faint-
hearted: dining room tables and rosewood tables cost
$16,000-$20,000.

Gerald D Katz
505 Royal Street, at St Louis Street (524 5050).
Bus 3 Vieux Carré, 55 Elysian Fields, 81 Almonaster,
82 Desire. **Open** 10am-5.30pm daily. **Credit** AmEx, MC, V.
Map 7 B2
The largest collection of antique and vintage jewellery in the
US, according to the owners, who, in old-fashioned shop-
keeper's style, live upstairs in this beautifully restored 1836
building. Half the collection is Victorian.
Website www.bijous.com

Keil's Antiques
325 Royal Street, at Conti Street (522 4552). Bus 3
Vieux Carré, 55 Elysian Fields, 81 Almonaster, 82
Desire. **Open** 9am-5pm Mon-Sat. **Credit** AmEx, MC, V.
Map 7 B2
An elegant store with friendly staff and diverse prices, spe-
cialising in eighteenth- and nineteenth-century French and
English antiques. New Orleans families have shopped here
since 1899. Fine gifts for under $100.

Find out what the future holds in store
for you at **Bottom of the Cup Tea Room**
& Gifts.

Lucullus
610 Chartres Street, at Wilkinson Row (528 9620).
Bus 3 Vieux Carré, 55 Elysian Fields, 81 Almonaster,
82 Desire. **Open** 9.30am-5pm Mon-Sat (summer closed
Mon). **Credit** AmEx, MC, V. **Map 7 B2**
From dining tables to porcelain fruit and vegetables, everything here is connected with food and eating. A clever concept and an imaginative collection.

Manheim Galleries
409 Royal Street, at Conti Street (568 1901).
Bus 3 Vieux Carré, 55 Elysian Fields, 81 Almonaster,
82 Desire. **Open** 9am-5pm Mon-Sat. **Credit** AmEx, Disc,
MC, V. **Map 7 B2**
This fourth-generation, family-owned business is housed in
a building designed by Benjamin Henry Latrobe, one of
the architects of the United States Capitol. There are five
floors of paintings, porcelain and furniture and a famous
jade room. The master carvers in the store's own cabinet
shop have produced custom-made furniture in walnut or
mahogany since 1898.

Moss Antiques
411 Royal Street, at Conti Street (522 3981).
Bus 3 Vieux Carré, 55 Elysian Fields, 81 Almonaster,
82 Desire. **Open** 9am-5pm Mon-Sat. **Credit** AmEx, MC,
V. **Map 7 B2**
A sister store to **Keil's Antiques** *(above)*, offering antique
and estate jewellery as well as French and English furniture.

MS Rau
630 Royal Street, at St Peter Street (523 5660).
Bus 3 Vieux Carré, 55 Elysian Fields, 81 Almonaster, 82
Desire. **Open** 9am-5.15pm Mon-Sat. **Credit** AmEx, MC,
V. **Map 7 B2**
In business since 1912 and in the present location since the
1930s, this is a third-generation, family-owned outfit. Look
out for the Reed and Barton 1920s sterling silver flatware set
– 296 pieces for $34,000 – which was originally displayed at
Marshall Fields department store in Chicago. There is also
an extensive cut glass collection.

Robinson's Antiques
329 Royal Street, at Conti Street (523 6683). Bus 3
Vieux Carré, 55 Elysian Fields, 81 Almonaster, 82
Desire. **Open** 10am-5pm Mon-Sat. **Credit** AmEx, DC,
Disc, MC, V. **Map 7 B2**
Owned by well-known antique dealer Henry Stern until his
death in 1993, this shop continues the high quality of merchandise and service for which he was known. You'll find
everything here: French and English furniture, silverware,
paintings, chandeliers and rugs.

Astrology & the occult

For palm readings at the **New Orleans Historic
Voodoo Museum**, *see page 91* **Museums &
Galleries**; for the Voodoo Spiritual Temple,
see page 50 **Sightseeing**.

Bottom of the Cup Tea Room & Gifts
732 Royal Street, at St Ann Street (523 1204).
Bus 3 Vieux Carré, 55 Elysian Fields, 81 Almonaster,
82 Desire. **Open** 10am-7pm daily. **Credit** AmEx, Disc,
MC, V. **Map 7 C2**
The grandmother of tearooms has been offering tarot and
tea leaf readings in the French Quarter since 1929. Audio-
taped readings are done in private – a 30-minute consulta-
tion costs $30 plus tax – and can be booked in advance.
There's also an assortment of tarot cards, crystals and astrological accessories on sale.
Branch: 616 Conti Street (524 1997).

Esoterica Occult Goods

*541 Dumaine Street, at Chartres Street (581 7711).
Bus 3 Vieux Carré, 55 Elysian Fields, 81 Almonaster,
82 Desire.* **Open** noon-9pm Mon-Thur, Sun; noon-
midnight Fri; 10am-noon Sat. **Credit** MC, V. **Map 7 C2**
Come here for crystal balls, candles, incense, oils and custom-made gris-gris bags (for holding voodoo charms). Self-
styled witches give tarot readings ($25 for 30 minutes) or
spiritual consultations ($40 for an hour). Walk-ins are wel-
come but it's better to make an appointment in advance. The
readings aren't recorded, but you're welcome to bring your
own tape recorder.

F&F Company

*801 N Broad Avenue, at Orleans Avenue (482 9142).
Bus 46 Canal.* **Open** 7.30am-6pm Mon-Sat. **Credit**
AmEx, Disc, DC, MC, V. **Map 4 F6**
Dubbed a spiritual church supply house, this shop has it all,
from statues of the saints to floorwash guaranteed to clean
out evil spirits. There are rows and rows of candles, and
jars of ancient herbs and roots for you to cook up your own
concoctions.

Golden Leaves Centre

*3242 Severn Avenue, at 17th Street, Metairie
(888 5208). St Charles Streetcar/bus 16 S Claiborne,
39 Tulane, 90 Carrollton, then E5 Causeway.* **Open**
10am-9pm Mon-Fri; 10am-7pm Sat; noon-6pm Sun.
Credit AmEx, Disc, MC, V.
This New Age and metaphysical bookstore and gift shop,
which has been in business since 1974, also offers taped
astrological readings ($55 plus $1 for the tape) and tarot readings ($45 plus $1 for the tape) in a private room. Book in
advance to guarantee an appointment.

Bookshops

Local branches of the big boys Barnes & Noble
and Bookstar are the places to find discounts on
bestsellers and recent hardbacks, but the inde-
pendents offer the best browsing, unusual finds
and expert assistance. Many have a good range
of books about New Orleans, including cook-
books. The only shop with an in-house café
is Barnes & Noble. The **Faubourg Marigny
Bookstore** has the most extensive collection of
gay and lesbian literature in New Orleans (*see
page 176* **Gay & Lesbian**). Visit the **Golden
Leaves Centre** (*see above*) has New Age and
spiritual books.

Afro-American Book Stop

*New Orleans Centre, 1400 Poydras Street, next to the
Louisiana Superdome (588 1474). Bus 16 S Claiborne.*
Open 10am-8pm Mon-Sat; noon-6pm Sun. **Credit** AmEx,
Disc, MC, V. **Map 6 B1**
An excellent selection of African-American and African
books, and knowledgeable, friendly staff. Author events are
held frequently.

B Dalton

*714 Canal Street, at St Charles Avenue (529 2705).
St Charles Streetcar/bus 41 Canal.* **Open** 9am-7pm Mon-
Sat; 11am-5pm Sun. **Credit** AmEx, Disc, MC, V.
Map 6 C1
A nationwide chain, with branches throughout the sub-
urbs, this is a good place for New Orleans maps, but in gen-
eral the selection is not as extensive as that at Barnes &
Noble or Bookstar. Check the phone book for your nearest
branch.

Barnes & Noble

*3721 Veterans Memorial Boulevard, near Lakeside
Shopping Center, Metairie (455 4929). St Charles
Streetcar/bus 16 S Claiborne, 39 Tulane, 90 Carrollton,
then E5 Causeway.* **Open** 9am-11pm daily. **Credit**
AmEx, DC, Disc, MC, V.
New Orleans's largest bookstore, with a full selection of local
subjects and authors, including self-published books.
Virtually indistinguishable from all other Barnes & Noble
superstores, but considered a good cruising spot for singles.

Beaucoup Books

*5414 Magazine Street, at Jefferson Avenue (895 2663).
Bus 11 Magazine.* **Open** 10am-6pm Mon-Sat; noon-5pm
Sun. **Credit** AmEx, Disc, MC, V. **Map 4 C9/10**
A classic neighbourhood bookstore, with excellent author
readings. The stock is small but carefully chosen, heavy on
literary fiction and New Orleans authors.

Best Seller Audio

*3501 Severn Avenue, at W Esplanade Avenue, Metairie
(455 0590). St Charles Streetcar/bus 16 S Claiborne,
39 Tulane, 90 Carrollton, then E5 Causeway.* **Open** 6am-
8pm Mon-Fri; 10am-8pm Sat; noon-6pm Sun. **Credit**
AmEx, DC, Disc, MC, V.
Stocks a comprehensive selection of books on tape, both
fiction and non-fiction.

Bookstar

*414 N Peters Street, at St Louis Street (523 6411).
Bus 3 Vieux Carré, 55 Elysian Fields, 81 Almonaster,
82 Desire.* **Open** 9am-midnight daily. **Credit** AmEx,
Disc, MC, V. **Map 7 B3**
Though part of a chain, this is arguably the city's best big
bookstore, particularly good on New Orleans and Louisiana
subjects, music books and fiction. It also stocks the best
selection of US and foreign periodicals in the city.

De Ville Books & Prints

*Riverwalk, 1 Poydras Street, at the Mississippi River
(595 8916). Riverfront Streetcar/bus 3 Vieux Carré,
10 Tchoupitoulas.* **Open** 10am-9pm Mon-Sat; 11am-7pm
Sun. **Credit** MC, V ($10 minimum). **Map 6 C1**
New Orleans distilled in a bookstore: urbane, charming,
eclectic and easygoing. Very knowledgeable staff oversee a
shop stocked with local favourites, an excellent history section and a very good collection of regional and local second-
hand books.
Branch: 344 Carondelet Street (525 1846).

Faulkner House Books

*624 Pirate's Alley, between St Peter & Orleans Street
(524 2940). Bus 3 Vieux Carré, 55 Elysian Fields, 81
Almonaster, 82 Desire.* **Open** 10am-6pm daily. **Credit**
AmEx, MC, V. **Map 7 B/C2**
Housed in the building where Nobel Prize winner William
Faulkner lived during his 1925 sojourn in New Orleans, this
shop specialises, of course, in Faulkner's books, including
rare and first editions. There's also a good selection of poet-
ry and literature, with a strong emphasis on local and
Southern writers.

Garden District Book Shop

*2727 Prytania Street, at Washington Avenue
(895 2266). St Charles Streetcar.* **Open** 10am-6pm Mon-
Sat; 11am-4pm Sun. **Credit** Disc, MC, V. **Map 6 A3**
Anne Rice's neighbourhood bookstore and a magnet for Rice
fans, who come for the autographed copies, special editions
and the author's appearance at special events.

Maple Street Bookshop

*7523 Maple Street, at Cherokee Street (866 4916).
St Charles Streetcar.* **Open** 9am-9pm Mon-Sat; 10am-6pm
Sun. **Credit** MC, V. **Map 4 B8**

Maple Street Bookshop's ubiquitous bumper sticker says 'Fight the Stupids', which it attempts to do from a rambling old house in Uptown stuffed with a good selection of fiction and non-fiction, many autographed by the authors. Next door (at No.7529) is Maple Street Children's Bookshop (861 2105).

Uptown Square Book Shop
200 Broadway Street, at River Road (865 8310). Bus 22 Broadway. **Open** 10am-6pm Mon-Sat; 1.30-5pm Sun **Credit** Disc, MC, V. **Map 4 A9**
Specialises in contemporary literature, including books on cassette, and has a good children's section.

Second-hand books

Beckham's Book Shop
228 Decatur Street, at Iberville Street (522 9875). Bus 3 Vieux Carré, 55 Elysian Fields, 81 Almonaster, 82 Desire. **Open** 10am-6pm daily. **Credit** Disc, MC, V. **Map 7 A3**
Two shabby floors of books, prints and pamphlets. A book lover's haven.

Great Acquisitions Books
8120 Hampson Street, at S Carrollton Avenue (861 8707). St Charles Streetcar. **Open** 10.30am-6pm Mon-Sat. **Credit** AmEx, Disc, MC, V.
The place for first editions and rare books. It has sections on art, music, photography, travel and history and is heavy on Louisiana and Southern literature. The helpful staff provide a free search service.

George Herget Books
3109 Magazine Street, at Eighth Street (891 5595). Bus 11 Magazine. **Open** 10am-6pm Mon-Sat; 11am-5.30pm Sun. **Credit** MC, V. **Map 6 A3/4**
Second-hand books, postcards and sheet music. It's musty, fusty, friendly and fun.

Kaboom Books
901 Barracks Street, at Dauphine Street (529 5780). Bus 3 Vieux Carré, 48 Esplanade. **Open** 11am-6pm daily. **No credit cards. Map 7 D1**
The character who runs this place will talk your ear off. There's a great assortment of classic and contemporary fiction, plus politics, philosophy and drama.

Cameras

New Orleans doesn't have a great selection of camera equipment, so don't hold out hopes of rock-bottom buys. Camera shops are usually small, with limited stock and scattered about various parts of the city. Although the string of camera and electronics stores along Canal Street, their windows filled to the brim, look tempting, they don't offer the reliability and expertise available in the smaller shops. If your camera needs mending, visit **AAA Camera Repair** (1631 St Charles Avenue; 561 5822).

Bennett's Camera & Video
3230 Severn Avenue, at 17th Street, Metairie (885 9050). St Charles Streetcar/bus 16 S Claiborne, 39 Tulane, 90 Carrollton, then E5 Causeway. **Open** 9am-6pm Mon-Sat. **Credit** AmEx, Disc, MC, V.
Bennett's aims to please. A good selection of many major brands of photographic tackle is stocked, plus darkroom supplies and digital imaging equipment.

Liberty Camera
337 Carondelet Street, at Poydras Street (523 6252). St Charles Streetcar. **Open** 9am-5.30pm Mon-Fri; 9am-2.30pm Sat. **Credit** AmEx, DC, Disc, MC, V. **Map 6 B1**
Stuffy but knowledgeable, with the usual brands – Nikon, Pentax, Minolta and Olympus – plus darkroom equipment and a small selection of second-hand cameras.

Wolf Camera & Video
Lakeside Shopping Center, 3301 Veterans Memorial Boulevard, at N Causeway Boulevard, Metairie (837 2665). St Charles Streetcar/bus 16 S Claiborne, 39 Tulane, 90 Carrollton, then E5 Causeway. **Open** 10am-9pm Mon-Sat; noon-6pm Sun. **Credit** AmEx, DC, Disc, MC, V.
A national chain that carries a decent selection of point-and-shoot cameras.
Branch: New Orleans Centre (581 6905).

Film processing

One-hour photo processing is available at drugstores Eckerd's and Walgreen's (check the phone book for your nearest branch), at most camera shops (including those listed above) and specialist labs. Check Sunday's *Times-Picayune* for discount coupons that can save you on film and developing. For expert colour processing, try **Primary Color Laboratory** near the Superdome (1116 Magnolia Street; 581 3444) or **Professional Color Service** in Metairie (604 Papworth Avenue; 835 3551).

Fox Photo
220 Baronne Street, at Common Street (523 4672). St Charles Streetcar/bus 41 Canal. **Open** 8am-5.30pm Mon-Fri. **Credit** AmEx, Disc, MC, V. **Map 6 B1**
One-hour photo developing within walking distance of the French Quarter. This branch is one of the only places, other than professional labs, that processes black and white film on the premises. Check the phone book for the location of the many other branches.

Computers

You're unlikely to be overwhelmed by the selection and level of assistance at most local computer dealers. Instead, consider buying a computer by mail from a reputable mail-order house such as **Dell** (1-800 472 3355), **Gateway** (1-800 846 2000) or **PC Connection** (1-800 846 0005).

CompUSA
8855 Veterans Memorial Boulevard, at David Drive, Metairie (468 3838). No public transport. **Open** 10am-9pm Mon-Sat; noon-6pm Sun. **Credit** AmEx, DC, MC, V.
This has the biggest selection (including a few Macs), with aisles of software, books and accessories and good prices. Fine if you know what you want but don't go to get educated about computers; the staff lack knowledge.

The Computer Shoppe
2125 Veterans Memorial Boulevard, between Bonnabel & N Causeway Boulevards (833 5100). St Charles Streetcar/bus 16 S Claiborne, 39 Tulane, 90 Carrollton, then E5 Causeway. **Open** 8am-6pm Mon-Thur; 8am-5pm Fri; 10am-4pm Sat. **Credit** AmEx, Disc, MC, V.
It's hard to find shops that sell or repair Macs in New Orleans, but this is probably the best place; it has been an Apple dealer since 1976.

The **French Market**: *selling fruit, veg and local produce through the night. For information on othe.*

PC Warehouse

*2222 Clearview Parkway, at I-10, Metairie (455 4699).
St Charles Streetcar/bus 16 S Claiborne, 39 Tulane, 90
Carrollton, then E5 Causeway.* **Open** 9am-6pm Mon-Fri.
Credit Disc, MC, V.
The store with the most knowledgeable sales staff, and no
hard sell. Prices are good, though not the cheapest.

Computer repair

A Prompt Computer Center

*1320 Veterans Memorial Boulevard, at Bonnabel
Boulevard, Metairie (830 3787). Bus 27 Louisiana,
40, 41 or 44 Canal, 48 Esplanade, then E1 Veterans
Memorial Boulevard.* **Open** 9am-5.30pm Mon-Fri.
Credit AmEx, Disc, MC, V.
Offers a 24-hour repair service for IBM-compatibles. Rentals
are also available.
Branch: 58 Westbank Expressway, Gretna (362 3922).

PC Tune-ups

*2716 Jefferson Highway, at S Causeway Boulevard,
Jefferson (828 9800). St Charles Streetcar/bus 16
S Claiborne, 39 Tulane, 90 Carrollton, then E5
Causeway.* **Open** 10am-7pm Mon-Fri; 10am-6pm Sat.
Credit AmEx, MC, V.
A helpful and accommodating mom-and-pop operation,
which builds and repairs computers – just tell them what
you want. Prices are competitive.

Dry-cleaning & laundry

In addition to the places listed below, you could
also try **Igor's Checkpoint Charlie** (*see page
204* **Nightlife**), a 24-hour music-club-cum-laun-
dromat, where you can listen to a band, play a
game of pool or grab a burger, all while your
clothes spin and dry.

...ers' markets, see page 159.

Washing Well Laundryteria

*841 Bourbon Street, at Dumaine Street (523 9955).
Bus 3 Vieux Carré, 55 Elysian Fields, 81 Almonaster,
82 Desire.* **Open** 7.30am-6pm Mon-Fri; 7.30am-2pm
Sat. **Credit** AmEx, Disc, MC, V.
Map 7 C2
The Washing Well offers citywide same-day pick-up and
return of laundry and dry-cleaning. Laundry is charged by
the load.

Hula Mae's

*840 N Rampart Street, at Dumaine Street (522 1336).
Bus 3 Vieux Carré, 48 Esplanade, 55 Elysian Fields,
57 Franklin, 81 Almonaster.* **Open** 7am-midnight daily.
Credit AmEx, MC, V.
Map 7 C1
A great place to watch the parade of the unwashed and
washed, both people and laundry. It offers delivery within
the French Quarter (10am-6pm Mon-Fri).

Fashion

Let's face it, New Orleans is not really the place
to spend time shopping for designer labels. The
department stores (*see pages 147-148*) are the
best places to find the major American and
European labels, with the most extensive collection being at Saks Fifth Avenue. You'll have
much more success searching out offbeat and
whimsical creations by local or small designers
from other American cities in the smaller stores
of the French Quarter or along Magazine Street
(*see page 73* **Sightseeing** for more details on
what else that street has to offer). For the popular fashion chains such as **Gap** and **Banana
Republic**, head for the large-scale malls (*see
page 147* **Shopping malls**).

Ann Taylor

Canal Place Shopping Center, 333 Canal Street,
at Decatur Street (529 2306). Bus 41 Canal. **Open** 10am-
6pm Mon-Wed, Sun; 10am-7pm Thur-Sat. **Credit** AmEx,
MC, V. **Map 6 C1**
Clean lines, good fabrics and neutral colours are the Ann
Taylor trademark. Prices are moderately expensive (jackets
for $200-$300), but these classics will last forever.
Branches: Lakeside Shopping Center (835 0843); New
Orleans Centre (835 0843).

Joan Vass of New Orleans

1100 Sixth Street, at Magazine Street (891 4502).
Bus 11 Magazine. **Open** 10am-5pm Mon-Sat. **Credit**
AmEx, DC, Disc, MC, V. **Map 6 A3**
This New York designer's signature line is cashmere-cotton
casual separates for women, in limited colours each season.
Pricey but good looking.

Nicole Miller Boutique

201 N Peters Street, at Iberville Street (581 9581). Bus 3
Vieux Carré, 41 Canal, 55 Elysian Fields, 81 Almonaster,
82 Desire. **Open** 10am-6pm Mon-Sat; noon-5pm Sun.
Credit AmEx, DC, Disc, MC, V. **Map 7 A3**
A saucy line of women's clothing from the designer known
for her clever silk fabrics and clothing. If you have long, lean
legs, the dresses here will show off your best assets. Plus
men's ties and boxer shorts in silk.

The Grace Note

900 Royal Street, at Dumaine Street (522 1513).
Bus 3 Vieux Carré, 55 Elysian Fields, 81 Almonaster,
82 Desire. **Open** 10am-6pm Mon-Sat; 11am-5pm Sun.
Credit AmEx, MC, V. **Map 7 C2**
This is a grace indeed, offering great local designs by owner
Libby Brighton, using vintage fabrics and *chibori*
(Japanese tie-dye) velvet. The hats are pretty special, too.

Le Fleur de Paris

712 Royal Street, at Pirate's Alley (525 1899). Bus 3
Vieux Carré, 55 Elysian Fields, 81 Almonaster, 82
Desire. **Open** 10am-6pm Mon-Sun. **Credit** MC, V.
Map 7 C2
The shop window on Pirate's Alley is an eye-catcher. There
are original pieces, copies of vintage designs by an in-house
designer and custom-designed *My Fair Lady*-style hats covered in ribbons and flowers. The clothes are very feminine
in a Lana Turner kind of way, and made to order, so fit is
never a problem.

Weinstein's

Canal Place Shopping Center, 333 Canal Street, at
Decatur Street (522 6278). Bus 41 Canal. **Open** 10am-
6pm Mon-Sat; 1-5pm Sun. **Credit** AmEx, MC, V.
Map 6 C1
Loyal customers shop at Weinstein's for its exclusive col-
lection of Italian and Belgian designer clothing for women.
Prices are high, but then so is the quality.

Children's clothing

All the major department stores have children's
departments, with the biggest selection at Macy's
in the Esplanade Mall. The malls are also the place
to look for branches of **Gap Kids** and **The
Limited Too**, the pre-adolescent and adolescent
version of women's clothing store The Limited (*see
page 147* **Shopping malls**).

Chocolate Soup

2030 Metairie Road, at Bonnabel Boulevard, Metairie,
(837 8314). Bus 27 Louisiana, 40, 41 or 44 Canal,

Pyschic readers

The ancient art of tarot – divining the truth
from symbolic images – has been taken up
by a small army of psychics and tarot readers
who have set up shop around the perimeter
of Jackson Square. You may spot Esperanza,
a redhead with blue nail polish, who turned
to tarot because 'retail was killing me' and
gives an enthusiastic, even passionate reading. Or Joy, an African-American from New
York with salt-and-pepper hair and eyes like
crystal balls, who hears angels, and gives
palm readings using a tiny flashlight. Or
there's Daniel, a green-haired young man
who admits that, although he's the best writer
in the world, he reads tarot when he's hungry
and needs some money.

Anyone who buys a city licence can set up
shop in a folding chair on Jackson Square.
There's no bar exam for psychic ability. You
won't be able to tell beforehand whether your
chosen reader turns out to be an intuitive type
or a complete huckster. Not surprisingly, readings can be uncannily accurate or completely
off the mark. Expect to pay $10-$20 for a reading that can last from 10 or 15 minutes up to
half an hour, and make sure you agree on a
price before you start.

48 Esplanade, then E4 Metairie Road. **Open** 9.30am-5pm
Mon-Sat; noon-5pm Sun. **Credit** MC, V.
An outlet store that carries its own line of appliqué clothing
as well as designer clothing, such as Rachel's Kids. Boys'
sizes go up to age 7 and girls' up to the age of 14.

Mignon

2727 Prytania Street, at Washington Avenue (891
2374). St Charles Streetcar. **Open** 10am-5pm Mon-Sat.
Credit AmEx, MC, V. **Map 6 A3**
This Garden District store carries the kind of children's clothing you either love or hate: heavy on the lace, appliqué, ruf-
fles and the Little Lord Fauntleroy look. Prices are high
(dresses cost from $100) for garments that will be outgrown
the next day. From toddler to age 4 (boys) and age 10 (girls).

Lollipop Shoppe

8125 Hampson Street, at Carrollton Avenue (865 1014).
St Charles Streetcar. **Open** 10am-5.30pm Mon-Fri; 10am-
4pm Sat. **Credit** MC, V. **Map 4 A8**
The name is telling: the emphasis here is on cute. Sizes run
from infant to age 14 (girls) and age 7 (boys).

Discount fashion

Catalog Collection

8141 Maple Street, at Dublin Street (861 5002).
St Charles Streetcar. **Open** 10am-6pm Mon-Sat.
Credit AmEx, MC, V. **Map 4 A8**
Casual wear for guys and dolls, including second-hand jeans
for under $20.

Stein Mart

*5300 Tchoupitoulas Street, at Napoleon Avenue
(891 6377). Bus 10 Tchoupitoulas.* **Open** 10am-9pm
Mon-Sat; noon-6pm Sun. **Credit** AmEx, DC, Disc, MC, V.
Map 4 D10
Designer fashions for men and women at rock-bottom prices
– though it can take some patience to unearth a real find.
Branch: 2840 Veterans Memorial Blvd, Metairie (831 0655).

United Apparel Liquidators

*3780 Veterans Memorial Boulevard, near Lakeside
Shopping Center, Metairie (455 7030). St Charles
Streetcar/bus 16 S Claiborne, 39 Tulane, 90 Carrollton,
then E5 Causeway.* **Open** 10am-9pm Mon Sat; noon-6pm
Sun. **Credit** AmEx, Disc, MC, V.
Good discounts on women's clothing and accessories, includ-
ing well-known labels such as Carol Horne, David Dart and
BCBG. Discovering a good find depends on luck.

Fashion accessories

Hats

New Orleans is not particularly famed for its hats
but hat shops seem to do well here – maybe it's the
Mardi Gras tradition of costuming along with a
generally casual and playful attitude to fashion.

Meyer the Hatter

*120 St Charles Avenue, at Canal Street (525 1048/
1-800 882 4287). St Charles Streetcar/bus 41 Canal.*
Open 10am-6pm Mon-Sat. **Credit** AmEx, DC, Disc, MC,
V. **Map 6 C1**
This dishevelled shop with 1950s décor is a family-run New
Orleans institution where men have been buying top labels
such as Dobbs and Stetson since 1894. Old-timers in the hat
business provide expert help and can tell a good story to
boot: ask about when the Marx Brothers shopped there.
Perfect for chaps who like caps.

New Orleans Hat Attack

*Jackson Brewery, 600 Decatur Street, at Toulouse Street
(523 5770). Bus 3 Vieux Carré, 55 Elysian Fields, 81
Almonaster, 82 Desire.* **Open** 10am-9pm Mon-Sat; 10am-
7pm Sun. **Credit** Disc, MC, V. **Map 7 B3**
Fulfill your costuming fantasies here. With 7,000 choices,
from novelty hats to garden party numbers, even the most
creative minds will find some suprises.

New Orleans Hat Company

*402 Chartres Street, at Conti Street (524 8792). Bus 3
Vieux Carré, 55 Elysian Fields, 81 Almonaster, 82
Desire.* **Open** 10am-5pm Mon-Thur; 10am-6pm Fri-Sun.
Credit AmEx, MC, V. **Map 7 B2**
Jazz Festers return here year after year for classic Panama
straw hats, jaunty berets and one-of-a-kind designs for
women. It also stocks unusual imported clothing and quirky,
hand-made jewellery.

RHINO Gallery

*Canal Place Shopping Center, 333 Canal Street, at
Decatur Street (523 7945). Bus 41 Canal.* **Open** 10am-
6pm Mon-Wed; 10am-7pm Thur-Sat; noon-6pm Sun.
Credit AmEx, Disc, MC, V. **Map 6 C1**
RHINO – 'Right Here In New Orleans' – is an artists' collective that showcases the best local artwork: glassware, pottery, wall hangings, photography, jewellery – and hats.
Tracy Thomson's creations sell like hot cakes at Jazz Fest,
while Dr Seuss's Cat in the Hat would purr over some of these
offerings, especially the deep purple velvet number with a
crown like a crooked stovepipe.

Jewellery

If you're looking for second-hand, family jewellery (usually known as 'estate' jewellery), the
French Quarter is your best bet, especially the
antique stores on Royal Street. However, all the
shopping areas have their share of jewellers,
both contemporary and antique, and most
department stores have collections of fine jewellery as well as costume pieces; Saks is a good
place to find striking contemporary designs.
Local artist Thomas Mann creates kooky jewellery; for details of his galleries, *see page 98*
Museums & Galleries. The **Watch & Clock
Shop** (824 Gravier Street; 525 3961) is a reliable
watch repairer located within walking distance
of the French Quarter.

Adlers & Sons

*722 Canal Street, at St Charles Avenue (523 5292).
St Charles Streetcar/bus 41 Canal.* **Open** 10am-5.45pm
Mon-Wed, Fri, Sat; 10am-7pm Thur. **Credit** AmEx, DC,
Disc, MC, V. **Map 6 C1**
This highly reputable store has everything in fine jewellery
for men and women. Locals have shopped here for years.

Bedazzle

*635 St Peter Street, at Royal Street (529 3248).
Bus 3 Vieux Carré, 55 Elysian Fields, 81 Almonaster,
82 Desire.* **Open** 10.30am-6pm daily. **Credit** AmEx, DC,
Disc, MC, V. **Map 7 B2**
Bangles and baubles if you want to sparkle.

Mignon Faget

*710 Dublin Street, at Maple Street (865 7361).
St Charles Streetcar.* **Open** 10am-5pm Mon-Sat.
Credit AmEx, Disc, MC, V. **Map 4 A8**
This New Orleans designer is well known for her striking,
elegant, nature-inspired designs in silver and gold. This
Riverbend shop also sells gifts such as linens, photo frames
and bath accessories.
Branches: Canal Place Shopping Center (524 2973);
Lakeside Shopping Center (835 2244).

Ruby Ann Tobar-Blanco

*3005 Magazine Street, at Seventh Street (897 0811/
1-800 826 7282). Bus 11 Magazine.* **Open** 10am-5pm
Mon-Sat. **Credit** AmEx, MC, V. **Map 6 A3/4**
A local designer who creates elegant, feminine designs with
an antique feel, using freshwater pearls, gemstones, coral,
wood and sterling silver.

Studio Diva

*1110 Antonine Street, at Magazine Street (899 0275).
Bus 11 Magazine.* **Open** 10am-5pm Tue-Sat. **Credit**
AmEx, Disc, MC, V. **Map 4 E9**
Smoked glass bead necklaces and earrings by New
Orleanian Wendy Ethridge, plus a reasonably priced assort-
ment of brooches, rings and earrings by up-and-coming local
jewellery makers.

Symmetry

*8138 Hampson Street, at Dublin Street (861 9925).
St Charles Streetcar.* **Open** 10am-5pm Mon-Sat (summer
closed Mon). **Credit** AmEx, Disc, MC, V. **Map 4 A8**
Handcrafted jewellery at reasonable prices by local
designers; if you have a design in mind, you can get it
made here. There's also a small collection of 1930s
watches by Bulova and Gruen. Staff are helpful and offer
expert jewellery repair.

Zoom Six

1229 Decatur Street, at Barracks Street (581 2880).
Bus 3 Vieux Carré, 48 Esplanade, 55 Elysian Fields,
81 Almonaster, 82 Desire. **Open** 11am-5pm daily.
Credit AmEx, Disc, MC, V. **Map 7 D3**
Small but interesting collection of hand-crafted 'symbolic jewellery' in sterling silver by British designer Mark Defrates.

Lingerie

Glamour pusses should check out the pricey peignoirs and boned foundation garments at **Le Fleur de Paris** (*see page 156*).

Victoria's Secret

Riverwalk, 1 Poydras Street, at the Mississippi River (522 1555). Riverfront Streetcar/bus 3 Vieux Carré, 10 Tchoupitoulas. **Open** 10am-9pm Mon-Fri. **Credit** AmEx, Disc, MC, V. **Map 6 C1**
The well-known chain that caters to gals that love satin.
Branches: New Orleans Centre (568 0223); Lakeside Shopping Center (843 2720).

Yvonne Lafleur

8131 Hampson Street, at Dublin Street (866 9666). St Charles Streetcar. **Open** 10am-6pm Mon-Wed, Fri, Sat; 10am-8pm Thur. **Credit** AmEx, Disc, MC, V. **Map 4 A8**
Sexy, expensive silk lingerie, including a decent selection in larger sizes, in surroundings reminiscent of a classy bordello. Take a look at the cocktail party dresses, imported wedding gowns and custom millinery.

Factory outlets

Factory outlet stores are the invention of retailers to get rid of over-ordered, slow-to-sell or last season's merchandise. They have had measured success in the New Orleans and Gulf Coast areas, and open and close with head-spinning speed. Before travelling so far from New Orleans, phone to make sure the outlet you want is still there.

The **Slidell Outlet** (646 0756) is about 30 miles (48 kilometres) east of New Orleans, off the I-10. and only worth a visit if you're in the area or are a die-hard shopper. **Gonzales Outlet Stores** (647 0521), also off the I-10, is 50 miles (80.5 kilometres) west of New Orleans and features Ann Klein, Aigner shoes, Nine West shoes, Levi's (jeans for under $20) and Eddie Bauer. You could combine a visit with a trip to the nearby plantation houses along the Mississippi (*see chapter* **Trips Out of Town**).

The newest outlet complex in the Gulf Coast area is **Gulfport Outlet Stores** (1-228 864 5223), on the Mississippi Gulf Coast, off the I-10 and about 75 miles (121 kilometres) east of New Orleans. It has the attraction of a Saks Fifth Avenue outlet, offering discounts of up to 40-50%.

Luggage

Rapp's Luggage & Gifts

604 Canal Street, at St Charles Avenue (568 1953). St Charles Streetcar/bus 41 Canal. **Open** 10am-6pm Mon-Sat. **Credit** AmEx, Disc, MC, V. **Map 6 C1**
In business since 1865 and on Canal Street since the 1920s, this store has plenty of luggage and leather briefcases as well as a small selection of purses, wallets, belts and gloves. Luggage brands include Hartmann, Tumi, Andimo, French of California, Halliburton and Samsonite. Leather and luggage repair is also available.
Branches: The Esplanade (467 8283); New Orleans Centre (566 0700).

Shoes

Feet First

5500 Magazine Street, at Octavia Street (899 6800). Bus 11 Magazine. **Open** 10am-6pm Mon-Sat; noon-5pm Sun. **Credit** AmEx, Disc, MC, V. **Map 4 C9/10**
Designer shoes for women (Kenneth Cole et al) at great discount prices.
Branch: 518 Chartres Street (566 7525).

Pied Nu

5521 Magazine Street, at Octavia Street (899 4118). Bus 11 Magazine. **Open** 10am-6pm Mon-Fri; 10am-5pm Sat. **Credit** AmEx, Disc, MC, V. **Map 4 C9/10**
Stocks a small but well-selected collection of shoes by Calvin Klein and Robert Clergervis, plus upmarket accessories such as beaded evening bags.

Saint Germain

Canal Place Shopping Center, 333 Canal Street, at Decatur Street (522 1720). Bus 41 Canal. **Open** 10am-6pm Mon-Wed; 10am-7pm Thur-Sat; 10am-noon Sun. **Credit** AmEx, Disc, MC, V. **Map 6 C1**
Sassy shoes from hot designers such as American Donald Pliner and Frenchman Luc Berjen, and handmade bridal shoes by British star Emma Hope. There is a small but well-chosen selection of accessories including leather belts and beaded evening bags.

Florists

Magazine Flowers & Greenery

737 Octavia Street, at Magazine Street (891 4356). Bus 11 Magazine. **Open** 10.30am-5.30pm Tue-Sun. **Credit** AmEx, DC, Disc, MC, V. **Map 4 C9/10**
This attractive store offers natural and unpretentious flower arrangements. You'll also find lots of orchids and flowering plants here.

Peter A Chopin

2800 St Charles Avenue, at Washington Avenue (891 4455). St Charles Streetcar. **Open** 8am-5pm Mon-Fri; 8am-4pm Sat. **Credit** AmEx, DC, Disc, MC, V. **Map 4 E9**
The grand master of florists in New Orleans, featured in Anne Rice's books and frequented by the folk of the Garden District. Arrangements are traditional and formal.

Planet Xeno

3818 Magazine Street, at Peniston Street (895 0807). Bus 11 Magazine. **Open** 10am-5pm Mon-Sat. **Credit** AmEx, DC, Disc, MC, V. **Map 4 D9/10**
If you're shopping on Magazine Street, stop at this brightly painted, double-shotgun cottage and investigate the cutting-edge florist's great sense of style – and wonderful selection of flowers and plants.

Food & drink

Central Grocery Co
923 Decatur Street, at St Philip Street (523 1620).
Bus 3 Vieux Carré, 55 Elysian Fields, 81 Almonaster,
82 Desire. **Open** 8am-5.30pm daily. **No credit cards.**
Map 7 C3
One of the few remaining Italian groceries in the city, packed
to the rafters with edible goodies. It sells great black olives
and the city's best muffuletta sandwich, a New Orleans original containing ham, cheese and olive salad.

Langenstein's
1330 Arabella Street, at Pitt Street (899 9283).
St Charles Streetcar. **Open** 8am-7pm Mon-Sat.
Credit MC, V. **Map 4 C3**
The best meat market in the city, dishing up a daily selec-
tion of home-made soups and a variety of frozen entrées.
Branch: 800 Metairie Road (831 6682).

Matassa's Grocery
1001 Dauphine Street, at St Philip Street (525 9494).
Bus 3 Vieux Carré, 57 Franklin. **Open** 6am-10pm daily.
Credit AmEx, DC, Disc, MC, V.
Map 7 C1
A small, late-opening neighbourhood store with a deli that
offers a daily lunch special and sandwiches. Delivery is avail-
able within the French Quarter.

Progress Grocery Co
915 Decatur Street, at St Philip Street (525 6627).
Bus 3 Vieux Carré, 55 Elysian Fields, 81 Almonaster,
82 Desire. **Open** 9am-5.30pm daily. **Credit** MC, V.
Map 7 C3
Another old-fashioned French Quarter grocery, which com-
petes with the **Central Grocery** (*above*) for the muffuletta
trade. Also sells sandwiches and various speciality foods
such as Italian sweets, black olives, Middle Eastern foods
and the best mozzarella in the city.

Beer & wine

You can buy beer, wine and liquor everywhere
in the city – in supermarkets, grocery stores, corner shops, even the major chain drugstores – so
there aren't very many specialist liquor shops.
Local beers Dixie and Abita (the latter brewed
on the North Shore) are popular, as are beers
imported from Britain, Ireland and Australia.
Unlike many US cities, you can also buy alcohol
on Sundays in New Orleans. You have to be 21
to buy (or drink) alcohol and you may be asked
to show photo ID.

Martin's Wine Cellar
See p135 **Restaurants** *for listings.*
Offers the best selection and prices on wine and imported
beer, plus a good deli and an assortment of gourmet treats
– such as grapes encased in Roquefort cheese and chopped
pecans – and party foods. It specialises in gift baskets.
Branch: 1200 Veterans Memorial Boulevard, Metairie
(896 7300).

Vieux Carré Wine & Spirits
422 Chartres Street, at St Louis Street (568 9463).
Bus 3 Vieux Carré, 55 Elysian Fields, 81 Almonaster, 82
Desire. **Open** 10am-10pm Mon-Sat; 10am-7pm Sun.
Credit AmEx, Disc, MC, V. **Map 7 B2**
The French Quarter's largest selection of wine and spirits.
It's open on Sundays and will deliver to local hotels.

Farmers' Markets

Sadly, the **French Market** (located on Decatur
Street, at the river) is a shadow of its former self,
and the souvenir stands outnumber the food
stalls, although you can still get fresh fruit and
produce and it is open all night. It's a good place
to buy New Orleans spices, hot sauce and pre-
packaged seasoned red beans. The **Crescent
City Market**, at the corner of Girod Street and
Magazine Street, operates on Saturday mornings
from 8am to noon. It sells locally produced
cheeses, fruit and produce and hosts culinary
demonstrations by local chefs.

Speciality & gift shops

If you want to take home the flavour of New
Orleans, Cajun and Creole spices, sugary pralines,
coffee, beignet mix and packaged red beans and
rice all travel well. You can find many of these at
grocery stores, but the following speciality shops
offer a wider selection and the convenience of having it all in one place.

Café du Monde Shop
800 Decatur Street, at St Ann Street (525 4544). Bus 3
Vieux Carré, 55 Elysian Fields, 81 Almonaster, 82
Desire. **Open** 24 hours daily. **Credit** AmEx, Disc, MC, V.
Map 7 C3
Across the street from the famous café (*see p142* **Cafés &
Coffeehouses**), the shop sells the house brand of coffee and
beignet mix and will ship overseas.

Louisiana Products
507 St Ann Street, at Jackson Square (524 7331).
Bus 3 Vieux Carré, 55 Elysian Fields, 81 Almonaster,
82 Desire. **Open** 9.30am-5.30pm Mon, Fri; 10am-6pm
Tue, Thur, Sat, Sun. **Credit** AmEx, Disc, MC, V.
Map 7 C2
The place for Cajun and Creole spices – such as Paul
Prudhomme blackening spices or the peppery coating for
fried fish made by the local Zatarain family. Choose from
pre-packaged gift boxes or get the staff to make one up for
you (prices range from $5 to $50).

Creole Delicacies Gourmet Shop
533 St Ann Street, at Chartres Street (525 9508).
Bus 3 Vieux Carré, 55 Elysian Fields, 81 Almonaster,
82 Desire. **Open** 9am-5pm daily. **Credit** AmEx, DC,
Disc, MC, V.
Map 7 C2
Another place that specialises in gift baskets containing
mixes and spices for Creole and Cajun cooking.
Branch: Riverwalk (523 6425).

Whole foods

Whole Foods Market
3135 Esplanade Avenue, at Ponce de Leon Street
(943 1626). Bus 48 Esplanade. **Open** 8.30am-9.30pm
daily. **Credit** AmEx, Disc, MC, V.
Map 5 E5
This small store on Esplanade Avenue is the only full-service
natural food supermarket in the city. It sells organic fruit and
vegetables and also stocks a good selection of herbal
remedies, food supplements and skin-care products. For
more on the food takeaway side, *see p139* **Restaurants**.

All dressed up

Mardi Gras, Hallowe'en, St Patrick's Day, St Anthony Day parades and even a raucous and camp celebration of Queen Elizabeth's official birthday – all provide an excuse for getting into costume. Dressing up is second nature in New Orleans and if you have the occasion and the opportunity to enter into the spirit of the city, shopping for a costume is part of the fun.

Vintage and second hand clothing stores – many of which are in the French Quarter, along Decatur Street – are a good place to start: that Hawaiian shirt could be the beginning of your costume or just a good thing to wear over shorts for Jazz Fest. And opportunities for Mardi Gras can be found in every second shop, in the cast-off costumes of satin and beads. Where else in the world would you be able to find a dress fit for a queen in a size 6 or 42?

On Decatur Street in the French Quarter, **Decatur Collectibles** (No.1224; 523 2345) has the best collection of Hawaiian shirts in the city, at reasonable prices. **Gargoyles** (No.1205; 529 4387) is the place to go for all things leather (Courtney Love shopped here before her conversion to designer labels), though prices are high. Look for labels such as Naughty Nola and check out its website (www.gargoylesleather.com). At **Jazzrags** (No.1215; 523 2942), the collection of vintage clothes from the 1940s to the 1970s is displayed in a user-friendly fashion. Prices are competitive and the staff are friendly.

La Garage (No.1236; 523 4467) has velvet trousers, beaded jackets and a selection of used army gear, khaki coats and bags. Prices are on the high side, but the sale rack has some bargains. **Masquerade Fantasy** (No.1233; 486 8854) sells leather masks decorated with feathers, beads and jewels, in non-traditional, spooky and frightening designs. A simple mask costs $25, the dollars mount up as the decorations increase. In a city with hundreds of marching clubs and carnival krewes, the market in second-hand costumes is flourishing: **One of a Kind** (No.1212; 486 5567) helps meet the demand with a plentiful and well-priced supply. At the far end of Decatur Street, by Esplanade Avenue, **Paisley Babylon** (No.1129; 529 3696) stocks a good and ever-changing selection of period pieces for costuming, plus satin dresses and velvet capes. Blanche Dubois would have loved it.

Also in the French Quarter, the **Mardi Gras Center** (831 Chartres Street; 524 4384) is the place to go for glitter and make-up and to get ideas for costumes. It's small, but packed with everything imaginable for the making of a party or celebration to remember.

Travelling uptown, **MGM** near the Garden District (1617 St Charles Avenue, at Euterpe Street; 581 3999) is the place to head for if you've ever longed to dress like Louis XIV or Marie Antoinette. The stage or movie costumes here cover every look from the Middle Ages to Southern Belle. They're custom-made and have been fitted for a particular actor or actress, so expect to have to search through the racks and try on garments to find the right fit. Hire prices

Gargoyles: *for all things leather.*

Lay in that over-the-top Mardi Gras number at the **Salvation Army Thrift Store***.*

range from $25 a day for a plain pirate outfit to around $400 for a Mardi Gras Queen's dress, hand-sewn with hundreds of glass beads. The shop is at its busiest at Hallowe'en.

There are several excellent vintage clothing stores on Magazine Street including **Mariposa** (No.2038, at Jackson Avenue; 523 3037), which sells both men's and women's clothes, mostly from the 1960s and 1970s, costing anything from $7 to $100. Further uptown, **Uptown Costume & Dancewear** (5533 Magazine Street, at St Joseph Street; 895 7969) is the busiest shop in town during carnival season. There are costumes, hats, wigs and make-up at prices that will encourage your sense of the outrageous: synthetic wigs cost $10 and packaged costumes start at $20.

At Riverbend, **On the Other Hand** (8126 Hampson Street; 862 0073) is an upmarket 'resale'

boutique, and nearby on Adams Street (No.714, at Maple; 862 0073) is a similarly funky shop.

To find the cheapest thrills available in the costume game, however, you'll have to travel out to 100 Jefferson Highway at Dakin Avenue, to the **Salvation Army Thrift Store** (837 5914), which sells cheap second-hand clothes and has a large selection of used carnival costumes. Search the costume barrel for the best bargains. There are no dressing rooms.

And finally, if you find yourself in need of a dinner jacket or full evening outfit, **Gentlemen's Quarterly** (232 Royal Street, at Iberville Street; 522 7139) hires out men's formal wear, in an extensive range of sizes, including shoes. One-day hire of a full outfit – jacket, trousers, shirt, cummerbund and bow tie – costs $79. It's open seven days a week and offers pick-up and delivery to Quarter hotels.

Health & beauty

Drugstores stock cosmetics but not many of the leading brands. For the higher-priced beauty products try the department stores **Maison Blanche**, **Macy's** and **Saks Fifth Avenue** (*see page 148*, all of which have large selections).

Hairdressers

Busta
752 Tchoupitoulas Street, at Julia Street (523 4645). Bus 10 Tchoupitoulas. **Open** 9am-7pm Tue Sat. **Credit** Disc, MC, V. **Map 6 C2**
Offers haircuts and body care – including massage (from $55), facial ($40), manicure ($20) and pedicure ($40) – and Aveda skincare products.

Eclipse Salon
536 Bienville Street, at Royal Street (522 3318). Bus 3 Vieux Carré, 55 Elysian Fields, 81 Almonaster, 82 Desire. **Open** 10am-6pm Mon-Fri; 10am-5pm Sat. **Credit** AmEx, MC, V. **Map 7 B2**
This full-service salon in the French Quarter provides haircuts for men ($25) and women ($35), make-up, nails and body treatments and sells beauty products such as Aveda and Paul Mitchell. A manicure costs $15, a pedicure £35, aromatherapy facials start at $35 and body wraps will set you back $55.

Opticians

St Charles Vision
138 Carondelet Street, at Common Street (522 0826). St Charles Streetcar. **Open** 9am-5pm Mon-Fri. **Credit** AmEx, Disc, MC, V. **Map 6 B/C1**
An optician with a same-day service and a large selection of designer frames. Check out the discount outlet stores (6900 Veterans Memorial Boulevard; 885 5555) and 837 S Clearview Parkway; 733 0406) for savings of up to 40% on frames.
Branches: 624 S Carrollton Avenue (866 6311); 3200 Severn Avenue, suite 102, Metairie (887 2020).

Perfume

Bourbon French Parfums
525 St Ann Street, at Decatur Street (522 4480). Bus 3 Vieux Carré, 55 Elysian Fields, 81 Almonaster, 82 Desire. **Open** 9am-5pm daily. **Credit** AmEx, Disc, MC, V. **Map 7 C3**
In business since 1843, this locally owned outfit offers custom-blended fragrances for men and women.

Hové Parfumeur
824 Royal Street, at St Ann Street (525 7827). Bus 3 Vieux Carré, 55 Elysian Fields, 81 Almonaster, 82 Desire. **Open** 10am-5pm Mon-Sat. **Credit** AmEx, MC, V. **Map 7 C2**
A local favourite. The tea olive scent is the quintessential New Orleans fragrance, capturing the smell of the sweet olive trees that bloom in spring and autumn all over the city. Also look out for the vertivier perfumes and soaps for men and women made from the scented root found in Louisiana.

Pharmacies (drugstores)

Several **Rite-Aid** drugstores are open 24 hours daily, including one in the Garden District (3401 St Charles Avenue, at Louisiana Avenue; 895 0344/prescriptions 896 4575) and one Uptown (4330 S Claiborne Avenue, at Napoleon Avenue; 895 6655/prescriptions 896 4570). The Mid City **Walgreens** branch (3311 Canal Street, at Jeff Davis Parkway; 822 8070) is also open 24 hours a day. The only pharmacy in the French Quarter is the **Royal Pharmacy** (1101 Royal Street; 523 5401) which is open 9am-6pm Mon-Sat.

Spas

See also **Mackie Shilstone Pro Spa** *page 221* **Sport & Fitness**.

Belladonna
2900 Magazine Street, at Sixth Street (891 4393). Bus 11 Magazine. **Open** 9am-8pm Mon-Fri; 9am-6pm Sat. **Credit** AmEx, MC, V. **Map 6 A3**
A complete day spa offering manicures ($15), massages (one-hour $60), facials ($55) and the largest selection of skin products in the city. Relax with a herb tea in the Japanese garden in between beauty treatments. There's no swimming pool but instead a Jacuzzi, steam room and sauna. Appointments can be hard to come by, so book well ahead.

Earth Savers
434 Chartres Street, at Conti Street (581 4999). Bus 3 Vieux Carré, 55 Elysian Fields, 81 Almonaster, 82 Desire. **Open** 10am-6pm Mon-Wed, Fri, Sat; 10am-8pm Thur; noon-5pm Sun. **Credit** AmEx, Disc, MC, V. **Map 7 B2**
Earth Savers has a complete line of 'earth-saving' products for the bath and the body (all are mineral oil-free and have not been tested on animals). A day of relaxation for $160 includes a manicure, pedicure, facial, one-hour massage and a light, healthy lunch. There are several branches, which tend to be small and rather sparse, including one in the French Quarter.
Branches: 5501 Magazine Street (899 8555); 3256 Severn Avenue, Metairie (885 5152); 200 Metairie Road, Old Metairie (828 1997).

Tattooing & body piercing

New Orleans is home to some of America's most renowned tattoo and piercing artists. Popular and easily reached from the Quarter are: **Above & Below Body Piercing** (521 St Philip Street, at Decatur; 598 2300); **Electric Expressions** (3421 S Carrollton Avenue, at Bienville; 488 1500); **Electric Ladyland Tattoo** (8106 Earhart Boulevard, at Carrollton (866 3859); **Orleans Ink** (610 Frenchman Street, at Chartres; 947 2300); and **Rings of Desire** (1128 Decatur Street, at Gov Nicholls; 524 6147).

Household, furniture & gifts

Artifacts Gallery
5515 Magazine Street, at Jefferson Avenue (899 5505). Bus 11 Magazine. **Open** 10am-5.30pm Mon-Sat. **Credit** AmEx, DC, Disc, MC, V. **Map 4 C9/10**
A interiors-cum-giftshop offering furniture made from vine branches and wooden pyramid cabinets in a primitive country style, plus unusual 'decorative hardware' – door knobs, drawer handles and such like. Work is often by young Louisiana artists.

Creative Concrete

*1700 Benefit Street, at Gentilly Boulevard, Gentilly
(949 5195). Bus 90 Carrollton.* **Open** 9am-5pm Mon-Sat.
Credit Disc, MC, V.
Tucked under the interstate in old Gentilly, you'll need directions to find this place. It sells yard art and statuary at great prices, all made on the premises, as well as a collection of Gentilly Balls ($29.95-$39.95). Now back in fashion, these decorative silver, gold or blue glass balls were so named in the 1950s because they could be found perched in gardens all over this working class neighbourhood.

Pottery Barn

*Canal Place Shopping Center, 333 Canal Street, at
Decatur Street (568 0011). Bus 41 Canal.* **Open** 10am-
6pm daily. **Credit** AmEx, DC, Disc, MC, V. **Map 6 C1**
Part of a nationwide chain, this beautiful store is packed with moderately priced, fashionable home furnishings and decorative accessories. It also has a studio where you can co-ordinate furniture, fabrics, window treatments and floor coverings.

Scriptura

*5423 Magazine Street, at Jefferson Avenue (897 1555).
Bus 11 Magazine.* **Open** 10.30am-6pm Mon-Sat. **Credit**
AmEx, MC, V. **Map 4 C9/10**
An absolutely gorgeous store packed with sophisticated, high-quality art papers, fine stationery, leather-bound journals and exquisite wrapping paper. The art paper comes mainly from Italy, London and Paris. Paper for lamp shades, Venetian glass pens, personalised wax seals made by a local bronze foundry are also available and there's a print shop for business cards and invitations.

Utopia

*5408 Magazine Street, at Jefferson Avenue (899
8488). Bus 11 Magazine.* **Open** 10am-6pm Mon-Sat;
noon-5pm Sun. **Credit** AmEx, DC, Disc, MC, V. **Map 4
C9/10**
Rummage around this cluttered shop to discover clothing – including the US family-run Flax label of simple cotton and linen designs – jewellery, photo frames and fancifully painted furniture by Texan David Marsh.

Ya-Ya

*628 Baronne Street, at Girod Street (529 3306). St
Charles Streetcar.* **Open** 9am-6pm Mon-Fri; noon-5pm
Sat. **Credit** AmEx, Disc, MC, V. **Map 6 B1**
The name stands for 'Young Aspirations, Young Artists' and it's a non-profit operation that provides a workspace and shop for local high school students and young adults to create and sell hand-painted furniture. Baby chairs cost $75-$175; chairs for adults are $175-$500. There are also tables, beds and hand-printed fabrics and pillows.

Musical instruments

International Vintage Guitars of New Orleans

*1011 Magazine Street, at Howard Avenue (524 4557).
Bus 11 Magazine.* **Open** 10am-6pm Mon Sat. **Credit**
AmEx, Disc, MC, V.
Walking into this store is a treat: the colours and shapes of the beautiful selection of vintage guitars are pure art. Local and visiting musicians flock here to check the ever-changing inventory, so you may run into Eric Clapton or Willie DeVille.

Werlein's

*214 Decatur Street, at Iberville Street (883 5080). Bus 3
Vieux Carré, 41 Canal, 55 Elysian Fields, 81 Almonaster,
82 Desire.* **Open** 10am-5.30pm Mon-Sat. **Credit** AmEx,
Disc, MC, V. **Map 7 A3**

Family-owned and operated since 1842, this is a New Orleans institution. The Superstore in Metairie has it all – new and used instruments (from violins to grand pianos), sheet music, software, sound systems and accessories. The store in the Quarter is smaller but has steel washboards and squeeze boxes for Cajun and zydeco musicians.
Branch: 3750 Veterans Memorial Boulevard, Metairie (883 5060).

Pets

And ToTo Too (901 Iberville Street, at Dauphine;
586 8686) is the place to go in the French Quarter
for all pet supplies.

Dr Mike's Animal House

*1120 N Rampart Street, at Gov Nicholls Street
(523 4455). Bus 3 Vieux Carré, 57 Franklin.*
Open 8am-6pm Mon-Fri; 8am-noon Sun. **No credit
cards. Map 7 D1**
Expect to pay $40 for a check-up for your pet and $25 for grooming at this vet. House calls are made and the staff are friendly.

Three Dog Bakery

*827 Royal Street, at Dumaine Street (525 2253).
Bus 3 Vieux Carré, 55 Elysian Fields, 81 Almonaster,
82 Desire.* **Open** 10am-6pm daily. **Credit** AmEx, DC,
Disc, MC, V. **Map 7 C2**
Adding a twist to the New Orleans tradition of creating food laden altars for St Joseph's Day in March (*see p19* **By
Season**), Three Dog's creates a canine St Joseph's altar. Home-made dog biscuits cost $4.95 per pound.

Records, tapes & CDs

Considering music is such an important part of New Orleans life, there is a surprising lack of good music shops. We've listed the best of the independent, specialist shops but you'll probably find the widest selection at the large chainstores, **Tower** and the newly arrived **Virgin. Beckham's** bookshop (*see page 153*) is worth visiting for second-hand classical recordings, including old vinyl.

Blockbuster Music

*231 N Carrollton Avenue, at Bienville Street (484 7200).
Bus 90 Carrollton.* **Open** 10am-10pm Mon-Fri; 10am-
11pm Sat; 11am-11pm Sun. **Credit** AmEx, Disc, MC, V.
Map 5 D5
Part of the national Blockbuster chain, the music side of things offers good prices on well-known national acts, but is weak on local and regional artists.
Branch: 5300 Tchoupitoulas Street (891 4026).

CD Warehouse

*8200 Hampson Street, at Carrollton Avenue (864 0444).
St Charles Streetcar.* **Open** 11am-9pm Mon-Sat; 1-6pm
Sun. **Credit** MC, V. **Map 4 A8**
They call themselves 'two seedy guys' and they sell nothing but CDs, many at cut-rate prices.

Jim Russell Records

*1837 Magazine Street, at St Mary Street (522 2602).
Bus 11 Magazine.* **Open** 10am-7pm Mon-Sat; noon-6pm
Sun. **Credit** AmEx, MC, V. **Map 6 B3**
An extensive, eclectic and strange collection of old 45s and LP vinyls, including some old Neville Brother albums. There's also a large selection of rap, soul and R&B.

Louisiana Music Factory

210 Decatur Street, at Bienville Street (586 1094). Bus 3 Vieux Carré, 41 Canal, 55 Elysian Fields, 81 Almonaster, 82 Desire. **Open** 10am-10pm daily. **Credit** AmEx, Disc, MC, V. **Map 7 B3**

This French Quarter store is chock full of music by New Orleans and regional artists, with extensive jazz and blues selections, bountiful bins of Cajun, zydeco, R&B and gospel, and helpful, knowledgeable staff. Rickety stairs lead vinyl collectors to an attic full of second-hand LPs. On weekends you might catch Tab Benoit, Snooks Eaglin or Ellis Marsalis in a live performance to celebrate a new release; call for the current schedule. Voted best record store by readers of *OffBeat* magazine.

Magic Bus

527 Conti Street, at Decatur Street (522 0530). Bus 3 Vieux Carré, 55 Elysian Fields, 81 Almonaster, 82 Desire. **Open** 11am-8pm daily. **Credit** AmEx, MC, V. **Map 7 B3**

The cool English guys who run this place offer some 15,000 titles in new and second-hand CDs and some rare vinyl – mainly rock and pop.

Musica Latina

4226 Magazine Street, at General Pershing Street (895 4227). Bus 11 Magazine. **Open** 10.30am-7pm Mon-Sat; 3-6pm Sun. **Credit** AmEx, Disc, MC, V. **Map 4 D10**

If your taste is for Latin sounds, this is the best place for salsa, merengue, boleros, tangos, flamenco et al. The staff are informative and helpful.

Mushroom

1037 Broadway, at Zimple Street (866 6065). Bus 22 Broadway. **Open** 10am-midnight daily. **Credit** AmEx, Disc, MC, V. **Map 4 B8**

Shop with the college-aged punters for 'import' (aka bootleg) CDs of live performances. Mushroom has a decent selection of local releases and indie music and also trades, buys or sells used CDs, LPs and cassettes.

Peaches

3129 Gentilly Boulevard, at Elysian Fields (282 3322). Bus 55 Elysian Fields. **Open** 10am-9pm Mon-Fri, Sun; 10am-10pm Sat. **Credit** AmEx, Disc, MC, V.

This the best place in town for rap and soul; Peaches has a good gospel section.

Rock & Roll Collectibles

1214 Decatur Street, at Gov Nicholls Street (561 5683). Bus 3 Vieux Carré, 48 Esplanade, 55 Elysian Fields, 81 Almonaster, 82 Desire. **Open** 10am-10pm daily. **Credit** AmEx, MC, V. **Map 7 D3**

Rock 'n' roll vinyl galore, along with plenty of blues, soul and jazz, including recordings by local musicians.

Tower Records

408 N Peters Street, at Conti Street (529 4411). Bus 3 Vieux Carré, 55 Elysian Fields, 81 Almonaster, 82 Desire. **Open** 9am-midnight daily. **Credit** AmEx, Disc, MC, V. **Map 7 B3**

The big daddy of music retail, with two floors offering up an impressive selection in most categories; serious music lovers should plan to spend time and money here. Tower also does a good job in stocking local artists. The video section (on the ground floor) is pretty thorough, too.

Underground Sounds

3336 Magazine Street, near Louisiana Avenue (897 9030). Bus 11 Magazine. **Open** noon-7pm Mon-Sat; noon-5pm Sun. **Credit** AmEx, Disc, MC, V. **Map 4 E9**

Head Underground for alternative and punk records and publications. The selection of new vinyl is surprisingly large.

Virgin Megastore

Jackson Brewery, 600 Decatur Street, at Toulouse Street (671 8100). Bus 3 Vieux Carré, 55 Elysian Fields, 81 Almonaster, 82 Desire. **Open** 10am-midnight Mon-Thur, Sun; 9am-midnight Fri, Sat. **Credit** AmEx, Disc, MC, V. **Map 7 B3**

The city's newest record giant opened in 1998. It's even bigger and better than **Tower** (*see above*) in the scope and depth of its selection, with three floors of CDs, tapes, videos, books and magazines housed in a neon-lit, utilitarian space. The second-floor coffeeshop is the best spot in the whole place because it's light and airy and overlooks the Mississippi.

Sport & fitness

For bicycle and rollerblading shops, see *chapter* **Sport & Fitness**.

Adventure Sports

333 N Service Road E, at Papworth Street, Metairie (835 1932). Bus 41 Canal. **Open** 10am-6pm Mon-Sat. **Credit** Disc, MC, V.

An outdoors outfitter with an emphasis on Southern weather conditions and the surrounding wilderness area. You'll find everything here – from tents, sleeping bags and hiking boots to rock climbing equipment – in all the major brands. There is a good selection of books and hiking maps and the staff are well informed and helpful.

Ticket agencies

Ticketmaster (522 5555) sells tickets for all major sporting and entertainment events in New Orleans. There are outlets in all the Blockbuster stores (*see below* **Video rental**) and the best-kept-secret location is in the Maison Blanche store on Canal Street (*see page 147* **Department stores**). The branch is only open during Maison Blanche store hours but when hot concert tickets go on sale, there is rarely a queue here, as there is elsewhere.

Video rental

The video selection at **Tower Records** (*see above*) is more diverse than at other chain rental stores, and it stocks more foreign titles than action and adventure movies.

Blockbuster Video

5330 Tchoupitoulas Street, at Valmont Street (897 9426). Bus 10 Tchoupitoulas. **Open** 10am-midnight daily. **Credit** AmEx, Disc, MC, V. **Map 4 C10**

This nation-wide chain has branches all over town, and stocks all the latest video releases as well as many of the classics. Check the phone book for the location of your nearest branch.

Video Alternatives

4725 Magazine Street, at Valence Street (891 5347). Bus 11 Magazine. **Open** 11am-10pm daily. **Credit** AmEx, Disc, MC, V. **Map 4 D10**

An Uptown shop that specialises in renting out foreign and classic films on video.

Entertainment

Children

Where to find the nosh, the novelties and the necessities for your nippers. We kid you not.

In a city where sugar-dusted beignets make an appropriate meal at any time of day and adults are happy to don costumes at the slightest excuse, children feel immediately at home. They're welcome almost everywhere and since bad behaviour falls loosely within the city's motto of 'let the good times roll', a temper tantrum is certainly no cause to pass on the bread pudding in the best of restaurants.

The disadvantage of visiting a city governed by the Inner Child is that you can't expect the adults around you to prevent your toddler from grabbing that pair of Mardi Gras beads sailing directly from a carnival float, or from selling alcohol to a youngster who might pass for 14. Although New Orleans is working hard to combat its dangerous reputation, the only way to be sure of your children's safety is to keep them under close supervision.

More information on local events can be obtained from the **New Orleans Welcome Center** in the French Quarter (*see page 168*).

Babysitting

You'll have to trust the agency to provide a responsible babysitter, as neither the city nor the state imposes rigorous licensing requirements on babysitting services. Both the agencies listed below claim to employ sitters over 21, with no criminal records and with prior experience. Nevertheless, careful screening of your sitter is recommended.

Accent on Children's Arrangements
Information 524 1227/pager 544 2818/fax 524 1229/ accentoca@accentoca.com. **Open** 8.30am-5pm Mon-Fri; on call 24 hours daily. **Cost** rates vary; call for more information. **Credit** AmEx, MC, V.
Accent provides a range of services, from daycare to city tours, for large groups only and by prior arrangement.

Dependable Kid Care
Information 486 4001/fax 486 5008/dnfc@dependable kidcare.com. **Open** 8am-5pm Mon-Fri; on call 24 hours daily. **Cost** from $9 a hour depending on number of children; call for more information. **Credit** AmEx, MC, V.

Sidle up to sharks at the **Aquarium of the Americas**. *See page 168.*

The firm will send a sitter to your hotel or lodging, even if your child is ailing. Phone a day or two ahead for family bookings; give two to three weeks' notice for a large group. *Website: www.dependablekidcare.com*

Eating out

New Orleans's justly famous cuisine isn't all raw oysters and zesty Cajun spices. There's plenty to please any child's more pedestrian palate. In the French Quarter, sample the beignets at **Café du Monde** (*see page 142*). For a more substantial meal, the French Quarter branch of **La Madeleine** (547 St Ann Street, at Jackson Square; 568 9950) offers wonderful pastries, soups and sandwiches. And if your youngsters won't brave the half-shell at **Acme Oyster House** (*see page 123*) or **Felix's Seafood Restaurant & Oyster Bar** (*see page 124*), tempt them with a fried oyster po-boy. The **Hard Rock Café** (*see page 134*) serves undistinguished fare but kids like the atmosphere and you'll like the prices. The **Louisiana Pizza Kitchen** (French Market Place, at Barracks Street; 522 9500) takes its pies to delectable culinary heights with toppings such as sun-dried tomato with roasted garlic, or gumbo ya-ya. If your meat lover craves a hamburger, **Port of Call** (*see page 126*) serves a great one, but avoid peak hours because there aren't many tables and service can be slow.

In the CBD, **New City Diner** (828 Gravier Street, at Baronne Street; 522 8198) and **Mother's** (*see page 128*) have cafeteria lines, offering finicky eaters a chance to look at the food before they commit to anything. Uptown, step into a 1950s diner at the **Camellia Grill** (*see page 131*) for an omelette and a slice of pecan pie, or share an enormous plate of pasta with your child at the local pasta chain **Semolina** (3242 Magazine Street, at Louisiana Avenue; 895 4260).

Fast-food outlets are everywhere, naturally, but New Orleans's own **Popeye's** (*see page 134*) has a few local specialities such as red beans and rice, fried chicken, and dirty rice that make a fine picnic meal if you can stomach the grease. Also, **Taco Bell**, located everywhere but downtown and open as late as your child can last, makes an earnest effort to include a few nutritional ingredients in each Tex-Mex dish (check the phone directory for your nearest branch).

Entertainment

General

Blaine Kern's Mardi Gras World

See p82 **Sightseeing** *for listings.*
Catch the ferry from the bottom of Canal Street to the Algiers side, where shuttle buses (9.30am-4.30pm daily) will whisk visitors to this warehouse where artists work all year round to create the floats for Mardi Gras parades. The fantastic exhibits can be viewed without the accompanying Mardi

Ooh, aah: the **Louisiana Children's Museum**.

Gras hubbub and kids can look at the spectacular floats instead of diving under the wheels in search of goodies thrown from them.

Ferry rides

See p82 **Sightseeing** *for listings.*
Ferry rides across the Mississippi offer an inexpensive view of the river and are great fun.

IMAX Theater

See p51 **Sightseeing** *for listings.*
A five-storey-high screen and booming digital sound system immerse the viewer in educational films, generally depicting natural themes. It's next door to the **Aquarium of the Americas** (*see p168*). Hours, show times and prices vary.

Louisiana Children's Museum

420 Julia Street, between Magazine & Tchoupitoulas Streets (523 1357). Bus 3 Vieux Carré, 10 Tchoupitoulas, 11 Magazine. **Open** *Sept-May* 9.30am-4.30pm Tue-Sat; noon-4.30pm Sun; *Jun-Aug* 9.30am-4.30pm Mon-Sat; noon-4.30pm Sun. **Admission** $5. **Credit** AmEx, MC, V. **Map 6 C2**
Well-conceived interactive exhibits teach the concepts of maths and science without preaching. Kids can create their own news broadcast, encase themselves in giant bubbles or watch the interplay of bones as a skeleton rides a bike. An especially welcome resource on rainy days.
Disabled: toilets. Website: www.lcm.org

Louisiana Superdome

See p60 **Sightseeing** *for listings.*
Frequent shows and athletic events are staged at the

Superdome, some of which are specially geared to children, such as the circus and *Disney on Ice*. If nothing is going on, your child might be consoled with a tour of the world's largest indoor arena; monitors offer glimpses of the events you've missed.

Streetcar rides

The St Charles Avenue streetcar runs from Canal Street to Carrollton and Claiborne Avenues, but the best sights are gone once the tracks turn on to Carrollton. For 10¢ more than the usual $1 fare, you can get on and off an unlimited number of times. Heading Uptown, disembark at First Street, go left one block to Prytania Street, then right five blocks for some of the prettiest sights the Garden District has to offer. At the corner of Washington Avenue and Prytania Street view the **Lafayette Cemetery** (*see p70* **Sightseeing**) and get some refreshment at **PJ's Coffee & Tea** (*see p142* **Cafés & Coffeehouses**) before reboarding the streetcar at Washington and St Charles. If the children need to stretch their legs, disembark again at **Audubon Park** (*see p74* **Sightseeing**). If they're wildly energetic, you can walk the mile to **Audubon Zoo** (*see below and p74* **Sightseeing**) at the back of the park. Reboard, and finally disembark at the Carrollton stop for a meal at the **Camellia Grill** (*see p131* **Restaurants**).

Animals & nature

Aquarium of the Americas

See p51 Sightseeing *for listings.*
The aquatic life of North and South America and the waters in between are explored here. Sharks get star billing. The **IMAX Theater** is next door (*see p167*).

Audubon Zoo

See p75 Sightseeing *for listings.*
Some 1,500 animals are kept in their natural habitats in these beautifully landscaped grounds in Audubon Park, a short walk from the St Charles streetcar stop. The award-winning Louisiana Swamp Exhibit has an impressive array of indigenous species. For the younger and tamer at heart, there's a petting zoo and a nice playground.

Global Wildlife Center

26389 Highway 40, Folsom (624 9453/796 3585).
Open *summer* 9am-4pm daily; *winter* 9am-3pm daily.
Admission free; wagon tour $10; $9 seniors; $8 2-11s.
Credit Disc, MC, V.
Admission to the centre is free, but you'll want to take the guided wagon tour around the 900 acres (365 hectares) populated by giraffe, zebra and other African grassland animals. It's about a 75-minute drive from New Orleans.
Disabled: toilets. Website: www.globalwildlife.com

French Quarter

Although it's most famous for its 24-hour adult entertainments, the French Quarter by day is a fascinating habitat for children. At weekends and on most other fair-weather days, street performers abound in **Jackson Square** (*see page 49* **Sightseeing**). A walk around the perimeter of the square can occupy several hours if the mime artists, balloon artists, psychics, musicians, tap dancers and portraitists are taken into full account. Most of the artists are amusing to watch and some are even talented. If you want one to undertake a pastel or caricature of your child, it's probably best to observe a work-in-progress, rather than relying on the artist's putative samples.

From the **New Orleans Welcome Center** on the square, brief walking tours head in almost every direction. These will take you down narrow streets overhung with wrought iron balconies. Even if the kids' stamina is flagging, try at least to coax them down **Pirate's Alley**, a charming two-block pedestrian walkway along the left side of St Louis Cathedral as you face it. Or cross Decatur Street and climb the steps leading to the **Moon Walk**, which overlooks the Mississippi River. From here, you can walk through **Woldenberg Riverfront Park** – which occupies 17 acres (7 hectares) of green space along the river between the French Quarter and Canal Street – to the **Aquarium of the Americas** (*see above*) and the **IMAX Theater** (*see page 167*).

Along the Decatur Street side of Jackson Square, horse-drawn **carriages** offer 35-minute tours of the French Quarter at a cost of about $40 per party (one to four people). The drivers give a brief, shallow but generally interesting commentary on architectural and 'historical' points of interest along the route. The fun of the ride usually keeps children quiet, if not attentive.

Musée Conti Wax Museum of Louisiana

See p91 Museums & Galleries *for listings.*
What tourist city would be complete without a wax museum? The Musée Conti takes the usual tabloid approach to history with tableaux that depict Napoleon signing away Louisiana while in his bathtub, frenzied voodoo dancers and slaves being whipped. Kids love it.

New Orleans Historic Pharmacy Museum

See p91 Museums & Galleries *for listings.*
This nineteenth-century apothecary shop has been preserved at its original site. The collection of jars, voodoo powders, gris-gris potions and containers for leeches will appeal to budding scientists.

New Orleans Welcome Center

529 St Ann Street, on Jackson Square (568 5661/fax 568 5664/parcher@linknet.net). Bus 3 Vieux Carré, 55 Elysian Fields, 81 Almonaster, 82 Desire. **Open** 9am-5pm daily. **Map 7 C2**
Come here for city maps, information and brochures (some offering discounts) on numerous local attractions.
Website: www.louisianatravel.com

Haunts for older children

The **Crescent Star Magick & Mystery Tour** (*see page 85* **Sightseeing**) is a good French Quarter walking tour for children aged 12 and up, strong on tales of witchcraft, voodoo and ghosts.

Haunted History Tour & Voodoo/Cemetery Tour

Tours leave from Rev Zombie's Voodoo Shop, 723 St Peter Street, between Bourbon & Royal Streets (861 2727). Bus 3 Vieux Carré. **Tickets** $15; $7 under-12s. **Credit** AmEx, Disc, MC, V. **Map 7 B2** (departure point)
The Haunted History Tour (2pm, 8pm daily) is a two-hour walking tour led by theatrical, storytelling guides. The Voodoo/Cemetery tour (10am, 1.15pm daily) takes you to New Orleans's oldest cemetery, St Louis Cemetery No.1, which contains the tomb of legendary voodoo queen Marie

Take your tot on a magical mystery ride at Storyland in **City Park** *(page 170).*

Laveau. Reservations are not required if you arrive 15 minutes before the tours start.
Website: www.hauntedhistorytours.com

Wearing them out

If your little angel has been perfectly attentive to each of the 660 collection objects at the **Cabildo** (*see page 89* **Museums & Galleries**) – or needs an inducement to behave tomorrow – try one of the treats below, all of which are found on the outskirts of the city. Don't go expecting any entertainment for yourself, although you might be pleasantly surprised.

Airline Skate Center

6711 Airline Drive, at David Drive, Metairie (733 2248). Bus 38 Airline. **Open** 1-9pm Mon-Thur; 1-11pm Fri, Sat; 1-10pm Sun. **Admission** around $6.50. **No credit cards.**
A gigantic new skating rink with rental skates, strobe lights and funky music.
Disabled: toilets.

Attack Shak Indoor Paint Ball Arena

1008 Jefferson Highway, at Causeway Boulevard, Kenner (835 8898). Bus Kenner Local. **Open** *Sept-May* 3-10pm Tue-Thur; 3pm-1am Fri; noon-1am Sat; 2-10pm Sun; *June-Aug* noon-11pm Tue-Thur; noon-1am Fri, Sat; 2-10pm Sun. **Admission** $14.50, $18.50, $24 packages (includes gun rental, mask & all-day field pass). **Credit** MC, V.
Takes laser tag one step further. Cloaked in protective gear, kids shoot at each other with paint pellets. The yuck factor usually makes this venue less popular with girls. Note that no under-10s are allowed.

Climb-Max

5304 Canal Boulevard, at City Park Avenue (486 7600). Bus 42 Canal/Cemeteries, 46 City Park. **Open** 3-9pm Mon; 3-11pm Tue-Fri; 9am-11pm Sat; 9am-9pm Sun. **Admission** $15 day pass (includes climbing gear and instruction). **Credit** MC, V. **Map 5 C5**
An indoor climbing gym where kids can exhaust themselves on rock walls of varying grades of difficulty without much risk of falling – you're expected to belay them.
Disabled: toilets.

Discovery Zone

3809 Veterans Memorial Boulevard, at Cleary Avenue, Metairie (885 1801). Bus E1 Veterans Memorial Boulevard. **Open** 11am-8pm Mon-Thur; 10am-9pm Fri, Sat; 11am-7pm Sun. **Admission** $7.99; $4.99 children under 38in (96cm) tall. **Credit** MC, V.
A temple to the hyperactive child. Bells and whistles delight the kids and put adults into a stupor that makes them sense less to the speed at which their dollars are flying away. Celebration Station (5959 Veterans Memorial Boulevard, at I-10; 887 7888) offers similar activities.
Disabled: toilets.

Laser Tag & Games

8916 Veterans Memorial Boulevard, between David Drive & Williams Boulevard, Metairie (469 7475). Bus E1 Veterans Memorial Boulevard. **Open** *Sept-June* 3-10pm Mon-Thur; 3pm-midnight Fri; 11am-midnight Sat; 11am-10pm Sun; *July-Aug* 11am-10pm Mon-Thur, Sun; 11am-midnight Fri, Sat. **Admission** $4 per game. **No credit cards.**
Kids love laser tag; they're armed with laser guns and dress up in shields that record the 'hits' on them in team warfare. For those aged 7 and above.
Disabled: toilets. Website: www.ltag.com

Outdoor activities

Parks

Audubon Park

See p75 **Sightseeing** *for listings.*
The Audubon covers 400 acres (162 hectares) in the heart of uptown New Orleans. It's closed to traffic, and a tranquil lagoon and thousands of ancient oaks make it a beautiful place for walking, skating or riding bikes. The **Zoo** is a must (*see p168*). There's limited playground equipment at the St Charles Avenue end. Unsafe after dark.

City Park

See p77 **Sightseeing** *for listings.*
City Park boasts 1,500 lovely acres (608 hectares) of land and several family-oriented amusements. **Storyland** playground's recreated scenes from nursery rhymes and fairy stories are wonderful for small children, who can sit in Cinderella's pumpkin coach or climb into the whale's mouth with Jonah. Nearby, there's an assortment of scaled-down carnival rides, an old-fashioned carousel, a miniature train, and canoe and boat rentals.

Louisiana Nature Center

5700 Read Boulevard, New Orleans East (581 4629/ 1-800 774 7394). Bus 72 Paris Road Express.
Open 9am-5pm Tue-Fri; 10am-5pm Sat; noon-5pm Sun. **Admission** $4.50; $3.50 seniors; $2.50 3-14s. **Credit** AmEx, MC, V.
Occasional overnight programmes, hikes and discovery activities are run for kids at this centre (20 minutes by car from the Quarter), which occupies 86 acres (35 hectares) of hardwood bottomland forest and has three miles (4.8km) of trails and a planetarium. In warm months, bring bug spray. *Disabled: toilets. Website: www.auduboninstitute.org*

Swamp tours

Swamp touring companies are as plentiful as cypress trees, but children generally appreciate those sites closer to town that can be explored by smaller craft. Most excursions take two hours and include a guide who will point out interesting flora and fauna. In summer, when the heat can be brutal, a morning tour is preferable and bug repellent a must. Reservations are required for the tours below, most of which offer transport from New Orleans for approximately double the listed rates. For other swamp tours, *see page 87* **Sightseeing**.

Mr Denny's Voyageur Swamp Tours

Information 643 4839. **Tours** 10am, 2pm, 7pm daily. **Tickets** *without transport* $20; $12 under-12s. **No credit cards.**
Groups of six are paddled through Honey Island Swamp in canoes. Overnight and moonlight cruises are also available.

Mockingbird Swamp Tours

Information 386 7902/1-800 572 3046. **Tours** 10am, noon, 2pm daily. **Tickets** *without transport* $17; $8 under-12s. **No credit cards.**
Mockingbird runs explorations of the Manchac Swamp, 45 minutes north-west of New Orleans. Booking required.

Shopping

For other children's clothes shops, *see page 156* **Shops & Services**.

Baby Gap/Gap Kids

Riverwalk, 1 Poydras Street, at the Mississippi River (522 5828). Bus 3 Vieux Carré, 10 Tchoupitoulas.
Open 10am-9pm Mon-Sat; 11am-7pm Sun. **Credit** AmEx, Disc, JCB, MC, V. **Map 6 C1**
Well-designed and rugged casual wear. There are branches in most of the other large shopping malls.
Website: www.gapkids.com

Disney Store

Riverwalk, 1 Poydras Street, at the Mississippi River (524 9192). Bus 3 Vieux Carré, 10 Tchoupitoulas.
Open 10am-9pm Mon-Sat; 11am-7pm Sun. **Credit** AmEx, Disc, MC, V. **Map 6 C1**
In the Riverwalk shopping mall, Disney's masterful marketing brings its characters as winsomely to lunch boxes, pyjamas and toothbrushes as to the silver screen.

Laura Ashley Mother & Children

Canal Place Shopping Center, 333 Canal Street, at N Peters Street (522 9403). Bus 3 Vieux Carré, 41 Canal. **Open** 10am-6pm Mon-Wed; 10am-7pm Thur-Sat; noon-6pm Sun. **Credit** AmEx, Disc, JCB, MC, V. **Map 7 A3**
Little girls who fancy Peter Pan collars and smocking will find the perfect dress here.

Maple Street Children's Book Shop

See p153 **Shops & Services** *for listings.*
A cosy cottage crammed with children's books, next door to a cosy cottage crammed with books for grown-ups. Picture books with a local flavour include *Cajun Night Before Christmas* by Trosclair; *Feliciana Feydra LeRoux* by Tynia Thomassie; and *Gumbo Goes Downtown* by Carol Talley.

The Nature Company

Riverwalk, 1 Poydras Street, at the Mississippi River (523 2981). Bus 3 Vieux Carré, 10 Tchoupitoulas.
Open 10am-9pm Mon-Sat; 11am-7pm Sun. **Credit** AmEx, Disc, MC, V. **Map 6 C1**
Geodes and whale music plus toys, games and puzzles inspired by nature fill the shelves here. If you don't want to dress your youngster in a Bourbon Street T-shirt, what about one with dinosaurs on it?
Website: www.natureco.com

Toys R Us

12250 I-10 Service Road, at Bullard Avenue, Metairie (245 8697). Bus 64 Lake Forest, 72 Paris Road Express.
Open 9.30am-9.30pm Mon-Sat; 11am-7pm Sun. **Credit** AmEx, Disc, MC, V.
A warehouse packed chock-a-block with virtually every brand name of toy. It's nirvana or it's a migraine, depending on your point of view, but the prices are unarguably good. *Website: www.toys.com*

Warner Bros Studio Store

Riverwalk, 1 Poydras Street, at the Mississippi River (524 9880). Bus 3 Vieux Carré, 10 Tchoupitoulas.
Open 10am-9pm Mon-Sat; 11am-7pm Sun. **Credit** AmEx, Disc, JCB, MC, V. **Map 6 C1**
A few doors down from the Disney Store, Tweety and Sylvester give the Lion King a run for his money. *Website: www.warnerbros.com*

The World's Best Toys

Canal Place Shopping Center, 333 Canal Street, at N Peters Street (558 0400/1-800 668 9639). Bus 3 Vieux Carré, 41 Canal. **Open** 10am-6pm Mon-Wed; 10am-7pm Thur-Sat; noon-6pm Sun. **Credit** AmEx, Disc, MC, V. **Map 7 A3**
A small but appealing selection, focusing on creative and educational, rather than mass-market toys.

Film

New Orleanians spend more time in front of the camera than in front of the screen. Here's where to see the city on film, and where to see films in the city.

The first three things people associate with New Orleans (after heat, humidity and mosquitoes) are Mardi Gras, music and food. Among locals, movie-going finds a place on the list of activities some way below that of partying, dining and partying some more. Per capita film attendance is lower than in most other American cities, and New Orleanians have access to a narrower range of movies than is available in cities of comparable size elsewhere in what Hollywood calls 'Flyover Land' – the great expanse between New York and Los Angeles where all films (except for Adrian Lyne's *Lolita*) get screened.

Still, what New Orleans misses is usually miss-able: second-rate Hollywood fare that performs poorly at the box office elsewhere. All the big US films, in both popular and artistic terms, enjoy a local release. And the city's aggressive art houses bring in a decent smattering of foreign films, including most of the films that garner Oscar nominations each year.

IT'S A WRAP

New Orleans has also proved an increasingly popular venue for film production. This is partly because Louisiana is a so-called 'right to work' state, which means production companies can hire non-union employees. Also, the prevailing wages and cost of living are lower in south Louisiana than in almost all other parts of the US. Films can be made for less money than elsewhere, and for decidedly less money than in heavily unionised California.

But, of course, New Orleans and the surrounding area have attractions that transcend the willingness of its labour force to work cheaply. The architecture of the city is distinctive: in the French Quarter, in the mansions of the Garden District and in the ornate Victorian homes Uptown. Plantations, like the ones at nearby Destrehan and Oak Alley, preserve the nineteenth century just a short drive up the Mississippi River. And all by itself, the forbidding beauty of the Louisiana swamp has attracted many a film-maker.

Head to the megaplex **Palace Theatre 20** *for mainstream viewing. See page 174.*

On location

America's enduring fascination with New Orleans as the country's 'most European city' has made the area the repeated subject of cinematic treatment. Today, the film industry is burgeoning in south Louisiana, which over the past decade has played host to nearly 100 movies, including a significant number of high-profile pictures by the world's leading directors and a glamorous array of stars.

A shortlist of the best recent films shot and set in or near New Orleans would include Tim Robbins's *Dead Man Walking* (1995), with Sean Penn and Susan Sarandon in her Oscar-winning role as New Orleans nun Helen Prejean; Neil Jordan's *Interview With the Vampire* (1994), with Tom Cruise as local author Anne Rice's vampire Lestat and Brad Pitt as his morose, bloodsucking companion; John Sayles's *Passion Fish* (1993), with Mary McDonnell in her Oscar-nominated

role as a paralysed and embittered former soap opera queen; Oliver Stone's *JFK* (1991), with Kevin Costner as crusading New Orleans district attorney and arch conspiracy theorist Jim Garrison; David Lynch's Southern Gothic *Wild at Heart* (1990), with Nicolas Cage and Laura Dern as lovers on the run; and Steven Soderbergh's Baton Rouge-filmed *sex, lies, and videotape* (1989), which won the Palme d'Or at Cannes.

The first New Orleans film to capture much notice was William Wyler's *Jezebel*, which starred Henry Fonda and won a 1938 best actress Oscar for Bette Davis as his scheming fiancée. Perhaps the finest film about the city was Elia Kazan's adaptation of the Tennessee Williams classic, *A Streetcar Named Desire* (1951, *above left*), won Oscars for Vivien Leigh, Kim Hunter and Karl Malden and a nomination for co-star Marlon Brando. Some critics, however (we're not among them), hold out for Kazan's earlier *Panic in the Streets* (1950), which starred Richard Widmark, Barbara Bel Geddes, Jack Palance and Zero Mostel in a thriller about an outbreak of bubonic plague. Many baby boomers, of course, retain fond memories of Dennis Hopper's *Easy Rider* (1969, *pictured opposite*), which starred Hopper and Peter Fonda as bikers looking for a place to settle down and made a star of Jack Nicholson as the daffy lawyer who tags along for a while.

Other locally set films of note include Anthony Quinn's *The Buccaneer* (1958), the story of the Battle of New Orleans, with Yul Brynner as Jean Lafitte and Charlton Heston as Andrew Jackson;

Until very recently, film companies had to go elsewhere to do all post-production, a fact that has no doubt kept a true colony of film-makers from settling in Louisiana. However, indigenous writer-directors Glen Pitre (*Belizaire the Cajun*) and Pat Mire (*Dirty Rice*) continue to live in the area, and they are joined by such distinguished part-time residents as film-makers Francis Ford Coppola (the *Godfather* trilogy), Taylor Hackford (*An Officer and a Gentleman*, as well as the locally set *Everybody's All-American*) and Ron Shelton (*Bull Durham* and *Blaze*), all of whom own property in the city. Helen Mirren (who is married to Hackford) and John Goodman (among his many credits) and TV performers Gerald McRaney and Delta Burke also spend long periods in the city. Perhaps the most powerful film person to live in New Orleans was the late Brandon Tartikoff, one-time president of Paramount Studios and before that head of programming at NBC.

A full-service production studio has opened recently in suburban Harahan. It provides sound stages for set construction and interior shoots, as well as state-of-the-art post-production facilities. Combined with the other advantages available locally, it might well lead to an increase in the number of film-makers and stars who call New Orleans home. Should this happen, newcomers will find a talented pool of locals trained in the cinematic arts at the **University of New Orleans**'s film programme. The **New Orleans Video Access Center** also supplies resources to local and regional professionals working primarily in video.

New Orleans Video Access Center
913 Magazine Street, New Orleans, LA 70130 (524 8626).

University of New Orleans
Department of Drama & Communications, University of New Orleans, New Orleans, LA 70148 (280 6317).

Martin Ritt's *Sounder* (1972), with Cicely Tyson, Paul Winfield and Kevin Hooks in a story about a Depression-era family of black sharecroppers; Walter Hill's *Hard Times* (1975), with Charles Bronson as a bare-knuckled streetfighter and James Coburn as his weaselly manager; Louis Malle's *Pretty Baby* (1977), with Brooke Shields in her début performance as a 12-year-old Storyville prostitute, Susan Sarandon as her corrupt mother and Keith Carradine as photographer Jacques Bellocq; Richard Tuggle's *Tightrope* (1984), featuring one of Clint Eastwood's finest performances as a sexually kinky New Orleans cop looking for a vicious serial killer; Andrei Konchalovsky's *Shy People* (1987), with Jill Clayburgh as a journalist writing an article about swamp-dweller Barbara Hershey; and Alan Parker's *Angel Heart* (1987), with Mickey Rourke as a private eye hired by an evil Robert De Niro.

Also of note are the Coen brothers' *Miller's Crossing* (1990), an existential gangster tale with Gabriel Byrne and Albert Finney (New Orleans here stands in for Depression-era New Jersey); and one of our favourites, Jim Jarmusch's *Down by Law* (1986), the story of three losers (including Italian star Roberto Benigni) who bond while serving time in a New Orleans jail.

And of enduring popularity, of course, is Jim McBride's *The Big Easy* (1986), a crime romance starring Dennis Quaid as a homicide detective and Ellen Barkin as the new DA. Well-made as this picture is, New Orleanians howl at Quaid's bizarre accent, which mixes, like oil and water, a Georgia drawl with some Cajun patois and includes not a dollop of the 'wheh yat, cap'n' Brooklynese far more likely to spring forth from the mouth of a real white New Orleans cop.

Perhaps the most intriguing movie about New Orleans, though, is one that is yet to be made, namely a film adaptation of John Kennedy Toole's Pulitzer Prize-winning *A Confederacy of Dunces*, once in development as a project for the late John Belushi, subsequently for the late John Candy. Producers are said now to be trying to develop the production for John Goodman. Since its publication in 1981, 'Confederacy' has been widely hailed as the definitive novel about New Orleans, a keen, affectionate and hilarious observation of the city and its colourful inhabitants. Goodman, who spends more time in New Orleans than perhaps any other Hollywood celebrity, would be a perfect choice if the proper script could be put together.

Cinemas

Movie-going has a long and interesting history in New Orleans. The first theatre anywhere in America dedicated exclusively to film programming opened in the city in 1896: Vitascope Hall, located at 623 Canal Street (at the corner of Exchange Place, and now occupied by a Burger King). It was the world's second movie theatre, preceded only by one in France. By the height of the silent era in the 1910s, Canal Street hosted more than a dozen cinemas, while others lined the streets in the downtown area.

By the mid-1920s, the first of the grand movie palaces began to appear. For the first year or so of its existence, the Loew's State (now the **State Palace**) did business as a vaudeville house, showing some films between the acts of its live programme. Across the street the magnificent **Saenger** opened exclusively as a venue for motion

pictures, as did the **Orpheum** around the corner. On rare occasions, all three theatres still show movies. The Orpheum sold out for a local production about New Orleans's restaurants (there's that food thing again), and Robert Redford showed up a few years ago for a benefit première of *Legal Eagles*. The State Palace has hosted travelling productions of the American Film Institute, and Carmine Coppola (Francis's father) led a 60-piece orchestra in a performance of his score for Abel Gance's silent masterpiece, *Napoléon*.

Ironically, all three of these gorgeous old theatres survive today as venues for live performance (*see chapters* **The Performing Arts** *and* **Nightlife** *for listings*). The Saenger hosts concerts, touring shows of Broadway musicals and other travelling stage productions; the Orpheum is the home of the Louisiana Philharmonic Orchestra; and the State Palace is booked mainly by music acts. Unrenovated as it is, the State Palace quickly reveals both its decayed splendour and the chilling spectre of the city's segregationist past. The inaccessible second balcony was once reserved for African-American patrons, who had to enter through a small separate entrance off Canal Street and buy their tickets at a separate box office. The other two theatres have been painstakingly renovated: the velvet seats are plush, the brass rails gleam. The Orpheum is beautiful, but the Saenger is nothing less than magnificent, as ornate and glamorous a movie house as was ever built anywhere.

Since the mid-1960s, in a phenomenon typical of mid-sized cities across the US, cinemas in Greater New Orleans have relocated from single-screen theatres downtown to shopping-mall multiplexes in the suburbs. Today, the area has 18 cinema sites. Only two of these are downtown, and only the **Joy** in Canal Street is regularly engaged in mainstream programming. In fact, of these 18 cinemas, only eight, with a total of 29 screens, are located in the municipality of New Orleans. By contrast, there are ten theatre operations with a total of 93 screens in the suburban areas of Jefferson and St Bernard Parishes.

A visitor to the city staying downtown will probably have to travel to one of three multiplexes in Jefferson Parish to view mainstream programming: the **Lakeside Cinema**, **AMC Galleria** or the megaplex **Palace 20**. Any of these three is an excellent choice. They are all comfortable, well managed and furnished with state-of-the-art equipment. You can reach them by bus but it's a long-winded process, so it's probably better to go by taxi or car (all have ample parking). The huge Palace 20 features raked stadium seating in each theatre, so sightlines are unimpeded even when screenings are sold out.

For fans of art cinema, the city has four theatres offering American independent and foreign film programming on 11 different screens. Most convenient for downtown is the **Landmark's Canal Place Cinema**. However, there's likely to be more choice at **Movie Pitchers** in Mid City, only two blocks off the Canal Street bus route. It normally offers two independent or foreign titles nightly on each of its four screens.

Other possibilities include the **Zeitgeist** (take the Magazine Street bus from downtown), which offers a wide range of films from the US and abroad and specialises in pictures with gay and lesbian themes. (It also presents performance art and avant-garde music and hosts art exhibitions.) The **Contemporary Arts Center** (see page 92 **Museums & Galleries**) also screens movies.

Finally, there's the vintage **Prytania Theatre**, just a short walk from the St Charles Avenue Streetcar line uptown. The city's last single-screen cinema, it opened as a neighbourhood movie house in the 1920s. In the 1970s it became the city's leading repertory cinema and in the 1980s the flagship art house. It has recently been renovated and currently offers eclectic programming with a speciality in English-language art films.

Daily listings for all area screens are available in the *Times-Picayune*. Reviews and other useful information can be found in the weekly *Gambit* and in the Picayune's Friday entertainment tabloid insert 'Lagniappe'.

In addition to the city's regular film offerings, each October the **New Orleans Film and Video Society** (225 Baronne Street, suite 1712, New Orleans, LA 70112; 523 3818) stages the New Orleans Film and Video Festival, a week-long series of premières and screenings focusing on American independent cinema. The festival includes workshops and panel discussions, plus features and shorts on 16mm film and video. Most screenings are held at the Canal Place Cinema and just a few steps away at the **Southern Repertory Theater** (see page 212 **The Performing Arts** for listings).

AMC Galleria 8 Theatre
1 Galleria Boulevard, suite 700, at Causeway Boulevard, Metairie (838 8309/8338). Bus Kenner Local to Causeway Boulevard, then Causeway bus. **Admission** $5.75; $3.75 under-12s, concessions, matinée; $3 twilight (4-6pm). **No credit cards.**

Joy Theatre
1200 Canal Street, at Elk Place (522 7575). Bus 41 Canal, 88 St Claude. **Admission** $5.75; $3.75 under-12s, concessions, matinée. **No credit cards. Map 7 A1**

Lakeside General Cinema
3301 Veterans Boulevard, at Severn Avenue, behind Lakeside Shopping Center, Metairie (833 2881). Bus Kenner Local or Veterans Memorial to Causeway Boulevard, then Causeway bus. **Admission** $6.25; $3.75 under-12s, concessions, matinée. **No credit cards.**

Landmark's Canal Place Cinema
Canal Place Shopping Center, 3rd floor, 333 Canal Street, at N Peters Street (581 5400). Bus 41 Canal, 55 Elysian Fields, 57 Franklin, 82 Desire. **Admission** $6.25; $4.25 under-12s, concessions, matinée. **No credit cards. Map 7 A3**

Movie Pitchers
3941 Bienville Street, at N Pierce Street (488 8881). Bus 40, 41, 42, 43 Canal, 90 Carrollton. **Admission** $5; $4 concessions, matinée. **No credit cards. Map 5 D5**

Palace Theatre 20
1200 Elmwood Park Boulevard, at South Clearview Parkway, behind Elmwood Shopping Center, Elmwood (734 2020). Bus Kenner Local to Elmwood Drive, then HP Long minibus. **Admission** $6; $3.50 3-12s, matinée. **Credit** MC, V.

Prytania Theatre
5339 Prytania Street, at Leontine Street (891 2787). St Charles Streetcar. **Admission** $6; $4-$5 under-12s, concessions. **No credit cards. Map 4 C9**

Zeitgeist Alternative Arts Center
2010 Magazine Street, at St Andrew Street (524 0064). Bus 11 Magazine. **Admission** $6; $5 concessions; $4 members. **No credit cards. Map 6 B3**

Gay & Lesbian

Extravagant celebrations, thriving bars and flamboyant costumes – queer New Orleans is worth getting dressed up for.

Gay New Orleans in many ways reflects the broader culture of this exciting city. In the past, homosexual behaviour fell easily into the customs established by illicit heterosexual relationships and continued to exist within society as long as certain rules were observed. Everyone understood that in the eye of the state, homosexual acts were criminal; that in the eye of the Church, homosexuals were sinners; and that all such practices must be in secret – in short, out of everyone's eye.

Within this framework of tacit tolerance, a vibrant homosexual culture developed in the French Quarter. Tennessee Williams came to terms with his sexuality there and found the freedom he needed to create his great body of work. Also seeking asylum in the Quarter were writers Truman Capote and Lyle Saxon, photographer Frances Benjamin Johnston and artist William Spratling. The same society that attracted artists and writers also found space for homosexual men and women in general.

After 250 years of New Orleans's history, the existing concept of homosexuality was challenged on all fronts by the arrival of the gay liberation movement of the late 1960s. As elsewhere, the tidal wave of the sexual revolution came crashing down on the old order. The new wave demanded that homosexuality should not be illegal and not deemed immoral. Furthermore, gay people had the right – no, the responsibility – to be visible, recognised and free from discrimination.

But gay liberation was slow to develop in New Orleans. This was due partly to the general culture of the South, which tends to be conservative and slow to change, and partly to the fact that New Orleans, despite its sizeable gay population, is not a large city and did not provide the anonymity afforded by bigger cities such as New York, Los Angeles, Chicago, Houston, Dallas or Atlanta.

Infamous anti-gay crusader Anita Bryant arrived in New Orleans shortly after her success in overturning Miami's gay rights ordinance in 1977, and her appearance provided the flame that ignited local gay political organising. Over the ensuing two decades, gay political activists have become a substantial force in city politics, helping to elect friendly city governments. Police harassment has diminished almost to the point of invisibility. The New Orleans City Council has passed an ordinance prohibiting discrimination based on sexual orientation, and inaugurated the process of registering same-sex domestic partnerships. In 1997 Mayor Marc Morial ordered spousal benefits for city employees registered as domestic partners.

Today, life is generally good for 'g/l/b/ts' (gay/lesbian/bisexual/transsexuals) in New Orleans. While discrimination in the workplace has not evaporated – nor are gay people always safe in public – the liberation movement has created a very different, and much better, world.

A few dos & don'ts

Orleanians are proud of their culture (sometimes to the point of chauvinism) and usually quite happy to share their hospitality, and the area's unique charms, with visitors – as long as visitors observe local cultural proprieties.

● Visitors are expected to be as enthusiastic about the city as natives are. If you like the city, tell everyone; if you're not happy in New Orleans, keep it to yourself.

● As in any major city, keep your wits about you while in the streets. Gay bashing is not a major problem in the Quarter, where there's a strong gay presence, but there are always

exceptions. Always be wary, particularly while drinking and particularly after dark.

● When travelling alone at night, it's best to catch a cab. Taxis are cheap and usually very prompt; any bar or restaurant will call one for you (*see chapter* **Directory** for a list of firms).

● Don't argue or question the police. Co-operate fully, even if you feel they are out of line. If there is any question as to their behaviour, quietly note their badge numbers and solve the problem later.

● Pace yourself. You cannot bar-crawl 24 hours a day, no matter what you think.

Wolfendales: *for DJ dancing and drag shows. See page 177.*

Despite the contributions of gay politics, New Orleans lesbian and gay culture is still more social than political. In the old French colonial culture, taverns were important gathering places; gay bars have picked up on the tradition and continue it. Likewise, the French custom of masked balls was copied by gay carnival clubs formed in the 1960s.

The oldest gay organisation of any kind in New Orleans is a private men's social gathering called the Steamboat Club, which has been entertaining its friends since 1953. A similar group of lesbians called the Gourmet Club dates from the early 1960s. But the oldest organised gay event, also private, is the Fat Monday Luncheon, held every year since 1949 on the day before Mardi Gras.

Information

There are three gay publications that will tell you what's going on and where. The oldest paper is *Impact* (522 8049/webmaster@ambushmag.com/ website: www.ambushmag.com), serving the community since 1977. Included in *Impact* is a supplement called *Eclipse*, which covers entertainment events. More of a 'bar rag' is *Ambush* (944 6722; gaymail@impactnews.com; website: www.impact news.com). Each comes out every

other week, so one or the other hits the streets every Thursday. The small, pocket-sized *Weekly Guide* (522 4300/ 525 1905) also appears on Thursdays. All three are free and widely distributed in gay bars and gay-owned and gay-friendly businesses.

There are two magazine-format, cable television shows aimed at the g/l/b/t audience – *A Krewe Production* (486 6304) and *Outlook Magazine* (366 7987). Schedules tend to vary so call for broadcast information.

Alternatives
907 Bourbon Street, at Dumaine Street (524 5222).
Bus 3 Vieux Carré, 48 Esplanade. **Open** 11am-7pm Mon-Thur, Sun; 11am-9pm Fri, Sat. **Credit** AmEx, Disc, MC, V. **Map 7 C2**
All manner of gay stuff such as cards, toys and clothing is sold at this shop, right in the centre of the Bourbon Street action. Staff will also provide information and directions.

Faubourg Marigny Bookstore
600 Frenchmen Street, at Chartres Street (943 9875).
Bus 82 Desire. **Open** 10am-8pm Mon-Fri; 10am-6pm Sat, Sun. **Credit** AmEx, Disc, MC, V. **Map 7 D2**
The South's oldest gay, lesbian and feminist bookstore. It also operates as an informal gay community centre.
Disabled: toilets.

Gay Heritage Tour
Information 945 6789. **Cost** $15. **Credit** AmEx, MC, V.
An entertaining and moving 2½-hour French Quarter walking tour that illuminates the vibrant lesbian and gay history

and culture of New Orleans. It departs from **Alternatives** (*see above*). Twice-weekly tours are held throughout the year, except December and January; phone for more details.

The Lesbian & Gay Community Center of New Orleans

816 N Rampart Street, at St Ann Street (522 1103).
Bus 88 St Claude. **Open** noon-7pm Mon-Fri; 9am-5.30pm Sat, Sun. **Map 7 C1**
Although the community centre is a small, volunteer based organisation providing limited activities, it's as useful a source for information, referrals and such like. Here, as well as in the gay papers, you'll find up-to-date information on cultural and social events, as well as details about health, religious, political and recreational activities.

The NO/AIDS Task Force

1407 Decatur Street, at Frenchmen Street (945 4000/ hearing-impaired 944 2492/statewide hotline 1-800 992 4379/944 2437/noaids@bellsouth.net). Bus 55 Elysian Fields, 57 Franklin, 82 Desire. **Open** 8.30am-5pm Mon-Fri; hotline noon-8pm daily. **Map 7 D3**
The Task Force provides information and a full range of educational, prevention and testing services.
Website: www.crescentcity.com/noaids/

Bars

Gay bars in New Orleans tend to be less specialised than in many other cities. This is largely due to two reasons: first, many are located near each other in the French Quarter and Faubourg Marigny; and second, local laws allow bar patrons to take alcoholic drinks on to the streets in plastic 'go cups'. Both these factors encourage locals to bar-hop, so the clientele, dress, attitude and so on will be a complete mixture at any given venue.

Solitary visitors should take care before walking from one location to another, especially if hopping from Quarter bars to Marigny bars, and especially at night and if already highly cocktailed. Bar staff will be happy to call a cab for you.

There's a large number of gay and lesbian bars and dance clubs, including a few scattered throughout the suburbs. Here are some of the most popular Quarter and Marigny hotspots. Most are open 24 hours and admission is free unless otherwise stated. For a more complete list of bars and clubs, *see chapter* **Nightlife**.

Bourbon Pub & Parade Disco

801 Bourbon Street, at St Ann Street (529 2107).
Bus 3 Vieux Carré, 48 Esplanade. **Open** *Bourbon Pub* 24 hours daily; *Parade Disco* from 9pm Mon-Sat; from 5pm Sun. **Admission** *Parade Disco* $2-$5. **No credit cards. Map 7 C2**
A very popular pub that plays music videos. The Parade Disco, upstairs, is open in the evenings: it's a great dance club, with great sound and a great balcony.
Website: www.bourbonpub.com

Café Lafitte & The Corral

901 Bourbon Street, at Dumaine Street (522 8397).
Bus 3 Vieux Carré, 48 Esplanade. **Open** 24 hours daily. **No credit cards. Map 7 C2**
In business since 1953, the Lafitte is among the oldest gay bars in America. Mostly men frequent the place, and it has a popular balcony in the attached Corral Bar, upstairs.

Charlene's

940 Elysian Fields Avenue, at N Rampart Street (945 9328). Bus 55 Elysian Fields, 57 Franklin. **Open** from 5pm daily. **Credit** MC, V.
Map 4 G6
One of the oldest lesbian bars in America, and, like Charlene herself, a local institution.

Good Friends Bar & Queen's Head Pub

740 Dauphine Street, at St Ann Street (566 7191).
Bus 3 Vieux Carré, 48 Esplanade. **Open** 24 hours daily. **Credit** MC, V. **Map 7 C1**
'Always snappy casual', they say of Good Friends. The upstairs bar, the Queen's Head Pub, is open most evenings and is as classy as gay bars get in New Orleans.
Website: www.goodfriendsbar.com

Mississippi River Bottom

515 St Philip Street, at Decatur Street (524 2558/efos@bellsouth.net). Bus 55 Elysian Fields, 57 Franklin, 82 Desire. **Open** 24 hours daily. **Credit** AmEx. **Map 7 C3**
Male dancers have taken to MRB, especially at weekends. There's a pleasant patio on which to cool off.

Oz

800 Bourbon Street, at St Ann Street (593 9491).
Bus 3 Vieux Carré, 48 Esplanade. **Open** 24 hours daily. **Admission** $3 Wed drag show; $5 Fri, Sat; $3 10pm-2am Sun. **No credit cards.**
Map 7 C2
Oz is opposite the Bourbon Pub, and the two are duelling discos. This is rated one of the best dance clubs in the US. A balcony is just one of the many features.
Website: www.gayneworleans.com/oz/

The Phoenix & The Men's Room

941 Elysian Fields Avenue, at N Rampart Street (945 9264). Bus 55 Elysian Fields, 88 St Claude. **Open** *The Phoenix* 24 hours daily.
The Men's Room 9pm-5am daily.
Both **No credit cards. Map 4 G6**
Home bar for the local leather club. The upstairs bar, open in the evenings, is called the Men's Room, which says it all.

Rawhide 2010

740 Burgundy Street, at St Ann Street (525 8106).
Bus 3 Vieux Carré, 48 Esplanade. **Open** 24 hours daily. **No credit cards. Map 7 C1**
Levi- and leather-clad males flock to Rawhide. The guys here can become very frisky late at night.
Website: www.rawhide2010.com

Rubyfruit Jungle

640 Frenchmen Street, at Royal Street (947 4000).
Bus 55 Elysian Fields, 82 Desire. **Open** 4pm-1am Mon-Wed; from 4pm Thur, Fri; from 2pm Sat; 2pm-1am Sun. **Admission** $3-$5. **Credit** AmEx, MC, V.
Map 4 G6
Young lesbians frequent this dance bar, which quite often has drag shows. Lesbians and drag shows? Only in New Orleans.
Disabled: toilets.

Wolfendales

834 N Rampart Street, between St Ann & Dumaine Streets (596 2236/efos@bellsouth.net). Bus 88 St Claude. **Open** 5pm-5am Mon-Sun. **Admission** $3 Thur-Sun. **No credit cards.**
Map 7 C1
Popular with African-American men, Wolfendales stages drag shows and dancing.

In and near the French Quarter there's an endless array of culinary opportunities, from a host of world-class restaurants to modest sandwich shops. Two moderately priced, take-out delis worth visiting are the **QuarterMaster Deli** (1100 Bourbon Street, at Ursulines Street; 529 1416) and **Verti Marte** (1201 Royal, at Gov Nicholls Street; 525 4767).

Popular, gay-owned restaurants (but not exclusively gay) include the **Clover Grill** (900 Bourbon Street, at Dumaine Street; 523 0904) for burgers and breakfast or **House of Bagels** (718 Orleans Street, at Bourbon Street; 525 5007) for bagels, sandwiches and salads. There's a fuller menu at **La Peniche** (1940 Dauphine Street, at Touro Street; 943 1460). **Petunias** (817 St Louis Street, between Bourbon & Dauphine Streets; 522 6440) specialises in crêpes.

Let the good times roll

'Laissez les bon temps rouler' echoes throughout south Louisiana. 'Let the good times roll' is the Cajun call to celebrate. This is a culture given to enjoying the pleasures of life. Any excuse for a party will do, particularly if it means dressing up in some manner. Everyone does it; gay people just seem to do it more extravagantly and better than anyone else.

The most famous celebration in New Orleans is, of course, **Mardi Gras**. For years it has provided gay people with the opportunity to wear masks, cross-dress and indulge in creative fantasy. While there are no gay parading organisations, four gay carnival clubs – Amon-Ra, Petronius, Armeinius and the Lords of Leather – present elaborate tableaux balls in the weeks preceding Mardi Gras. In the past, attendance at these balls was by personal invitation only, but in recent years all except Amon-Ra have sold tickets to the public. Traditionalists frown on this practice, but it provides visitors with the chance of a glimpse at what was for decades totally private. Ticket information, when available, is published in the gay press in the weeks leading up to Mardi Gras. Be warned, however: each club has a strict dress code for those attending. This varies from club to club, but might include formal evening wear, drag, leather – or a combination of all three.

The madness culminates on Fat Tuesday (Mardi Gras day), which is the only day that costumes are worn in the street. Many of the grandest are those created for the gay balls, and the costume judging at noon is the best place to see the gay finery. The event is still called the Bourbon Street Awards, but it now takes place on Burgundy Street, in front of **Rawhide 2010** (*see page 177*).

The other major gay craziness is **Southern Decadence**, held on the weekend before Labor Day. Started as a little party in 1972, it is now a major gay event – and one that is still entirely a gay phenomenon. Mostly, it's an excuse to dress up in genderfuck drag (on the Sunday before Labor Day itself) and careen drunkenly from bar to bar. Although this spectacle is called a 'parade', it has less in common with polite parades than it has with the running of the bulls in Pamplona.

Other gay celebrations include **Hallowe'en**, which is commemorated with a large circuit party on the Saturday night closest to 31 October, as well as with a number of smaller activities before and after the day. The event is funded by a large group of sponsors and all revenues are donated directly to Lazarus House, an AIDS hospice.

The **New Orleans Lesbian & Gay Pride Festival** is celebrated in autumn (usually late September or early October) with a parade and two days of festival activities in a park – usually Washington Park but 1998's event was transferred to Armstrong Park. Visitors are often surprised that Gay Pride is not a very large-scale event in New Orleans, although support for the celebration has been growing in recent years. For more information on all these events, *see chapter* **By Season**.

The great number of people crowding the streets around popular gay bars during the large celebrations has created a very festive atmosphere, but the laid-back attitude in New Orleans has been misinterpreted by some visitors to mean that, literally, anything goes. Local gay community activists and business owners have begun to put up signs urging people to respect the neighbourhood, and posters warn that public urinating, nudity and sexual acts are liable to lead to arrest. Visitors are reminded that all these activities can take place quite satisfyingly in appropriately interior spaces.

Some people prefer to avoid the crowds and visit New Orleans during quieter times. They discover that the party never really stops, not even during Lent. The good times, like Old Man River, just keep rolling along.

Accommodation

Almost all the large chain hotels are represented in New Orleans, but many visitors prefer the local feel of a smaller guesthouse in the French Quarter or Faubourg Marigny. Demand exceeds supply during major events such as Mardi Gras or Jazz Fest, when you should book well in advance. Most hotels, large or small, charge extra at holidays, and usually require a minimum stay. The businesses we list here are gay-owned, but welcome everyone. For a fuller list of hotels in the city, *see* chapter **Accommodation**.

Bourgoyne Guest House
839 Bourbon Street, at Dumaine Street, New Orleans, LA 70116 (524 3621/525 3983). Bus 3 Vieux Carré, 48 Esplanade. **Rates** $70.50-$160.50. **Credit** MC, V. **Map 7 C2**
An 1830s townhouse with antique-filled rooms and a charming courtyard. The location's great: plumb in the middle of the Bourbon Street bars.

The Claiborne Mansion
2111 Dauphine Street, at Frenchmen Street, New Orleans, LA 70116 (1-800 449 7327/949 7327/ fax 949 0388). Bus 82 Desire. **Rates** $150-$300. **Credit** AmEx, MC, V. **Map 4 G6**
Quite a posh residence, the Claiborne boasts luxurious furnishings and a swimming pool. Rooms have TVs, video machines and private telephones with voicemail. Breakfast is included in the room price.
Disabled: rooms.

La Dauphine Guest House
2316 Dauphine Street, at Marigny Street, New Orleans, LA 70117 (948 2217/fax 948 3420/LaDauphine@ aol.com). Bus 3 Desire, 55 Elysian Fields. **Rates** $65-$110. **Credit** Disc, MC, V. **Map 4 H6**
One for the budget traveller. Room prices include airport pick up and bicycle hire. The minimum stay is three nights. No smoking. No attitude.
Website: www. ladauphine.com

French Quarter Reservation Service
940 Royal Street, suite 263, New Orleans, LA 70116 (523 1246/1-800 523 9091/fax 527 6327/fqrsinc@ linknet.net). **Credit** AmEx, Disc, MC, V.
A booking service that handles a range of accommodation, from B&Bs to private condos.
Website: www.neworleansgay.com

Lafitte Guest House
1003 Bourbon Street, at St Philip Street, New Orleans, LA 70116 (581 2678/1-800 331 7971/fax 581 2677). Bus 3 Vieux Carré, 48 Esplanade. **Rates** $99-$189. **Credit** AmEx, DC, Disc, MC, V. **Map 7 C2**
The location's perfect, the décor's elegant and the price includes continental breakfast, afternoon wine and snacks.
Website: www.lafitteguesthouse.com

Macarty Park Guest House
3820 Burgundy Street, at Alvar Street, New Orleans, LA 70117 (943 4994/1-800 521 2790/faxmehard@ aol.com). Bus 82 Desire. **Rates** $59-$115. **Credit** AmEx, Disc, MC, V.
In a lovely quiet setting, 25 blocks from the French Quarter, Macarty Park offers a heated pool, private gym, cable TV and off-street parking. Price includes breakfast.
Website: www.macartypark.com

The bare necessities in Faubourg Marigny.

Over C's Guest House
940 Elysian Fields Avenue, at N Rampart Street, New Orleans, LA 70117 (943 7166). Bus 55 Elysian Fields, 57 Franklin. **Rates** $90. **Credit** MC, V. **Map 4 G6**
A guesthouse above Charlene's, one of America's oldest lesbian bars. The one-bedroom apartments include a microwave, fridge, cable TV, phone and sun deck. Men are welcome.

Royal Barracks Guest House
717 Barracks Street, between Bourbon & Royal Streets, New Orleans, LA 70116 (529 7269/1-888 255 7269/ fax 529 7298/phillips@getus.net). Bus 3 Vieux Carré, 41 Canal. **Rates** $75-$140. **Credit** AmEx, MC, V. **Map 7 D2**
In a quiet part of the Quarter, the Barracks boasts a courtyard with a hot tub. Other features include cable TV, private phones and free coffee and juice.

Sports clubs

Club New Orleans
515 Toulouse Street, at Decatur Street (581 2402). Bus 55 Elysian Fields, 57 Franklin, 82 Desire. **Open** 24 hours daily. **Admission** guest pass $6. **Credit** MC, V. **Map 7 B3**
A men's bath, with full gym, spa, steam room and sauna. You can also hire rooms (from $16.50) and lockers ($11).

The Country Club
634 Louisa Street, at Royal Street (945 0742). Bus 82 Desire. **Open** Apr-Sept 10am-6pm daily. **Admission** $5. **Credit** AmEx, MC, V.
This swimsuit-optional swimming club is about 20 blocks from the French Quarter and welcomes men and women. Day membership is available. Note that the club is closed during the winter.

Media

In a city that devotes an entire media outlet to 'the print-impaired', readers and newshounds have to read between the lines or hear it on the grapevine.

If you don't expect much interest in the news in a place that proudly calls itself 'the city that care forgot', you would be correct. New Orleans is in many ways an overgrown village. There's a deep-rooted conviction that everybody knows what's going on, so further commentary in the press would be superfluous. On local television, the fishing report often gets as much airtime as the latest municipal scandal, sometimes more. Big local stories are often first reported by out-of-town newspapers and on network television. The local media then unblushingly follows up, often not very thoroughly. Where New Orleans media does shine is in radio, particularly its innovative non-commercial station, WWOZ, devoted to local music. Other stations play more jazz, blues and roots music than you'll hear in any other American city.

Newspapers & magazines

Daily newspapers

Like the rest of the United States, New Orleans has seen a shrinkage of the daily press. In 1980 the afternoon *States-Item* was merged with the morning *Times-Picayune*, leaving the city with one daily newspaper, initially called the *Times-Picayune/States-Item*. Mercifully, the name has been shortened to the *Times-Picayune*, often called 'the TP' around town.

Unlike other metropolitan areas where suburban daily papers dot the richer, whiter commuter towns, New Orleans doesn't have a second tier of small newspapers nipping at the heels of the dominant daily. The relative poverty of Louisiana, combined with a low literacy rate and the quirky geography of the New Orleans urban area, conspire against it being a strong newspaper town like Miami, Chicago or San Francisco.

As the leviathan of the news, the *Times-Picayune* (50¢, $1 Sunday) is a reasonably professional newspaper that covers the basics. It prides itself on being a Pulitzer Prize winner, but its most recent award came, tellingly, for editorial cartoons by the talented Walt Handelsman, rather than reporting or writing. The paper is big on 'only in New Orleans' colour stories. It covers subjects such as gardening (with special attention to the city's problematic climate), interior design and non-controversial local history with depth and flair. On more serious subjects, such as the environment, the city's crumbling infrastructure, the local power structure and racial politics, the *Times-Picayune* is circumspect if not wilfully oblique.

On the plus side, columnists Lolis Eric Elie, James Gill and Bill Grady sometimes take their readers into the genuine complexities and conflicting realities of New Orleans without the usual journalistic pieties. The weekend entertainment tabloid, 'Lagniappe', comes with the Friday edition and is a handy guide to forthcoming musical and other events. The art critic, Chris Waddington, points readers towards small but exciting galleries and exhibitions. All literary coverage is shoehorned into two or maybe three Books pages at the back of the Travel section on Sunday. Look here for the weekly calendar that lists readings and author appearances. This is practically the only guide to literary events in the city and certainly the most comprehensive and timely.

For in-depth news coverage of the US and the world, look for the *New York Times* ($1, $4.25 Sunday), the *Wall Street Journal* (75¢) and *USA Today* (50¢), all of which are readily available from coin-operated boxes around town.

Weekly & monthly newspapers

Just as there is one daily newspaper in New Orleans, so there is one alternative newspaper (or, as they're becoming known in the US, 'city weekly'). Liberally distributed to cafés, coffeehouses, shops and bars on Sunday night, the free *Gambit Weekly* is primarily an arts and entertainment vehicle. Political news often leads the tabloid but its reporting is as bland as the *Times-Picayune*'s. Gambit's editorial stance is a clubby left-of-centre view as opposed to the TP's stuffy moderate conservatism. The listings are good for music, art and restaurants.

City Business ($1.25) is a fortnightly newsprint magazine covering the local business scene. It's better for its lively features on people and unusual businesses than for hard-nosed reporting.

New Orleans also has three African-American newspapers, the *Louisiana Weekly*, the *New Orleans Data News Weekly* (both free) and the monthly *New Orleans Tribune* (50¢). All are heavy on social life and intent on imparting uplifting messages. None offers much in the way of serious

Reading between the lines on the St Charles Avenue Streetcar.

reporting or even writing about the realities of contemporary New Orleans.

The gay community is covered by the every-other-Thursday free newspaper *Impact*. It has smartened up in the past couple of years, dismissing campy writers peeping out from behind noms de plume, in favour of straightforward reporting on issues such as the city's careless handling of AIDS funding. However, the saucy *Eclipse* magazine is folded into every issue of *Impact*. *Eclipse* columnists, who cover leather bars, beauty contests and local gossip, are often difficult to decode but provide an unfiltered look at local gay life. For other gay media, *see page 176* **Gay & Lesbian**.

Magazines

Happily, New Orleans's genius for music has a print companion, the free monthly newsprint magazine *OffBeat*. It is nearly comprehensive in its attention to the roots and popular music of New Orleans and Louisiana. Regular columns and in-depth features examine jazz, R&B, brass bands and Cajun music, plus the artists who make the music. *OffBeat* is valuable for its calendar of WWOZ radio as well (*see page 182*).

New Orleans Magazine ($1.95) is a slick monthly that takes a leisurely look at local celebs, newly decorated houses, restaurants and forthcoming events. Definitely uninterested in being on the cutting edge, the magazine is nevertheless stylish and well written. It also includes a programme guide for WYES-TV, channel 12, the PBS (Public Broadcasting System) outlet in New Orleans (*see page 182*).

Tribe ($2.50), the city's other slick magazine, is still settling on a personality while providing a monthly showcase for fashion, music personalities and antic humour. Over-designed to the point of unreadability, *Tribe* sometimes delivers stories with the flair that the design promises, such as a guide to the Beats accompanied by a strong interview with William Burroughs.

New on the scene is *Café Progresso* (free), a publication the size of a greetings card. Appearing 'approximately every 13 to 28 days', this free-spirited little rag informs readers about non-mainstream events and publishes writing from anyone with an opinion. It also lists poetry events in New Orleans and Baton Rouge.

Outlets

As there isn't a dense media community in New Orleans, it follows that there aren't many newsstands. The best place for finding out-of-town and foreign publications is **Lakeside News**, off Severn Avenue, Metairie. Located in a strip mall behind the Lakeside Shopping Center (next door to the 24-hour Morning Call coffee stand), the newsstand is open 24 hours, has no phone and is well stocked with US publications and UK and European magazines and newspapers.

The **Bookstar** bookshop in the French Quarter (414 N Peters Street, at Conti Street; 523 6411), has a good magazine selection but is thin on European magazines and carries only a few newspapers. Also in the Quarter is **French Quarter News** (700 Decatur Street, opposite Jackson Square; 569 8700). The **Lenny's News** chain at one time stocked a very good selection of European and US newspapers but has cut back sharply on its volume. It has two outlets in Uptown (622 S Carrollton Avenue, at St Charles Avenue, 866 2364; and 5420 Magazine Street, at Jefferson Avenue, 897 1183).

Media websites

For a list of other New Orleans-related websites, see chapter **Directory**.

City Business *www.neworleans.com/citybusiness*	**Times-Picayune** *www.nolalive.com*	**WVUE-TV** *www.Fox8.net*
Gambit Weekly *www.bestofneworleans.com*	**Tribe** *www.tribemagazine.com*	**WWL-TV** *www.wwl.tv.com*
Impact *www.impactnews.com*	**WDSU-TV** *www.wdsu.com*	**WWOZ Radio** *www.gnofn.org/~wwoz*
OffBeat *www.offbeat.com*	**WGNO-TV** *www.ABC26.com*	

Television

The New Orleans television menu is similar to that of every American city. The three major networks are represented – ABC on **channel 26**, **WGNO**; NBC on **channel 6**, **WDSU**; and CBS on **channel 4**, **WWL** – while the new Fox and WB networks are making steady gains. What is unusual is the proliferation of religious programmes. New Orleans has two religious channels, **WLAE-TV**, **channel 32**, run by the Catholic Church, and freelance **WHNO**, **channel 20**, where you will see evangelists ranging from the dethroned Jimmy Swaggart to a female dwarf who confesses she is an ex-lesbian while pleading for universal love and donations to stay on the air. On **channel 32**, an archbishop anchors a putative news show with a vivacious blonde co-hostess. Guests are often earnest nuns and priests discussing modern miracles and the authentication of the Shroud of Turin.

Local TV stars include two New Orleans characters who speak in the distinctive New Orleans 'Yat' accent. Both are on **channel 4**, and enjoy taking pot shots at one another in their spots during the local news. One is an energetic fisherman and chef named Frank Davis who delivers the fishing report and a daffy interlude called 'Naturally N'awlins'. He alternates with Ronnie Virgets, a grizzled ironist who delivers essays on everything from New Orleans's famously bad drivers to the headaches of book promotion (his own, of course).

PBS station **WYES**, **channel 12**, provides some of the best locally produced programmes with its Friday night line-up of *Steppin' Out* and *Informed Sources*. The former is a round-table discussion of music, food, theatre and other entertainment events, and the latter a review of local news by a changing panel of reporters and editors.

New Orleans does have local cable programmes but their effect and audiences are minimal. For television listings, check the *Times-Picayune* or pick up the ever-popular *TV Guide* ($1.19).

Radio

In **WWOZ** (89.9 FM) New Orleans has not only one of the most unusual radio stations in the US, but also one of the best. This non-profit-making enterprise is dedicated to New Orleans music. The station is staffed by volunteers, often dedicated music collectors and fans who bring in their own records and CDs. Programmes include traditional jazz, contemporary jazz, Latin music, R&B, zydeco, Cajun, Caribbean, African, gospel and even brass bands. Interviews with musicians are frequent events, rambling and fascinating. As one sage put it: 'This isn't radio, it's music paradise.'

The city's National Public Radio outlet, **WWNO** (89.9 FM), offers all the NPR news shows, *Morning Edition*, *All Things Considered* and *Marketplace*, as well as Garrison Keillor's *Prairie Home Companion* (every Saturday) and daily mini-interviews about local arts and entertainment. It is also the city's classical music station.

Also on the A-list is Tulane University's student-run **WTUL** (91.5 FM), which can be annoyingly amateurish, yet is also wide-ranging and mostly good-natured. Programming segments might include medleys of 1970s TV show theme songs followed by an all-Mozart interlude, followed by cuts from an unknown garage band.

WRBH (88.3 FM) is a non-profit all-talk station. Billed as 'radio for the blind and print-impaired', the station marshals a small army of volunteers who read the daily newspaper (including ads), national magazines and books in half-hour and hour blocks. The readers are uneven in skill but the book and magazine segments can often be a pleasure, especially when you're driving.

Among its other 50-odd radio outlets, New Orleans has the usual mix of rock, country, easy listening, religious and talk stations. Try **WWL** (870 AM) for talk, **WNOE** (101.1 FM) for country, **KHOM** (104.1 FM) for rock. **WYLD** (98.5 FM and 940 AM) is the main African-American station.

Nightlife

The nights are long and the opportunities endless, in a city with 24-hour licensing hours and an inexhaustible supply of clubs and bars.

Bars

'Nightlife' in New Orleans tends to mean one of, or a combination of, two things: live music and alcohol. For years, people have speculated whether New Orleans has more bars per capita than any other city in the United States. It's probably a safe assumption, even though, since so many are tiny, neighbourhood places, there are no accurate statistics to substantiate the speculation. Bar owners go to great lengths to give their bar a unique feel and appearance in New Orleans. There are few 'theme' bars, yet each bar is different in its décor, type of drinks offered and the clientele it attracts. There are college bars, just as there are corner neighbourhood bars and tourist establishments in the French Quarter, but in most cases each bar has something unique to offer, making bar-hopping an unfailingly intriguing – and essential – activity.

Given the sheer number of bars, an all-inclusive list would be impossible to amass, let along publish. Here, then, is a list of the city's more interesting bars; for a list of music clubs and larger venues, *see page 199*. We've largely ignored the tourist-packed Bourbon Street bars, but chances are you'll find them if that's what you're looking for – but remember that the city has much more to offer than Bourbon Street and to spend more than

one night amid its strip clubs and karaoke bars would be to miss the real attractions of the city's nightlife. For details of classical music and the performing arts, including spoken word events, *see chapter* **Performing Arts**, and for yet more bars and dance clubs, *see chapter* **Gay & Lesbian**.

ALCOHOL & THE LAW

Local laws make drinking in New Orleans unique. First and foremost, bars are not required to close or stop serving alcohol at any time, resulting in numerous late-night bars that are open until after the sun comes up (although not many bars, in fact, take full advantage of the licensing laws and stay open 24 hours). Many bars open at a particular hour but have no set closing time; usually, they'll remain serving as long as there are still people wanting to buy drinks. Although the opening times listed below were accurate at the time of going to press, it's always a good idea to check if a venue is still up and running before going out of your way to visit it.

It is also legal to walk out of a bar and down the street while carrying your drink, provided you pour it into a plastic cup. Although the bartender or doorman of the next bar will usually make you finish your drink before letting you in, the 'go cup' phenomenon makes traipsing from one joint to the next more enjoyable than in most cities.

Pick of the best...

... bars

The Abbey: a rare local in the tourist-clogged Quarter (*p185*).
Columns Hotel: for comfortable, intimate booths and illicit nooky (*p197*).
Cooter Brown's Tavern & Oyster Bar: New Orleans's mecca for beer fans (*p197*).
F&M Patio Bar: go and toast the sunrise with a Bloody Mary (*p197*).
Polo Lounge at the Windsor Court: for Martinis by the pitcher in swank surroundings (*p191*).
R Bar: quirky décor, a hip crowd and centipedes behind the bar (*p191*).
Saturn Bar: air-conditioner repair shop by day, atmospheric dive by night (*p199*).
Snake & Jake Christmas Club Lounge: for music gossip late into the night (*p198*).

... music clubs

Carrollton Station Bar & Music Club: rock, funk, folk and fusion and a colourful history (*p209*).
Dragon's Den: for experimental jazz and poetry slams (*p204*).
Dream Palace & Reality Grill: where the Radiators started out (*p204*).
Funky Butt at Congo Square: some of the best contemporary jazz and Creole cooking (*p201*).
House of Blues: where to hear the big names and the best sound system (*p203*).
Maple Leaf Bar: simply unmissable (*p209*).
Snug Harbor: catch an impromptu jam session at the city's pre-eminent jazz club (*p204*).
Tipitina's Uptown: legendary shrine to Professor Longhair (*p209*).

Don't bet on New Orleans

Although gambling has been pronounced a failure in New Orleans, three casinos still exist in the metro area. Actually, it didn't exactly fail, it just didn't live up to the gargantuan expectations of the gambling industry. Instead of glitzy Las Vegas-on-the-bayou, legalised gambling turned out to be a low-roller, blue collar diversion, a variation on parish bingo nights.

The casinos are heavily weighted toward slot machines and video poker. The more sophisticated games of poker, roulette, blackjack and baccarat are offered but barely. Bally's, for instance, has 1,216 slot machines and two roulette tables. Entry to all the casinos is free but restricted to those aged 21 and over. Be prepared to show photo ID.

Because of the tortured politics surrounding New Orleans gambling (*see chapter* **New Orleans**

Today), all the casinos are on boats and are legally obligated to 'sail' several times a day. In fact, the boats hardly ever leave dock and then only under extreme pressure from the authorities. However, if you're pressed for time it's a good idea to find out when the next departure is so you won't miss your plane because the *SS Craps* is in the middle of Lake Pontchartrain at flight time.

Bally's Casino *Lake Pontchartrain, next to Lakefront Airport, 1 Stars & Stripes Boulevard (248 3200). Bus 60 Hayne Boulevard.* **Open** 24 hours daily.

Boomtown Casino *(on the West Bank), 4132 Peters Boulevard, Harvey (366 7711).* **Open** 24 hours daily. *Website: www.boomtowncasinos.com*

Treasure Chest Casino *Lake Pontchartrain, 5050 Williams Boulevard, Kenner (443 8000/1-800 298 0711). Bus Kenner Loop.* **Open** 24 hours daily.

Finally, while the current law prohibits anyone under the age of 21 from purchasing or consuming alcohol in bars, anyone aged 18 or over can enter and hang out in a bar, so the crowd, particularly at college bars, tends to be younger than in many other US cities. Bars that offer occasional live music may charge admission, but it's rarely more than $5.

SAFETY

Since bar- and club-hopping is *de rigueur* in New Orleans, it's best to take a cab at night, particularly if you're venturing out of the Quarter (and we recommend you do). *See chapter* **Directory** for a list of local companies.

French Quarter

The Abbey
1123 Decatur Street, between Gov Nicholls & Ursulines Streets (523 7150/ubbeybar@webtv.net). Bus 55 Elysian Fields, 57 Franklin, 82 Desire. **Open** 24 hours daily. **No credit cards. Map 8**
Three years ago, the Abbey had a reputation as the place where visiting sailors and merchant marines went to get falling-down drunk. Since then, under the guidance of a bartender from London, it has reinvented itself as the most comfortable and interesting bar on the Decatur Street stretch. The owner (who relocated to New Orleans from Boston in the 1970s) takes pride in the amount of Wild Turkey bourbon consumed here, while the bartenders insist they can keep up with any shot-drinking patron. On Sundays, the Abbey shows old B-movies to a regular local

Stand your round at the disconcertingly revolving **Carousel Bar** *inside the Monteleone Hotel.*

crowd and on Thursday nights a DJ spins drum 'n' bass. The walls are covered with random bar paraphernalia and a few years' dust, but this all adds to the feel of a bar well liked by locals and shunned by tourists – a rare find in the French Quarter.
Disabled: toilet.

Carousel Bar & Lounge at the Monteleone Hotel
214 Royal Street, at Iberville Street (523 3341). Bus 3 Vieux Carré. **Open** 11am-2am daily. **Credit** AmEx, DC, Disc, MC, V. **Map 8**
This eccentric bar, located off the lobby of the Monteleone Hotel in the heart of the French Quarter, caters largely to guests or tourists looking for an after-dinner drink. Weirdly, the bar is decorated as an antique carousel, and the bar stools and counter actually revolve around the bartender, taps and bottles. If you prefer to get your spins from drinking rather than while doing it, there are tables by the large windows and a back room lit only by small lights on the ceiling, creating a simulated view of the cosmos that usually outdoes the often overcast night sky of New Orleans. Drinks are priced higher than at many places, but not unreasonably so and while there's no dress code, the crowd tends to be older and smarter than at other places. Worth trying once.
Disabled: toilet.

The Chart Room
300 Chartres Street, at Bienville Street (522 1708). Bus 3 Vieux Carré, 42 Canal. **Open** 11am-4am daily. **No credit cards. Map 8**
This quiet, dimly lit bar is one of the few in the French Quarter that caters predominantly to a local crowd. Decorated with nautical charts, fishing nets, sextants and other seafaring paraphernalia, it is at its busiest just after work. Both the beer and bar selections are limited and, without any pool tables or food, there's little reason to visit except for the cheap drinks – which is enough for the middle-aged regulars who call this home. Walk a few more blocks to find a more stimulating atmosphere.

For big-name acts and local hotshots, head to the **House of Blues** (above and left). Page 203

Coop's Cajun Kitchen
1109 Decatur Street, at Ursulines Street (525 9053).
Bus 57 Franklin, 55 Elysian Fields, 82 Desire. **Open**
11am-4am daily. **Credit** AmEx, DC, Disc, MC, V. **Map 8**
Blurring the line between bar and restaurant, Coop's is one
of the better places to grab a bite on Decatur Street. The food
(served from before noon till 3am) is largely south Louisiana
fare – many say the gumbo, thickened with a dark roux, is
among the best in New Orleans. Still, this is not a formal sit-
down dining establishment, and about 20 bottled beers and
six draughts, along with a pool table and jukebox, make
Coop's a good afternoon joint. Evenings are pretty slow, but
that can be a welcome change.

The Dungeon
738 Toulouse Street, at Bourbon Street (523 5530).
Bus 3 Vieux Carré, 41 Canal. **Open** from midnight Tue-
Sun. **Admission** $3 Fri, Sat, holidays. **Credit** MC, V.
Map 8
The Dungeon is legendary, mainly due to its hours of operation and half-hidden entrance (it's down a narrow alleyway),
and scares most tourists away by not opening until midnight. The crowd is mostly younger French Quarter residents, and the red-lit interior and labyrinthine rooms and
hallways make the place feel like a medieval submarine –
surrealism is the order of the day here. If there are indeed
vampires in New Orleans, it's a good bet that the Dungeon
is their preferred hangout.

The Hideout
1207 Decatur Street, at Gov Nicholls Street (529 7119).
Bus 57 Franklin, 82 Desire. **Open** 24 hours daily.
Credit AmEx, Disc, MC, V. **Map 8**
Decatur Street is known as a congregation point for New
Orleans's seedier characters, from high-school goth kids
draped in black satin to bikers bedecked in black leather.
And of all the bars on Decatur that cater to this clientele, the
Hideout prides itself on attracting the most extreme cases.

The bar smells particularly unsavoury, and when games of
pool spin off into arguments, it's common to see the cliché
'Let's take it outside' actually put into use. Most of the skirmishes are between the younger goths and the older bikers,
so fear of bar brawls or a few menacing glances shouldn't
keep you away. But apart from witnessing this particular
side of New Orleans, there's not much reason to go, either.
Disabled: toilet.

Lafitte's Blacksmith Shop
941 Bourbon Street, at St Philip Street (523 0066).
Bus 3 Vieux Carré, 48 Esplanade. **Open** from noon daily.
Credit AmEx, Disc, MC, V. **Map 8**
In any other city in the US, the ancient building that houses
Lafitte's would have been committed to historical preservation years ago. In New Orleans, however, it continues to function as a bar – in fact, it's reputed to be the oldest structure
in the country used as a bar, and is lit only by candlelight.
It's also far enough down Bourbon Street to escape much of
the tourist traffic. The beer selection is limited, but the bar
is well stocked and the crowd refreshingly local and usually
jovial. *See also p39* **Architecture**.
Disabled: toilet.

Marie Laveau's Voodoo Bar
*Historic French Market Inn, 509 Decatur Street, at
St Louis Street (522 7225). Bus 55 Elysian Fields,
57 Franklin, 82 Desire.* **Open** 11am-3am daily.
No credit cards. Map 8
In the middle of the T-shirt stands hoping to squeeze the last
dollar out of the thousands of tourists who visit this stretch
of Decatur Street is the surprisingly comfortable Voodoo Bar.
The room is tiny, with about four tables, a small bar serving
local brews and images of voodoo rituals painted on the
walls. The bar takes its name from New Orleans's most
famous voodoo practitioner, and perhaps in hopes of chan-
nelling the spirit of Madame Laveau, you can have your palm
read in a booth opposite the bar.

Molly's at the Market

1107 Decatur Street, at Ursulines Street (525 5169).
Bus 57 Franklin, 82 Desire. **Open** 10am-6am daily.
Credit AmEx, MC, V. **Map 8**
Of all the Decatur Street bars, none go through as complete
a transformation from day to night as does Molly's.
Afternoons find it crowded with tourists visiting the French
Quarter; in the evening, it's packed with pierced and tattooed
twentysomethings. There's a rather homogenised feel
despite all the effort to look different – think of it as generic
eclecticism. The political press clippings on the walls seem
completely out of place for the apathetic crowd, but Molly's
does offer a decent beer selection and a good jukebox. It's
also the kick-off point for the first St Patrick's Day parade
(*see chapter* **By Season**).
Disabled: toilet.

The Napoleon House

500 Chartres Street, at St Louis Street (524 9752).
Bus 3 Vieux Carré, 41 Canal. **Open** 11am-midnight
Mon-Thur; 11am-1.30am Fri, Sat; 11am-7pm Sun.
Credit AmEx, DC, Disc, MC, V. **Map 8**
While many French Quarter bars have able bartenders, few
employ a staff as knowledgeable, capable and commend-
able as the Napoleon House – and it's one of the few bars in
town to garnish a Pimm's Cup with a slice of cucumber. The
building that houses the bar was built at the beginning of
the nineteenth century as the home of the mayor of New
Orleans; popular myth has it that in 1821, it was offered to
Napoleon, then living in exile and hoping to be sprung and
liberated to New Orleans by the privateer Jean Lafitte.
Napoleon died before enacting his escape, but the building
retained his name and is now a confortable, dark bar with
a large grill menu and an outdoor courtyard.

Pat O'Brien's

718 St Peter Street, at Bourbon Street (525 4823/1-800
597 4823/huricane@patobriens. com). Bus 3 Vieux
Carré, 41 Canal. **Open** 10am-4am Mon-Thur, Sun; 10am-
5am Fri, Sat. **Credit** MC, V (piano bar & patio bar only).
Map 8
This is probably the granddaddy of French Quarter bars
and few tourists leave the city without stopping at Pat O's
on at least one occasion. Its signature drink is the Hurricane,
a saccharine concoction of fruit juices and rum (if the alcohol doesn't give you a hangover, the sugar will) served in a
tall glass that you can take home as a souvenir – for a price,
of course. There are three bars within the complex, and
entrances on both Bourbon and St Peter Streets. The main
patio, with its flaming fountain, draws the biggest crowd,
while the piano bar is full of cheesey, sing-along types.
Drinks are fairly expensive, but there are a number of
unique concoctions beyond the Hurricane to sample. As a
landmark, Pat O's is a must-see, but as a cool bar to spend
an evening, it's as representative as the French Quarter is
of all New Orleans.
Disabled: toilet. Website: www.patobriens.com

Port of Call

838 Esplanade Avenue, at Dauphine Street (523 0120).
Bus 3 Vieux Carré, 48 Esplanade. **Open** 11am-1am Mon-
Thur, Sun; 11am-3am Fri, Sat. **Credit** AmEx, MC, V.
Map 8
A somewhat dingy, dark bar bordering the French
Quarter, Port of Call is best known for its grill which,
many locals say, serves the best hamburgers and baked
potatoes in town. It attracts an even mix of locals and
tourists and has recently become a favourite haunt of
Ruthie the Duck Lady, a French Quarter eccentric known
for raising ducklings that follow her on her walks through
the Quarter. The beer list and drink selection are only average, but it's comfortable and a great place for random bar-
room conversation.

Lafitte's Blacksmith Shop. *See page 187.*

Ryan's Irish Pub

241 Decatur Street, at Bienville Street (523 3500).
Bus 41 Canal, 57 Franklin, 55 Elysian Fields, 82 Desire.
Open 11am-8am daily. **Credit** AmEx, Disc, MC, V.
Map 8
Ryan's is a great place to spend your setbreaks while at
shows at the House of Blues, just down the street. Prices are
a little high, but the selection is good and so is the company.
You can also play billiards. Paintings and photos of Irish
poets and writers adorn the walls.
Disabled: toilet.

Turtle Bay Bar & Grill

1119 Decatur Street, at Ursulines Street (586 0563).
Bus 57 Franklin, 82 Desire. **Open** 11am-4am daily.
Credit MC, V. **Map 8**
Extensive beer selections are rare in the French Quarter, so
Turtle Bay is trying to fill the void by establishing itself as
the only beer bar on Decatur Street. With 24 taps and a large
selection of bottled beer, it draws an older crowd and the
prices serve to keep out the area's gutter punks.
Unfortunately, it feels rather antiseptic, with little distinctive décor and almost no atmosphere of its own. The grill
serves a standard, if limited, menu until 1am. A decent place
to stop for a good beer during the afternoon while touring
the Quarter, but not a final, or even important, destination.

Faubourg Marigny

Apple Barrel

609 Frenchmen Street, at Chartres Street (949 9399).
Bus 82 Desire. **Open** 11am-2am daily. **No credit cards.**
Map 8
The Apple Barrel is best used as a break from the crowds on
Frenchmen Street on busy nights. It's small, often crowded

HOUSE OF BLUES

New Orleans' Premier Restaurant and Entertainment Venue

Live Music 7 Nights a Week

Club Hours:
8pm-til

Casual to eclectic dining in an exciting Juke Joint atmosphere. Restaurant open daily at 11am

Get the coolest threads at the HOB Company Store. Retail Stores open daily at 10am

LIVE MUSIC HOUSE OF BLUES® 7 NIGHTS A WEEK

Unity in Diversity™
225 Decatur Street in New Orleans
Concert and Info Line: 504-529-BLUE
Discount validated parking available at Canal Place
VISIT US AT HTTP://WWW.HOB.COM

and offers a decent beer and drink selection, all for a fair price. You can also play darts. There's a small crowd of regulars, but most of the business seems to be made up of spillover from the surrounding music clubs.

R Bar

1431 Royal Street, at Kerlerec Street (948 7499/heto@ wisdom.com). Bus 82 Desire. **Open** 3pm-5am Mon-Thur, Sun; 3pm-6am Fri, Sat. **Credit** AmEx, MC, V. **Map 8**

Relatively unknown to Uptown revellers and locals, the R Bar quickly became popular with off-work bartenders, waiters and other service industry types. Word spread and the crowds became larger but remained young and hip. Prices are reasonable, there's a pool table crammed in one corner, and the décor is film-inspired rather than the aged, dingy look usual in New Orleans' bars. Where else can you sit in an antique barber's chair while sipping a cocktail, or gaze up at a motorcycle perched on top of a beer cooler above the bar? Ask the bartenders for a look at the preserved aquatic centipedes in jars behind the bar.

CBD

Audubon Hotel

1225 St Charles Avenue, at Erato Street (568 1319). St Charles Streetcar. **Open** 24 hours daily. **Credit** MC, V. **Map 6 B2**

To really get a whiff of the underbelly of New Orleans's nightlife, try the Audubon. Despite its location on St Charles Avenue, mere blocks from some of the city's swankier restaurants, it's dingy, dark and deliciously hedonistic. Favoured by just-off-duty bartenders and strippers, the Audubon's melancholy, regulars only daytime feel metamorphoses into utter weirdness after midnight. It's a late-night hangout, ideal if you're out for the long haul and looking for a wildly eclectic crowd to drink with. There's a full bar but the beer selection is pretty limited. No matter: if you're at the Audubon at 4am, you'll be on to harder stuff anyway.

Polo Lounge at the Windsor Court

300 Gravier Street, at Tchoupitoulas Street (523 6000). Bus 10 Tchoupitoulas. **Open** 11am-11.45pm daily. **Credit** AmEx, DC, Disc, MC, V. **Map 6 C1**

The Windsor Court is annually selected as one of the top hotels in the country, and the Polo Lounge undeniably lives up to the hotel's high reputation. A brightly lit room with paintings of polo ponies on the walls, a few cocktail tables, couches and a small bar, the room is top-shelf, from its liquor to the nuts served with the cocktails. A dress code is not strictly enforced, but most patrons are well dressed. Drinks are expensive (average $9), but you get what you pay for: the signature drink, the Polo Martini, comprises gin or vodka, champagne and bitters served in a small pitcher. Fridays and Saturdays feature a jazz trio of some of the best players in town; on other nights a pianist plays

Sazerac Bar at the Fairmont Hotel

123 Baronne Street, at Canal Street (529 4733). Bus 41 Canal. **Open** 5-10pm Tue-Thur; 5-11pm Fri, Sat. **Credit** AmEx, DC, MC, V. **Map 6 C1**

Situated next to the Sazerac restaurant in the lobby of the Fairmont Hotel, the classy, art deco Sazerac Bar won international fame after a bartender concocted the Sazerac cocktail in the early 1900s. It's staffed by confident, qualified bartenders who expertly spin glasses in the air to coat them with a local absinthe substitute used in the namesake cocktail and is popular with the pre- and post-theatre crowd (the Fairmont is across the street from the Orpheum theatre and only a few blocks from the Saenger). Given the opulence of the room, drinks are surprisingly reasonably priced. By the way, the Sazerac cocktail also contains rye whiskey, sugar and bitters – and is definitely worth trying.
Disabled: toilet.

*A cure for the blues? The **Red Room** (p206).*

Top of the Mart

World Trade Center, 33rd floor, 2 Canal Street, at the Mississippi River (522 9795). Bus 41 Canal. **Open** 10am-11pm Mon-Thur; 10am-midnight Fri; 11am-1am Sat; 2-11pm Sun. **Credit** AmEx, DC, Disc, MC, V. **Map 6 C1/2**

Sitting atop the World Trade Center next to the Mississippi, Top of the Mart is a slowly revolving circular room that provides a panoramic view of the French Quarter, the river and Algier's Point on the West Bank. The bar itself doesn't live up to the view, however. Red velvet and gold curtain ties and tassels create the ambience of a tacky, out-of-town steakhouse. Drinks are expensive, the menu limited and the clientele not particularly friendly. The view makes it worth a visit, but limit yourself to one drink or one rotation of the room, whichever comes first. And don't leave your drink on the window sill, or you'll find yourself chasing it around the room.
Disabled: toilet.

Whisky Bar

730 Common Street, at St Charles Avenue (525 6660). St Charles Streetcar. **Open** from 5pm Mon-Fri; from 9pm Sat. **Credit** AmEx, DC, Disc, MC, V. **Map 6 C1**

Probably the most upscale bar in the city. The crowd at the Whisky Bar is appropriately well dressed and relatively unfriendly. Bartenders are quite knowledgeable and the quality of brands is top-notch, but expect to pay for it. The interior is exquisite, with polished surfaces everywhere, vases laden with roses, subtle lighting and comfortable chairs and couches. The two bathrooms, with their black-lacquered surfaces and two locks on the doors, seem purpose-built for illicit drug-taking or sexual encounters.
Disabled: toilet.

Warehouse District

Aprés Cigar & Martini Bar

709 St Charles Avenue, at Girod Street (566 7000). St Charles Streetcar. **Open** *from 5pm Tue-Fri; from 9pm Sat.* **Credit** AmEx, MC, V. **Map 6 B/C1**
Catering to a well-dressed, deep-pocketed crowd, Apres opened on the edge of the Warehouse District in 1996. Stylised glass and wrought iron furniture create a nice looking, if not entirely cosy ambience. Although Martinis are the most common order, they're generally not what we'd consider the best in the city. For commanding such high prices, the owners must trust that their patrons will value the bar and the other people in it over the ability of the staff – on one evening, a bartender not only didn't know how to make a Manhattan but didn't have a recipe book on hand to cover for her lack of competence.
Disabled: toilet.

Ernst Café

600 S Peters Street, at Lafayette Street (525 8544). Bus 3 Vieux Carré, 10 Tchoupitoulas. **Open** *11am daily.* **Credit** AmEx, DC, MC, V. **Map 6 C2**
This small bar in the Warehouse District does much of its business by hosting private parties in an upstairs room. Downstairs, Tuesdays and Saturdays are most popular, thanks to Ladies' Night drink specials. Drink choices are limited to a few beers and cocktails, although there are free hors d'oeuvres for the Friday happy hour (4-7pm).

Lucy's Retired Surfer's Bar

701 Tchoupitoulas Street, at Girod Street (523 8995/ 523 9198). Bus 3 Vieux Carré, 10 Tchoupitoulas. **Open** *from 11am daily.* **Credit** AmEx, DC, Disc, MC, V. **Map 6 C1**
Lucy's is popular with local Warehouse District dwellers and yuppie suburbanites. While weekend nights are the busiest, food (mostly Mexican-inspired) and drink specials keep the bar relatively crowded most nights; it's best as an early evening venue. There's a large dining room in the back and the bar offers a number of fruity, frozen drinks along with a limited beer selection. For reasons seemingly only thematic, there are surfboards hanging over the bar and tropical décor throughout.
Disabled: toilet.

Red Eye Bar & Grill

852 S Peters Street, at Julia Street (593 9393). Bus 3 Vieux Carré, 10 Tchoupitoulas. **Open** *11am-5am Mon-Sat; 6pm-4am Sun.* **Credit** AmEx, DC, MC, V. **Map 6 C2**
Located just half a block from the **Howlin' Wolf** music club (*see p206*), the Red Eye cashes in on setbreak crowds and a noticeably younger clientele, who for reasons unknown (lax carding at the door, maybe?), make this their home. Prices are below average and there is a late-night grill, but, as with many bars, the food is best relied upon only when you're desperate. Pool is big among the younger patrons, and the two tables are always busy.
Disabled: toilet.

Garden District

Balcony Bar & Café

3201 Magazine Street, at Harmony Street (895 1600/ 891 2800). Bus 11 Magazine. **Open** *5pm-4am daily.* **Credit** AmEx, Disc, DC, MC, V. **Map 6 A4**
Opened as a bar and po-boy shop, the Balcony recently expanded into a large space downstairs from the original bar. The menu now contains more than lunch fare and the balcony overlooking one of the busier stretches of pedestrian traffic on Magazine Street provides a nice change of pace from smoky rooms. Downstairs, 75 taps offer mega- and micro-brewed beers from across America and the world. Unfortunately, the compressed air draught system used can result in stale and flat beer – definitely ask for a small taste before ordering. There's a projection TV for larger sporting events, and two pool tables.
Website: www.neworleans.com/balconybar

Catch zydeco night on Thursdays at the **Mid City Lanes Rock 'n' Bowl.** *See page 210.*

New Orleans'
Legendary
Live Music Club

The club called Tipitina's was created in the mid-1970's by a group of local music enthusiasts, and quickly became home to dozens of New Orleans rhythm & blues artists. Its patron saint was Henry Roeland Byrd, better known as Professor Longhair, who was the most colorful and influential piano stylist to emerge from New Orleans since Jelly Roll Morton.

Recent years have seen the emergence of Tipitina's as one of the premier music clubs in the world. It has been the setting for movies ("The Big Easy"), videos (The Neville Brothers), and many great nights on the dance floor for everyone from local rock stars to Hollywood actors.

Some say Tipitina's is filled with magic. Some say it's plain haunted by the spirit of Professor Longhair, who inspires the musicians with an excitement and energy that will always keep the custom of great music alive. Whatever you choose to believe, after experiencing a night at Tipitina's, you will be a part of the legacy and the magic of an inspired New Orleans tradition.

Lunch and dinner served at the French Quarter location

**Original Uptown Location: 501 Napoleon Avenue
French Quarter: 233 N. Peters
Warehouse District: 310 Howard Avenue
For tickets and information: 504-895-8477
Fax 504-523-3527 • Email: mwalker@communique.net
www.tipitinas.com**

*The very discreet Victorian Bar at the **Columns Hotel**. See page 197.*

The Bulldog
3236 Magazine Street, at Louisiana Avenue (891 1516).
Bus 11 Magazine. **Open** noon-2am Mon-Sat; 2pm-2am
Sun. **Credit** AmEx, Disc, MC, V. **Map 6 A3**
One of New Orleans's three bars with an extensive beer selection, the Bulldog offers 50 beers on tap plus a wide bottled beer list. The draught beer is fresher than at the Balcony but not as good as **Cooter Brown's** (*see p197*), primarily because the Bulldog's clientele tends to stick to mega-brewed swill like Miller and Budweiser. It can get packed later in the evening with suburbanites and yuppies on their way home from work. On slower nights, such as Sundays, a small but loyal group of trivia buffs does battle on a nationally networked trivia game.

The Half Moon
1125 St Mary Street, at Sophie Wright Place (522 0599).
Bus 11 Magazine. **Open** 11am-4am daily. **Credit** AmEx,
Disc, MC, V. **Map 6 B3**
Tucked in a relatively empty section of town between the Lower Garden District and downtown, the Half Moon's business is secured by a late afternoon/early evening crowd of young professionals heading home. After 1am, it's sparsely populated. The beer selection is surprisingly good, and two back rooms offer pool and football tables and plastic-tipped darts. There's a great jukebox, but the usual customers make some horrible selections – feed the machine a few dollars to keep AC/DC out of rotation.
Disabled: toilet.

Igor's Lounge
2133 St Charles Avenue, at Jackson Avenue (522 2145).
St Charles Streetcar. **Open** 24 hours daily. **Credit**
AmEx, MC, V. **Map 6 B3**
The first of Australian Igor Margan's four bars and, like the other three, also a laundromat. Exceedingly greasy burgers and french fries are available from the grill, and there are pool tables at the back of the bar and in a small upstairs room. Nestled among three of the larger hotels on St Charles Avenue, Igor's draws crowds of tourists looking for nightcaps. The bar practically exists on the profits made during Mardi Gras, when every Uptown parade rolls by its front

doors and both drinks and bathrooms are in huge demand. If you're fond of Igor's, try his other bars, Lucky's (1625 St Charles Avenue; 523 6538) or the Buddha Belly (4437 Magazine Street; 891 6105) – both are near copies of the original. Igor also owns **Checkpoint Charlie's** (*see p204*).
Disabled: toilet.

Parasol's Restaurant & Bar
2533 Constance Street, at Third Street (897 5413).
Bus 11 Magazine. **Open** 11am-10pm Mon-Thur, Sun;
from 11am Fri, Sat. **Credit** AmEx, MC, V. **Map 6 B3**
This small, neighbourhood bar in the Irish Channel is ground zero for St Patrick's Day celebrations (*see chapter* **By Season**). On the day itself (17 March), the streets surrounding Parasol's are closed to traffic and when the parade rolls, on the Saturday closest to the holiday, it's packed until the wee small hours. Parasol's lunch business keeps the place going the rest of the year, and a regular crowd of older locals maintains a lively, relaxed and comfortable atmosphere.

Rocky's Bar & Pizza Joint
3222 Magazine Street, at Pleasant Street (891 5152).
Bus 11 Magazine. **Open** 11.30am-11pm Mon-Thur, Sun;
11.30am-12.30am Fri, Sat. **Credit** AmEx, DC, Disc, MC,
V. **Map 6 A4**
While it could be argued that Rocky's is a restaurant that happens to have a bar, the drink specials certainly allow for the retort that this is a bar that happens to serve pizza. Early evenings find the restaurant pulling in most of the business, primarily from the crowd of 20- and 30-year-olds traversing the coffeeshops, restaurants and bars along this stretch of Magazine Street. Later on, as the diners thin out, the bar draws a crowd that ranges from relaxed and quiet to packed and boisterous. On Tuesday and Thursday nights, from 9pm until everyone goes home, there is a two-for-one drink special, and even the occasional draw of free pizza slices (on Thursday nights).
Disabled: toilet.

Samuel's Restaurant & Beer Pub
1628 St Charles Avenue, at Euterpe Street (581 3777).
St Charles Streetcar. **Open** from 11am daily. **Credit**
AmEx, DC, Disc, MC, V. **Map 6 B2**

You won't go thirsty at **Cooter Brown's Tavern & Oyster Bar**. See page 197.

One of the newer bars in town and on a section of St Charles Avenue currently experiencing a revival, Samuel's has quickly become the prime after-work hangout for young professionals. Although it promotes itself as a big beer bar, the selection pales in comparison to Cooter Brown's, Bulldog's or Balcony's – and it's pricey. Still, the beer is better than your average swill, and there are pint specials on early Tuesday and Thursday evenings. The menu in the adjoining dining room is also better than usual; there are hamburgers, po-boys, salads, pizzas and seafood platters.
Disabled: toilet. Website: www.samuelspub.com

Uptown

Audubon Tavern II

6100 Magazine Street, at Webster Street (895 9702).
Bus 11 Magazine. **Open** 11am-9pm Mon, Sun; 11am-1.30am Tue-Thur; 11am-3.30am Fri, Sat. **Credit** AmEx, MC, V. **Map 4 B9**
ATII's is the bar of choice among fraternity and sorority members at Tulane University – this fact alone should serve to steer most people away. It has little to offer other than a haven for its drunken, sometimes belligerent regulars. Drinks are cheap but not very good, the grill has one item people make an effort to come here for (cheese fries with roast beef gravy) and the rest is pretty bland. Fights have been known to break out, so drop by only if you want to see what you don't miss about being in college.

Le Bon Temps Roulé

4801 Magazine Street, at Bordeaux Street (895 8117).
Bus 11 Magazine. **Open** 11am-3am daily. **Credit** AmEx, Disc, MC, V. **Map 4 C10**
A long-time favourite of both college students and locals, Le Bon Temps is one of the most established bars in New Orleans, a city where some places last only a matter of months. It's comfortable, with wooden floors and furniture and a recently added patio. In the front room are two pool tables and one of the best jukeboxes in town, while the back

room houses the **House of Dues** music club (really just a small stage, *see p209*) and an excellent late-night grill. Prices are a bit high, but the beer selection (draught and bottled) wide. Nightly specials include cheap Abita (from the local microbrewery) beer on Monday nights and free oysters on Friday afternoon.
Website: www.brecht.com/lebontemps/

The Boot Bar & Grill

1039 Broadway, at Zimple Street (866 9008).
Bus 22 Broadway. **Open** 11am-6pm daily. **Credit** AmEx, Disc, MC, V. **Map 4 B8**
Across the street from one of the Tulane University buildings and two blocks from the university library, the Boot is strictly a college bar. Occasionally a professor or three may stop by, but the crowd is predominantly made up of undergrads, who, due to lack of transport or adventure, have little option other than bars near campus. Once in a rare while a band will play inside the bar or outside on the patio, but a music venue the Boot is not. Plenty of draught beer is served, including a dozen choices on tap that are better than the usual college bar swill. The pool tables are always in high demand. Hormone levels run high, but the meat market is generally limited to classmates.

Bruno's

7601 Maple Street, at Hillary Street (861 7615).
Bus 22 Broadway/St Charles Streetcar. **Open** 3pm-3am Mon-Thur, Sun; noon-5am Fri, Sat. **Credit** AmEx, DC, Disc, MC, V. **Map 4 B8**
Bruno's is across the street from **TJ Quills** (*see p199*) and about four blocks from Broadway, where many students live. Freshmen usually stick closer to campus, but it's popular with older undergrads. Drinks are nothing special and the beer list limited, but prices are cheap and the free popcorn sometimes becomes a meal when students miss dinner at the campus dining halls. Pool tables and darts allow for some entertainment besides talking to classmates, but there are plenty of better places to go, some only blocks away.
Disabled: toilet.

The Club/Ms Mae's

*4336 Magazine Street, at Napoleon Avenue (895 9401).
Bus 11 Magazine, 24 Napoleon.* **Open** 24 hours daily.
No credit cards. Map 4 D10
Popular with older barflies and college students, the Club is
one of the few bars to take full advantage of New Orleans's
lax liquor laws, staying open 24 hours a day. Wednesday
nights are particularly popular with the younger crowd,
thanks to a two-drinks-for-a-dollar special. This is also one
of the few bars within walking distance of Tipitina's (about
five blocks), so if it's an exceedingly crowded night at Tip's,
this can be a nice place to take a breather, shoot a game of
pool or darts and drink cheaply.

Columns Hotel

*3811 St Charles Avenue, at Peniston Street (899 9308).
St Charles Streetcar.* **Open** 3pm-midnight Mon-Thur;
3pm-2am Fri; 11am-2am Sat; 11am-midnight Sun.
Credit AmEx, MC, V. **Map 4 D9**
The stately, old Columns Hotel houses one of the more comfortable bars in the city. With dark wood, booths, small
tables and a large porch overlooking St Charles, the
'Victorian Lounge' is frequented by older students and professionals on their way home from work. It's busiest during
afternoon happy hour. The staff are friendly and knowledgeable, and rumour has it that the hotel is a favourite place
for illicit affairs among local politicians, professors and poets.

Cooter Brown's Tavern & Oyster Bar

*509 S Carrollton Avenue, at St Charles Avenue (866
9104). Bus 34 Carrollton Express/St Charles Streetcar.*
Open 11am-2am Mon-Wed, Sun; 11am-4am Thur-Sat.
Credit DC, Disc, MC, V. **Map 4 A8**
For beer fans, Cooter Brown's is the mecca of New Orleans
bars. It offers over 65 draught beers and over 350 brands of
bottled beer from throughout the world, and if a beer is distributed in New Orleans, it will be at Cooter's. To keep all
this draught beer fresh, Cooter's uses a carbon-dioxide tap
system to prevent contact between the beer and the air. The
crowds are generally middle-aged, sometimes annoying but

usually not. It also has one of the best grills in town, a raw
oyster bar, two pool tables, a dartboard and numerous TVs
for sports fans.
Website: http://turnipseed.com/cooter_browns

Dos Jefes Uptown Cigar Bar

*5535 Tchoupitoulas Street, at Joseph Street (891 8500).
Bus 10 Tchoupitoulas.* **Open** 5pm-2am Mon-Thur, Sun;
5pm-4am Fri, Sat. **Credit** AmEx, DC, Disc, MC, V.
Map 4 C10
Contrary to the stuffy atmosphere of many establishments
that cater to an older crowd, Dos Jefes is a comfortable place,
tucked away in an Uptown neighbourhood along the
Mississippi River. There is a large cigar humidor (an excellent ventilation system keeps the room from getting overly
hazy), a wide selection of ports, brandies, scotches and bour-
bons, a good choice of beer, a short wine list and a small
menu of appetisers. You can play a quiet game of billiards
in the back room, and a recently opened outdoor patio has
swings in place of bar stools and hammocks hung from the
rafters. Jazz bands and soloists play from Thursday to
Saturday night.

F&M Patio Bar

*4841 Tchoupitoulas Street, at Lyons Street (895 6784).
Bus 10 Tchoupitoulas.* **Open** 1pm-4am Mon-Thur, Sun;
1pm-6am Fri, Sat. **Credit** V. **Map 4 C10**
For years F&M's was known for two things: as the place
to go after shows at **Tipitina's** (*see p209*) and as the best
place for late-night romantic encounters. The pool table in
the front room became so popular as a dance surface that
another was added on the patio for those actually wanting
to play. It has a decent beer selection and some of the best
staff in town – bartenders are efficient and know their
drinks. Crowds can be overwhelmingly dense on weekend
nights. There is a grill, but the food's not great; still, if it's
getting close to dawn and your energy is waning, a plate
of cheese fries or quesadillas may be the lift you need.
Better yet, skip the food and order a Bloody Mary to toast
the sunrise.

It's a bar, but not as we know it: **Snake & Jake's Christmas Club Lounge**, *page 198.*

Rock 'n' roll out to Jefferson Parish for the **Rivershack Tavern**. *See page 199.*

Fat Harry's
4330 St Charles Avenue, at Napoleon Avenue
(895 1045). Bus 24 Napoleon/St Charles Streetcar.
Open from 9am daily. **Credit** AmEx, Disc, MC, V.
Map 4 D9
College students venturing to Fat Harry's for the first time
are often jokingly warned to bring boxing gloves. This is
sage advice, as many of the young local crowd at Fat's consider this bar to be their territory. Nevertheless, it draws a
large population of local and visiting students; college networks mean it's one of the best known bars at schools
throughout the country. The bar is open late and serves grill
food until early in the morning. Weekend nights are particularly busy. If a large, dense crowd of college students in a
dimly lit room is what you're looking for, Fat Harry's is
worth a visit. If not, stop by on a sunny afternoon while
exploring Uptown.
Disabled: toilet.

Madigan's
800 S Carrollton Avenue, at Maple Street (866 9455).
St Charles Streetcar. **Open** from 3pm daily. **Credit**
AmEx, MC, V. **Map 4 A8**
Far Uptown near Riverbend, Madigan's is a small bar with
reasonable prices and a pool table, which caters primarily to
older college students and young professionals. There's little
to hold people here, however: it's more a place to meet friends
and decide where to go for the rest of the evening than a bar
to stay in for hours.
Disabled: toilet.

Phillip's Restaurant & Bar
733 Cherokee Street, at Maple Street (865 1155).
Bus 22 Broadway/St Charles Streetcar. **Open** 3pm-2am
daily. **Credit** AmEx, Disc, MC, V. **Map 4 B8**
Long a favourite with Tulane University graduate students,
Phillip's has a strict enough door policy to keep drunken
undergrads out of the way. Dimly lit with a well-staffed bar
and cocktail waitresses, it has pool tables and dartboards for
gamers, and for those patrons looking for a study partner

who may just happen to be of the opposite sex, there is a
cleverly placed mirror above the bar, allowing you to look
around the room without drawing attention to yourself. The
real fun comes when eye contact is made through the mirror.
Disabled: toilet.

St Joe's
5535 Magazine Street, at Joseph Street (no phone/stjoes
@bellsouth.net). Bus 11 Magazine. **Open** from 5pm
daily. **Admission** free. **Credit** AmEx, MC, V. **Map 4**
C9/10
Formerly Ms Mae's Place, a seedy hangout for local lushes,
this bar reinvented itself in 1997 as St Joe's, drastically
changing its look and the regular crowd demographics.
While still long and narrow, the bar's ceiling was raised,
making for a less claustrophobic space. The flavoured
vodkas for the extensive 'Martini' menu cater to the new
clientele, mainly Tulane graduate students and young professionals. There's also a pool table, above-average beer list
and a good selection of top-quality liquors.

Sitting Duck Café
5130 Freret Street, at Valmont Street (895 1400).
Bus 15 Freret. **Open** from 9pm Tue-Sat. **Admission**
$3-$5 for occasional live music. **Credit** AmEx, DC, Disc,
MC, V. **Map 4 C8**
Frequented by under-age college and high school students,
the Sitting Duck's largest claim to fame is its relatively
obscure location for a college bar, closer to the undesirable
neighbourhoods surrounding Freret Street than to either
Loyola or Tulane. The bar specialises in serving sweet,
liqueur-laden shots, popular with students looking for a buzz.
Pool tables and dartboards in the back room make for a more
interesting scene than the dark front room.
Website: www.comm.net/~pvp2

Snake & Jake's Christmas Club Lounge
7612 Oak Street, at Hillary Street (861 2802).
Bus 22 Broadway/St Charles Streetcar. **Open** from 9pm
daily. **No credit cards. Map 4 B8**

A tiny neighbourhood bar, Snake's first caught on with the music club crowd due to its late hours of operation – it doesn't open until 9pm and rarely closes before dawn. Soon, word of mouth spread about this hole-in-the-wall joint and it grew into a bar that is always busy, especially on weekend nights. The interior is dark, the décor looks like it's been preserved since the 1950s, the bartenders are notoriously slow – yet everyone who's been at a music show seems to end up at Snake's, comparing notes on that evening's bands. Prices are average, though the crowd is anything but, ranging from students to local journalists and musicians.

TJ Quills

7600 Maple Street, at Hillary Street (866 5205).
Bus 22 Broadway/St Charles Streetcar. **Open** from 3pm
Mon-Sat; from 7pm Sun. **Credit** AmEx, Disc, MC, V.
Map 4 B8
The last stop on the Tulane/Loyola University stretch, Quills is reputed to be the best place to meet Loyola co-eds. Not surprisingly, it's full of students and the drinks are cheap and not very good, but specials allow for vast quantities to be consumed on a student's budget. Pool tables and video games are provided for the rare few not looking to hook up with a member of the opposite sex, and while brief skirmishes among male patrons are common, the bouncers are quick to quell any altercations and toss people off the patio at the front of the bar.

Waldo's Restaurant & Bar

7130 Freret Street, at Broadway (861 0236).
Bus 15 Freret, 22 Broadway. **Open** from 6pm Mon-Thur,
Sun; from 2pm Fri, Sat. **Admission** $5 Wed for Penny
Pitchers. **Credit** AmEx, Disc, MC, V. **Map 4 B8**
Second only to the Boot in its appeal to undergrads, Waldo's is only two blocks from Tulane and in the middle of the fraternity/sorority row that is Broadway. There's a large patio and rooms with pool tables on either side of the main bar. In one of the rooms, frozen drink machines churn out Daiquiris. Probably the highlight at Waldo's is the occasional Drink or Drown special where patrons pay one price at the door and can then order as much of any drink as they want.

Bywater

Saturn Bar

3067 St Claude Avenue, at Clouet Street (949 7532). Bus
88 St Claude. **Open** 2pm-2am daily. **No credit cards**.
The Saturn Bar is one of the city's most out-of-the-way and unusual drinking holes. Located out on St Claude Avenue, far from tourists limited to getting around on foot, it's a locals' place that functions as an air-conditioner repair shop in the daytime. The beer selection is surprisingly large, but don't try to order any fancy cocktails, or you'll probably be chastised by the cantankerous bartenders. Worth a trip, especially late in the evening when it's usually packed with service industry workers off their shifts in the French Quarter bars and restaurants.

Further afield

Rivershack Tavern

3449 River Road, at Shrewsbury Road, Jefferson (834
4938). Bus Kenner Local to Shrewsbury. **Open** from
11am daily. **Credit** AmEx, DC, Disc, MC, V.
Stuck way out on River Road on the Mississippi River levee in Jefferson Parish, the Rivershack is home to metro New Orleans area bikers. On any night and especially on Wednesdays, the small parking lot is filled with beautifully chromed and hand-painted motorcycles. Inside is a small stage (where blues bands play on Saturday nights), a pool table, a good selection of draught beer, one of the city's better grills and the best collection of bizarre barstools and tacky ashtrays anywhere in the state. The crowd is distinctly middle-aged and can be territorial, but if you make it this far out of town, it's worth dropping in.

Music clubs

Few cities in the world are as defined by music as New Orleans is. It's appropriate, then, that the number of venues for live music is so extensive, and the clubs themselves so diverse. New Orleans is most famous, of course, for being the birthplace of jazz. At the turn of the century, when country blues played by African slaves in the South met European instrumentation, this new music – played largely for patrons at the legendary Storyville brothels – was created. New Orleans jazz is still played nightly at some clubs around town, but there is much more to the live music scene than various styles of jazz. Local musicians have the luxury of drawing on a number of musical traditions: from early jazz to music for marching brass bands, country Cajun two-steps to funky R&B, New Orleans is a home to almost every style of live music imaginable.

Like the bands and musicians whose sound is often hard to pigeon-hole, New Orleans clubs are difficult to classify. Witness the **House of Blues** *(page 203)*, where, despite its name, blues is usually offered only one day of the week. There are a few clubs that stick exclusively to one format, but, for the most part, checking local club listings for a band's style is the only way to tell what type of music will be happening at a particular club on a given night.

Club patrons more accustomed to canned music or DJs may feel out of place in New Orleans – the club scene here is rooted in live performance and, luckily, the number of talented musicians in town keeps each club booked most nights of the week with top-notch local talent and the occasional touring band. Cover charges are usually very reasonable, making visiting more than one club in one night not only feasible but sometimes necessary when trying to take in as many good bands as possible.

The best time of the year for music clubs is undoubtedly during Jazz Fest, with Mardi Gras, New Year's Eve and Hallowe'en other big times *(see chapter* **By Season** *for details)*. But whatever the time of year, whatever the day of the week, there'll be a band playing somewhere in town you'll want to see.

Given the number of clubs in the city, a complete list would be too long to include here. Noticeably absent from our list are music venues on Bourbon Street, but these usually book cover bands and are so close to one another that the prerequisite tourist stroll down Bourbon will give you a taste of what's to be heard (or seen). All clubs listed are easily accessible by streetcar, bus or taxi from anywhere within New Orleans. Don't overlook smaller, out-of-the-way places, as these are the real gems of the local music scene and often leave the most lasting memories of New Orleans as a unique city for live music.

All that jazz

New Orleans offers more musical diversity, history and legend than any other city in the States. While the 'birthplace of jazz' label is the city's largest claim to fame, New Orleans and southern Louisiana have also been instrumental in the development of blues, rock, R&B, brass bands, Cajun and zydeco. At any moment in the city's history, it has held a unique place in popular music worldwide. Even now, when so many people are quick to affix the 'roots' label to the local scene and claim nothing new or innovative is happening there, New Orleans rapper/producer Master P is scoring gold on every record he has a hand in, and a burgeoning Afro-Cuban and Latin jazz scene is attracting music fans from all over the country.

Jazz, born in New Orleans at the turn of the century, was a music performed largely for patrons of the famous Storyville brothels. The city's position as a prominent port and its diverse cultural mix allowed country blues and African poly-rhythms sung by slaves to meet ragtime and European music forms and instrumentation. The result would forever change popular music, and even this earliest form of jazz, Dixieland, is still performed and enjoyed worldwide. Early jazz musicians such as Buddy Bolden, Jelly Roll Morton, King Oliver and Louis Armstrong (*pictured*) live on eternally through their music.

In the 1950s, the R&B scene in New Orleans churned out a huge number of now legendary artists, among them Earl King, Fats Domino, Professor Longhair and James Booker. The latter three artists were instrumental in developing the distinct New Orleans piano sound, later picked up by Dr John, Art Neville, Harry Connick Jr and countless others. Art Neville, along with brothers Aaron, Charles and Cyril, went on to form New Orleans's 'first family of funk', the Neville Brothers, one of the city's many recent international stars. Art Neville's earlier band, the Meters, continues to play to a growing fanbase as the 'funky Meters'. The Radiators, one of New Orleans's biggest rock bands, celebrated its twentieth anniversary in 1998 and shows no signs of slowing down, to the delight of thousands of 'Fishheads' across the country, whose devotion to the Rads rivals that of the Deadheads at the height of the Grateful Dead's popularity.

Outside the city, Cajun music developed as a cultural expression of country life in the bayous

Top spot for contemporary jazz: the **Funky Butt at Congo Square**.

of the bands that play them. Cajun and zydeco bands perform regularly in New Orleans. The jazz scene continues as strong as ever, with almost every style – Dixieland, swing, big band, bop, fusion and avant-garde – played at clubs throughout the city. The bars and clubs of **Frenchmen Street** are the home of Latin, Cuban and reggae music, while **Donna's Bar & Grill** (*see page 201*) hosts brass bands nightly – New Orleans's unique party music, which has its orgins in the music played at jazz funerals. Legends Dr John, the Neville Brothers, the Meters, Allen Toussaint, Irma Thomas, Pete Fountain and many more play bigger clubs such as the **House of Blues** (*page 203*) and **Tipitina's** (*page 209*) a few times a year, and almost all famous New Orleans musicians get a chance to perform for the throngs of fans at the city's annual Jazz Fest

of south Louisiana. With most songs sung in Cajun French, the music has contributed to the preservation of the dialect, once facing extinction. Also from outside the city came zydeco, music developed by the black Cajuns, and which shares much of its instrumentation with Cajun music, including accordions and rub-boards, but has a stronger beat and a funkier, more contemporary sound. It has become a favourite dance music among Louisiana music fans.

The beauty of all this musical history for a visitor to New Orleans is the regularity with which all forms are played, and the high quality

In fact, it's hard not to find something appealing happening in New Orleans, no matter what time of year. The city cherishes its reputation as the home of such a thriving live music scene, and just as the number of performing bands continues to grow, so does the number of venues to showcase them – three more large downtown clubs were in the planning stages as the 1998 Jazz Fest approached.

If live music is your passion, then there is nowhere better in the world to satisfy it than in New Orleans.

French Quarter

Crescent City Brewhouse

527 Decatur Street, at St Louis Street (522 0571). Bus 55 Elysian Fields, 57 Franklin, 82 Desire, 92 Express. **Open** 11am-midnight (food served until 10pm) Mon-Thur, Sun; 11am-1am (food served until midnight) Fri, Sat. **Admission** free. **Credit** AmEx, DC, Disc, MC, V. **Map 8**
One of New Orleans's only two brewpubs, Crescent City offers jazz and Latin combos in the early evening and oldies' cover bands later, plus a good, moderately priced menu (*see p114* **Restaurants**). The bands play on the ground floor at street level, so the best seats are at the front of the main bar. Because of its French Quarter location, the Brewhouse draws more tourists than locals, but the good beers make it well worth an hour's visit.
Disabled: toilet.

Donna's Bar & Grill

800 N Rampart Street, at St Ann Street (596 6914/ donnascom@aol.com). Bus 3 Vieux Carré, 13 Esplanade, 57 Franklin, 82 Desire. **Open** from 8.30pm Mon, Wed-Sun. **Admission** $5. **No credit cards. Map 8**
Donna's is the city's hotspot for brass bands, with performances nightly. Located directly across from the entrance to Louis Armstrong Park on the northern boundary of the French Quarter, it draws a predominantly local crowd. You can order food from the bartenders until late and the cover charge is reasonable, but don't forget to tip the band if the hat is passed around. A word of caution: although the lights outside Armstrong Park make it look inviting in the evening,

restrict your visits there and to the surrounding Tremé neighbourhood to daylight hours.
Disabled: toilet.

Funky Butt at Congo Square

714 N Rampart Street, at Orleans Street (558 0872). Bus 31 St Claude. **Open** 8pm-3am daily; noon-3am during Jazz Fest, Mardi Gras. **Admission** free-$15. **Credit** MC, V. **Map 8**
A few doors down from Donna's, the Funky Butt has, in only two years, come to rival Snug Harbor as the city's top spot for contemporary jazz. Located in a former restaurant with a refurbished art deco interior and named after the home club of early New Orleans jazz legend Buddy Bolden, the club serves up hot music and Creole cooking in swanky surroundings with a laid-back atmosphere. Cover charges can be high, but the talent is top-notch and the setting intimate enough to put you only a few feet from some of the city's best jazz players.
Disabled: toilet. Website: www.funkybutt.com

Hog's Breath Saloon

339 Chartres Street, at Conti Street (522 1736). Bus 55 Elysian Fields, 57 Franklin, 82 Desire. **Open** 11am-3am daily; closed Christmas week. **Admission** free. **Credit** AmEx, Disc, MC, V. **Map 8**
In the heart of the French Quarter, this Hog's Breath Saloon is number three of three (the first was opened in Fort Walton Beach, Florida, and the second and most famous in Key West). The biggest crowds (mainly tourists) stroll in on weekend afternoons and evenings when blues bands play in the back room. There's a large, copper-topped bar with booths opposite, and a few small tables at the back. The place

plays off the success of the Key West Hog's Breath – T-shirt sales probably account for as much business as the limited beer selection or the average grill menu. Walls and ceiling are covered with patrons' graffiti, many of whom climb on top of the bar to leave their mark.
Disabled: toilet. Website: www.hogsbreath.com

House of Blues

225 Decatur Street, at Iberville Street (529 2583). Bus 55 Elysian Fields, 57 Franklin, 82 Desire. **Open** *music hall* 8pm-3am daily; *store* 10am-10pm Mon-Thur, Sun, 10am-midnight Fri, Sat; *restaurant* 11am-midnight Mon-Thur; 11am-midnight Fri, Sat; *gospel brunch* (phone for reservations) 9.30am, noon, 2.30pm, Sun. **Admission** $6-$25. **Credit** AmEx, Disc, MC, V. **Map 8**

Practically a household name in the US, the New Orleans House of Blues was the second in this music club chain (the first was in Cambridge, Massachusetts). The project was led by Isaac Tigrett (who also created the Hard Rock Cafés) and much of the financial backing came from Harvard University, so the club had the largest budget of any local music venue – and it shows. Other celeb backers include Dan 'The Blues Brothers' Ackroyd, James Belushi and Aerosmith. Big-name national acts play regularly, as do local hotshots like Dr John, the Neville Brothers and the Radiators. Cover charges are high (often over $20 or more), and the club's name and location draw a large number of tourists. Still, great acts play here – from gospel for Sunday brunch to alternative rock, and everything in between – and the room is comfortable, with the best sound system and live engineer in town. HoB also cashed in on New Orleans's lack of dance clubs, and on Monday, Thursday, Friday and Saturday nights the live music ends by 2am and DJs spin till near-dawn.
Disabled: toilet. Website: www.hob.com

Jimmy Buffett's Margaritaville Café & Storyville Tavern

1104 Decatur Street, at Ursulines Street (592 2565). Bus 55 Elysian Fields, 57 Franklin, 82 Desire. **Open** 11am-midnight Mon-Thur, Sun; 11am-12.30am Fri, Sat. **Admission** free. **Credit** AmEx, DC, MC, V. **Map 8**

Founded by musician and 'boat drink' fanatic Jimmy Buffett after he'd opened a club in Key West, Margaritaville offers live music seven days and nights a week. Blues and R&B bands start at 2pm in the club's smaller bar room; bigger acts play in the main room later in the evening. This is not a place to find Jimmy Buffett cover bands – he's made a point of drawing on original, local talent. Admission is always free, and tables and cocktail waitresses in the main room accompany the faux Key West décor. The Jimmy Buffett association and the club's site, next to the French Market, draw a predominantly tourist crowd, but this is a good place for an afternoon break when touring the French Quarter.
Disabled: toilet. Website: www.margaritaville.com

Kerry Irish Pub

331 Decatur Street, at Conti Street (527 5954). Bus 55 Elysian Fields, 57 Franklin, 82 Desire. **Open** 2pm-4am daily. **Admission** free. **Credit** AmEx, Disc, MC, V. **Map 8**

One of the better places for acoustic folk music, Kerry Irish Pub does indeed offer traditional Irish music but also features ex-Alarm frontman Dave Sharp, who plays on Sunday nights (often the most popular). Despite the bar's location in the French Quarter, it manages to accommodate a regular local crowd as well as tourists, probably because there is free live music nightly. A small bar at the front leads to small

There's no bar, few seats and no air-conditioning, but plenty of hot jazz and an essential slice of New Orleans history.

tables and a pool table at the back, with the stage along the back wall. Paintings and photos of Irish and Irish-American musicians adorn the walls and ceiling. Bartenders expect a one-drink minimum when a band is playing.
Disabled: toilet.

O'Flaherty's Irish Channel Center

514 Toulouse Street, at Decatur Street (529 1317). Bus 55 Elysian Fields, 57 Franklin, 82 Desire. **Open** noon-3am daily. **Admission** $3-$5 Ballad Room. **Credit** AmEx, Disc, MC, V. **Map 8**

O'Flaherty's is in the French Quarter not the Irish Channel, but it is the largest and most Irish-influenced Irish bar in New Orleans, and the centre for Irish bar-goers, whether local or tourist. A large complex housing three bars, a small court-yard and a giftshop, it offers a wide selection of British, Irish and Scottish beers and stouts, a number of Irish and Scotch whiskies and Irish food. Traditional Irish ballads are per-formed for dancers at 8pm in the Informer Room, while the larger Ballad Room features Irish bands later in the evening. On crowded weekend nights the Aengus Lounge, above and looking down on the Ballad Room, is opened for customers or private parties.
Website: www.CelticNationsWorld.com

Original Tropical Isle

738 Toulouse Street, at Bourbon Street (525 1689). Bus 3 Vieux Carré, 41 Canal. **Open** noon-3am daily. **Admission** free. **No credit cards. Map 8**

With two locations in the French Quarter, the Tropical Isle books blues, folk and cover bands nightly. The décor is tacky and Caribbean-influenced, and the crowd predomi-nantly tourist plus a few students on weekend nights. The bar's signature drink is the bright green Hand Grenade, which it claims is the strongest in the city – it's certainly the most toxic-looking. There are better places in the French Quarter (let alone the rest of the city), but if blind blues guitarist and singer Bryan Lee happens to be play-ing, it's worth a visit.
Branch: **Tropical Isle Bourbon** 721 Bourbon Street, at Orleans Street (529 4109).

Palm Court Jazz Café

1204 Decatur Street, at Gov Nicholls Street (525 0200). Bus 55 Elysian Fields, 57 Franklin, 82 Desire. **Open** 7-11pm Wed-Sun. **Admission** $5. **Credit** AmEx, Disc, MC, V. **Map 8**

Second only to Preservation Hall as the best place for tradi-tional jazz, the Palm Court (unlike that older club) offers a full menu and bar, with the restaurant opening at 7pm and music beginning at 8pm. You'll find more tourists than locals, but this isn't a cheesy tourist joint, as the live music attests. An adjoining warehouse sells trad jazz LPs, CDs and cassettes.
Disabled: toilet.

Preservation Hall

726 St Peter Street, at Bourbon Street (24 hours 522 2841/8pm-midnight 523 8939). Bus 3 Vieux Carré, 42 Canal. **Open** 8pm-midnight daily. **Admission** $4. **Credit** AmEx, MC, V. **Map 8**

As old as the traditional jazz played here, Preservation Hall serves as a living testament to turn-of-the-century New Orleans. Bands play two sets (9pm and 11pm), and a queue usually starts forming outside shortly after 8pm and stretches half a block down St Peter Street to Pat O'Brien's. Inside, amenities are kept to a minimum – there's no bar (bring your own booze), food, toilets or air-conditioning, and seating is limited, but that doesn't keep the musicians, some of whom are well over 80 years old, from playing hot sets. Despite the almost exclusively tourist crowd, to miss Preservation Hall while on a visit to the French Quarter is to miss a part of New Orleans history.
Website: www.preservationhall.com

Tipitina's French Quarter

233 N Peters Street, at Iberville Street (529 1980).
Bus 55 Elysian Fields, 57 Franklin, 82 Desire.
Open 11am-3am daily. **Admission** $5-$15 evening.
Credit AmEx, DC, MC, V. **Map 8**

The latest Tipitina's venture, overlooking the Mississippi River and about one block from the **House of Blues** (*see p203*). The main music hall occupies one half of the club; a merchandise shop and restaurant the other. The club has committed itself to booking local bands and musicians almost exclusively, keeping larger, touring bands at the **Uptown** (*see p209*) and **Big Room** (*p206*) venues. Showcase nights are hosted by local music luminaries such as Cyril Neville, Allen Toussaint and Henry Butler, and a Sunday brunch features local cuisine and trumpeter/vocalist Kermit Ruffins and his Big Band.
Disabled: toilet.

Faubourg Marigny & Tremé

Café Brasil

2100 Chartres Street, at Frenchmen Street (947 9286).
Bus 55 Elysian Fields, 82 Desire. **Open** 6pm-2am Mon-Thur, Sun; 6pm-4am Fri, Sat. **Admission** $5. **No credit cards. Map 8**

Located in the heart of Faubourg Marigny, three blocks from Esplanade Avenue and the edge of the French Quarter, Café Brasil hops on weekend nights with one of the hipper crowds in New Orleans. Friday nights usually feature Latin bands, with funk, rock, jazz and hip hop bands on Saturdays and throughout the rest of the week. On more popular nights, the crowd often spills out on to Frenchmen Street, creating a block-party atmosphere, and there's an adjoining bar for those unwilling to pack into the main room or pay the $5 cover charge. The beer selection is limited and there's no grill, but if you're in the mood to dance to live music you'll be hard pressed to find a better crowd.
Disabled: toilet.

Dragon's Den

435 Esplanade Avenue, at Frenchmen Street (949 1750). Bus 55 Elysian Fields, 82 Desire. **Open** 6pm-4am daily. **Admission** $2-$5. **Credit** AmEx, MC, V. **Map 8**

A small, dark, intimate room that doubles as a dining room for Thai restaurant Siam Café, the Dragon's Den has recently established itself as one of the top places to catch younger, experimental jazz bands and poetry slams. There's no stage to speak of and the crowd on the small dancefloor practically merges with the band. Patrons range from college students to ageing hipsters. Covers, when charged, rarely exceed $5 – easily manageable when doing the Frenchmen Street club crawl. On free nights, it's completely packed. *See p214* **Performing Arts** for details of spoken word events.

Dream Palace & Reality Grill

534 Frenchmen Street, at Chartres Street (945 2040).
Bus 3 Vieux Carré, 82 Desire. **Open** 7pm-3am daily.
Admission $5-$7 1st floor; free 2nd floor. **Credit** AmEx, Disc, MC, V. **Map 8**

The lore of the Dream Palace is as impressive as the club itself. The Radiators, perhaps the biggest rock band to come out of New Orleans, got their start at this midsized music hall, located across the street from Café Brasil. While three-set, dance-until-daylight Radiators shows are rare these days (although the band did celebrate its twentieth anniversary here in January 1998 with just such a show), the Dream Palace is a comfortable place to catch Latin, rock and traditional and experimental jazz bands (usually Wednesday to Saturday). Upstairs, the Reality Grill offers

a full menu and occasional folk and acoustic shows, plus a balcony overlooking the throngs of weekend revellers on Frenchmen.

Ernie K-Doe's Mother-In-Law Lounge

1500 N Claiborne Avenue, at Columbus Street (947 1078). Bus 29 St Bernard. **Open** 5pm-4am daily.
No credit cards. Map 4 G6

In an area short of music clubs, this small room is owned and run by R&B singer Ernie K-Doe, whose song 'Mother-In-Law' was a hit 30 years ago. The bar is usually open but live performances happen sporadically; when they do, K-Doe himself is more than likely to join the band. One of the city's bigger eccentrics in a town filled with them, while on stage he is apt to sell boxer shorts emblazoned with a likeness of his face and his catchphrase, 'I'm cocky, but I'm good'.
Disabled: toilet.

Faubourg Center

508 Frenchmen Street, at Decatur Street (949 0369).
Bus 55 Elysian Fields, 57 Franklin, 82 Desire.
Open times vary; phone for details. **Admission** varies.
No credit cards. Map 8

The pre-eminent dive of New Orleans music clubs, the Faubourg Center is open sporadically for ska, punk and hardcore shows. The crowd is decidedly young – most shows are for all ages and there's no bar, so high school kids are the most common patrons. Plan on walking down to Checkpoint Charlie's if you want a drink. The Faubourg Center is also a prime location for rave parties, but these are rarely promoted or advertised. Chances are, if you follow a group of tattooed and pierced teenagers down Frenchmen Street on a weekend night, they'll lead you here.

Igor's Checkpoint Charlie

501 Esplanade Avenue, at Decatur Street (949 7012).
Bus 55 Elysian Fields, 57 Franklin, 82 Desire. **Open** 24 hours daily. **Admission** free. **Credit** AmEx, MC, V. **Map 8**

Established by Australian ex pat Igor Margan, Checkpoint is on the edge of the Faubourg Marigny and presents rock, metal and punk bands nightly. As well as pool tables and a grill that serves hamburgers until about 3am, Checkpoint has a coin-operated laundromat behind the stage – although it seems rarely used by the unwashed punk crowd. When all the Frenchmen Street clubs are booked with great bands and large crowds, this is a good place to relax with a beer – even if the music itself isn't relaxing. Resort to the grill only as a last hope – better to head a block down Esplanade to the Siam Café for late-night Thai food.
Disabled: toilet.

Snug Harbor

626 Frenchmen Street, at Royal Street (949 0696).
Bus 82 Desire. **Open** 5pm-3am daily; shows 9pm, 11pm.
Admission $5-$25. **Credit** AmEx, MC, V. **Map 8**

New Orleans's leading jazz club, Snug Harbor offers the city's best contemporary jazz musicians in an intimate setting, seven nights a week. Cover charges can be high, but are well worth paying if jazz is your thing. It's a sit-down venue, with tables and benches spread across the floor and right up to the stage. Crowds are generally quiet, respectful of the musicians and intense listeners. It's not at all uncommon for players not scheduled to perform to join the band on stage, leading to some of the best impromptu jazz jam sessions anywhere in the world. Outside the main music room is a bar and adjoining restaurant.

Tipitina's Uptown *headquarters (see page 209): shrine to Professor Longhair and unmissable venue.*

CBD

Michaul's Live Cajun Music Restaurant

840 St Charles Avenue, at Julia Street (522 5517).
St Charles Streetcar. **Open** 11am-1pm, 5-10pm, Mon-Fri;
6-11pm Sat; closed most Catholic holidays. **Admission**
free. **Credit** AmEx, DC, Disc, MC, V. **Map 6 B2**
A popular misconception is that New Orleans is full of Cajun
culture and music. In fact, most Cajuns live in areas of
Louisiana south and west of the city, but Michaul's caters
for the tourist looking for Cajun food and music. Wood
rafters, stuffed and mounted animals and swamp décor are
as transparent in their attempt to look authentic as are the
plate glass windows overlooking the streetcars on St Charles
Avenue. The crowd comes mainly for dinner, but Cajun
bands play nightly in front of an under-used dancefloor.
Disabled: toilet.

Mulate's Cajun Restaurant

201 Julia Street, at Convention Center Boulevard (522
1492). Bus 3 Vieux Carré, 33 Tchoupitoulas. **Open**
11am-11pm daily. **Admission** free. **Credit** AmEx, DC,
Disc, MC, V. **Map 6 C2**
Like Michaul's, Mulate's caters to an almost exclusively
tourist crowd intrigued by Cajun cuisine and music. The
place feels more authentic than Michaul's, though, and usually has higher-calibre Cajun bands, good enough to keep the
small dancefloor relatively busy. There's no cover charge for
music, but both dinner and bar prices are high. A large souvenir shop makes it easy for tourists to take home a bit of
Mulate's, but this doesn't alter the fact that this is a sanitised
version of the true Cajun culture of Acadiana.
Disabled: toilet. Website: www.mulates.com

Warehouse District

Howlin' Wolf

828 S Peters Street, at Julia Street (523 2551). Bus
3 Vieux Carré, 10 Tchoupitoulas. **Open** from 3pm Mon-
Sat. **Admission** $5-$15. **Credit** AmEx, Disc, MC, V.
Map 6 C2
Until recently the city's top spot for touring alternative rock
groups, the Howlin' Wolf is in the process of reinventing itself
to offer more jazz and local bands. Recently renovated, it has
a balcony area (open for larger shows), an excellent sound
system, a pool table at the back and an impressive (for a
music club) beer selection. The Wolf still draws a largely college-aged crowd, but due to its proximity to the Convention
Center and a number of hotels, tourists often wander in. On
Monday, there's an acoustic open-mike night; on Tuesdays
the sound engineer plays CDs but there's no live music.
Disabled: toilet.

Mermaid Lounge

1100 Constance Street, at John Churchill Chase Street
(524 4747). Bus 10 Tchoupitoulas, 11 Magazine. **Open**
9pm-3am Tue-Sat. **Admission** $2-$7. **No credit cards.**
Map 6 C2
Perhaps the most out-of-the-way club in New Orleans, this
hole-in-the-wall is a haven for twenty- and thirtysomething
hipsters. Like the Dragon's Den, there is no real stage and
bands play in one corner of the L-shaped club. Expect
mostly experimental jazz and funk, with occasional appearances by rockabilly and klezmer bands. Bar service can be
painfully slow, but at least the mermaid décor provides a distraction while you're waiting. There's also a small art gallery
in an adjoining room and a sculpture garden on the lawn.

Tipitina's Big Room

310 Howard Avenue, at S Peters Street (529 1980). Bus
3 Vieux Carré, 33 Tchoupitoulas. **Open** times vary;
phone for details. **Admission** $10-$30. **Credit** AmEx,
MC, V. **Map 6 C2**

The first of Tipitina's expansions away from the **Uptown**
club *(see p209)*, the Tip's Big Room was created as a space
for larger-name national bands too popular for the smaller
clubs in town. Originally a yuppie dance club called City
Lights, much of the flashy décor remains at the back, while
the main music hall is a large space with an enormous balcony. Music from the main room is piped into the former
dance club area, so when the place gets too crowded, it's easy
to settle down with a drink and still hear the music.
Disabled: toilet.

True Brew Coffeehouse

200 Julia Street, at Fulton Street (524 8441). Bus
3 Vieux Carré, 33 Tchoupitoulas. **Open** 7am-8pm Mon,
Thur, Sun; 7am-11pm Tue, Fri, Sat. **Admission** $5-$10.
No credit cards. Map 6 C2
A small coffeeshop/bar/theatre/music club in the Warehouse
District that offers folk and jazz bands in the main room and
plays in an adjoining theatre. You'll find a full selection of
coffee (it's an offshoot of the True Brew coffeeshop in Mid
City) as well as pastries, a small beer selection, wines by the
glass and speciality cocktails. Theatre and music perfor-
mances take place on Thursday to Saturday evenings.
Disabled: toilet.

Vic's Kangaroo Café

636 Tchoupitoulas Street, at Girod Street (524 4329/
vics@satchmo.com). Bus 3 Vieux Carré, 33
Tchoupitoulas. **Open** 11.30am-4am daily; opens at 5pm
during major holidays. **Admission** free. **Credit** AmEx,
DC, Disc, MC, V. **Map 6 C1**
Founded by an Australian ex pat in 1992, Vic's has managed to escape much of the hipness of the Warehouse
District. This is probably attributable to the club's insistence that only local blues bands are allowed to grace the
small corner stage. Bands play on Thursday, Friday and
Saturday nights to a mix of local blues fans and occasional
conventioneers en route to their hotels. There are some 15
beers on tap – though this may be a few too many given its
sometimes poor quality. There are also a few dozen bottled
beers, a small grill menu, Australian-theme décor and comfortable chairs and benches in the main room. You can play
pool and darts (plastic- or steel-tipped) in the newly added
upstairs room.
Disabled: toilet.

Garden District

Red Room

2040 St Charles Avenue, at Josephine Street
(528 9759). St Charles Streetcar. **Open** 5pm-2am Mon-
Sat. **Admission** free. **Credit** AmEx, DC, MC, V.
Map 6 B3
The latest venue to latch on to the current revival in 1920s-
and 1930s-style swing clubs, the Red Room caters to an older
crowd waxing nostalgic for times past and a younger, hip
crowd looking for something new. The room is decorated in
red throughout – red carpet, red chairs, red velvet curtains
and red jackets on the waiters. Jazz bands play older swing
and big band ballads and standards, and the small dancefloor is usually packed with dancing couples. A full menu
makes for a dinner club atmosphere, with tables on the main
floor, but the bars on either side do a good business, too.
Prices are high, the crowd is too trendy and the feel is more
Los Angeles than New Orleans, but thanks to the supply of
great musicians in the city, at least the music is good – even
if most of the crowd is only partially paying attention to it.
Disabled: toilet.

There's something worth catching every
night of the week at the Uptown
Maple Leaf Bar *(see page 209).*

Maple Leaf Bar
PRESENTS
MON.
TUES.
WED.
THURS.
FRI.
SAT.
SUN.
MAS MAMONES
HENRY BUTLER
SMILIN' MYRON

Uptown

Carrollton Station Bar & Music Club

8140 Willow Street, at Dublin Street (865 9190).
St Charles Streetcar. **Open** 3pm-3am daily. **Admission**
$5-$8 Fri, Sat. **Credit** AmEx, MC, V. **Map 4 B7**
Boasting one of the better beer selections of the town's
music clubs, Carrollton Station is a relaxed, small room
that hosts rock, funk, folk and fusion bands from
Thursdays to Sundays. Located far Uptown, it's across the
street from Jimmy's Music Club and only blocks from the
Maple Leaf, so perfect for club-hopping. The crowd is usually an older one, and the few tables and benches in front
of the stage fill up quickly. On non-performance nights, it's
a good place to play darts. With some gentle prodding, the
bartenders will tell you about the bar's multiple addresses
– there are four permanently closed doors from when owners used to run illegal numbers games: once one address
was shut down, another door would be cut out in the same
building under a new address – or about the now-defunct
'Chicken Drop'.

House of Dues/ Le Bon Temps Roulé

4801 Magazine Street, at Bordeaux Street (895 8117).
Bus 11 Magazine. **Open** 11am-3am daily. **Admission**
free. **Credit** AmEx, Disc, MC, V. **Map 4 C10**
In the back of popular Uptown bar Le Bon Temps Roulé
(from the popular Cajun cry 'Let the good times roll', see
p196), the House of Dues is a small stage area presenting
local jazz, rock and blues bands a few nights a week, usually
with no cover. It also has one of the better late-night grills in
town, and if the music doesn't move you or you need a diversion during setbreak, there are pool tables in the front room.
On crowded nights (usually only during Mardi Gras and Jazz
Fest), it gets pretty hot and sticky, so don't dress to the nines
if this is your destination.
Website: www.brecht.com/lebontemps/

Jimmy's Music Club

*8200 Willow Street, at Dublin Street (866 9549/concert
line 861 8200). St Charles Streetcar.* **Open** 8pm-3am
Tue-Sat. **Admission** up to $20. **Credit** AmEx, Disc, MC,
V. **Map 4 C10**
Celebrating its twentieth anniversary in August 1998,
Jimmy's is the longest continuously operating music club in
the city. The speakers have been pushed beyond their years,
but the layout is one of the best, with a raised area in front
of the bar overlooking the large dancefloor. Expect every
type of music, from Latin dance nights to hip hop to the occasional surprise Nine Inch Nails show (Trent Reznor lives and
has a studio in New Orleans). Crowds and cover charges vary
from non-existent and free to jam-packed and expensive.
Jimmy's has also become the somewhat unlikely home of the
local roots reggae scene, with the New Orleans Reggae
Coalition hosting monthly shows.
Disabled: toilet.

Kemp's Lounge, Restaurant & Bar

2720 LaSalle Street, at Washington Avenue (891 2738).
Bus 15 Freret, 27 Louisiana. **Open** 6am-2am daily.
Admission $3 Thur. **No credit cards.**
Map 6 A2
North of the Garden District and a block from the rather
dodgy Magnolia housing project, Kemp's is a decidedly local
place that few tourists venture to. Thursday night is usually
the only night for live music, when the ReBirth Brass Band's
midnight sets create a scene unique to New Orleans. Mardi
Gras Indian tribes practise their chants and songs here prior
to Mardi Gras, and on Super Sunday in March (when all the
Indian tribes march and do battle with each other), Kemp's

is a prime location to see the Uptown tribes before they make
their way to Armstrong Park.
Disabled: toilet.

Maple Leaf Bar

*8316 Oak Street, at Dante Street (866 9359). St Charles
Streetcar.* **Open** 3pm-4am daily. **Admission** $5-$16.
No credit cards. Map 4 A7
New Orleans music magazine *OffBeat* once claimed that
'no musical tour of New Orleans is complete without a stop
at the Maple Leaf – and it's true. The back of the stage
abuts a plexiglass window overlooking Oak Street, and on
hot nights drummers often open a door in the window for
air. Inside, there are red-painted, pressed-tin walls and the
dancefloor is long and narrow, running back to a rear bar,
chess and pool tables and an outdoor patio. The place
jumps when the city's top brass, funk, R&B and zydeco
bands play. Located in Carrollton near Tulane and Loyola
Universities, the Maple Leaf draws a perfect mix of college
students and older music fans, black and white – if there is
any example of cultural harmony through mutual appreciation of music, this is it. Tuesday nights, when the ReBirth
Brass Band plays, are magical and not to be missed.
Admission averages $6, but never tops $16. *See p214*
Performing Arts for details of the spoken word events
held here on Sundays.

Neutral Ground Coffeehouse

*5110 Danneel Street, at Soniat Street (891 3381/ngch@
supernews.com). St Charles Streetcar.* **Open** 8pm-
midnight Tue-Thur, Sun; 8pm-1am Fri, Sat. **Admission**
free. **No credit cards. Map 4 C9**
The top spot for acoustic folk. Not far from the Tulane and
Loyola campuses, the Neutral Ground draws younger kids
(who can't get into most bars) and a number of ageing
folkies. You can play chess and backgammon when bands
aren't playing, which isn't often since three separate acts
perform most nights. The talent is usually local acoustic
musicians and spoken word poetry, but when nationally
known folk acts come through town, this is their most
likely venue.
Disabled: toilet. Website: www.acadiacom.net/ngch/

Tipitina's Uptown

*501 Napoleon Avenue, at Tchoupitoulas Street
(895 8477). Bus 26 Napoleon, 33 Tchoupitoulas.*
Open 5pm-3am daily. **Admission** $5-$12. **Credit**
AmEx, DC, MC, V. **Map 4 D10**
Prior to the opening of the House of Blues in 1995, Tipitina's
was the premier club for both local greats and nationally
touring bands. It still offers some of the best live music in
the city. Established as a shrine to New Orleans pianist and
music legend Professor Longhair (Henry Roeland Byrd),
the club bears the name of one of his songs and contains a
bust of the 'Fess' inside the front door and a banner over
the stage with his likeness. The place is legendary, and
recent additions – including air-conditioning and a fantastic new PA system – make it a must on any music lover's
itinerary. Everyone from local brass bands to international
reggae stars is welcome at Tip's. A large balcony overlooks
the stage and dancefloor, and there's a grill for late-night
meals. On Sundays, you'll find there is usually a Cajun Fais
Do-Do dance.
Disabled: toilet. Website: www.tipitinas.com

Mid City

Acadian Beer Garden

*201 S Carrollton Avenue, at Iberville Street
(483 9003). Bus 34 Carrollton Express.* **Open**
2pm-midnight Mon-Thur; 2pm-2am Fri; 1pm-2am Sat;
1pm-midnight Sun. **Admission** $3-$4 Sat. **Credit**
MC, V. **Map 5 D5**

The newest brewpub in New Orleans features fresh beer nightly and live music from Thursday to Sunday. The room is small, so performances are often solo and acoustic: guitarists or keyboard and accordion players. Sunday nights usually feature Grateful Dead cover bands, and often draw the biggest crowds. There are only a few tables and booths, so space is limited, but the huge L-shaped bar has seating, even if it isn't right in front of the band. The Acadian is a good distance from downtown, so the crowd is almost exclusively local.
Disabled: toilet.

Mid City Lanes Rock 'n' Bowl

4133 S Carrollton Avenue, at Tulane Avenue (482 3133/ rocknbowl@bellsouth.net). Bus 34 Carrollton Express, 39 Tulane. **Open** noon-2am daily. **Admission** $5; $10 special events. **Credit** AmEx, DC, MC, V. **Map 4 D5**

If Checkpoint Charlie's distinguishes itself as the only music club in town with a laundromat, the Rock 'n' Bowl ups the ante as the only club in town with a full bowling alley – ten lanes' worth. Somewhat out of the way – take a cab or drive along Tulane Avenue from downtown – and in a strip mall, this is a hidden gem that such rock luminaries as Mick Jagger have sought out. As well as the hottest zydeco night in town (Thursdays), Rock 'n' Bowl offers rockabilly, R&B and blues bands most nights. The club has recently expanded into the space a floor below the bowling alley, and for one cover charge (usually $5), you can go back and forth between the two and catch as many as six bands in one night. If you're in town for Jazz Fest, don't miss the Zydeco Showdown (usually on both Sunday nights of the festival) when Louisiana's hottest zydeco bands vie for the crown of King of Zydeco.
Disabled: toilet.

Sandbar

Student centre, University of New Orleans, off Elysian Fields (280 6039). Bus 55 Elysian Fields, 56 Elysian Fields Express, 60 Hayne. **Open** 8-11pm Wed during academic year (Sept-Dec, Feb-May). **Admission** $5. **No credit cards.**

The University of New Orleans has one of the best jazz studies courses in the world (directed by Ellis Marsalis, the patriarch of the famous Marsalis family), so it should come as no surprise that its Sandbar club offers some of the hottest young players in contemporary jazz (Wednesdays only), most of whom are students at the school. The ambience is like that of most bars in college facilities – nothing special – but the music is stellar, making the club worth the trek. The best way to find the bar is to get to the UNO campus, look on a campus map for the student centre – and then ask.
Disabled: toilet.

Bywater

Vaughan's Lounge

800 Lesseps Street, at Dauphine Street (947 5562). Bus 82 Desire. **Open** 11am-3am daily. **Admission** $5 Thur night. **No credit cards.**

Located way down in the Bywater neighbourhood and best reached by cab or car, Vaughan's is a small bar that became a local music lovers' haven when it started booking trumpeter Kermit Ruffins and his Barbeque Swingers (on Thursday nights). At first, there was no cover charge and free red beans and rice was served at setbreak. Now, with a modest $5 admission, the place still jumps on Thursday nights, packed to the street with a decidedly local crowd. Even such lofty jazz players as New Orleans native Wynton Marsalis have been known to drop by and play with Kermit at these intimate sets.

Contemporary Arts Center

See p92 **Museums & Galleries** *for listings.*

Used as a music venue mainly during Mardi Gras and Jazz Fest, the adjoining warehouse space to the Contemporary Arts Center has become, in the past two years, a hotspot for big-name jazz, funk and rock bands. Amenities are limited to what the production company sets up for each show, but usually include a few full-service bars, food from local caterers and portable toilets in the parking lot. The shows are seasonal, so the crowds are often determined by the event: college-aged revellers for the Mardi Gras funk shows and serious music lovers of all ages and backgrounds for the Jazz Fest concerts.
Disabled: toilet. Website: www.cacno.org

State Palace Theatre

1108 Canal Street, at N Rampart Street (522 4435/ robert@statepalace.com). Bus 41 Canal. **Admission** $5-$8. **Credit** AmEx, MC, V. **Map 7 A1**

This beautifully ornate old theatre reinvented itself as a midsized music venue for concerts by nationally touring rock and rap artists. The State Palace seats about 4,000 in four areas: in an orchestra pit in front of the stage, on the main floor and on two balconies. In the past, it has come under fire from local high school parent groups for hosting large rave parties. After a recent touring rave with the Crystal Method several fans who had adjourned to an Uptown park for a post-rave party were arrested and charged with possession of Ecstasy and crystal methamphetamine. Security is always increased at the venue during such events, however, and the management has no intention of stopping future raves.
Website: www.statepalace.com

Louisiana Superdome

Sugar Bowl Drive, at Poydras Street (box office 587 3800/ tour information line 587 3808). Bus 16 S Claiborne. **Open** 9am-4pm daily; tours hourly depending on other scheduled events. **Credit** MC, V. **Map 6 A/B1**

With seating capacity close to 80,000, the New Orleans Superdome is one of the biggest venues in the country, hosting only the largest international rock stars, such as the Rolling Stones and U2. With it's covered ceiling and giant size, the cavernous dome can make for some of the worst sounding shows in the city, but the staging is typically brilliant, and fans of stadium rock rarely complain. For the past few years, *Essence* magazine has hosted its 'Essence Fest' here over the 4 July weekend, offering big-name talent like Stevie Wonder and Barry White in the main room and smaller bands like the Ohio Players and Cameo in 'superlounges' throughout the venue (*see chapter* **By Season**). *See also chapter* **Sightseeing.**
Disabled: toilet. Website: www.superdome.com

UNO Lakefront Arena

6801 Franklin Avenue, at Leon C Simon Drive (280 7171/arena@uno.edu). Bus 14 Franklin, 17 Hayne, 92 Express. **Open** box office 10am-6pm Mon-Fri. **Admission** $15-$65. **Credit** MC, V.

New Orleans's home of arena rock and country and western bands too popular to play clubs, Senator Nat G Kiefer University of New Orleans Lakefront Arena (to give it its full name) is like most sports arena/music venues. Lots of cement makes the sound ear-piercingly bright if not mixed properly and, with a capacity of over 6,000, it's anything but intimate. But if arena rock is your thing and you'd rather stand in front of an uncomfortable plastic bleacher chair than pack into a club, that's what you'll find here.
Disabled: toilet. Website: www.uno.edu/~lfar

The Performing Arts

Dance, theatre and classical music are no big deal in the Big Easy, but the stage is set for prime local talent.

Let's face it, just about everybody who comes to New Orleans on holiday is more interested in beer and blues than in Beethoven and ballet. Perhaps that is the reason the city's theatre, classical music and dance scenes are fairly small and limited, compared to less classical entertainments. To be honest, the quality of performing arts in New Orleans is about what you'd expect in an American city of less than a million people – mostly mediocre.

There are two types of theatre in New Orleans – large, Broadway roadshows that pass through town about once a month; and small, local theatre groups. The touring shows are a little weary by the time they reach New Orleans. The city tends to attract the most mainstream of Broadway plays, probably in an effort to draw in a large suburban crowd: Andrew Lloyd Webber's Broadway musical *Cats*, for instance, has visited New Orleans no less than nine times.

The city's large theatres, the **Saenger Theatre** and the **Orpheum Theatre**, occupy magnificent nineteenth-century buildings whose elaborate details make a trip to them an event in itself. Locals tend to dress up for these shows and linger over wine in the elegant marble lobbies. The smaller theatres are usually modern and less formal and are where the most creative and unusual performances are to be found.

Local theatre groups vary widely in terms of quality and adventurousness. Suburban theatres stick to the more predictable pieces such as Thornton Wilder's *Our Town*, or *Meet Me in St Louis* or *Showboat*. Urban theatre groups tend to concentrate on more innovative and modern works, and the level of talent can be quite high. Local universities, especially, can put on some of the most creative and impressive local productions.

Of all the performing arts, orchestral music is perhaps best covered. New Orleans has a high-class ensemble in its **Louisiana Philharmonic Orchestra**, one of few orchestras in the country that is owned by its musicians. The result of this egalitarian arrangement is a strong group of talented and enthusiastic musicians who work closely with audiences to create popular performances. Ticket prices for concerts are among the best arts deals in town. As an added incentive, performances are held in the beautiful and historic Orpheum Theatre.

Theatres

Contemporary Arts Center

See p92 **Museums & Galleries** *for listings.*
Inside a converted warehouse, the CAC forms the heart of the city's alternative theatre. The ambience is warehouse chic; the building's historic exterior belies its thoroughly modern insides. In addition to visual art space, the Center houses three auditoriums of various sizes that are regularly used for local theatrical productions as well as dance performances and concerts.

Jefferson Performing Arts Center

400 Phlox Street, between W Metairie Avenue & Hwy 61, Metairie (885 2000/fax 885 3437/jpas@iamerica.net). Bus 38 Airline. **Admission** varies. **Credit** AmEx, MC, V.
Located in New Orleans's nearest suburb, this venue is home to the Jefferson Performing Arts Society, which regularly attracts less well-known travelling productions and groups than those frequenting the Saenger, although the Vienna Boys Choir is a regular. The Center specialises in mainstream offerings designed to please the whole family, except, perhaps, unruly teenagers.
Disabled: toilet. Website: www.jpas.com

Loyola University

Marquette Theatre & Lower Depths Theatre, 6363 St Charles Avenue, at Calhoun Street (box office 865 3824/Department of Drama & Speech 865 3840). St Charles Streetcar. **Admission** $8; $6 concessions. **No credit cards. Map 4 B/C8**
While it stages fewer offerings than **Tulane University** (*see p212*), Loyola cannot be counted out completely. Performances at these two theatres are not always cutting edge, but they're generally solid.
Disabled: toilet in Marquette Theatre. Website www.loyno.edu

Mahalia Jackson Theater of the Performing Arts

Armstrong Park, 801 N Rampart Street, at St Ann Street (565 7470/fax 565 7477). Bus 88 St Claude. **Admission** varies. **Credit** MC, V. **Map 7 C1**
In recent years, this theatre has become a valuable alternative to the Saenger, particularly in its staging of innovative local and national ballet and opera productions. It's located in Armstrong Park, adjacent to the Municipal Auditorium and just outside the French Quarter.
Disabled: toilet.

The splendid – and recently restored – **Saenger Theatre**.

North Star Theater

*347 Gerard Street, Mandeville (626 1500). By car:
take the Pontchartrain Causeway, then Hwy 190.*
Admission varies. **No credit cards**.
Sited across Lake Ponchartrain from New Orleans, this little
theatre is fast becoming the North Shore's cultural centre.
Performances concentrate on local talent, and the theatre has
been taking more chances recently than in years past. Worth
keeping an eye on.

Orpheum Theatre

*129 University Place, at Common Street (524 3285).
Bus 3 Vieux Carré, 41 Canal.* **Admission** varies.
Credit MC, V. **Map 7 A1**
This lovely Gothic building, with its grand old lobby, is
the home of the **Louisiana Philharmonic Orchestra**
(*see p213*). The building is beginning to crack around the
edges and needs a good coat of paint, but the acoustics are
good, and the theatre is the perfect environment for any
classical performance.
Disabled: toilet.

Le Petit Théâtre du Vieux Carré

*616 St Peter Street, at Chartres Street & Jackson Square
(522 2081). Bus 3 Vieux Carré, 55 Elysian Fields, 57
Franklin, 82 Desire.* **Admission** varies. **Credit** AmEx,
MC, V. **Map 7 B2**
One of the oldest non-professional troupes in the country, Le
Petit specialises in new productions of mostly familiar plays.
Oscar Wilde does well here, as do musicals like *The Sound
of Music*. The theatre, which is housed in a historic building
on the edge of Jackson Square, lures in more tourists and
families than local Quarterites.

Saenger Theatre

*143 N Rampart Street, at Canal Street (524 2490).
Bus 41 Canal.* **Admission** varies. **Credit** AmEx, MC, V.
Map 7 A1
First opened in 1927, the Saenger was considered world-class
in its time. Even today, the building is a beautiful structure

lush with unique details. The ceiling in the auditorium is
designed to resemble a night sky, with clouds passing twink-
ling stars. The décor is mostly inspired by Renaissance
Florence, with Greek and Roman sculpture, marble statues
and cut-glass chandeliers thrown in for good measure. Such
theatres are increasingly rare in the US, and most have been
replaced by sleek modern structures. New Orleans loves its
Saenger, and recently restored it to its current shining state.
The theatre is generally used for touring Broadway shows
and the occasional concert.
Disabled: toilet.

Southern Repertory Theater

*Canal Place Shopping Center, 3rd floor, 333 Canal
Street, at N Peters Street (861 8163). Bus 41 Canal,
55 Elysian Fields, 57 Franklin, 82 Desire.* **Admission**
$8-$17. **Credit** MC, V. **Map 7 A3**
Southern Rep showcases the works of Southern talent – both
playwrights and actors – in a theatre that is intimate and
modern. Though the space is located on the third floor of the
ritzy Canal Place Shopping Center, it hasn't that 'in-a-mall'
feel. The theatre shows work from young writers in its sporadic New Playwrights series, which runs throughout the
year. Otherwise, it hosts new and old, creative, professional
work by regional talent.

Tulane University

*6823 St Charles Avenue (Dixon Hall 865 5267/McAlister
Auditorium 865 5196). St Charles Streetcar/bus 15
Freret, 22 Broadway.* **Admission** varies. **No credit
cards. Map 4 B8**
This private university has two medium-sized theatres on
its campus, both of which provide wonderful venues for
plays and musical performances. Dixon Hall is the smallest
of the two and is frequently the site of classical music events.
McAlister Auditorium seats about 1,000 in a sprawling and
comfortable environment and usually hosts plays and musical performances, among other events.
*Disabled: toilet at Dixon Hall. Website: www.tulane.edu/
index.html*

Zeitgeist Alternative Arts Center

2010 Magazine Street, at St Andrew Street (524 0064). Bus 11 Magazine. **Admission** $6; $5 concessions; $4 members. **No credit cards. Map 6 B3**

An upstart, in-your-face alternative theatre that takes no prisoners, Zeitgeist occupies an echoing, ramshackle, two-storey building among the antique stores of the Lower Garden District. Starkly modern art lines its walls. The theatre has a mission to provide a home for the most alternative pieces, particularly those that wouldn't find a venue elsewhere in New Orleans. In addition to mostly local plays, independent films are also regularly shown here (*see p174* **Film**).

Theatre groups

In the late 1980s and early 1990s, dozens of small theatre groups performed in the New Orleans area. Recently, their numbers have declined. Today, just a handful of groups regularly perform together as a troupe. Most of these stick to traditional plays designed, as they say, to please the whole family. By keeping a watch on what's listed in the *Times-Picayune* and *Gambit Weekly*, however, visitors can stumble upon new and creative groups as they form.

Dog & Pony Theatre Company

PO Box 71234, New Orleans, LA 70172-1234 (897 2466/fax 529 5403).

A regular contributor to the local theatre scene, Dog & Pony produces plays that range from the predictable to the unusual. Its season is not scheduled far in advance, so check the papers for listings, or phone for the current show schedule. Performances are at various city venues.

Summer Stages

Summer Stages office (833 8748).
Performances at First Unitarian Universalist Church, 2903 Jefferson Avenue, at S Claiborne Avenue (598 3800). Bus 3 Vieux Carré, 41 Canal. **Admission** $8; $5 concessions. **No credit cards.**

This group puts on regular performances during the summer months between June and August. Recently, Summer Stages has offered creative performances of Shakespeare plays at brilliantly chosen locations in City Park. Past shows have included *Julius Caesar* performed at the Romanesque Peristyle structure, with its huge columns providing the perfect backdrop to the drama.
Disabled: toilet.

Tulane University

Several Tulane groups produce annual series of performances. Among these is the **Summer Lyric Theatre** (865 5269/865 5271), which produces plays throughout the summer months, and Tulane's **Summer Shakespeare Festival** (865 5105), which generally includes a series of three Shakespeare plays, some performed outdoors.

Classical music

Though New Orleans doesn't have many performances of classical music, what it does offer is high quality at bargain prices. The **Louisiana Philharmonic Orchestra** is professional and innovative and performs regularly throughout the year. The local opera company is another respected organisation. It stages fewer productions than the Philharmonic Orchestra, and tickets are a bit pricier. In addition, local universities and small musical groups offer a wide variety of good classical performances.

Louisiana Philharmonic Orchestra

305 Baronne Street, suite 600, New Orleans, LA 70112 (523 6530/fax 595 8468).
Performs at the Orpheum Theatre, see p212.
Tickets $11-$48; $7 students.

Until the early 1990s, this was the New Orleans Symphony. But in what turned out to be an extraordinary battle of wills, the musicians rebelled against their own board of directors – composed primarily of local business leaders – over pay and budget structures. When the board refused to back down after a very public battle, the Symphony disbanded. Within a few months the players reformed as the LPO. Musician-owned, and musician-run, the orchestra struggled financially for several years, but has recently moved into the black. It performs virtually all year round. Ticket prices are a bargain, with cheap seats going for as little as $11. The lower- priced seats are in the highest balconies, but sitting there is hardly a burden in the gracious if somewhat battered Orpheum Theatre, and the orchestra is reliably good.
Website: www.gnofn.org/lpo

Newcomb College

Dixon Hall, Tulane University, 6823 St Charles Avenue (865 5267/caccini@ mailhost.tcs.tulane.edu). St Charles Streetcar/bus 15 Freret, 22 Broadway. **Tickets** free. **Map 4 B8**

A division of Tulane, Newcomb College stages regular, high-quality performances by students, faculty and guest professionals on the Tulane and Newcomb campuses. Throughout the school year, Newcomb stages its Music at Midday programme, with classical music performed weekly at noon. The college also has an annual Concert Piano Series and a Classical Guitar Series, which run between August and May, along with a long list of performances by visiting classical players. Check local newspapers for listings, or phone for more information.
Website: www.tulane.edu/`music

New Orleans Musica da Camera

1035 Eleonore Street, New Orleans, LA 70115 (865 8203/musica@gnofn.org). **Tickets** free.

Concentrating on early music performed on original instruments, this group provides an unusual and beautiful alternative to the city's other classical offerings. Musica da Camera plays in churches and halls throughout the region; for concert dates and venues, check local listings or phone the number above.
Website: www.gnofn.org/`musica/

New Orleans Opera Association

305 Baronne Street, suite 500, New Orleans, LA 70112 (529 2278/fax 529 7668).
Performs at the Mahalia Jackson Theater of the Performing Arts, see p211. **Tickets** $30-$70; $10 discount for students.

Opera and New Orleans go way back. The city was first home to an opera company in the early 1800s, and by the 1890s, opera was hugely popular. A glorious French Opera House was built, just for the purpose of showcasing opera performances. Tragically, the building burned to the ground in 1919. This effectively ended local opera production until the 1940s, when the Opera Association was formed. The company performs only a handful of times each year at the Mahalia Jackson Theater, and the season is not widely publicised in advance. But the shows are highly professional, and feature stars from around the country in lead roles.
Website: www.neworleansopera.org

Spoken word

Like so many elements of New Orleans life, a storied past is a fine substitute for a vibrant present. As literary tours of the French Quarter and the annual Tennessee Williams Festival make clear, New Orleans has a rich tradition of literature, but that doesn't mean creative writing is particularly well supported today. Poetry has never become much of a spectator sport in New Orleans; when the poetry slam caught on in other cities, it found its way down the Mississippi River a year or two later, and then only as a novelty and not as implied poetics.

Still, New Orleans is probably like most cities in most relevant ways. It's cliquey, with each group sharing its own vision of poetry, and each clique tends to be associated with a venue. The groups aren't insular, but they're sceptical of each other. Since, like other cities, writers dominate the audiences at readings, the catty whisperings at the back of the room are often as entertaining as the poetry on stage.

As coffeehouses spring up and look for customers, venues for spoken word events increase; when a scene gets tired, it dies. Ironically, both can happen in a very short span of time, so today's hot spots may be tomorrow's blues joints. Check the *Times-Picayune*, *OffBeat* and *Gambit* for the most current listings.

Community Book Center

217 N Broad Street, at Bienville Street (822 2665). Bus 97 Broad. **Open** 10am-7pm Mon-Sat; open-mike evenings every 2nd Fri. **Admission** free. **Map 4 E6**

Just outside the French Quarter, the Community Book Center is a based in a shotgun house that serves as an African-American bookstore during the day. At night, the organisation hosts poetry readings and other creative writing events, including open-mike evenings. Those interested in reading may wish to call ahead and try to get on the schedule.

Dragon's Den

See p204 **Nightlife** *for listings.*

Located upstairs from a Thai restaurant at the Faubourg end of the French Quarter, the Dragon's Den is *the* poetry venue every Thursday night. 'The Mad Poet Express', as it's called, fills the room with old hippies, tangle-headed punks, junkies, whores, grad students and other members of the Culturally Marginal. It's an open-mike reading, and after some months of limping along, there are now more readers than there is time for. The poetry, like the audience that now jams the place, is varied to say the least. Serenade and improvised babble are just as at home as verse that reflects effort and craft, and clothes are always optional.

Hi-Ho Lounge

2239 St Claude Avenue, at Marigny Street (947 9344). Bus 88 St Claude. **Open** 5pm-5am Mon-Fri; 7pm-5am Sat, Sun. **Admission** $3-$5. **No credit cards.** **Map 4 H6**

The Hi-Ho features one of the newer reading series in town, and one with unique solutions to open-mike problems. The anxiety of being the last on the list is alleviated because the reading is sequenced by drawing names out of a hat. Similarly, writers who consider their introductory lectures and monologues separate from their reading time learn that the clock starts when they hit the stage, and those who overstay their welcome are shot with squirt guns. The poetry is genuinely varied, but those bored by it don't have to suffer too much: the Hi-Ho puts board games on the tables.

Maple Leaf Bar

See p209 **Nightlife** *for listings.*

The Maple Leaf is a perfectly New Orleans landmark. It is physically humble, it has tradition, and it comes with its own patron saint. Everette Maddox, whose skills at writing poetry and drinking scotch ran neck and neck, began what is the longest-running regular poetry reading series in the South. Every Sunday afternoon for the past 20 years, people have gathered at the Maple Leaf for beer and poetry. Even before Maddox's death in 1989, the tone of the readings had changed, and the days of free-for-alls had largely passed, being replaced with pleasantly informal literariness. Audiences can be very kind and patient, and the poets are similarly moderate in their manner and material; no one is likely to fall to the floor shrieking about the sins of mommy and/or daddy. If someone did, people would applaud politely.

Dance

This is the tiniest of New Orleans's performing arts offerings. The city has little to offer in the way of classical performances, as the ballet company performs only two or three times a year, and no other dance groups of substance are based in the city. Visiting contemporary dance troupes usually perform at the Saenger Theatre. Look for dance elsewhere.

New Orleans Ballet Association

305 Baronne Street, suite 700, New Orleans, LA 70112 (522 0996/fax 595 8454).

Performs at the Mahalia Jackson Theater of the Performing Arts, see p211. **Tickets** $20-$65; $13-$58 concessions.

A small but accomplished troupe that merged several years ago with the Cincinnati (Ohio) Ballet. The result of this marriage is a good flow, back and forth, of gifted dancers, plus a new creative fire for the local group. While the choice of ballets is generally predictable (*Swan Lake* and *The Nutcracker* almost every year), the dancers are talented and the shows worthwhile. The ballet season is changeable, but generally runs from autumn to spring.

Elizabeth Futral sings Delibes' 'Lakmé' for the **New Orleans Opera Association** *(page 213).*

Sport & Fitness

Gone fishin': the lowdown on your sporting options in New Orleans, such as they are.

Spectator sports

It is a sad reflection on the state of sport in the US that because New Orleans is not a particularly large television market, professional sports leagues have little interest in locating teams in the city. When the New Orleans Jazz left to play basketball in jazzy Utah, the Saints – the local football team – became the city's only major league team. And since their history has been one of mediocrity interrupted by flickers of competence, the city's relationship with the team has been an uneasy one, consisting of Saints bashers, Saints fanatics and few people in between. In fact, this level of intensity characterises New Orleanians' involvement with any sport.

INFORMATION

The *Times-Picayune* is the most reliable source of information on local sports and schedules of events. It is not, however, the most complete source of sports information, since sports not played in New Orleans receive little coverage. Sports junkies will probably want to supplement their morning reading with *USA Today*'s sports page.

Perhaps the number one source for Saints news is Buddy Diliberto, who hosts a nightly sports talk show (6.15-10pm) on WWL (870 AM) as well as a show before Saints' games and 'Hap's Point After' after games. Buddy D, as he's known, has been intimately associated with the Saints since he was inspired by yet another loss to suggest that fans wear paper bags over their heads to show the team they were ashamed to be seen at a game. His joke took off, people wore bags and the 'Aints' were born (*see chapter* Sightseeing for the Saints Hall of Fame). Buddy D could only be a celebrity in New Orleans, where his speech impediment and overeager delivery make him a dubious hero. What his callers lack in coherence and logic, however, they make up for in pure mania. There is nothing in radio quite like it.

TICKETS

Ticketmaster is the giant in New Orleans that it is everywhere else, so tickets for almost every sporting event in the New Orleans area can be purchased by phoning them on 522 5555. You pay a service charge. Tickets are also generally available from the teams' ticket offices, usually without extra charge.

If you want to get tickets through less official channels, talk to hotel concierges, many of whom act as unofficial ticket brokers. Though this isn't the most reliable way to get tickets and is rarely the most economical, creative concierges can find oversubscribed tickets more easily than lost luggage.

You can also buy tickets from scalpers, but tread carefully and make sure the tickets you are being offered are for the right date and game before handing over any money. And always haggle a little first: if a lot of scalpers are selling tickets, it's a sure indication of a buyer's market and the patient buyer can get a good deal. Even though there are risks involved in dealing with scalpers, the results can be fruitful: frustrated Saints season-ticket holders can often be found dumping their tickets for below face value in a bad season.

LOUISIANA SUPERDOME

For the giant home to the Saints and host of other major events, sporting or otherwise, *see page 218* **Saints**. Tours of the building are available daily, and there's a website with more information (www.superdome.com).

Baseball

Despite the lack of a major league franchise, New Orleans is a good baseball city. The New Orleans Zephyrs, a Triple-A farm team for the National League's Houston Astros, plays at Zephyr Field in Metairie, and even though summer isn't a great time to be outdoors in New Orleans, the Zephyrs draw well. The field is as pleasant a place to watch a game as can be found away from an air-conditioner. The beer is cheap, the chairs are comfortable and the rows of seats leave leg-room. Sure, you've never heard of the ball players, but then they've never heard of you either.

More important than the Zephyrs' farm league baseball is college baseball, particularly **Louisiana State University** baseball. LSU is an hour west of New Orleans in Baton Rouge (*see page 227* **Trips Out of Town**), but LSU alumni are everywhere and now that the baseball team has won four College World Series championships in the 1990s, everybody's proud of their alma mater. Home games are played at Alex Box Stadium in Baton Rouge. It's a comfortable place to watch a game but the Southeastern Conference doesn't allow beer at ball games, so thirsty fans may

*Win or lose, everyone follows the **Saints**.*

prefer to wait until LSU comes to New Orleans to play the **University of New Orleans** (UNO) or **Tulane**, both of which regularly field competitive teams.

The professional season runs from mid-April to early September, the college season from early February to early June.

Louisiana State University

Alex Box Stadium, S Stadium Drive, Baton Rouge (information 334 4578/box office 388 2184). **Open** *box office 8am-5pm Mon-Fri.* **Tickets** $4-$6. **Credit** MC, V. *Disabled: toilet.*

New Orleans Zephyrs

Zephyr Field, 6000 Airline Highway, between Transcontinental & David Drives, Metairie (734 5155). Bus E2 Airport. **Open** *9am-6pm Mon-Fri; 10am-4pm Sat.* **Tickets** $6-$8; seniors, under-12s $1 discount. **Credit** AmEx, MC, V.

Tulane University

Turchin Stadium, Tulane University, at Claiborne Avenue (information 862 8239/box office 865 5810). St Charles Streetcar. **Open** *8.30am-5pm Mon-Fri.* **Tickets** $3-$6. **Credit** AmEx, MC, V. **Map 4 C8**

University of New Orleans

Privateer Park, at Leon C Simon Drive & Press Drive (information 280 6100/box office 280 6284). Bus 58 Franklin Express. **Open** *box office 8am-noon, 1-4.30pm, Mon-Fri.* **Tickets** $2-$6. **Credit** AmEx, MC, V. *Disabled: toilet.*

Basketball

The New Orleans Jazz professional team is a fond memory, so basketball fans dream of a pro team returning to the city and meanwhile focus on local college basketball. The National Collegiate Athletic Association (NCAA) season runs from early December to early March, when the NCAA Tournament determines the national champion. **LSU**, having produced stars like 'Pistol' Pete Maravich and, more recently, Shaquille O'Neal, commands the most attention, but **Tulane** and **UNO** also have strong programmes. Both have appeared in the NCAA Tournament in the 1990s, which is impressive considering their situations – UNO is a commuter school whose players are often junior college transfers and Tulane's programme, which was ended after a point-shaving scandal, was only restarted in the 1990s.

Women's basketball is growing nationwide and in some places, women's games draw as big a crowd as men's games. Recently, both Tulane and LSU's women's teams have been doing well, but diehard fans might want to take the road trip to northern Louisiana to Ruston, the home of Louisiana Tech, a perennial powerhouse in the women's game. Doubleheaders, featuring a women's and a men's game, are good deals.

The basketball season runs from early November to early March.

Louisiana State University

Pete Maravach Assembly Center, N Stadium Drive, Baton Rouge (information 334 4578/box office 388 2184). **Open** *box office 8am-5pm Mon-Fri.* **Tickets** $10. **Credit** MC, V. Weekend games are usually sold out. *Disabled: toilet.*

Tulane University

Foggelman Arena, Tulane University, at Freret Street (information 865 5505/box office 865 5810). St Charles Streetcar. **Open** *box office 8.30am-5pm Mon-Fri.* **Tickets** $8-$16. **Credit** AmEx, MC, V. **Map 4 B8** *Disabled: toilet.*

University of New Orleans

UNO Lakefront Arena, 6801 Franklin Avenue, at Leon C Simon Boulevard (information 280 6100/box office 280 6284). Bus 14 Franklin, 17 Hayne, 93 Express. **Open** *box office 8am-noon, 1-4.30pm, Mon-Fri.* **Tickets** $4-$16. **Credit** AmEx, MC, V. *Disabled: toilet.*

Football

American football has a heroin-like grip on the nation, so much so that even highlights from high school games make the evening television news. In New Orleans, only **Tulane** fields a college football team, and they play in the Louisiana Superdome before a gathering of fans small enough to learn each others' names. The **Sugar Bowl** (every 1 or 2 January) is an intercollegiate game, part of the end-of-season invitational series that is supposed to determine the best college team in the country. If you're in town for it, it's good fun.

Saints games, also played at the Superdome, are more raucous events, not surprisingly. Fans possess an inexhaustible supply of dark humour and can find fun and laughs in the midst of the most inept moments. Because they know what it's like to be laughed at by others, Saints fans are pretty tolerant of other teams' fans. Note that the Superdome box office (on ground level, facing Poydras Street) does not accept phone bookings, only ticket purchases in person.

The most complete football event in the area is an **LSU** game in Baton Rouge. The LSU campus starts to become RV city on the Friday night before a Saturday game, and by Saturday, tents, shelters, barbecues and pick-up trucks are strewn all over campus, all surrounded by people preparing for the game. Exactly why a game requires five, even ten hours of preparation is unclear, but beer and hamburgers seem crucial to fuelling fandom. The scene is impressive in its rawness and enthusiasm, and eventually a football game is played. Tickets are often sold out.

The professional season runs from the end of August to the end of December, the college season from September to December.

Louisiana State University

Tiger Stadium, N Stadium Drive, Baton Rouge (information 334 4578/box office 388 2184). **Open** *box office* 8am-5pm Mon-Fri. **Tickets** $26. **Credit** MC, V.
Disabled: toilet.

Saints

Louisiana Superdome, Sugar Bowl Drive, at Poydras Street (Superdome box office 587 3800/Saints 731 1700). Bus 16 S Claiborne. **Open** *Superdome box office* 9am-4.30pm Mon-Fri; open at weekends for special events. *Saints* 8.30am-6pm Mon-Fri; 8.30am-1pm Sat. **Tickets** $27-$53. **Credit** MC, V. **Map 6 A/B1**
Disabled: toilet. Website: nfl.com

Tulane University

Louisiana Superdome, Sugar Bowl Drive, at Poydras Street (Superdome box office 587 3800/Tulane information 865 5355/Tulane box office 865 5810). Bus 16 S Claiborne. **Open** *Superdome box office* 9am-4.30pm Mon-Fri; open at weekends for special events. *Tulane box office* 8.30am-5pm Mon-Fri. **Tickets** $18; $16 under-18s. **Credit** *Superdome* MC, V; *Tulane* AmEx, MC, V. **Map 6 A/B1**
Disabled: toilet.

Horse racing

New Orleans's horse racing fans suffered a tragic loss on 13 December 1993 when the New Orleans Fair Grounds' grandstand, at that time the second oldest in the US, burned down. Racing was unaffected but the atmosphere of the place was – not that it bothered real gamblers, many of whom wouldn't mind a bear trap on their leg if they were ahead a few bucks. Those who have been to Jazz Fest will be amazed at how different the Fair Grounds look without tents, food booths and tens of thousands of people. The horse racing season runs from Thanksgiving to the end of March and the opening day of the season is a festive event (*see p23* **By Season**).

Fair Grounds Racecourse

1751 Gentilly Boulevard, near Esplanade Avenue (944 5515/fgno@accesscom.net). Bus 48 Esplanade. **Open** Mon, Thur-Sun but hours vary; call for details. **Map 5 E/F5**
Disabled: toilet.

Ice hockey

The **New Orleans Brass** are a part of hockey's great southward migration, and they are demonstrating what executives everywhere are starting to learn – that people don't have to have grown up skating on frozen ponds to enjoy ice hockey. The Brass are a minor league team, but their games still sell out regularly. When the new stadium being built next to the Superdome is complete, it will be the home of the Brass, but for now, games are played at the Municipal Auditorium in Armstrong Park. The season runs from mid-October to early April.

New Orleans Brass

Municipal Auditorium, 1201 St Peters Street, at N Rampart Street (box office 565 8081/Brass information 522 7825/nobrass@cmq.com). Bus 57 Franklin. **Open** *box office* 9am-5pm Mon-Fri; noon-5pm Sat. **Tickets** $6-$15. **Credit** AmEx, MC, V. **Map 7 B1**

Soccer

Soccer audiences are composed of those who have grown up with the game – therefore usually members of the international community – and suburban kids. America's more regular participation in international soccer has increased interest, but the game moves a little too slow for people accustomed to the way American football doles out brief, intense bursts of action – so tickets are often available. Moving the game out of the Tad Gormley Stadium in Mid City to suburban Metairie's Zephyr Field may bring in larger crowds. The new **Storm** team are a farm team for the Dallas Burn in the Major League. The season runs from March to August.

New Orleans Storm

See p217 **New Orleans Zephyrs** *for listings.*

Active sports

Louisiana car licence plates announce the state as a 'Sportsman's Paradise'. Archaic, gender-specific name aside, there is a lot the outdoor-minded can do in the New Orleans area, but the heat and humidity do demand respect. During July, August and September it gets hot early, peaks in the high 90s°F in the mid-afternoon, then stays hot into the

82 Desire. Open 10am-6pm daily. **Bike rental**
$4.50 per hour; $16.50 per business day; $20 24 hours;
$35 for 2½ days. **Credit** MC, V. **Map 7 C3**

Joe's Bike Shop
2501 Tulane Avenue, at N Rochblave Street (821 2350).
Bus 39 Tulane. Open 8am-5pm Mon-Fri; 8am-4pm Sat.
Bike rental $12 per day; $35 per week; $25 per
weekend. **Credit** AmEx, Disc, MC, V. **Map 4 E6**

Olympic Bike Rentals
1618 Prytania Street, at Euterpe Street (522 6797/
olympic@bicycle expeditions). *St Charles Streetcar.*
Open 9am-5pm daily. **Bike rental** $15 24 hours.
Credit MC, V. **Map 4 F8**
Free delivery and pick-up to area hotels. You can also
arrange sightseeing bicycle tours ($30-$65).

Fishing

The world is divided into three types of people:
those who find fishing a colossal bore, those who
find the boredom of fishing therapeutic and those
who find every element of fishing fascinating.

Those who fear that their bobber going under
means they'll have to stop drinking and do something will not want to fish in Louisiana, where the
bayous and the Gulf of Mexico provide a variety
of game fish and a fair amount of action. In the
inland waters, you can catch largemouth bass,
striped bass, flounder, speckled trout and redfish;
in the mouth of the Mississippi, you'll find red
snapper, amberjack, grouper, copia, tarpon, shark,
white trout, barracuda and trigger fish.

Fishing charters are easily arranged. Look in
the *Yellow Pages* or online (www.rodnreel.com/rrw
05.htm) or ask your hotel concierge. Prices range
from $115 to $150 a person a day, depending on the
size of the party, services offered, length of journey
and current demand for charters. Two reputable
charters are **Capt Nick's** (361 3004/1-800 375
3474) and the family-run **Bourgeois Charters**
(341 5614; website: www.neworleansfishing.com).

For information on **fishing licences**, call the
Louisiana Department of Wildlife and Fisheries on
1-888 765 2602. A one-day licence usually costs
$5.50 and a three-day licence $20, but prices vary
depending on the kind of fishing being done

Gulf

During the 1970s oil boom, it was thought that the
unconscionably wealthy didn't have quite enough
ways to spend their money, so new golf courses
were built for them. When the boom ended and the
money went to Texas, the New Orleans area was
left with a number of fine golf courses – though they
aren't always in the shape they should be due to the
lack of money for maintenance and the long, hot
summers. Inevitably, most courses are outside the
city centre, so the best way to reach them is by car.

English Turn, a Jack Nicklaus-designed
course on the West Bank, hosts an annual PGA
event and is the Cadillac of the area's courses. It is

Fishing: fun for all the family.

late evening. The heat and humidity is hard to
imagine for those who haven't experienced it, so
those interested in high-exertion activities should
take precautions for their health. Wear a hat,
drink plenty of water and maintain a reasonable
perspective. Smart tennis players don't try to
replay one of Bjorn Borg and John McEnroe's five-
set Wimbledon marathons in late August.

Cycling

New Orleans is not a particularly good city for
cycling. Its flatness is appealing, but its potholes
and narrow streets aren't. Those who wish to ride
need to be very alert or should head to City Park
or Audubon Park, both of which are safely out of
traffic's way. You can rent bikes from **Joe's Bike
Shop** and **Olympic Bike Rentals**. In the French
Quarter, try **French Quarter Bicycles** or
Bicycle Michaels (which also organises tours)
in nearby Faubourg Marigny.

Bicycle Michaels
622 Frenchmen Street, between Royal & Chartres Streets
(945 9505). Bus 3 Vieux Carré, 48 Esplanade, 55
Elysian Fields. Open 10am-7pm Mon-Sat; 10am-5pm Sun.
Rates $12.50 per day plus $5 helmet. **Credit** AmEx,
Disc, MC, V. **Map 4 G6**

French Quarter Bicycles
522 Dumaine Street, at Decatur Street (529 3136).
Bus 3 Vieux Carré, 55 Elysian Fields, 81 Almonaster,

*Stepping out at the **New Orleans Athletic Club**, the oldest gym in town.*

a private club, but hotel concierges can usually get a tee time for those willing to pay the $150 green fees. The fairways are playable for the average club member, but the two- and three-tiered greens will embarrass all but the best putters.

In New Orleans East, **Eastover** (off I-10) is an attractive course that is generally kept in good condition and is more moderately priced. If you don't mind the 30-minute drive to Slidell, **Oak Harbor** has one of the most interesting layouts, where few tee shots are as simple as they look. Since it is near Lake Pontchartrain, the wind is often strong and unpredictable.

Those who don't want to pay a lot of money to discover that their swings are no better in New Orleans than they are at home will enjoy the **Bayou Oaks Golf Course** in City Park. The prices are very reasonable and both the West and East courses are fair tests, the East being a little more interesting. There isn't any rough and each hole could use one more sand trap, but shots that drift too far right or left will end up under very large oaks, forcing players to take shots that resemble Wayne Gretzky more than Tiger Woods. Duffers and those with time constraints may prefer the North course, which is shorter and more open. There's also a very cheap course in Audubon Park, but it's not really worth playing.

Bayou Oaks Golf Course

City Park, 1040 Filmore Avenue, near Wisner Boulevard (483 9397). Bus 43 Canal. **Open** 6am-8pm Mon-Fri; 5.30am-8pm Sat, Sun (hours vary according to season; usually dawn to dusk). **Rates per round** $5-$17; discounts for seniors. **No credit cards.** Map 5 E2

Eastover

5889 Eastover Drive, at Lake Forest Boulevard, New Orleans East (245 7347). No public transport.

Open 8am-6pm Mon-Fri; 7am-6pm Sat, Sun (hours vary according to season). **Rates per round** $95.92 (includes cart, green fee and taxes). **Credit** AmEx, DC, MC, V.

English Turn Golf & Country Club

1 Clubhouse Drive, off English Turn Parkway, West Bank (391 8018). No public transport. **Open** *summer* 6am-7pm, *winter* 7am-6pm, Tue-Sun. **Rates per round** $150. **Credit** AmEx, MC, V. Note that you must be a guest of a member or go through a hotel concierge to play here. *Disabled: toilet.*

Oak Harbor

201 Oak Harbor Boulevard, at Pontchartrain Drive, Slidell (254 0830). No public transport. **Open** 7am-6pm daily. **Rates per round** $37 Mon-Fri; $47 Sat, Sun; discounts after 3pm. **Credit** AmEx, Disc, MC, V. *Disabled: toilet.*

Gyms

The following gyms offer day membership. For spas, *see page 162* **Shops & Services.**

Downtown Fitness Centers

3800 One Canal Place, at Decatur Street (525 2956). Bus 41 Canal. **Open** 6am-10pm Mon-Fri; 9am-6pm Sat, Sun. **Map 7 A3**
Le Meridien Hotel, 8th floor, 814 Canal Street, at St Charles Avenue (527 6750). St Charles Streetcar/ bus 41 Canal. **Open** 6am-9pm Mon-Fri; 9am-9pm Sat, Sun. **Map 7 A2**
Both **Rates** $10 per day (three-day and weekly passes also available). **Credit** AmEx, Disc, MC, V.
The One Canal Place site has free weights, Nautilus and other weight machines, the usual assortment of treadmills, and tanning beds. At Le Meridien there is a swimming pool, a whirlpool, Nautilus machines and a massage therapist. Both offer daily aerobic classes.

Elmwood Fitness Center Downtown

701 Poydras Street, at Carondelet Street (588 1600). Bus 16 S Claiborne. **Open** 5.30am-9pm Mon-Fri; 8am-4pm Sat. **Rates** $10 per day; $35 per week. **Credit** AmEx, MC, V. **Map 6 B1**

Offers weights, cardiovascular equipment, a sauna, a whirlpool and aerobics classes.
Disabled: toilet.

Mackie Shilstone Pro Spa
Avenue Plaza Hotel, 2111 St Charles Avenue, at Josephine Street (566 1212). St Charles Streetcar. **Open** 6am-9pm Mon-Fri, 8am-6pm Sat, Sun. **Rates** from $30 an hour. **Credit** AmEx, DC, Disc, MC, V. **Map 4 F8**
Mackie Shilstone is a legend in the athletic world, developing sport-specific workouts that have pushed boxers to championship level and rehabilitated arm-sore basketball pitchers. Shilstone, a hyperactive pixie of a man, doesn't limit himself to professionals or even stars: he's happy to work out training programmes for weekend golfers and teenage football players. For anyone serious about a sport, working with Shilstone is like an opera buff being invited onstage at La Scala. To schedule an evaluation and have a personalised workout plan created for you, contact Shilstone well in advance. For drop-in workouts, Shilstone-trained coaches put clients through a first-rate session or clients can work on their own. The spa also has daily aerobics classes.

New Orleans Athletic Club
222 N Rampart Street, at Bienville Street (525 2375). Bus 3 Vieux Carré, 57 Franklin. **Open** 6am-10pm Mon-Fri; 6am-6pm Sat; 8am-6pm Sun. **Rates** $20 per day. **Credit** AmEx, MC, V. **Map 7 B1**
The only gym with any history, being 125 years old. It offers the usual assortment of weight machines and cardiovascular equipment as well as free weights, a swimming pool, basketball and racquetball courts, saunas, steam rooms and a dizzying array of fitness classes.
Disabled: toilet.

Rivercenter Racquet & Health Club
New Orleans Hilton, 6th floor of parking garage, 2 Poydras Street, at Convention Center Boulevard (556 3742). Bus 16 S Claiborne. **Open** 5.30am-9pm Mon-Fri; 7am-7pm Sat; 7am-5pm Sun.

Admission $8 one day; $15 two days; $22 three days; $29 four days; $36 five days. **Credit** AmEx, Disc, MC, V. **Map 6 C1**
The centre has indoor tennis, racquetball and squash courts, Nautilus machines and cardiovascular equipment. There isn't a swimming pool, but there is a sauna, whirlpool and aerobics classes.

Horse riding

Cascade Stables
700 East Drive, at Magazine Street (891 2246). Bus 11 Magazine. **Open** 9am-4pm daily. **Rates** $20 trail ride; $20 group lesson; $25 private lesson. **Credit** MC, V. **Map 4 B9**
These stables next to Audubon Park offer a 45-minute trail ride within the park.

City Park Stables
Marconi Boulevard, at Filmore Street, City Park (483 9398). Bus 48 Esplanade. **Open** *office* 9am-5pm Mon-Fri; 9am-6pm Sat, Sun; *lessons* 3-7pm Mon-Fri; 9am-6pm Sat, Sun. **Rates** $20 group lesson; $25 ½hour private lesson; $50 1-hour private lesson. **No credit cards. Map 5 D2**
The stables are near the golf course in City Park. You can have private or group lessons, including jumping, but no trail rides. Book in advance for weekend sessions.

Ice skating

Ice skating is not the activity most commonly associated with New Orleans, but since the Municipal Auditorium in Armstrong Park has become home to a minor league ice hockey team, the surface is usually open for skating on weekend afternoons – though it's a good idea to phone first to check.

At **Cascade Stables** *you can take a trail ride through Audubon Park.*

Municipal Auditorium
1201 St Peters Street, at N Rampart Street (522 7825).
Bus 57 Franklin. **Open** 1-3pm Sat, Sun. **Rates** $6;
$4 children, students. **No credit cards. Map 7 B1**

Rollerblading

The challenges that New Orleans poses for cyclists
also apply to rollerbladers. The safest and most
pleasant place to rollerblade is on the road that
weaves through **Audubon Park**. This is also a
popular walking, running and cycling path, but
everyone co-exists peacefully, mocking the golfers
hacking their way around Audubon's pasture-like
golf course. **City Park** doesn't offer the same
amusing distractions or sense of community, but
its trees and size make it a more solitary and
romantic place to rollerblade.

Blade Action Sports
341 N Hennessey Street, at Conti Street (486 8889).
Bus 41 Canal, 90 Carrollton. **Open** 10am-8pm daily.
Rates $6 per hour (day rates also available). **Credit**
AmEx, Disc, MC, V. **Map 5 D5**
A few blocks from City Park, this is the place to rent
rollerblades. It also has an indoor skate park ($14 one-day
membership) for rollerbladers and skateboarders.

Running

Considering New Orleans's drivers, there is something appropriate about New Orleanians referring
to the grassy traffic medians as 'neutral grounds'.
Not only do they keep cars safely separated, but
they provide a nice place for runners who want to
get a feeling for the city.

One of the busiest neutral grounds is the one
on **St Charles Avenue**, which runs from the
uptown side of Lee Circle away from the downtown area, past Audubon Park and on to the
Riverbend and Carrollton Avenue. Taking the neutral grounds to the park, running its loop and heading back home makes for a nice run. In Mid City,
City Park provides a pleasant, shady place to run
– and shade can be crucial in the summer.

Twice a year, the city hosts the **Crescent City
Classic**, a 10km (6.2 mile) road race from the
French Quarter, through the Central Business
District and along Prytania Avenue uptown to
Audubon Park. The race used to be a spring event,
but has become so popular among both competi-
tive and recreational runners that it is now held
in spring and autumn. The **New Orleans Track
Club** (482 6682) administers road races and pro-
vides information on upcoming running events.

Swimming

New Orleans has few public swimming pools. New
Orleanians who want to swim make friends with
people who have pools at home, but visitors without such useful contacts should check out gyms (*see
page 220*) and the YMCAs (*see below*). Do not go to

Lake Pontchartrain for a swim. Although the water
is getting cleaner, it is still unsafe to swim in.

Tennis

For the most part, tennis clubs in New Orleans are
private, but the **City Park Tennis Center** and
the **Audubon Park** courts are open to the public,
well kept and well lit.

Audubon Park Tennis Courts
*6320 Tchoupitoulas Street, at Calhoun Street (895
1042). Bus 19 Nashville Express.* **Open** 8am-7pm daily.
Rates $6 per hour. **No credit cards. Map 4 B10**

City Park Tennis Center
*City Park, between Victory Avenue & Dreyfous Drive
(483 9383). Bus 48 Esplanade.* **Open** 7am-10pm Mon-
Thur; 7am-7pm Fri-Sun. **Rates** $5.50 day session; $6.50
evening session. **No credit cards. Map 5 D4**

Watersports

Although boat-owning locals crowd the flat (and
still polluted) waters of Lake Pontchartrain, there
are limited options for visitors wanting to indulge
in some watery sports. **Murray Yacht Sales/
Boat Rentals** (283 2507), on the edge of the lake,
charters 26-foot (8m) sailing boats and also runs
weekend sailing courses ($185 per person).
Otherwise, you can rent canoes and paddle-boats at
weekends and explore the lagoons of **City Park**
or try one of the canoe treks offered in **Jean
Lafitte National Historical Park & Preserve**
(*see chapter* **Sightseeing** *for both*). Outside the
city, there are plenty of **fishing** options (*see page
219*) and you can always take a **swamp tour** (*see
chapter* **Sightseeing**).

YMCAs

There are three YMCAs in New Orleans, two in the
downtown area, one in Metairie. The downtown
ones are in novel sites, one flanked by Lee Circle
and the Contemporary Arts Center and the other
in the Superdome. After you've finished your
workout at the former, check out the lunch counter,
which doesn't look like much but is one of the
secret gems of the Warehouse District.

Lee Circle YMCA
*920 St Charles Avenue, at Howard Avenue (568 9622).
St Charles Streetcar.* **Open** 5am-9pm Mon-Fri; 7am-5pm
Sat; 12.30-5pm Sun. **Admission** $5 per day. **Credit** MC,
V. **Map 6 B2**
Offers more than the Superdome site, with a basketball court,
track, sauna, steam room, racquetball courts, free weights,
cardiovascular and weight machines, plus aerobics classes.

Superdome YMCA
*Louisiana Superdome, Sugar Bowl Drive, at Poydras
Street (568 9622). Bus 16 S Claiborne.* **Open** 5.45am-
7pm Mon-Fri. **Admission** $5 per day. **Credit** MC, V.
Map 6 B1
Primarily a workout facility, limited to different types of
weight machines, free weights, cycles, treadmills and stair-
masters. There are also aerobics classes.

Trips Out of Town

Trips Out of Town

It's time to leave the Topless Metropolis and discover the grand plantation houses, Cajun wetlands, pristine white beaches and historic towns a few hours' drive away.

Apart from its cuisine, New Orleans has little in common with the rest of the state. Most of Louisiana is rural, and the people are of French and Native American descent. Although much of the state is dirt-poor, its residents have learned over the centuries how to make the most of what they have. The result is a strange, joyous, multi-lingual mixture of towns and villages filled with music, art and food, scattered along the bayous and highways. From the Cajuns and Creoles in Acadiana around Lafayette, to the descendants of the grand English land barons in St Francisville, to the distinctive political heritage of Baton Rouge and the casinos and beaches of southern Mississippi, there is much to discover within a few hours' drive of New Orleans. It is a rare Louisiana town that doesn't welcome visitors with open arms, so hit the road – you never know what you might find.

TRANSPORT

The good news is that travelling around Louisiana is easier now than ever before. The state lagged behind the rest of the country in building highways, and just 60 years ago the trips described in this chapter would have taken days rather than a few hours. It was the efforts of the controversial, populist, former state governor Huey Long that resulted in the construction, in the 1930s and 1940s, of an elevated highway system that passes alongside and above the swamps that once regularly flooded the old dirt roads.

The bad news is that public transport is a rare and slow thing. There is no passenger train service to most of Louisiana, and although a bus service (via **Greyhound**) is available, most of these towns are rural farming communities spread over dozens of miles, and walking between them is simply not feasible. The best way to travel is the American way – by car. There are plenty of car rental outfits in New Orleans (*see chapter* **Directory**), and prices can be reasonable if you plan in advance. Even if you rent a car for only one day, you can see a great deal if you plan carefully. If you're a member of an affiliated organisation

such as the British AA, contact the wonderful **AAA** for maps and help on planning your trip (*see chapter* **Directory**).

For coverage of south-east Louisiana, *see* **Map 1** at the back of this guide; for details of the River Road plantations, *see* **Map 2**.

Amtrak
Information (1-800 872 7245/528 1610). Trains depart from New Orleans's Union Passenger Terminal, 1001 Loyola Avenue, at Howard Avenue. **Map 6 B1** *Website: www.amtrak.com*

Greyhound
Information (1-800 231 2222). Buses depart from the Union Passenger Terminal (see above). Website: www.greyhound.com

---

Heading North

The Great River Road

There was a time when the Great River Road lived up to its name. Running on both sides of the Mighty Mississippi, this road once offered extraordinary views of the largest North American river and awe-inspiring marshes and plantations. But after a number of devastating floods in the early twentieth century, the US Government built what amounts to a Great Wall of Louisiana – an enormous dirt levee system lining the river throughout the state. The levee is almost never breached and has stopped the seasonal flooding that once destroyed homes and killed dozens of people every year. It has also ruined the view.

But driving down the River Road you can still get the feeling of what it once must have been like. Columned plantation houses surrounded by huge

Bastions of the Great River Road: **San Francisco** *(top),* **Houmas House** *(middle) and* **Oak Alley** *plantation houses. See pages 226-7.*

Giant's causeway: to head north, cross the world's longest bridge over Lake Pontchartrain.

oak trees draped in languid Spanish moss appear in the distance like ghosts. 'Once upon a time,' they seem to say, 'this place was really something.'

Touring the plantations on the river is a lesson in contrasts: the plantations of old surrounded by their modern-day equivalents – chemical plants. The result is a tragic and ruined landscape hanging on to the remnants of its beauty, like a faded film star plastered in make-up, peeking out of the window of an industrial nursing home.

Although the landscape is far from pristine, it underscores for visitors the reasons why a bitter battle is developing between residents and the powerful chemical industry, which has long had free run of the place. Cancer and disease rates are high and residents have begun fighting the development of new industry, even though they desperately need more jobs.

One way they're doing this is through the promotion of tourism as an alternative to industry. More than a dozen plantations along the river are open to the public, and many are well worth the trip. The buildings are rather scattered about and each tour costs $5-$10, so seeing more than three in a day can get pricey and be repetitive: target a couple that appeal to you.

These homes are noteworthy because of their sheer size, their grand restoration and sometimes the collection of antiques inside. Most tours concentrate on the real history of the land and the families who built lives at a time when simply doing that was a heroic effort, battling floods, disease, heat and deprivation. However, very few plantations maintain much to indicate how the farms actually operated – in other words, the homes and lives of the slaves are not similarly restored and celebrated. Little is said about just how that indigo was harvested, or the sugarcane or the rice: it certainly wasn't the landowner out there digging. But the landowners themselves aren't always portrayed in a positive light: their weaknesses or flirtations with brutality are often described in vivid detail (particularly at the Myrtles Plantation; *see page 232*). Bear in mind that the tours are likely to be one-sided and lacking some critical details, and look around for clues; for example, buildings described as 'out-buildings' were usually in fact slave quarters.

The closest plantation to New Orleans is also the oldest intact structure, though not the most impressive. **Destrehan Plantation** (13034 River Road; 764 9315) was constructed in West Indies-style in 1787 by a free man of colour. It is of interest for being so old, and for the hand-hewn cypress timbers used in its construction and the insulation in its walls, made of bousillage (a mixture of Spanish moss and horse hair). About a mile from Destrehan is **Ormond Plantation** (13786 River Road; 764 8544; website: www.plantation.com), also a late eighteenth-century West Indies colonial house, which has been only recently restored. While a relatively small house, Ormond is known for its collection of antiques and its tiny B&B on the upper floor ($125 per night with tour).

About 30 minutes' drive further upriver is one of the area's most fanciful plantations, **San Francisco**

(535 234; website: www.sanfranciscoplantation. org;
located on River Road in Reserve, it has no numbered street address so look for the signs). Painted
in vivid Victorian azure hues and with two huge,
onion dome-topped cisterns on either side of the
building adding an Eastern look, it is unique among
the state's plantations and was used as a model by
Louisiana novelist Frances Parkinson Keyes for her
book *Steamboat Gothic*. The house's name stems
from the moniker originally given the structure by
its first owner, Edmond Bozonier Marmillion, who
was said to be so impoverished by the expense of
construction that he nicknamed his money pit 'Sans
Frusquin', French slang for being penniless.

The house was gorgeously, authentically renovated in the 1980s when it was purchased by the
Marathon Oil Company, which owned a nearby
chemical plant (several of the plantations are now
the non-profit, tax-deductible property of major
petrochemical companies). Its elaborately frescoed
ceilings and lushly decorated pocket-doors are
worth the visit alone.

Just upriver from San Francisco on the north
edge of the tiny town of Convent is one of the area's
best seafood restaurants, and a great place to stop
for lunch. **Hymel's Restaurant** (8740 Highway
44/River Road; 562 7031) is extremely casual and
usually packed with locals, all of whom know each
other. When things get busy, some customers lend
a hand setting and clearing tables, while others
pour their own drinks. Country music trickles out
of the jukebox, and the motherly waitress is sure
to call you darlin'. This is an almost tourist-free
establishment, so you may attract some attention,
but it is a welcome alternative to other restaurants
in the area, which tend to be packed with tour bus
parties. The raw oysters are the biggest and freshest you're ever likely to see, short of a radioactive
accident, and are the speciality, along with fried
seafood. Most dishes cost under $10.

Nearby is the **Tezcuco Plantation** (3138
Highway 44/River Road, Darrow; 562 3929),
another building with impressive grounds. It's a
sprawling property with original outbuildings
including a chapel and a blacksmith's shop, which
now serve as an antique store and a small but interesting Civil War museum, respectively. There's
also an African-American History Museum, but it's
very rarely open. The interior of the main house,
though small, is beautifully furnished, and the educational tour makes the most of the antiques with
an interactive discussion of the use of some of the
more extraordinary period pieces and devices.

The best thing about Tezcuco is its B&B accommodation, particularly the 11 period cottages, most
with fireplaces. Prices range from as little as $65
a night for the smallest, up to $170 for a two-bed-
room suite in the main house. Some of the cottages
are of brick-between-post construction and many
are original outbuildings. Book in advance.

Less than five miles (eight kilometres) upriver
from Tezcuco is another impressive house that has
been immortalised by Hollywood – in the Bette
Davies film *Hush, Hush, Sweet Charlotte*. **Houmas
House** (40136 Highway 942/River Road, Darrow;
474 0480) is actually two houses connected by a
carriageway. The rear structure is older, dating
from the eighteenth century, while the front Greek
Revival structure was built in 1840. Formal gardens surround the buildings, and it's a short stroll
up the levee to see the river.

Take the Sunshine Bridge to the south side of
the river to find one of the area's jewels. The
grounds around **Oak Alley Plantation** (3645
Highway 18/River Road, in Vacherie, 1-800 442
5539; website: www.oakalleyplantation.com) are
among the most beautiful in the South. Dozens of
enormous and ancient live oak trees line either side
of the grand entrance to the pale pink, columned
plantation building. The house and grounds have
been the setting for a dozen Hollywood films, and
for good reason. It is breathtaking. It is so easy to
picture how it once looked, with the pathway
between the oaks sloping down to the lazy river,
that the levee is an outrage here. The grounds and
exterior are considerably more impressive than the
interior and you can wander the grounds for free,
so consider saving your money for tours of other
buildings. You can also stay in guest cottages here;
prices range from $95-$125.

Three miles (five kilometres) downriver from
Oak Alley, **Laura Plantation** (2247 Highway 18,
Vacherie; 265 7690; website: www.laura.com)
offers a different kind of plantation tour. The main
house is modest compared with many of the River
Road showplaces, but owner Norman Marmillion
has established a landmark of a different kind at
this former Creole sugar plantation. Tours by
unusually knowledgeable guides inform visitors
about the day-to-day life of the plantation, giving
appropriate weight to the lives of the slaves who
made the wealth of the 'big house' possible.

Laura is unusual in that it was run by women for
three generations – not merely because the men were
off at war but because they were better managers.
The plantation dates from the late eighteenth century and belonged to the French Locoul family for
more than 150 years. It was named Laura after the
last owner, Laura Locoul Gore. Her father thought
that if the plantation bore her name she would never
leave it, but she did, selling out to a German Creole
family in the early twentieth century, so that she
could marry and live in St Louis, free of the responsibility of running a large agricultural business.

Since it was bought by preservationist
Marmillion and a group of investors, Laura is
being slowly returned to its old beauty – but it was
always a spare, unglamorous kind of beauty. The
main house is a spacious, raised Creole villa rather
than a large mansion.

The slave cabins here were the birthplace of the famous Brer Rabbit stories. The slaves translated these, which had their roots in West African folktales, into their new language, French, and adapted them to their new world. Louisiana historian and folklorist Alcee Fortier wrote them down in the late nineteenth century and his friend, writer Joel Chandler Harris, used them for his *Uncle Remus* dialect stories for children. The tales finally made their way into a 1946 Walt Disney cartoon film, *Song of the South*, and became really famous.

Madewood Plantation (4250 Highway 308, Napoleonville; 369 9848 – follow the signs from River Road) is a sumptuous, columned house in the best *Gone With the Wind* tradition. Its 21 rooms were constructed in 1846 and are elegantly furnished with antiques. It's worth visiting, but if you have the money its exclusive B&B will give you an even better look at the place. Included in the $200 per night price tag is a multi-course dinner, coffee in bed in the morning and a huge Southern breakfast. Relaxation is key here, so there are no telephones or televisions.

Nearing the end of plantation row now, the next structure upriver is considered the ultimate Louisiana plantation. **Nottoway Plantation** (30970 Highway 405, White Castle; 369 7151; website: www.louisianatravel.com) has been dubbed the 'wedding cake' plantation; it's a huge building that seems to drip around the edges like lace, blurring the lines between gorgeous and gaudy. The architect who designed Madewood, Henry Howard, also built this structure; clearly, he had a lot more money and freedom on the Nottoway project. Built in 1859, it has 22 columns, 64 rooms, 200 windows and occupies 50,000 square feet. So solid was the workmanship that it is still sheltered by the original slate roof and the original crystal chandeliers still hang in the ballroom. The name is said to stem from the workers who built it, who, on seeing the plans for the building, said there was 'not a way' it could be done.

You can also spend the night here – there's a B&B inside the main house. For $125-$250 a night you can sleep in the lap of luxury and tour the mansion and plantation.

Getting there

By car
From New Orleans, head west on I-10 and take the exit marked 'Geismar/Lutcher Bridge'. Follow it to Hwy 44, the Great River Road. Destrehan Plantation is about 25 minutes from New Orleans.

By bus
A number of local tour companies offer day-long plantation tours, including Quarter Charter of New Orleans (522 2489). *See also chapter* **Sightseeing**.

Baton Rouge

Poised on the edge of Acadiana, 80 miles (129 kilometres) north of New Orleans, the capital of Louisiana is the centre of the state's infamous and controversial political culture. Baton Rouge was founded in 1699 when an expedition led by two French explorers – Pierre le Moyne, Sieur d'Iberville, and his brother Jean Baptiste le Moyne, Sieur de Bienville – stumbled upon an area of high bluffs on the Mississippi River. The diaries of the two explorers tell of their discovery of a pole stained with animal blood that served as the dividing line between two factional Indian tribes. It is from this bloody 'red stick' that the city received its name.

In 1999, the city celebrates its 300th anniversary. Most of the festivities will take place from 5-7 March, with outdoor parties including a performance by the Baton Rouge Symphony, a laser and fireworks show, and local music, food and entertainment. Call 383 1825 for more information.

Today, Baton Rouge is a rapidly growing burg with fairly serious traffic congestion problems, especially on the I-10. Luckily, the most interesting parts of the city are in its highly centralised downtown area, which can be easily explored on foot.

Don't miss the **State Capitol Building** (383 1825), constructed under the auspices of former state governor Huey Long. It is jokingly called 'the house that Huey built', and its phallic shape has led to some less-than-polite comparisons to parts of Long's own anatomy. Whatever his intentions, the building is unique in its art deco styling and size and considered to be one of the most architecturally significant of the country's state capitols. (To reach the building from I-10, turn onto I-110, then take the North Street exit and turn right onto N Fourth Street, which ends at the Capitol.)

It is said that Long wanted the Capitol to be the tallest in the country and so it is, standing 450 feet (137 metres) high with 34 floors, built grandly of limestone and marble in 1932-33 – a time when the country was deep in the mire of the Great Depression. The entrance is via a grand staircase with 48 steps (one for each of the US states at the time). Two enormous statues flank the stairs – on the left is 'The Patriots', depicting a soldier and mourners of a warrior slain in battle; on the right, 'The Pioneers' represents the state's original settlers. The inside is just as grand as the exterior. There's a great view from the observation deck on the 27th floor, from which the city, the river and the surrounding countryside open up in a verdant green vista – which is absolutely destroyed on the north side by dozens of chemical plants.

The greatest attraction of the Capitol is really its greatest tragedy. Long was assassinated as he walked down a main hallway on the first floor in

*The house that Huey built: Louisiana's **State Capital Building** in Baton Rouge.*

1935, and most visitors are at least partly drawn here to see the murder site. A large display case has recently been erected on the precise location of the shooting; it contains articles and photos relating to the incident and shows where Long and his bodyguards were standing at the time. The bullet holes in the marble floors and walls have never been filled in; look carefully and you'll probably find a few. The incident remains clouded in mystery: although a New Orleans doctor was accused of the crime – and killed by Long's bodyguards – precisely who shot the governor, and why, has never been fully determined.

Long was buried in front of the Capitol, beneath a massive statue of himself. The local kids are quick to point out that if you stand behind and to the right of the statue, it appears that the former governor is extending his middle finger. Somehow this seems appropriate.

The **State Governor's Mansion** (342 5855) is only a few blocks from the Capitol. (Follow the slope of the parking lot as it curves around past the Capitol Lakes – note the 'No Fishing' signs, even these lakes are polluted – that becomes Lake Drive. The mansion is on the right.) It was constructed in 1963 and an outside view is probably enough for most visitors (if you want to see inside, tours are conducted by appointment only, Monday to Friday). Until 1997, the property was ungated and passers-by could stroll to the door if they chose. But the current governor, Mike Foster, disliked the unusual accessibility that has over the years resulted in some extraordinary meetings

between governors and their electorate, and ordered the erection of the 10-foot (three-metre) fence that now encloses the mansion.

Return downtown via N Fifth Street and it will take you directly to downtown Baton Rouge's other famous site, the **Old State Capitol** (100 North Boulevard; 342 0500; open 10am-4pm Tue-Sat; noon-4pm Sun). Until Long built the current Capitol, this was the centre of Lousiana government. It was built in 1847, burned in the Civil War and restored in 1882.

Over the years its neo-Gothic architecture has elicited both admiration and ridicule. Mark Twain is supposed to have described the building, which sits on the bluffs above the river, as 'the ugliest building east of the Mississippi'. An unidentified Natchez travel writer wrote in 1855: 'At a distance, its white appearance and bulk give it the look of an iceberg.' Still, a recent renovation has left it looking its best, with impressive stained-glass windows and extensive carved mahogany trim as glossy as the day they were built.

At the foot of the bluffs in front of the Old Capitol is the **Louisiana Arts and Science Center** (100 S River Road, at North Boulevard; 344 5272; open 10am-3pm Tue-Fri; 1-4pm Sat, Sun), a small and inexplicably beloved local museum with a permanent exhibition of Ancient Egyptian artefacts. The USS Kidd, a restored World War II destroyer, is now part of the **Louisiana Naval War Memorial Museum** (305 S River Road; 342 1942; open 9am-5pm daily). The museum also contains some American World War II memorabilia.

If you've had enough history by now, walk a block downriver to a different kind of sea-going vessel: casino boats. Two boats – the **Belle of Baton Rouge** and **Casino Rouge** – sit on the river near the Old State Capitol. Both are busily taking the money of locals, and will undoubtedly welcome yours with hands extended. Try your luck at slots, blackjack and craps 24 hours a day. Nearby is Catfish Town, a large, enclosed mall of shops, restaurants and bars that keeps the fun and money flowing.

Also in Baton Rouge is the state's largest university, **Louisiana State University**, located on a sizeable campus several miles from downtown.

(To get there, follow St Ferdinand Street away from downtown until it becomes Highland Road, which eventually enters the campus at the main gates.) Shaded by huge oak trees, the campus is a pleasant if uneventful place to wander: most of the fun is to be found on the periphery. Do what the students do – hang out at the shops and bars around the intersection of Highland Road and Chimes Street. Park and walk through the stores, coffeeshops and bars that make up college life. This is the best place in town to grab a quick bite to eat, or to experience the local bar scene.

Join the local crowd at **The Chimes** (3357 Highland Road; 383 1754). It's a casual, friendly

Highway 61 revisited

The 290-mile (467-kilometre) stretch of US 61 between Natchez, Mississippi, and Memphis, Tennessee, is known as the 'Blues Highway'. The road is so dubbed because it was a direct route from the Mississippi Delta, the birthplace of many of the country's greatest blues players, to Memphis, where they all wanted to play and record. Such greats as BB King, Muddy Waters, Willie Dixon and Robert Johnson all grew up in the Delta.

Just driving through the Delta, long considered the single most impoverished section of the US, gives you a feeling for why they sang the blues in the first place. Things change, but somehow the Delta stays the same. Tarpaper shacks have been replaced by rotting wooden shacks. The antebellum plantations have been replaced by simple farms and factories. But there remains a sense of sadness and a beauty that belies the poverty, which helps even casual visitors develop some sense of how residents have lived for centuries – and why it gives them the blues.

At the centre of it all is Clarksdale, a Delta town that most blues aficionados believe is the true heart and soul of the life of the blues. But before and after Clarksdale, the road winds through the small towns and farms, where the masters of the blues lived out their youths, and past the small roadhouses where they honed their skills. The route is geared toward blues travellers: sites are generally clearly marked and the Mississippi Visitors Centers, located on major highways at all the state borders – including the one outside St Francisville – offer helpful maps and brochures to guide visitors on a blues hunt.

From Natchez, the first stop is the Civil War town of **Vicksburg**. There's no blues here, not the musical kind anyway. But the emotional kind

is a different story. This was the site of the 47-day battle and siege of Vicksburg, one of the Civil War's critical conflicts and longest sieges. You can learn about the event at the **Vicksburg National Military Park** (1-601 636 0583), which has a museum and 1,800 acres of hills, trenches and bluffs.

From Vicksburg, continue up the River Road to **Greenville**, a town inextricably intertwined with the local arts: blues and literature. Pick up information at the **River Road Queen Welcome Center** (1-601 332 2378), at the intersection of US 82 and Reed Road in Greenville, an unusual structure built to resemble a paddle-wheel riverboat. Greenville is the site of the annual **Delta Blues and Heritage Festival** in September (1-601 335 3523/1-888 812 5837). This is the quintessential Mississippi blues festival, packed with the best music the region has to offer, along with great local food. If you miss the festival but still want some blues, stop by the **Flowing Fountain** (816 Nelson Street; 1-601 335 9836), one of the best music spots in town.

The **Greenville Writers' Exhibit** (341 Main Street, at the William Alexander Percy Memorial Library; 1-601 335 2331; open Mon-Sat) is also worth visiting. The exhibition showcases the works of the extraordinary number of writers produced by this sleepy little town, among them historical writer Shelby Foote and his lifelong friend Walker Percy, as well as Hodding Carter, Beverly Lowry, Bern and Franke Keating and Clifton L Taulbert.

From Greenville, the next stop is the main blues destination on the route: **Clarksdale**, a mecca for blues lovers throughout the world. Start at the **Delta Blues Museum** (114 Delta Avenue; 1-601 627 6820), which is jam-packed with memorabilia and minutiae related to the

restaurant with a good menu that runs the gamut from sandwiches to crawfish étouffée and also specialises in beers from around the world. Next door is **The Varsity**, Baton Rouge's best live music venue, attracting local and national acts nightly.

For a more laid-back experience, walk down Chimes Street half a block to **The Bayou** (124 W Chimes Street; 346 1765). A long-standing local alternative bar, The Bayou became famous among American college students after it was featured in the movie *sex, lies and videotape* (director Steven Soderbergh is a local). The speakers pump the latest indie cuts, the beer is cheap and the pool tables are plentiful. Drop a word with the too-cool bartenders

blues, from videos, photographs and sound-and-slide shows to musical instruments and sheet music.

If you want to take home some of those blues, visit the famous **Stackhouse Delta Record Mart & Rooster Blues** (232 Sunflower Avenue; 1-601 627 2209). This local record store has become a repository for obscure and vintage blues recordings, and is also a central clearing-house for information on area blues clubs and music tours.

A couple of other sites in the area worth noting include **Muddy Waters' Cabin** – or what's left of it. Six miles (9.6 kilometres) out of Clarksdale (take Highway 6 west to Highway 322, then south on to Highway 1), this is the site on Stovall Road where McKinley Morganfield (aka Muddy Waters) grew up; it's marked by a plaque. There is no access to the property, and no building anymore, really, as the cabin itself is now 'on loan' to the House of Blues nightclub chain. Damn Dan Akroyd – don't Hollywood just give you the blues?

Another home without a home is that of **WC Handy**, who was born in 1873 and is regarded by many as the 'Father of the Blues'. From 1903 to 1905, he lived with his family at 317 Issaquena Avenue, Clarksdale. While there Handy collected and later published much of the local blues music that was a hallmark of the area. A plaque marks the site of his former home.

Clarksdale is also the site of two popular festivals: the **Delta Jubilee** (1-601 627 7337) held in June and the **Sunflower River Blues and Gospel Festival** (1-601 627 6820) in August. Both are centred around two local favourites: music and food.

that you're from out of town, and they'll hook you up with locals who will fill you in on anything you ever wanted to know about the city.

Directly behind The Bayou is the best 24-hour diner in the state, **Louie's** (209 W State Street; 346 8221). After midnight it is crammed with inebriated partygoers; during the day it's considerably more staid. The menu is basic – eggs, sandwiches and hamburgers – but good and cheap.

Tourist information

Baton Rouge Convention & Visitors Bureau
730 N Boulevard, between Napoleon & Jackson Streets, Baton Rouge (383 1825/1-800 527 6843); mailing address PO Box 4149, Baton Rouge, LA 70821. **Open** 8am-5pm Mon-Fri.

Where to stay

Accommodation in Baton Rouge is plentiful if unimaginative: your best bet is probably one of the major hotels. At the low-end, try **La Quinta Inn** (2333 S Acadian Thruway; 924 9600), where a double room costs $71. At the **Radisson Hotel & Conference Center of Baton Rouge** (4728 Constitution Avenue; 925 2244), expect to pay $60-$135 a night. This has the benefits of more extensive business facilities, including conference rooms, fax service and modems.

If you can swing it, however, visit Baton Rouge during the day and spend the night at one of the River Road plantations or one of the B&Bs in nearby St Francisville (*see below*).

Getting there

By car
From New Orleans, take I-10 west: it's 80 miles (129km) to Baton Rouge. Take the I-110 north exit, and then the North Street exit to downtown.

By bus
Greyhound offers frequent shuttles to Baton Rouge (round-trip $20 Mon-Thur; $21 Fri, Sat). The trip takes 1½-2½ hours, depending on whether you catch the express bus. However, note that the Baton Rouge bus station is not centrally located, and cabs can be difficult to find there, especially on weekends. Amtrak also runs a Thruway Bus service (3 buses daily).

St Francisville

A 45-minute drive north from Baton Rouge, St Francisville is one of Louisiana's true treasures. Once a centre of farming life, today it is a quiet country town with tourism its principal trade. The plantations that once thrived on crops of indigo or cotton are now museums and inns, serving as mementoes of the state's antebellum past. There are more 200-year-old silver pieces, Sèvres porcelain and French mahogany in these houses than anywhere else in the state. Whereas the River Road plantations are largely part of the state's French history, St Francisville is where the English settled, and its architecture, antiques and the emphasis of its history are considerably different from those of the old homes downriver.

Driving up US 61 from Baton Rouge, the landscape changes as you move from the city's modern urban accoutrements to the chemical plants at the edge of town, then suddenly you're on a two-lane highway surrounded by thick forest. This is West Feliciana Parish, a peaceful, tree-filled stretch of country, and home to dozens of plantation houses.

So varied is the wildlife here that the noted naturalist and artist John James Audubon spent nearly two years sketching the flora and fauna, painting 80 of his famous folios. The town has never forgotten it. The annual **Audubon Pilgrimage** (635 6330), held on the third weekend in March, commemorates his memory with a festival and tour of buildings and areas related to his time in St Francisville. Local residents take part dressed, of course, in period costumes.

Follow the well-placed signs that direct you off the highway to St Francisville's historic downtown and stop on the main avenue at the **West Feliciana Historical Society Museum** (11757 Ferdinand Street; 635 6330). Stock up on free maps and brochures guiding you to the plantations scattered through the area, as well as historical books and other information.

Head back to the highway, where signs will direct you to the turn-offs for the plantations. If you like to think big, stop first at **Rosedown Plantation** (635 3110). Its 28 acres of sculpted gardens frame an enormous white columned house stocked from top to bottom with antiques, china and silver. It is generally considered the most complete of the area's plantations. It is also the most expensive – just getting inside the gate costs $10 per person.

If size doesn't matter, just peek at Rosedown through the white arched gateway, then head back up the road to **Catalpa Plantation** (635 3372), which has long been home to the descendants of the original owners of Rosedown. This gracious if small house, located at the end of a long, tree-shaded drive, stands under gnarled oak trees draped in Spanish moss. It is still owned by members of the family that built it. Until 1997, nonagenarian owner 'Miss Mamie' Thompson would personally guide guests through her home, past the priceless silver and china, all the while relaying stories of her family and frequently plying her visitors with sherry.

After she died, her daughter Mary Thompson took over the responsibility of handling visitors: 'My mother would have wanted us to keep the house open,' she said during a recent visit. A tour of Catalpa is the most up-close and personal look you will get at a plantation, with family dogs wandering in and out while you get to know Mary Thompson's ancestors as if they were your own. When you look at the silver and rare china you might wish they were. Included in the collection is the still-dented silver, damaged when the family retrieved it from its hiding place in the mud underneath a nearby pond at the end of the Civil War.

Mary, who is also a local school teacher, can tie up genealogical loose ends from your visit to other houses in the area and has an encyclopaedic knowledge of St Francisville history. She will also offer you sherry as you tour her dining room.

Another plantation considered crucial to any visit to the area is **Oakley House** (635 3739), where Audubon made a living by teaching the family's daughter, Eliza Pirrie, for a brief time in 1821. Although Audubon is supposed to have called the area 'the happy land', it wasn't always that happy – when Eliza became ill and was unable to take lessons for several months, her father refused to pay the artist and tutor, so he quit. Now part of the State Park system, Oakley House was patterned after the homes of the West Indies, raised to catch every breeze, with a sleeping porch and wide gallery and is filled with antiques and portraits.

If you are in St Francisville in the spring or summer, don't miss the **Afton Villa Gardens**, a restored classical garden built around the ruins of a 40-room Gothic mansion – and the most celebrated garden in the area. If you're lucky enough to visit in March, you can catch Daffodil Valley at its height, when 100,000 daffodils burst into bloom. Nature lovers should contact local naturalist and artist **Murrell Butler** (635 6214). He offers informative birdwalks on his property, and a checklist of 138 area species to look out for – 78 of which nest on his land.

If you've had your fill of nature and the more conventional history of the area, turn into the darkly shaded drive that leads to the **Myrtles Plantation** (635 6277). This is a completely different kind of plantation house, both in its physical appearance and in its paranormal reputation — for more than 20 years the Myrtles has been known as the most haunted house in America.

The house is eerily perfect. The exquisite plaster frieze work for which it is renowned is more than 200 years old and has apparently never been renovated and it matches the blue colour of the lacy wrought ironwork on the porch. The tour is spooky and lively, an entertaining mix of rumour and history – it is said that somebody from every family that has lived here has been violently killed.

The most horrible story is that of the second owners. A West Indian slave is both the culprit and the victim in this tale: she eavesdropped on her owners, who punished her by cutting off her ear. Outraged, she retaliated at a birthday party for the owners' children, feeding them cake laced with the poisonous juice of the oleander plant. Both children died, and the slave was executed for the crime. All three are said to haunt the house today – the slave in her turban, the little girl in petticoats and the boy in short trousers.

The Myrtles was formerly a bed and breakfast, but the owners closed the visitor rooms after repeated incidents in which they arrived in the morning to find their terrified guests sleeping in their cars. They reported hearing noisy parties, complete with string quartets, in the empty main house throughout the night.

Parts of the 1980s US television version of William Faulkner's *The Long Hot Summer* were filmed in the house. Another story goes that the crew rearranged the parlour furniture for one scene, then stopped for lunch. Upon their return, the furniture had been painstakingly returned to its prior location – presumably by pernickety spirits.

The weird theme continues if you turn off US 61 onto the road simply marked 'Angola'. This is Highway 66 and in about 15 miles (24 kilometres) it will take you directly to the gates of the infamous **Louisiana State Prison Farm** at Angola (655 4411). The prison, surrounded on three sides by swamp and river and on the fourth by massive fences, is said to be inescapable.

During the early part of this century the prison was among the most brutal in the nation and was known as 'the bloodiest prison in the South' due to both inmate and guard violence. Under federal court order, its more inhumane conditions were alleviated but today it still requires inmates to work in the fields, escorted by mounted guards toting hunting rifles. The prison featured in Tim Robbins' 1995 film *Dead Man Walking* and also in Oliver Stone's *JFK*. Every Sunday in October the prison holds the Angola Prison Rodeo in which inmates compete, and which is open to the public.

For a less intimate but still informative look at the prison, visit the **Angola Museum** (also 655 4411), just outside the prison gates. Admission is free and it houses everything from log books from the 1940s listing prisoners' crimes and sentences to the actual electric chair replaced several years ago by lethal injection. The prison's dark history is outlined in startlingly honest fashion and terrific prison records are displayed on such famous criminals as the blues singer Leadbelly, including his admission papers – with a notation indicating he was arrested for manslaughter and released after writing a song for the prison warden.

Where to stay

After a day of touring, there's no reason to leave St Francisville because the area has some of the best B&Bs in the state; contact the **West Feliciana Historical Society** (635 6330) for a complete list. Expect to pay $60-$110 for a double.

One of the most unique and relaxing B&Bs is the **Shadetree Inn** (1818 St Ferdinand Street; 635 6116). Owner KW Kennon has restored this once-abandoned house to splendid, rustic beauty. Three private suites, each with a separate entrance and none coming into contact with another, are decorated in an elegant, simple style, with polished wooden floors, stained glass and dozens of windows overlooking the bluffs that lead down to the river. No detail is overlooked: there's a spot for visitors to build their own campfire, wide porches with rocking chairs, even aromatherapy products in the bathrooms. Expect to pay $145-$195.

Shadetree offers a relaxing view of the bluffs but for an even higher perspective, walk about a block down Ferdinand Street to Our Lady of Mount Carmel Catholic Church, which is perched on the highest hill in the area and offers a really great view.

Another, larger B&B nearby is the **Butler Greenwood Plantation** (8345 US 61; 635 6312; $65-$100), which has five modern cottages scattered around the grounds and a peaceful pond where ducks float placidly. Each cottage is decorated differently, and most have fireplaces. A tour of the main house, conducted by owner Anne Butler, a seventh-generation plantation resident, is included in the price.

Where to eat

St Francisville is a small town, so eating opportunities are somewhat limited and generally based around seafood, fried and boiled.

The locals gather for lunch at **Magnolia Café** (635 6528) at the corner of Ferdinand and Commerce Streets, which has friendly, no-frills service and familiar, home-made food such as soups, meatloaf and turkey divan.

A favourite spot is **Mattie's House Restaurant** at the Cottage Plantation (10528 Cottage Lane; 635 3674). Mattie's offers a wide variety of entrées including chicken marsala and fresh orange roughy (a large saltwater fish) with a garlic and herb sauce. It's open daily for dinner. For more upmarket dining, try the restaurant at the **Myrtles Plantation** (635 6276) where the chef prepares lunch and dinner from Wednesday to Sunday in a building behind the spooky house. Reservations are recommended.

Getting there

By car

From New Orleans, take I-10 west to Baton Rouge (80 miles/129km). Exit onto I-110 north, then follow it until it turns into Hwy 61 north. Follow the signs to St Francisville.

By bus

Greyhound runs 2 buses a day; the round trip costs $40.50.

Mississippi

About 30 minutes north of St Francisville over the Mississippi border in Wilkinson County is the **Clark Creek Natural Area**, known locally as Tunica Falls. Popular with local outdoor types, it is made up of steep hills and ravines, walking trails and several beautiful waterfalls. The area is vast and a good map essential (pick up one at the West Feliciana Historical Society Museum in St Francisville; *see page 232*). The area is known for its wildlife as well as its beautiful trails, but the hiking can be difficult, so wear proper footwear.

A somewhat easier, if less wild alternative is the **Mary Ann Brown Nature Preserve**, a 109-acre preserve in the Tunica Hills that has only recently opened to the public. Run by the Nature Conservancy of Louisiana, a two-mile (3.2-kilometre), well-blazed trail passes through a hardwood forest dominated by magnolia and beech trees, and traverses shallow ravines. The preserve also includes butterfly and humming bird gardens.

Natchez

Sixty miles (96.5 kilometres) north of St Francisville on US 61 in Mississippi lies the historic town of Natchez. This small, distinctly Southern community sits like a jewel on the high, hazy bluffs overlooking the Mississippi River.

Unusually, the integrity of Natchez's historic neighbourhoods has been largely preserved, with new construction relegated to the outskirts of town. The community lies on the site of an ancient village belonging to sunworshipping Natchez Indians. Bienville, the same pioneering Frenchman who settled New Orleans, established Fort Rosalie on the bluffs above the river in 1716. The Indians fought for their home, taking the fort in 1729 and killing or capturing most of the colonists, but France sent the full strength of its army to put down the tribe, destroying them in the process. Eventually the town took the name of the tribe it had displaced.

Natchez residents made their huge wealth during the early 1800s, when the town was the only port on the Mississippi between the mouth of the Ohio River and New Orleans and the development of the steamboat trade made fortunes for local speculators. It is the result of that money that most people come to Natchez to see.

The most famous event is the **Natchez Spring Pilgrimage** (1-601 446 6345), held annually in March. You can visit the historic houses as well as a number of private homes not usually open to the public. The locals participate enthusiastically, dressing in antebellum clothes and guiding visitors on a variety of tours, which are colour-coded to make it easier to choose which houses to visit.

Start at the **Natchez Convention & Visitor Bureau** (640 S Canal Street, by the river; 1-800 647 6724; open 8.30am-5pm or 6pm daily) to collect maps and brochures. There are so many extraordinary houses to see here it is best to do some research first and do some picking and choosing. Any trip to the area, however, should include some of the following homes.

Rosalie (Orleans Street, at Canal Street; 1-601 445 4555) was built in 1820 on the Mississippi bluff near the site of Rosalie Fort. It's a modest, red-brick mansion with white columns built in a restrained style, with the ribbon-like wrought iron fence that surrounds it adding most of the frills. It is easy to see why the site attracted armies: from its perch high above the river you can see for miles in every direction. Appropriately, Rosalie was the headquarters of the Union Army during the Civil War.

Dunleith (84 Homochitto Street; 1-601 446 8500) is a magnificent Greek Revival mansion built in 1856. It sits on 40 acres of landscaped parkland, and you will pass it as you come into town. It is one of the most striking homes in the area, completely surrounded by colonnaded galleries, and includes an 11-room B&B (rooms $95-$140).

Stanton Hall (401 High Sreet; 1-601 447 6282) is worth touring not because of the furnishings, but because of its sheer size. Original owner Frederick Stanton constructed four enormous Corinthian columns in the front gallery, imported Italian marble for the fireplaces, built 19-foot (six-metre) ceilings into the first floor and developed a vast hallway as the grand entrance. The huge bronze, Gothic chandeliers in each of the downstairs rooms are rare and detailed enough to merit the $6 tour fee.

The house with possibly the oddest history in the South is **Longwood** (140 Lower Woodville Road), a tragedy in brick. Built in the Byzantine style, the eight-sided building topped with an onion-shaped dome is unique among Southern mansions. Its original owner, cotton magnate Dr Haller Nutt, planned the house in 1859 as a permanent home for his family. Nutt's timing was disastrous. Work began on the house in 1860 and stopped a year later at the outbreak of the Civil War. Most of the artisans he had hired to build his dreamhouse were from Pennsylvania, and they left on the last boat out of Mississippi before the war.

The house was intended to have six storeys encircling a massive central gallery, and 32 rooms. Nutt, who had a weakness for science, designed an intricate system of mirrors and windows to bring light to the rooms on the inside of the circle. But the building was never finished. By the middle of the war, Nutt's fortunes were ruined. Although he

The carefully recreated Arcadian village of **Vermilionville** *could show Disney a thing or two. See page 237.*

Cajun country: a trapper's cabin tucked away in the Acadian wetlands.

was a Union sympathiser, the Yankees took no pity on him and destroyed his farms. He died a few years after the war, a broken man. No member of his family ever took the initiative to complete his dream or picked up the tools, abandoned by the Pennsylvania workers, to make good on the promise of the glorious exterior of the massive home. Instead, Nutt's descendants lived on the ground floor of the extraordinary house for more than 100 years, in what is described as near-poverty, before donating it to the Pilgrimage Garden Club (which also owns Stanton Hall) in 1970.

The tour includes the impressive (though incomplete) portion of the house, which still contains the tools left behind by the fleeing Northern workers. Longwood is a spacious white elephant and as a national landmark is destined never to be completed; instead it will stand as a monument to the strange but beautiful dreams of poor Nutt.

Both Stanton Hall and Longwood are on the route of Natchez Pilgrimage Tours (1-601 446 6631/1-800 647 6742).

Where to stay

The best accommodation is to be found in the extensive collection of B&Bs in historic houses throughout the area. Most are affordable, with rooms costing $60-$150 a night. The **Natchez Convention & Visitors Bureau** (1-601 445 4611) has a brochure listing the B&Bs (with a photo of each). Reservations are required at all, so plan ahead.

One of the most sought after B&Bs is at **Monmouth Plantation** (36 Melrose Avenue; 1-601 442 5852), which has 28 rooms and suites in the main house and the surrounding outbuildings. Its lush gardens, blue ponds dotted with quaint wooden bridges, gazebos, marble statuary and lovely, croquet-friendly lawn will explain why it has been voted one of the most romantic places in the US by several American newspapers and magazines. Rooms cost $135-$265 during the high season (March-May and October), which includes a tour of the white columned mansion and a full Southern breakfast.

Harper House (201 Arlington; 1-601 445 5557) is a smaller B&B, with just a few guest rooms inside a large Victorian home. The owners live in the building, and prices include a tour of the house. You can relax on the wide verandah and, when the weather permits, breakfast is served in the gazebo. A double room costs $80-$100.

For a less expensive option, the **Howard Johnson Lodge** (45 Sargent S Prentiss Drive; 1-601 442 1691) will put you up in normal hotel style for $35-$75 a night.

Where to eat

When you ask locals for advice on a good place to eat, notice how they hesitate. This is because there is really not much in the way of good food in Natchez: most of the dining options here run the very short gamut between heavy and fried. A lighter option is **Clara Nell's Downtown Deli**

(412 Main Street; 1 601 445 7779), which offers home-made soups, sandwiches and salads for under $6. The coffee is great, too.

For dinner, head to **Under-the-Hill**, the area under the bluffs at the very edge of the Mississippi. The restaurants here are touristy, but the food is hearty and the view great. The **Wharf Master's House** (57 Silver Street; 1-601 445 6025) spe-cialises in char-broiled steaks and seafood, prices range from $6 for lunch to $15 for a main course at dinner.

For upscale dining, **Monmouth Plantation** (*see page 236*) offers a five-course dinner nightly in its grand dining room ($37 per person, not including wine). The menu changes daily and places are limited, so book in advance.

Getting there

By car
From New Orleans, take I-10 west to Baton Rouge (80 miles/129km). Exit onto I-110, which turns into Hwy 61 and leads directly to Natchez. Follow the signs to downtown. It's a 2hr drive from New Orleans.

By bus
Greyhound buses run twice daily to and from Natchez and Baton Rouge. A round trip costs $33.45 and the journey takes 2 hours. The trip from New Orleans takes over 5 hours and costs $68 return.

Heading West

Acadiana

French-speaking Acadians – known as Cajuns – are the cultural heart of Louisiana and Cajuns con-sider **Lafayette** to be their *de facto* capital. Located about 120 miles (193 kilometres) west of New Orleans, Lafayette is a booming oil town sur-rounded by swamps, farms and crawfish ponds. It is the centre of Cajun activity, and where you must go to find what some consider the 'real Louisiana'.

After a lengthy effort by the local government throughout the twentieth century to wipe out the French language here (ask any Cajun over 40 about it, and they will tell you stories of being beaten for speaking French in school), a massive movement is underway to restore the language to prominence. Cajuns today are revelling in their his-tory. They've received support from a new, more culturally aware America. Cajun music, food and art is now known the world over, and the intensive tourist interest in Acadiana has bolstered their self-confidence. These days Cajuns are so proud to be Cajuns it's almost annoying.

Most Cajuns from the more rural communities surrounding Lafayette still speak French in their homes, and local restaurants and shops have begun offering weekly 'L'états Françaises' – a

morning or evening during which only French is spoken. Particularly in the small villages around Lafayette, you're almost as likely to hear 'bonjour' as 'hello' from passing strangers. A tourist with passable French skills could find themselves warmly embraced and invited to a local *boucherie* (basically a pig slaughter and barbecue) – Cajuns are that friendly.

Once you've got your bearings, start with the past and work your way forward. **Vermilionville** (1600 Surrey Street; 1-318 233 4077) is a museum of Cajun history in the form of a recreated Acadian village. Sprawling over 23 acres, Vermilionville invites visitors to experience Cajun life as it was a century ago. The town has houses, a one-room schoolhouse, church, bakery and blacksmith shop. The buildings, with steeply peaked roofs and stairways to the second floor located on the front porch, are typical examples of Acadian architec-ture. Workers and guides wander about in cos-tume and French is widely spoken. Regular activities include Cajun bands and cooking, art and dance instruction. It's very well done and not at all tacky or Disneyesque.

On the way to Vermilionville, visit the **Acadian Cultural Center** (1-318 232 0789; open 8am-5pm daily) just outside the village. This is an informa-tive museum filled with photos and information on the history of the Acadians and the lives of the area's earliest settlers.

After getting educated, head downtown to wan-der among the old buildings, restaurants and shops. Lafayette is a largely utilitarian place, but it has charming touches and winding streets. The best nightclub in town, **Grant Street Dance Hall** (1-318 237 2255) is in the middle of down-town, and offers local and regional acts nightly.

Although central Lafayette is pleasant, the best sites lie in the surrounding territory, so head about 15 miles (24 kilometres) south to see the property of one of the area's more quixotically successful families. **Avery Island** (1-318 365 8173 – off US 90, follow the signs) is a barrier island in the Louisiana wetlands and has long been the home of the McIlhenny and Avery families, creators of Tabasco sauce and numerous other spicy things, as well as collectors of unusual animals.

The areas of Avery Island that are open to the public are actually a tiny percentage of the space and activity on the island. The rest is home to the family and its pepper farms and factories. The island itself is an oddity, sitting as it does on a salt mountain (known as a salt dome) hundreds of feet tall. The public cannot visit the salt mines on the island, which are said to contain tunnels more than 100 feet high and a mile wide, but you can tour the factory and see the process by which Tabasco is made, with bushels of salted peppers mashed and set in oak barrels to age.

*A resident of the **Atchafalaya Swamp Basin** awaits the next tour party.*

The island's other attraction is its 200-acre wildlife park, **Jungle Gardens**, refuge to hundreds of species of bird, another fixation of early twentieth-century McIlhenny patriarch Edmund McIlhenny, who fancied himself a naturalist. The park is walled with bamboo, and features alligator ponds and bird-nesting platforms absolutely crowded with endangered species. However, McIlhenny's love of unusual animals has had some unfortunate repercussions.

He imported nutria – a large South American swimming rat – to the island many years ago in an attempt to balance his eco-system. Some of the animals escaped and set up homestead elsewhere and spread like wildfire. Today, these voracious vegetarian creatures are blamed for devouring the area's wetlands and are considered a menace to the conservation of the state's marshes and swamps. Attempts to popularise nutria fur and meat in order to encourage hunters to kill the huge rats have been, so far, unsuccessful, and they are gradually munching their way through southern Louisiana.

Head back on US 90 toward Lafayette and stop off at another salt dome island. **Jefferson Island** is famous for its breathtaking gardens, which trail around the top and sides of the salt dome that rises out of Lake Peigneur. The island was founded by a nineteenth-century actor, Joseph Jefferson, who constructed a fantastic house at its peak, with wide porches and Moorish details in a style locally known as Steamboat Gothic. The house (1-318 365 3332) is full of antiques and open for tours, while

the gardens are ablaze in spring and summer with flowers that swirl around ponds, gazebos and sculptures. Statues of Buddha and Hindu gods dot the landscape, rabbits hop across the path and exotic birds hover overhead.

Despite its beauty, the island is most famous in local lore for a bizarre accident that occurred in 1980. An oil rig in the lake punctured the ceiling of the vast salt mine below the water, triggering a massive whirlpool that dragged down the drilling rig, 11 barges, tugboats, houses, 65 acres of land and all the water in the lake. Much of the incident was captured in an astounding video that can be viewed at the island. In what seems a miracle, nobody was killed in the incident. The lake itself remained completely dry until the tide came in 12 hours later.

Nature lovers will be seduced by the nearby **Atchafalaya Swamp Basin** – if you're travelling from Baton Rouge, an elevated section of I-10 travels right through the swamp. Its wild look attracts boaters and fishing aficionados from around the world and there are numerous swamp tours and alligator-watching expeditions; for details check the adverts in the weekly *Times of Acadiana* newspaper and the brochures at local hotels and the **Lafayette Convention & Visitors Commission**.

If you want to combine sightseeing with lunch, one of the best restaurants in the area is just a few miles from Lafayette in nearby **Breaux Bridge**. (Signs along the Evangeline Thruway near downtown will direct you to shortcuts to this small town; otherwise head back on I 10 east to the Breaux Bridge exit). Breaux Bridge is a charming town that retains its original downtown buildings along with elevated sidewalks and old wooden shopfronts. Restored Victorian homes in the surrounding neighbourhood make for a pleasant drive through town. Several antique stores in downtown are worth a browse, but your real destination should be **Café des Amis** (110 E Bridge Street; 1-318 332 5273).

This is one of the best places in the area and its small dining room is often packed – for good reason. The food is excellent and at about $15 per person, reasonably priced. Catfish, crawfish and shrimp with creative sauces are a speciality and the fried eggplant (aubergine) is the best in the South. The atmosphere is festive, with wide windows thrown open on warm days, wooden floors, antique furniture and local art decorating the walls.

After leaving Breaux Bridge, head south on Highway 31 about 12 miles (19.3 kilometres) to another quaint bayou town with historic charm, **St Martinville**. This little community is home to several legends. It is central to Longfellow's poem *Evangeline,* which tells the tale of star-crossed Acadian lovers Evangeline and Gabriel, who were cast out with their people from Canada, but sent away on different ships. They were reunited only in middle age when Evangeline had become a nun and Gabriel was near death. The poem ends with him dying in her arms.

The story was so popular that another legend grew up to prove it was based on real-life lovers. Although historians roll their eyes, everyone in St Martinville will tell you that the 'real' Evangeline and Gabriel met at last under the **Evangeline Oak** in the middle of St Martinville. You'll find it behind the Presbytere of St Martin de Tours church on the banks of Bayou Teche. Nearby is a statue of Evangeline, modelled on 1930s Hollywood filmstar Dolores del Rio, who played the Acadian heroine in the film *The Romance of Evangeline.*

St Martinville was also a favoured refuge for French aristocrats fleeing the French Revolution. So elegant was the town that it became known as 'Petit Paris' and many of its more impressive homes were constructed during that period. For more information, visit the **Petit Paris Museum** (131 S Main Street; 1-318 394 7334) next door to the church, which offers visual and written information on the history of the town.

One of the best restaurants in the area is located 15 minutes' drive north of Lafayette in the tiny burg of **Grand Coteau**. **Catahoula's** (1-318 662 2275) is located at the only traffic light in town, directly across the street from Grand Coteau's biggest attraction, the peaceful, historic convent Academy of the Sacred Heart. Elegant and creative

versions of local cuisine cost about $15 for an entrée, there's a surprisingly good wine list and a pleasant atmosphere. The walls are decorated with large photos of the restaurant's namesake – the strange-looking Catahoula hound that is the official state dog. It's a welcome change from the sometimes overly enthusiastic Cajun restaurants that predominate in the area.

If you don't feel like making the drive to Grand Coteau, **Evangeline Seafood & Steakhouse** (2633 SE Evangeline Thruway; 1-318 233 2658) offers great food in the middle of Lafayette. Main courses, such as fried tilapia with crab meat sauce, cost around $15.

Tourist information

Lafayette Convention & Visitors Commission

1400 NW Evangeline Thruway, off I-10, Lafayette (1-318 232 3737/1-800 346 1958); mailing address PO Box 52066, Lafayette, LA 70501. **Open** 8.30am-5pm Mon-Fri; 9am-5pm Sat.
Website: www.lafayettetravel.com

Where to stay

Tourism is still a relatively recent phenomenon in Acadiana, so the selection of places to spend the night is limited. However, a handful of B&Bs have opened in recent years, providing a welcome alternative to the mainstream hotels.

One of the best is **Alida's Bed & Breakfast** (2631 SE Evangeline Thruway; 1-318 264 1191; website: www.alidas.com), located in a pleasant historic house off the busy central road through Lafayette. Run by Tanya and Douglas Greenwald, it has four large guest rooms ($60-$80 a night), furnished with antiques and each with a TV and telephone. If you want to talk to locals and get their insight into the community, this is the place to go. Breakfast is a sit-down affair with all the guests together and conversation is lively.

Alternatively, try the **Old Castillo Hotel** in St Martinville (220 Evangeline Boulevard; 1-318 394 4010; $50-$80), a large B&B on the banks of the Bayou Teche directly under the branches of the Evangeline Oak. The rooms in the nineteenth-century building – formerly a girls' school – are spacious and comfortable, and offer the best view in town. Photos of past pupils line the walls in the small restaurant.

For an upscale, mainstream hotel, the **Courtyard by Marriott** in Lafayette (214 E Kaliste Saloom Road; 1-318 232 5005) has everything you could hope for, including a location near downtown; rooms cost $62-$129. Those on a budget should head for **Motel 6** (2724 NE Evangeline Thruway; 1-318 233 2055), which offers nondescript but serviceable rooms with televisions. Expect to pay $28-$55.

Getting there

By car
From New Orleans, follow I-10 west through Baton Rouge, over the spectacular Atchafalaya Swamp and take exit number 103-A, which will deposit you on the Evangeline Thruway. The Lafayette Convention & Visitors Commission is a couple of miles down the road.

By bus
Greyhound runs frequent daily services to Lafayette from New Orleans. A round trip ticket costs $34 and the journey takes 3-4 hours.

Heading South

Grand Isle

Many people who know Grand Isle's reputation through literature often take the trouble to seek out this barrier island at the tip of Louisiana, 110 miles (177 kilometres) from New Orleans. In Kate Chopin's 1889 novel *The Awakening*, a conventional nineteenth-century wife begins to find herself during a summer on Grand Isle. Famous New Orleans writer Lafcadio Hearn wrote a lyrical novel and many adoring articles about the place 'where finally all the land melts down into desolations of sea-marsh'. Today the sandy, six-mile- (9.7 kilometre-) long island bears little resemblance to the languid resort described by earlier writers, but Grand Isle is still an entertaining side-trip from New Orleans, in some ways more interesting for the trip itself than the destination.

The drive to Grand Isle from New Orleans is a pleasant tour of the wateriest part of Cajun Country, where farms give way to the maritime world of commercial fishing, offshore oil work, charter boats, ship-building and ship-repair businesses. At Raceland, 50 miles (80 kilometres) south-west of New Orleans on US 90, the Grand Isle tour truly begins when you turn due south on Highway 1. This two-lane road runs alongside Bayou Lafourche (pronounced 'La-Foosh'), a busy navigable waterway that runs down to the Gulf of Mexico. The bayou is known as 'the longest street in the world' because it is the main thoroughfare and point of reference for this part of south Louisiana.

While Highway 1 runs on the west side of Bayou Lafourche, Highway 308 runs parallel to the east side. The area is thickly populated, with the towns of Lockport, Larose, Cut Off, Galliano, Golden Meadow and Leeville blending into one another. Large Catholic churches are the dominant municipal structures, a reminder that Cajun Country, for all the tourism hoopla, is a very real place, rooted in family and church. Points of interest along the way include religious shrines, stores and restaurants.

In Cut Off, there's the **Louisiana Catalogue Store** (14839 W Main Street; 693 4100/1-800 375 4100), a combination bookstore and Louisiana emporium run by filmmaker Glen Pitre (maker of *Belizaire the Cajun*). It sells a wide range of Louisiana-connected items such as records, food, spices, crafts, souvenirs and folk art.

For large-scale folk art, look out in Golden Meadow for an impressive, hand-made, outdoors shrine to the Virgin Mary. Located on the Highway 1 side of Bayou Lafourche, beside the Golden Meadow police department, this is a pocket park of Catholic devotion with a larger-than-lifesize Mary in a glassed-in refrigeration unit (so that fresh flowers can be left and won't wilt), white-washed cement pews and guest books/prayer lists thoughtfully sheltered in purpose-built cases. After Leeville, the land really begins to 'melt down' and the rest of the drive is rather bleak.

Look for a tiny church on the east side of Highway 1. Measuring a scant 10 by 14 feet (3 by 4.3 metres), **Smith's Chapel** was built by a local couple as a memorial to their two sons, one who died of a childhood disease and one who died in a knife fight. It's never locked (if the door is closed, lift the bolt and go in) and there are always candles burning at the minuscule altar. Paper and pens are left for visitors to write messages to God ('Thank you God!! Clean and sober for 24 hours!', 'Please tell my Mom hello up there'). Mrs Noonie Smith, who built the chapel, lives across the road and operates an 'adult novelties' business in a trailer. She sees no contradiction between her X-rated adult videos and the chapel, and is happy to greet visitors at either site.

Grand Isle floats off the tip of Louisiana like a footnote, connected to the mainland by the causeway-like highway and sheer determination. In 1893 one of the worst hurricanes on record swept the island clear of hotels, casinos, fishermen's cottages and the landscape that gave Lafcadio Hearn heart palpitations ('imposing groves of oak, its golden wealth of orange trees, its odorous lanes of oleander, its broad grazing meadows yellow-starred with wild camomile… its loveliness is exceptional'). Alas, Grand Isle's great beauty has faded, but not its seaside allure. Despite Louisiana's considerable coastline, there's hardly any beach in the state. When New Orleanians want real beach, they go east to Mississippi, Alabama or Florida. When they want immediate beach or fishing beach, they head to Grand Isle.

The island is home to a small group of year-round fishermen, oil-rig workers and their families but the population swells as the weather gets warmer. Most summer visitors come for the fishing, which is excellent, from piers or by boat. The island is full of modest summer homes, usually simple frame cabins on stilts, painted garish colours and given humorous names.

Oddly for a place that promotes itself as a seaside playground, access to the water is limited. For those who aren't staying in a summer house or a motel, just about the only way to get to the water is through the **Grand Isle State Park** (787 2559; entrance $10 per vehicle) at the eastern tip of the island. Relatively new, the park has very good facilities and is a favourite with those who enjoy no frills camping. The beach is reached by a long, elevated walkway past the scrubby landscape; while this isn't the sparkling white sand beaches of the rest of the Gulf Coast, it does have sand, picnic tables and a mile of beach.

The 400-foot (122-metre) fishing pier is the main draw for the park but a small beachside campground is popular too. It's primitive, meaning no running water or electricity. All facilities are a five-minute walk away but the rusticity is the attraction for most campers who bring tents or sleep in their vehicles. There is a $10 per night camping fee and a $2 per car entrance fee to use the park.

Though Grand Isle is mostly a laid-back resort with no nightlife, things change during the annual Tarpon Fishing Rodeo in August when thousands of fishing fanatics crowd the island. This is not a time when Grand Isle lives up to its reputation as a place of quiet retreat.

Tourist information

Lafourche Parish Tourist Commission
Mailing address: PO Box 340, Raceland, LA 70394 (537 5800/cajun@ lafourche-tourism.org). **Open** 9am-4pm Mon-Fri; 10am-3pm Sat.
This very handy tourist office is at the junction of US 90 and Hwy 1 in Raceland, and clearly signposted.

Grand Isle Tourist Commission
Mailing address PO Box 817, Grand Isle, LA 70358 (787 2997). **Open** 8am-4pm Mon-Fri.
Phone or write; there isn't an office to visit.
Website: www.sportsmans-paradise.com/grandisle/html

Where to stay & eat

Cigar's Cajun Cuisine (Highway 1, Grand Isle; 787 3220) offers seafood (most entrées under $12) and a bar and is open seven days a week. Year-round residents and weekend visitors gather at Cigar's compound, which includes a marina and a motel. **Randolph's Restaurant** (806 Bayou Drive, Golden Meadow; 1-601 475 5272) is a landmark, dating from the 1930s. It's famous for its seafood dishes, cooked in the local Cajun style, at moderate prices. Depending on the season, there are also fruit stands along the way.

Seabreeze Cottages (3210 Highway 1, Grand Isle; 787 3180) is a pleasant compound of small, two-bedroom cottages with kitchenettes. Prices range from $56-$100 a night depending on the time of year; there's a two-night minimum during summer. If you want to rent a private fishing camp

(usually a summer house with water access) the **Grand Isle Tourist Commission** (787 2997) keeps a list of local rentals.

Getting there

By car
You need a car to get to Grand Isle. From New Orleans, take US 90 west. At Raceland, turn south on Hwy 1, which ends at Grand Isle.

Heading East

'I'm going to the Coast,' say New Orleanians as the weekend approaches, their faces softening and their voices taking on a happy lilt. The weekend exodus out of the city (all year round) is a mystery to New Orleans-bound travellers who can't wait to get to the city. But the residents of New Orleans need a respite from the endless parties and party-planning of Planet Hangover. Carnival and Jazz Fest may occupy just a few weeks a year but locals spend hundreds of hours in meetings, conferences, costume-fittings and working lunches planning the damn things. 'The Coast' is their release from the pressure of having fun in New Orleans.

'The Coast', as defined in New Orleans terms, means the seaside areas of the Gulf of Mexico that are within a day's drive. It stretches from the almost-suburb of Bay St Louis, Mississippi, to the quintessential beach town of Panama City, Florida. For visitors to New Orleans the coast is an alluring trip, too. Travelling east, the mossy, laid-back seaside towns of Mississippi give way to 'the poor man's New Orleans' of old coastal cities Mobile and Pensacola and then to the gorgeous beaches of the Gulf of Mexico. New Orleans is an easy drive from some of the best beaches in North America. From roughly Mobile Bay to Panama City, the coast is a paradise of white, sugary sands edged by warm, blue-green waters.

Of course, no paradise is complete without its serpent. The Gulf Coast, alas, has several. Once the coast was practically a secret playground for Southerners. Until fairly recently it was a collection of lightly populated waterside towns characterised by old-fashioned guesthouses, lazy fishing villages and untouched beaches. Today the Mississippi coast (known as the Redneck Riviera) sometimes seems to be one big gambling casino while the magnificent beaches of south Alabama and northwestern Florida have been discovered by condo-crazed developers.

Yet the beauty and the charm of the Gulf Coast somehow overwhelm the tawdriness that has been inflicted upon it by mega-casinos and appalling condo architecture. From the arty little towns in Mississippi to the gorgeous pure white sand beaches of the Florida Panhandle, the coast offers rich rewards to travellers. And it's not just a summertime place. With the mild, semi-tropical climate, swimming is possible from March to October and beach walking, birdwatching, fishing and boating are year-round activities.

Travel by car is the only realistic way to see the Gulf Coast. There is train and bus transportation from New Orleans to Mobile, Pensacola and Mississippi coast towns, but local public transport (when there is any) doesn't tie into the major train or bus routes. Amtrak schedules are incredibly inconvenient, putting east-bound travellers into Mobile and Pensacola in the early morning hours when long waits for taxis are the norm. Once in Mobile or Pensacola, the local bus systems are poorly organised and limited in scope. Hitchhiking among younger travellers isn't unknown but isn't recommended.

Mississippi Gulf Coast

If your priority is beaches, keep going. While there are some pleasant public beaches along US 90, they are poor substitutes for the sparkling white sands another hour to the east. The barrier islands that line the Mississippi coast intercept the best sand and the clearest water, making the state's 80-mile (129 kilometre) coastline a pale imitation of the better coastal spots.

But the Mississippi coast has its attractions, from the wannabe-Las Vegas casinos to the likeable little beach towns. The attractions, old and new, are nicely summarised by **Bay St Louis**, 60 miles (96.5 kilometres) east of New Orleans on US 90 (and several exits off I-10). Bay St Louis has a big casino, **Casino Magic** (1-800 562 4425; website: www.casinomagic.com), but it is thankfully not located in the adorable little village beside the quiet waters of the bay that gives the town its name. The old town is centred around Beach Avenue and Main Street, both heavily populated with antique shops, second-hand stores, art galleries and cafés.

Of particular interest is the **Serenity Gallery** (126½ Main Street; 1-600 467 3061), which specialises in local and regional artists. Old rock-'n'rollers will want to stop by **Dock of the Bay** restaurant (119 N Beach Boulevard; 1-601 467 9940) owned by former Blood, Sweat & Tears guitarist Jerry Fisher. He still keeps a hand in the music biz, playing great old blues and rock songs with a pick-up band most Saturday nights. Food at the Dock, by the way, is some of the best on the Mississippi coast, particularly the grilled fish; entrées cost $2.95-$19.95.

To be honest, most of the crowds heading for Mississippi aren't interested in cute towns or dusty second-hand stores. They are gamblers in search of the elusive big strike. Gambling is growing rapidly – more than a dozen large casinos operate along the coast, with more planned for the near future – in defiance of the size of the actual communities, which are tiny. Neither **Biloxi** nor **Gulfport** has a real downtown, and the hottest restaurants in town are pizza joints. It's a strange juxtaposition, but Mississippi is welcoming the gambling world, warts and all, with open arms.

And the casinos are no cheap Southern imitation. This is the real thing. Casino companies are spending hundreds of millions of dollars on their casino-hotel complexes: seven have more than 300 rooms, while the President Casino has an 850-room hotel. The latest developer, Mirage Resorts, spent more than $475 million on its 1,800-room Beau Rivage casino-hotel in Biloxi – larger than any in Atlantic City. The gambling revenues from Mississippi casinos amount to $1.72 billion a year: third in the nation behind gaming facilities in Nevada and New Jersey. So roll the dice and take your chances, if gambling is your vice.

For those in search of beach-oriented fun, Mississippi has a **26-mile man-made beach** stretching from Pass Christian, just over the Louisiana border, to Ocean Springs. But the biggest surprise of Mississippi beach life isn't to be found on the main shoreline; instead, it is a brief ferry ride away from Gulfport Yacht Harbor. The ferry takes travellers 12 miles (19.3 kilometres) across the Gulf to **Ship Island** (1-601 864 1014), a barrier island that is part of the Gulf Islands National Seashore.

A wooden boardwalk crosses the island, linking the swamps with a wide, breezy beach. The best area of beach, which is pristinely maintained, is on the far side of the island where the sand is as white and the water as blue as any Florida beach. The row of barrier islands blocks the muddy water of the Mississippi River from sullying the ocean, as it does elsewhere, creating an oasis that verges on tropical paradise. Note that visitors are allowed only between March and October and from morning until sunset. Tickets cost $16, concessions $8-$14.

While Mississippi is geared mainly for visceral pleasures, art lovers will be happy to learn that there are also a couple of unusual and worthwhile art museums in the area. The **George E Ohr Arts & Cultural Center** in Biloxi (136 George Ohr Street; 1-601 374 5547; open 9am-5pm Mon-Sat) displays the work of the turn-of-the-century 'Mad Potter of Biloxi'. Ohr was known for his two-foot-long moustache as well as his unique take on pottery, which is no simple, elegant affair but designed to look as though it is constantly in motion. His teapots, with impossibly curling handles, seem to jig, while his bowls twist and turn in oddly graceful ways.

Ohr was never appreciated in his lifetime, and it is said that one day he just up and quit. He packed large crates with his favourite work, hauled them out to Biloxi's back bay and buried

*One of the conservative **Mobile**'s more modern offerings. See page 245.*

them in the mud. He then gave up pottery forever and opened a Cadillac dealership. Nobody has ever found the buried pottery, which is a shame – especially as a quality Ohr pot now sells for about $35,000 at auction.

The other art museum is in nearby **Ocean Springs**, a few miles east of Biloxi. The **Walter Anderson Museum of Art** (510 Washington Avenue; 1-601 872 3164) showcases the work of New Orleans-born Walter Anderson, another magnificent lone artist. Ranked as one of the best small museums in America, it deftly blends world-class art and smalltown intimacy.

Anderson (1903-1965) was a classically trained artist-turned-visionary who painted an intensely personal world of sun, sky, sea, wildlife and light. He rarely sold or exhibited his work during his lifetime, which was punctuated by bouts of mental illness. He lived a hermit's life among his artistic family, often avoiding his wife and children and working at his brothers' famous art pottery workshop only when he needed money. The extent of his work and vision was discovered after his death when his family was finally free to look through his work. They discovered Anderson's masterwork, a dazzling mural of the earth's creation that covered the walls and ceiling and floor of one locked room of his small cottage.

'The Little Room' has been painstakingly reassembled within the museum. The panoramic vision is echoed in the community centre wing of the museum. During a period of clarity in 1951, Anderson volunteered to paint the interior of the Ocean Springs Community Center. He created another masterpiece in his vivid, powerful colours and forms, this one describing the Mississippi Gulf Coast's flora and fauna as well as its Indian past and European conquest. The museum was built adjacent to the community centre and displays Anderson's paintings, watercolours, pottery and other artefacts.

The Anderson family's **Shearwater Pottery** (102 Shearwater Drive; 1-601 875 7320) is still operating and worth a visit. It's only a few minutes' drive from the museum (open 9am-5.30pm Mon-Sat; 1-5.30pm Sun).

Tourist information

Mississippi Gulf Coast Convention & Visitors Bureau

135 Courthouse Road, at 16th Street, Gulfport (1-601 896 6699); mailing address PO Box 6128, Gulfport, MS 39506-6128. **Open** 8am-5pm Mon-Fri. *Website: www.gulfcoast.org*

Where to stay

A huge number of hotels have sprung up in Southern Mississippi in recent years to keep up with the increasing tourism, so finding a room is rarely a problem.

In the moderate size and price range, try the **Best Western Oak Manor Motel** (886 Beach Boulevard, Biloxi; 1-601 435 4331). The rooms ($75-$145) are simple and pleasant, and all have cable TV. For a true casino-hotel experience, sample the

500-room **Grand Casino Biloxi Hotel** (245 & 280 Beach Boulevard, Biloxi; 1-601 432 2500; $99-$189 a night), complete with all the casino bells and whistles. The glitz must be seen to be believed. Budget travellers should consider the **Econo Lodge** in Gulfport Beach (40 E Beach Boulevard; 1-601 863 2666). Rooms cost $40-$85.

Where to eat

Plenty of restaurants, mostly chains, dot the area, but a careful search can turn up a few good ones and the number of worthwhile eateries is growing as tourism and gambling bring in more visitors.

For an upmarket experience, **Mary Mahoney's Old French House** in Biloxi (1-228 374 0163) specialises in seafood, particularly shrimp dishes. In Ocean Springs, the **Blow-Fly Inn** (1-601 896 9812) offers a nice view of a nearby bayou and traditional Southern cooking – barbecue ribs are the mainstay. Also in Ocean Springs, **Aunt Jenny's Catfish Restaurant** (1-601 875 9201) is a downhome place in a beautiful historic house on the shores of the back bay. All-you-can-eat specials of seafood and chicken cost under $12.

Getting there

By car
From New Orleans, take I-10 east (about 45 mins). Large signs indicate the exits to Biloxi and Gulfport. Follow the signs to Hwy 1, a scenic road that follows the ocean.

By bus
Greyhound runs daily buses to Biloxi from New Orleans; a round trip costs $42. Several area casinos also provide shuttle services for New Orleans gamblers.

Mobile

Older than New Orleans by more than a decade, **Mobile**, Alabama, is often looked on as the poor man's New Orleans. Located 120 miles (193 kilometres) east of New Orleans on the deep-water port of Mobile Bay, the city was founded by the same French Le Moyne brothers (Iberville and Bienville) who were to be the mainstays of early New Orleans. Mobile (pronounced 'MOE-beal' – citizens will correct anyone saying 'Mo-bull') underwent the same chaotic French and Spanish colonial history but was in the hands of the British for long stretches, which gave it a more Anglo character than New Orleans. Although the city has many of the same street names (Conti, St Ann, Royal, Dauphin, Iberville, Bienville and so on), its own fully fledged Mardi Gras and even flashes of the same colonial architecture, the city is far more conservative, Protestant and American Southern than New Orleans.

Bellingrath Gardens, *designed for the Coca-Cola magnate, are a seasonal delight.*

Visitors interested in the city will find plenty of written information and plenty of Southern hospitality at the **Visitor Center** at Fort Conde, a reconstructed 1711 French fort (150 South Royal Street; 1-800-252-3862).

Two of the Mobile area's biggest tourist draws are both interesting enough to merit stopovers. **Bellingrath Gardens and Home** (1 334 973 2217), 20 miles (32 kilometres) south of Mobile, has more than 800 acres of carefully designed gardens and woodlands, with changing seasonal displays. The estate started out as a hunting camp in 1917 for Coca-Cola magnate Walter Bellingrath and his wife Bessie. The place evolved into their full-time home, with a vaguely Mediterranean manor house that is stuffed with antiques that the Bellingraths bought off Southern gentry impoverished by the Depression.

The battleship **USS 'Alabama'**, permanently anchored in Mobile Bay (Battleship Parkway off I-10; 1-800 426 4929), was one of the workhorse ships of World War II. It's now a walk-through museum and a big favourite with kids. It was used as a location in the 1992 Steven Segal-Tommy Lee Jones movie *Under Siege*.

Civil War buffs will be interested in the two historical sites at the tip of Mobile Bay. **Fort Gaines** (1-334 861 6992) is on the west side, on Dauphin Island, a barrier island south of Mobile connected to the mainland by bridge (at the east end of Bienville Boulevard). Its mirror image across the bay is **Fort Morgan** (1-334 540 7125), at the end of Highway 180. As Confederate strongholds, they kept out the Union Navy until Admiral David Farragut overwhelmed them with his 1864 assault and famous battle cry: 'Damn the torpedoes! Full steam ahead!'. They are among the coastal fortifications that the US built in the 1840s, many of which were in use through World War II. Both forts often host Civil War re-enactments. A car ferry (1-334 540 7787) runs daily between Fort Gaines and Fort Morgan, but though fun it's notoriously unreliable.

Where to eat

Mobile is not a good restaurant town despite its reputation. Two long-time local favourites are **Rousso's** (166 S Royal Street, next to Fort Conde; 1-334 433 3322), where the seafood is reliable and the service first rate, and **Wintzell's Oyster House** (605 Dauphin Street; 1-334 432 4605), a colourful ramshackle seafood restaurant downtown.

Getting there

By car
The fastest method is to take I-10 east. It's almost a straight line from New Orleans to Mobile and, barring a lane-closing traffic pile-up, the 120-mile (193-km) trip will take 2½hrs or less.

Alternatively, you can take the scenic route via US 90, a favourite with locals when they can spare the time.

*The battleship **USS Alabama** lies at anchor in Mobile Bay. See page 245.*

Take Broad Street/Gentilly Boulevard east, travelling through New Orleans east. The old highway goes through suburban Gentilly and out along the Chef Menteur highway, finally dwindling to two lanes winding through fishing camps and small towns. US 90 hits all the populated areas along the Mississippi Gulf Coast before going into Mobile through the back door.

By bus

Greyhound runs several buses a day. The journey takes 3¾ hours and the round trip costs $56.

By train

Amtrak (1-800 872 7245/528 1610) runs between New Orleans and Mobile but the service is inconvenient: trains arrive and leave in the middle of the night and the Mobile train station is isolated and taxis difficult to find.

Alabama Gulf Coast

Alabama has a minuscule coastline compared with Florida's hundreds of miles of beaches. But for the New Orleans-based traveller, the Alabama coast is attractive because it is a quick trip without giving up any beach quality.

The beachside town of **Gulf Shores** is the orientation point for the Alabama coast. Highway 59 (exit off I-10 east of Mobile) dead-ends in Gulf Shores, where it intersects 'the beach highway', Highway 180. The main public beach is located at the end of Highway 59. There is plenty of free parking, good facilities and an excellent beach, with

lifeguards on duty during the summer. The beach is ground-zero for teenagers and college students on spring break or summer vacation; the mood is usually 'Party down dude!' in thick Southern accents. A public fishing pier lies a mile or so east of the public beach on Highway 182. There are also several public access areas along this road, with parking areas an easy walk from the beach.

Gulf Shores has little of the raffishness associated with most beach towns, in part because of Alabama's Deep South prudery. For years it was illegal to call drinking establishments 'bars' or 'saloons' and bizarre laws made serving mixed drinks a legal maze. Yet the area has two of the most famous bars on the Gulf Coast.

On the beach, the **Pink Pony Pub** (948 6371) has live music, an unapologetic pick-up scene and reasonably good seafood. The **Flora-Bama** (predictably located on the Alabama-Florida stateline, on Highway 182) is a beach bar crossed with a country juke-joint. Pick-up trucks usually outnumber convertibles, but the free-flowing spirits, loud music and its reputation for outrageousness have kept customers coming for over 30 years.

Shopping is a major draw for the area because of the **Riviera Center Factory Stores** (2601 Highway 59 south; 1-800 523 6873) in nearby Foley. Riviera has more than 100 outlet shops, selling everything from high-end brand names to large-size clothing for women to kitchenware. Prices are said to be 20-70 per cent off regular prices, but it depends on the season and luck.

East of Gulf Shores is **Perdido Key** (regularly voted one of the best beaches in the US) and the Florida stateline. The area on both sides of the line is called Perdido Key, but the Alabama side seems to have the bigger and uglier condo resorts.

Tourist information

Alabama Gulf Coast Visitors & Convention Bureau

3150 Gulf Shores Parkway (Hwy 59), Gulf Shores 36542 (1-334 968 7511). **Open** 8am-5pm Mon-Fri.

Where to stay

Renting a beach house for a few days or a week is the best way to visit the Gulf. There's a huge word-of-mouth network but newcomers can usually find a place through agencies such as **Kaiser Realty** (1-800 225 4853/website: www.kaiserrealty. com); **Bender Realty** (1-800 528 2651/website: www. gulftel.com/~bender); and **Meyer Real Estate** (1-800 824 6331/website: www.gulfbeach. com). Expect to pay around $700 per week for a two-bedroom beach house in summer ($400 in winter); minimum stay is one week.

Hotels and motels tend to be big and impersonal, dominated by the usual chains. The **Gulf State Park Resort Hotel** (1-334 948 4853) is a low-rise development to the east of Gulf Shores; a double room costs $49-$105 depending on the season.

For beach camping, nothing on the Gulf Coast is better than **Rosamond Johnson Beach** (1-334 934 2623), a white sand paradise on Perdido Key. It's actually on the Florida side of the key, off the Beach Highway (Highway 292), part of the Gulf Islands National Seashore. While there's a very nice daytime-use beach, the real jewel in the crown of the park (if not the entire Gulf Islands Seashore) is the seven-and-a-half miles (12 kilometres) of untouched island that is open to primitive camping. That means you have to hike in with all your supplies, but the bonus is a pristine beach with no cars, no roads, no condos, no noise.

Where to eat

The **Oar House Café** (540 7991) in Fort Morgan Marina, at Mile Marker 2 on Fort Morgan Road, is a casual waterside eatery, more a convenience for the fishermen and boaters who dock their vessels here than a commercial restaurant. It does good grilled fish. You could also try **Live Bait** (1-334 974 1885, on the Beach Highway, Romar Beach, east of Gulf Shores). **Doc's Seafood Shack & Oyster Bar** (1-334 981 6999, Highway 189, Orange Beach, east of Gulf Shores), caters to the unrepentant consumers of traditional Southern-cooked seafood: 'If it ain't deep-fried, it ain't worth eating'.

Getting there

By car

From Mobile, Gulf Shores is about 40 miles (64.4km) southeast via Hwy 59.

*The perfect antidote to the Redneck Riviera: Orange Beach, just east of **Gulf Shores**.*

Florida Gulf Coast

The north-west corner of Florida, usually called the Panhandle, was long seen as the state step-child, more hick Alabama and Georgia than sophisticated Palm Beach and Miami. But now that South Florida is seriously overbuilt and crime continues to be a major worry, the Panhandle is coming into its own. The 'real' Florida the residents like to call it. The Panhandle has its own problems with over-building but a large military (mostly naval) presence has kept many prime waterfront lands in government hands, making for far more unspoiled coastline than other parts of the state.

Pensacola, 60 miles (96.6 kilometres) east of Mobile on I-10, is another Gulf Coast city with colonial roots similar to Mobile and New Orleans. While there are some museums and restored houses, the two main places of interest for the passing traveller are Pensacola Beach and the **National Museum of Naval Aviation** (1-800 327 5002/website: www.naval-air.org).

The Navy Museum, as most locals call it, is a well-designed, airy building that will interest even non-militarists. Restored aircraft and vintage navy memorabilia are on display and a new addition is an IMAX cinema that practically puts viewers in the cockpit of an F-18 fighter jet. The museum is on the grounds of the Pensacola Naval Air Station: take exit 2 off I-10, or follow Navy Boulevard south, which leads to the NAS.

Pensacola Beach is actually separate from the city; it's on **Santa Rosa Island**, the barrier island in Pensacola Bay. From the city, take US 98 east across the three-mile (five-kilometre) Pensacola Bay Bridge to the neighbouring community of Gulf Breeze, then follow signs marked 'Beaches' to the toll bridge to the island. The beach has plenty of public access and even some traces of its old beach-comber personality with a handful of family-owned, one-storey motels and non-theme bars. There's plenty of parking for day-trippers and good facilities such as bathrooms and showers.

Santa Rosa Island also has two other beaches worth exploring. **Navarre**, a less crowded but beautiful beach, is on the east end of the island, while **Fort Pickens** (1-800 365 2267), a National Seashore Park, is at the western tip. Fort Pickens has drive-up camping spots and the old fort is famous for being the prison of Geronimo, the American Indian guerrilla leader. The jetties off Fort Pickens are a prime spot for Gulf Coast snorkelling.

From Santa Rosa Island to Panama City, the coast is an almost unbroken development of condos, villas, resorts and strip malls. Two places stand out in the frenzy for tourist dollars. The village of **Grayton Beach**, 50 miles (80.4 kilometres) south of Pensacola off Alternate US 98 (also called Florida Road 30-A), is the Gulf Coast answer to Brigadoon. This sleepy little town of modest cottages, beach houses and shacks is a throwback to the 1950s that has somehow managed to opt out of the development maw. While a few gaudy villas have begun to rise at the edge of the beach, the town is firmly committed to the past.

Pensacola Beach – *the 'real' Florida.*

White silver sands

Geologists and holidaymakers agree: America's best beaches are on the Gulf of Mexico. The University of Maryland's Laboratory for Coastal Research annually rates US beaches – and Florida's **Grayton Beach** (*pictured*) is usually number one. **Perdido Key**, in Alabama, is another Gulf Coast beach that always ranks highly.

The researchers use more than 40 criteria to make their decision, including physical facts such as water temperature, water quality, currents, wave size, softness of sand, width of beach and cultural considerations such as views, crime and crowd levels. The Top 10 list is usually split between Hawaii and Florida. California, with its rocky coast, damp sand and freezing water is notably absent – except on the 'worst beaches' list.

The gorgeous beaches of the Gulf Coast are the result of millions of years of earth works. The beautiful white sands started off aeons ago as quartz rocks in the Appalachian Mountains. Post-Ice Age flooding moved bits of quartz through the rivers (this took thousands of years) and into what is now the Gulf of Mexico. As the current-day coastline began to form about 5,000 years ago, the quartz chips, now ground down to shining bits of blindingly white sand, were deposited along the shoreline. The sand is so fine that it actually squeaks when it's walked on.

*Ready for those tourist dollars: **Fort Walton**, between Santa Rosa Island and Panama City.*

Just south of Grayton Beach, also on 30-A, is the most influential beach town in America, **Seaside**. Begun in the 1980s as a revolt against high-rise condoism, Seaside is a planned community that keeps a firm grip on design, mandating a nineteenth-century look. Approaching the thickets of pastel neo-Victorian houses and picket fences is like driving into a Walt Disney movie. Innovative in its beginnings, Seaside now has a rather precious feel about it. Yet the shops, cafés and services are very good and it's an easy place to be.

Tourist information on Grayton Beach and Seaside is available through the **South Walton Tourist Development Council** (1-800 822 6877/website: www.beachesofsouthwalton.com).

Where to stay

At Pensacola Beach, the **Best Western** motel (16 Via De Luna; 1-800 934 3301) on the beach side, has its own pools, comfortable rooms and good prices. Rooms cost $59-$79 in winter, $119-$139 in summer. **Tiki House** (17 Via De Luna; 1-850 934 4447) is an old-fashioned, one-level motel where a double room costs $45-$65 a night. Some rooms on the less desirable north side, facing Santa Rosa Sound, have kitchenettes. For condo and beach house rentals, contact **Gulf Coast Accommodations** (1-800 239 4334/website: www.juxta/com/juxta/beachside) or **Tristan Realty** (1-800 445 9931).

There are no hotels or motels at Grayton Beach, but rentals are available through **Rivard Realty** (1-800 423 3215/website: www.rivardnet.com). A couple of miles down 30-A, **Grayton Beach State Park** (1-850 231 4210/website: www.dep.state.fl.us/parks) offers good daytime facilities, a campground and several miles of perfect, white sand beaches and beautiful blue-green Gulf waters. You can rent cottages in Seaside through a central agency; phone 1-850 231 4224 for details.

Where to eat

Boy on a Dolphin (400 Pensacola Beach Boulevard; 1-850 932 7954) offers seafood with a Greek emphasis and is a longstanding favourite among Pensacola citizens. There's also **Flounder's** (800 Quietwater Beach Road, Pensacola Beach; 1-850 932 2003), which has good seafood, an attractive outdoor beach bar and a dancefloor.

Since 1949, hearty Southern meals have been served at **Hopkins Boarding House** in Pensacola (900 North Spring Street; 1-850 438 3979) a rambling old house near downtown. It's an unpretentious place and the food is marvellous.

Getting there

By car
If you're coming from Mobile, Pensacola is 60 miles (96.6km) east on I-10. If you're travelling from Gulf Shores, you can take Hwy 59 and US 98 or go along the coast on smaller roads.

By bus
Greyhound runs several buses a day. The journey takes just over 5 hours and a round trip costs $56.

Directory

Directory

For information on abbreviations used in this guide, *see page vi* **About the Guide**.

If you're phoning from outside New Orleans but within the US, dial 1 + area code 504 before the numbers listed in this guide, unless otherwise stated. All 1 800 numbers can be called free of charge, although many hotels add a surcharge for use of their phones, whatever number you call.

Getting Around

Without a doubt, New Orleans is a walking city. But to get from one section of town to another can be daunting because of the distance. For example, from Uptown to the edge of the French Quarter is over 30 city blocks. As a visitor, your best bets for moving from one place to another are bus, streetcar or taxi. Although finding a car parking space is fairly easy – except in the Central Business District (CBD) and the French Quarter – there are countless rules about parking in New Orleans, and the city makes a tidy profit from issuing tickets and impounding cars.

For bus schedule information, phone the Regional Transit Authority's RideLine on **248 3900**. Tell the person who answers the phone where you want to pick up a bus and where you want to go. Public transport – generally used only by those who don't have a car – is fairly dependable, although if there is a breakdown you might have to wait anywhere from 30 to 60 minutes for a bus, even on a heavily used route. After all, New Orleans is a provincial city that isn't in a hurry to get anywhere.

The taxi system is also quite good. In the CBD, along Canal Street, lines of waiting cabs can be found in front of the major hotels. As a rule, the taxi operators are friendly and helpful: the city even sent most of them to a special school to make sure they understood the concept of good customer service recently.

Cycling around New Orleans is quite possible and easier than in many cities because of the flatness of the landscape. The only time you'll need those powerful lower gears will be to traverse the overpasses to get across the I-10 expressway. But beware: not only do many local cyclists complain loudly of the attitude of local drivers toward the rules of the road, but New Orleans is seventh highest in the nation for bicycle traffic fatalities. The huge potholes to be found everywhere don't help, either. Maps are available with suggested bike routes, though these routes are designed more for recreational biking than for destination-bound riding.

To & from the airport

You have three transport options after arriving at the airport (assuming you are not renting a car): the airport shuttle, a bus and taxis. All three will deliver you to the city – but if you want to go beyond downtown to Mid City or Uptown, you should spend the extra money and take a cab.

By bus

Louisiana Transit (737 9611) provides a bus that runs from the airport to the CBD, two blocks away from the French Quarter. You'll need the exact fare ($1.50) and only carry-on luggage is allowed. Buses run to and from the airport from 6am-midnight daily. From 6-9am and 3-6pm, a bus leaves the airport every 10-15 minutes; otherwise they leave every 20 minutes.

The bus will take you to Tulane Avenue and Elk Place, which is about four blocks from the heart of the CBD and just above the French Quarter, until 6.30pm. After 6.30pm, it will stop at Carrollton and Tulane Avenues, about 15 blocks from Tulane and Elk, where you can catch an RTA bus (39 Tulane-CBD).

You can catch the bus back to the airport from Tulane and Elk from 6am-6.30pm. From 6.30pm-midnight, the bus picks up at Carrollton and Tulane. There is no service to or from the airport between midnight and 6am.

By shuttle

The airport provides an excellent **shuttle service** (465 9780), which costs $10 (cash or credit card) per person one-way to most downtown hotels. The service is available as soon as planes arrive at the airport, and runs until the last plane has arrived. Shuttles depart from the airport every ten minutes. Most luggage items can be put on the shuttle but be prepared for an extra charge if you have oversized luggage or numerous items.

It you want the shuttle to collect you from your hotel and take you to the airport, phone 522 3500 the day before you want to be picked up and make a reservation.

By taxi or limousine

There is always a long queue of taxis at the airport waiting to whisk you into the city. Expect to pay $21 from the airport to almost anywhere in New Orleans for up to two passengers. For three or more passengers, the cost is $8 per person. Taxis are probably the quickest and most efficient way of getting to and from the airport – though not the cheapest.

New Orleans
International Airport
Information 464 0831

For domestic and other international airlines, consult the *Yellow Pages*.

AirTran
1-800 825 8538
American Airlines
1-800 433 7300
British Airways
1-000 247 9297
Continental Airlines
1-800 523 3273
Delta Air Lines
1-800 221 1212
Northwest Airlines
Domestic 1-800 225 2525
International 1-800 447 4747
Southwest Airlines
1-800 435 9792
Trans World Airlines (TWA)
Domestic 1-800 221 2000
International 1-800 892 4141
USAirways (USAir)
1-800 428 4322
United Airlines
1-800 241 6522

Public transport

The public transport system in New Orleans is run by the **RTA** (Regional Transit Authority). RTA operates all the Orleans Parish buses and streetcars, including the famous St Charles Streetcar, the longest continuously operating rail car line in the nation. The fare for all lines, except express buses and the Riverside Streetcar, is $1, plus 10¢ for a transfer. Transfers must be purchased when you board the bus and are not good on the same bus route from which they are purchased. The fare for express buses and the Riverfront Streetcars (known as the Red Ladies) is $1.25.

Travel passes

Known as VisiTour Passes, these come in two denominations: one-day ($4) and three-day ($8). Good for full fares on any RTA vehicle, they are an excellent bargain if you plan on being out and about most of the day. Available from most hotel concierges and tourist information booths.

Bus stops

The bus will stop only at the bus stop – not a block before or a block after. Some stops are sheltered from the weather, some are not.

Taxis & limos

Taxis are a great way to get around New Orleans if you don't have a car. They are, without a doubt, the safest way to travel late at night.

If you are downtown during the day you won't have a problem finding one. You can flag down a taxi on Decatur Street, other parts of the Quarter and on Canal near the large hotels; otherwise, your best bet is to find a big hotel and go to the first taxi in line outside. If you are in Uptown,

Mid City or Carrollton, just call the local number and one will arrive shortly. Driving a cab in New Orleans is a pretty good way to make a living, so there isn't any shortage of available hires. If you are at a bar, restaurant or store, ask the staff to call one for you.

Regular meter fares begin at $1.70 and increase 20¢ every one-fifth of a mile or 40 seconds. There is an additional charge for each extra passenger. A tip of $1 for a normal ride is the norm. If you have packages, tip a dollar more. In the unlikely event that you have any complaints about a cab, driver or the service provided, phone the **Taxicab Bureau** on 565 6272.

Local taxicab companies include: **United Cabs** (522 9771), **White Fleet** (948 6605) and **Checker-Yellow Cabs** (943 2411).

If you have the money, limo services include **New Orleans Limousine Service** (529 5226), **Blue Moon Limousine** (525 6281) and **Orleans Limousines** (288 1111).

Driving

Driving a car in New Orleans can be a thrill, especially if you are from a place that has plenty of driving rules that are obeyed and enforced. In New Orleans few local drivers pay heed to traffic lights. Always look both ways before pulling into an intersection – even if your light is green. There will almost always be some fool who will blast through their red light at the last second.

Also, if you park your car on any street near downtown or the French Quarter, look carefully for signs telling you when and where you can park. The signs are not always easy to find, but the parking authorities know where they are and will tow your car away in a heartbeat. Never waste your time or energy arguing with a meter maid. They are made of stone and will not pay attention to you. Meekly accept your fine and move on.

Car rental

You will need a valid driver's licence and a major credit card (American Express, Discover, MasterCard, Visa) to rent a car in New Orleans. Since the car rental business is very competitive, it's worth phoning two or more agencies to compare prices.

National rental companies include **Avis** (1-800 331 1212), **Budget** (467 2277), **Enterprise** (1-800 736 8222), **Hertz** (1-800 654 3131) and **National** (1-800 227 7368).

American Automobile Association (AAA)

3345 N Causeway Boulevard, at 14th Street, Metairie (838 7500). **Open** 8.30am-7pm Mon, Wed; 8.30am-5.15pm Tue, Thur, Fri.

The AAA has piles of maps and a treasure trove of travel tips – all free to members, including those belonging to affiliated clubs such as the British AA. You can also contact the local AAA chapter – or any other branch – by phoning 1-800 596 2228 and choosing from the automated menu.

Breakdown services

AAA Emergency Road Service

1-800 222 4357. **Open** 24 hours daily.
Members including members of affiliated clubs such as the British AA – receive free towing and roadside service.

The Auto Clinic

Recorded information 840 7710. Offers a free tow and delivery service included in the price of repairs.

Doody & Hank's

522 5391/524 0118. **Open** 7.30am-5.30pm Mon-Fri.
Located in the CBD, Doody & Hank's provide road service in that and surrounding areas.

Expert Auto Service

895 4345. **Open** 9am-5pm Mon-Fri. Located Uptown.

Parking

Allright Parking

522 9434.
This national company operates about 30 parking lots and garages around the city. Rates range from $3.50 to $10 for 12 hours.

Downtown Parking Services

529 5708.
Event parking for small and large vehicles. Valet services are available.

Louisiana Superdome

Sugar Bowl Drive, at Poydras Street (587 3805). **Map 6 B2**
There are four parking garages at the Superdome where you pay a flat rate of $5 from 6am-2pm, then an hourly rate until 9pm. Daily, weekly and monthly rates are also available.

Bicycle rental

See page 219 **Sport & Fitness.**

Directory A-Z

Business

The convention industry is one of the city's primary sources of revenue. For information on conventions, contact the **New Orleans Metropolitan Convention & Visitors Bureau** (*see page 264* **Tourist information**).

Ernest N Morial Convention Center

900 Convention Center Boulevard, at Julia Street (582 3027). Bus 3 Vieux Carré, 10 Tchoupitoulas. **Not open to the public.** **Map 6 C2**
With its recent expansion, the centre is now the fourth largest in the US and local planners are hoping it will provide enough space to take care of the 1.5-2 million conventioneers who pour into the city every year for upwards of 2,000 conventions and meetings.

Courier services

Local and national messenger and delivery services include:

A Plus Courier Service 467 1080. Provides 24-hour 'hot shot' service.
Federal Express 1-800 463 3339. Phone for opening hours and pick-up places.
United Cab 522 9771. A taxi company with desk-to-desk delivery 24 hours a day.
UPS 1-800-742-5877. Phone for the opening hours and pick-up places of this national service.
US Postal Service 1-800 222 1811. Priority mail service to 27 countries.

Office services

Kinko's

Downtown: *762 St Charles Avenue, at Julia Street (581 2541). St Charles Streetcar.* **Open** 24 hours daily. **Map 6 B2**
Uptown: *1140 S Carollton Avenue, at Oak Street (861 8016). St Charles Streetcar.* **Open** 24 hours daily. **Map 4 B7**
Services include on-site use of computers, Internet access, typesetting, printing, photocopying and faxing. Check the phone directory for the location of other branches.
Website: www.kinkos.com

Mail Pack & Ship

6003 Bullard Avenue, near David Street, Metairie (245 7885). **Open** 9am-6.30pm Mon-Fri; 9.30am-4pm Sat.
FedEx, UPS and US Postal Services are available.

Consulates

All embassies are located in Washington, DC. There is an Honorary Consulate for Great Britain in New Orleans (524 4180); the nearest consular offices for all other English-speaking countries are in Washington. Phone directory assistance on 1-202 555 1212 for their location and phone numbers.

Consumer information

Better Business Bureau

24-hour information line 581 6222.
The BBB has information on almost every company in the city. If you

Business facts

With the second largest port in the world in size and tonnage after Amsterdam, New Orleans has always been a natural at business. Its strategic location – poised on the edge of the Gulf of Mexico and at the mouth of the Mississippi River – is also conducive to a relationship with the petrochemical industry.

But, with typical New Orleans quirkiness, nothing is ever completely as it should be, and these days the city is no world business hub. In fact, at times in the past ten years, the city's downtown has felt like a ghost town. Businesses aren't likely to locate their headquarters in cities with a weak economy, bad infrastructure, poor schools and high crime rates – and New Orleans has them all. The volatile weather doesn't help, either.

The single biggest hurdle between the city and corporate success is overwhelming poverty. The average annual household income in Lousiana is a mere $15,000 and the state consistently ranks 49th in the country in terms of wealth (only Mississippi is poorer). In New Orleans itself, more than 40 per cent of the residents are below the official poverty line.

Never mind that both the poverty and the pollution in the area could be blamed, in part, on industry, which treats the state as a dumping ground. The huge chemical plants that dot the Louisiana landscape have left virtually every waterway tainted, yet none of the companies operating these plants locates headquarters in the area, a situation that economists say keeps the money flowing out of the state, while saddling it with a heavy environmental burden.

There have been better times, of course. In the heady oil boom days of the 1970s and 1980s, the city did see a huge growth of local business, as oil money flowed through the region like the muddy water down the Mississippi. Most of the downtown skyscrapers were built then – among them the Texaco building on Camp Street, One

Shell Square on Poydras Street and a handful of others. But when the price of oil fell hard and long in the late 1980s, so did the city's downtown.

Those shining new buildings emptied fast as businesses closed in droves, driven out of work by the hard times. It has been more than a decade since the oil bust and the city has not yet recovered. Stand in the middle of the CBD and look around you – nearly half of those buildings are empty.

Even as the oil market has improved in recent years, it has not brought much to New Orleans. Major oil companies have centralised their regional operations in nearby Houston. So, even as the economy is improving, New Orleans businesses have been shutting down. One of the most recent losses, Louisiana Land & Exploration Co, the largest New Orleans-based oil company, was sold in 1997 to a Houston-based competitor and is closing its local offices.

The city's saving grace, in addition to the port, is tourism. Thank God for the French Quarter, locals say. Of the city's annual ten million visitors, around eight million are tourists, bringing in money the city brags is 'clean', meaning it does not damage the environment like the pollution-spouting petrochemical facilities upriver. The convention industry is also on the rise, with up to two million people attending conventions in New Orleans each year.

A full half dozen of those empty downtown office buildings are in the early stages of conversion to hotels, as dozens of hotel chains vie for the opportunity to open largely upscale structures in the area.

The service industry is the city's biggest employer these days, with tens of thousands of New Orleanians working in hotels, restaurants and bars. The downside of that, though, is that wages in the service industry are notoriously low. Tourism may be the city's goldmine, but few New Orleanians reap the profits.

have a complaint about a product or service in New Orleans, give the BBB a call and it will make a report. If you want to know if a complaint has already been registered against a company, the BBB will tell you.

Consumer Product Safety Commission

1-800 638 2772.

Louisiana Attorney General's Office of Consumer Protection

1-800 351 4889.
Call the LA Attorney General's Office to make a complaint regarding consumer law enforcement or any other agency.

Disabled access & information

New Orleans is a very lax place when it comes to the disabled. Many of the federally mandated accessibility laws seem to have been ignored and

Dodging bullets

Or, surviving your stay in the Big Easy.

Once the home of pirates and still an infamously favourite spot for those on the run from the law, New Orleans's darker side is nothing new. The city's nicknames – the Big Easy and Fat City – refer as much to the takings to be had from the unaware as to the city's status as a party town.

It could be said the city's corrupt heritage started at the very beginning with one of its founders, John Law, the Scottish entrepreneur who swindled so much money from the French to bankroll the settling of New Orleans that he almost bankrupted that nation. He also convinced thousands of Europeans to buy expensive pieces of worthless swamp and many moved to the area only to see their dreams of utopia shattered by the mosquito-infested reality.

Ever since then, part of the attraction of New Orleans has been its air of danger. Today the city is home to hustlers all talking a cool game like Mississippi riverboat gamblers a century before them. They will rap, sing, recite poetry and practise street-corner voodoo — all on Bourbon Street at 2am. Many of them are legitimate street performers, but others will remove your watch from your arm while they shake your hand and they'll do it so smoothly you'll still be talking about how nice they were when you realise it's gone.

The city's crime rate has always been relatively high, with the local police force well known for its corruption and lackadaisical attitude toward crime. But in the early 1990s, the crime level reached heights that were quite shocking even to cynical locals. Tourists were often singled out by criminals who found they could be counted on to be carrying large quantities of cash. In 1992-4 New Orleans' per capita homicide rate eclipsed that of every other city in the US, and it earned the dubious distinction of being rated the murder capital of the country – murders averaged one a day.

But things have improved. A new city administration brought in tougher rules and a new police chief. In addition, a crackdown by federal authorities on the New Orleans Police Department resulted in a massive wave of firings of officers considered incompetent.

As a result, the crime rate is down and police presence, particularly in the Quarter, is up. But that does not mean travellers should let their guard down. This is still a big American city, with all the inherent problems that brings.

When wandering the city, pay attention to where you are walking. If you notice things looking seedy, do not hesitate to turn on your heel and go the other way. Lingering on a dodgy corner looking at a map is not a wise move if you want to keep your travellers' cheques on your person.

Should you be so unlucky as to be mugged, be aware that guns are a dime a dozen in New Orleans and you cannot fight a bullet. Promptly give the criminal your cash and travellers' cheques, plus any jewellery and/or clothing that catches your hold-up person's fancy. At the first opportunity, **call the police by dialling 911** from any pay phone.

Carry only the amount of money that you expect to use while you're out. Use credit cards as much as possible and consider separating your money and credit cards into a variety of pockets, bags or even socks. Odds are that emptying one pocket will be enough for the thief. You could even be left with enough money to go out later and have a drink to steady your nerves. And you'll have one hell of a story to tell the bartender.

---

the historic nature of most buildings precludes making structural changes (adding elevators, constructing entrance ramps and so on). More restaurants and hotels are becoming 'friendly' to people with disabilities, but, again, many are in old buildings. Always phone your destination first to check. When finding a hotel room, the best solution for anyone with impaired mobility

is a new hotel, one that has been designed with a barrier-free mindset.

Getting around the city is a little easier. All regional city buses on fixed routes are equipped with lifts, can 'kneel' to make access easier and have handgrips and spaces designed for wheelchair users. RTA also provides people who are mobility-impaired with a special pick-up bus service

Paratransit (827 7433) – but you must book two weeks in advance and provide medical certification of your condition to use it. Availability of the Paratransit system is best during non-rush hours (10am-3pm weekdays).

For full details of the Paratransit system, as well as information concerning just about any aspect of navigating New Orleans if you have a disability, contact **Citizens With Disabilities**.

Citizens With Disabilities
Katherine Hoover, Disability Affairs Specialist, 1221 Elmwood Park Boulevard, suite 306, Harahan, LA 70123 (736 6086/fax 731 4520/ access3@communique.net).
Make sure you put 'Citizens With Disabilities' in the subject line of your e-mail.

Deaf Action Center
523 3755. **Open** 8am-4.40pm Mon-Fri.
Information on interpretation and local resources. Catholic Charities will pick up the phone and then connect you to the Deaf Action Center – there is no direct line.

National Federation of the Blind of Louisiana
1-800 234 4166. **Open** 8am-5pm Mon-Fri.
The Federation can provide resource information such as a guide to restaurants with Braille menus.

WRBH (88.3 FM)
899 1144.
This radio station reads the daily newspaper for the blind and print handicapped (7am-10am, 6.30-8pm). On Saturdays (9.30-11am), the *Times-Picayune*'s entertainment guide, 'Lagniappe', is read.

Electricity

Rather than the 220-240V, 50-cycle AC used in Europe, the United States uses a 110-120V, 60-cycle AC voltage. Except for dual-voltage, flat-pin plug shavers, you will need to run any small appliances you bring with you via an adaptor, available at airport shops, pharmacies and department stores.

Bear in mind that most US videos and TVs use a different frequency from those in Europe: you will not be able to play back camcorder footage during your trip. However, you can buy and use blank tapes.

E-mail & websites

The major problem in checking your e-mail is that you will need a computer with access to the Internet to do it. If you don't

want to risk carrying your laptop around, the best method is to log on to the Internet from a computer in a local library or cybercafé and use one of the free e-mail services on the World Wide Web.

Before you leave, set up a free e-mail account at **Yahoo** (mail.yahoo.com), **MailCity** (www.mailcity.com) or **Hotmail** (www.hotmail.com). In fact, it might be a good idea to set up an account at all three just in case one is down when you log on. All instructions for creating an e-mail account are at the WWW sites.

Once you are in New Orleans, phone the information desk at the **New Orleans Public Library** (596 2570) and ask which branch is closest to you. Call the branch and make sure its computer is up and running. Stop by, log on and check your account. The same applies to the **cybercafés** listed below. Of course, they will charge you a small sum for the amount of time you are online, but they do offer drinks and things to eat, which the libraries do not.

See chapter **Accommodation** for hotels that offer modem or dataport facilities (*listed under* **Room services**) if you want to check mail via your laptop.

You could also try the **Kinko's** branch at 762 St Charles Avenue (*see page 254*), which has nine workstations. Expect to pay 17¢ per minute. Kinko's is hooked up to America Online (AOL), so if you already have an AOL e-mail account, you can check it there.

Cybercafés

New Orleans is a low-tech city. The focus on entertainment and tourism and the high poverty rate have prevented much of the populace from becoming active netizens. However,

whether the Big Easy likes it or not, technology, specifically the Internet, is making inroads. Cybercafés are springing up, and beginning to enjoy community attention.

There are three cybercafés that appear to have the customer traffic required for continued existence.

CyberCafe@the CAC
900 Camp Street, at Howard Street (523 0990). **St** Charles Streetcar. **Open** 7am-8pm Mon, Tue, Sun; 7am-11pm Wed-Sat. **Map 6 B/C2**
The Contemporary Arts Center (CAC) houses a new cybercafé that provides free Internet access from five computer kiosks with Windows-based computers adorned with mini-speakers. There's a full coffee bar selling pastries and light lunches, a full liquor bar (this is New Orleans), and, depending on the day you visit, a 2-for-1 cocktail happy hour. You can also hear poetry read by local writers, be instructed in the art of buying a new computer or pick up tips on building a website. With free parking for patrons, this is the number one choice for visitors seeking to check their e-mail.
Website: www.cacno.org

Java Bit
225 Baronne Street, at Common Street (527 5282). St Charles Streetcar/bus 3 Vieux Carré. **Open** 8am-5pm Mon-Fri. **Map 6 B1**
Located in the heart of the CBD, Java Bit hosts state-of-the-art, super-cool computer kiosks replete with cup holders, 20in (50.8cm) monitors and shape-conforming chairs. Full video conferencing is available, thanks to the T3 connection provided by the ISP (baileylink.net) on the other side of a glass partition and every high-tech game you can think of is ready to go. Frankly, the whole place looks out of place in laid-back New Orleans. The rates are $7.50 per hour, $60 for ten hours, $250 for 50 hours (at which point a T-shirt and mug are thrown in for long-service). There is a full coffee bar with pastries and light lunches are also available.
Website: www.javabit.com

Realm of Delirium
941 Decatur Street, at St Philip Street (586 8989). Bus 3 Vieux Carré, 55 Elysian Fields, 81 Almonaster, 82 Desire. **Open** 10am-midnight Mon-Thur, Sun; 10am-2am Fri, Sat. **Map 7 C3**
This cybercafé is probably the most atmospheric of the lot. It's located in the upstairs loft of Kaldi's coffeeshop and coffee museum in the heart of the French Quarter. The ROD sports four

Emergencies

Ambulance, Fire Brigade or Police
911 (toll-free from any phone booth).

BellSouth (telephone)
Automated hotline 557 7777/557 6500.

Entergy Corporation (gas & electricity)
Information hotline 1-800 368 3749.

Poison Control Center
Emergencies 1-800 256 9822.

Sewerage & Water Board of New Orleans
Emergency service 529 2837.

---

workstations, a red velveteen bordello-style couch and a very Big Easy style. You can use the machines for a full hour for $7.63. For those who try their damnedest to look dangerous, this is without a doubt the hip place to log on and geek with. Downstairs, Kaldi's can supply you with every imaginable caffeine concoction.
Website: www.RealmofDelirium.com

New Orleans online

Since New Orleans is not a hi-tech city the Internet is still not used by a lot of businesses and services. Here is a selection of sites providing information about the city.
See also page 182 **Media**.

The Ditka Altar
www.slonet.org/~bbanducc/ditka.html
A tribute to the New Orleans Saints and their coach, 'Iron' Mike Ditka.

Historic New Orleans Collection
www.hnoc.org/
Information about the history and culture of New Orleans, including exhibitions, lectures, publications and historic buildings.

Love New Orleans
www.loveneworleans.com/
Upcoming events in the city. Sign up for a weekly e-mail newsletter and weather reports for New Orleans and the surrounding area.

Mayor Marc H Morial
www.neworleans.com/government/morial.html
The Mayor's picture and a welcome message.

New Orleans Bicycle Club
www.gnofn.org/~nobc/

Dedicated to the promotion of bicycling in New Orleans.

New Orleans City Council
www.nocitycouncil.com/
Check on the antics of local politicos.

New Orleans Film & Video Festival
www.neworleansfilmfest.com/
This festival is highly regarded by film buffs. View a listing of the films that will be shown at this year's event.

New Orleans Metropolitan Convention & Visitors Bureau
www.neworleanscvb.com

New Orleans Public Library
www.gnofn.org/~nopl/

New Orleans Weather
www.neworleans.com/weather.html
Get a four-day forecast.

New Orleans Zephyrs
www.zephyrsbaseball.com/
Official site of New Orleans's baseball team.

NOLA Live – New Orleans Home Page
www.nolalive.com/
Headlines from the *Times-Picayune*.

Tennessee Williams/ New Orleans Literary Festival
www.gnofn.org/~twfest/
Tenn would be proud of this site. A schedule of the events, including plays, is provided.

University of New Orleans
www.uno.edu/Welcome.shtml
A nicely built site introducing various student projects.

Ursuline Academy
www.gnofn.org/~ursuline/
The first school for girls in the United States.

Vampire Sightings
www.nolalive.com/annerice/vsight.html
The Unoffical Anne Rice Worship Page.

WWOZ radio station
www.wwoz.org
The sounds of New Orleans.

Health & medical
Clinics

In New Orleans, the **Charity Hospital** system provides access to medical care in almost every imaginable area. Charity's Trauma Care Unit is rated the best in the country. In the unlikely and unlucky event that you are on the receiving end of a gunshot, Charity Hospital's Emergency Room is the place you want to wind up.

You will have to pay for emergency treatment. If you are a foreign national, contact the emergency number on your travel insurance before seeking treatment if you can, and you will be directed to a hospital that will deal directly with your insurance company.

For referral to a doctor, contact the **Tulane University Professional/Physicians Referral Group** (588 5800).

Charity Hospital Campus
1532 Tulane Avenue, at Lasalle Street (568 3723). Bus 39 Tulane. **Open** *Emergency Room 24 hours daily.* **Map 6 B1**

Children's Hospital
200 Henry Clay Avenue, at Tchoupitoulas Street (899 9511). Bus 10 Tchoupitoulas. **Open** *Clinic 8.30am-4.30pm Mon-Fri; Emergency Room 24 hours daily.* **Map 4 B10**

Clinics

Acupuncture Clinic
4212 Teuton Street, off Houma Boulevard, Metairie (288 1303). Bus E5 Causeway. **Open** 8am-3pm Mon, Wed, Fri.

Daughters of Charity Health Center
3900 S Carrollton Avenue, at Palmetto Street (482 0084).
Bus 90 Carrollton. **Open** 8am-6.30pm Mon-Fri; 10am-2pm Sat.
Map 4 C6
Care for the entire family is provided, including a pharmacy and counselling services. A sliding fee scale is operated.

Dentists

NO Dental Association
834 6449. **Open** 9am-5pm Mon-Fri.
The place to call for referrals to a dentist; outside office hours, a recorded message will direct you to an emergency number.

Pharmacies (24-hour)

For pharmacies, including ones open 24 hours daily, *see page 162* **Shops & Services**.

Helplines & agencies
AIDS/HIV

NO/AIDS Task Force
945 4000. **Open** 8.30am-5pm Mon-Fri.
Outside office hours, you can leave a message on an answering machine.

AIDS/HIV Hotline
944 2437. **Open** noon-8pm daily.

AIDS/HIV Teen Hotline
944 2437. **Open** noon-4pm Sat.
Phones are staffed by teenagers at this service aimed at teenagers with questions about AIDS and the HIV virus.

Alcohol/drug abuse

Alcoholics Anonymous Central Ofice
779 1178. **Open** 9am-4.45pm Mon-Fri.
Outside office hours, an answering service will take your number and someone will call you back.

Narcotics Anonymous
899 6262. **Open** 24 hours daily.
Call for a recorded list of meeting times and locations.

Child abuse

Child Protection Hot Line
483 4911. **Open** 24 hours daily.

Psychiatric emergency services

DePaul-Tulane Behavioral Health Center
899 8282. **Open** 24 hours daily.
This excellent psychiatric hospital provides outpatient and evening treatment. A sliding scale is operated for fees.

Rape

Rape Crisis Line
483 8888. **Open** 24 hours daily.

Suicide

Suicide Prevention
523 2673. **Open** 24 hours daily.

Immigration & Customs

Few international flights arrive in New Orleans: you will usually have to transfer to a domestic flight at another US city, and will go through Immigration and Customs there. This means that you can't check your baggage straight through: you will have to reclaim it at the transfer airport, take it through Customs and then check it in again.

The airlines try to make this a painless process by having a transfer check-in desk just outside Customs at most major transfer airports; however, you will have to make your own way to the domestic departures terminal. Connection times do take account of this and the fact that

Hurricane watch

A hurricane coming out of the Gulf of Mexico is a serious business. The storm can cause flooding and considerable material damage, although New Orleans is far enough inland to escape the very worst, usually. The hurricane season lasts from May to November, with most activity occurring between August and October.

A Scale 1 hurricane involves sustained winds of 74-95mph, while a Scale 5 hurricane (the severest and fortunately very rare) yields winds of over 155mph.

There are two distinct warning stages. If you hear a **Hurricane Watch** (issued when a hurricane *may* strike within the next 36-48 hours), fill your car tank with gas, secure loose items and, if flooding threatens, leave the area if you can. If a **Hurricane Warning** is issued (the storm is expected to strike within 24

hours), monitor a TV or radio for information and stay indoors.

You will have three options if a hurricane hits the city during your visit.

● Stay where you are. If you are in a large hotel, you will be directed to a place of safety by the staff and management.
● Follow the evacuation signs out of town. These signs are located on all the roads designated as major evacuation routes. Follow the directions of state police and local law enforcement officals manning the routes. Listen to them – they know what they are doing.
● Listen to the radio or TV for directions to the nearest shelter. Go immediately to the shelter.

American Red Cross
586 8191. **Open** 24 hours daily.
Provides information on disaster preparedness.

Weather information
Recorded information 828 4000. **Open** 24 hours daily.

you may have to queue at Immigration, but we recommend that you go through the transfer process and check in for your New Orleans flight before you take any time to relax.

Standard immigration regulations apply to all visitors. Be prepared to wait when you arrive at Immigration for up to an hour. During your flight, you will be handed an immigration form and a customs declaration form to be presented when you land at the airport.

Expect to explain the nature of your visit (business and/or pleasure). If you don't have a return ticket and are planning a long visit, you will be questioned closely.

Usually, you will be granted an entry permit to cover the length of your stay. For information on visas, *see page 264.*

US Customs allows visitors to bring in $100 worth of gifts ($400 for returning Americans) duty free, 200 cigarettes or 50 cigars and one litre of spirits (liquor). No plants, fruit, meat or fresh produce can be taken through Customs. For more detailed information, contact your nearest US embassy or consulate.

UK Customs & Excise allows returning travellers to bring in £145 worth of gifts and goods and an unlimited amount of money, as long as you can prove it's yours.

Insurance

It's advisable to take out comprehensive insurance cover before arriving in the United States: it's almost impossible to arrange once you are there. Make sure that you have adequate health cover since medical expenses can be high. *See page 258* **Health & medical** for a list of New Orleans hospitals and emergency rooms.

Libraries

New Orleans Public Library (main library)
219 Loyola Avenue, at Tulane Avenue (596 2570). Bus 39 Tulane. **Open** 11am-6pm Mon-Thur; 11am-5pm Sat. **Map 6 B1**

Broad Library
4300 S Broad Street, at Fontainebleau Street (596 2675). Bus 21 Fontainebleau. **Open** 11am-8pm Mon, Wed; 11am-6pm Tue, Thur; 11am-5pm Sat; 1-5pm Sun. **Map 4 C7**

Gentilly Library
3000 Foy Street, at Gentilly Boulevard, Gentilly (596 2644). Bus 51 St Bernard/Lake Terrace. **Open** 11am-8pm Mon, Wed; 11am-6pm Tue, Thur; 11am-5pm Sat.

Latter Memorial Library
5120 St Charles Avenue, at Soniat Street (596 2625). St Charles Streetcar. **Open** 11am-6pm Mon-Thur; 11am-5pm Sat. **Map 4 C9**

Nix Library
1401 S Carrollton Avenue, at Willow Street (596 2630). St Charles Streetcar. **Open** 11am-6pm Mon-Thur; 11am-5pm Sat. **Map 4 B7**

Money

The US dollar ($) equals 100 cents (¢). Coins range from copper pennies (1¢) to silver nickels (5¢), dimes (10¢), quarters (25¢) and half dollars (50¢). Coins worth $1 come in two sizes – very large and very small – but are now rare since the US public decided the large ones weighed too much to ride comfortably in the pocket and no vending machines would accept them; and the small ones (Susan B Anthonys) looked and weighed too much like quarters. However, the large and small $1 coins are still in circulation, so check your change every so often.

Paper money (bills) is confusingly all the same size and colour. It comes in denom-inations of $1, $5, $10, $20, $50 and $100. The design of the $100 bill was recently altered by the US Treasury. Many of the old $100 bills are still in circulation and are still good,

so don't be surprised if you have two $100 bills that look radically different. The new $100 bills feature a picture of Ben Franklin on steroids. Since counterfeiting of $50 and $100 bills is a booming business, many small shops will not accept them. It is best to restrict your paper money to denom-inations of $1, $5, $10 and $20.

Banks & bureaux de change

Most banks are open from 9am-5pm Mon-Fri. Some banks stay open until 6pm and most banks are open from 9am-noon on Saturdays. You will need photo identification, such as a passport, to transact any business such as cashing travellers' cheques or obtaining cash from a credit card. Note that there aren't as many bureaux de change (exchange offices) in New Orleans as in other tourist meccas such as San Francisco and New York.

If you arrive in New Orleans after 5pm, change money at the airport or, if you have US dollars travellers' cheques, buy something in order to get some change. If you want to cash travellers' cheques at a shop, ask first if a minimum purchase is required. Most banks and shops in New Orleans accept travellers' cheques in US dollars.

You can also obtain cash on a credit card account from certain banks. Check with your credit card company before you leave, and be prepared to pay interest rates that vary daily.

American Express Travel Services
201 St Charles Avenue, at Canal Street (586 8201). St Charles Streetcar/bus 41 Canal. **Open** 9am-5pm Mon-Fri. **Map 6 C1**

Bank One
201 St Charles Avenue, at Canal Street (558 1164). St Charles Streetcar/bus 41 Canal. **Open** 8am-2pm Mon-Fri. **Map 6 C1**

Branch: *2 Canal Street, at Poydras Street (569 0483). Bus 41 Canal.* **Open** 9am-3pm Mon-Fri. **Map 6 C1**

First National Bank of Commerce
210 Baronne Street, at Common Street (561 8500). St Charles Streetcar/bus 3 Vieux Carré. **Open** 8am-3pm Mon-Fri. **Map 6 B1**

Hibernia National Bank
313 Carondelet Street, 12th floor, at Gravier Street (533 5471). St Charles Streetcar. **Open** 9am-5pm Mon-Fri. **Map 6 B1**

Travelex
465 9647. **Open** 6am-7pm daily. Handy for when you arrive, this bureau de change is located in the main lobby at the airport.

Western Union
1-800 325 6000.
Western Union has been around for what seems like forever, but it still works if you are in need of cash. You can get advice on how to get money wired to you and where to pick it up at one of the dozen or so locations in New Orleans. You can also wire money to anyone outside the state over the phone using a Visa or MasterCard. Phone the number above, or check the phone book for the location of the nearest branch.

ATMs

Automated Teller Machines (ATMs or cashpoints) are everywhere. Most accept American Express, MasterCard and Visa provided you have an affiliated PIN number. There will be a usage fee, of course – as with almost every convenience, cash on demand has its price.

You can get directions to the nearest ATM location by calling **Plus System** (1-800 843 7587) or **Cirrus** (1-800 424 7787). If you have forgotten your PIN number or have de-magnetised your card, most banks will dispense cash to card holders; try **Bank One** (*above*), which offers advances at any of its branches.

Credit cards

Less of a hassle to lose than cash if you're robbed and accepted almost everywhere, credit cards are required by almost all hotels,

car rental agencies and airlines. They are also accepted by restaurants, petrol stations, many taxicabs and, of course, shops. Without a doubt, your stay will be made much more pleasant if you 'don't leave home without them'.

The five major credit cards most often accepted in the US are **American Express**, **Discover**, **Diners' Club**, **MasterCard** and **Visa**.

Lost or stolen credit cards

American Express
1-800 992 3404.

Diners' Club
1-800 525 9150.

Discover
1-800 347 2683.

MasterCard
1-800 307 7309.

Visa
1-800 336 8472.

Lost or stolen travellers' cheques

American Express
1-800 221 7282.

Thomas Cook
1-800 223 7373.

Visa
1-800 227 6811.

Postal services

Most post offices are open from 8.30am-5pm Mon-Fri, with limited hours on Saturday. Phone **1-800 725 2161** for information on your nearest branch and mailing facilities. Stamps can be bought at any post office as well as at many hotels, grocery stores and convenience stores.

Central Post Office
701 Loyola Avenue, at Girod Street (589 1143). Bus 88 St Claude. **Open** 7am-11pm Mon-Fri; 7am-8pm Sat; noon-5pm Sun. **Map 6 B1**
Open later than any other post office in the city, and by far the best place for sending foreign mail.

Poste Restante (General Delivery)
If you need to receive mail in New Orleans and you're not sure where you will be staying, have it marked General Delivery and posted to the Central Post Office (*above*). Mail is kept ten days from receipt and you must have photo ID to collect it.

Vieux Carré Post Office
1022 Iberville Street, between Burgundy and N Rampart Streets (524 0072). Bus 3 Vieux Carré, 40 Canal. **Open** 8.30am-4.30pm Mon-Fri. **Map 7 A1**

Western Union
1-800 325 6000.
Telegrams are taken over the phone and charged to your phone bill (not available from pay phones). For getting money via Western Union, *see p260* **Banks & bureaux de change**.

Public toilets/ Restrooms

Finding a toilet has been a problem in New Orleans forever and a day. During Mardi Gras hundreds of people, male and female, are arrested for public urination. In the French Quarter, especially during a big event such as Mardi Gras or Jazz Fest, you will see signs in almost every establishment to the effect that only customers can use the facilities. Buy a drink from a café or restaurant so that you can use their toilet without restraint.

There are public toilets opposite Jackson Square on Decatur Street.

Religion

There is no lack of places to worship in New Orleans, regardless of your faith or beliefs. Here is a very brief selection; look in the *Yellow Pages* for the location of countless others.

Coliseum Place Baptist Church
1376 Camp Street, at Terpsichore Street (525 4809). Bus 11 Magazine. **Map 6 B2**

Student life

In early 1996, the loophole in the Louisiana drinking law that made it legal for those over 18 years of age to purchase alcohol (as compared to 21 for the rest of the country) was closed for good. Despite this change in the law, out-of-state university enrollment has yet to suffer, surely a testament to the quality of education New Orleans's colleges have to offer.

Where to study

Delgado Community College
501 City Park Avenue (483 4216).
Delgado's mostly working-class students look at the two-year technical programmes as a passage to well-paying jobs, while the more ambitious position themselves for four-year colleges. The college also offers many non-credit fun courses such as pottery, local history, computers, ballroom dancing and barbecuing.

Dillard University
2601 Gentilly Boulevard (283 8822).
Founded in 1869 to educate former slaves, Dillard is one of the old-line African-American universities. It's green, relaxed campus in Gentilly (east of City Park), populated by some of the South's top black students, reminds many of the popular TV sitcom *A Different World.*

Loyola University
6363 St Charles Avenue (865 2011).
Located adjacent to Tulane on St Charles Avenue, Loyola's Jesuit heritage is apparent in a strong student bent toward social justice causes and activism. It's a sophisticated activism that puts students on picket lines attacking corporate greed and Third World exploitation rather than harassing abortion clinic clients. Known for its law school, business school, sociology and theology faculties.

Southern University at New Orleans
6400 Press Drive (286 5000).
Developed in the same way as the University of New Orleans – as a branch of a larger school, in this case, Southern University in Baton Rouge. SUNO opened in 1959 when Louisiana colleges were still segregated by race. It's primarily a black institution but has become increasing multiracial. Strong on education and night school courses.

Tulane University
6823 St Charles Avenue (865 5000).
Rich, old and social, Tulane is the school of choice for Eastern students who think it will be easier than Ivy League schools and Southerners who want to live in New Orleans. The law school is much sought after for making connections while the business school, Latin American studies and architecture are nationally recognised.

University of New Orleans
Lakefront (280 6000).
The classic commuter school success story. Originally a branch of Louisiana State University, UNO is now the largest college in New Orleans with an enrollment of 16,000. Popular with returning students, people who work full-time and non-New Orleanians who want cheap tuition and a Big Easy degree. Unlike many commuter schools, UNO has developed some first-class academic programmes including creative writing, jazz studies (headed by Ellis Marsalis) and the study of World War II.

Central Congregational United Church of Christ
2401 Bienville Street, at Tonti Street (822 3223). Bus 41 Canal.
Map 4 E6
St Louis Cathedral
725 Chartres Street, on Jackson Square (525 9585). Bus 55 Elysian Fields, 82 Desire. **Map 7 C2**
St Luke's Methodist Church
5875 Canal Boulevard, at Brooks Street (486 3982). Bus 41 Canal.
Map 5 C3
St Patrick's Church
724 Camp Street, at Julia Street (525 4413). St Charles Streetcar.
Map 6 C2
The Hispanic Apostolate
3368 Esplanade Avenue, at Maurepas Street (486 1983). Bus 48 Esplanade. **Map 5 E5**
Zen Center of New Orleans
784 Camp Street, at Julia Street (523 1213). St Charles Streetcar.
Map 6 C2

Safety

See page 256 **Dodging bullets.**

Smoking

According to anecdotal evidence, the citizens of New Orleans smoke a lot of tobacco. Except for hospitals, federal buildings, large shopping malls and a few upmarket restaurants, you may light up at will. Most small restaurants have smoking and non-smoking sections. In fact, you may have to walk through the smoking section to get to the non-smoking section.

Naturally, the current awareness of the dangers of passive smoking make it incumbent upon smokers to step outside to fire one up. If you smoke, keep an eye out for no smoking signs.

Telephones

The telephone system in New Orleans is cheap and reliable. A local call costs 35¢. Pay phones accept only nickels, dimes and quarters (watch out you don't put a Susan B Anthony $1 coin in a pay phone). Always check for a dial tone before parting with your money.

Xavier University
7325 Palmetto Street (486 7411).
The only Catholic university (as opposed to college) founded for African-Americans in the US. Xavier has found a niche in the healthcare field with a very competitive pharmacy degree programme and a hugely successful pre-med programme. The small campus hosts many African, Third World and black cultural events.

Hanging out

It is a profound testament to the seductive nature of New Orleans that a large number of out-of-town students choose to take up residence in the city after graduation. When you add this group to the steady influx of young musicians, artists and assorted eccentric others, you get the gradual gentrification of formerly blighted neighbourhoods.

LOWER GARDEN DISTRICT
One of these emerging areas is the Lower Garden District, dubbed by the alternative press digest *Utne Reader* 'the coolest neighbourhood in America'. Judge for yourself.

Places worth checking out include the **Half Moon** bar (*see page 195* **Nightlife**), which offers arguably the best and largest hamburgers in New Orleans. Alternatively, **Juan's Flying Burrito** (2018 Magazine Street; 569 0000), is an extremely popular and vegetarian-friendly Mexican eatery featuring the kinds of burritos that require a serious commitment to finish. **The Balcony Bar & Café** (*see page 193* **Nightlife**) offers 70-plus draught beers and, best of all, second-storey outdoor seating, while **Rue de la Course** is an excellent coffeehouse with two branches on Magazine Street (*see page 143* **Cafés & Coffeehouses**).

UPTOWN
The primary college neighbourhood, however, is still the Uptown area around Tulane and Loyola universities. These adjacent colleges boast a higher concentration of Cabriolet convertibles, Jeep Cherokees and BMWs than any other campus in New Orleans. You'll also find a higher concentration of non-New Orleans natives here.

The tightest cluster of bookstores, bars, restaurants and cafés can be found on a six-block stretch along **Maple Street**, between Broadway and Carrollton Avenue. Broadway itself features popular student watering holes the **Boot Bar & Grill** (*see page 196* **Nightlife**) and **Waldo's Restaurant & Bar** (*page 199*), which has been rated one of the top 100 college bars in America by *Playboy* magazine. The **F&M Patio Bar** (*page 197*) really gets going after midnight, when the pool table becomes a dance floor and its late-night kitchen will satisfy your cheese fry cravings.

For breakfast specials and local art, try the **Bluebird Café** at 7800 Panola Street (865 7577). It has another branch at 3625 Prytania Street (895 7166). Venture into residential convenience store **Adams Street Grocery & Deli** (1309 Adams Street; 861 1120) to pick up one of the best and most inexpensive shrimp po-boys in New Orleans.

Finally, while Uptown, listen to **WTUL** (91.5 FM) for the most eccentric playlist in the city and to find out what's on every night.

A fairly new item in the New Orleans long-distance phone industry is the phone card. These can be purchased at almost any retail outlet and range in price from $5 to $50. They are probably the best and most convenient way of making international calls since they can be used on pay phones or hotel phones. You can also use your MasterCard with **AT&T** (1-800 225 5288) or **MCI** (1-800 269 2255).

Directories are divided into *Yellow Pages* (classified) and *White Pages* (business and residential) listings. These are available at most public phones and in hotels. If you can't find one, dial directory assistance and ask for your listing by name.

Toll-free calls generally start with 1-800 or 1-888, while expensive pay-per-minute calls (gambling tips and phone sex) usually start with 1-900 or 1-976. Don't get them mixed up.

Operator assistance
dial 0
Emergency (police, ambulance, fire)
dial 911
Directory assistance
1 + area code + 555 1212
Dial 1 + 504 if you're in New Orleans and want a local number. If you want a number in another area, dial that area code. Calls are free from pay phones.

Area codes
The area code for the city of New Orleans and Orleans Parish is 504.

International calls
Dial 011+ country code. Codes include: **UK** 44, **Australia** 61, **New Zealand** 64. If you need operator assistance with international calls, dial 00.

Direct dial calls
If you are using a pay phone and will be paying for the call with change, dial 1 + area code (if outside New Orleans) + phone number. An operator or recorded message will tell you how much change to deposit. If you are using a phone card to pay for the call, follow the instructions on the card.

Collect calls
Dial 0 + area code + phone number. If things become too confusing for words, simply dial 0 and fall on the mercy of an operator.

Time & dates

New Orleans is on Central Standard Time, which is two hours ahead of Pacific Standard Time (California), one hour behind Eastern Standard Time (New York) and six hours behind the UK. Daylight Saving Time (which is almost concurrent with British Summer Time) runs from the first Sunday in April to the last Sunday in October, when the clocks are rolled ahead one hour.

In the US, dates are written in the order of month, day, year; therefore 2.5.99 is the fifth of February 1999, not the second of May.

Tipping

The tourism industry in New Orleans employs a large part of the local labour force and many depend on gratuities for part of their income, so you should tip accordingly. Most sit-down restaurants will automatically add 15 per cent to a table of six or more diners. If you receive good service in a restaurant, tip generously; if you receive bad service, tip poorly and report it to the management on your way out. Here's a rough guideline:

Bellhops & baggage handlers $1-$2 per bag; **hotel maids** $1 a night; **hotel concierges** $3-$5; **bartenders** 15% of the bill; **cabbies, waiting staff, hairdressers & food delivery staff** 15%-20% of the total bill; **valets & counterstaff** $1-$3, depending on the size of the order and any special arrangements required.

Visas

Under the Visa Waiver Program, citizens of the UK, Japan, Australia, New Zealand and all West European countries (except for Portugal, Greece and the Vatican City) do not need a visa for stays in the United States of less than 90 days (business or pleasure) – as long as they have a passport that is valid for the full 90-day period and a return ticket. An open standby ticket is acceptable.

Canadians and Mexicans do not need visas but must have legal proof of their residency.

All other travellers must have a visa. Full information and visa application forms can be obtained from your nearest US embassy or consulate. In general, send in your application at least three weeks before you plan to travel. Visas required more urgently should be applied for via the travel agent booking your ticket.

US Embassy Visa Information Line

Recorded information in the UK
0891 200 290.

Work

The employment situation in New Orleans is unstable at best. There is very little in the way of a middle-income population, thus making the availability of decent paying employment scarce and undependable. As one ex-chief of police put it, 'There are two classes of employment in New Orleans:

Tourist information

New Orleans Metropolitan Convention & Visitors Bureau
1520 Sugar Bowl Drive, at Poydras Street (566 5011/1-800 672 6124). Bus 16 S Claiborne. **Open** 8.30am-5pm Mon-Fri. **Map 6 B1**
Website: www.neworleanscvb.com

French Quarter office
529 St Ann Street, at Jackson Square (566 5031). Bus 3 Vieux Carré, 55 Elysian Fields, 81 Almonaster, 82 Desire. **Open** 9am-5pm daily.
Map 7 C2
This is a beautiful little office located in the heart of the French Quarter opposite Jackson Square. Maps, general directions, tour information, local history and hotel and restaurant recommendations can be obtained here.

Visitor information hotline
566 5003. **Open** 24 hours daily.
Recorded information about the city.

people who work in the hotels, and people who own the hotels.' Further, New Orleans is recognised as having an employment shortage. This means that honest officals of the government admit there are simply not enough jobs to go around.

Every employer wishing to stay within the law is required to have a prospective employee declare in writing that he or she is a genuine American citizen with a right to work in this country.

If you find a US firm that will attempt to convince the Immigration Department that you can do a particular job better than any American alive, you will be provided with an H-1 visa allowing you to work in America for five years.

For more information while you are visiting New Orleans, phone the **Louisiana Department of Labor** (568 7239).

If you are a student, you should check out **Study Abroad** (phone in the UK 0171 801 9699/ www.study abroad.com/) to see if you qualify for a work/study programme.

Further Reading & Listening

Music

Louisiana

Alex Chilton: *High Priest* (1987); *A Man Called Destruction* (1995).
Charlie Daniels Band: 'Sweet Louisiana' (1976).
Dr John: *(pictured on p266)* 'Louisiana Lullabye' (1979).
Emmylou Harris: 'Leaving Louisiana in the Broad Daylight' (1978).
Gil Scott Heron: 'Angola, Louisiana' (1978).
Maria McKee: 'This Property's Condemned' (1989).
NRBQ: 'Boozoo, That's Who!' (1989) – a tribute to zydeco's Boozoo Chavis.
The Old 97's: '504' (1994).
Kid Ory: *Kid Ory's Creole Jazz Band, 1954*
Tom Petty & the Heartbreakers: 'Louisiana Rain' (1979).
Paul Revere & the Raiders: 'Louisiana Redbone' (1969).
Muddy Waters: 'Louisiana Blues' (1950).
Victoria Williams: *Happy Come Home* (1987). Originally from Opelousas, Williams is an art-folkie whose songs have a feel for small town life, particularly 'Opelousas (Sweet Relief)'.

New Orleans

Louis Armstrong: *The Hot Fives, Vol. 1* (1988) – Satchmo's earliest work from 1925 and 1926; *Let's Do It* (1995) – a collection of his later vocal work, much of it with Ella Fitzgerald.
Sidney Bechet: *New Orleans Jazz; Spirits of New Orleans*
Gary US Bonds: 'New Orleans' (1960).
Freddy Cannon: 'Way Down Yonder in New Orleans' (1957).
Fats Domino: 'Walking to New Orleans' (1960).
Dr John: *Gris Gris* (1968); *Dr John, The Night Tripper (The Sun, Moon and Herbs)* (1971); *Gumbo* (1972); 'I Thought I Heard New Orleans Say' (1979).
Gottschalk: *Classics of the Americas Vol 4: Piano Works* (Georges Rabol, piano)
Johnny Horton: 'Battle of New Orleans' (1959).
Invisible Cowboy: *Unsafe Trigger (at the White Trash Discotheque)* (1990).
John Kay: 'Down in New Orleans' (1978).
Led Zeppelin: 'Royal Orleans' (1976).
The Meters: *Funkify Your Life: The Meters Anthology* (1995).
John Mooney: *Dealing With the Devil*
Jelly Roll Morton: *The Complete Jelly Roll Morton 1926-1930*
The Neville Bros: *Treacherous: A History of the Neville Bros. Vol. 1* (1986); *Treacherous: A History of the Neville Bros. Vol. 2* (1990).
Maceo Parker: *Southern Exposure* (1993). James Brown's sax player with New Orleans bands.
Elvis Presley: 'New Orleans' (1958).
Professor Longhair: 'Mardi Gras in New Orleans' (1950); *New Orleans Piano* (1972); *Crawfish Fiesta* (1980); *The Last Mardi Gras* (1982); *Rock'n'Roll Gumbo* (1985).
Michael Ray & the Cosmic Krewe: *Michael Ray & the Cosmic Krewe* (1994).
Redbone: 'Witch Queen of New Orleans' (1971).
REM: 'New Orleans Instrumental No.1' (1992).
Shirley and Lee: *The Legendary Masters Series* (1990).
Silver Jews: 'New Orleans' (1994).
Swingin' Haymakers: *For Rent* (1995).
Thousand $ Car: *Big Shot* (1997).
The Tractors: 'Trying to Get to New Orleans' (1995).
Tom Waits: 'I Wish I was in New Orleans' (1977).
Wild Magnolias: *They Call Us Wild* (1975).
Wild Tchoupitoulas: *The Wild Tchoupitoulas* (1976).
Compilations: *Cajun Dance Party: Fais Do-Do* (1994); *The Mardi Gras Indians Super Sunday Showdown* (1992).

Writing

Non-fiction

John M Barry: *Rising Tide*
Gripping and elegantly written account of the great Mississippi flood of 1927.
Christopher Benfey: *Degas in New Orleans*
Degas' stay on Esplanade Avenue is placed in the context of 1870s New Orleans.
Jason Berry, Jonathan Foose & Tad Jones: *Up From the Cradle of Jazz: New Orleans Music Since World War II*
Insights into the succeeding generations of musicians such as Fats Domino and the Neville Brothers, who took New Orleans music in new directions.
John Broven: *Rhythm & Blues in New Orleans*
History of R&B in the city, written by an Englishman.
John Churchill Chase: *Frenchmen, Desire, Good Children and Other Streets of New Orleans*
Definitive and delightful history (written in the 1950s) of the city though its streets, by former *Times-Picayne* cartoonist.
Randolph Delahanty: *New Orleans: Elegance and Decadence*
A satisfying examination of New Orleans through its houses and cultural history
Robert Florence: *New Orleans Cemeteries: Life in the Cities of the Dead*
Cemetery guide-historian Florence weaves together history, myth, culture and the present in this beautifully illustrated volume.
James Gill: *Lords of Misrule: Mardi Gras and the Politics of Race in New Orleans*
British transplant Gill turns a sharp yet not unsympathetic eye on the intertwined history of Mardi Gras and New Orleans's identity.
Jeff Hannusch: *I Hear You Knocking*
The Sound of New Orleans R&B by a local music journalist.
Lafcadio Hearn: *Creole Sketches*
Hearn's plummy tales of 1880s New Orleans are probably more invented than fact-based experience – but this is the way life should have been.
John R Kemp: *New Orleans: An Illustrated History*

Large illustrated overview of New Orleans's history.
Richard S Kennedy (ed): *Literary New Orleans*
A scholarly but engaging study of major New Orleans
writers and an enquiry into the nature of the city's
literary community.
John Maginnis: *The Last Hayride*
Entertaining coverage of the notorious 1991
gubernatorial campaign by top Louisiana political
reporter.
Tim Pickles: *New Orleans 1815*
Written by an Englishman living in New Orleans, this
slim volume is part of the Osprey Military Campaign
Series, and illuminates the Battle of New Orleans and the
War of 1812. Superb maps and illustrations.
Henri Schindler: *New Orleans Mardi Gras*
Outstanding recent book about Mardi Gras by native
New Orleanian, lavishly illustrated.
Michael P Smith: *Mardi Gras Indians*
The first book to examine the culture of the black Indians
of New Orleans. Superb photos.
Gasper J Stall: *'Buddy': Buddy Stall's New Orleans*
Classic book by popular local historian and speaker.
Mary Ann Sternberg: *Along the River Road: Past and
Present on Louisiana's Historic Byway*
Useful for visitors exploring the River Road and its
plantations.
Robert Tallent: *Voodoo in New Orleans*
Like the title says – a history of the religion that
originally hailed from Haiti.
Roulhac Toledano: *The National Trust Guide to New
Orleans Architectural and Cultural Treasures*
Toledano's 1996 guide is small and portable, an excellent
companion to walks and rides around the city.
Christina Vella: *Intimate Enemies: The Two Worlds of
the Baroness Pontalba*
Masterful biography of one of New Orleans's mythic
women and one of the best histories of colonial New
Orleans available.
New Orleans Architecture Series
A seven-volume set, written by various architects, writers
and preservationists. Lavishly illustrated, each volume is
devoted to a different district of the city.

Fiction

Nelson Algren: *A Walk on the Wild Side*
A classic American novel set in the French Quarter.
George Washington Cable: *Old Creole Days*
Cluttered with Creole and black dialect, slowed down by
the elaborate descriptive style of the Victorian era,
Cable's 1879 stories are nevertheless entertaining tales.
Kate Chopin: *The Awakening*
Chopin's 1899 novel of a sexually and spiritually frustrated
Creole wife is told with dreamlike softness but is startlingly
contemporary in its understanding of gender roles.
Tony Dunbar: *Shelter from the Storm*
The best of a series of mysteries by a New Orleans
attorney, featuring hapless lawyer-cum-gourmand Tubby
Dubonnet.
William Faulkner: *Pylon; Absolom, Absolom!; The
Wild Palms*
New Orleans is a marginal but significant setting in
many of Faulkner's books. Only his apprentice novel
Pylon is completely set in the city.
Ernest Gaines: *A Gathering of Old Men*
The old men are black, and they gather on decrepit
porches in rural Louisiana to recount stories shot through
with wisdom.
Ellen Gilchrist: *Victory Over Japan; In the Land of
Dreamy Dreams*
Gilchrist's stories of bored Uptown divorcees, sexually
ravenous teenagers and Irish Channel adventurers are
best told in her early books.
Shirley Ann Grau: *Keepers of the House; The House
on Coliseum Street*

A Pulitzer Prize winner delves into post-World War II,
pre-Civil Rights movement New Orleans.
Everette Maddox: *American Waste; Bar Scotch; The
Everette Maddox Songbook*
Maddox was a poet whose books of romantic barfly
poetry capture life in the Riverbend area.
Walker Percy: *The Moviegoer*
Troubled Catholic Binx Bolling navigates upper-crust
New Orleans by retreating to lower-middle-class Gentilly
and searching for meaning in movies.
Anne Rice: *Lasher; The Feast of All Saints; Interview
With the Vampire*
New Orleans is the stage for Anne Rice's fertile
imagination.
John Kennedy Toole: *A Confederacy of Dunces*
Definitive and hilarious tale of New Orleans, which won
the author a posthumous Pulitzer prize.
Tennessee Williams: *A Streetcar Named Desire*
Read the play or watch a production, but don't miss the
Marlon Brando/Vivien Leigh film.
Margaret Woodward: *No Place Called Home*
A suspenseful walk on the darker side of New Orleans, in
the company of a seven-year-old boy.

Index

Center 62, **254**
Esplanade Avenue 42-43, 58, **78**, *80*
Essence Music Festival 20
Evangeline (Longfellow) 239
Expedite, Saint 58

f

Fair Grounds Racecourse 78, **218**
Fairmont Hotel
  Sazerac Bar 191
  Sazerac restaurant 126
Fashion Café New Orleans 53, 134
Faubourg Marigny 58
  accommodation 108
  bars 189-191
  cafés 142-143
  music clubs 204
  restaurants 125-126
Faubourg Tremé 57-58
  music clubs 204
Faulkner, William **33-34**, 53, 233
  Pirate's Alley Society 34
Faulkner House Books *33*, 34, **152**
festivals 19-24
  Audubon 24, 232
  birdwatching 85
  film 174, 258
  gay & lesbian 21, 178
  literary 34-35
  music 20-21, 22, 24, 84, 230, 231
film festivals 174, 258
film industry 171-172
film locations 68, 71, 111, **172-173**, 227, 231, 233, 245
Fire Department
  emergencies 258
  Museum 91
First Street 68-69
fishing 77, 83, **219**, 240-241
Florida Gulf Coast 248-250
florists 158
food 18, 115, 124-125
  festivals 24
  shops 78, **159**, 263
football (soccer) 218
football, American 217-218
  Sugar Bowl 23, 217-218
  see also Saints
Fort Gaines 245
Fort Morgan 245
Fort Pickens 248
Fort Walton *250*
French Market **49**, *154-155*, 159
French Quarter **47-58**, 145

accommodation 103-108
architecture 37-39, 41-42
art galleries 95-97
bars 185-189
cafés 142-143
children's attractions 168
festival 20
music clubs 201-204
restaurants 114-125
tourist information 264
tours 85-87
Frenchmen Street 58
Funky Butt at Congo Square *200*, 201
furniture
  designers 98
  shops 162-163

g

Gabrielle 125, **137**
Galatoire's 120
Gallier Hall 7, 42, 59, **60**
Gallier House 56
Gambit Weekly 180
gambling 15-16
  casino boats **185**, 230
  Gulf Coast casinos, 242, 243-245
Garden District 43, *43*, **68-72**
  accommodation 109-113
  bars 193-196
  cafés 143
  Red Room club 72, *191*, **206**
  restaurants 131
  tour 87
  see also Lower Garden District
gardens 232, 238, 245
  Audubon Pilgrimage 24, 232
  Botanical 77
gas emergencies 258
gay & lesbian New Orleans 56, 58, **175-179**
  accommodation 107, 108, **179**
  festivals 21, 178
  heritage tour **86**, 176
  publications 176, 181
ghosts 50, 56, 168, 232-233
Gilchrist, Ellen 32, **36**
glass studios & galleries 94-95
Global Wildlife Center 85, 168
Go 4th on the River 20
Golden Meadow 240
golf 219-220
  courses 74, **220**
Grand Boutique Hotel 109
Grand Coteau 239
Grand Isle 240-241
Grau, Shirley Ann 35
Grayton Beach 248, 249, 250

Great Louisiana Bird Fest 85
Great River Road 224-228
Greenville 230
Greyhound buses **224**, 231, 233, 237, 240, 245, 246, 250
Gulf Coast 241-250
Gulf Shores 246
gyms **220-221**, 222

hairdressers 162
  in Hotel Intercontinental 108
Half Moon 73, **195**
Hallowe'en **21**, 178
Handy, WC 231
Hard Rock Café 53, **134**, 167
health 258-259
  spas **162**, 221
Hearn, Lafcadio 14, 18, **33**, 240
Hellman, Lillian 34
helplines 259
Hermann-Grima Historic House 56, **57**
Higgins Shipyard 11
'Highway 61' **230-231**, 232, 233
Hi-Ho Lounge 214
Historic New Orleans Collection (HNOC) 53, **90-91**
  website 258
  Williams Research Center 92
  see also Merieult House
history 4-13
  key events 13
  twentieth century 11-18
HNOC *see* Historic New Orleans Collection
Holditch, Kenneth 33
  literary tour 34, **87**
holidays, national 19
Honey Island Swamp 85
  tours 87
horse racing 23, 78, **218**
horse riding 75, 77, 84, **221**
hospitals 258
Hotel Intercontinental 108
  Veranda (restaurant) 126
Hotel Maison de Ville 103
  Bistro 116
hotels 101-113
  chains 111
Houmas House 227
House of Blues 53, *186*, *187*, **203**
Howard-Tilton Memorial Library 76
Howlin' Wolf (club) 62, **206**
Hummingbird Hotel 59
hurricanes 259

Advertisers' Index

Please refer to the relevant sections for addresses/telephone numbers

Maps

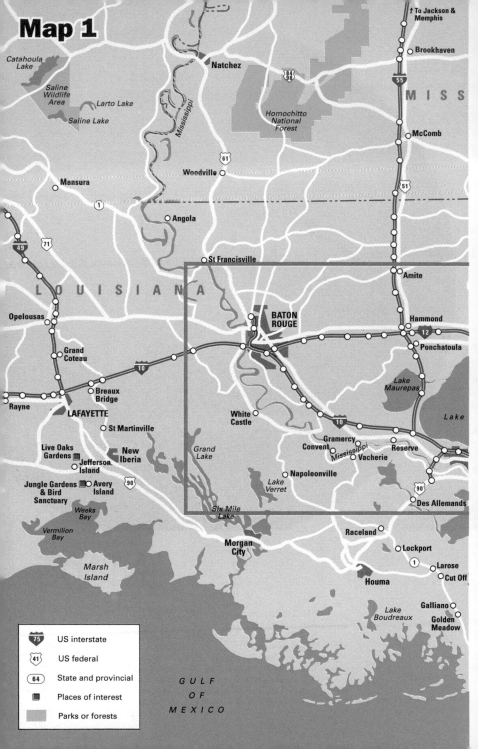

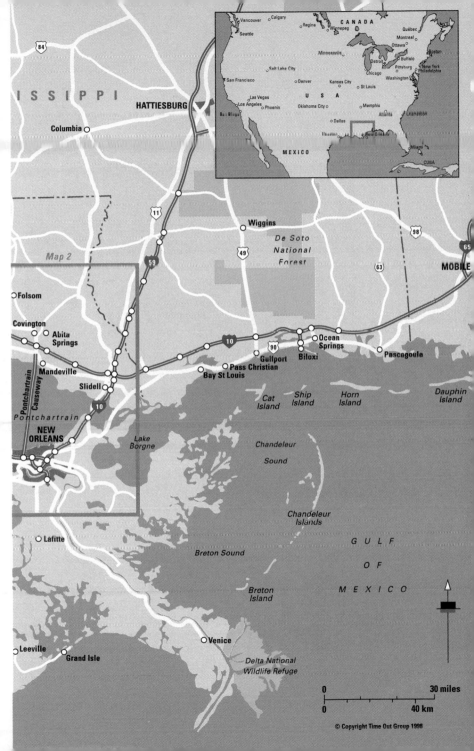

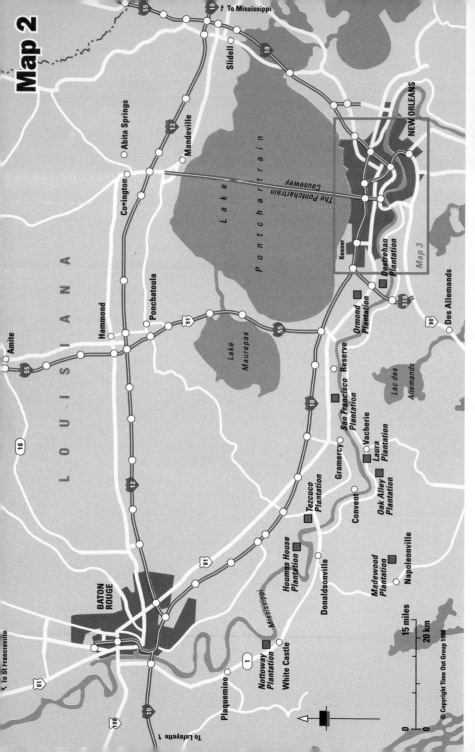

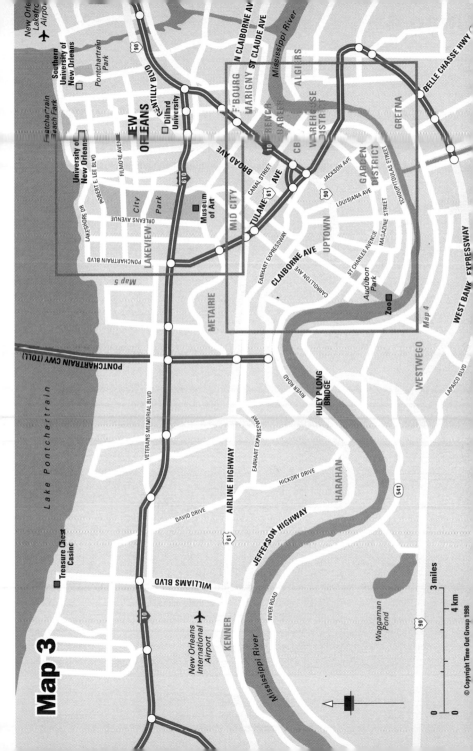

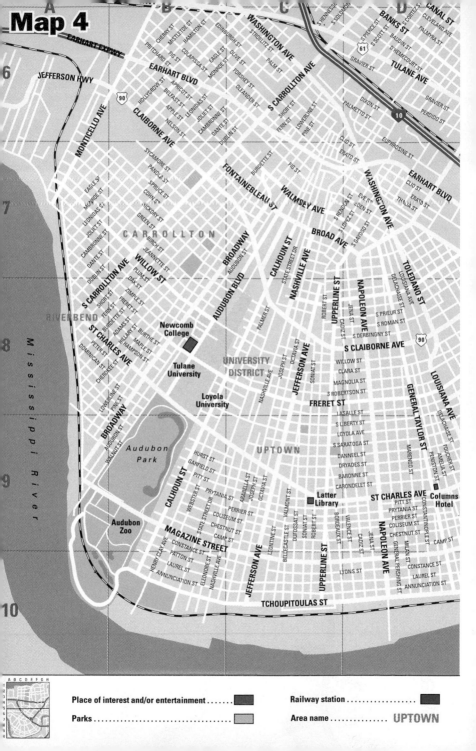

Map 4

Place of interest and/or entertainment .... ▮

Parks .... ▮

Railway station .... ▮

Area name .... UPTOWN

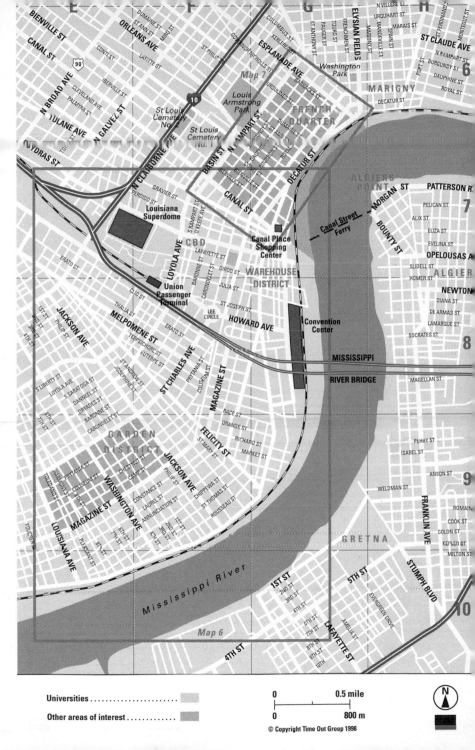

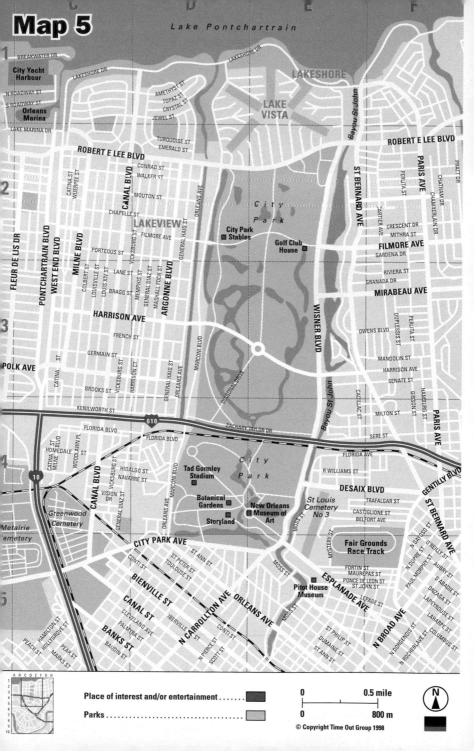

Map 5

Lake Pontchartrain

LAKESHORE

LAKE VISTA

City Yacht Harbour

Orleans Marina

N ROADWAY ST
S ROADWAY ST
LAKE MARINA DR
BREAKWATER DR
LAKESHORE DR
LAKESHORE DR
LAKESHORE DR

ROBERT E LEE BLVD
ROBERT E LEE BLVD

AMETHYST ST
TOPAZ ST
CRYSTAL ST
JEWEL ST
TURQUOISE ST
EMERALD ST

PARIS AVE
PRATT DR
PERLITA ST
CHATHAM DR
CHAMBERLAIN DR

ST BERNARD AVE

Bayou St John

City Park

CONRAD ST
WALKER ST
MOUTON ST
CHAPELLE ST

CANAL BLVD

LAKEVIEW

City Park Stables

Golf Club House

FILMORE AVE
CRESCENT DR
CARTIER AVE
MITHRA ST
GARDENA DR
RIVIERA ST
GRANADA DR

MIRABEAU AVE

FILMORE AVE

ORLEANS AVE

GENERAL HAIG ST

ARGONNE BLVD

MILNE BLVD

WEST END BLVD
PONTCHARTRAIN BLVD

FLEUR DE LIS DR

PORTEOUS ST
COLBERT ST
LOUISVILLE ST
LOUIS XIV ST
MEMPHIS ST
GENERAL DIAZ ST
MARSHALL FOCH ST
BRAGG ST
LANE ST

HARRISON AVE

FRENCH ST

GERMAIN ST

CATINA ST

VICKSBURG ST

HARRISON CT

BROOKS ST

GENERAL HAIG ST

ORLEANS AVE

MARCONI BLVD

WISNER BLVD

OWENS BLVD

DUPLESSIS ST
PERLITA ST

MANDOLIN ST
HARRISON AVE
SENATE ST

GIBSON ST

CADILLAC ST

HAMBURG ST

PARIS AVE

POLK AVE

KENILWORTH ST

610

DIAGONAL DRIVE

ZACHARY TAYLOR DR

MILTON ST

SERE ST

FLORIDA BLVD
FLORIDA BLVD

HOMEDALE ST
WOODLAWN PL

CANAL BLVD
MILNE
CATINA ST
BLVD

10

VICKSBURG ST
HIDALGO ST
NAVARRE ST

VISION DR

GENERAL DIAZ ST

Greenwood Cemetery

Metairie Cemetery

ORLEANS AVE

MARCONI BLVD

Tad Gormley Stadium

City Park

Botanical Gardens

Storyland

New Orleans Museum of Art

FLORIDA AVE

R WILLIAMS ST

DESAIX BLVD
TRAFALGAR ST
CASTIGLIONE ST
BELFORT ST

St Louis Cemetery No 3

GENTILLY BLVD

ST BERNARD AVE

N GAYOSO ST
N DUPRE ST
N PRIEUR ST
PAUL MORPHY ST
N GALVEZ ST

O'REILLY ST
AUBRY ST
D'ABADIE ST
ONZAGA ST

CITY PARK AVE

CONTI ST

ST PETER ST
TOULOUSE ST

ST ANN ST

BIENVILLE ST

CANAL ST

CLEVELAND AVE
PALMYRA ST

N CARROLLTON AVE

ORLEANS AVE

IBERVILLE ST

CONTI ST

MOSS ST

MOSS ST

MYSTERY ST

Fair Grounds Race Track

FORTIN ST
MAUREPAS ST
PONCE DE LEON ST
ST JOHN ST

LEPAGE ST

ESPLANADE AVE

Pitot House Museum

N BROAD AVE

LAPEYROUSE ST
LAHARPE ST

N DORGENOIS ST
N ROCHEBLAVE ST
N COLUMBUS ST

HAMILTON ST
HOLLYGROVE ST

BANKS ST

PEACH ST
MARKS ST
PALM ST

BAUDIN ST

N PIERCE ST

SCOTT ST

ST PHILIP ST

DUMAINE ST

ST ANN ST

Place of interest and/or entertainment

Parks

0   0.5 mile
0   800 m

N

© Copyright Time Out Group 1998

Map 6

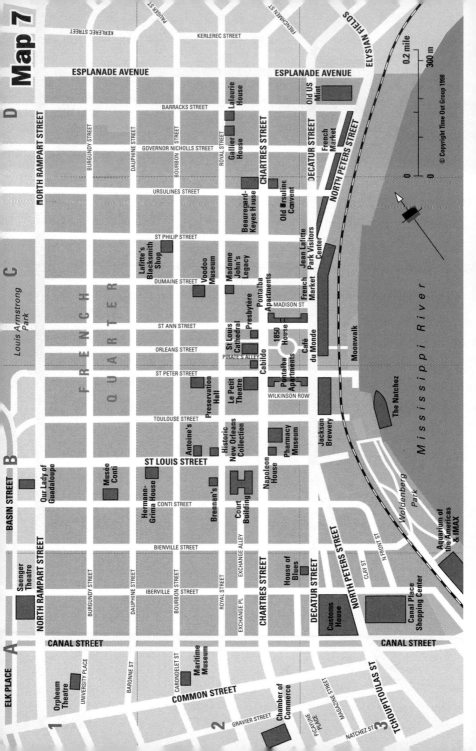

Map 7

© Copyright Time Out Group 1998

ELK PLACE

Orpheum Theatre

University Place

BARONNE ST

NORTH RAMPART STREET

BURGUNDY STREET

DAUPHINE STREET

BOURBON STREET

ROYAL STREET

CHARTRES STREET

DECATUR STREET

NORTH PETERS STREET

CANAL STREET

Maritime Museum

CARONDELET ST

COMMON STREET

Chamber of Commerce

GRAVIER STREET

MAGAZINE STREET

PICAYUNE PLACE

NATCHEZ ST

TCHOUPITOULAS ST

Saenger Theatre

BASIN STREET

Our Lady of Guadaloupe

Musée Conti

Hermann-Grima House

Brennan's

Antoine's

CONTI STREET

Court Building

ST LOUIS STREET

Historic New Orleans Collection

Napoleon House

Pharmacy Museum

TOULOUSE STREET

Preservation Hall

Le Petit Theatre

ST PETER STREET

WILKINSON ROW

Jackson Brewery

Pontalba Apartments

Cabildo

PIRATE'S ALLEY

St Louis Cathedral

Presbytère

1850 House

Café du Monde

ORLEANS STREET

ST ANN STREET

Pontalba Apartments

MADISON ST

French Market

Jean Lafitte Park Visitors Center

Moonwalk

FRENCH QUARTER

Louis Armstrong Park

Lafitte's Blacksmith Shop

ST PHILIP STREET

Voodoo Museum

Madame John's Legacy

DUMAINE STREET

Beauregard-Keyes House

Old Ursuline Convent

URSULINES STREET

GOVERNOR NICHOLLS STREET

Gallier House

Lalaurie House

BARRACKS STREET

Old US Mint

ESPLANADE AVENUE

KERLEREC STREET

PAUGER ST

FRENCHMEN ST

ELYSIAN FIELDS

French Market

DECATUR STREET

NORTH PETERS STREET

CHARTRES STREET

House of Blues

EXCHANGE ALLEY

EXCHANGE PL

ROYAL STREET

BOURBON STREET

DAUPHINE STREET

BURGUNDY STREET

IBERVILLE STREET

BIENVILLE STREET

DECATUR STREET

NORTH PETERS STREET

CLAY ST

N FRONT ST

Customs House

Canal Place Shopping Center

CANAL STREET

Aquarium of the Americas & IMAX

Woldenberg Park

The Natchez

Mississippi River

0.2 mile

300 m

0

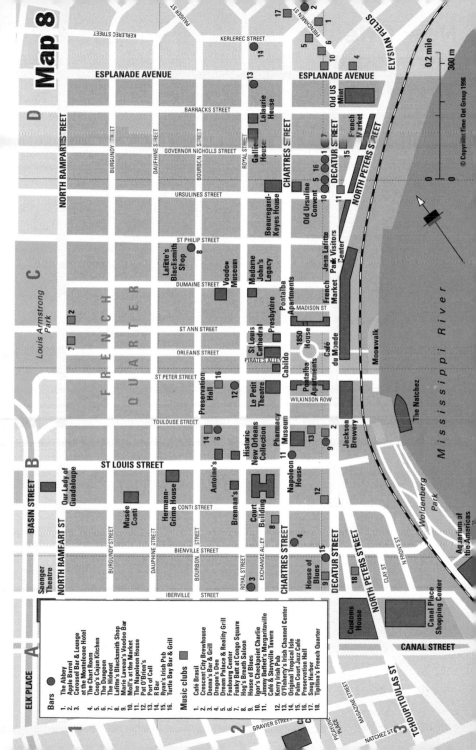

Map 8

ELK PLACE

Saenger Theatre

BASIN STREET

Our Lady of Guadaloupe

NORTH RAMPART ST

Musée Conti

Hermann-Grima House

Antoine's

Brennan's

Court Building

Historic New Orleans Collection

Pharmacy Museum

Napoleon House

House of Blues

Jackson Brewery

Customs House

Canal Place Shopping Center

Aquarium of the Americas

CANAL STREET

NORTH PETERS STREET

DECATUR STREET

CHARTRES STREET

BOURBON STREET

DAUPHINE STREET

BURGUNDY STREET

ROYAL STREET

IBERVILLE STREET

BIENVILLE STREET

CONTI STREET

ST LOUIS STREET

TOULOUSE STREET

ST PETER STREET

ORLEANS STREET

ST ANN STREET

DUMAINE STREET

ST PHILIP STREET

URSULINES STREET

GOVERNOR NICHOLLS STREET

BARRACKS STREET

ESPLANADE AVENUE

KERLEREC STREET

KERLEREC STREET

PAUGER ST

FRENCHMEN ST

ELYSIAN FIELDS

Louis Armstrong Park

FRENCH QUARTER

EXCHANGE ALLEY

PIRATE'S ALLEY

Preservation Hall

Le Petit Theatre

Lafitte's Blacksmith Shop

Voodoo Museum

Madame John's Legacy

Beauregard-Keyes House

Old Ursuline Convent

Galller House

Lalaurie House

Old US Mint

French Market

Jean Lafitte Park Visitors Center

Pontalba Apartments

St Louis Cathedral

Presbytère

Cabildo

1850 House

Café du Monde

Pontalba Apartments

WILKINSON ROW

MADISON ST

NORTH PETERS STREET

Moonwalk

The Natchez

Woldenberg Park

The Mississippi River

CLAY ST

N FRONT ST

GRAVIER STREET

NATCHEZ ST

PICAYUNE PLACE

MAGAZINE STREET

TCHOUPITOULAS ST

0 | 300 m
0 | 0.2 mile

© Copyright Time Out Group 1998

Bars
1. The Abbey
2. Apple Barrel
3. Carousel Bar & Lounge at the Monteleone Hotel
4. The Chart Room
5. Coop's Cajun Kitchen
6. The Dungeon
7. The Hideout
8. Lafitte's Blacksmith Shop
9. Marie Laveau's Voodoo Bar
10. Moll's at the Market
11. The Napoleon House
12. Pat O'Brien's
13. Port of Call
14. R Bar
15. Ryan's Irish Pub
16. Turtle Bay Bar & Grill

Music clubs
1. Café Brasil
2. Crescent City Brewhouse
3. Donna's Bar & Grill
4. Dragon's Den
5. Dream Palace & Reality Grill
6. Faubourg Center
7. Funky Butt at Congo Square
8. Hog's Breath Saloon
9. House of Blues
10. Igor's Checkpoint Charlie
11. Jimmy Buffett's Margaritaville
12. Kerry Irish Pub
13. O'Flaherty's Irish Channel Center
14. Original Tropical Isle
15. Palm Court Jazz Café
16. Preservation Hall
17. Snug Harbor
18. Tipitina's French Quarter

New Orleans Transport

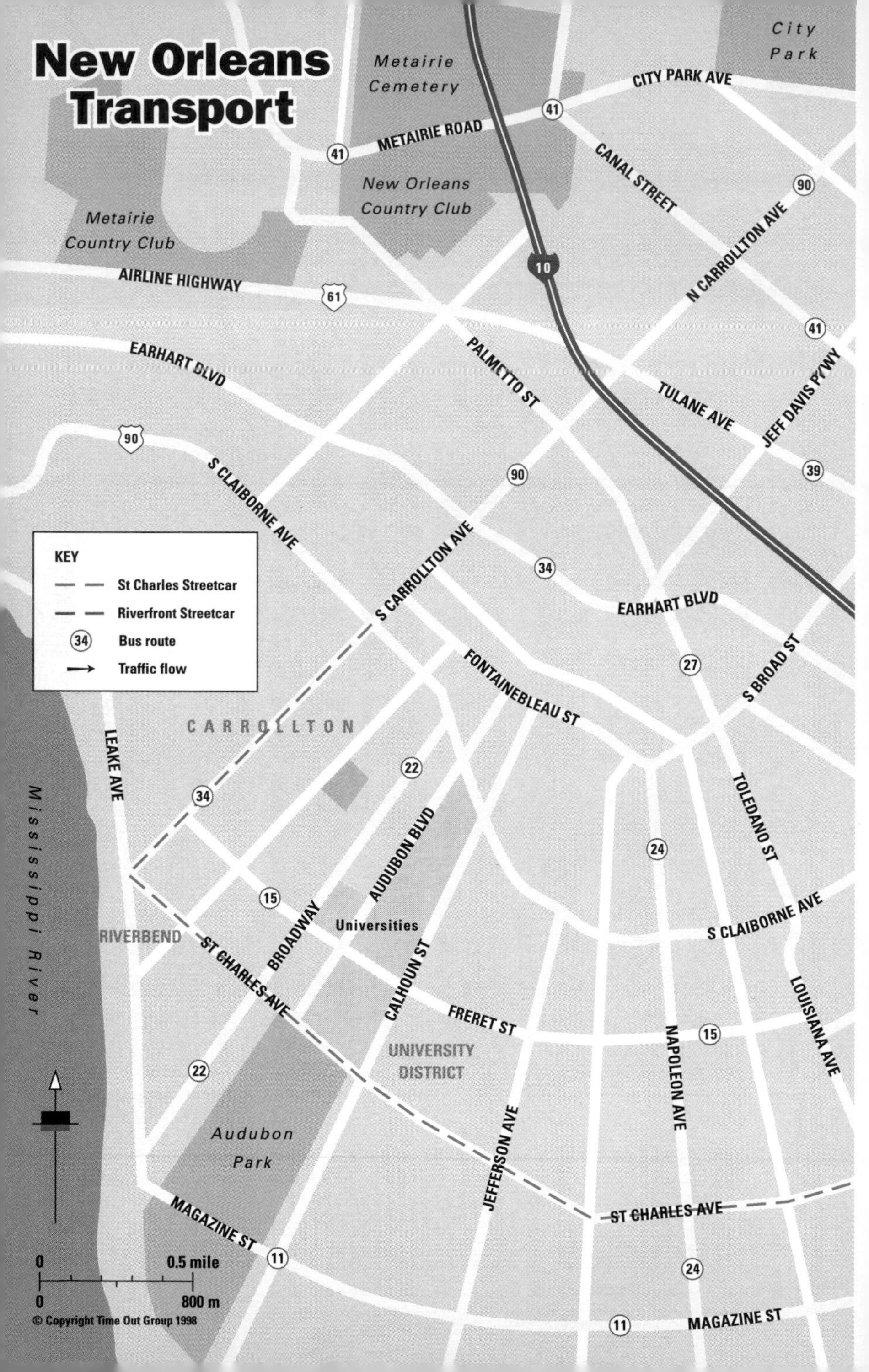

Metairie Cemetery
City Park
CITY PARK AVE
41
METAIRIE ROAD
41
CANAL STREET
New Orleans Country Club
90
Metairie Country Club
N CARROLLTON AVE
10
AIRLINE HIGHWAY
61
41
EARHART BLVD
PALMETTO ST
TULANE AVE
JEFF DAVIS P'WY
90
S CLAIBORNE AVE
90
39
S CARROLLTON AVE
34
EARHART BLVD
KEY
St Charles Streetcar
Riverfront Streetcar
34 Bus route
Traffic flow
FONTAINEBLEAU ST
27
S BROAD ST
CARROLLTON
LEAKE AVE
22
TOLEDANO ST
Mississippi River
34
AUDUBON BLVD
24
15
BROADWAY
Universities
S CLAIBORNE AVE
RIVERBEND
ST CHARLES AVE
CALHOUN ST
LOUISIANA AVE
FRERET ST
15
NAPOLEON AVE
UNIVERSITY DISTRICT
22
JEFFERSON AVE
Audubon Park
ST CHARLES AVE
MAGAZINE ST
11
0
0.5 mile
24
0
800 m
11
MAGAZINE ST

© Copyright Time Out Group 1998

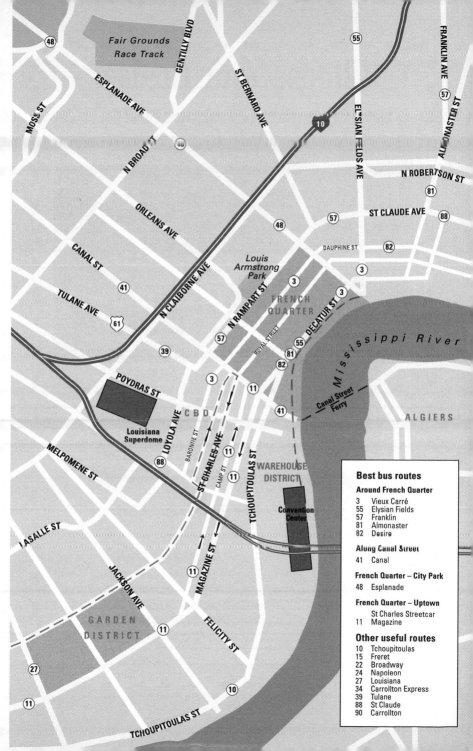

48
Fair Grounds
Race Track
GENTILLY BLVD
ST BERNARD AVE
55
FRANKLIN AVE
ESPLANADE AVE
57
ALMONASTER ST
MOSS ST
N BROAD ST
10
ELYSIAN FIELDS AVE
N ROBERTSON ST
ORLEANS AVE
48
57
ST CLAUDE AVE
81
88
CANAL ST
41
DAUPHINE ST
82
N CLAIBORNE AVE
Louis
Armstrong
Park
3
TULANE AVE
61
FRENCH
QUARTER
3
N RAMPART ST
Mississippi River
57
ROYAL STREET
DECATUR ST
3
39
55
3
POYDRAS ST
81
82
11
CBD
Canal Street
Ferry
41
ALGIERS
Louisiana
Superdome
LOYOLA AVE
BARONNE ST
ST CHARLES AVE
CAMP ST
88
MELPOMENE ST
11
TCHOUPITOULAS ST
WAREHOUSE
DISTRICT
11
Convention
Center
MAGAZINE ST
LASALLE ST

Best bus routes

Around French Quarter

3	Vieux Carré
55	Elysian Fields
57	Franklin
81	Almonaster
82	Desire

Along Canal Street

| 41 | Canal |

French Quarter – City Park

| 48 | Esplanade |

French Quarter – Uptown

| | St Charles Streetcar |
| 11 | Magazine |

Other useful routes

10	Tchoupitoulas
15	Freret
22	Broadway
24	Napoleon
27	Louisiana
34	Carrollton Express
39	Tulane
88	St Claude
90	Carrollton

JACKSON AVE
27
11
GARDEN
DISTRICT
11
FELICITY ST
10
11
TCHOUPITOULAS ST

Street Index

Kenilworth St - Map 5 C4/D4
Kepler St - Map 4 H9
Kerlerec St - Map 4 G6,
  Map 7 D1/2

Lafayette Sq - Map 6 C1
Lafayette St - Map 4 F7/G7
Lafayette St (Gretna) - Map 4
  G10
Lafitte St - Map 4 E6/F6
Laharpe St - Map 5 F5
Lake Marina Dr - Map 5 B2/C2
Lakeshore Dr - Map 5
  C1/D1/E1
Lamarque St - Map 4 H8
Lane St - Map 5 C3/D3
Lapeyrouse St - Map 5 F5
Lasalle St - Map 4 C8/D8,
  Map 6 A2/B1
Laurel St - Map 4
  B10/C10/D10/E9/10/F9
Laurel St - Map 6 A4/B3
Lee Circle - Map 4 F8,
  Map 6 B2
Leonidas St - Map 4 A7/B6/7
Leontine St - Map 4 C9/10
Lepage St - Map 5 E5/F5
Louis XIV St - Map 5 C2/3
Louisiana Ave - Map 4
  D7/8/9/E9/10, Map 6
  A3/4
Louisville St - Map 5 C2/3
Lowerline St - Map 4
  A9/B7/8/C6/7
Loyola Ave - Map 4
  C9/D9/E8/F7, Map 6 B1
Loyola St - Map 6 A2/3
Lyons St - Map 4 C10/D10

Madison St - Map 7 C2/3
Magazine St - Map 7 A3
  Map 4 A9/B9/C10/
  D10/E9/F9/8,
    Map 6 A3/4/B2/3
Magellan St - Map 4 H8
Magnolia St - Map 4 C8/D8/E9,
  Map 6 A2
Mandeville St - Map 4 H6
Mandolin St - Map 5 F3
Maple St - Map 4 A7/8/B8
Marais St - Map 4 G6/H6
Marconi Blvd - Map 5 D2-4
Marengo St - Map 4 D8-10
Marigny St - Map 4 H6
Market St - Map 4 F9/G9,
  Map 6 C3
Marks St - Map 5 C5
Mashall Foch St - Map 5
  D2-4
Maurepas St - Map 5 E5/F5
Melpomene St - Map 4 E8/F8
  Map 6 A2/B2
Memphis St - Map 5 C3/D2
Milan St - Map 4 D8-10
Milne Blvd - Map 5 C2-4
Milton St - Map 4 H10,
  Map 5 E4/F5
Mirabeau Ave - Map 5 E3/F3
Miro St - Map 4 F6
Mistletoe St - Map 4 B6
Mithra St - Map 5 F2
Monroe St - Map 4
  A7/B6/7/C6
Montegut St - Map 4 H6
Monticello Ave - Map 4
  A6/7/B6
Morgan St - Map 4 H7
Moss St - Map 5 E4/5
Mouton St - Map 5 C2/D2
Mystery St - Map 5 E4/5

N Broad Ave - Map 4 E6,
  Map 5 F5
N Carrollton Ave - Map 5 D5
N Dorgenois St - Map 5 F5
N Dupré St - Map 5 F5
N Front St - Map 7 A3/B3
N Galvez St - Map 4 E6/7/F6
N Gayoso St - Map 5 F4/5
N Peters St - Map 7
  A3/B3/C3/D3
N Pierce St - Map 5 D5
N Rampart St - Map 4
  F7/G6/H6, Map 6 B1,
    Map 7 A1/B1/C1/D1
N Roadway St - Map 5 B1/C1
N Rocheblave St - Map 5 F5
N Villere St - Map 4 G6/H5
Napoleon Ave - Map 4 D7-10
Nashville Ave - Map 4 B10/
  C7-9
Natchez St - Map 7 A3
Navarre St - Map 5 C4/D4
Nelson St - Map 4 B6/7/C7
Newton St - Map 4 H8

O'Keefe Ave - Map 4 F7
O'Reilly St - Map 5 F5
Oak St - Map 4 A7/B7/8
Octavia St - Map 4 C7-10
Oleander St - Map 4 B6/C6
Olive St - Map 4 B6/C6
Onzaga St - Map 5 F5
Opelousas Ave - Map 4 H7
Orange St - Map 4 F9/G9,
  Map 6 B3/C3
Orleans Ave - Map 4 E6/F6,
  Map 5 D2-5/E5
Orleans St - Map 7 C1/2
Owens Blvd - Map 5 E3/F3

Palm St - Map 4 C6
Palmer St - Map 4 C8
Palmetto St - Map 4 C6/D6
Palmyra St - Map 4 D6/E6/F7,
  Map 5 C5/D5
Panola St - Map 4 B7
Paris Ave - Map 5 F1-4
Patterson Rd - Map 4 H7
Patton St - Map 4 B9/10
Pauger St - Map 4 G6,
  Map 7 D2
Paul Morphy St - Map 5 F5
Peach St - Map 5 C5
Pear St - Map 5 C5
Pelican St - Map 4 H7
Peniston St - Map 4 D8/9
Perdido St - Map 4 D6/E7/F7,
  Map 6 A1/B1
Perlita St - Map 5 F2/3
Perrier St - Map 4 B9/C9/D9
Perry St - Map 4 H9
Peter St - Map 4 A8/B8
Philip St - Map 4 E8/F9,
  Map 6 A2/3/B3
Picayune Pl - Map 7 A3
Pine St - Map 4
  A9/B7/8/C6/7
Pirate's Alley - Map 7 C2
Pitt St - Map 4 B9/C9/D9
Pleasant St - Map 4 E9/10,
  Map 6 A3/4
Plum St - Map 4 A7/B7/8
Polk Ave - Map 5 C3/D3
Polymnia St - Map 6 B2
Ponce de Leon St -
  Map 5 E5/F5
Pontchartrain Blvd -
  Map 5 C2/3
Port St - Map 4 H6
Porteous St - Map 5 C2/D2
Poydras St - Map 4 E7/F7,

Map 6 A1/B1/C1
Pratt Dr - Map 5 F2
Pritchard St - Map 4 B6
Prytania St - Map 4
  B9/C9/D9/E9/F8/9,
  Map 6 A3/B2/3

R Williams St - Map 5 E4
Race St - Map 4 F8/9/G9,
  Map 6 B3/C3
Richard St - Map 4 F9/G9,
  Map 6 C3
Riviera Ave - Map 5 E3/F3
Robert E Lee Blvd -
  Map 5 C2/D2/E2/F2
Robert St - Map 4 C7-10
Romain St - Map 4 H0
Rousseau St - Map 4 F9,
  Map 6 B4/C4
Royal St - Map 4 G6/7/H6,
  Map 7 A2/B2/C3

S Carrollton Ave -
  Map 4 A8/B7/C6
S Cortez St - Map 4 D6
S Derbigny St - Map 4 D8
S Galvez St - Map 6 A1
S Gayoso St - Map 4 D7
S Hennessey St - Map 4
  C6/D5
S Liberty St - Map 4 C9/D9/E8
  Map 6 A2
S Lopez St - Map 4 D7
S Pierce St - Map 4 D6
S Prieur St - Map 4 D8
S Rampart St - Map 4 F7
S Rendon St - Map 4 C7/D7
S Roadway St - Map 5 B1/C1
S Robertson St - Map 4
  C8/D8/E9
S Robertson St - Map 6 A2
S Roman St - Map 4 D8,
  Map 6 A1
S Saratoga St -
  C9/D9/E8/9,
    Map 6 A2/3
S Scott St - Map 4 D6
S Solomon St - Map 4 C6/D5
Scott St - Map 5 D5
Senate St - Map 5 E3/F3
Sere St - Map 5 E4/F4
Short St - Map 4 A8/B7/8/C6
Simon Bolivar St -
  Map 6 A2/B2
Slidell St - Map 4 H7
Socrates St - Map 4 H8
Solon St - Map 4 H9
Soniat St - Map 4 C8-10
Sophie Wright Pl -
  Map 6 B3
Soraparu St - Map 6 B3/4
S Peters St - Map 6 C1/2
Spain St - Map 4 H6
Spruce St - Map 4 B7
St Andrew St - Map 4 E8/F8/9
  Map 6 A2/B3/C3
St Ann St - Map 4 F6/G6/7,
  Map 5 D5/E5,
    Map 7 C1/2
St Anthony St - Map 4 G6
St Bernard Ave - Map 5
  E1-3/F4/5
St Charles Ave - Map 4
  A8/B8/9/C9/D9/E9/F8,
    Map 6 A3/B2/3/C1
St Claude Ave - Map 4 H6
St Ferdinand St - Map 4 H6
St John St - Map 5 E5/F5
St Joseph St - Map 4 B8/G8
St Louis St - Map 7 B1-3
St Mary St - Map 4 F8/9,

Map 6 B3/C3
St Peter St - Map 5 D5/E5,
  Map 7 B1-3
St Philip St - Map 4 F6/G6,
  Map 5 D5/E5,
    Map 7 C1/2
St Thomas St - Map 4 E10/F9,
  Map 6 A4/B3/4/C3
State Street Dr - Map 4
  B9/10/C6-9
Stroelitz St - Map 4 C6
Stumph Blvd - Map 4 H10
Sugar Bowl Dr - Map 6 A1/B1
Sycamore St - Map 4 B7

Tchoupitoulas St -
  Map 4 B10/C10/D10,
  Map 6 A4/B4/C2/3,
  Map 7 A3
Terpsichore St - Map 4 E8/F8,
  Map 6 B2/C3
Thalia St - Map 4 D7/E7/8/F8,
  Map 6 A1/B2
Toledano St - Map 4
  D7/8/E9/10,
    Map 6 A3/4
Tonti St - Map 4 E6/7/F6
Topaz St - Map 5 D1
Toulouse St - Map 5 D5/E5,
  Map 7 B1/2
Touro St - Map 4 G6
Trafalgar St - Map 5 E4/F4
Tulane Ave - Map 4
  D6/E6/7/F7,
    Map 6 B1
Turquoise St - Map 5 D2

Union St - Map 6 B1
University Pl - Map 7 A1
Upperline St - Map 4 C8-10
Urquhart St - Map 4 G6/H6
Ursulines St - Map 4 F6/G6
Ursulines St - Map 7 C1-3

Valence St - Map 4
  C8/9/D9/10
Valmont St - Map 4 C8-10
Vicksburg St - Map 5 C3/4/D2
Vision Dr - Map 5 C4

Walker St - Map 5 C2/D2
Walmsey Ave - Map C7
Walnut St - Map 4 A9/B9
Washington Ave - Map 4
  C6/D7/E8/9/F10,
    Map 6 A2/3/B4
Webster St - Map 4 B9
Weldman St - Map 4 H9
West End Blvd - Map 5 C2/3
Wilkinson Row - Map 7 B2/3
Willow St - Map 4
  A7/B7/8/C8/D8,
    Map 6 A2
Wisner Blvd - Map 5 E2-4
Woodlawn Pl - Map 5 C4
Wuerpel St - Map 5 C2/3

Zachary Taylor Dr - Map 5
  D4/E4
Zimple St - Map 4 A7/B8